T0181609

Lecture Notes in Computer Science 14060

Founding Editors

Gerhard Goos
Juris Hartmanis

The series Lecture Notes in Computer Science (LNCS), including its subseries Lecture Notes in Artificial Intelligence (LNAI) and Lecture Notes in Bioinformatics (LNBI), has established itself as a medium for the publication of new developments in computer science and information technology research, teaching, and education.

LNCS enjoys close cooperation with the computer science R & D community, the series counts many renowned academics among its volume editors and paper authors, and collaborates with prestigious societies. Its mission is to serve this international community by providing an invaluable service, mainly focused on the publication of conference and workshop proceedings and postproceedings. LNCS commenced publication in 1973.

Panayiotis Zaphiris · Andri Ioannou ·
Robert A. Sottilare · Jessica Schwarz ·
Fiona Fui-Hoon Nah · Keng Siau · June Wei ·
Gavriel Salvendy
Editors

HCI International 2023 – Late Breaking Papers

25th International Conference on Human-Computer Interaction
HCII 2023, Copenhagen, Denmark, July 23–28, 2023
Proceedings, Part VII

 Springer

Editors
Panayiotis Zaphiris
Cyprus University of Technology
Limassol, Cyprus

Robert A. Sottilare
Soar Technology, Inc.
Orlando, FL, USA

Fiona Fui-Hoon Nah
City University of Hong Kong
Hong Kong, Hong Kong

June Wei
University of West Florida
Pensacola, FL, USA

Andri Ioannou (iD)
Cyprus University of Technology
Limassol, Cyprus

CYENS
Nicosia, Cyprus

Jessica Schwarz
Fraunhofer FKIE
Wachtberg, Germany

Keng Siau
City University of Hong Kong
Hong Kong, Hong Kong

Gavriel Salvendy
University of Central Florida
Orlando, FL, USA

ISSN 0302-9743 ISSN 1611-3349 (electronic)
Lecture Notes in Computer Science
ISBN 978-3-031-48059-1 ISBN 978-3-031-48060-7 (eBook)
https://doi.org/10.1007/978-3-031-48060-7

This Springer imprint is published by the registered company Springer Nature Switzerland AG
The registered company address is: Gewerbestrasse 11, 6330 Cham, Switzerland

Paper in this product is recyclable.

Foreword

Human-computer interaction (HCI) is acquiring an ever-increasing scientific and industrial importance, as well as having more impact on people's everyday lives, as an ever-growing number of human activities are progressively moving from the physical to the digital world. This process, which has been ongoing for some time now, was further accelerated during the acute period of the COVID-19 pandemic. The HCI International (HCII) conference series, held annually, aims to respond to the compelling need to advance the exchange of knowledge and research and development efforts on the human aspects of design and use of computing systems.

The 25th International Conference on Human-Computer Interaction, HCI International 2023 (HCII 2023), was held in the emerging post-pandemic era as a 'hybrid' event at the AC Bella Sky Hotel and Bella Center, Copenhagen, Denmark, during July 23–28, 2023. It incorporated the 21 thematic areas and affiliated conferences listed below.

A total of 7472 individuals from academia, research institutes, industry, and government agencies from 85 countries submitted contributions, and 1578 papers and 396 posters were included in the volumes of the proceedings that were published just before the start of the conference. Additionally, 267 papers and 133 posters were included in the volumes of the proceedings published after the conference, as "Late Breaking Work". The contributions thoroughly cover the entire field of human-computer interaction, addressing major advances in knowledge and effective use of computers in a variety of application areas. These papers provide academics, researchers, engineers, scientists, practitioners and students with state-of-the-art information on the most recent advances in HCI. The volumes constituting the full set of the HCII 2023 conference proceedings are listed on the following pages.

I would like to thank the Program Board Chairs and the members of the Program Boards of all thematic areas and affiliated conferences for their contribution towards the high scientific quality and overall success of the HCI International 2023 conference. Their manifold support in terms of paper reviewing (single-blind review process, with a minimum of two reviews per submission), session organization and their willingness to act as goodwill ambassadors for the conference is most highly appreciated.

This conference would not have been possible without the continuous and unwavering support and advice of Gavriel Salvendy, founder, General Chair Emeritus, and Scientific Advisor. For his outstanding efforts, I would like to express my sincere appreciation to Abbas Moallem, Communications Chair and Editor of HCI International News.

July 2023   Constantine Stephanidis

HCI International 2023 Thematic Areas
and Affiliated Conferences

Thematic Areas

- HCI: Human-Computer Interaction
- HIMI: Human Interface and the Management of Information

Affiliated Conferences

- EPCE: 20th International Conference on Engineering Psychology and Cognitive Ergonomics
- AC: 17th International Conference on Augmented Cognition
- UAHCI: 17th International Conference on Universal Access in Human-Computer Interaction
- CCD: 15th International Conference on Cross-Cultural Design
- SCSM: 15th International Conference on Social Computing and Social Media
- VAMR: 15th International Conference on Virtual, Augmented and Mixed Reality
- DHM: 14th International Conference on Digital Human Modeling and Applications in Health, Safety, Ergonomics and Risk Management
- DUXU: 12th International Conference on Design, User Experience and Usability
- C&C: 11th International Conference on Culture and Computing
- DAPI: 11th International Conference on Distributed, Ambient and Pervasive Interactions
- HCIBGO: 10th International Conference on HCI in Business, Government and Organizations
- LCT: 10th International Conference on Learning and Collaboration Technologies
- ITAP: 9th International Conference on Human Aspects of IT for the Aged Population
- AIS: 5th International Conference on Adaptive Instructional Systems
- HCI-CPT: 5th International Conference on HCI for Cybersecurity, Privacy and Trust
- HCI-Games: 5th International Conference on HCI in Games
- MobiTAS: 5th International Conference on HCI in Mobility, Transport and Automotive Systems
- AI-HCI: 4th International Conference on Artificial Intelligence in HCI
- MOBILE: 4th International Conference on Design, Operation and Evaluation of Mobile Communications

Conference Proceedings – Full List of Volumes

https://2023.hci.international/proceedings

25th International Conference on Human-Computer Interaction (HCII 2023)

The full list with the Program Board Chairs and the members of the Program Boards of all thematic areas and affiliated conferences of HCII2023 is available online at:

http://www.hci.international/board-members-2023.php

HCI International 2024 Conference

The 26th International Conference on Human-Computer Interaction, HCI International 2024, will be held jointly with the affiliated conferences at the Washington Hilton Hotel, Washington, DC, USA, June 29 – July 4, 2024. It will cover a broad spectrum of themes related to Human-Computer Interaction, including theoretical issues, methods, tools, processes, and case studies in HCI design, as well as novel interaction techniques, interfaces, and applications. The proceedings will be published by Springer. More information will be made available on the conference website: http://2024.hci.international/.

General Chair
Prof. Constantine Stephanidis
University of Crete and ICS-FORTH
Heraklion, Crete, Greece
Email: general_chair@2024.hci.international

https://2024.hci.international/

Contents – Part VII

eCommerce, Digital Marketing and eFinance

Learning Technologies and Learning Experiences

Curiously: Supporting Young Children and their Caregivers Create Meaningful Learning Adventures in Nature

Carolina Alí Fojaco[✉]

Boston College, Chestnut Hill, MA 02467, USA
carolina.alif@gmail.com

Abstract. Our planet is facing critical challenges and systemic changes that demand an urgent attention to educational and technological solutions that empower people to take care and protect our home. But, how can we protect something that we don't love? Curiously provides resources and support to help caregivers and families with young children (ages 2–6) create playful and engaging learning adventures in nature together, promoting meaningful emotional bonding. It includes a mockup of an app that helps parents and caregivers plan such adventures and, eventually, will include a functionality that allows them to share their ex-presences with other families while developing a community that deepens the engagement with the platform and develops emotional bonding with the natural world. This paper describes in detail the systematic design process that was followed, including design insights from the literature and from user-soaked interactions.

Keywords: Learning Engineering · Learning Design · UX/UI design · Early Childhood · Learning Technologies · Nature · Sustainability · Outdoor learning · Family engagement

1 Introduction

Our planet is facing critical challenges and systemic changes. The World Economic Forum (2023) presented some of the imminent risks we face at a global level and with local consequences: some are climate change, loss of biodiversity, and water and food crises affecting our health in many different ways. The survival of humanity depends on the way we interact with the environment and on being able to protect it (Haines-Young and Potschin 2010).

Moreover, childhood is a critical stage of life for learning and development. James Heckman, Nobel prize in economics, stated that quality interventions at this stage of life have long-term benefits across a person's lifespan and also have the greatest economic return (Heckman 2013). Building from a social and cognitive perspective, providing a range of high-quality experiences in the early years is imperative (OECD 2019).

Thus, childhood has moved indoors, leaving kids disconnected from the natural world. Louv (2005, 2016, 2019), co-founder and chairman emeritus of the Children &

P. Zaphiris et al. (Eds.): HCII 2023, LNCS 14060, pp. 3–23, 2023.
https://doi.org/10.1007/978-3-031-48060-7_1

Nature Network has written about the metaphor "Nature-deficit disorder", for describing some of the human costs of alienation from nature, such as *"diminished use of the senses, attention difficulties, higher rates of physical and emotional illnesses, a rising rate of myopia, child and adult obesity, Vitamin D deficiency, and other maladies."* The author also has written about the imperative need of *raising children that build a personal and meaningful relationship with nature,* and how parents, educators and the community play a crucial role.

Numerous research has found that connecting young children to nature has many long-term benefits related to health (Strife and Downey 2009) cognitive, socio-emotional aspects (Johnstone et al. 2022) school readiness (Fjortoft 2001), and pro-environment behaviors (Wells and Lekies 2006). According to Bouton and Thomas (2022) outdoors play benefits schema development since *"movements are greater, creativity is deeper, and schemas are overtly witnessed during outdoor play, where the self-governance of the play itself enables schematic development".*

As David Sobel (2008) quoted *"If we want children to flourish, to become truly empowered, let us allow them to love the earth before we ask them to save it".* How can we ask our youth to love and protect nature, our home planet earth, when we offer few possibilities for playing outdoors, having shared and collaborative experiences of wonder and awe for creating meaningful connections with the natural world?

With the foundations cited above, the design challenge was to design a series of experiences that children and their caregivers could have to build together rich learning experiences in nature and over time. A design constraint that was important was that the experience could be revisited and explored so that families could reflect together on it. For that to happen, supports have to be provided, and a constraint was that they could be offered through a technology that could afford to hold all of these desirable interactions.

The idea started with a mock up an of an app that families could use in different key moments (before, during, and after going outdoors) and providing them ideas, resources, and tools for planning, wondering, creating, sharing, documenting, and learning about their adventures outdoors in nature.

2   Method

Curiously provides resources and support to help caregivers and families with young children (ages 2–6) create playful and engaging learning adventures in nature together, promoting meaningful emotional bonding.

It includes a mockup of an app that helps parents and caregivers plan such adventures and, eventually, will include a functionality that allows them to share their experiences with other families while developing a community that deepens the engagement with the platform and develops emotional bonding with the natural world. The app is intended to be available in both English and Spanish, as a start. In Curiously, children and their caregivers explore, discover and learn together in and from nature, lifting the weight on parents to "know everything", rather showing curiosity and wonder, essential dispositions for lifelong learning.

The app design is intended to help parents, children, and other caregivers plan "learning adventure journeys" through three phases: planning and preparation before the adventure begins, the nature adventure itself, and sharing and storytelling after the nature adventure.

Along the design process, during the final iteration, a "caregivers" guide was created as a complement to the experience.

Embodiment of App Mockup: *Learner's Adventure Journey*

The embodiment of the learning design is reflected in across different features of an app in three main stages; before (Prepare and Wonder), during (Explore Outdoors) and after (Create and Share) the experience (See Fig. 1).

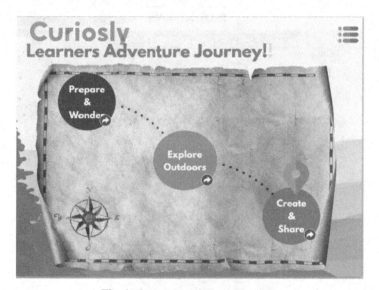

Fig. 1. Learner's Adventure Journey

Prepare and Wonder- Before the Adventure Begins: Children and their caregivers plan the adventure together at home. Its context could be any experience outdoors together, ranging from visiting their local park or even their backyard, a hike in the woods, a visit to a pond, or going on a trip to the beach. Families can choose which place they are visiting in each adventure (See Fig. 2). The app provides maps to find relevant venues for their next adventure and encourages conversation around which location to choose based on the range of activities, seasons, or weather. The app also provides a library of appropriately curated storybooks to read before the outing, organized by age, language, and setting. Prompts are provided to create a conversation around the story stimulating wonder and curiosity. A family can even use the story's foundation to their activity plan around some of its elements. This might be accessed through a computer, tablet, or phone.

Key Features of the "Prepare and Wonder" section:

- Families can select and explore possible venues to visit through a map feature that help caregivers and kids situate the adventure and find interesting natural places nearby. Also, they can select the season they are going to and the day. (See Figs. 2 and 3)

Fig. 2. Feature for selecting the venue for the adventure.

Fig. 3. Map feature for selecting venue based on location.

- A curated storybook library to help families select stories to read and learn together about the place they are going and wonder about it. Books are curated based on the chosen place. Age group and language of the users. (Fig. 4)

- Conversation guides for each storybook are provided as scaffolding to promote meaningful conversations around the storybook and promote curiosity through open-ended questions (Fig. 5).

Explore Outdoors- During the Adventure: While the main purpose in this stage is to engage fully with nature, the app would offer caregivers prompts for modeling exploration, encouraging kids to be mindful and explore with their senses, marking relevant concepts and vocabulary, and referencing the book they read. Parents might also pack a sketchbook for children to use to sketch what they are seeing and experiencing, sketches of their discoveries. Mostly, the adventure is about exploring the site, noticing and sharing interesting and fascinating phenomena. The app might be used by children to taking and collecting pictures of specimens (e.g., leaves, shells), making drawings, recording

Fig. 4. Curated library of storybooks based on the chosen venue.

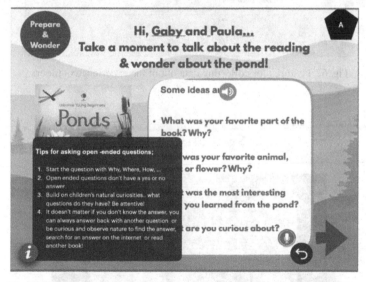

Fig. 5. Storybooks' scaffolding prompts for asking open-ended questions

videos play-pretending to be an animal, audios of narrations, stories or sounds, among other data. Families might play games they planned before arriving or spontaneously create games while there. For the most part, the app, to be run on a phone while in the outdoors, will be used for collecting data such as photos, audio, and video.

Key Features of "Explore Outdoors" section:

- Suggestions of activities and tips for families to go out in nature and play, engage with their senses and wonder about scientific phenomena.
- Features for documenting their adventures together such as taking videos and pictures, making drawings and sketches, and recording audios (Figs. 6 and 7).

Fig. 6. Features for collecting data out of the experience outdoors.

Fig. 7. "Spot an animal"- Feature for taking pictures, a camara tool is embedded.

Create and Share- After the Adventure: On this last section, three main features are provided for reflecting and sharing the experience (Fig. 8). Reflection is crucial in learning-from-experience in informal learning settings, building on previous research, supporting reflection using technology tools can take the functions of *"amplifying obser-vations for deliberative noticing, organizing processes of exploration to support revisit-ing them, and, compare, extend and explain what learners know throw representations or new data"* (Land et al. 2013). Considering these key supports for learning, the app will create moments for families to engage in retrospective moments about the adventure (e.g., what did they learn? what was their favorite part? what would they do differently next time?).

Fig. 8. Create and Share section menu. Three main features; revisit "our collections", "Create a new adventure story" and visualize your "library of adventures".

Also, important to learning from experience is the expression of what was learned. After the adventure, the app helps children create meaningful digital artifacts with the data collected to share with friends and other family members (e.g., grandparents, cousins, aunts, and uncles). Curiously helps them create storybooks, photo albums, mini-movies, mini-podcasts, or songs and save what they create into their library of adventures to share. Such activities give children a chance to reflect on, discuss and express their experiences while also bringing family members who live far away together (they can add family members into their "family rooms" and through a private and safe space and have videocalls with them). Deepening bonds between family members and help youngsters create meaningful emotional bonds with the natural world (Chawla 2007).

Key Features of "Create and Share" section:

- Features include prompts for looking up to the "data collected" and remembering and reflecting on the experience (Fig. 9).
- Inspired by the *"low-floor, wide walls and high-ceilings"* constructionist approach (Resnick 2016) (Dasgupta and Mako 2018), on designing learning technologies. The

Fig. 9. "Collections" of data gathered outdoors.

app should have multiple canvases, templates, art and multimedia tools and features that afford learners to create a digital artifacts that reflects their learning experience and play "mix and match" the data they collected to create the digital artifact as a persoal project they care about (open options could be; a storybook, a photo album, a card, music, mini-podcast, a minimovie, etc.). For novice users, the feature of creating an automated photo album is optional as a sandbox experience (Figs. 10, 11 and 12).

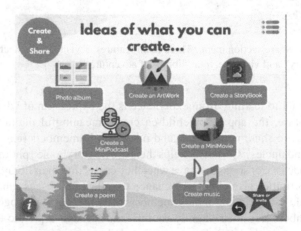

Fig. 10. Menu of ideas for creating digital artifacts.

- A *sharing* feature connects children with a significant family member (grandparents, for example) to share and present their artifacts and what they learned in their adventure in nature. This could be either sent as a pdf format or link to the app, and/or a build-on just-in time videocalling function (Fig. 13).

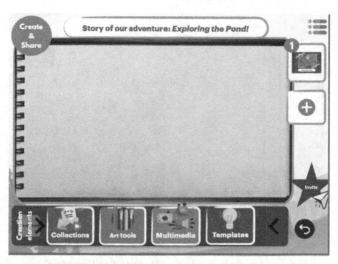

Fig. 11. Creating a digital artifact menu with creation elements available: Collections (data collected), art tools, multimedia features and templates.

Fig. 12. Creating a digital artifact sub-menu with drag-and-drop interactions for pulling in data collected: pictures of animals.

- *Library of Adventures.* Library of finished or ongoing digital projects. Based on user's insights alongside the design process, I found that parents enjoy keeping memories of their child's creations and pictures in the same "space." And this could be one of the main affordances of building the experience on an app (Fig. 14).

Caregivers and children can access any section of the experience whenever it is more convenient for them and use the resources that best fit their needs. The tools are meant

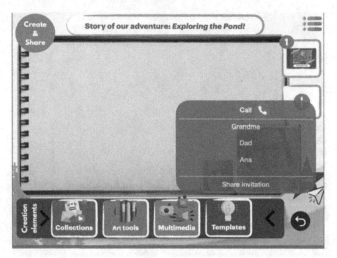

Fig. 13. Example of "sharing" feature- "call grandma".

Fig. 14. Library of Adventures

to support playful experiences, not a burden of "mandatory things they have to do in order to have a learning experience". Additionally, scaffolding support is given so that every family can engage in the learning process at their own pace.

2.1 Design Process

Overview of the Design Process
The design process implied different iterative steps, from understanding the challenge and the context for learning, including conducting a literature review that guided design decisions, empathizing and co-designing some features with the targeted learner population. It was critical for the design to engage with caregivers during the ideation part of

the design process since they shared their needs, wants, and struggles regarding going outdoors with young kids and using technology in early childhood. Along the design process, I discussed and tested ideas with parents and caregivers and went outdoors to playtest some key interactions with kids and families (Fig. 15).

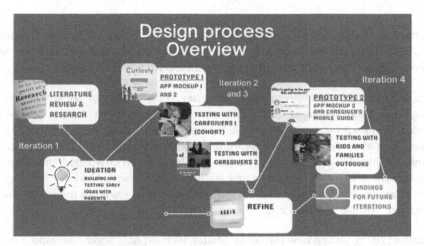

Fig. 15. "Curiously"- Design process overview

Through four iterations, prototypes and tests were made to improve the design of technology features, scaffolded prompts, and suggested learning activities with different stakeholders. The final products designed were a final app mockup prototype & a digital guide for caregivers.

A design journal was kept along the process to document key insights, ideas and design- decisions.

Design Lenses: Theoretical Framework that Informed the Design
The design process was informed by different design lenses from the Learning Sciences. Prior to designing it was important to conduct a literature review with the purpose of understanding and gathering ideas based on evidence and/or previous research.

In addition, it included a review of similar applications designed to support learning outside with mobile applications. For example, Zimmerman and Land (2014) developed a mobile design guideline for place-based education and applied it to its "Tree Investigators" outdoor science learning project, principles of the mobile design guideline for place-based education that were inspiring for Curiously were; *"Facilitating participation in disciplinary conversations and practices within personally relevant places, amplify observations to see the disciplinary-relevant aspects of a place, and connect local experiences to those of general, disciplinary concerns through exploring new perspectives, representations, conversations, or knowledge artifacts"*.

Curiously is meant to be design in a mobile app learning environment. And as Klopfer et al. (2002) described, mobile computing or handheld computing as they referred to at the time, have unique properties produce unique educational affordances: portability, social interactivity, context sensitivity, connectivity and individuality. *These affordances suggest an array of unique modes of interacting, such as distributed, collaborative investigations, peer-to-peer networking or coupling physical space with virtual space in instruction (Klopfer 2007).*

Other applications that served as inspiration for their success in designing for kids were;

- Scratch Jr, one of the most widely used introductory coding learning environments explicitly designed for children ages 5–7, for its successfully integration of the "low-floor, high celings" principles in designing an app for young children;

    "Low Floor and (Appropriately) High Ceiling: Make it easy to get started with ScratchJr programming. Provide room to grow with concepts varying in complexity, but keep the tool manageable for the range of users. Wide Walls: Allow many pathways and styles of exploration, creation, [expression] and learning. Tinkerability: Make it easy to incrementally build up creations and knowledge by experimenting with new ideas and features. Conviviality: Make the interface feel friendly, joyful, inviting, and playful, with a positive spirit of exploration and learning" (Blake and Bers 2023).

- Caribu (2023), an app now owned by Mattel, its interphase served as inspiration for its library feature and "invite family members feature". Although, in Curiously, the books in the library are all related to nature and are curated based on the place the family is visiting, the activities that kids can do in the app are more are open-ended, following the "low-floor, high celings approach" and not "predetermined activity sheets" and are not related to a particular character.

Building Islands of Expertise (Crowley and Jacob 2002)

The overarching inspirational idea design is based on Crowley and Jacob's (2002) research paper on Island of Expertise. An island of expertise is a topic in which children happen to become interested and in which they develop relatively deep and rich knowledge. A typical island emerges over weeks, months, or years and is woven throughout multiple family activities. Because of this, developing islands of expertise is a fundamentally sociocultural process.

"Through the joint activity, guided by a combination of children's and parent's interests, families can build deep, shared domain-specific knowledge bases, which we can refer to as islands of expertise" - Crowley and Jacob's (2002).

Based on this approach, on Crowley and Jacob's (2002) the learning conjecture is that through rich conversations embedded in a family environment, and the interaction with the natural environment, and the use of complementary tools found embedded in the app families would share time building islands of expertise related to a topic that a child is curious about.

David Sobel's Design Principles for Children and Nature

The "Design principles for Children in Nature" by David Sobel (2008) provided a great framework for the design. Mainly because Sobel draws has identified seven key "play motifs" that are commonly observed in all children while cultivating relationships with nature. Sobel states that it is during these kinds of play that transcendental experiences occur. A design decision was to consider those natural interactions account for providing scaffolding and advice for caregivers to help children learn from nature.

"Spend time at a safe, woodsy playground, and you'll find children (1) making forts and special places; (2) playing hunting and gathering games; (3) shaping small worlds; (4)developing friendships with animals; (5)constructing adventures; (6) descending into fantasies; (7)and following paths and figuring out shortcuts.". - Sobel (2008).

Table 1. Curiously Design decisions based on Sobel's (2008) *Children and Nature. Design Principles for Educators.*

Principle	Description	Design Decisions for Curiously
Adventure	*"Environmental education needs to be kinesthetic, in the body"*	• Activities and experiences are framed as "let's go for an adventure, prepare for the adventure, explore..." • The scaffolding prompts for engaging during the adventure provide examples of physical activities that could be done outdoors, including exploring with the five senses also and activities for gross motor skills development such as jumping, climbing, etc."
Fantasy- Imagination	*"Young children live in their imaginations... Stories are preferred media for early childhood"*	Before going outdoors, preparation activities include story books embedded in the app so caregivers and children can read them together to build prior knowledge, foster imagination, curiosity, and wonder about the place they are visiting
Animal Allies	*"If we aspire to developmentally appropriate science education, then the first talk is to become animals, to understand them from the inside out, before asking children to study them or save them"*	The stories integrated into the app would be curated to highlight and mark special animals of the ecosystem the families decided to explore. Kids might want to dig further and dig *islands of expertise* around these animals

(continued)

Table 1. (*continued*)

Principle	Description	Design Decisions for Curiously
Maps and Paths	*"Children have an inborn desire to explore local geographies. Developing a local sense of place leads organically to a bioregional sense of place and hopefully a biospheric consciousness."*	A map feature is integrated into the preparation and planning (before) part of the experience, with the purpose that families choose together where they want to go. Exploring the map together and having prompted conversations around it can help learners sense the place they are visiting and wonder how to explore it together
Special Places	*"Children like to find and create places where they can hideaway and retreat into their found or constructed spaces."*	Prompts in the caregivers´ guide include modeling dispositions towards wonder and curiosity during adventure by asking questions while following their children's natural curiosity to explore freely and build a sense of place. Taking pictures and making sketches are encouraged to record and keep memories of those special places that further on can be compared and contrasted
Small Worlds	*"Almost everyone remembers a fort, den, treehouse, or hidden corner in the back of a closet. Especially between ages eight and eleven, children like to find and create places where they can hideaway and retreat into their own found or constructed spaces."*	Developing a sense of belonging to planet earth and to the natural world/ place they are visiting is encouraged from the preparation activities before the experience, the prompts for caregivers during the exploration, and the reflective and creation activities post- the adventure. Especially in the "after" activities, children are encouraged to create a mini artifact as a "mini representation" of the adventure (a photo album, video, mini-podcast, storybook, artwork, etc..) to recall, share and revisit with significant caregivers

(*continued*)

Table 1. (*continued*)

Principle	Description	Design Decisions for Curiously
Hunting and Gathering	" *From a genetic perspective, we are still hunting and gathering organisms. Gathering and collecting anything compels us; searching for hidden treasure or the Holy Grail is as recurrent mythic form. Look at the success of 'Where's Waldo'. How do we design learning opportunities like treasure hunts?"*	Children are invited to gather and collect pictures, videos, audio, sketches, and special artifacts during the experience as "treasure hunts", the feature in the app the families can keep these archives is named after this principle. The archives are used later to remix them in creative mini projects

Each of these principles, guided some of the design decisions taken into account for developing "*Curiously*". (Table 1).

Conjecture Map as Tool for Systematic Learning Design

These theoretical frameworks provided a solid background in making design decisions, refining ideas, and bringing all the app elements together. An adaption of the Conjecture Map tool (Sandoval 2014) was made for mapping out the learning and engagement conjectures and how these led to desired interactions and particular features in the learning design (Fig. 16).

Conjecture maps were design as "*a means of specifying theoretically salient features of a learning environment design and mapping out how they are predicted to work together to produce desired outcomes*" (Sandoval 2014) (Fig. 17).

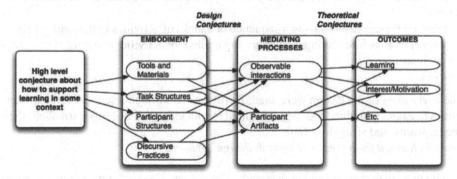

Fig. 16. Conjecture Mapping as a tool for systematic educational design research, from Sandoval (2014)

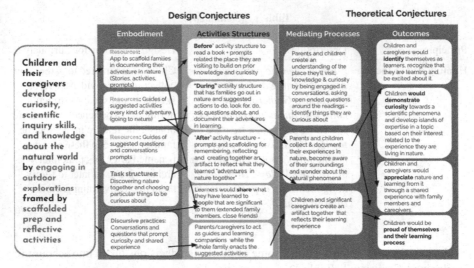

Fig. 17. Conjecture Mapping for systematic decision-making while designing "Curiously", based on Sandoval (2014)

3 Discussion

3.1 Design Process: First Iteration

For the first iteration, initial ideas from parents and caregivers were taken into account for the early stages of the design. One valuable finding was that parents and caregivers appreciated having "strong foundations" to consider for the design of learning technologies, as some of them shared with me that the design of apps for children should be grounded in evidence and that they value the theories that back up the ideas of the design.

Testing these ideas of having a sequence or chunks of activities in the main stages of the experience (before, during, and after) and a subset of activities and critical resources for each section.

Process:

The early ideas of the design were shared with parents through a semi-structured interview via Zoom with three moms (individually) with kids aged 3–11 to learn about their needs, wants, and struggles (Table 2).

Lessons learned from these iteration & design decisions:

- The need of empathize and understand the needs and wants of some parents in going outdoors in nature, as well as the variability between families. This experience helped to build personas.

   The need of creating a prototype that reflected the ideas in a clear visual way for shared understanding.
- The suggestion of adding a map in the planning section was interesting to all. They also provided suggestions on ideas of activities, features and prompts that could be integrated along with the map.

Table 2. Semi-structured interview questions to caregivers

Interview Questions to caregivers:
- What do you do with your child to help them learn about nature?
- How do you help your child explore their interests? Can you tell me an example of something your child is interested in?
- Would they be interested in using a kit that helps your child intentionally explore nature?
- How would they use it?
- What would they want help with in implementing such a kit?

3.2 Design Process: Second Iteration

For the second iteration, a prototype was tested through two cycles of testing a first mock-up of the app that visually reflected the desirable interactions of each stage.

For the first testing of the second prototype, the mock-up was shared with colleagues for peer feedback and critique; they gave written comments on each screen and overall comments in a focus group format. Some of the colleagues are uncles, aunts, or even grandmothers of young kids.

Some of the insights of this testing were recorded on a design journal (Table 3).

Table 3. Personal notes on Design Journal after testing the app mock-up with caregivers.

Personal notes on Design Journal- Prototype Revisions

Changes and why:
- Change the design of the scaffolding for parents and
- Add more activities based on the age range and season and specifically tailored to the location
- Change menu buttons
- Hide some tools following the human-computer interaction design

How this will affect the functions of the design:
- This will help to make a coherent journey of interactions that will sustain engagement for both parents and children
- Interactions will be smoother, and the user experience will be better

The changes will provide for high-quality interactions concentrating on learning with a more personalized experience according to age, season, and location

---

3.3 Design Process: Third Iteration

After integrating some changes based on my peers´ and professors´ comments, I presented and tested the prototype to 5 families/caregivers (via zoom and in person) in a semi-functional mock-up with an iPad. The location, culture, and background of the caregivers varied. A test of the prototype was made with a playtest and semi-structured interview to caregivers from the following cultural and geographical background:

- An aunt of a 6-year-old and 2-year-old nephews in Quéretaro, México. (Virtual)

- A Chilean mom of two girls, one 4-year-old and one 2-year-old living in Boston (in person)
- A Chinese mom of a boy of 6 and a girl of 11 in Boston (In person)
- A Mexican couple, parents of two young boys, a one-year-old and a 4-year-old - Mérida, Mx (Virtual)
- An Uruguayan mom and an American aunt of a 3-year-old in Boston. (In person)

Observations of the interactions with the mock-up were made, and recording of their their comments though a talk-out-loud protocol. Afterwards, a semi-structured interview was conducted to learn more about what they liked, what they didn't like, what they found useful or relevant and why, on each main section (before, during and after). In addition, form that they could answer any time after the testing session was provided.

Lessons learned from this iteration & design decisions:

- Caregivers have different priorities and time availability; constraining the experience to have a fixed order might be overwhelming for some caregivers. So a decision was made to give recommendations on the order of doing the activities without restricting access or navigation across the different stages so that caregivers can access them based on their goals.
- One of the parents mentioned the need to be more explicit in integrating Universal Design for learning (UDL) principles and addressing variability among learners (for example, changing the wording of "engage with your five senses, to engage with your senses").
- Parents appreciate and value well-thought technologies and applications for children backed up by the literature and have a purpose for their development. I had to make David Sobel's (2003) principles, for example.

3.4   Design Process: Fourth Iteration

For the fourth iteration, I a guide for caregivers with scaffolding prompts and simulated expected interactions of the app was created to be used across the different stages of the experience outdoors as a prototype of the design. The caregiver's guide complements the app. Prompts were designed to simulate the main desired interactions before, during, and after the experience in nature. The goal was to test if the prompts, suggestions, and tips are helpful for families for meaningful interactions at each stage and connections across the different locations.

Process: To test the guide, it was sent to two families with kids of different ages, one with a two-year-old and the other with a seven-year-old; along with the guide, books were curated and sent an age-appropriate digital storybook about the pond. Then, we went outdoors to a local Boston area pond. Lastly, a photo album with pictures we took during the adventure at the pond was sent so that they could continue the conversation at home and create a digital photo album if they wanted.

The objective of testing the guide was to learn if these prompts are useful to parents to then think about ways that in future app development could be embedded. Also, the guide could always be accessible through the menu in the app section of "tips for parents".

For gaining user feedback observations outdoors with the selected families were conducted during the family engagement. A survey via email was sent to gain more concrete user's feedback (Table 4).

Table 4. Wrap-up questions for feedback sent through an email survey.

---

* How did the reading/preparation phase (planning and reading a book and questions) help/influence you and your kid in your experience outdoors? What would you change/remove?
* How well did the guide help you/give you ideas on things to point out activities or tips for implementing outdoors? What would you remove, add or change?
* How did the recall/reflection or creation/sharing activities work out? Did you and your child find them helpful, meaningful, or engaging to look back at the adventure outdoors? What would you change/remove or add?
* Do you consider that you and your kid created learning insights and connections across the three main stages of the experience? Yes/no, why?
* Please let me know about any other comments or suggestions for improvement!

Lessons Learned from this Iteration and Design Decisions

Two-year-old family insights:

* Two-year-olds can be very engaged with the activity, they might not document the experience as much or draw lots of connections across the three stages, but adaptations could be made so that discovering, playing, and using their senses are encouraged outdoors. High-quality interactions were noted, activities, and connections that caregivers and the child did naturally.
* Such as open ended questions, "are you jumping like a frog?", "where does this come from, maybe from the tree?" comparing and contrasting "stand next to the baby tree and see who is taller," "look, the size of that rock is like a whale," and "We can hear the water," "look at this rock," marking vocabulary of particular species and elements of nature; "listen, woodpeckers!" "These are blossoms," and reinforcing identity building, "you are an explorer"!
* The importance of Sobel's principles were confirmed as an excellent framework for designing experiences in nature with children; treasures, animal allies, unique places, using their body, using their senses, and adventure time, among others... The child loved playing, finding unique rocks, and throwing them to the pond to compare the different sizes of splashes. They also walk in rocks, walk on a bridge,

Seven-year-old testing insights:

* He used his body a lot; he had lots of energy and was moving from one thing to another, skated, climbed a hill, play with the playground tubes.
* He had a specific goal or interest in mind: turtles! But he was also playing and enjoying the day outdoors overall.
* He got excited about the app; "Mom, show me the app" "we are doing what the app said"

Findings from suggestions from the caregiver on the app design:

- There could be two kinds of adventures: With a specific goal or learning objective in mind. Maybe this is for older kids, and in the preparation phase, they could do mini-research as an alternative option for reading the storybook.
- With no specific target, follow natural curiosity and ask questions to expand interest. (some kids cannot focus on something specific for a long time)
- The app's recording feature would help keep track of insights, questions, and curiosities and then reflect or investigate more about them at home.
- "That's why we need your app because we do many reflections outdoors, but we forget them. It would be very useful. Older kids can also record their observations, visit the place several times, and keep track". – Mom

3.5 What Worked on This Design

- Addressing variation among learners: Involving a variation of parents and caregivers since the idea's conception helped me a lot to do mini-cycles of refinement of the learning design along the way, given the time constraints. But, again, listening was crucial for not constraining the experience to be restricted to a fixed order and instead having suggestions of activities to do in each stage and suggestions on order.
- A good decision was to find families with age variation (2-year-old and 7-year-old) to test how the learning design was helpful and supportive for addressing the learning goals and how it could be improved/personalized for each targeted age group. It was also a good idea to simulate curating storybooks based on their developmental level and sending them to them as a preparation resource along with prompts for parents.
- Supporting mental model building; It was an excellent structure to chunk the activity into three main stages. Chunking is a way of helping learners build mental models, as they can systematically process the information through big categories of interactions and content. It gives opportunities to grow the learning over time and to "come back" to recall, reflect and learn from the experience "bit by bit." Also, this decision helped me identify the desirable critical interactions of each stage and the expected mediating processes that could lead to the learning outcomes and then design the right resources and supports to make that happen.

3.6 Improvements on the Design for Future Iterations

- Talking with more young children since the design conception and including them and their families as co-designers could've given insights based on their interests and perspective and addressing social justice and accessibility issues. Unfortunately, given the time and logistical constraints, it was hard to find them, but more of their views could've been incorporated more actively.
- For further iterations it would be important to test the creation features of the design with young children and their families, maybe having a video with their grandparents and creating something that reflected their learning after the adventure outdoors and sharing it with them to learn if the right supports for sustaining engagement and motivation across the whole process are given.

References

Blake-Westa, J.C., Bers, M.U.: ScratchJr design in practice: low floor, high ceiling. Int. J. Child-Comput. Interact. (2023). ISSN 2212-8689. https://doi.org/10.1016/j.ijcci.2023.100601

Boulton, P., Thomas, A.: How does play in the outdoors afford opportunities for schema development in young children? Int. J. Play 11(2), 184–201 (2022). https://doi.org/10.1080/21594937.2022.2069348

Caribu. Mattel (2022). https://caribu.com/

Chawla, L.: Childhood experiences associated with care for the natural world: a theoretical framework for empirical results. Children Youth Environ. 17(4), 144–170 (2007). https://doi.org/10.7721/chilyoutenvi.17.4.0144

Dasgupta, S., Mako, B.: How "Wide Walls" can increase engagement: evidence from a natural experiment in scratch. In: Proceedings of the 2018 CHI Conference on Human Factors in Computing Systems (CHI 2018), Paper 361, pp. 1–11. Association for Computing Machinery, New York (2018). https://doi.org/10.1145/3173574.3173935

Fjortoft, I.: The natural environment as a playground for children: the impact of outdoor play activities in pre-primary school children. Early Childhood Educ. J. 29, 111–117 (2001)

Haines-Young, R., Potschin, M.: The links between biodiversity, ecosystem services and human well-being. In: Raffaelli, D., Frid, C. (eds.) Ecosystem Ecology: A New Synthesis, Ecological Reviews, pp. 110–139. Cambridge University Press, Cambridge (2010). doi:https://doi.org/10.1017/CBO9780511750458.007

Heckman, J.J.: Giving Kids A Fair Chance. MIT Press, Cambridge (2013)

Johnstone, A., et al.: Nature-based early childhood education and children's social, emotional and cognitive development: a mixed-methods systematic review. Int. J. Environ. Res. Public Health 19(10), 5967 (2022). https://doi.org/10.3390/ijcrph19105967

Klopfer, E., Squire, K., Jenkins, H.: Environmental detectives: PDAs as a window into a virtual simulated world. In: Paper Presented at International Workshop on Wireless and Mobile (2002)

Klopfer, E., Squire, K.: Environmental Detectives—the development of an augmented reality platform for cnvironmental simulations. Educ. Tech. Research Dev. 56, 203–228 (2007). https://doi.org/10.1007/s11423-007-9037-6

Technologies in Education, Vaxjo, Sweden

Land, S.M., Smith, B.K., Zimmerman, H.: Mobile technologies as mindtools for augmenting observations and reflections in everyday informal environments. In: Learning, Problem Solving, and Mindtools: Essays in Honor of David H. Jonassen, pp. 214–228. Taylor and Francis (2013). https://doi.org/10.4324/9780203111062

Louv, R.: Last child in the woods: Saving our children from nature-deficit disorder. Algonquin, Chapel Hill (2005)

Resnick, M.: Designing for wide walls. Design Blog: MIT Scratch Team, MIT Media Lab (2016)

Sandoval, W.: Conjecture mapping: an approach to systematic educational design research. J. Learn. Sci. 23(1), 18–36 (2014). https://doi.org/10.1080/10508406.2013.778204

Sobel, D.: Childhood and Nature: Design Principles for Educators. Stenhouse Publishers, Grandview Heights (2008)

Strife, S., Downey, L.: Childhood development and access to nature: a new direction for environmental inequality research. Organ. Environ. 22(1), 99–122 (2009). https://doi.org/10.1177/1086026609333340

Wells, N.M., Lekies, K.: Nature and the life course: pathways from childhood nature experiences to adult environmentalism. Child. Youth Environ. 16, 1–25 (2006)

World Economic Forum. Global Risks (2023). https://www3.weforum.org/docs/WEF_Global_Risks_Report_2023.pdf

Zimmerman, H.T., Land, S.M.: Facilitating place-based learning in outdoor informal environments with mobile computers. Techtrends Tech Trends 58, 77–83 (2014). https://doi.org/10.1007/s11528-013-0724-3

3D Animation to Address Pandemic Challenges: A Project-Based Learning Methodology

Diana Carvalho[1,2] (iD), Maria Cabral[2,1], Tânia Rocha[1,2] (iD), Hugo Paredes[1,2] (iD), and Paulo Martins[1,2(✉)] (iD)

[1] UTAD - University of Trás-os-Montes e Alto Douro, Quinta de Prados, 5001-801 Vila Real, Portugal
{dianac,trocha,hparedes,pmartins}@utad.pt
[2] INESC TEC, Rua Dr. Roberto Frias, 4200-465 Porto, Portugal
maria.i.cabral@inesctec.pt

Abstract. The use of 3D animations in medical education is becoming increasingly popular. Indeed, animations are an efficient way to present complex information, reducing time spent reading textbooks. Thus, in the educational contexts, animations can help students learn more efficiently, retain and better understand information. In addition to improving the learning experience, medical education is a highly important and necessary endeavor, as it can directly affect the lives of patients. These videos can be useful in emergency care instructions and provide information about how to administer CPR to a patient or help in forensic reconstructions; a doctor might explain a medical term to a patient in a friendly way, and they can also help patients understand complex procedures. We find it important to understand if students and schools, when challenged, take a role in their community preparedness for major health problems. Projects led by schools are addressed within educational scenarios focused on STEM education and developed under a relevant public health issue through their continuous engagement in open schooling approach. By implementing an educational scenario with a focus on 3D animation, and thus potentiate the use of this technology, we intend to help raise awareness on the public health theme.

Keywords: Public Health · Project-based Learning · Open Schooling · Design Thinking · Interaction Design · Human-Computer Interaction · 3D Animation · Multimedia

1 Introduction

Highly engaging educational content is essential to improving the overall learning experience [1]. A plethora of data exists that confirms what many health care professionals know intuitively: that multimedia content, including animation in education, is superior to text-based or static image education content [2]. When culturally suitable images and language are added, the efficacy is increases and the outcomes improve [3]. This scenario supports science and ICT teachers in exploring 3D animation, and the learning experience supports youths in understanding how Art and Technology may contribute to have high-quality 3D models useful for public health purposes [4, 5].

P. Zaphiris et al. (Eds.): HCII 2023, LNCS 14060, pp. 24–33, 2023.
https://doi.org/10.1007/978-3-031-48060-7_2

Indeed, 3D animation can be a useful resource to study and convey typical objects that otherwise could not be visually perceived, creating a visual explanation of things based on different media (i.e., multimedia contents) that could be difficult for people or even students to understand or build a mental model of, with only text or still imagery content [6]. As such, there is a need to enhance the readiness of communities in the public health perspective, thus strengthening the level of responsibility and proactiveness of young people and citizens in participating in public health-related measures. This will also improve the collaboration between stakeholders, schools and their communities to the benefit of education and wellbeing.

The COVID-19 pandemic has shown that scientific research and innovation can be a complex and slow process, with fundamental unpredictability in research findings and its own adoption by society. The collective challenges caused by the COVID-19 pandemic, amplified by the population modest health literacy [7], puts public health education in the spotlight, as it can boost awareness about risk factors, individual behaviors, determinants of health, and their relationship with living environments. It is crucial to promote science education to help communities be ready and better manage public health risks, in collaboration with stakeholders, schools, students and their families.

Project-based learning may help students address these themes. Indeed, by motivating students with hands-on projects, we can inspire students at low secondary level make informed choices regarding their health and, in the process, strengthen the schools' capacity to promote Science, Technology, Engineering, Mathematics (STEM) learnings with a focus on public health. In partnership with community stakeholders, such as local companies or laboratories, students may feel more integrated in their surroundings, thus advocating for an open schooling framework.

Our goal is to develop and implement an educational scenario regarding 3D animation that uses project-based learning to address these topics, strengthening the capacity of students in low secondary level and their schools to promote Science, Technology, Engineering, Mathematics (STEM) learning with a focus on public health issues. The scenario supports 8th grade science and ICT teachers in exploring 3D animations and environments using updated scientific/technical evidence. The learning experience supports youths in understanding and reaching high-level comprehension on how STEM may contribute to address these issues, contributing to evidence-based personal decision-making, and public policy.

Finally, we find it important to understand if students and schools, when challenged, take a role in their community preparedness for major health problems. By implementing an educational scenario with a focus on 3D animation, and thus potentiate the use of this technology, we intend to help raise awareness on the public health theme. This paper is organized as follows: Sect. 2 presents a background on project-based and inquiry-based learning and contexts of use of 3d animation; Sect. 3 provides a description of the educational scenario's topics and the methodology, how project-based learning is addressed, and how the scenario is enacted; Sect. 4 brings up the conclusions of the article and future work.

2 Background Overview

The use of 3D animations in medical education is becoming increasingly popular: animations can help students learn more efficiently, retain and better understand information [6]. A lot of content has been created for various disciplines or professional trainings: from galleries to simulations, animation provides a complementary learning experience [18].

Indeed, animation is becoming more and more popular in education. Many educational research demonstrate the effectiveness of animation for the cognitive recognition of artifacts, and how vision aids the thinking process [19]. 3D animation can be a useful resource to communicate typical objects that would otherwise not be visually perceived. For example, healthcare students present difficulties in achieving a conceptual understanding of 3D anatomy; also, misconceptions about physiological phenomena are persistent and hard to address. Thus, 3D animation has facilitated the understanding of complex phenomena [20].

By creating a visual explanation of things with more than only text or still imagery content, users can comprehend abstract concepts or complex artifacts more efficiently [18]. Realistic feeling, immersiveness and interactivity are always regarded as the criteria of choosing 3D animation content.

2.1 Project-Based Learning

Research has demonstrated that project-based learning is a valid approach to the development of critical thinking. When students are able to partake in problem-solving activities in real-world challenges, they present a high degree of responsibility, autonomy, and unsupervised work time when engaging in the projects [8]. This approach embraces a driving question, collaboration among students, communication skills, and interdisciplinary learning, continuously highlighting the importance of critical thinking [9, 10].

Indeed, teachers have an important role in motivating the students, launching focused queries but always providing a suitable distance for students to work freely. Through this goal-directed process for problem resolution, the tasks are carried out by students autonomously, having continued feedback from not only their peers, but also from experts [8].

Evidence suggests that project-based learning is capable of engaging and motivating middle grades learners [11, 21]. In fact, when students are allowed to choose a topic of their interest or relevance to their personal lives, they become naturally driven to commit to the work and aim for high quality results [12]. Even when compared to traditional educational approaches focused on long-term knowledge retention, project-based learning proves to be more effective [13], positively influencing students' performance, recollection, awareness and self-efficacy across different educational levels [14].

Also, for STEM-related disciplines, project-based learning is considered a powerful approach for learning due to the inclusion of realistic tasks [15]. This brings some challenges, e.g.: students taking responsibility for the learning process by setting goals and sustaining their motivation, the need of positive interdependence, individual accountability, equal participation, and social skills [16, 17].

3   Educational Scenario

The educational scenario is an integrated instructional and learning unit that propose a structured way for organizing the teaching-learning process. Following inquiry and project-based learning as key approaches for skills development, it engages students, teachers and the entire school community in research projects developed under a major public health topic: 3D animation to address pandemic challenges. The scenario includes learning goals, digital learning objects, a teaching-learning script with lessons plans, assessment methods, supplementary learning activities and a guide for school-based projects under the topic. The script brings STEM professionals to the classroom (e.g., researchers, public health specialists, engineers, project managers) and challenges students to manage projects and present their results in an open-schooling event.

3.1   Target Audience

The educational scenario was developed with a focus on basic education: 8th graders (14-year-old students). ICT classes are preferred to be the ground for the scenario enactment. However, it can be implemented not only by ICT teachers, but also these teachers can integrate other colleagues in the enactment of the scenario (e.g., ICT, visual education, science and English teachers), as it aims to be interdisciplinary.

3.2   Learning Goals/Competences

There are specific key STEM-related competences worth of mentioning, as well as those connected with 3D animation and innovation. Overall, the educational scenario expects key competences acquired within three scopes: knowledge, skills (abilities/competences), beliefs (attitudes/behavior). Also, there are explicit outcomes related to 3D animation.

Learning Goals. Expected overall outcome assessment:

- Uses tools for 3D animation.
- Analyzes 3D models.
- Identifies 3D environments and basic features.
- Animates basic elements in a 3D environment.
- Exports animations.

Knowledge. Expected outcome assessment regarding overall 3D animation concepts:

- Knows 3D animations' technical principles and workflows.
- Knows tools for creating 3D animations.
- Knows the shortcuts for fast animations.
- Understands the importance of 3D animations to address public health.
- Understands the 3D animation technical principles and workflows.
- Recognizes software basic features regarding rendering.
- Understands the importance of 3D animations to address pandemic challenges.

Skills. Expected outcome assessment regarding 3D animation basics, imagination, creativity:

- Animates 3D elements by combining process knowledge, computational design tools and application requirements.
- Technically uses 3D animation software.
- Recognizes appropriate proficiencies necessary for 3D animation.
- Understands the virtual environment.
- Identifies the differences of multiple 3D animation software.
- Can animate specific 3D objects.
- Recognizes that 3D animation can improve public health.

Beliefs. Expected outcome assessment regarding affective, attitudes and behaviours:

- Makes use of intellectual curiosity to solve problems.
- Makes use of creativity skills on new technologies in the development process of the solution.
- Makes use of imagination for designing real tools and materials.
- Believes that it is important to raise awareness on how 3D animation can help the community.
- Has intention to continue extending the skills and knowledge regarding 3D animation.
- Is aware of the democratization of 3D animation for public health.
- Believes that it is important to improve one's own personal capabilities.

3.3 Estimated Duration

The scenario is divided in different sessions and scope: 7 inside-classroom sessions of 40–45 min each (lesson 1 – lesson 7), plus 4 outside-classroom sessions of 40–45 min each (lesson 8 – lesson 11), for supplementary learning activities and the school project.

3.4 Teaching-Learning Activities (Lesson Plan)

Lesson 1: Introduction of 3D Animation. The teaching-learning script starts with a question "what is a 3D animation"? Students are divided into groups and asked to share their thoughts on what 3D animation means. This activity will contribute to reveal the students' initial ideas of the topic, helping teachers understand their skills and knowledge on the subject. Also, this activity should be presented to the students as a theoretical background of the 3D animation and its practical applications, and will be important for teachers to introduce the subject on what involves 3D animation and the current limitations of scientific evidence. Examples: level of skill required for professional and complex animations, 3D animations can be more limiting regarding styles and shapes than 2D ones in some situations, the resource consumption of the rendering process. A pedagogical glossary for technical terms and definitions is granted and distributed. Also, an introduction of 3D animations with several examples in different fields of study is presented: Architectural 3D Animations; 3D Character Animation; 3D Graphics; 3D Product Visualizations; Website 3D Animated Intros. Furthermore, several videos made with 3D objects in 3D environments are be demonstrated.

Lesson 2: The Democratization of 3D Animation. Brainstorming on the question "what can 3D animations represent"? Students are asked to Google, in groups, key definitions of a 3D animation and in which situations it can be used. Each group should produce at least three different sentences and examples; read them and select the main keywords for sharing, regarding the areas of expertise where 3D animations can be used. Then, they go to the flipchart or whiteboard and write the main keywords. The next step is a video presentation about the different types of animations. After, a discussion is mandatory about their previous definitions and keywords and their recent new knowledge about the topic learned. After a short conversation about the previous lesson, 3D animation and approaches are presented to be discussed. Also, this activity is important to provide awareness on public health challenges, their impact on STEM and their interactive parameters with specific examples, presenting ideas on how to tackle these issues resorting to 3D animation.

Lesson 3: The Key Principals of 3D Animation. The principles for 3D animation will be presented: from concept and storyboards, compositing and special VFX, to editing and final output. Simple exercises will be done, and replicated by the students, demonstrating the steps for creating an animation. Later, a debate will occur: "How can we 3D animate this object? E.g., a car engine". The aim is to show different basic objects and discuss and reveal which basic elements can be used to animate the objects shown.

Lesson 4: 3D Animation Basic Features (Rigging and Skinning). The teaching-learning script starts with the presentation of the animation rigging process, providing an individual hands-on approach. A video tutorial about 3D animation rigging is shown. Also, a step-by-step video on how to complete the rigging process will be presented. Following, individually, students will replicate the basic functionality in the computer. The same process occurs about skinning, with a 3D animation video tutorial about skinning being given. After a first approach on object rigging, a simple step-by-step tutorial will be provided explaining the skinning process and students will autonomously and individually do it. A debate will arise around the questions: "What does rigging do?"; "Why is the process of rigging important?"; "How can we complete the skinning process?".

Lesson 5: 3D Animation Basic Features (Animation Parameters). Students are introduced to parameters in 3D animation: types of parameters (video tutorial) + step-by-step tutorial. A group work is expected (the availability of laptops or tablets for group work is required). Students are organized in groups (1 group – 1 Animation) and invited to create simple daily objects animation. After, they will present their work to the colleagues.

Lesson 6: 3D Animation Basic Features (Camera Angles and Techniques). Students are introduced to camera angles and techniques in 3D animation. A series of video tutorials are presented regarding camera settings: students are shown the different settings to mimic real camera features, as focal length, depth of field, etc. A step-by-step tutorial on filming techniques is presented, as other options for moving a 3D camera are similar to those in movie making, including truck, dolly, motion blur, orbit and pan. A group work is expected (the availability of laptops or tablets for group work is required).

Lesson 7: 3D Animation Basic Features (Exporting/Rendering). To finalize the first complete exercise in the 3D animation environment, students will learn what is the process of export/render, which differs from the normal process regarding 3D modelling. A manual is granted and students are invited to explore the software's different render settings. Later, a presentation and group activity takes place (also works as qualitative assessment): students must present their animated objects and for each presentation, in groups, the other students identify which features were used or which other solutions may have been used to improve the present work.

Lesson 8 – Onward. After building and presenting their work, students are challenged to model other 3D objects in groupwork. This is the School Project described next.

3.5 School Project and Supplementary Educational Activities

The final school research project focuses on the following topics: importance of 3D animation; technical features and principles of 3D animation; possible applications of 3D animation in public health topic. Supplementary educational activities are expected during this stage. devoted to the preparation of the school project, these activities include (but are not restricted to):

- Teleconference with STEM professionals (e.g., engineers, designers, medical doctors, researchers). Students make questions to experts with a particular focus on: a) future academic choices and career paths; b) identifying new professions in new fields of industry 4.0.
- Visits to field-related laboratories (e.g., FABLABs). Students are shown the working environment and dynamic of a FABLAB. Here, students are provided with the opportunity to make questions to experts within the laboratory, see the processes and go along with the working dynamic. These activities are relevant for students' connections with STEM curriculi, careers and professionals.

The school project's goal is to animate a 3D object to address communicable diseases challenges.

Method. Lesson 8 to 11 will be dedicated to the school research project. Students are organized in groups; each group addresses one object based on the daily pandemic challenges lived. The project challenges each group of students to: 1) identify and represent their progress in the form of essay responses and using Likert scales to show their improvement from the first lesson to the last; 2) animate and present an object with what they have learned throughout the teaching-learning sequences and the ideas that emerged during the teleconference with experts. A competition and reward for the best 3D objects will take place at the final open-schooling event.

Teaching-Learning Process Milestones. There are defined milestones for the final project: 1) Students will be able to propose solutions for 3D animation of basic objects; 2) Students will be able to communicate the findings, motivations and limitations of various 3D animations considered in the work process; 3) Students will be able to identify and communicate the importance of 3D animation to address pandemic challenges but also the role Innovation; 4) Students will be able to use technical argumentation to justify policy choices.

Organization of the Open Schooling Event. At the end of the lessons and development of the school project, an open-schooling event is organized. Each project output (3D animation) is presented by the students in a community setting (e.g., exposition center, municipality, garden, museum, science fair) in a 3D prepared environment (all apparatus included). Students will prepare a pitch on how 3D animation can address pandemic challenges and technical speeches to motivate peers to new technologies and environments will occur. Students, parents, school community and relevant local stakeholders may attend the event and are introduced on the topic on how 3D animation can be used to address pandemic challenges. Furthermore, the scenario has a multidisciplinary approach, such as in art, design, engineering and mathematics. The final results of the competition and reward for the best 3D objects will take place, as well as the dissemination of evidence recommendations via social, community and conventional media. The goal is to formulate a final public debate around the topic at hand.

3.6 Assessment Method

The outcome assessment if twofold: qualitative and quantitative. The qualitative approach involves the student's final school project itself: the creation of a 3D animation within a STEM context. As for the quantitative approach, a series of questionnaires need to be implemented, focusing on the impact assessment in terms of students' knowledge, skills, attitudes and behaviors.

The process assessment – assessment of the teaching-learning sequence – will comprise an observation grid: reaching the target audience, and extent; implementation of the scenario as planned; learning scenario enactment as expected; organizational issues to be solved; duration of the teaching-learning sequence; number of people exposed; score for likeability regarding students, schools, parents, stakeholders.

4 Conclusion

Regarding the 3d animation educational scenario, teachers will need to identify the different levels of expertise amongst students, as to guarantee that the less experienced ones have higher support, either from teachers or colleagues. As this is an extremely technical program and deals with third-party software, with subjects being presented that are out of the school national curriculum, students will not be as comfortable with the topics at hand and may need further support and motivation.

Indeed, in the proposed educational scenario, students have an active voice in the entire learning process. By participating in doing projects, not only do they go beyond provided information, but the learning process also takes place outside of the classroom environment. Indeed, students share the results of their work with other students, their parents, local community members, community leaders and policymakers. This approach creates opportunities for building an open schooling ecosystem. That means students need to develop autonomy and, to do so, they must decide the paths to follow in their projects, combining the teacher's guidance. This brings some challenges, e.g.: students taking responsibility for the learning process, the need of positive interdependence, individual accountability, equal participation, and social skills. This encourages communication and leadership, while encouraging them to evolve into next projects. Indeed, project-based learning in school environments supports the strategy to create high-quality inquiry projects related to public health education that guide students in collecting evidence and thus engaging the local community in open discourse processes.

After the piloting of the educational scenario in the current year within educational hubs, these will be evaluated and refined. Results will be presented and discussed, and novel iterations will be proposed.

Acknowledgements. This project has received funding from the European Union's Horizon 2020 research and innovation programme under grant agreement No 101006468.

Disclaimer: The sole responsibility for the content on this publication lies with the authors. It does not necessarily reflect the opinion of the European Research Executive Agency (REA) or the European Commission (EC).

References

1. Almara'beh, H., Amer, E.F., Sulieman, A.: The effectiveness of multimedia learning tools in education. Int. J. Adv. Res. Comput. Sci. Softw. Eng. **5**, 761–764 (2016)
2. Liu, C., Elms, P.: Animating student engagement: the impacts of cartoon instructional videos on learning experience. Res. Learn. Technol. **27**, 1–31 (2019). https://doi.org/10.25304/rlt.v27.2124
3. Knapp, P., Benhebil, N., Evans, E., et al.: The effectiveness of video animations in the education of healthcare practitioners and student practitioners: a systematic review of trials. Perspect. Med. Educ. **11**, 309–315 (2022). https://doi.org/10.1007/s40037-022-00736-6
4. Dhulipalla, R., Marella, Y., Katuri, K.K., Nagamani, P., Talada, K., Kakarlapudi, A.: Effect of 3D animation videos over 2D video projections in periodontal health education among dental students. J. Int. Soc. Prev. Community Dent. **5**(6), 499–505 (2015). https://doi.org/10.4103/2231-0762.170526. PMID: 26759805; PMCID: PMC4697236
5. Kapoor, K., Singh, A.: Veterinary anatomy teaching from real to virtual reality: an unprecedented shift during COVID-19 in socially distant era. Anat. Histol. Embryol. **51**, 163–169 (2022). https://doi.org/10.1111/ahe.12783
6. Hansen, M.: Versatile, immersive, creative and dynamic virtual 3-D healthcare learning environments: a review of the literature. J. Med. Internet Res. **10**(3), e26 (2008). https://doi.org/10.2196/jmir.1051
7. Mheidly, N., Fares, J.: Leveraging media and health communication strategies to overcome the COVID-19 infodemic. J. Public Health Pol. **41**, 410–420 (2020). https://doi.org/10.1057/s41271-020-00247-w
8. Thomas, J.W.: A Review of Research in Project-Based learning. Autodesk Foundation, San Rafael (2000)
9. Unaizahroya, I., Maryani, E., Ratmaningsihn, N.: curriculum integration across subjects in secondary schools through project-based learning. Sainteknol J. Sains dan Teknol. **20**(1), 13–19 (2022)
10. Shahrizoda, T.: Project-based learning as an effective teaching method. J. Ethics Divers Int. Commun. **2**(2), 54–56 (2022)
11. Yetkiner, Z.E., Anderoglu, H., Capraro, R.M.: Research summary: project-based learning in middle grades mathematics (2008). http://www.nmsa.org/Research/ResearchSummaries/ProjectBasedLearninginMath/tabid/1570/Default.aspx

12. De Vivo, K.: A new research base for rigorous project-based learning. Phi Delta Kappan **103**(5), 36–41 (2022). https://doi.org/10.1177/00317217221079977
13. Strobel, J., van Barneveld, A.: When is PBL more effective? a meta-synthesis of meta-analyses comparing PBL to conventional classrooms. Interdisc. J. Probl. Learn. **3**(1) (2009). https://docs.lib.purdue.edu/ijpbl/vol3/iss1/4
14. Bilgin, I., Karakuyu, Y., Ay, Y.: The effects of project based learning on undergraduate students' achievement and self-efficacy beliefs towards science teaching. EURASIA J. Math. Sci. Technol. Educ. **11**(3) (2015). https://www.ejmste.com/article/the-effects-of-project-based-learning-on-undergraduate-students-achievement-and-self-efficacy-4397
15. Capraro, R.M., Scott, S.W.: Why PBL? why STEM? why now? an introduction to STEM project-based learning: an integrated science, technology, engineering, and mathematics (STEM) approach. In: Capraro, R.M., Capraro, M.M., Morgan, J.R. (eds.) STEM Project-Based Learning: An Integrated Science, Technology, Engineering, and Mathematics (STEM) Approach, pp. 1–5. SensePublishers, Rotterdam (2013). https://doi.org/10.1007/978-94-6209-143-6_1
16. Kagan, S.: Cooperative Learning. Kagan Cooperative Learning, San Clemente (1994)
17. Johnson, D.W., Johnson, R.T., Holubec, E.J.: Circles of learning. Interaction Book Company (1993)
18. Xiao, L.: Animation trends in education. Int. J. Inf. Educ. Technol. **3**(3), 286–289 (2013)
19. Card, S.K., Mackinlay, J.D., Schneiderman, B.: Readings in Information Visualization: Using Vision to Think. Academic Press, San Diego (1999)
20. Silén, C., Wirell, S., Kvist, J., Nylander, E., Smedby, Ö.: Advanced 3D visualization in student-centred medical education. Med. Teach. **30**(5), e115–e124 (2008). https://doi.org/10.1080/01421590801932228
21. Santos, C., et al.: Science education through project-based learning: a case study. Procedia Comput. Sci. **219**, 1713–1720 (2023). ISSN 1877-0509. https://doi.org/10.1016/j.procs.2023.01.465

Data Collection and Feedback Preparation in Virtual Reality Training Systems

Arnis Cirulis[(⊠)] [iD], Lauris Taube, Toms Amsons, and Alvis Sokolovs

Faculty of Engineering, Vidzeme University of Applied Sciences, Valmiera, Latvia
{arnis.cirulis,lauris.taube,toms.amsons,alvis.sokolovs}@va.lv

Abstract. Nowadays virtual reality (VR) technologies are considered an increasingly important part of the educational process, especially in areas where practical work in laboratories is essential. It even helps students test situations that are impossible to perform in a real laboratory. Such training environments save costs, improve results and reduce training time. Thanks to visualisation technologies and special effects, it is possible to depict phenomena, like magnetic fields, radio waves etc. to better understand a topic. To achieve meaningful results with the use of virtual reality technologies, it is important that the designed training environment is capable of generating tasks and evaluating results instead of just instructing the participant to follow predefined operations based on a tutorial. This paper describes a training system that provides evaluation based on LEAN principles, so the gathered data and generated feedback at the and of a training session provide information in various levels of detail, including correct/incorrect operations, sequence, time spent, distance walked, score and suggestions. With this approach, the instructor can more accurately evaluate the trainee's knowledge level, and the trainee is more engaged and takes greater responsibility for the subject due to the active learning experience, as opposed to step-by-step training.

Keywords: virtual reality · mechatronics training · interactive assignments · evaluation

1 Introduction

Virtual reality (VR) technologies are becoming more and more accessible to all of us, providing interactive and immersive 3D content. But interactive content is not enough, especially in the field of education. Interaction should be merged with environmental intelligence. Existing VR technologies and the displayed content ensure high quality, allowing for visualization of real workplaces while minimizing the symptoms of cybersickness and ensuring longer periods of operation within the VR experience. What's more, in addition to replicas of real workplaces, there is an opportunity to develop virtual workplaces of the future, where trainees can freely experiment and learn without endangering their health and damaging expensive laboratory equipment. Environmental intelligence describes what level off action can be taken during the training process and what feedback the trainee receives after training sessions, and how the next session is prepared.

P. Zaphiris et al. (Eds.): HCII 2023, LNCS 14060, pp. 34–46, 2023.
https://doi.org/10.1007/978-3-031-48060-7_3

Virtual reality (VR) training systems provide various benefits like the visualization of scenarios that cannot be replicated in real life and captured in training videos. With interaction techniques participants can navigate through predefined instructional scenes and gain knowledge by reading, listening and watching. The next level of the training process is the practical execution of instructions using guided tutorials. This is important for industrial training where different assembly, disassembly and maintenance tasks play a major role. While this approach is commonly used in training systems, it may not provide the necessary skills, highlighting the need for improved training methodologies.

Training participants need to receive feedback on accomplished tasks. That is why assignments and task evaluation should be integrated in VR training systems to provide a full training cycle. The VR-Mech system was designed and developed to implement the concept of assignments and evaluation. This system is intended for the practical work of mechatronics studies and provides three scenes: training, practice and assignment. The VR-Mech solution runs on the standalone Oculus Quest 2 head-mounted display and is utilized in courses for the mechatronics study program "Production and Service Organization" and "Electric Drive" at Vidzeme University of Applied Sciences. The VR-Mech assignment mode provides six criteria for evaluation. The system was fully completed and implemented into courses, thus providing the research team with valuable information on user experience, the participant training process and evaluation accuracy in comparison to a real instructor. Several techniques for improving interaction were developed and implemented. This research paper presents information on the design and development of the VR-Mech system, as well as its results from testing and implementation. These findings are crucial for the development of similar systems in the future, as the widespread use of the metaverse will increase the availability of VR training environments to society, providing greater accessibility to interactive content and improving the acquisition of skills during the training process.

2 VR Environment Complexity and Training Methods

Before a virtual reality (VR) system is designed and developed, it is important to assess its need, as well as the format in which the activity in the virtual environment will take place. Studies show that there is no fundamental difference whether the 3D experience is used in desktop mode, or in VR mode with VR glasses [1]. There are a number of nuances that affect it. It should be determined whether the virtual learning experience is in a static place or if there is a need to move around in it. Implementation of movement depends on several factors, including the duration of the experience, the required actions, and the level of physical effort required.

We classify three basic modes in the implementation of actions (see Fig. 1). In the introductory scene, in which the experience mode is chosen, the participant has the opportunity to learn the types of controllers and interaction, choose a full body avatar, change movement and other parameters. The first mode is the training mode, where participants are presented with a sequence of actions along with descriptions in the environment. The participant is an observer who chooses the next/previous step of the instruction with the simplest possible dialogue windows, then observes the animations and reads the explanatory information about each of the steps. The VR-Mech tutorial consists of seventeen steps with adjustable animation speed and the ability to connect a three-phase electric motor to electricity at the end of the scenario, turn on the controller, start the motor, adjust the revolution speed, visualize the operation of the motor in cross section (transparency), turn on magnetic field visualizations.

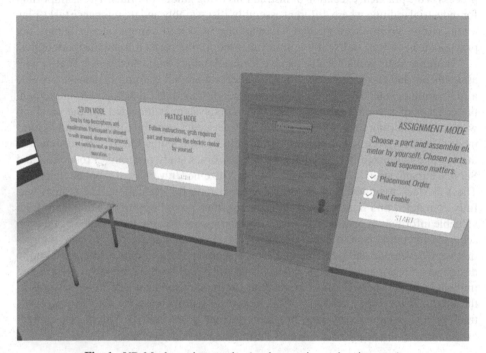

Fig. 1. VR-Mech runtime modes (study, practice and assignment).

In practical mode, each assembly step is presented as a task. The trainee gets familiar with the task and follows detailed instructions for its execution. Instead of watching animations, the learner must take the motor parts from a table and put them in the correct position. The parts that need to be picked up are identified.

The assignment (test) mode is like an exam in which a summary of the assignment is given, but there is no indication as to how it should be performed. The student must come up with the correct sequence and parts to be used. All parts are located in warehouse cabinets, parts boxes. The only feedback received by the participant during assembly is information on whether the correct part is inserted into the engine. It is measured when the part is released at the moment of insertion. Since the sequence is imperative, it is important to perform the operation as long as the correct part is inserted. In assignment mode, an alternative mode is available where no feedback is given and the participant can assemble the parts in the wrong order and then take a specific part out if it interferes with the execution of subsequent steps.

All previously-mentioned modes can be implemented on different VR equipment. The results of the VR experience are also influenced by VR equipment kits and application areas, and, as technologies develop, the most suitable equipment kits for a single experience can change [2]. Currently, the VR-Mech solution prioritizes experience availability and ease of use, utilizing the Meta Quest 2 VR glasses. In this case, greater attention is paid to graphics optimization, therefore visually the result will not be as good as if a computer with a powerful graphics card is used for rendering. Controllers are utilized for interaction to facilitate precise operations, as they are more effective and convenient compared to hand tracking. Hand tracking is not suitable for movement in space. However, if the physical space is large enough, movement on foot is possible. Since room dimensions are often limited, teleportation or controller-based movement should be utilized.

The next chapter will provide a detailed discussion of the technical execution and functionality of VR-Mech, which is essential in assessing and planning the amount of work, team size, and budget required for the time-consuming process of designing and developing the environment. The training mode is predefined and static, so its development is not complex. The practical mode adds the use of controllers. The most extensive and complex to realize are the assignment scenarios, since the environmental intelligence is higher, and the program scripts must take into account a lot of conditions, measure, log, compare all actions, carry out evaluations, provide feedback and recommendations if any operations are implemented incorrectly.

3   Prototype Model for Assignment and Data Management

This section describes the approaches and technologies used in the development of VR-Mech core logic. Object assembly setup is achieved as follows. The chosen object model needs to be edited in a specific way in Blender 3D modelling software before it can be imported into Unity. Depending on the object that needs to be assembled, it has to be divided into sets of parts, for example – an electric motor needs to be divided into two sets as the covers of the motor can be assembled separately. This way the model is more optimized for use in a 3D environment. When the cover is assembled, the separate parts get disabled and a set model is enabled. These actions are only necessary for parts that can be assembled separately from the object's main body, for example, the motor's frame (see Fig. 2).

When the model is divided into necessary sets, it can be imported into the Unity engine. The first script that needs to be added to the model is "Correct order tests" (see Fig. 3).

It has four functions:

- Fill list – gets all the divided parts into a list.
- Clear list – Clears current list.
- Export list – exports the current list to a.txt file for editing outside Unity (Can be found in Assets/Scripts/SortedList.txt
- Import list – User can import the list from the.txt file.

When a list is filled, it can be sorted into the correct order by dragging and dropping list elements (see Fig. 4).

Fig. 2. Object 3D model set and separate parts.

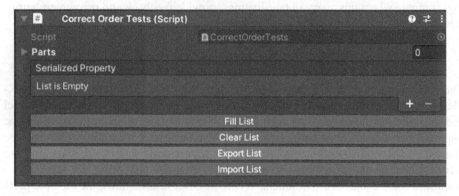

Fig. 3. Correct order tests script.

The list UI (user interface) also has one integer field and two Boolean fields. The integer field is for sorting the motor parts into sets. These also have to be in order starting from zero. With these sets the model can also be divided into more sets, but not necessarily separate models. This is for training purposes, so the user does not get confused when assembling the object. These sets just disable the next set placement points (see Fig. 5).

The first Boolean field needs to be set to "true" for parts that need to have the same ID when sorting. For example, screws. The second Boolean value needs to be "true" if there are multiple parts in a row that should have the same ID when sorting (see Fig. 6).

The second script that needs to be added after the list is sorted is the System Generator script (see Fig. 7).

Fig. 4. Correct order tests script filled list.

Before pressing the buttons, Socket (Placement point) material needs to be added. This script has several functions:

- Generate Sockets – This button generates sockets (Placement points) for all the separate parts and sets (Only the 3D divided sets) for the object.
- Add Parent constraint – Adds parent constraint component to parts of the object and sets the source to corresponding socket.
- ObjectID – Adds a script to parts and a unique ID for the part if the first Boolean is "false" in correct order, if it is "true" for several components in a row, the first part's ID is given to the rest of the parts.
- Generate Colliders and Grabbables – Adds colliders and grabbable scripts to objects.
- Place Set sockets – Automatically places the required sockets for the 3D separated sets.
- Add outlines – Adds outline script for parts.
- Clear – Clears all actions.

Fig. 5. Placement points.

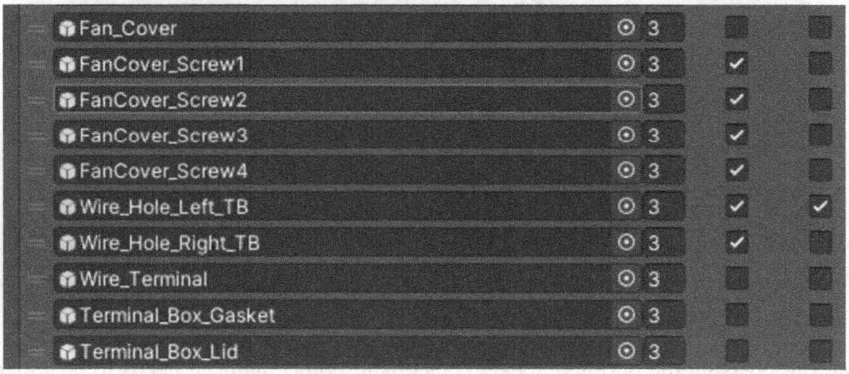
Fan_Cover
FanCover_Screw1
FanCover_Screw2
FanCover_Screw3
FanCover_Screw4
Wire_Hole_Left_TB
Wire_Hole_Right_TB
Wire_Terminal
Terminal_Box_Gasket
Terminal_Box_Lid

Fig. 6. Boolean values.

These buttons should be pressed one by one starting from Generate Sockets. The Clear button should only be pressed if all the added components and scripts need to be removed.

Assembly grading is done with the Grading controller script. This one script is responsible for all grading functionality and all the visual effects that are associated with grading, like displaying the end results, showing +1 or −1 point effects and other things.

All of the lists shown after the experience are compared to the original list that was made in the Correct order tests script. The grading is based on how the user places the object. These lists are created while the user is playing the experience and each action is logged in the corresponding list (see Fig. 8).

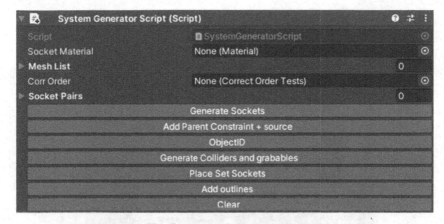

Fig. 7. System generator script.

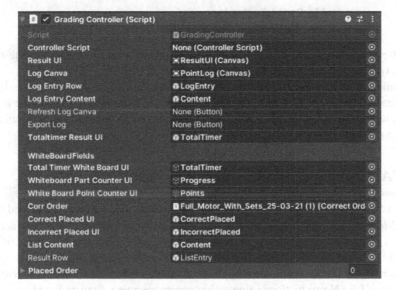

Fig. 8. Grading controller script.

The point system (assignment evaluation) adds a point for every part that is placed in the correct order and subtracts a point for a part that is placed in the incorrect order.

There are three UIs that appear when the task is completed:

- First UI shows all parts placed and how many times each part has been picked up and how long it has been held (see Fig. 9).
- The second UI shows points gained and subtracted from the total score and for what part.
- The third UI shows the Total timer, how many parts are placed and how many are left to place, total point count, teleport count, distance teleported, distance walked.

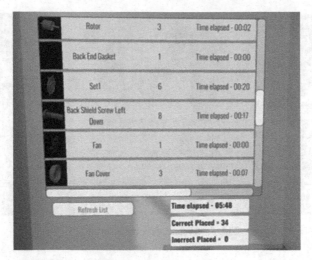

Fig. 9. Feedback at the end of assignment session.

In the first two UIs the part list is displayed in the placed order. Both of these lists can be exported to a.txt document and saved in the build folder.

Detailed result logging is necessary to help learners apply good practices from LEAN principles in organizing the production process during practical activities. In the following chapter, the need for LEAN will be outlined, as the VR-Mech solution offers much more than just learning motor assembly.

4   LEAN Principles and Feedback Provision

The term "LEAN production" originated in Japan in the 1950s and was developed by the Toyota Motor Corporation. It is considered a philosophy and approach to manufacturing that aims to eliminate waste, reduce costs, and increase efficiency by optimizing the value-adding activities in a production process. Nowadays LEAN philosophy is applied to different fields of activities including services and education [3–5]. There are five main principles of LEAN production: value, value stream mapping, flow, pull and perfection. Value – identifying the value that a product or service provides to the customer and ensuring that every step in the production process adds value. Value stream mapping: analysing the steps involved in delivering a product or service and identifying areas of waste and inefficiency in the process. Flow: ensuring that the production process flows smoothly, with minimal interruption or delay. Pull: producing goods only when they are needed, based on customer demand, rather than in anticipation of demand. Perfection: continuously striving to improve the production process through the elimination of waste and the pursuit of efficiency. Implementation of LEAN principles can reduce production costs, improve product or service quality, and increase customer satisfaction. This makes Lean philosophy attractive to many companies including small and medium size businesses, but it demands a company-wide commitment to continuous improvement, involving all employees in the process of identifying and eliminating waste and improving processes. As new industries develop in the Vidzeme region in the upcoming years, there is a predicted increase in demand for professionals with knowledge and skills in LEAN principles. Hence there is a demand from industry, particularly from medium-sized and large manufacturing companies, to include LEAN principles in the study curriculum. Including more content regarding LEAN in study courses can have overall benefits for students, such as the development of problem-solving and data analysis skills, as well as fostering a continuous self-improvement mindset. In the mechatronics study programme at ViA the general Lean production principles are presented to students during the "production and service management" course, where students have practical game-based production planning and execution training. However more practical and reality-based training should be considered to give students an insight into different production processes and services to be able to apply obtained skills in different situations.

VR-Mech collects essential criteria to be able to organize the study process according to LEAN principles. The collected criteria include time used, distance travelled, incorrect and unnecessary actions, frequency of use of the warehouse, working environment and others. The collected data allows the instructor to better evaluate the student's performance. Furthermore, groups of students are able to compare results with each other in a valuable way, to conduct analyses and discussions about the potentially best and most successful action in process organization. To achieve reasonable use of LEAN principles in virtual reality, user experience is crucial, as well as user openness and readiness to use virtual reality. The fifth and last section provides user feedback from training sessions.

5   Project Implementation and Study Results

To gather user opinions, questionnaires were administered after each individual study session, with participation from students and teachers in the mechatronics study program. For most users it was their first virtual reality experience. In order to more successfully prepare students for VR sessions, an approximately 4-min-long educational video was prepared and sent out, which gave a first glimpse of what the students can expect and will have to do. This is important to remove the fear of the unknown and inform about the tasks to be performed and the skills required to carry them out. This video explains the basic operations and use of the controllers, as well as the basics of each learning mode and how they are selected (see Fig. 10).

In the initial phase, it is difficult to statistically assess the benefits of using LEAN principles in VR mode, because no long-term data has been collected in the relevant study courses. However, the detailed information obtained through the facilitated supervision is an essential aid for instructors to more accurately evaluate the participants' performance and the effectiveness of the VR-Mech system in teaching LEAN principles. Additionally, the experience is important for the participants as it allows them to become more familiar with the learning objectives, tasks, and tests, which are designed to be easy to use and closely mimic real-life scenarios. The participants were asked to evaluate their experience with VR-Mech through a questionnaire consisting of nine questions. Figure 11 shows the six most important results:

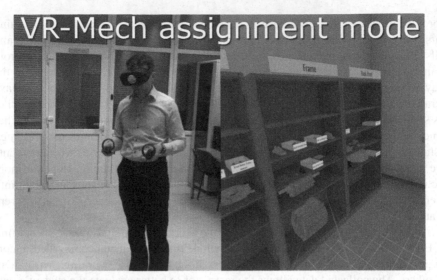

Fig. 10. Video tutorial for use of all training modes.

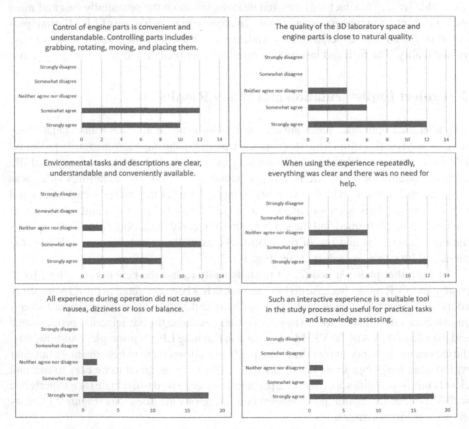

Fig. 11. Survey results from experience users (mechatronics students).

- Control of engine parts is convenient and understandable. Controlling parts includes grabbing, rotating, moving, and placing them.
- The quality of the 3D laboratory space and engine parts is close to reality.
- Environmental tasks and descriptions are clear, understandable and conveniently available.
- When using the experience repeatedly, everything was clear and there was no need for help.
- The experience did not cause any nausea, dizziness or loss of balance during operation.
- Such an interactive experience is a suitable tool in the study process and useful for practical tasks and assessing knowledge.

6 Conclusions

The development of a virtual reality learning system is a labour-intensive and time-consuming process, so in the beginning it is important to define the stages of project development and the tasks to be performed at each stage. In the case of VR-Mech, these are the different levels of use of the system. The development team began with the implementation of the simpler levels and progressed to the more technically complex levels.

It is important that the system includes actions and activities that are useful in various specialized courses, as well as allows any type of user to get to know the possibilities of virtual reality. In addition to mechatronics students, schoolchildren and students of other study programs also participated in system trials.

Mitigating cybersickness is crucial for any VR learning system to ensure user safety and a positive experience. This is necessary to prevent participants from experiencing discomfort and negative effects, which could ultimately discourage them from using similar learning systems in the future.

The knowledge and lessons acquired during the development of the VR-Mech system are valuable for the creation of other related training systems, particularly in terms of implementing various levels, ranging from basic instructions to assessment scenarios with an evaluation mechanism. This is crucial for expediting the development of such systems in the future and facilitating the adaptation of current systems.

Ensuring cross-platform support is crucial for the successful implementation of VR systems in education. While the availability of virtual reality headsets in educational institutions has increased, it is still important to ensure that these systems can be accessed on traditional computer systems. Additionally, it is important to consider the compatibility of the system with the next generation of VR glasses. This requires dedicating resources to system maintenance and resolving compatibility issues to ensure seamless and consistent use of the system across various platforms.

The VR-Mech prototype and scripts can be reused in other training experiences without much investment and advanced programming skills.

Although the VR-Mech system is fully functional and survey results confirm that it can be used in the study process, certain goals have been set for the improvement of this system in the future. This training system is intended to be supplemented and improved, providing simultaneous multi-user access, integrating a free roam test mode, and also continuing to integrate good practice in the use of LEAN principles in production processes.

Acknowledgements. This work is a part of Next Generation Micro Cities of Europe project finished in 2021 and funded by the European Regional Development Fund. Activity 5.2.4 name was Virtual reality training solution for mechatronics studies. Research and development activities took place at the Faculty of Engineering at Vidzeme University of Applied Sciences, and specifically, in the Virtual Reality Technologies laboratory (ViA VR-Lab). The laboratory was established in 2009 in cooperation with the Fraunhofer Institute Virtual Reality Training and Development Centre (Magdeburg, Germany) and the University of Agder (Kristiansand, Norway), pointing to its long history and years of experience. ViA VR-Lab specializes in virtual and augmented reality system design and development for various fields (industry, medicine, safety training, education, tourism etc.) by developing technological innovations in multi user environments, large scale position tracking, simulation visualization, content management, evaluation and assignments, cloud-based rendering, sensors, IoT and digital twins, wearable sensors and training therapy, artificial intelligence.

References

1. Bailey, S.K., et al.: Using virtual reality for training maintenance procedures. In: Proceedings of the Interservice/Industry Training, Simulation and Education Conference (2017)
2. Xie, B., et al.: A review on virtual reality skill training applications. Front. Virtual Real. **2**, 645153 (2021)
3. Gil Vilda, F., Yagüe-Fabra, J., Sunyer, A.: From lean production to lean 4.0: a systematic literature review with a historical perspective. Appl. Sci. **11**, 10318 (2021). https://doi.org/10.3390/app112110318
4. Khomyakov, N.V., Cheremukhina, Yu.Yu.: Toyota production system: the origins of lean manufacturing. Qual. Innov. Educ. 37–41 (2022). https://doi.org/10.31145/1999-513x-2022-5-37-41
5. Helmold, M., Yılmaz, A.K., Flouris, T., Winner, T., Cvetkoska, V., Dathe, T.: Lean management in higher education (LHE). In: Helmold, M., Yılmaz, A.K., Flouris, T., Winner, T., Cvetkoska, V., Dathe, T. (eds.) Lean Management, Kaizen, Kata and Keiretsu: Best-Practice Examples and Industry Insights from Japanese Concepts, pp. 229–238. Springer, Cham (2022). https://doi.org/10.1007/978-3-031-10104-5_17

The Autonomous Platform Using the Markov Chain

Karim Elia Fraoua[1]([envelope]) and Amos David[2]

[1] Université Paris Est Marne-La-Vallée, Equipe Dispositifs d'Information et de Communication à l'Ere Numérique (DICEN IDF), Conservatoire national des arts et metiers, Paris-Est Paris-Ouest, EA 7339 Serris, France
fraoua@u-pem.fr
[2] Université Lorraine, Equipe Dispositifs d'Information et de Communication à l'Ere Numérique (DICEN IDF), Conservatoire national des arts et metiers, Paris-Est Paris-Ouest, EA 7339 Serris, France

Abstract. This work focuses on the use of the Markov chain to optimize the learning path for learner. We observe that most of them during their online courses can be are victims of boredom which pushes them to give up their courses and consequently do not obtain the certificate, of which they had the ambition to obtain the formation and the diploma. We based our works on Q-Learning methods that seem to meet our need to satisfy students' demand for titles and certificates without getting bored.

Keywords: E-learning · Markov Chain · Q-Learning · Adaptative learning

1 Introduction

Our approach is part of an attempt to improve online and distance learning courses in order to allow everyone to follow an adapted and motivating training course. These two forms of course organization to which we will return largely reflect the efforts made by the scientific community to improve the quality of online training. Several communities and disciplines contribute to this effort. There is the community of pedagogical engineers who make efforts without it being part of a pedagogical school. Indeed very often focus on the use of tools and their variations, which in itself is certainly useful, but we note at least in university education in the master's cycle, that this does not correspond to the expectations of many students. We have, in an unpublished survey on the use of online course platforms without interaction with teachers, found that many adapt to this situation and follow the course on platforms like Moodle because this is done within the framework of their curricula, without the scripting taking into account the differentiated levels of the learners. Moreover, the connection figures show a very high rate since the connection is also a tool for measuring attendance, which de facto is the reality in physical class, since the student, although present, can do something else just like during remote lessons even when the camera is on. It is therefore important to understand the reasons for this attitude on the part of students and what constitutes boredom during

P. Zaphiris et al. (Eds.): HCII 2023, LNCS 14060, pp. 47–57, 2023.
https://doi.org/10.1007/978-3-031-48060-7_4

the course, and to propose alternative solutions in order to increase the effectiveness of online training. Indeed for various reasons, these trainings are more and more present, either because companies wish to perform their collaborators because of developments of tools, methods, processes... or because the same collaborators wish to follow distance training, to improve their skills, and do them according to their own availability, which makes it possible not to physically mobilize the presence of the speakers during the dispensation of the course. We have, like others, proposed the use of Chatbot, which have human capacities, particularly from an emotional point of view, even if this does not seem crucial except in the case of intervention in the class forum. [1].

We have borrowed concepts from several disciplines to justify this use, first of all affective computing [2] to think about this Chatbot and its contribution to exchanges. To achieve this we took into account two aspects, the profile of the learner. This approach remains fundamentally important in the definition of the scripting of the course and the tutoring that must be provided to them. The second point is that we believe it is important to reproduce another aspect of the training, namely the role of the teacher who, by his knowledge of the students, responds in a differentiated way because he knows well the emotional character of the latter. The second aspect is that according to our reading of decision-making models of learning from neuroscience, and based on the work of Damasio, that the emotional character has an important aspect. This is consolidated by the work of which shows that taking charge of this emotional aspect can improve learning abilities [3]. Dehaene's work clearly shows the place of neuroscience in learning process [4].

The contributions of the concepts of information and communication are also very useful. Some of our work and the work that inspired us, were based on it [5], just like the choices made by the learners and the place of cooperation in this learning space [6], whether this space itself or its artefacts, by already developing the idea of the reward which is perceived here as being the diploma, and also the acquisition of the skills associated with this diploma. The emotional aspect to consolidate our previous remarks has been the subject of an interesting look by Martin-Juchat [7].

The objective of this work is to build a platform capable of taking into consideration the choice of the student on the basis of an autonomous course built in such a way as to ensure at least a base of skills necessary to obtain the diploma or the certification. Since the appearance of the concept of ITS (intelligent tutoring system), the world of online training has evolved a lot [8]. Initially, it was a question of setting up a device allowing learners to follow online courses supposed to reproduce the courses that took place in person. This gave rise to this vision with the emergence of models which have since continued to develop, with the implementation of educational scenarios with the ADDIE (Analysis Design Development Implementation Evaluation) [9] or SAM (Successive Approximation Model) [10]. All these models have been extensively reviewed and improved in order to provide learners with the tools necessary for their development. Other educational capsules have also been developed and have made it possible to improve the effectiveness of online training, by including serious games [11].

We see that learning materials are increasingly available on the web, making it an excellent source of educational information, with the introduction of recommendation systems to encourage course selection. Several training courses are now offered and often in connection with renowned universities. In the context of technical training that promotes the acquisition of skills, learners seem to be motivated, even if the attrition rate measured between the number of learners following the training and those who pass the exam or certification, is significant. According to our surveys of our students, it is possible that students are not sure of their acquisitions because it seems to us that the training path is not so simple. Based solely on the recommendation system, even if it is interesting, it does not necessarily meet the student's profile. The risk is that based on the recommendation, we could have learners who would be bored in this course even if it is less. Indeed, the lack of sufficient knowledge of the learning domain means that learners are unable to build the best path to achieve the learning objectives. Moreover, as part of our Master Data training, we support our students in this certification process, supported for this by the fact that we ourselves are certified in many areas, whether on Amazon, Microsoft or Google. The uses and techniques assume a good knowledge of the domain and therefore it leads to this abandonment, if a learner takes courses that are not adapted to his profile, his level of knowledge, or if the student is not aware of the difficulties encountered. There is too much knowledge that students are often unaware of and that also exists, except that it is not proposed in the implementation of the course.

We have noticed that some platforms are offering more and more modules or capsules integrated as part of a course. Some, however, already have some relevant knowledge that allows them to acquire these new skills, and can without following all of these courses lead to these objectives. In the case of a traditional face-to-face course, the learners generally have homogeneous knowledge, which is not necessarily the case for learners following an online course. In this regard, we wish to build a collection of didactic courses and other sources of knowledge which could be recommended to learners at the start of their journey through a Quiz analysis and which do not seem necessary to us in our way of thinking. This approach will be dynamic in the sense that at each course, various choices will be available with the benefit/risk that is displayed if the learner chooses a new module if he has completed the current task or prefers to skip it. This idea is based on the principle of the Markovian process, within the framework of the Q-Learning model [12]. Q-learning is a machine learning technique based on reinforcement programming theory. It learns by trying to maximize the reward obtained for each action. Q-learning is an algorithm that can be used in many applications. The letter 'Q' designates the function that measures the quality of an action performed in a given state of the system.

This will make it possible to recommend a training course to learners, and its improvement during the course by offering learners the best collection to acquire, to make their course the best possible to achieve their goal without getting bored.

2   Identify Emotions in the Text

A recommendation system is a system whose objective is to support a user in making a decision on the consumption of a good and that he can make this choice with help thanks to this system [13]. Basically, he must from the information left by users in order to advise him of the courses that have a great chance of interesting him to better meet his final objective. Here we find the idea of recommendation by peers when they have the same profile.

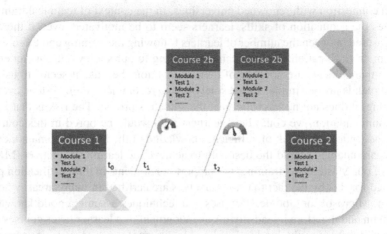

Fig. 1. Proposal of modules according to the results of in-situ tests in each course

We assume that each course has a place in the course and which would come from a function r which associates a user and a course (u,c). Such a system is represented by a function r which, to a couple (user, course) associates a note corresponding to the interest that the user could have for the item:

$$r : U \times C \to R$$

where U is the set of users and C the set of courses.

Knowing then the efficiency of r, of the course c followed by the user u, we can predict the rate which would be attributed to this course c by the user uj who would be interested in the course c. For this we must know all the users u_s having graded the course c, as well c_u which are the rated course by u.

This mapping is then a good starting point to predict the grade that our learner should give to courses that could accompany him. We can map his training path, and then he can decide if he wants to do this or that course, indicating each time the place of this course in view of his results on the previous course, or during the course itself in order to avoid him getting bored.

This may correspond in some respects to Adaptive Learning Design, which has been reviewed by Fonseca among others with a view to improving [14]. Research in adaptive learning dates back to the 1990s. One of the main areas of research in adaptability in e-learning is mainly centered on learner modeling. Learner modeling is the foundation of adaptive learning [15].

The improvement approach to allow better efficiency of online courses is studied and implemented such as constructivism, socio-constructivism, network theory, connectivism and many others [16, 17]. Some scholars have developed schemas to make constructivist or social constructivist models more effective. Tools, capsules or content have been structured to make these models more suitable [18].

There is a plethora of works on constructivist or socio-constructivist models, and in the latter case it is recognized that online group work promotes these interactions, which allow learners to learn from their peers, the trainer becomes more a facilitator than a transmitter of awareness. The constructivist views learning as the process of constructing knowledge by building understanding on the basis of past experiences, and inputs, moving from teaching to guiding learners so that learners themselves construct their knowledge [19].

The underlying difficulty of the Adaptive Learning Design approach is that it is necessary to know the profile of the learner as well as his mental state, ... It is for this reason that we recommend this approach where the learner decides on its own, by observing the state of the system, where it is in its learning path, the "recommendations" on a complementary, alternative or next course to achieve its objective based on the reward to be achieved (see Fig. 1).

To summarize our action and our model, we must design our platform on a Markovian approach where the MDP (Markov Decision Process) is a tuple $\{S, A, P, r, \gamma\}$ which will be explained below.

The training course at the start is given by the expert. We are experimenting with this approach ourselves in the context of setting up courses on the Datacamp platform and in which we observe recommendations from the students themselves to say to their classmates: "I recommend this or that course to you". Students with access to course content can determine which resources are likely to be of interest to another user. We encourage students to post their badges or certifications on LinkedIn afterwards. This approach that we have put in place allows us to structure a recommendation process based on the idea of reward and which has already been obtained by peers.

The latter is offered at each moment of the course in order to allow the achievement of the final objective without risk and without boredom. Markov decision processes are defined as controlled stochastic processes satisfying the Markov property, assigning rewards to state transitions.

They are defined by a set (S, A, T, p, r) where:
S is the state space in which the process evolves;
A is the space of actions ai that control the dynamics of the state;
T is the space of time t;
p() are the transition probabilities between states;
r() is the reward function on transitions between states (Fig. 2).

Fig. 2. Markov process

In this process, we see that the learner can be deviated from his main trajectory at any time, without his choice depending on the previous choice, which was not necessarily foreseen at the beginning. In this process, the learner is no longer in a state of risk or uncertainty, the future choice depends only on the achievement of his goal, based on rational choices, driven only by the knowledge base he has at a given time.

The prospect theory can be used here to build a training plan with the least amount of risk [20]. However, this approach can be time-consuming and forces the learner to follow a course set in advance. Our approach is rather the opposite, namely to reduce the training time and make it an à la carte training adapted to the learner's profile with the least possible risk for the learner in his perspective of obtaining the diploma. It is in this perspective that the Markov chain seemed relevant to us and also because it fits well with the Q-Learning approach.

The Markov process is an efficient process for modeling a particular class of discrete states space systems. It suffices to know the result of an action on an agent in information asymmetry and the reward of this action to form an incentive action. However, he can take a risk of try-ing another course by estimating the loss he may have with regard to the time required for the training. These losses can be modeled with the criteria of Laplace, Hurchwitz, Wald, Minimax or Savage that we will recall. This situation is resumed here (Table 1):

Table 1. Matrix of regrets

	Initial state	Final state
Situation 1	−1	3 with choice 1
Situation 2	−1	0 with choice 2
Situation 3	−1	1 with choice 3

2.1 Optimist Criterion

In this behavior, the student selects the best final state possible. We maximize the gain; so that the best choice is the first situation (take course 2) with a gain of 3 which is the rate allocated to the course [21].

2.2 WALD's Criterion

In this criterium, the behavior of the student is more regret driven than gain driven. It is a classical MaxMin strategy, the decision consists in minimizing the regret. In this case, the best choice is situation 2, the student being afraid to express regret [21].

2.3 LAPLACE's Criterion

In this reward model, the agent maximizes an average regret. This criterion supposes that the student considers that the states are equiprobable.

Choice 1 leads to a gain of: $(-1+3)/2 = 1$

Choice 2 leads to a gain of: $(-1-0)/2 = -0, 5$
Choice 3 leads to a gain of: $(-1+1)/0 = 0$

The best choice is situation 1.

2.4 HURWICZ's Criterion

In the Hurcwicz's approach, we ponder the gain by a coefficient α which is applied to the strategy. The more strong regret is pondered by the α coefficient while the lowest is pondered by $(\alpha - 1)$ [21].

For example, with $\alpha = 0, 6$ (optmistic approach) we obtain:

Course 2 the gain is: $-1*0.4 + 3*0.6 = 1, 4$
Course 3 the gain is: $-1*0.4 + 0*0.6 = -0.4$
Course 4 the gain is: $-1*0.4 + 1*0.6 = 0, 2$

The best choice is situation 1 in this situation.

2.5 SAVAGE's Criterion

In this situation, and for each state of nature, one seeks the strongest regret. We will obtain the matrix of regrets on the basis of a calculation for each decision in each state of nature, the regret that is to say the difference between the strongest regret retained and the expected regret [21].

Savage advises to choose the strategy that makes minimum regret possible. We then take the decision that minimizes the maximum regret and therefore we try to minimize the shortfall. It is based on the gain matrix, and it holds for each state of nature the decision the one that ensures the best gain and it subtracts from each column the other gains made (Table 2).

Table 2. Matrix of regrets

Regret value for each situation
MAX – VALUE i.e. 3- V
3–3 = 0
3–0 = 3
3–1 = 2

The best decision is therefore 1 where the minimum is 0 because the student must choose a course and cannot stay on the spot.

We recommend the installation of a gauge allowing to visualize at each moment the risk incurred, if the learner chooses to do another course (Cf. Fig. 1). The objective for us is to direct it towards maximizing gains.

We can represent a Markov process as an influence diagram. At each instant t, the action a is applied in the current state st, influencing the process in its transition to the state st + 1. The reward rt is emitted during this transition. This choice is called a policy. We see here that if a learner is in Si and that he sees the reward he has by taking this course that can encourage him to take this course, before going to the next course, and the risk he can take, if he takes the next course without having this policy. The chain consists of a set of courses which the learner can access at any time by skipping the intermediate courses, knowing the risk taken and which will be measured according to the various criteria mentioned above. The advantage here is that the learner can take any course, at any time by integrating into their approach the optimization of their course, according to their profile and their level of knowledge.

3   The Learning Style

Some learners prefer visual content to textual content, just as they are guided by three elements that come from the affective domain, namely BDI (Belief, Desires and Intentions) [22]. For this, it is necessary to understand the learning styles to allow an adapted creation and the development of more effective educational path. Determining learning styles is therefore an important step, because it gives us useful indications of their specific preferences. For this we can base ourselves on the Felder and Silverman questionnaire to establish a profile of each learner beforehand to better design the educational content [23].

4   What is Q-Learning?

Q-Learning is an approach proposed by Watkins to solve Markov Decision Processes (MDP) with incomplete information [24], it is considered an adaptive method, and it is based on Q learning. The principle is based as in the Markovian equation that by performing an action a, the agent moves from a state s to a new state s and receives a reward r. In this context, the learner will seek to maximize his total reward, namely obtaining the diploma or certification without getting bored or taking the risk of skipping a step at the risk of failing in the final step. We therefore indicate to each learner, the optimal action in each stage based on the greatest reward over the long term and which is the weighted sum of the mathematical expectation of the rewards of each future stage from the state current. Which then gives the following equation:

$$Q : S \times A \to \mathbb{R}$$

By initializing the Q function, the learner will see at each step and during this step, the reward and the new state (which depends on the previous state and the current action). This gives in terms of equation:

$$Q[s, a] := (1 - \alpha)Q[s, a] + \alpha(r + \gamma \frac{Max}{a'} Q[s', a']$$

where s' is the future state, s is the previous state, a is the action chosen by the agent among the proposed actions, r the reward received, a is between 0 and 1, called learning factor, and g is the discount factor.

Here we see two important factors that appear, the learning factor and the discount factor. For the learning factor, namely a, it varies from 0 to 1 and denotes the learning of a person during the course. If the value is zero then there has been no learning and when this value reaches 1 then the agent still ignores everything it has learned so far and will only consider the latest information. The discount factor γ determines the size of future rewards.

We therefore see that it is a method of reinforcement learning which is based on the search for the optimal policy of a Markov decision process (MDP). Learning is done in episodes, where each episode begins in an initial state which is chosen by the expert in this case and which can be reviewed by the learner, then reach another state with the condition of obtaining the trajectory necessary to reach the end state. This condition is defined by the designer of the learning system. This allows you to establish an optimal strategy by knowing what action should be taken to optimize your journey independently (Fig. 3).

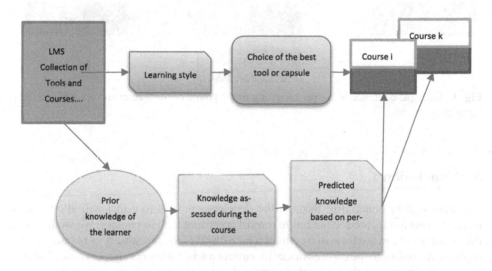

Fig. 3. Definition of the autonomous training process

This learning method makes it possible to establish a strategy, and to know what action can be taken in each state of the system in order to optimize its course with the condition of succeeding in the final step. The designer can set up various actions to inform the learner about his future chances of success.

We thus define a state-action value function denoted Q which makes it possible to determine the potential gain, that is to say the long-term reward, Q[s,a], brought by the choice of an action a in a state s following an optimal policy. Here we find the principle of the Markovian model of optimizing a journey according to future gains. We support this approach with the risks of losses and by an optimal choice which takes into account these calculations of loss. We see through this example, the underlying idea of our method.

We see that Q-learning makes it possible to compare the probable rewards in each action and that is why we have integrated the risk calculation in order to eliminate the loss of course as much as possible, for a learner who considers that he can go faster and take accessible actions to optimize your strategy. This progression of formation by following all the states or skipping some of them, can give this kind of configuration (A, V1, V2, D3, F) (Fig. 4).

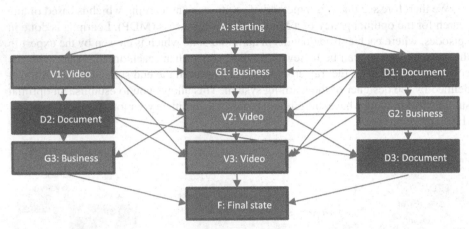

Fig. 4. Example of choice of course according to the profile of the learner and according to his knowledge

5   Conclusion

Our approach to materialize through the development of a tool that will allow each learner, at each stage, to see the future reward according to their choices. We would like this display to be in the form of a counter which displays the probability of obtaining the diploma according to the choices made, in particular when a learner chooses to accelerate his course, but also to show him that certain choices are useless because they do not do not allow you to optimize your future earnings in order to avoid boredom.

References

1. Fraoua, K.E., Leblanc, J.-M., David, A.: Use of an emotional chatbot for the analysis of a discussion forum for the improvement of an E-learning platform. In: Zaphiris, P., Ioannou, A. (eds.) HCII 2020. LNCS, vol. 12206, pp. 25–35. Springer, Cham (2020). https://doi.org/10.1007/978-3-030-50506-6_3
2. Picard, R.W.: Affective Computing. MIT press, Cambridge (2000)
3. Elias, M.J., Zins, J.E., Weissberg, R.P.: Promoting social and emotional learning: guidelines for educators. In: ASCD (1997)

4. Dehaene, S.: How We Learn: The New Science of Education and the Brain. Penguin, UK (2020)
5. Qazi, A., Hardaker, G., Ahmad, I.S., Darwich, M., Maitama, J.Z., Dayani, A.: The role of information & communication technology in elearning environments: a systematic review. IEEE Access **9**, 45539–45551 (2021)
6. Wahlstedt, A., Pekkola, S., Niemelä, M.: From e-learning space to e-learning place. Br. J. Edu. Technol. **39**(6), 1020–1030 (2008)
7. Dumas, A., Lépine, V., Martin-Juchat, F.: Le tournant affectif dans les études en communication organisationnelle. Commun. Organ., 75–93 (2023)
8. Nwana, H.S.: Intelligent tutoring systems: an overview. Artif. Intell. Rev. **4**(4), 251–277 (1990)
9. Allen, W.C.: Overview and evolution of the ADDIE training system. Adv. Dev. Hum. Resour. **8**(4), 430–441 (2006)
10. Jung, H., Kim, Y., Lee, H., Shin, Y.: Advanced instructional design for successive E-learning: based on the successive approximation model (SAM). Int. J. E-Learn. **18**(2), 191–204 (2019)
11. Fraoua, S.C., Zara, G., David, A.: Learning by serious game: case study. In : ICERI2020 Proceedings, pp. 5643–5650. IATED (2020)
12. Hammoudeh, A.: A Concise Introduction to Reinforcement Learning. Princess Suamaya University for Technology, Amman (2018)
13. Jannach, D., Zanker, M., Felfernig, A., Friedrich, G.: Recommender Systems: An Introduction. Cambridge University Press, Cambridge (2010)
14. Alier, M., Casañ Guerrero, M.J., Amo, D., Severance, C., Fonseca, D.: Privacy and E-learning: a pending task. Sustainability **13**(16), 9206 (2021)
15. Chrysafiadi, K., Virvou, M.: Student modeling approaches: a literature review for the last decade. Expert Syst. Appl. **40**(11), 4715–4729 (2013)
16. Sangrá, A., Raffaghelli, J. E., & Guitert-Catasús, M.: Learning ecologies through a lens: ontological, methodological and applicative issues. a systematic review of the literature. Br. J. Educ. Technol. **50**(4), 1619–1638 (2019)
17. Bower, M.: Pedagogy and technology-enhanced learning. In: Design of Technology-Enhanced Learning, pp. 35 63. Emerald Publishing Limited (2017)
18. Hammad, R., Khan, Z., Safieddine, F., Ahmed, A.: A review of learning theories and models underpinning technology-enhanced learning artefacts. World J. Sci. Technol. Sustain. Dev. **17**(4), 341–354 (2020)
19. Bada, S.O., Olusegun, S.: Constructivism learning theory: a paradigm for teaching and learning. J. Res. Method Educ. **5**(6), 66–70 (2015)
20. Trepel, C., Fox, C.R., Poldrack, R.A.: Prospect theory on the brain? toward a cognitive neuroscience of decision under risk. Cogn. Brain Res. **23**(1), 34–50 (2005)
21. Zaraté, P., Belaud, J.P., Camilleri, G. (eds.): Collaborative Decision Making: Perspectives and Challenges, vol. 176. IOS Press (2008)
22. Sinhababu, N.: The desire-belief account of intention explains everything. Noûs **47**(4), 680–696 (2013)
23. Ortigosa, A., Paredes, P., Rodriguez, P.: AH-questionnaire: an adaptive hierarchical questionnaire for learning styles. Comput. Educ. **54**(4), 999–1005 (2010)
24. Watkins, C.J., Dayan, P.: Q-learning. Mach. Learn. **8**, 279–292 (1992)

From Spoken Words to Prompt Triggers: Technical Iterations of a Semi-Intelligent Conversational Agent to Promote Early Literacy

Brandon Hanks[1]([✉]) [iD], Grace C. Lin[1] [iD], Ilana Schoenfeld[1] [iD], and Vishesh Kumar[2] [iD]

[1] Massachusetts Institute of Technology, Cambridge, MA 02139, USA
{bhanks,gcl,ilanasch}@mit.edu
[2] Northwestern University, Evanston, IL 60201, USA
vishesh.kumar@northwestern.edu

Abstract. AI technology is rapidly evolving and has vast potential for educational applications. This paper focuses on the technical iterations that took place as our project team developed a semi-intelligent conversational agent (CA) that uses speech recognition to fire spoken prompts to promote caregiver-child interaction as they read books aloud together. Situating this work in a design-based research methodology, the technical iterations reported here are part of the iterative "build" phase. (Easterday et al., 2018; Hoadley & Campos, 2022). The CA app promotes conversations between caregivers and children by listening to the human dyads as they read, matching their spoken words to marker words that would pinpoint the page of the storybook the dyads are reading, and playing a prompt corresponding to the page. The dynamic system that supports the app involves multiple components: web accessible services, data processing services, and human outputs, and it has gone through a combined seven iterations in three prototypes. Though a very small part of the DBR cycle, the technical iterations presented here have the potential to inform others interested in incorporating text-to-speech and other AI technologies into educational applications. We close with considerations for future directions.

Keywords: Educational Technology · Early Literacy Software · Conversational Agent

1 Introduction

Decades of research have shown that back-and-forth conversations between more advanced readers, such as the parents, and novice readers, such as children, are essential for children's early literacy development [1–3]. These conversations can take place as caregivers and their children shop at the grocery store [4, 5] or as they read books aloud together. In fact, strategies have been developed to help caregivers engage children in dialogic reading practices [6–8]. For example, as caregivers read a book to their child, they may pause and ask children questions related to what they have been reading. These questions might include asking the child what they see on the page (e.g., "Do you seen an elephant?"), explaining vocabulary words (e.g., "What does the word vegetarian

© The Author(s), under exclusive license to Springer Nature Switzerland AG 2023
P. Zaphiris et al. (Eds.): HCII 2023, LNCS 14060, pp. 58–69, 2023.
https://doi.org/10.1007/978-3-031-48060-7_5

mean?"), or relating to something in their everyday life to a picture they are seeing in the book (e.g., "What did you do the last time you went to the playground?").

This backdrop of dialogic reading practices is the inspiration behind our educational technology app. In this paper, we will highlight how we sought to promote dialogic reading practices through innovative technologies. Specifically, we will begin by establishing the methodology with which we carried out our work. We will then describe how the app works from both the user's perspective and, to get a sense of the dynamic system, from the perspective of a datum. We will also highlight the various challenges that surfaced in our rounds of technical iterations. Finally, we will conclude with the future directions.

2 Design-Based Research

Adhering to the advice of Reeves [9] that educational technology researchers should make the goals more explicit, our work presented in this paper focuses on the development goals and follows the iterations of development research. Specifically, the design and development of the dialogic reading app is grounded in design-based research (DBR; [10, 11]). DBR is a methodology used by educational researchers, designers, and developers to design and test out innovative approaches or technologies to improve learning. The process of DBR often involves multiple cycles and iterations, often beginning and ending with design principles and values [9–11]. After identifying our design values and providing a general overview of how the app is supposed to function, we highlight the iterations during the "build and test" phases of the DBR cycle.

2.1 Objectives and Design Values

Once "dialogic reading practices" had been identified as a goal, the team went on to establish design principles/values for the app. In particular, the team decided that the app must be:

- Easy to use
- Neither a distraction nor the centerpiece of the experience
- Accessible

In particular, the concept is to have the technology scaffold caregivers who otherwise may not be following best-practices of dialogic reading while reading with their children. It should generate dialogue between the pair, and should neither be a distraction nor the centerpiece of the experience. We envisioned caregivers and children reading a physical book together while a conversational agent (CA) listened and guided the conversations they were having. The human dyads' conversations are the focal point the app serves to promote. Therefore, unlike eBooks where the human dyads had to directly interact with the technology (e.g., touch the screen to move on to the next page), we did not want the caregivers or the children to stare at a screen/device. Because of the notably lower language and literacy levels of students from socioeconomically disadvantaged backgrounds [12], we also settled on targeting families with lower annual household income. With this in mind, the technology must be accessible to most people (i.e., no AR or VR that requires a high-end phone).

3 The App: How It Works

3.1 Overview of the User's Experience

To use the app, the caregiver (or the child) first chooses a physical book they want to read (see Fig. 1). They select the book on the app and start the session. Once the "Start" button is pressed, the CA starts listening in. When they read to a page with a preset prompt, the device will play a chime sound alerting the human dyads that the CA is about to speak. Following the chime, the CA will fire the audio prompt. These prompts are meant as conversation starters between the caregiver and the child (i.e., the CA is not meant to engage in a conversation with the dyads). The prompts also serve to model for the caregivers the types of dialogic questions they could ask. For example, as a caregiver reads page 4 of Corduroy where the writer describes how Corduroy was sad as Lisa (a child in the story) and her mom walked away, a chime will sound followed by the CA asking, "Why did Corduroy feel sad?" The human readers will then talk about what it means to feel sad, why Corduroy was sad, etc., before they resume reading the book.

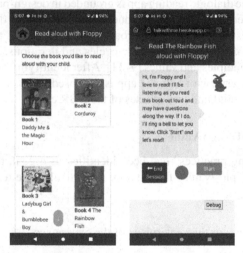

Fig. 1. Screenshots of the app. On the left, we see the book selection screen. On the right, we see the screen (Prototype 3 Iteration 7) once the participant selected *The Rainbow Fish*.

3.2 Architecture

For the CA to work, a dynamic system was designed to connect the various moving pieces (see Fig. 2). The system involves multiple components: web accessible services (represented by ovals in Fig. 2), data processing services (rectangles in Fig. 2), and human outputs (diamond in Fig. 2). An essential feature of the system, marker words were created using n-grams: The books' texts are first sent to the backend, where a script written by our developer automatically determines the types (e.g. bi-grams, tri-grams) and density of n-grams on each of the books' pages. N-grams unique to individual pages are then identified as potential marker words. Content developers wrote dialogic questions for the pages of the books containing unique marker words and then sent both text and audio-recordings of the questions to the backend. These questions were then ready to be played aloud any time a user's recorded spoken words matched a recognized marker word.

Let's track the journey of a snippet of voice data to understand the system's connections better. When a caregiver and a child want to read with the app, the caregiver opens the app, grants microphone access, selects a book, and starts reading out loud. The voice data snippet originates when the caregiver presses the "start" button on the app, and leaves the front end immediately. When it reaches the backend, the snippet is appended to a short mp3 file that then travels to Google and is transcribed into text. The text returns to the backend, which converts it into an n-gram and tries to match it against n-gram marker words. If a matching n-gram marker word is found, the prepared audio prompt from the content developers is triggered and sent to the user-facing frontend, where it is played on the caregiver's device. Seemingly simple, this entire process continues until the reader decides to pause or end the read-aloud session. A final copy of the entire mp3 audio file is sent to a secure archive. Along the way, metadata are created to indicate session information, e.g. the time the caregiver accessed the app, the book selected, and other de-identified details about the user. These metadata are also sent via the backend to the secure archive.

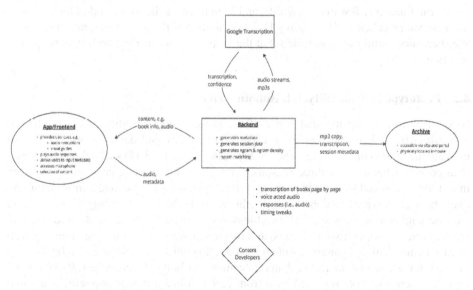

Fig. 2. Interconnected system for the conversational agent app.

4   The App: Technical Development Iterations

The system was not built all at once. Three prototypes that went through a combined seven iterations were created prior to testing the app in usability and efficacy studies. The first prototype, for example, used a robotic voice for the dialogic reading questions, but had all of the essential functions. The second prototype iterated on the user interface, swapped the robotic voice for a human recorded voice, and addressed feedback from educational and literacy experts. The third and final prototype was the one deployed for testing. Following, we detail the technical iterations from the Proof of Concept to the final prototype (see Table 1 for an overview).

4.1   Proof of Concept

The initial proof-of-concept was a Python script that used PyAudio [13] to capture audio, Google Cloud to transcribe it, and a system call to mpg321 [14] to play MP3 files. A second Python script was written to identify unique words in a body of text which could be used to determine when to play the MP3 files. That second script would then associate these unique words, aka "markers," with book pages and associated MP3 files. Next, some sentences were written as filler content, and converted to MP3 files via Google Text-To-Speech. Finally, the second script was run against a test book, The Very Hungry Caterpillar, which had been transcribed to a text file. We immediately discovered that the book contained very few unique words, and so to increase the likelihood of having more markers we switched to The Snowy Day and added unique word pairs, aka "bigrams." We then successfully demonstrated that the entire process worked both in concept and practice.

4.2   Prototype 1: Scalability, UI, Robotic Voice

Next, to both increase the scalability of the process, compatibility across platforms, and minimize disk use (which is at a premium on low-end devices), we decided to migrate the system onto the web. (See Table 1, Iterations 1 ~ 3.) For a back-end, we used Django with Channels for three reasons. First, since the proof-of-concept was written in Python, it allowed for simple porting of the demo codebase. Second, while streaming over the web is typically done via something like RTMP, constraining all of the data and messaging to a websocket allowed less system complexity. This allowed our tiny team of one developer, two designers, and two researchers to minimize maintaining web infrastructure. Third, Django is full- featured, allowing for development to be focused on the interfaces and data, rather than on the nuts-and-bolts of webservers. PyAudio and mpg321 were also both replaced by a front-end vanilla JavaScript app which captured audio via the browser's getUserMedia [15] method and played audio by loading MP3s into HTML audio elements. The MP3 responses were generated algorithmically from written text which had been sent to Google Text-To-Speech for voice synthesis, and stored in the back-end for transmission over the websocket. These responses consequently sounded robotic, due to their synthetic nature.

We then collaboratively generated user stories for three groups of users: reading dyads, researchers, and content experts. Web apps were then written to support the three

Table 1. Technical Iteration Descriptions. Each major prototype is separated by a line. After the Proof of Concept, Prototype 1 went through iterations 1 ~ 3, Prototype 2 went through iterations 4 ~ 6, and Prototype 3 is currently on the 8th iteration.

Iteration #	Description	Feedback or Issues	Revisions
0	Proof of Concept	Not scalable	Moved to web architecture
1	Robotic voice with simple questions in browser	Needed more UI	Added more dyad UI, such as ability to pause recording and animated character
2	More dyad UI	Not enough books Prompts were not triggered well Needed better artifact capturing	Added interface to easily add more content Better n-gram matching and filtering
3	Researcher/Content Creator interfaces	Dyad UX issues such as how interruptive the voice was	Added chime, more indicators (markers), and debug messages for the dyad
4	Dyad UX enhancements	Questions were too simple or too complicated (depending on age of the kid) Timing of prompts not great	Created new questions Implemented new timing mechanism
5	Human-recorded voice	Timing issues remain	Added another timing mechanism Experimented with new books with more markers per page
6	Content creator timing tweaks	Audio not playing correctly in certain browsers	Migrated to standardized Android devices
7	Android devices/Usability Study	Requested repeat button Some prompts fired at the wrong place	Android App Repeat functionality added Revised n-gram lists
8	Android App/Efficacy Study	Data analysis is currently underway	Stay tuned

use cases, and an SFTP research repository was created to store session artifacts (such as MP3s) from the system. While a monolithic app, such as a Single Page Application (SPA), would likely have made the system feel more cohesive, we chose this approach both to separate the roles further and make it easier to iterate on features specific to those roles. For example, adding blinking lights to the dyad interface could be done without touching any of the other user groups' interfaces.

4.3 Prototype 2: UX Enhancement, Human Voice, and Tweaks

We completed an initial user test following the first prototype. Based on feedback, we enhanced the user experience by polishing the questions asked and swapping out the robot voice with human voice. We also uncovered technical problems with prompt timing and frequency during this initial test (see Table 1, Iterations 4–5). To address these issues, we experimented with two alternative mechanisms for transcribing the audio. The original mechanism involved streaming the audio directly from the back-end to Google, which would return a transcript upon speakers' natural pauses. The new second mechanism had Google return transcriptions immediately, though it had similar issues since it often contained errors and low confidences. The new third mechanism would create MP3s from the audio stream on a fixed interval of 8 to 13 s for submission to Google, which seemed to improve both the frequency and reliability of responses. A toggle was created to select which mechanism was to be used per book, and we tested each to determine which worked best. For most books, mechanism three with intervals of 8, 9, or 10 s worked well, though the original mechanism was retained for two of the test books.

Our subsequent user testing revealed yet another technical obstacle (Table 1, Iteration 6). At this point, the app had been solely an in-browser app to minimize hard-drive space. However, this benefit was not able to be realized since we found that some Chrome browser versions were preventing the audio files from playing successfully. Specifically, the anti-spam measures built into the browsers were the culprit. To solve the issue with media blocking, we moved the front-end into our standalone coaching app, which was built in Expo/React for Android devices.

4.4 Prototype 3: Android App and Continued Iterations

The third prototype was then created as an Android app to address these compatibility issues. Due to our values of accessibility and the belief that the technology should work even on low-end devices, we acquired older versions of Android phones for use in our first formal usability test. We standardized each device, ensuring that each phone had identical installs, operating systems, and permissions set. Since we were intending to deploy only into browsers at this time, this allowed us to minimize issues that might arise that were not related to our technology. It also allowed us to focus our attentions specifically on the technology, and not on attempting to troubleshoot with a distant user. To be specific, once the user clicked on a book in the app (see Fig. 1 left), they were taken to the browser-based page (see Fig. 2 right) where they could then start their reading session.

After the installation, we mailed the phones (with return envelopes) to the 20 participating families (18 mothers, 2 fathers; 10 boys and 10 girls) in our formal usability study. The dyads read with and without the app in remote Zoom sessions as well as at-home reading sessions. During the first Zoom session, participants first read without using the app. We then introduced them to the app and dialogic reading strategies. They then read again with the app. After providing feedback to the team, we asked the participants to read at home using the app before their next session scheduled 2–4 weeks later. The second Zoom session repeated largely the same procedure, though families no longer needed the app introduction.

After gaining the extended exposure to the app, the families revealed that the app was easy to use (see [16] for a more detailed report of the usability results). However, they also echoed our findings from previous iterations, such that the timing of the conversational agent could be off. Some participants even thought that it was because of their own reading pace. Because they occasionally missed a question prompt, multiple participants asked for a repeat button on the app.

We built the repeat function into the newest iteration of the app (see Fig. 3) and addressed the timing concern this time by manually checking the auto-generated unique n-grams and removing the ones that were not so unique after all (e.g., "shimmer" was a marker word on page 3 of The Rainbow Fish while "shimmery" was a marker word for page 18).

In playtesting the new set of marker words, we also discovered a rarely occurring bug in which two sessions could cross-communicate triggers, due to how the temporary MP3s that were being sent to Google Cloud were stored. For example, one dyad could be reading a book at the same time as another dyad, which might trigger incorrect prompts to be activated in the second dyad's session. Similarly, dyad 2's reading could trigger the incorrect prompts for dyad 1. While we did not observe this happening in any studies, it may have been responsible for some of these early timing issues that we encountered during in-house testing. To ensure future users do not encounter prompts from the wrong books, we resolved the issue by implementing additional codes to prevent collisions among the temporary MP3s.

Additionally, because, among other things, we wanted to investigate how the app could function on participants' own devices, this newest version is completely contained within the app (see Fig. 3); participants are no longer taken to a browser page to start their reading session. The newest version had now been implemented in an efficacy study on whether the educational app could help caregivers improve their dialogic reading practices. Data analysis from the efficacy study is still underway, though the analyses from the usability participants' reading sessions with the app suggest the conversational agent indeed promoted conversations between caregivers and children [17].

5   Discussion

One persistent issue that gave us a lot of trouble was the timing of the responses by the agent. This is a commonly recognized challenge in the design and creation of conversational agents [18, 19], especially balancing the tension between processing speech inputs, deciding on appropriate responses, in a way that feels natural to the ongoing conversation. Corroborating similar work, we also experienced difficulty triggering prompts from the CA fast enough and with enough frequency. For the former, parents would sometimes have turned the page and would need to return to the previous one to have the discussion with the child. For the latter, if the agent was not responding often enough the parents would assume a technical issue had occurred and would turn their attention to the screen. This was exacerbated by our decision to ensure the technology would be

Fig. 3. Screenshot of the newest version of the literacy app. The "Repeat" button is displayed on the bottom, and participants are no longer taken to a browser page while reading.

deployable on low-end devices. As a result, given our resource constraints we decided to switch to an Android app rather than build out a technology stack that could respond with increased optimal timing. As recommended by other conversational agent design work, possible solutions include developing backchannels for feedback so that users are aware of the agent's intent to participate in a more conversationally natural manner, though this also brings up a tension with our design where we did not want the conversation to be conducted with our agent itself but only augmented with one way prompts [18, 19].

On a positive note, the simple design of the tech stack made it possible for such a small team to make a tool that ultimately families enjoyed using. Using just websockets made it straightforward to switch to an Android app. It also made it easy to add and modify both content and how that content was used by the front-end, since no API endpoints needed to be configured to support the change.

Additionally, the decision to use the low-end devices in the first formal test with remote users turned out well. First, we were able to ensure that the technology worked even with phones that were not that fancy. Second, by standardizing each device and the installation, we were able to concentrate on the usability of our technology. For example, browser plug-ins that change website functionality, system permissions incorrectly set to block microphone access, or having the audio volume turned off could have prevented the technology from working. Although the setup and mailing process was time-consuming, it helped us avoid encountering issues that may be irrelevant to the application we were developing.

Some lingering issues remain with regard to our literacy app's content. We tested 15 books throughout development, and only eight seemed to have enough unique markers to allow prompts frequent enough to engage the parents. Children's books often contain repetitions to help children get into the rhythm of reading and reinforce learning concepts [20]. This pattern makes it challenging at times to identify books that work well with the app as they must contain unique marker words to trigger the types of dialogic reading prompts we wanted to target. There is also a copyright-related issue related to scaling the app for public usage. The app requires the uploading of the full, exact text of each of the books to be read aloud. Copyright permissions for popular children's books are often difficult and/or costly to obtain. Books also go out of print at times, making it harder to obtain hard copies.

To address aforementioned issues, one potential solution could involve the creation of a dedicated series of children's books designed to seamlessly integrate with the application. Furthermore, future endeavors could leverage recent advancements in both artificially generated art and conversation. For example, the current version of the conversational agent relied on prewritten prompts. Therefore, a promising avenue for future research could involve exploring whether new and different dialogic prompts that are generated each time the same book is read aloud might maintain a higher level of novelty and engagement in the caregiver-child dyad's reading experience over time (as it is common for young children to want to read the same story over and over again).

6 Conclusion

We developed a semi-intelligent conversational agent who asked questions related to children's books that caregiver-child dyads read aloud. The questions were meant to both model the dialogic reading strategies for caregivers as well as prompt conversations between the human dyads. Throughout development and multiple iterations of playtesting and formal testing, we uncovered various kinks and attempted to address them while adhering to our design principles/values of having the technology be accessible, easy to ease, and not the centerpiece of the experience. As we continue our exploration, we hope this technology can do its part in promoting early literacy, and that this paper can be helpful to others pursuing similar lines of work.

Acknowledgment. This work was funded by the Chan Zuckerberg Foundation as part of the Reach Every Reader project. We would like to thank all the playtesters in and out of The Education Arcade who gave valuation feedback throughout the development process. We would also like to give special shout-outs to Louisa Rosenheck, who led the project early on and established the design values and principles, Scot Osterweil, who designed and created the character that embodied the conversational agent, Melissa Callaghan, who, besides being an exceptional researcher and designer, also voiced the first iteration (human version) of the conversational agent, and Dr. Cigdem Uz-Bilgin, without whom the formal usability testing would likely have fallen apart. Finally, the work would not have been possible without Dr. Kathryn Leech, whose dialogic reading strategies are the basis of our early literacy app, and Dr. James Kim, who provided invaluable insights toward the prompts the conversational agent should ask.

Author Contributions. Brandon Hanks developed the literacy app and performed writing – original draft and conceptualization of this paper. Grace Lin performed writing – original draft and conceptualization of this paper. Ilana Schoenfeld and Vishesh Kumar performed writing – review and editing.

References

1. Towson, J.A., Fettig, A., Fleury, V.P., Abarca, D.L.: Dialogic reading in early childhood settings: a summary of the evidence base. Top. Early Childhood Spec. Educ. **37**(3), 132–146 (2017). https://doi.org/10.1177/0271121417724875
2. Arnold, D.S., Whitehurst, G.J.: Accelerating language development through picture book reading: a summary of dialogic reading and its effect. In: Dickinson, D.K. (ed.) Bridges to literacy: Children, families, and schools, pp. 103–128. Blackwell Publishing, Malden (1994)
3. Doyle, B.G., Bramwell, W.: Promoting emergent literacy and social-emotional learning through dialogic reading. Read. Teach. **59**(6), 554–564 (2006). https://doi.org/10.1598/RT.59.6.5
4. Hirsh-Pasek, K., Golinkoff, R.M.: Put your data to use: entering the real world of children and families. Perspect. Psychol. Sci. **14**(1), 37–42 (2019). https://doi.org/10.1177/1745691618815161
5. Bustamante, A.S., et al.: More than just a game: transforming social inter-action and STEM play with Parkopolis. Dev. Psychol. **56**(6), 1041–1056 (2020). https://doi.org/10.1037/dev0000923
6. Leech, K.A., Rowe, M.L.: An intervention to increase conversational turns between parents and young children. J. Child Lang. **48**(2), 399–412 (2021). https://doi.org/10.1017/S030500092000252
7. Leech, K.A., Wei, R., Harring, J.R., Rowe, M.L.: A brief parent-focused intervention to improve pre-schoolers' conversational skills and school readiness. Dev. Psychol. **54**(1), 15–28 (2008). https://doi.org/10.1037/dev0000411
8. Leech, K.A., Haber, A.S., Jalkh, Y., Corriveau, K.H.: Embedding scientific explanations into storybooks impacts children's scientific discourse and learning. Front. Psychol. **11**, 1016 (2020). https://doi.org/10.3389/fpsyg.2020.01016
9. Reeves, T.C.: Socially responsible educational technology research. Educ. Technol. **40**(6), 19–28 (2000)
10. Anderson, T., Shattuck, J.: Design-based research: a decade of progress in education research? Educ. Res. **41**(1), 16–25 (2012). https://doi.org/10.3102/0013189X11428813
11. Barab, S., Squire, K.: Design-based research: putting a stake in the ground. J. Learn. Sci. **13**(1), 1–14 (2004)
12. Linder, S.M., Ramey, M.D., Zambak, S.: Predictors of school readiness in literacy and mathematics: a selective review of the literature. Early Childhood Res. Pract. **15**(1) (2013). https://eric.ed.gov/?id=EJ1016152
13. Pham, H.: PyAudio: cross-platform audio I/O with PortAudio. Accessed 01 Aug 2019. https://people.csail.mit.edu/hubert/pyaudio/
14. Drew, J.: mpg321. Accessed 01 Aug 2019. https://mpg321.sourceforge.net/
15. MediaDevices: getUserMedia() method - Web APIs|MDN. https://developer.mozilla.org/en-US/docs/Web/API/MediaDevices/getUserMedia
16. Thompson, M., Lin, G.C., Schoenfeld, I., Uz-Bilgin, C., Leech, K.: Taking advice from a virtual agent: usability of an artificially intelligent smart speaker app for parent and child storybook reading. In: Filipiak, D., Kalir, J.H. (eds.) Proceedings of the 2022 Connected Learning Summit, pp. 100–108. Carnegie Mellon University, ETC Press, Virtual (2022). https://doi.org/10.57862/tg5r-ck86

17. Lin, G.C., Schoenfeld, I., Thompson, M., Xia, Y., Uz-Bilgin, C., Leech, K.: "What color are the fish's scales?" Exploring parents' and children's natural interactions with a child-friendly virtual agent during storybook reading. In: Interaction Design and Children, pp. 185–195. ACM, Braga (2022). https://doi.org/10.1145/3501712.3529734

18. Smith, C., et al.: Interaction strategies for an affective conversational agent. In: Allbeck, J., Badler, N., Bickmore, T., Pelachaud, C., Safonova, A. (eds.) IVA 2010. LNCS (LNAI), vol. 6356, pp. 301–314. Springer, Heidelberg (2010). https://doi.org/10.1007/978-3-642-15892-6_31

19. Smith, C., et al.: Interaction strategies for an affective conversational agent. Presence **20**(5), 395–411 (2011). https://doi.org/10.1162/PRES_a_00063

20. Boutte, G.S., Hopkins, R., Waklatsi, T.: Perspectives, voices, and worldviews in frequently read children's books. Early Educ. Dev. **19**(6), 941–962 (2008). https://doi.org/10.1080/10409280802206643

Real-Time Lighting Analysis for Design and Education Using a Game Engine

Luis Hernandez-Ibáñez(✉) ⓘ and Viviana Barneche-Naya ⓘ

Universidade da Coruña, A Coruña, Spain
{luis.hernandez,viviana.barneche}@udc.es

Abstract. Real-time lighting analysis is a crucial aspect of architectural design, as it allows designers to evaluate the lighting conditions of a space and identify potential problems or issues that may impact the appearance or function of the space. In this paper, we present an interactive tool for real-time lighting analysis using a game engine. Our tool provides users with a range of features for assessment of lighting conditions, using real-time global illumination, physically based materials, and post-processing techniques such as tonemapping and color grading provided by the game engine. This allows users to study the effect of different lighting conditions on the appearance of the space, and to identify areas of the space that may be too bright or too dim. Users can change the reflection properties of materials, the light characteristics of every luminaire, including intensity, color profile, color temperature, and IES photometric web. The user can walk interactively inside the virtual space to see how these changes affect the lighting distribution in the scene and/or the effect along a specific viewing direction. Light orientation can also be changed, including incoming sunlight. In addition to its usefulness for architects and lighting designers, our tool has the potential to be an educational tool for students in architecture. By allowing students to interactively modify the lighting conditions of space and study the effects of these changes, our tool can provide a valuable hands-on learning experience that helps students to understand better the principles of lighting design and analysis and the human visual perception system.

Keywords: lighting design · educational tools · game engine

1 Introduction

1.1 Background

"Architecture is the masterly, correct and magnificent play of masses brought together in light"

This famous quote by Le Corbusier perfectly describes the importance of light, not only in the perception of space and form in architecture but also in its genesis from them. Light catalyzes the essence and presence of masses and voids, puts them into relationship with each other, and endows them with expressive capacity. However, buildings, and the

P. Zaphiris et al. (Eds.): HCII 2023, LNCS 14060, pp. 70–81, 2023.
https://doi.org/10.1007/978-3-031-48060-7_6

built environment in general, are not just beautiful sculptures displayed in an illuminated setting. As the same famous architect also said, a building is a machine for living. It must fulfil the function of facilitating human activities inside it that require certain visibility conditions and visual comfort to be carried out.

Therefore, lighting design becomes an essential task in designing built environments both indoors and outdoors. Lighting conditions have a significant impact on multiple aspects of people's lives, well-being, and health [1]. Furthermore, environmental lighting affects performance when carrying out tasks [2, 3]. That is why an adequate formulation of a lighting design should consider objectively sufficient luminaire contribution qualitatively suitable without losing sight of subjective perceptual emotional satisfaction aspects for users. In addition to this consideration are others related to aesthetics aimed at improving spatial expressiveness through light.

Lighting design requires considering the following:

- The use of natural light sources, such as sunlight or sky glow, and artificial in the form of lamps grouped according to a specific organization, and even a combination of both.
- The choice of materials whose nature responds specifically to incident light in terms of color, reflectivity and brightness. Those parameters influence how they are perceived and their contribution to scene lighting through the indirect illumination produced by the light they reflect.
- Perceptual criteria, derived from the different perceptions of the same illuminated environment based on viewer location and orientation in the room, pupil accommodation to exposure, contrast and dynamic range. Thus, the perception of a room's lighting is not the same for an individual when facing a window as when they have their back towards it.

Regarding having reference values for interior lighting design for various uses, specific regional regulations such as UNE-EN 12464.1 [4] regulate aspects such as the amount of light each type of surface should receive depending on its use or tolerable glare limits.

Various programs used in architectural design analysis and calculation take into account applicable standards such as UNE EN 12464-1, which must be complied with in lighting projects for both indoor and outdoor spaces. However, these recommendations based on guaranteeing minimum illumination (illuminance) levels in spaces are ineffective at predicting visual appearance if the materiality of elements is not considered, especially surface reflectivity, reflection anisotropy or purely perceptual aspects like observer pupil adjustment or perceived scene dynamic range.

There is, therefore, a dichotomy between complying with minimum values for supplying light within scenes, something that most software available allows us to verify [5], versus projected environmental appearance. Although realistic appearance can be simulated using widely distributed rendering methods, it falls short because of inherent limitations within existing display technology. Those technical limitations make it impossible for current computer screens to reproduce the capability of the human visual system to adapt to different light configurations with the necessary accuracy and dynamic range (for example, physical annoyance from reflections in a rendered image or causing a glare when contemplating an area of an image on screen).

1.2 Lighting Metrics

To better understand how the lighting of an environment can be measured and analyzed, it is important to comprehend the significance and differences between the various metrics used in evaluating lighting (see Fig. 1).

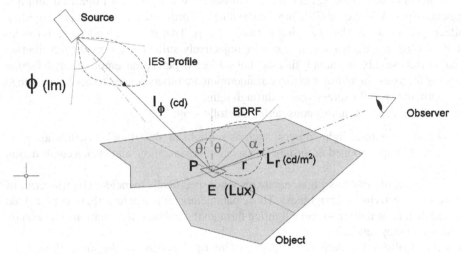

Fig. 1. Metrics involved in photometric analysis

Luminous flux ϕ: In photometry, luminous flux is the measure of perceived luminous power. It differs from radiant flux, the measure of total emitted power, as it is adjusted to reflect human eye sensitivity to different wavelengths. Luminous flux comprises all power a lamp emits, regardless of its emission profile geometry. Its unit of measurement in the International System of Units is the lumen (lm).

Luminous intensity I_ϕ: Luminous intensity measures the power weighted by wavelength emitted from a light source in a specific direction per unit solid angle. It can also be defined as the amount of luminous flux emitted by a source per unit solid angle. Its unit of measurement in the International System of Units is the candela (cd).

Iluminance E: This metric indicates the density of incident luminous flux on a surface. Due to the simplicity of its empirical measurement, illuminance is commonly used to analyze light adequacy in lighting standards regarding various human activities [6]. This metric is independent of surface characteristics as it indicates the amount of luminous energy that impacts but not the effect it produces on vision, which is also conditioned by material reflectivity characteristics and the geometry of the bidirectional reflection function (BDRF), among other aspects. Its unit of measurement in SI is lux (lx) (1 lx = 1 lm/m^2).

Luminance L_r: Luminance indicates the amount of luminous flux emitted per unit area in a particular direction. Recently, High Dynamic Range Imaging (HDRI) sensors have been used to obtain this value and methodologies for obtaining luminance distribution on surfaces of interest [6] have been introduced, which are applied to small-extent elements such as windows, furniture or walls, and large extent elements such as the entire visual field, daytime hemisphere or terrain. Although crucial for studying glare, few studies have evaluated this metric regarding performance in human activities [7, 8]. This metric depends on the nature of the surface being measured - whether emitting or reflecting - anisotropic reflection for illuminated surfaces, defined by its BDRF, and, therefore, it also depends on viewing direction. Its unit in SI is cd/m^2.

1.3 Perception and Representation of the Illuminated Environment

The contemplation of an illuminated environment by a human spectator involves interpreting the luminous energy that emanates from emitting surfaces if observed directly, and more importantly, to understand the environment, the energy that reaches their eyes through light reflection on object surfaces. Although the behaviour of luminous energy is fundamentally linear, the human perceptual system is nonlinear. Humans can distinguish low-intensity tones more remarkably than very bright ones. Our scotopic vision can see details in lighting as low as moonlight, but we cannot distinguish between highly illuminated surfaces. In fact, we are designed to avoid looking at surfaces that dazzle us.

On the other hand, the human eye has an iris which acts as a diaphragm limiting light entry into the retina, allowing people to adapt to wide variations in luminance levels. Adaptation requires time, so transitioning from dark environments to brighter ones may cause discomforting glare, while moving from bright settings into darker ones causes excessive darkness sensation [10]. For this reason, when taking photographs or videos of an environment, it's necessary to consider aspects regulating how much light your device can capture, such as aperture setting, ISO sensitivity or exposure time.

The vast majority of images and video material formats used today only capture a fraction of the information visible to our visual perception system. The limiting factor is not resolution since most cameras can take higher resolution images than what screens can display but rather limited colour gamut and even more limited tonal dynamic range (contrast) captured by most cameras and shown by image/video formats available today [9] (Fig. 2).

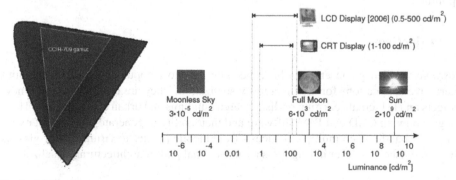

Fig. 2. Left: colour gamut frequently used in traditional imaging (CCIR-705), compared to the full visible colour gamut. Right: real.world luminance values compared with the range of luminance that can be displayed on CRT and LDR monitors. Source: [11]

To reproduce colour and contrast accurately, digital images must display the luminance range as closely as possible to real-life scenes. In this sense, High Dynamic Range Image (HDRI) technology) [12, 13] represents the luminance range encompassing both photopic (daytime) and mesopic (twilight) vision. Additionally, it enables representing ubiquitous visual phenomena such as self-illuminated objects (sun, light fixtures), bright specular reflections or visual glare due to sudden increases in light levels (e.g., going from an indoor setting to a brightly illuminated outdoor environment with sunlight).

Along with the development of graphics cards, video game developers were among the first to adopt this technology. Nowadays, most game engines provide specialized implementations of real-time global illumination techniques and accurate soft shadow creation, significantly enhancing environmental visual quality. HDRI allows the creation of much more realistic environments thanks to its ability to represent fine details in high-contrast lighting situations.

However, HDRI rendered by game engines differs in some characteristics from real-life scenes' HDRI due to approximations used in the models employed. The number of colors present in rendered content is lower than what can be perceived in real life and generated luminance values concentrate on relatively smaller ranges within a high dynamic range.

Despite efforts towards creating increasingly realistic content, means for displaying them are not yet fully matched. New generations of LCD and plasma screens improve display colour gamut and dynamic range compared to old cathode ray tube displays (CRT). Currently, available monitors incorporate wider dynamic ranges leading standards proposals such as those presented by VESA certification programs [14], HDRI10, HDRI10+ and Dolby Video [15].

However, many displays still have technical limitations related to contrast and maximum luminance reproduced, preventing them from showing the full dynamic range captured by rendered HDRI. To visualize HDRI content adapted to current display standards, techniques like tone mapping [16] reduce the amount of information in the image. This technique allows for preserving essential details without losing too much visual information enabling enjoying games with great visual detail without requiring advanced equipment.

2   Objectives

Nowadays, video game engines have become the most popular tool for developing interactive applications for architectural visualization. They are used to showcase new projects and to recreate existing or disappeared buildings and urban environments. Their integration with CAD and BIM software and their ability to generate virtual visit experiences of buildings on multiple devices - from mobile phones to virtual reality glasses - has established these authoring tools as an essential part of architectural visualization.

High-end video game engines such as Unreal Engine calculate perceived luminance by working in High Dynamic Range with 16bits pixel depth. Although graphic output can be adapted for the latest HDR displays (commonly using 10 and 12 bits pixel depth), most commonly used monitors cannot display the necessary dynamic range and precise colours. Therefore, the scene lighting values, calculated internally in HDRI, are remapped into low dynamic range values (LDR) to be displayed on regular screens and stored in standard image and video formats. This remapping process, called tone mapping, transforms lighting values expressed in 16-bit floating-point linear format into integer values of 8 bits per colour channel adapted to monitor nonlinear (gamma) behaviour.

The tool described here seeks to provide users with information about the real luminance of a scene in parallel with its LDR visualization. In this way, it is possible not only to know luminance values for any point in the scene but also to highlight areas that may contain uncomfortable or harmful reflections that are not appreciable under LDR or identify essential variations in the lighting of dark areas.

Logically, since these variations cannot be appreciated through simple observation of image brightness alone, luminance information and its variation throughout the scene are shown using a false-colour scale, so differences between apparently equal brightness levels coded differently can be better appreciated.

Through the use of this tool, people who use video game engines in their work related to architectural design and visualization can:

- Better control environment lighting for lighting design purposes, not just based on the appearance of rendered images but also taking into account effects such as glare that are not perceptible on a monitor or seem much less apparent when viewed through VR glasses than in reality.
- Control the effect of material characteristics, especially specular reflection, on excessive brightness and dazzling reflections
- For virtual production and other post-production works where real images must be mixed with computer-generated ones, identify virtual scene luminance values, so they can apply them in the real scene illumination that will be mixed later.
- In architectural education, the tool allows for immediate illustration of the effect of variations in the elements that compose the illuminated environments, supported by numerical values. It can also be included in any interactive digital architecture presentation tool made with Unreal Engine.
- In applied education for generating virtual environments like video game development or virtual production training courses, this tool helps students understand and manage High Dynamic Range Imaging concepts.

3 Methodology

The tool is developed on Unreal Engine, using version 4.27. This environment calculates images using Physically Based Rendering algorithms with Physically Based Materials and Lighting, emulating the real physical behaviour of light and materials. UE4 can be programmed using both C++ and a Visual Scripting system called Blueprint.

Any element in a scene - an object, a light, or the surrounding environment - can be easily programmed to change various parameters that control their response to light or their ability to generate it in real-time during simulation. Our tool allows displaying the effect of these changes on HDR values of the scene also in real-time, facilitating interactive design. Values are immediately updated when there are changes in the geometry and position of objects, colour characteristics, reflectivity properties of materials as well as modifications made to luminaires such as intensity level, emission geometry or colour temperature.

The tool is created by combining specific elements from Unreal Engine programmed through Blueprint Visual Scripting which include:

- Postprocess volumes: A postprocess volume generally applies changes to the characteristics of an already calculated image to obtain multiple correction effects on pixel-level graphic information. These changes can range from modifying saturation or global lighting effect to adjusting exposure or dynamic range over which exposure adjustment effect applies. The latter is precisely one of the mechanisms we work with as it allows deciding minimum and maximum luminance values that constitute limits between which illumination values should be remapped for presentation. Thus, we can consider the value Lmin as the minimum luminance value that the scene must display and a value Lmax as the value beyond which pixels are displayed with maximum brightness available on the device. These magnitudes' values may differ significantly depending on whether it is an interior lighting, exterior lighting scene or a combination of both. One such postprocessing volume is placed in a scene allowing us to control its overall visual adjustment. The same values will be used in post-processing materials explained later on.

- Postprocessing Materials: A postprocessing material is a specific type of shader that allows applying all kinds of operations to pixels in the scene within a postprocessing volume. It can take various kinds of data as input, such as those associated with the position of the point being processed within the scene, such as its depth relative to the camera or lighting data, such as pixel luminance. This latter information is especially relevant since it is what our tool operates on. The pixel's luminance value, in cd/m^2, is remapped into [Lmin, Lmax] range to obtain a value [0, 1], which is transferred as U coordinate in UV coordinates assigned to a false-color ramp image. This image consists of an 8-bit chromatic gradient between hue values [0, 1]. Thus smaller lighting values are assigned to lower hue colours (blues), while larger ones are mapped to higher hues (reds).

  In the general process for preparing final images displayed on screen, luminance calculations performed in linear 16-bit color space must be corrected using tonemapping algorithms before their presentation on display devices. The postprocessing material described above is used to replace the tonemapper during the rendering of the final image sent to a render target. In this way, instead of sending HDR transformed into LDR image it transforms it into false color with a linear distribution hue, thus allowing for measurement purposes.

- Render Targets: To display the scene's luminance information in HDR superimposed on its LDR view; this tool uses a render target, a secondary framebuffer to which data captured by a secondary camera can be sent or drawn at runtime. The image generated in the render target is shown by overlaying it with the main camera image on the screen interface, occupying the same extension and with variable transparency so that both real and false-color images can be combined for a better appreciation of the effect.

The values of Lmin and Lmax can be modified at runtime, so the resulting gradation can represent different ranges of values depending on the specific luminance range of the scene (Fig. 3).

Fig. 3. Combined display of lighting values and realistic rendering. Left: HDRI values. Right: LDR rendered image. Centre: Mix of both visualization modes.

4 Results

Applying the tool to examples of architecture makes it easy to identify problem areas for correction, such as materials that generate annoying reflections (Fig. 4), and allows their modification by interactively showing the result until they are eliminated (Fig. 5).

The tonal variation marked by the limits Lmin and Lmax allows for a better explanation of the concept of dynamic range to students since it visualizes the significant differences between perceptible lighting levels, such as those found between interior and exterior spaces in a building (Fig. 6), or the human perceptual system's ability to distinguish very low luminance levels (Fig. 7).

The displayed luminance values can be useful in the design of real architectural environments. However, they are especially interesting for the design of digital scenography for virtual production, such as those employed in television studios and virtual sets for film production. In these environments, knowledge of the virtual environment's luminance is crucial for planning the lighting of the real-world elements that will combine.

The tool allows its use with any image output device, from monitors to virtual reality headsets.

Fig. 4. Above: An indoor space where sunlight causes an annoying glare effect on the floor, evident from the luminance levels shown in the analysis image below.

Fig. 5. Removal of glare effect by correcting the roughness characteristics of the floor material.

Fig. 6. Test building model (Ville Savoye) displaying the tonal extreme variations among luminance levels.

Fig. 7. Effect of the variation of the values of Lmin and Lmax in the lighting analysis node in a dark, shadowed area.

5   Conclusions

Until now, the visualization of architectural environments has been based on generating images with a realistic appearance. However, those images have much lower precision in describing the luminance range and colours the human perceptual system can perceive.

Although devices that display high dynamic range images have appeared in the last years, they are not yet widely used nor applicable to every technology, such as virtual reality. Therefore, effects like glare are beyond the capabilities of most display systems.

The use of a tool that permits the graphical display of luminance HDR values on the scene not only quickly identifies these problems while virtually walking through the building but also instructs architects and designers of virtual environments about the challenges associated with the computer-based representation of lighting conditions in an environment, especially when compared to the capacity of human visual perception.

References

1. Boyce, P.R.: Human Factors in Lighting. CRC Press (2014)
2. Boyce, P.R., Berman, S.M., Collins, B.L., Lewis, A.L., Rea, M.S.: Lighting and human performance: a review. National Electrical Manufacturers Association (NEMA) and Lighting Research Institute, Washington (DC) (1989)
3. Konstantzos, I., Sadeghi, S.A., Kim, M., Xiong, J., Tzempelikos, A.: The effect of lighting environment on task performance in buildings–a review. Energy Build. **226**, 110394 (2020)
4. UNE, Asociación Española de Normalización. UNE-EN 12464-1:2022. Light and Lighting. Lighting of work places. Asociación Española de normalización, Madrid (2022)
5. Su, M., Wu, J., Wang, H.: A comparative analysis of lighting design software. In: 2021 International Conference on Culture-oriented Science & Technology (ICCST), pp. 585–589. IEEE (2021)
6. Veitch, J.A., Newsham, G.R.: Determinants of Lighting Quality II: Research and Recommendations (1996)
7. Van Den Wymelenberg, K., Inanici, M.: A critical investigation of common lighting design metrics for predicting human visual comfort in offices with daylight. Leukos **10**(3), 145–164 (2014)
8. Sturr, J.F., Kline, G.E., Taub, H.A.: Performance of young and older drivers on a static acuity test under photopic and mesopic luminance conditions. Hum. Fact. **32**(1), 1–8 (1990)
9. Osterhaus, W.: Recommended luminance ratios and their application in the design of daylighting systems for offices. In: 35th Annual ANZAScA Conference, November 2002 (2002)
10. Hunt, R.W.: Light and dark adaptation and the perception of color. J. Opt. Soc. Am. **42**(3), 190–199 (1952)
11. Mantiuk, R.: High dynamic range imaging: towards the limits of the human visual perception. Forsch. Wiss. Rechnen **72**, 11–27 (2007)
12. Seetzen, H., et al.: High dynamic range display systems. In: ACM SIGGRAPH 2004 Papers, pp. 760–768 (2004)
13. Debevec, P.E., Malik, J.: Recovering high dynamic range radiance maps from photographs. In: ACM SIGGRAPH 2008 Classes, pp. 1–10 (2008)
14. VESA: Vesa Certified Display HDR. https://displayhdr.org/. Accessed June 2023
15. Rtings.com: Differences Between HDR10, HDR10+, and Dolby Vision (2022). https://www.rtings.com/tv/learn/hdr10-vs-dolby-vision#differences-between-hdr10-hdr10-and-dolby-vision. Accessed June 2023
16. Mantiuk, R., Daly, S., Kerofsky, L.: Display adaptive tone mapping. In: ACM SIGGRAPH 2008 Papers, pp. 1–10 (2008)

Enhancing Interactive Art and Design Education Through CIMA-I Studio-Based Teaching Strategy

Yiyuan Huang[(✉)] and Chenze Yuan

Beijing Institute of Graphic Communication, Beijing, China
yiyuan.huang@bigc.edu.cn

Abstract. Interactive art & design is a rapidly emerging field that combines artistic expression with technology and interaction. This study aims to enhance the deployment and practice of interactive art & design education by proposing a comprehensive teaching strategy CIMA-I. Drawing on an analysis of related researches and theories, this strategy emphasizes critical thinking, interactive storytelling, materials & styling, automation, and integration as key areas of focus. The strategy promotes collaboration, innovation, and problem-solving skills, preparing students to navigate the complex landscape of interactive art & design and contribute to its ongoing growth and development. By incorporating interactive, collective and cognitive approaches, tailoring the learning experience to students' prior knowledge, our teaching strategy offers an integrated framework for interactive art & design education.

Keywords: Interactive art & design education · Studio-based teaching strategy · Collaboration and innovation

1 Introduction

Interactive art is a collaboration of human and computer that requires a unique set of skills and knowledge. Engagement and experience are central to current Human Computer Interaction (HCI) thinking [1]. Creators of interactive art & design must possess critical thinking abilities, interactive storytelling techniques, familiarity with materials, proficiency in automation and integration. Unlike traditional art and design, interactive creators must be adept at both artistic expression and engineering principles while understanding narrative and user experience. Interactive art are the strategies organizing fields of activity for the receivers-participants. They can be understood as scores that project the interactive behavior of the receivers [2]. With the advancement of technology and aesthetics, the demand and market share for interactive art are experiencing exponential growth. Collaboration between technologists and artists frequently creates new forms of interaction and visualization: it also promotes thinking about new ways of programming such systems [3].

This trend is evident in the increasing number of international educational institutions that offer interactive art & design courses. Many of them adopt studio-based teaching

P. Zaphiris et al. (Eds.): HCII 2023, LNCS 14060, pp. 82–99, 2023.
https://doi.org/10.1007/978-3-031-48060-7_7

approaches that closely align with industry requirements. Lawson's questions about creativity, how deterministic and how it could be measured were central to shifting the attention of the design studio to the students' learning process [4]. At the core of this process is creating active and exchange environments and communities that embody positive and progressive approaches to learning [5, 6]. The focus is on imparting practical theoretical knowledge and fostering creative methods. Concerning the studio-based teaching method, in many accounts it is "a practicum, a virtual world that represents the real world of practice but is relatively free of its pressure, distraction and risks" [7].

However, it is important to acknowledge that educational models and methodologies in this field of interactive art & design teaching are still developing. While scientific knowledge and practical applications are equal components of the student's learning process [8]. Therefore, it is a mistake to perceive design as separate from design implementation. The two must go together, because it is only during the implementation phases that the reality of the world imposes itself most strongly, requiring revisiting and changing many design decisions. And this discovery and reconsideration is why designers must consider implementation a part of design [9]. This study aims to address this gap by proposing a strategy to enhance the deployment and practice of interactive art & design education and improve the training system. It also incorporates related models and outcomes from cognitive psychology.

2   Related Works

Due to the scarcity of well-established interactive art & design education models or approaches, our research primarily focuses on classical teaching-learning models, including general higher education, practical education, and art and design education. We should help our students pay close attention to the design process, idea generation and their thinking, rather than focusing only on readily available facts and procedures [10]. Thus, in this chapter, we categorize these models into three specific areas: Interactive Teaching, Learning and Cognition, and Self-Directed Study. We aim to identify the factors and variables that align with the characteristics of interactive art & design and explore the potential of studio-based education.

2.1   Interactive Teaching

In 2016, Mohamed Gamal Abdelmonem proposed a teaching model for the design studio, emphasizing the distinct nature of design [11]. He highlighted that in studio practice, the teacher possesses fixed knowledge and experience, acting as a constant. On the other hand, students bring variables such as differing experiences, access to information, cultural backgrounds, interests, and abilities. Traditional teaching methods often involve the teacher imparting constant knowledge and experience to students in a unidirectional manner, with students passively receiving it. However, it remains uncertain whether these constants can be uniformly absorbed by different variables. Unlike mathematical theorems or formulas, design is a creative and emotional process where outcomes are not standardized. Consequently, understanding how variables absorb constants becomes vital necessitates an instructional design strategy that centers around students. Abdelmonem suggests that teachers should collaborate as knowledge facilitators, while students actively contribute to knowledge by providing resources, diversity, talents, and more. This mutual exchange forms a continuous cycle of knowledge production and processing. Studio-based teaching should be an interactive process, where students whose expectations combined with academic training becoming producers and contributors rather than consumers (See Fig. 1).

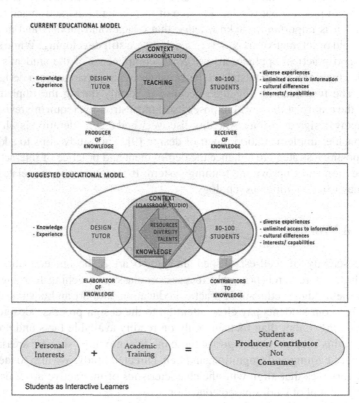

Fig. 1. Models of teaching and communications in the design studio proposed by Mohamed Gamal Abdelmonem (Figure captured from the paper *From propagation to negotiation of ideologies in the architectural design studio: Critical insights in student-centered strategies for interactive learning,* credit to Mohamed Gamal Abdelmonem)

Through Abdelmonem's interactive teaching model, we observe that design, unlike other disciplines, embraces students' characteristics such as resources, diversity, and talent, which are not confined by professional abilities. This understanding forms the basis for teachers and students to engage in effective collaboration, fostering innovation in art and design. In this context, both students and teachers possess equal abilities. Teachers' advantage lies in their grasp of rules, processes, technical methods, and other constant factors that guide students in transforming their own characteristics into refined works.

2.2 Learning and Cognition

In 1990, Derry proposed a cognitive model of learning and memory in teaching [12]. This model explains how new information and prior knowledge are integrated during the learning process from a cognitive standpoint. New information and prior knowledge enter working memory to undergo information processing, searching for connections. As the new information becomes part of the knowledge network, the learning process commences, resulting in meaningful and practical knowledge. The new knowledge may merge with the existing network or reshape it. Once the learning process concludes, the newly acquired knowledge becomes prior that can be extracted to solve problems or construct new knowledge deduced from the network (See Fig. 2).

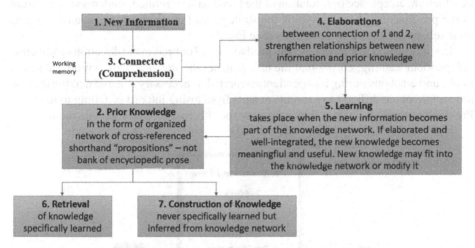

Fig. 2. Cognitive Model of Learning proposed by Sharon J. Derry

Prior knowledge refers to students' academic backgrounds, encompassing their diverse experiences, information access, cultural backgrounds, interests, and abilities. According to the relationship between learning and cognition, teachers need to assess students' learning situations, considering their cognitive characteristics. This assessment guides the determination of the teaching direction and facilitates the connection between new information and students' prior knowledge. Ultimately, new knowledge becomes a part of the network (prior experience), requiring expansion through further learning to validate its effectiveness.

2.3 Self-directed Study

In 2003, Zimmerman and Campillo proposed a model for self-directed learning and problem-solving in their study on Motivating Self-Regulated Problem Solvers [13]. As the practical teaching involves cooperation between teachers and students, it is crucial to leverage the advantages of constant quantity and variables in cooperation, foster innovation, and solve art and design problems, which inevitably leads students to experience the process of independent learning and mutual research.

Zimmerman and Campillo divided the process of self-directed learning and problem-solving into three phases: pre-thinking, practice, and self-reflection. The pre-thinking phase consists of task analysis and self-motivation, with a focus on identifying goals and designing strategies. Self-motivation is an intrinsic factor affecting the effect of funded learning, and includes an individual's self-efficacy, expectations, intrinsic interests (values), and goals. The practical phase involves self-control and self-discovery, where self-control focuses on the formation of a realistic picture, independent research, and guidance of the practical process, concentration of attention, and strategies for implementing tasks. Self-discovery involves the encoding of knowledge by the self and autonomous experimentation. The self-reflection phase involves self-judgment and reaction, including self-assessment and attribution analysis for self-judgment, emotional satisfaction, acceptance or refutation of the final result. If refuted, students should return to the pre-thinking phase to rethink the strategy until the problem is solved and meets their self-psychological expectations (See Fig. 3).

In studio-based teaching, teachers need to control or predict the direction of students' independent learning, ensure that the task matches the students' expectations, abilities, goals, and emotions during independent research. It is necessary to avoid making the task too simple or too difficult to prevent students from losing interest or failing to improve. Pre-evaluation of students is thus necessary for effective guidance and instruction.

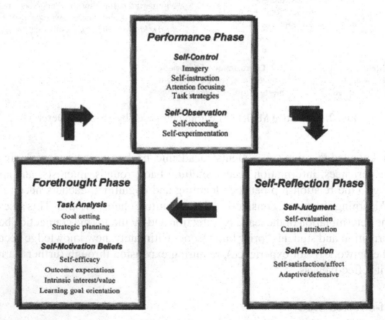

Fig. 3. Phases and subprocesses of self-regulation proposed by Barry J. Zimmerman and Magda Campillo (Figure captured from the article *Motivating Self-Regulated Problem Solvers,* credit to Barry J. Zimmerman and Magda Campillo)

3   CIMA-I Studio-Based Teaching Strategy

The undergraduate course starts with building knowledge and applying basic skills, developing into deep understanding and creative assemblage, and ending up with an intuitive position demonstrated through comprehensive art and design tasks [14].

According to the creative characteristics of interactive art & design, we have categorized the teaching content into five aspects: critical thinking, interactive storytelling, materials & styling, automation, and integration. Refer to the prior related works' analysis, we have designed the teaching strategy considering three key elements: the cognitive learning process, teaching rules and methods, and independent practice process.

3.1   Critical Thinking

Creative thinking can aid to enrich and develop the abilities needed to tackle ill-defined processes, and generate exceptional solutions [15]. Brian Lawson's book How Designers Think offers valuable insights on the design process as an inquiry about critical thinking as an objective and accumulative research task [16]. Carlo Argan emphasized that "when one designs, consciously or unconsciously he is attached or detached to the existing typologies" [17]. Thus, "design success" means critical understanding first. Students need to be exposed to different methods and experiences. Imposing styles that do not meet students' personal desires may affect their creative mindset. Critical thinking is a ritual yet transparent event that is designed as a "rite of passage" – a process of critical insights that celebrate creative thinking diversity but also in reality can make or break [18].

In the **cognitive learning process**, untrained undergraduates, being non-professionals, often rely on habitual thinking patterns. At this stage, new knowledge should be introduced to students as a means of training them to discover new perspectives or uncover hidden aspects within familiar concepts. Emotionally, informationally, and functionally valuable research should be emphasized. Establishing connections between prior experience and new knowledge requires identifying common factors, often referred to as "known things." Therefore, it is reasonable to interpret students' prior knowledge from alternative angles and explore the other side of concepts (See Fig. 4).

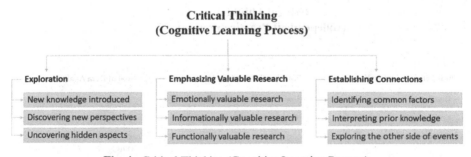

Fig. 4. Critical Thinking (Cognitive Learning Process)

Teaching rules and methods are centered around questioning, researching, and proving. Students are encouraged to question their initial concepts and explore alternative perspectives. Hypotheses are then proposed. Research is conducted to prove or disprove these hypotheses. This reciprocal dialogue between ambition and critique helps the student's agenda to develop and progress [19]. Regardless of the outcome, students gain a more comprehensive understanding of the concept through the research process and discover its multifaceted nature (See Fig. 5).

Critical Thinking
(Teaching Rules and Methods)

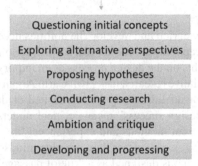

Fig. 5. Critical Thinking (Teaching Rules and Methods)

In the **independent practice process**, students' motivation lies in discovering new value. They continuously collect data and analyze it. However, students' abilities may be limited in the early stages, so teachers should provide guidance on information retrieval methods and assist in data analysis. The goal is to demonstrate, through data analysis, whether the concept's hypothesis holds true and establish new findings. Emotionally, students should test whether the new concept fulfills their own needs (material or spiritual) and engage in discussions with others to assess its universality (See Fig. 6).

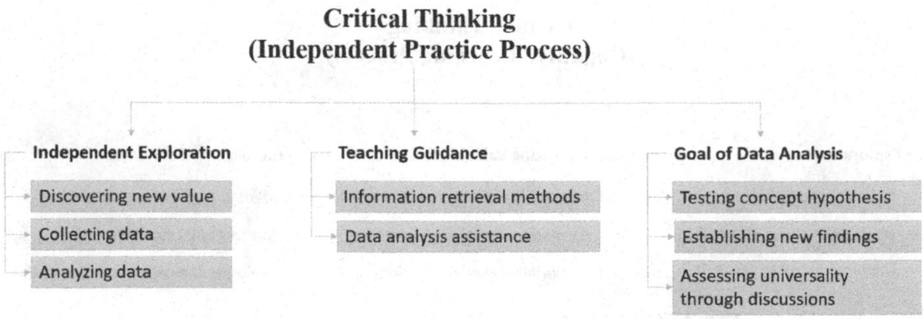

Critical Thinking
(Independent Practice Process)

Independent Exploration	Teaching Guidance	Goal of Data Analysis
Discovering new value	Information retrieval methods	Testing concept hypothesis
Collecting data	Data analysis assistance	Establishing new findings
Analyzing data		Assessing universality through discussions

Fig. 6. Critical Thinking (Independent Practice Process)

3.2   Interactive Storytelling

A portion of digital interactive storytelling creators recognized the essential role of considering their audience's cultural background, to enhance the design and development of narratives. It was found that, to understand how to make changes that align more closely with an audience's cultural background, remains the most challenging aspect for creators. Considering this there are common issues that arose when creators attempted to improve their work, such as inappropriately using cultural elements, or not having a thorough understanding of their audience' s background. These factors can result in ineffective improvements to digital interactive storytelling. It is crucial for creators to be aware of these specific manifestations as they strive to improve and enhance their work [20].

Interactive art & design employs interaction to convey information and create holistic experiences. Given its temporal and spatial nature, narrative plays an integral role in interactive art & design, enhancing sensory perception and aesthetic experiences. Interactive storytelling encompasses the entire dynamic storyline and the framework planning of the work. It concretizes critical thinking concepts, provides structure for interaction engineering, and establishes multimedia symbols.

In the **cognitive learning process** of interactive narrative ability, students' prior experience often reflects "director" and monotonic thinking. "Director" thinking is characterized by strong subjective perspectives, where creators focus on their own cognition without considering or unilaterally considering the audience's perspective. This approach often leads to a mismatch between interactive scenario and audience actions, hindering comprehension. In interactive storytelling, it is important to view the audience as directors (without speaking) and the creators as actors. Creators should anticipate the audience's expectations and align with their preferences. Monotonic thinking refers to the repetition of interaction points with the same mechanism or similar outcomes, leading to decreased interest and sensitivity. To combat this, temporal design should optimize the audience's perceptual experience through interaction, drawing inspiration from film and television narrative techniques (See Fig. 7).

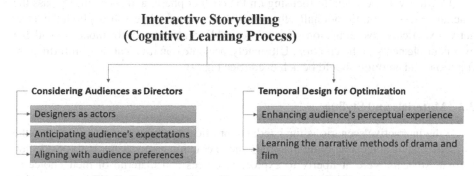

Fig. 7. Interactive Storytelling (Cognitive Learning Process)

Teaching rules and methods can be guided by the Modified SCQA framework, which supports interactive narrative creation. In 2022, D. Huang proposed this theoretical framework which offers a set of methods to assist in the narrative design of interactive art, taking inspiration from film narration and cognitive psychology [21]. By utilizing this framework, lecturers can effectively guide students in constructing the four stages of Situation, Complication, Question, and Answer. These stages contribute to the assessment of aesthetic fluency, interest persistence, conceptual accuracy, and experiential immersion throughout the interactive experience process. With the aid of Modified SCQA, students will progressively cultivate an understanding of how concept, content, medium, interaction, and experience seamlessly integrate into a cohesive and dynamic whole within interactive art & design (See Fig. 8).

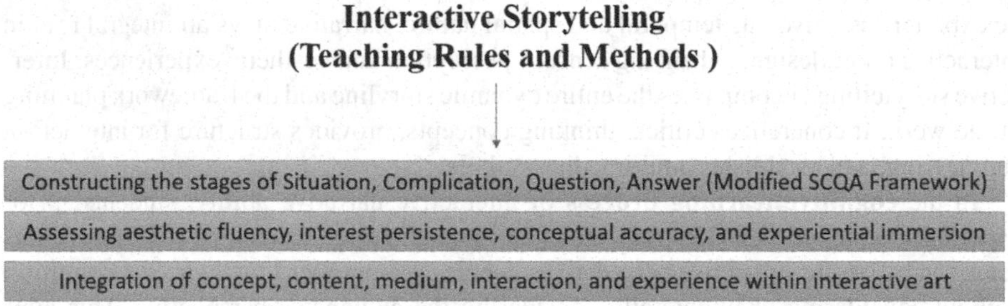

Interactive Storytelling
(Teaching Rules and Methods)

Constructing the stages of Situation, Complication, Question, Answer (Modified SCQA Framework)

Assessing aesthetic fluency, interest persistence, conceptual accuracy, and experiential immersion

Integration of concept, content, medium, interaction, and experience within interactive art

Fig. 8. Interactive Storytelling (Teaching Rules and Methods)

In the **independent practice process**, students are expected to convey critical thinking through their works, incorporating information, function, and emotion. The application of the Modified SCQA framework demonstrates their competence. As students may still be relatively new to Modified SCQA, close collaboration between teachers and students is necessary to guide the integration of independent research with the framework. The goal is to complete the design of interactive narratives following the Modified SCQA framework, especially focusing on the conflict phase, and successfully pass the teacher's assessment. Emotionally, the aim is to maintain freshness throughout the interactive experience, avoiding monotony, while enabling the audience to empathize with the events or elements in the creation. Ultimately, accurate communication of information, function, and emotion should be achieved (See Fig. 9).

3.3 Materials and Styling

Once the interactive scenario is finalized, the practical teaching process moves into the implementation stage, involving materials and interaction engineering. In the workshop format, students were at liberty to explore resources and material of their choice as the medium of inquiry [22]. The first aspect is styling and material selection, which includes the shape, texture, and symbolic expression of the work, as well as the material foundation. Therefore, the focus of teaching is to emphasize the control of symbols and characteristics.

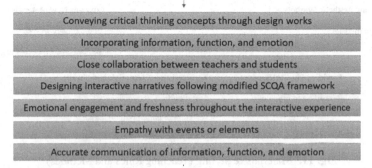

Fig. 9. Interactive Storytelling (Independent Practice Process)

In the **cognitive learning process**, students often rely on figurative and intuitive thinking, without considering the aesthetic and symbolic properties of materials. Consequently, their design is based on everyday materials, lacking in textural quality that aligns with the intended artistic expression. Furthermore, the physical properties of the materials may not adequately support the engineering design requirements, resulting in roughness or deformation of the work. Moreover, students may overlook the symbolic abstraction of the characteristics of objects and incorporate unnecessary elements, compromising simplicity and aesthetic value. To address these issues, it is essential to cultivate students' analytical skills in materials and shapes, enabling them to accurately abstract and refine their concepts (See Fig. 10).

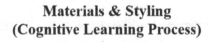

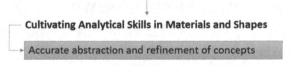

Fig. 10. Materials & Styling (Cognitive Learning Process)

Teaching rules and methods can be explored from two perspectives: stimulating aesthetic symbols based on the medium's characteristics and providing physical support according to the medium's properties. The teaching content can be divided into two aspects. Firstly, introducing the characteristics of materials based on the desired effects and feelings, facilitating the selection of appropriate materials and the creation of suitable forms. Secondly, exploring new materials and determining their compatibility with specific shapes to achieve desired performance effects (See Fig. 11).

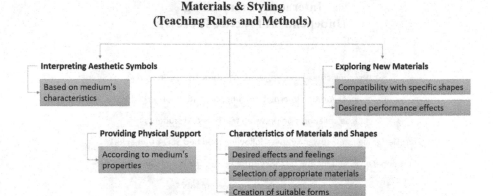

Fig. 11. Materials & Styling (Teaching Rules and Methods)

During the **independent practice process**, students are expected to effectively convey the message and concept of their work through materials and symbols, while ensuring engineering adaptability. Their ability will be demonstrated through exploring materials and shapes, analyzing their characteristics, and deconstructing concepts. The goal is to accurately grasp the material's characteristics, deconstruct symbols, and reconstruct aesthetically pleasing results. Emotion should be reflected in the final result, which needs to be profound, unique, simple, and characterized (See Fig. 12).

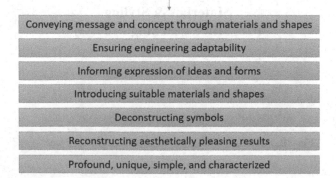

Fig. 12. Materials & Styling (Independent Practice Process)

3.4 Automation

The realization of interaction relies on automation, involving sensors, output devices, programming knowledge, and artificial intelligence. While materials and styling represent visible aesthetics, the interaction processes support dynamic experiences. At this stage, the interaction processes outlined in the interactive scenario need to be refined and implemented using engineering techniques. For art students, automation may be an unfamiliar concept, making this part of the teaching a completely new training experience without prior knowledge. However, if students have a background in science and engineering or are familiar with sensors and programming, this part will be relatively easy. To maximize instructional design, we specifically target art students without a science and engineering background.

In the **cognitive learning process**, students' pre-knowledge and experiences could contribute significantly to their learning processes, according to studies in other educational fields [23]. However, students may lack prior knowledge of automation. Therefore, the new knowledge primarily focuses on sensors, output devices, and programming. Unlike computer science students, art students, at the early stage of interactive art creation, can initially approach automation as an operational aspect, where the interactive functions of the work can be realized without delving into complex programming theories or circuits. To introduce students to the subject matter effectively, bridges can be built between figurative concepts and abstract automation engineering. In most interactive art creations, operations can be categorized as "switches" and "communications." A switch refers to a digital or analog variable that triggers an interaction mechanism when it reaches a certain threshold, while communication involves transmitting signals to subordinate structures (See Fig. 13).

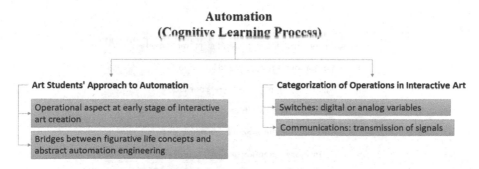

Fig. 13. Automation (Cognitive Learning Process)

Since the focus is on realizing the work rather than the underlying principles, **teaching rules and methods** can revolve around modular systems and graphical programming tools. For example, Arduino and related modular components can be used, allowing students to drive structures through plug-ins and simple programming. Additionally, visual programming interfaces such as TinkerCAD can be utilized to enable students to implement interactive functions without requiring extensive programming knowledge. However, it is still essential for students to grasp basic programming and control logic (See Fig. 14).

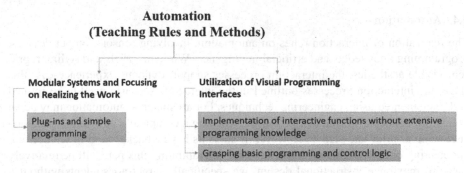

Fig. 14. Automation (Teaching Rules and Methods)

During the **independent practice process**, the desired performance is expected to achieve the intended interaction effect. Students' ability will be demonstrated through the application of logical thinking. They should identify the required sensor modules, establish connections with Arduino, TinkerCAD, Touchdesigner, Unity, etc., and successfully operate the program architecture through trial runs. The goal is to achieve interactive engineering by establishing connections between logic, hardware, and programming, ensuring the system runs smoothly. Emotionally, students should experience a sense of achievement, fostering their interest and confidence in science and engineering, even as art students (See Fig. 15).

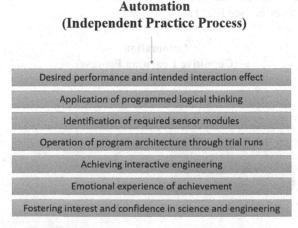

Fig. 15. Automation (Independent Practice Process)

3.5   Integration

Integration entails the combination of four components: critical thinking, interactive storytelling, materials & styling, and automation. The process of integration is interwoven

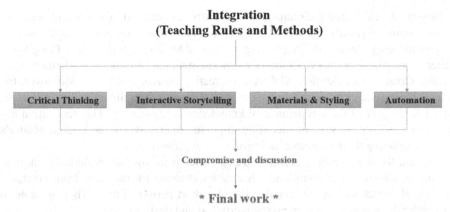

Fig. 16. Integration - combination of four components

throughout each stage, with each stage building upon the foundation laid by the previous ones (See Fig. 16).

For instance, the positioning and concealment of sensors in automation depend on the properties of materials and plastic designs. Time delays and errors in the interaction process may impact the expression of the interactive scenario. Visual representations in materials and shapes may not effectively inspire the audience's emotions and understanding of the message conveyed in critical thinking. These situations necessitate compromise and discussion at every stage. Ultimately, the objective is to find a series of changes that encompass the four stages. Sometimes, art must adapt to technology, and vice versa. Through compromise, the works can be integrated into a cohesive whole, considering the expression of ideas, artistic aesthetics, accessibility, and the interactive experience. For finally evaluation of student's outcome, one strategy is to allow for student-led reviews to gain more weight in the evaluation process. This is a familiar approach of 'self and peer assessment' which, according to Nicol and Pilling, helps students to develop their skills for lifelong learning [24].

4   Early Experiments

In order to evaluate the CIMA-I studio-based teaching strategy, we conducted an experimental class with 20 students in 2021. This class spanned five semesters, corresponding to the five stages outlined in the model, starting from the sophomore year.

Currently, the first experimental class has reached the fifth stage, and the data gathered from this class provides valuable insights. It has revealed several challenges within the program, such as effectively imparting knowledge within limited time, simultaneously training creative thinking ability, art & design skills, electronic programming proficiency, and material processing skills, while respecting individual personality and desires. Additionally, it must explore a series of effective training plans for different types of students and effectively address the specific issues they encounter. Furthermore, the COVID-19 pandemic forced us to switch to online teaching, which significantly impacted the studio-based teaching strategy.

Despite the challenging circumstances, the artworks created by the first experimental class achieved significant acclaim, receiving prestigious awards such as the British Ecological Design Award, Beijing Collegiate Digital Media Design Contest, Hong Kong Contemporary Design Award, Golden Crown International Design Award, Britain International Creative Competition, G-CROSS Creative Award, and more. Moreover, the students have gained a profound understanding of the interdisciplinary nature of interactive art & design and the significance of knowledge accumulation. This realization has led to over 90% of the students deciding to pursue Interactive Art & Design Master's studies, furthering their academic and professional growth.

Overall, the studio-based teaching strategy effectively stimulates students' motivation and builds their self-confidence. It enables students to transition from amateurs to practical talents with professional skills in a short period of time. They are able to independently design and complete interactive art and design works.

The second experimental class is currently in its second semester. With the conclusion of the COVID-19, improved facilities, and lessons learned from the first class, the training program has been significantly enhanced. Additionally, we are placing greater emphasis on the use of intelligent tools and fostering intelligent development. In the evolution and creation of interactive and intelligent digital art, artificial intelligence and machine learning are playing a highly positive role. Art developed with the use of these approaches is capable of conveying human emotions and sentiments precisely and correctly [25]. Artificial intelligence not only expands the possibilities of interaction but also enhances production efficiency.

Given the atypical nature of the data from the first experimental class due to the impact of COVID-19, we plan to rely on data from the second class as the official sample for a comprehensive and objective evaluation of the strategy. Therefore, this paper does not include formal evaluation and testing chapters, as the evaluation will be conducted after the second experimental class graduates.

5   Discussion and Conclusion

In this study, we have explored the field of interactive art & design education and proposed a strategy to enhance the deployment and practice of interactive art & design teaching. Meanwhile, as Akin's argument, we criticized precedent-led studios and the easy route of reproducing the past, through skillful imitation in new forms [26]. It turned the studio into a 'game without written rules' where the staff knew the rules but the students "could only discover them by breaking them and being criticized" [27].

Therefore, by focusing on five key areas—critical thinking, interactive storytelling, materials & styling, automation, and integration—we aimed to address the unique challenges and requirements of interactive art & design studio education. The specific use of material space, project-based learning, learning-by-doing and the requirement for students to experience physical, temporal and cultural immersion. These features support the central purpose of the studio; developing independent and/or professional creative practitioners [28]. The studio is not just a space marked studio; it is a way of thinking and learning [29].

Through an analysis of related researches, we have identified the importance of the teacher-student relationship, teaching models, and cognitive processes in interactive art education. Drawing on these insights, we have developed a teaching strategy that incorporates interactive and collaborative approaches, aligning with the characteristics of interactive art and fostering innovation and problem-solving skills in students.

In the strategy, critical thinking plays a central role, emphasizing the exploration of new perspectives and uncovering valuable aspects within a given context. Interactive storytelling enables students to effectively convey information and create immersive experiences, while materials and styling focus on the aesthetic and symbolic properties of the work. Automation provides the means to realize interactive functions, and integration ensures a cohesive and harmonious combination of all elements.

By implementing this teaching strategy, educators can guide students in developing the necessary skills and knowledge for interactive art & design creation. The strategy encourages students to actively contribute to the knowledge production process, fosters independent learning and research, and promotes collaboration between teachers and students. It also takes into account students' prior knowledge and cognitive characteristics to tailor the learning experience effectively.

Furthermore, the CIMA-I teaching strategy addresses the challenges of the rapidly evolving field of interactive art & design. It enables students to adapt to emerging technologies, stay abreast of advancements, and develop a versatile skill set that combines artistic expression and engineering principles. By emphasizing the five key areas, students are equipped to navigate the complex landscape of interactive art and contribute to its ongoing growth and development.

It is worth noting that interactive art & design education is still a relatively new field, and the CIMA-I represents one possible strategy. Further research and experimentation are necessary to refine and expand upon this strategy, taking into account evolving technologies, pedagogical advancements, and feedback from educators and practitioners.

In conclusion, the deployment and practice of interactive art & design courses can be enhanced through the adoption of a comprehensive teaching strategy. The design studio should no longer act as an isolated universe inside which students are trained as industrious professionals in isolation from the reality of their daily social world [30]. By fostering collaboration, innovation, and problem-solving skills, CIMA-I studio-based teaching strategy prepares students to become proficient interactive artists and designers, capable of creating engaging and immersive experiences. Through exploration and refinement, interactive art & design education can evolve to meet the demands of a rapidly changing digital landscape, ensuring the growth and success of this dynamic and exciting field.

Acknowledgments. This research is supported by Beijing Institute of Graphic Communication: the Beijing Association of Higher Education Project in 2022 (No. 22150223016) and the program of The Characteristic Talent Training and Innovation Practice Of "ZhiXing" (No. 22150323004).

References

1. Edmonds, E.A.: Human computer interaction, art and experience. In: Candy, L., Ferguson, S. (eds.) Interactive Experience in the Digital Age. SSCC, pp. 11–23. Springer, Cham (2014). https://doi.org/10.1007/978-3-319-04510-8_2

2. Kluszczynski, R.: Strategies of interactive art. J. Aesthetics Cult. **2**(1) (2010)
3. Edmonds, E., Turner, G., Candy, L.: Approaches to interactive art systems. In: Proceedings of the 2nd International Conference on Computer Graphics and Interactive Techniques in Australasia and South East Asia, pp. 113–117 (2004)
4. Lawson, B.: What Designers Know. Architectural Press, Oxford (2004)
5. Okada, T., Simon, H.A.: Collaborative discovery in a scientific domain. Cogn. Sci. **21**(2), 109–146 (1997)
6. Seidel, A.: Teaching environment and behavior: have we reached the design studios? J. Archit. Educ. **34**(3), 8–13 (1981)
7. Schon, D.: Toward a marriage of artistry & applied science in the architectural design. J. Archit. Educ. **41**(4), 4–10 (1988)
8. Schon, D.: The architectural studio as an exemplar of education for reflection-in-action. J. Archit. Educ. **38**(1), 2–9 (1984)
9. Meyer, M.W., Norman, D.: Changing design education for the 21st century. She Ji J. Des. Econ. Innov. **6**(1), 13–49 (2020)
10. Li, Y., et al.: Design and design thinking in STEM education. J. STEM Educ. Res. **2**(2), 93–104 (2019). https://doi.org/10.1007/s41979-019-00020-z
11. Abdelmonem, M.: From propagation to negotiation of ideologies in the architectural design studio: critical insights in student-centered strategies for interactive learning. J. Des. Res. **14**(1), 1–21 (2016)
12. Derry, S.J.: Learning strategies for acquiring useful knowledge. In: Jones, B.F., Idol, L. (eds.) Dimensions of Thinking and Cognitive Instruction, pp. 347–379. Lawrence Erlbaum Associates, Hillsdale (1990)
13. Zimmerman, B.J., Campillo, M.: Motivating self-regulated problem solvers. In: The Psychology of Problem Solving (2003)
14. ARB Criteria: Standard Criteria for the Prescription of Qualifications in Architecture, at Part I and Part II by Architects Registration Board and the Royal Institute of British Architects. http://www.arb.org.uk/ARB-criteria-within-ARB-criteria. Accessed 04 May 2015
15. Casakin, H., Wodehouse, A.: A Systematic review of design creativity in the architectural design studio. Buildings **11**(1), 31 (2021)
16. Lawson, B.: How Designers Think: The Design Process Demystified. Elsevier, London (2006)
17. Gulgonen, A., Laisney, F.: Contextual approaches to typology at the Ecole de Beaux-Arts. J. Archit. Educ. **35**(2), 26–28 (1982)
18. Anthony, K.H.: Design Juries on Trial: The Renaissance of the Design Studio. Van Nostrand Reinhold, New York (1991)
19. Abdelmonem, M.G.: Portrush Architecture for the North Irish Coast. Ulster Tatler, Belfast (2013)
20. YinZhu, R.: The impacts of audience contexts on interactive storytelling: exploring how cultural backgrounds and personal preferences influence the design and development of interactive narratives. JESSS **7**(1), 51–66 (2023)
21. Huang, Y., Ji, C., Chen, C.: Modified SCQA framework for interactive scenario design. In: Rauterberg, M., Fui-Hoon Nah, F., et al. (eds.) HCI International 2022 – Late Breaking Papers, LNCS, vol. 13520, pp. 20–38. Springer, Heidelberg (2022). https://doi.org/10.1007/978-3-031-18158-0_2
22. Schneider, T., Till, J.: Beyond discourse: notes on spatial agency. Footprint **4**, 97–111 (2009)
23. Butler, J.: From didactic expert to partner in learning. In: O'Reilly, C., Cunningham, L., Lester, S. (eds.) Developing the Capable Practitioner, pp. 33–42. Routledge, London (1999)
24. Nicol, D., Pilling, S.: Architectural education and the profession: preparing for the future. In: Changing Architectural Education. Spon Press, London (2000)
25. Wenjing, X., Cai, Z.: Assessing the best art design based on artificial intelligence and machine learning using GTMA. Soft. Comput. **27**(1), 149–156 (2023)

26. Akin, Ö.: Case-based instruction strategies in architecture. Des. Stud. **23**(4), 407–431 (2002)
27. Doidge, C., et al.: The Crit: An Architecture Student's Handbook. The Architectural Press, Oxford (2000)
28. Corazzo, J.: Materialising the Studio. A systematic review of the role of the material space of the studio in art, design and architecture education. Des. J. **22**(Suppl. 1), 1249–1265 (2019)
29. Maitland, B.M.: Problem-based learning for an architecture degree. In: Boud, D., Feletti, G. (eds.) The Challenge of Problem-Based Learning. Kogan Page, London (1991)
30. Abdelmonem, M.G.: The Architecture of Home in Cairo: Socio-Spatial Practice of the Hawari's Everyday Life. Ashgate, Farnham (2015)

Data Privacy in Learning Management Systems: Perceptions of Students, Faculty, and Administrative Staff

Jialun Aaron Jiang[1] iD, Fujiko Robledo Yamamoto[2] iD, Vaughan Nagy[2],
Madelyn Zander[2] iD, and Lecia Barker[2(✉)] iD

[1] Meta, Menlo Park, CA, USA
[2] University of Colorado Boulder, Boulder, CO, USA
lecia.barker@colorado.edu

Abstract. Some software platforms are exempt from regulations to protect personal data privacy, including learning management systems (LMS) used by postsecondary educational institutions. LMS collect, process, and store extensive amounts of personally identifiable information. LMS use is required, but students are provided with few or no privacy management features, further compounding a highly asymmetric power relationship. The survey study presented here examines a random sample of students', faculty members', and administrators' perceptions of student data privacy in LMS with the goal of improving the design of systems with inherent power imbalances. Respondents answered access questions with some degree of accuracy, but consistently overestimated the privacy of certain types of data. All three groups assumed LMS data were protected, but differed significantly in perceptions of how frequently student data is accessed and used, including for predictive analytics. Compared to the other groups, students viewed their data as less private and secure and had less knowledge of LMS data practices. In open-ended comments, faculty and students frequently asked for the correct answers about data access. All respondent groups expressed concerns regarding the unethical use of student data, compliance with regulations, lack of knowledge of what was done with the data, and inability to withdraw consent. The findings are interpreted through the lens of Nissenbaum's theory of contextual integrity, which highlights norms of appropriateness of disclosure and distribution as informed by particular use contexts. The authors recommend that designers explicitly and visibly integrate norms of appropriateness and distribution into LMS interfaces.

Keywords: Learning Management Systems · Data Privacy · Higher Education

1 Introduction and Related Works

To mitigate privacy risks, companies and platforms have called for transparency about data collection, storage, and processing/sharing practices, while also providing users with fine-grained control of their privacy settings. Recent legislative attempts to regulate the collection and use of personal data like the European Union's General Data Protection

P. Zaphiris et al. (Eds.): HCII 2023, LNCS 14060, pp. 100–115, 2023.
https://doi.org/10.1007/978-3-031-48060-7_8

Regulation (GDPR) and California's California Consumer Privacy Act (CCPA) impose greater obligations for data controllers and processors, while attempting to provide users with increased ownership over their personal data. These frameworks emphasize principles of transparency, accountability, data minimization, and opt-in/opt out rights. The GDPR requires companies to obtain approval from users before collecting personally identifiable data, while the CCPA requires companies to notify users that their data is being collected and allow them to opt out [1, 2].

Learning management systems (LMS) collect, process, and store extensive amounts of personally identifiable student information. Indeed, vendor-hosted cloud-based LMS have become extremely popular among institutions of higher learning because these institutions can avoid the often-arduous task of ensuring that software is up to date [3]. LMS can gather an abundance of student data such as course materials accessed, time spent viewing materials, and academic performance. Students are required to use LMS to access and engage with course materials, forcing them to comply with potential access, collection, and use of their data by other parties. Additionally, students are provided with little to no privacy management features, and may not know what data is harvested, for what purposes, or for whom, further compounding a highly asymmetric power relationship [4, 5]. This lack of agency is not unique to higher education; in fact, similar situations exist with regards to both governmental and healthcare data systems.

LMS vendors are required to comply with data privacy regulations, but regulations often do not address modern age situations. For example, in the U.S. the 1974 Family Educational Rights and Privacy Act (FERPA) was developed when student data was mostly limited to physical records stored in structured databases. Today, information is more easily accessed and manipulated. Data can be combined, placed in automated sorting algorithms, and transferred from one location to another without reflection about privacy implications. In addition, FERPA is only enforceable for federally-funded educational institutions, and not the vendors of LMS software themselves, who are generally only subject to the contracts they initiate with these institutions.

Most students and faculty are unaware of the terms of service for the LMS they use and have little knowledge of how their personal information is being used [4]. While regulation of data privacy is essential with contemporary technical systems, current frameworks rely on a 'notice and consent' model, which simply requires individuals to be notified about information practices through privacy policies and to provide consent to use a service or access a website [6]. Privacy policies are often presented in vague and complex language, which most people do not read or understand [6].

Prior research has found four dimensions of concern among students, faculty members, and university staff's perceptions of student data privacy [7, 8]. These include collection, errors, unauthorized secondary use, and improper access [9]. Other research has focused on student data privacy in the context of learning analytics. Learning analytics refers to using both individual and aggregate student data to predict performance, measure retention rates, understand learning behaviors, and improve student learning and performance. Predictive analytics have the potential to guide student learning and retention, support development of adaptive learning courseware, and improve institutional quality [10]. However, ethical issues surrounding the use of learning analytics have been raised based on student lack of familiarity, resulting inability to give informed consent, and potential use and misuse in a networked setting [11]. In a recent qualitative study, students desired to be informed of how their data was being used and to be involved in decisions/processes surrounding learning analytics [12]. In another qualitative study, students expressed concerns about increased surveillance, and recommended that the use of their data for learning analytics should be voluntary [13]. These concerns may be unfounded, given faculty members' uncertainty about what data is important for predictive analytics [14].

Few studies have focused on privacy in LMS, despite their being a primary data source for learning analytics. The study presented here contributes to the understanding of LMS data privacy by examining students', faculty members', and administrators' perceptions of student data privacy in LMS. Our research questions are:

- How do stakeholders perceive access to student data in LMS? How do these compare with actual system configurations?
- How do stakeholders perceive student data privacy and protection in LMS?
- How do stakeholders perceive the frequency of use and access of student data?
- What concerns, if any, do stakeholders have about using LMS?

2 Methods

2.1 Survey Design

To understand LMS users' perceptions of access, protection, and use of student LMS data, we distributed a survey to students, faculty, and administrators across four campuses of a large state university system in the western U.S. We first reviewed scholarship on student data privacy and developed a preliminary set of survey items. We then conducted short, informal interviews with 18 students and nine faculty members to explore their conceptions of "data" in LMS and their thoughts about data privacy, use, and protection in LMS. We used these interviews to refine our survey questions. We also conducted in-depth interviews with head information technology specialists at each of the four university campuses to understand privacy policies and data collected, including which personnel have access to student data and why. Relevant LMS included Blackboard, Desire to Learn (D2L), and Canvas. Each individual university campus controls data access settings for its LMS, so there are correct answers to each data access question on the survey. Based on the qualitative data, we constructed closed-ended survey items within the three broad categories using Likert-style scales. The three categories, their questions, and response categories are:

- Data access: Fourteen questions about who can view different types of student data (e.g., course grade, assignment submission, discussion posts, etc.). Response categories: 7-point scale ranging from nobody (most private) to the general public (most public), with "I don't know" outside the scale.
- Data protection: Four questions asking the level of agreement with different statements about student data protection. Response categories: strongly disagree, disagree, agree, strongly agree, don't know.
- Data use frequency: Five questions about how frequently different groups of people access student data for different purposes. Response categories: never, rarely, sometimes, always.

Additionally, we included demographic questions and one open-ended item at the end of the survey intended to collect comments about student data privacy in LMS.

Our survey design adhered to the documented approach of providing term definitions for clarity and priming respondents for active reflection [15]. Respondents were asked to bring a single LMS into working memory to answer the subsequent survey items. Most questions measuring our three concepts of interest were identical between each of the three surveyed groups, although on some questions, faculty and administrators were asked questions regarding their personal use of data, as both groups have the ability, as well as potential incentives, to access and use student LMS data.

The initial question all respondents encountered asked them to indicate with which LMS they were most familiar. Respondents who had never used an LMS were not allowed to continue the survey. To avoid ambiguity, the names of the "most familiar" LMS were piped into survey questions. We piloted the survey to refine the questions before distribution and to determine the time it would take to complete.

2.2 Sample Selection and Profile

To develop the sample, we randomly selected email addresses of two faculty members in every department on all four campuses. The list of administrators included all relevant personnel with access to student data on each campus. The student sample included only undergraduates, since graduate students can also be instructors. First, we contacted leaders of major student organizations on all four campuses through email, asking them to forward the survey link to all the members of their corresponding group. We also sent a link to faculty teaching large enrolment courses on each campus, requesting that they ask their students to participate. Each group was offered a pre-incentive in the form of random drawings for gift cards, ranging from fifty to one-hundred dollars. All told, 586 participants provided complete responses to the survey, including 283 students, 265 faculty, and 38 administrators.

2.3 Analysis

We generated descriptive statistics for each group. To compare groups, we used the Kruskal-Wallis H-test, as the responses are ordinal and do not follow a normal distribution. We also performed a thematic analysis of the open-ended comments in the survey. All authors collaboratively came to consensus on four broad themes.

3 Results

Quantitative findings are presented by the survey's three main question categories: access, protection, and frequency of use of LMS data. Qualitative findings from open-ended thematic analysis are discussed to add additional insight into respondents' attitudes towards and concerns about LMS data privacy.

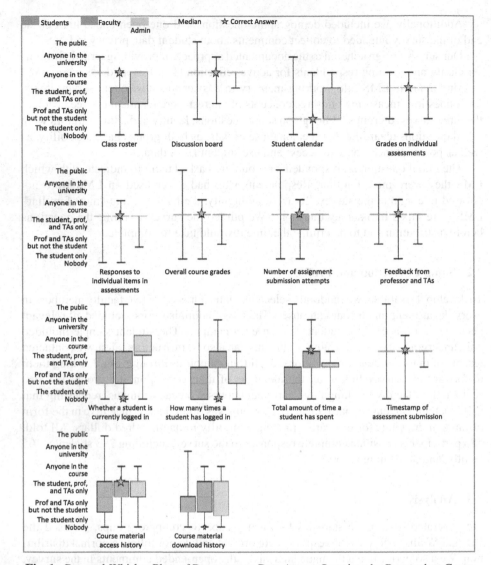

Fig. 1. Box-and-Whisker Plots of Responses to Data Access Questions by Respondent Group

3.1 Perceptions of Data Access

Figure 1 shows box and whisker plots for each data access item by respondent group. Plots of student, faculty, and administrator responses for each question are shown from left to right respectively. Red lines denote median values. A single red line without a box means the second quartile only contains the median value. The correct answer provided by central information technology (IT) units in the university system is shown with a star. As denoted by median responses for survey items regarding LMS data access, respondents answered more than half of the survey items correctly. However, particular data types, including material download history, whether students are currently logged in, and the number of times students log in, were consistently overestimated in terms of their publicity. For many items, the range of student responses was greater than faculty or IT staff, suggesting greater uncertainty.

Table 1 shows the results of Kruskal-Wallis H tests identifying significant differences between groups, as well as pairwise post-hoc Dunn's tests to determine which groups are different. All p-values were adjusted using the Holm-Bonferroni method for multiple comparison. For questions whose median responses are equal across all three groups, significant results indicate differences between distributions, instead of medians. Only one item, access to the class roster, showed significant differences between all three groups. For access to discussion boards and overall grades, students tended to view the relevant information as more private than did faculty. Students also differed significantly between faculty and administrators in terms of their perceptions regarding course material download history and how many times a student has logged into the LMS. In most questions addressing access to LMS data, all three groups' perceptions are consistent. Where significant differences exist, students almost consistently viewed access as more private than faculty and administrators.

Table 1. Differences Between Students, Faculty, and Administrators on Data Access Items

Who can see the...	Kruskal-Wallis H	p	Pairwise Dunn post-hoc tests		
			Student: Faculty	Student: Admin	Faculty: Admin
Class roster	140.63	<.01	<.01	<.01	<.01
Discussion board	10.67	<.05	<.01	n.s.	n.s.
Overall course grades	18.97	<.01	<.01	n.s.	n.s.
Discussion board	10.67	<.05	<.01	n.s.	n.s.
Overall course grades	18.97	<.01	<.01	n.s.	n.s.
Course material download history	17.41	<.01	<.01	<.05	n.s.
Whether a student currently logged in	10.70	<.05	n.s.	<.01	<.01
How many times a student is logged in	34.43	<.01	<.01	<.05	n.s.
Total time a student has spent	53.01	<.01	<.01	<.01	n.s.
Timestamp of assessment submission	16.79	<.01	<.01	n.s.	n.s.

n.s. = not significant.

3.2 Perceptions of Data Protection

Figure 2 shows the box-and-whisker plots of participants' responses, and Table 3 shows Kruskal-Wallis H and post-hoc Dunn's test results comparing groups' responses to data protection questions.

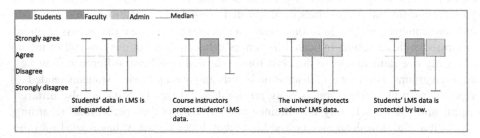

Fig. 2. Box-and-Whisker Plots for Data Protection Items by Respondent Group

All three stakeholder groups expressed consensus around the protection of student data in LMS. However, judging by the middle quartiles on response distributions, students were less apt to "strongly agree" with survey items regarding data protection than the other groups, suggesting greater levels of uncertainty regarding LMS security. We found significant differences across groups for all four data protection items (Table 2).

Table 2. Differences Between Students, Faculty, and Administrators on Data Protection Items

Survey Item	Kruskal-Wallis H	p	Pairwise Dunn post-hoc tests		
			Student: Faculty	Student: Admin	Faculty: Admin
Student data in LMS is safeguarded	29.86	<.01	<.01	<.01	n.s.
Course instructors protect students' LMS data	25.58	<.01	<.01	n.s.	n.s.
The university protects students' LMS data	28.98	<.01	<.01	<.01	n.s.
Students' LMS data is protected by law	45.58	<.01	<.01	<.01	n.s.

n.s. = not significant.

3.3   Perceptions of Frequency of Data Access and Use

Figure 3 shows the box-and-whisker plots of participants' responses, and Table 3 shows the results of Kruskal-Wallis H-tests and the post-hoc Dunn's tests on responses to the data use frequency questions. Across all four questions on data use frequency, significant differences exist among all three groups.

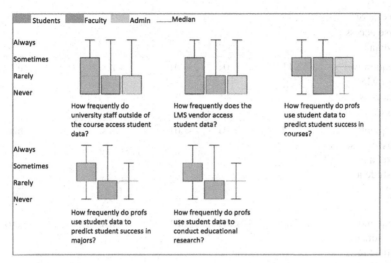

Fig. 3. Box-and-Whisker Plots for Frequency of Data Use Items by Respondent Group

Both students and administrators believed that faculty used student data for predicting student success and conducting educational research with greater frequency than faculty responses indicated actually occurred. However, faculty and administrators generally agreed that student data is infrequently accessed by staff. Students overestimated the frequency with which their data was accessed and used.

3.4   Thematic Analysis of Open-Ended Responses

Ninety-one respondents wrote comments prompted with the question, "Please use this box for any comments you have about student data privacy in learning management systems." The survey was clearly provocative, leading respondents to realize that a tool they regularly used might be used in ways they had no control over, that they lacked knowledge and wished to be informed, a desire for more control, and that privacy concerns were less important than other concerns.

Some commonly expressed student criticisms pertained to the lack of information regarding LMS data access and use, as well as the lack of a choice to opt out. One student wrote, "[I] Didn't think others had much access to my CANVAS portal or would use it as research data? Confused about the legal parameters of that?" While faculty members' open-ended comments tended to convey greater faith in the security of LMS than students, their criticisms also tended to be more negative, and were often focused on

Table 3. Differences Between Students, Faculty, and Administrators on Frequency of Data Use

Survey Item	Kruskal-Wallis H	p	Pairwise Dunn post-hoc tests		
			Student: Faculty	Student: Admin	Faculty: Admin
How frequently do university staff outside of the course access student data?	18.13	<.01	<.01	<.01	n.s.
How frequently does the LMS vendor access student data?	52.11	<.01	<.01	n.s.	n.s.
How frequently do professors use student data to predict student success in courses?	24.72	<.01	<.01	n.s.	n.s.
How frequently do professors use student data to predict student success in majors?	115.35	<.01	<.01	n.s.	<.01
How frequently do professors use student data to conduct educational research?	174.09	<.01	<.01	n.s.	<.01

n.s. = not significant.

limitations to their practices. Issues addressed included inability to adequately protect LMS data, lack of adequate data access in LMS, and the use of LMS data to perform faculty evaluations. For example, one faculty member suggested that our study didn't go far enough, writing,

> You should also be concerned about faculty protection, and what access administration, etc. have to grades, scoring, course materials, other intellectual property, etc. Faculty should know if their Canvas presence and student interactions are used to conduct faculty evaluations. Please extend your research to this important question.

Most administrators assumed lower levels of privacy for LMS data relative to the other two groups. One administrator expressed deep concern about ethical oversight, writing,

> My main critique is of using LMS data for predictive analytics i.e., student success. We've launched a huge campaign that does this without any ethical oversight. These programs have the potential for systematic discrimination and the multiple times I've brought this up has been ignored. Furthermore, there's no regulation on how these companies use student data in their products, research, or services beyond FERPA, which doesn't cover the scope of the kind of abuse that can be done with student data.

Students expressed greater uncertainty regarding their LMS data than faculty or administrators and a desire to be more informed. For example, "The truth is that I am not exactly sure to what extent my data gets used by either my professors, the school, or anyone affiliated with Canvas" and "How would we go about learning this information?" Faculty also confessed a lack of knowledge and a desire to become more informed. One wrote,

> This survey has made me feel terrible about how little I know about who can see what and where the data is saved. I assume only the student and I can see information when really I don't know. Thank you for doing this work, and can you please let us know the real answers at some point?!

Despite the uncertainty, however, several students and faculty members assumed that their data was safely handled. A student wrote, "I really have no idea about my data security in D2L, but I trust it's well-kept." Similarly, a faculty respondent wrote, "I think we do a good job of protecting data."

Several students wished for more control over their personal data, proposing a policy against data commodification. One wrote,

> I think a lot of details about student data privacy in Canvas is unknown to the students using it. Since we don't really have a choice about whether or not we can have all of this data exposed to administrators or the people maintaining Canvas we should at the very least be educated about exactly how much data privacy we are granted.

Similarly, some faculty brought up specific policy recommendations regarding data access for research, greater measures to inform users, standards for different course types, and greater oversight over agreements made with LMS companies. Administrators' comments addressed ethical oversight, predictive analytics, integration of outside vendors, institutional compliance with FERPA, and implications for the future of policy review. For example,

The expectations for privacy may change substantially with GDPR, CCPA (and the other developing state standards). The increasing use and dependence on distance learning mechanisms supporting global constituencies will require significant alignment of priorities to achieve a declarable position to many of these questions.

A few students asserted that LMS data do not present risks to student wellbeing. One wrote, "I have no comments about student data privacy, because we are in a public university I don't think it matters that much." Some faculty members suggested that more important issues had their attention, such as "actually teaching, assessment, committees, research, mentoring."

4 Discussion

The focus of research on student data privacy in higher education has mainly been on predictive analytics, and not the LMS systems that students are required to use every day. In this section, we discuss our findings through the lens of Nissenbaum's theory of contextual integrity, assess the efficacy and potential of pre-existing and novel legal infrastructure regarding data regulation, and discuss potential design implications. Conclusions made in this study might be broadened to suit a variety of other systems that offer users few choices when it comes to the collection and use of their personal data.

4.1 Summary of Results by Research Question

How do stakeholders perceive access to student data in LMS? How do these compare with actual system configurations? Respondents answered data access-related questions with a reasonable degree of accuracy, though they consistently overestimated the privacy of certain data types, including material download history and student log-in data. Students estimated data to be less accessible than did faculty and administrators, and administrators estimated data as more accessible than did the other two groups.

How do stakeholders perceive student data privacy and protection in LMS? All three groups assumed some level of protection over LMS data. However, students believed their data to be less secure than did faculty and administrators. It should be noted that as a group, students also had lower levels of knowledge of LMS data practices than the other two surveyed groups.

How do stakeholders perceive the frequency with which their data is accessed and used? All three groups showed significant differences in their perceptions of how frequently student data is accessed and used. Both students and administrators overestimated the frequency with which faculty actually used student LMS data for predictive analytics, but this discrepancy did not exist with regards to staff access/use. In relation to the other groups, students tended to view their data as less private, overall.

What concerns, if any, do stakeholders have about using LMS? All three surveyed groups expressed concerns regarding the unethical use of their data. Students were particularly concerned that they had no idea what was done with their data and that they had no ability to withdraw their consent. Faculty shared such concerns as well, but different, as makes sense given the context. Faculty were more concerned about the use of student data to perform faculty evaluations but often assumed a high level of data security for students. Administrators expressed concern related to compliance with the U.S. FERPA and related laws, specific policy implementation, and the ethical treatment of data.

4.2 Results Through the Lens of Nissenbaum's Theory of Contextual Integrity

Nissenbaum's theory of contextual integrity [16] provides an ideal framework for understanding the findings of this study. This framework is based on the norms of appropriateness of disclosure and distribution as informed by particular contexts. Norms of appropriateness prescribe what information is appropriate to reveal in a particular context, and a violation would occur if certain information is revealed outside of the specific context within which it is meant and/or appropriate to be revealed. Norms of distribution govern the flow of information; if one party receives information with an expectation of confidentiality, and then decides to communicate it outside of that relationship of exchange, a violation of privacy might be constituted. Our survey found that a universal consensus did not exist amongst respondents regarding these norms, particularly when it came to certain data types.

Respondents' perceptions of norms of appropriateness might best be summarized by their responses to information-access questions; in other words, those that asked which parties had access to which kinds of LMS data under normal circumstances. Alternatively, norms of distribution might best be summarized by responses to security-related questions which inquired about the degree to which LMS data is protected and whether certain parties adhere to their roles in maintaining its confidentiality. Both norms of appropriateness and distribution are addressed in questions pertaining to the frequency of access and use of data, because they allude to relevant aspects of both security and access permissions. In terms of information access, there was relatively high consensus amongst respondents, but perceptions varied substantially with regards to specific data types. Norms of distribution had lower consensus overall, largely because students often viewed their data as being accessed and used to a greater extent than it was. Faculty and administrators answered more similarly to each other on the frequency of access questions, but substantial differences existed, particularly in their perceptions of how often faculty used student data for predictive analytics. All groups tended to agree that LMS data was secure but expressed concerns. Taken together, these perceptions suggest a lack of clear norms of both appropriateness and distribution for student LMS data. With no clear effort on behalf of LMS companies and their policies to convey such norms in a transparent manner, it becomes difficult to achieve contextual integrity within these systems.

4.3 Results Through the Lens of Regulations

Education records contain sensitive, personally identifiable information such as grades and test scores, contact information, and course and attendance records. These bits of personal information are collected and stored with ease through learning management systems and may be shared by LMS vendors with third party entities, used in university studies, or for evaluative purposes without a student's explicit knowledge. The U.S. FERPA law indicates that schools may not disclose student education records without students' written consent apart from certain conditions (e.g., to school officials with legitimate educational interest, organizations conducting certain studies on behalf of the school, or specified officials for audit or evaluation purposes [17]. Further complicating the issue, LMS contain personal information distinct from traditional education records in that a much broader range of data can be harvested. Used unethically and without the explicit consent of a student, this data could be used for surveillance, to make highly personal inferences about individual students, or to predict student success outcomes leading to discriminatory sorting [4, 10]. Though students have consented to a privacy policy, it is not clear whether they are sufficiently and transparently informed of the many uses of their LMS data traces.

Even if there are regulations in place to check the actions of entities with regards to their confidential information practices, prior research has noted several concerns about LMS vendor compliance with FERPA, particularly in regard to data sharing and use [11]. Because few users take the time to read privacy policies or can understand the complex legalese with which they are often written, users are placed at an inherent disadvantage. If students are required to use LMS and other systems for their enrolment and learning but are unable to access or understand the privacy policies to which they are subject, the question of whether or not they have consented to the access and use of their data becomes less clear-cut. Stripped of the ability to make autonomous decisions with their data, students find themselves the disadvantaged party in an imbalance of power, an imbalance not mitigated by FERPA, because it allows disclosure of personal educational information to 'certain parties', 'under certain conditions', or 'legitimate educational interests' without consent. Finally, FERPA fails to guide those who benefit from the use of LMS data with a lack of ethical oversight or what constitutes appropriate use.

Also using a contextual integrity lens, Rubel and Jones (2016) argue that it is important to consider student data privacy with respect to those collecting and accessing data, along with the nature of the data itself [18]. This argument assumes that there are clearly established and accepted norms surrounding the optimal handling of student data within different contexts. However, our survey results demonstrate a general lack of awareness of the access, protection, and use of student data with leaves clearly established norms to be understood and upheld. As might be expected in adherence to Nissenbaum's framework, lack of trust was commonly expressed by respondents, when asked to consider the privacy of LMS data. Respondents in our study expressed concern that their data could be misused or shared with little regard for the data subjects. However, these sentiments were not universal. Many respondents, despite their lack of knowledge, chose to assume that LMS were upheld securely, and some even provided legal arguments for why this might be the case, such as that FERPA should be sufficient to formulate a set of clear norms surrounding the access, use, and transmission of student LMS data. However, FERPA only provides baseline protection for student privacy: according to the U.S. Department of Education, it is the "floor" for protecting the privacy of student records, and not the "ceiling" [17].

Although most of our policy analysis here has focused on FERPA, other preeminent data privacy regulations include the GDPR and CCPA. These newer pieces of data privacy legislation inform our policy recommendations for improving FERPA to better align with LMS. The GDPR and CCPA are currently global leaders with regards to contemporary data privacy frameworks. While they share a number of similar regulatory provisions, there are substantial differences in how they each choose to approach data privacy. Under the GDPR (after which the CCPA was modelled), if a business collects and/or manages "any information relating to an identified or identifiable natural person (data subject), directly or indirectly, in particular by reference to an identifier," that individual must be notified prior to the collection/management of this data and must give their consent. The GDPR is highly expansive and applies to anybody within the European Union boundaries, regardless of citizenship. The CCPA is more limited in scope; under this legislation, only residents of the state of California are affected. Companies are required to provide users with a notification on their websites that informs them that their data is being collected and used and provide users with the ability to opt out. Unlike the provisions laid out by the GDPR, the CCPA allows businesses to collect users' personal data without prior approval; however, users have the right to know what is being done with their data and can make independent decisions [1, 2].

5   Implications for LMS Design

We suggest that contextual integrity within LMS is difficult to maintain due to an absence of shared norms of appropriateness and distribution. We recommend that designers explicitly integrate these norms into LMS interfaces. More specifically, designers should consider displaying access policies for each data type displayed within system interfaces. Creative designers might consider collapsible tables, featuring interactive visual icons that display relevant information, bots that notify students of who will be able to uploads or posts, and other methods. While it might be argued that such information is laid out or alluded to in systems' terms of service or privacy policies, prior research indicates that users often interpret them incorrectly, highlighting the need for a more effective means of communication [5, 19].

6   Conclusions

The complexity, sensitivity, and contextual nuance of data in LMS coupled with the ease of opportunity for data portability, sharing, and its subjection to several potential uses demonstrates a stark need for re-evaluation and reform of practices and laws that govern data in LMS and other educational systems/databases. Regulatory provisions outlined in laws that protect educational information should require transparency and the regular dissemination of information amongst stakeholders. While in many systems users can gain agency over the privacy of their personal data through privacy settings or can opt out of their use, neither of these choices is available to student users of LMS. This study examined stakeholders' perceptions and concerns of student data privacy and use in LMS. We found that LMS users had diverse and sometimes contradicting opinions about who has access to what data, whether student data is protected by different parties, and how often the data was used for different purposes. In the absence of effective regulation, we argue that these findings demand a normative approach to privacy in Nissenbaum's contextual integrity framework and recommend that designers carefully consider user data privacy when designing systems that users are required to use, building into systems transparency about data privacy.

References

1. State of California Department of Justice: California Consumer Privacy Act (CCPA). https://oag.ca.gov/privacy/ccpa. Accessed 11 May 2022
2. OneTrust: Understanding the 7 Principles of the GDPR. https://www.onetrust.com/blog/gdpr-principles/
3. Edutechnica: 4th Annual LMS Data Update. http://edutechnica.com/2016/10/03/4th-annual-lms-data-update/
4. Prinsloo, P., Slade, S.: Big Data, higher education and learning analytics: beyond justice, towards an ethics of care. In: Daniel, B.K. (ed.) Big Data and Learning Analytics in Higher Education, pp. 109–124. Springer, Cham (2017). https://doi.org/10.1007/978-3-319-06520-5_8
5. Slade, S., Prinsloo, P., Khalil, M.: Learning analytics at the intersections of student trust, disclosure and benefit. In: Proceedings of the 9th International Conference on Learning Analytics & Knowledge, pp. 235–244. Association for Computing Machinery, New York (2019). https://doi.org/10.1145/3303772.3303796
6. Susser, D.: Notice after notice-and-consent: why privacy disclosures are valuable even if consent frameworks aren't. J. Inf. Policy 9, 148–173 (2019). https://doi.org/10.5325/jinfopoli.9.1.0148
7. Alexander, P., Brown, S.: Attitudes toward information privacy: differences among and between faculty and students. In: AMCIS 1998 Proceedings (1998)
8. Earp, J.B., Payton, F.C.: Data protection in the university setting: employee perceptions of student privacy. In: 2001 Proceedings of the 34th Annual Hawaii International Conference on System Sciences, p. 6 (2001). https://doi.org/10.1109/HICSS.2001.927152
9. Smith, H.J., Milberg, S.J., Burke, S.J.: Information privacy: measuring individuals' concerns about organizational practices. MIS Q. 20, 167–196 (1996). https://doi.org/10.2307/249477
10. Ekowo, M., Palmer, I.: The Promise and Peril of Predictive Analytics in Higher Education: A Landscape Analysis. New America (2016)
11. Esposito, A.: Research ethics in emerging forms of online learning: issues arising from a hypothetical study on a MOOC. Electron. J. e-Learn. 10, 286–296 (2012)
12. Sun, K., Mhaidli, A.H., Watel, S., Brooks, C.A., Schaub, F.: It's my data! Tensions among stakeholders of a learning analytics dashboard. In: Proceedings of the 2019 CHI Conference on Human Factors in Computing Systems, pp. 1–14. Association for Computing Machinery, New York (2019). https://doi.org/10.1145/3290605.3300824
13. Ifenthaler, D., Schumacher, C.: Student perceptions of privacy principles for learning analytics. Educ. Tech. Res. Dev. 64, 923–938 (2016). https://doi.org/10.1007/s11423-016-9477-y
14. Arnold, K.E., Sclater, N.: Student perceptions of their privacy in learning analytics applications. In: Proceedings of the Seventh International Learning Analytics & Knowledge Conference, pp. 66–69. Association for Computing Machinery, New York (2017). https://doi.org/10.1145/3027385.3027392
15. Dillman, D.A., Smyth, J.D., Christian, L.M.: Internet, Phone, Mail, and Mixed-Mode Surveys: The Tailored Design Method. Wiley, Hoboken (2014)

16. Nissenbaum, H.: Privacy as contextual integrity. Wash. Law Rev. **79**, 119 (2004)
17. The Family Educational Rights and Privacy Act: Guidance for Reasonable Methods and Written Agreements (2015)
18. Rubel, A., Jones, K.M.L.: Student privacy in learning analytics: an information ethics perspective. Inf. Soc. **32**, 143–159 (2016). https://doi.org/10.1080/01972243.2016.1130502
19. Fiesler, C., Lampe, C., Bruckman, A.S.: Reality and perception of copyright terms of service for online content creation. In: Proceedings of the 19th ACM Conference on Computer-Supported Cooperative Work & Social Computing, pp. 1450–1461. Association for Computing Machinery, New York (2016). https://doi.org/10.1145/2818048.2819931

Designing an Adaptive Instructional System for Financial Literacy Training

Cheryl I. Johnson(✉) and Jennifer L. Solberg

Quantum Improvements Consulting, LLC, Orlando, FL 32803, USA
drcherylijohnson@gmail.com

Abstract. Adaptive instructional systems (AIS) provide instruction tailored to an individual's abilities and/or needs to meet their educational goal. AISs have been shown to improve learning and performance outcomes and reduce time in training relative to traditional approaches. Typical AISs that are documented in training and education research involve use cases in which the educational objective is to maximize a learner's understanding of a topic or performance on a task and employ different instructional techniques based on the learner's performance during training. This paper aims to explore another method of adaptation to promote adult learning or workplace training where it may be more relevant to focus interventions that personalize content for learners. Personalization can help learners find information they need quickly and is theorized to increase motivation to learn by having content more directly related to a learner's personal experience. Using financial literacy as a use case, we discuss how we used this personalization approach to design a mobile-based AIS to train U.S. service members about personal finance topics.

Keywords: Adaptive Training · Adaptive Learning · Mobile Learning · Personalization

1 Introduction

Over the past decades, adaptive training technology has emerged from laboratory settings into broad use in education and the workplace. Research and practice have shown that adaptive instructional systems (AIS) provide benefits to learners, including the ability to tailor content to the individual learner's strengths, weaknesses, and interests, increase engagement, improve learning outcomes, and the ability to evaluate and track learner performance continuously. For organizations investing in AIS, benefits such as improved learning efficiency, reduced training time, and improved job performance are driving factors. The rise of artificial intelligence and related capabilities has enabled the content designer to deliver tailored content to an individual learner with minimal effort. Many off-the-shelf learning management systems (LMS) now feature some adaptive training capabilities. To enable adaptation, these systems feature learner profiles based on demographic information, preferences, and performance. Adaptation is often achieved by adjusting content based on level of difficulty, by providing additional examples and resources, or through personalized learning paths. Often, these systems learn

P. Zaphiris et al. (Eds.): HCII 2023, LNCS 14060, pp. 116–127, 2023.
https://doi.org/10.1007/978-3-031-48060-7_9

themselves and, through interactions with learners, improve their recommendations to become increasingly effective with use.

As adaptive training has entered the learning and development industry vernacular, so has confusion about what an AIS is. Marketing is partly to blame for this confusion, as "adaptive" is currently an industry buzzword. However, throughout the history of AIS research, the definition of adaptation itself has been cloudy. Adaptive training has been discussed on the macro- and micro-levels [23], which roughly correspond to tailoring content outside and inside the learning experience. Consequently, the phrase "adaptive training" has been used to describe everything from assigning students to different classes based on aptitude to adjusting content based on physiological responses. Adding to the confusion is the term "personalized learning," which is often used synonymously with adaptive training. While some use these terms interchangeably, as adaptive training is inherently personalized, some argue for a broader definition of personalization to include interests and other factors that may not directly relate to domain knowledge but may be relevant to a learner's willingness to engage in training.

The purpose of this paper is not to propose a new framework for describing adaptive training but to provide a discussion of how and when certain adaptive and personalized approaches may work in practical workplace settings. Often, we as researchers tend to argue that a training solution should only be expected to be beneficial when data supports it. However, the converse is not always true; just because an approach has been supported by data does not mean it is the optimal solution in a practical setting. We will discuss this distinction by first summarizing our understanding of AISs and their effectiveness. Next, we describe limitations of frequently researched AIS approaches in organizational settings. We discuss the role of personalization in tailored learning contexts and provide an example from our work to illustrate the distinction between adaptive and personalized training systems. We argue that ideally, AIS should include both types of approaches to maximize learning and engagement.

2 Adaptive Instructional Systems

2.1 What is an Adaptive Instructional System?

For decades, one-on-one tutoring has been considered the gold standard for education and training. Bloom [4] found that students who received one-on-one tutoring performed two standard deviations higher on achievement tests compared to those taught with conventional classroom methods [c.f. 33]. As a result, he urged researchers to explore teaching methods for groups that were as effective as one-on-one tutoring, which he called the "2 Sigma problem." One-on-one tutoring is believed to be so effective because human tutors can identify what a student knows about the domain, understand what gaps there are in the student's knowledge, and apply their knowledge of instructional strategies to constantly adapt their approach on the fly as the student progresses [4, 16]. Given advances in technology, it is now possible for computers to emulate these strategies employed by human tutors at scale, in which algorithms can assess and respond to students' needs and adapt accordingly during a learning episode.

Although researchers have referred to this technology by different names, the general theme of these definitions is the same. For example, Park and Lee [23] define "adaptive instructional systems" as "educational interventions aimed at effectively accommodating individual differences in students while helping each student develop the knowledge and skills required to learn a new task" (p. 651). Shute and Zapata-Rivera [28] define an "adaptive system" as one that "adjusts itself to suit particular learning characteristics and the needs of the learner" (p. 269). Vandewaetere et al. [32] define "adaptive learning environments" as instructional technology that "accommodates different learning needs and abilities of the learners" (p. 119). Finally, Landsberg et al. [14] take a more specific approach and define "adaptive training" as "training interventions whose content can be tailored to an individual learner's aptitudes, learning preferences, or styles prior to training and that can be adjusted, either in real-time or at the end of a training session, to reflect the learner's on-task performance" (p. 9). Taken together, all of these definitions include making adjustments during the learning episode to help learners achieve their educational goals. For this paper, we will use the term *adaptive instructional system* (AIS) to refer to this educational technology approach since it is the broadest term that encompasses both "adaptive learning" and "adaptive training" and is more descriptive than "adaptive system." Bringing together components of these definitions, we define AIS as technology that is used to tailor instruction to an individual's abilities and/or needs to meet their educational goal.

The complexity of AISs can be considered a continuum, ranging from simple to complex. On the simple side of the spectrum, a course may adapt the information presented to the learner based on pre-test performance, such that only the material the student answered incorrectly is delivered to them. On the complex side of the spectrum, adaptive decisions are driven by some form of artificial intelligence (e.g., an intelligent tutoring system). For instance, a math intelligent tutoring system presents a particular set of problems to a student next based on an assessment of the student's competency compared to an expert model.

2.2 How Do AISs Work?

There are three core capabilities that AIS must possess to function and each of these elements can vary in its level of complexity [6, 10] (see Fig. 1). The first capability is to *Observe*, which is how the AIS collects information about the learner, such as behaviors, certain characteristics, or physiological measures. As a simple example, the AIS can collect survey responses from the learner or collect behavior data, such as the timestamps of when learners click and where they are clicking on the screen. A more complex example is collecting the learner's gaze pattern data, physiological data (e.g., heart rate variability, EEG recordings), or other information such as facial features or posture.

The second essential capability of an AIS is to *Assess*, in which the AIS makes determinations about the learner based on the inputs collected from the Observe stage, which can include simple evaluations about a learner's traits or behaviors, or several measurements can be aggregated to create a complex student model. Based on the student's responses to a survey, the AIS can assess state and trait characteristics of the learner, such as their motivation, goal orientation, or self-efficacy. Likewise, based on their responses on a pre-test, the AIS can ascertain their level of prior knowledge, and this assessment can also vary in its granularity. For example, the assessment could be at the level of an overall score, or the student's responses to each item could be used to assess their knowledge of individual learning objectives. Using data on the student's interactions with the system, such as button clicks and typed responses, the system can determine if the student completed the task sequence correctly or with errors. If the AIS collects heart rate variability data from the learner, it can assess the learner's stress level. Likewise, using eye tracking data, the system could assess whether the learner was attending to the right information on the display at the right time. Taken together, some combination of data can be aggregated meaningfully to form a learner model, a digitized representation of the learner that can include both cognitive and noncognitive information [28]. The student model could determine the learner's competency level for a particular concept, remember a student's preferences and traits, and classify a student's affective state (e.g., boredom, confusion, excitement, etc.), which could be used to drive adaptation decisions.

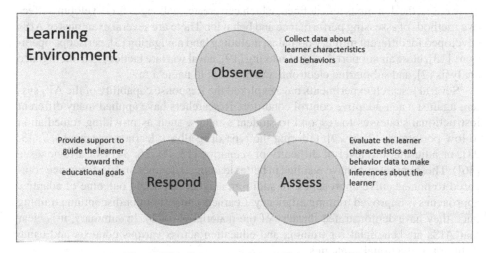

Fig. 1. The three essential capabilities of an AIS.

Finally, the third essential capability of an AIS is to *Respond*, which is how the AIS responds to help the learner meet their educational goal. A simple example is providing instruction for only items students missed on their pre-test. A more complex example is having a natural language dialogue with the student to help them overcome conceptual misconceptions. Adding another layer of complexity would allow the AIS to respond differently based on its assessment of the student's cognitive and affective states. For instance, when the system detects the student's frustration, it responds with more direct feedback and assertions. When the system detects the student is bored, it responds in a way that generates more interest, such as providing more challenging exercises or options of choice [8].

Depending on the AIS's complexity, these Observe-Assess-Respond processes can happen once or continuously throughout the learning episode. However, it is important to underscore that the AIS examples discussed above generally concern the educational goal of helping the learner to achieve mastery of a topic or skill, where the objective is for learners to gain competency or reach a certain level of performance (e.g., score 80% on an evaluation). A growing literature base demonstrates the effectiveness of adaptive techniques for improving learning and performance outcomes.

2.3 Are AISs Effective?

In general, AISs have been developed most often for education and military contexts and there are many successful examples. Within education, AISs have been developed to teach students science [7, 9], math [1, 11], and programming [15, 24], all of which are usually well-defined domains with clear goals and clear paths to obtain those goals. This research has generally demonstrated improved learning outcomes in both laboratory and classroom settings (for reviews, see [12, 18, 30, 33]). Similarly, AISs have also been applied in military training contexts to teach service members the skills necessary to perform complex tasks to become qualified operators in a given domain. In many of these cases, the domain is less defined, which can create challenges for developing effective methods of assessing performance and behavior. There are several examples of AISs developed for different military domains, including land navigation [5], periscope operations [13], close air support decision-making [19], naval warfare tactics [31], intelligence analysis [2], and submarine electronic warfare [34] to name a few.

Several research experiments have explored the Response capability of the AIS system against a non-adaptive control condition. Researchers have applied many different instructional strategies to respond to student's inputs, such as providing remediation to low performers [2, 5, 29], tailoring the type of feedback learners receive [3, 7, 13, 27], or adjusting the level of difficulty of scenarios [13, 20, 26, 34] (for a review see [36]). These approaches have resulted in better learning outcomes and performance compared to non-adaptive approaches. In addition, another important outcome of adaptive approaches is improved training efficiency. Learners can test out or discontinue training once they have demonstrated mastery of the material [13, 21]. In summary, it is clear that AISs are beneficial for training and education across various contexts and using different instructional strategies.

These examples share some commonalities that are important to consider when thinking through the design of AIS systems. First, the educational goal was to improve mastery of a particular concept or skill, so the AIS was designed to assess the learner's performance during the learning episode and adjust how the information was presented in some way based on that assessment. Second, for the most part, learners may use these systems once or a few times during a particular course. Rarely would most of these systems be used beyond the scope of a course or over extended periods. Once learners have demonstrated their knowledge or proficiency, they are unlikely to use it again, except perhaps for refresher training. For the military examples in particular, it is unlikely that the students would have access to these tools outside of the context of the schoolhouse.

2.4 What Are the Limitations of Current Approaches?

As we previously discussed, AISs are defined by three component processes which serve to observe the behavior of a trainee, conduct an ongoing assessment of their performance, and respond by providing adjustments to training content, feedback, or other aspects of the training environment to optimize performance. Historically, adaptive training has been discussed on macro- and micro-levels and includes a variety of approaches to maximize learning outcomes. The difference between macro- and micro-level adaptive training approaches in part speaks to the distinction between *personalized* and *adaptive* training. *Personalization* describes tailoring content to the individual based on known characteristics and needs of the trainee or student. According to the U.S. Dept. of Education [22], personalized learning "refers to instruction in which the pace of learning and the instructional approach are optimized for the needs of each learner. Learning objectives, instructional approaches, and instructional content (and its sequencing) may all vary based on learner needs. In addition, learning activities are meaningful and relevant to learners, driven by their interests, and often self-initiated" (p. 9). *Adaptation*, on the other hand, often involves adjusting content and feedback based on an ongoing performance assessment and can be accomplished without prior knowledge of the trainee or regard to their preferences, interests, or individual needs. Ideally, an AIS would enable both personalization and adaptation, although often the focus of both design and research into AIS has focused on the adaptive capability of the system.

The distinction between personalization and adaptation is relevant when training systems are considered outside of a classroom or controlled setting and implemented in adult learning contexts. As a result of recent advances in artificial intelligence, the adult learning technology market has seen an influx of adaptive training products. The global adaptive training market is estimated to be nearly $3.5 billion in 2023 and is projected to increase to nearly $9 billion in 2028 [25]. These technologies often focus less on real-time adaptation of content and more on personalization. The reason for this is that providing content that is relevant to an individual and their role in an organization is more valuable in terms of efficiency than providing content that varies based on learning progress. Interestingly, while this approach has been adopted by global markets, it is far less well researched in educational settings.

Personalized training provides content to an individual based on their job description, role, background, social groups, and interests. These approaches provide benefits above traditional AIS because, in part, they speak to the motivational aspects of training. AISs have been conceptualized to maintain the trainee in what Vygotsky [35] (1978) described as the "zone of proximal development" wherein the level of difficulty provides enough of a challenge to keep them engaged. However, this approach presupposes the trainee is motivated to engage in learning the content in the first place. In adult learning situations, the learning process is not necessarily inherently motivational, and trainees often prefer to perform their jobs, socialize, or do anything other than take training mandated by their employer. Personalizing the learning experience helps increase motivation by providing content tailored to maximize personal relevance. Presumably, if the content is provided based on topics that matter to you, you will be more motivated to learn.

In addition, adult training situations often require self-directed learning approaches. On the job, an employee may find themselves in situations in which they do not know how to perform a task, particularly if it is a task they perform infrequently or one that changes often. If resources are available to them at the point of need, they will seek out the answer to their question. An employee may want to learn a new skill for purposes of advancement or sheer curiosity. Some employees may want to share information they have learned with their colleagues or learn based on a recommendation from another. Personalized content facilitates this self-directed learning process, whereas simply adapting training to performance would not.

Another instance of traditional AIS approaches being limited in adult learning contexts is how content libraries are often constructed. Adaptive training approaches frequently depend on content that builds on itself or varies in difficulty. Adult learners are often presented with a wide variety of content, but it may not differ in complexity or challenge; therefore, the typical adaptive methods of adjusting scaffolding or increasing difficulty based on performance would not apply. Well-designed instructional content in an organization should be readily accessible to all who require it. In these cases, it is far more useful to the trainee to have content prescribed to them that is more personally relevant than increasingly difficult.

Personalization and adaptation are not mutually exclusive; an ideal AIS would accomplish both goals of maintaining relevance through personalization and optimizing learning through adaptation. Increasingly, commercially available AIS include both instructional approaches in their delivery mechanisms, and this trend should continue as the barriers to implementing AIS are reduced through advances in artificial intelligence, machine learning, and related technologies.

To illustrate the distinction between these two approaches, we describe our approach to developing a mobile learning application for a complex topic relevant to everyone – financial literacy.

3 Use Case: Financial Literacy

3.1 Financial Literacy

Despite its importance in our daily lives, many people never receive formal education or training in personal finance. People regularly make important decisions and experience life events that profoundly affect their finances, such as starting a new job, getting married, or buying a home. Financial literacy training makes a good use case for taking a different approach to adaptive training. Financial literacy is the ability to understand fundamental financial skills (e.g., personal financial management, budgeting, and investing) and to apply that knowledge to make informed financial decisions. When people are financially literate, they make effective decisions about managing their money confidently, such as paying their bills on time, borrowing responsibly, saving their money, and planning and investing for retirement and other financial goals. Yet research has shown across the world that people fail to understand three fundamentals of financial literacy – interest rates, inflation, and risk diversification [17]. Critically, these skills are required throughout your lifetime, not just during a particular course or for a specific job. Your financial needs change throughout your life, so the information pertinent to you also changes over time. Further complicating matters is that the financial landscape is ever-changing with new methods to make payments and borrow money, new financial products and services promising users new ways of managing and investing their money, and new investment opportunities (e.g., cryptocurrency) popping up all the time, making it difficult to keep up and make sound decisions about whether these new technologies and opportunities are worth pursuing and how to employ them effectively to meet your financial goals.

For a recent project, we focused on financial literacy training for U.S. military service members and their families. The U.S. Department of Defense (DoD) defines financial readiness as a state of successful management of a service member's financial responsibilities that supports them in carrying out their wartime responsibilities, and the DoD considers this a critical component of mission readiness. Financial decisions and major life events can be especially challenging for military service members and their families to navigate since their jobs may require keeping unpredictable schedules and several relocations across their career span. In addition, service members are often targets of predatory loan practices and other financial schemes, so it is important to provide them with resources to quickly make informed decisions about their finances. Furthermore, the large body of content relevant to financial wellness can be overwhelming for many. Therefore, making this information easy for learners to find is key. To support these training objectives, our team developed a mobile-based AIS to provide financial literacy training to service members and their families. We chose a mobile platform for this AIS because that would be the most convenient method to reach our target users. Since many service members do not have access to a computer in their everyday job or may be on deployment, it was important to provide a resource they could use on the go.

3.2 Design Considerations for Financial Literacy Training for Service Members

To develop an AIS for financial literacy training, we had to tackle several design issues. The first issue was that there is a plethora of resources on personal finance topics, from books to websites to companies offering services, and not all of them are reliable. A critical objective for the design of this training was to be able to provide people with reputable resources to help answer their questions quickly. This approach differed from traditional eLearning or other AISs because the training objective is not necessarily that the user needs to master personal finance topics to reach their educational goals but rather that they need to learn enough information to make educated decisions. Therefore, the focus was on developing, organizing, and presenting the content in such a way as to support finding the information that learners need when they need it, rather than on designing an AIS that assesses for understanding and adjusts instructional strategies based on learner performance.

Yet another issue was that service members have different needs throughout their careers, and some of their financial realities are not tied directly to their employment. Recognizing these needs, the DoD has codified a financial literacy training requirement at critical times in a service member's career and personal life in 10 U.S. Code § 992. These include during initial entry training, at their first duty station, upon promotions, when they are vested in the federal savings and investment plan, during leadership training, during pre- and post-deployment training, at significant life milestones (e.g., marriage, divorce, birth of a first child, disabling sickness or condition), and upon separation from the service. Some events, such as getting deployed or changing duty stations, are job-related, but other events, such as whether they get married or have children, are not job-related. As a result, we chose to organize topics in terms of "touchpoints," which are key milestones in a service member's career, and "major life events" which depend on the member's lifestyle choices.

A third design issue to overcome was that financial literacy content is generally not inherently interesting to service members. They may not see an immediate use for the information, and many people lack interest in learning about personal finance on their own time. Therefore, part of the personalized learning approach was to provide the most pertinent information as quickly as possible without wading through a sea of resources, trying to determine what is relevant. When users log in to the app, they select touchpoints relevant to their career and finance topics they are interested in learning about. From here, the AIS uses a recommendation engine to present content the learner would be most interested in. Learners can rate the usefulness of the content and update their touchpoints and topics at any time. Over time, the recommendation engine can use this information in addition to the learner's interactions in the app along with the same data from other learners using the app to recommend additional content. In this way, learners will not have to search through irrelevant content to find something that interests them at that particular time.

A related issue is that the personal finance content changes all the time. For instance, tax laws can change on a yearly basis, new methods of investing become available, and investment strategies may need to be updated as a result. Consequently, our design strategy had to be flexible and modular enough to handle these periodic changes in such a way that the whole system would not break if the content was updated.

A final design issue concerned people's sensitivity to financial problems in general. As previously mentioned, service members with serious financial problems can lose their security clearance, jeopardizing their job. Members may be hesitant to talk to others about financial matters, particularly within their chain of command. This particular issue also informed our data strategy choices. In addition, our use case required the collection of very limited personal information about our learners due to security concerns. For example, some financial wellness apps access users' bank accounts to track their personal spending and savings habits, which they use to advise users on how to save more money or invest. Although such access to user data would allow for more personalized content, maintaining the learner's privacy was paramount, and user-specific financial data were not collected.

4   Conclusion

This paper described a different approach to the design of adaptive instructional systems for adult learners. Typical AISs documented in the training and education literature have been designed with a mastery approach in mind, where the educational goal is to perform to a set standard or score a certain value on an exam. In these cases, a typical AIS observes the learner's characteristics and behaviors, assesses the learner's performance, and responds with an instructional strategy designed to improve their understanding or performance. A growing body of research evidence shows the benefits of this sort of adaptive instruction for promoting learning and performance outcomes. By diagnosing learners' strengths and weaknesses, the training can target gaps in the learners' knowledge or skills. Although adaptation based on performance is effective, it may not always be practical. Personalization is a different but complementary approach to adapting content for learners, and it is particularly popular in workplace learning contexts, where the educational goal is to provide timely information at the point of need. Learning is an inherently effortful process, and it can be difficult for adult learners at work to engage in training. Personalizing training content can be a powerful method to motivate learners by presenting information relevant to their interests and needs. This approach seems well-suited for situations with a great deal of content, when the content is updated frequently, and when the information is not needed often. Indeed, these adaptive and personalized learning approaches are not mutually exclusive and could be used together to maximize training time and learner engagement. Future research is needed to determine how effective personalization approaches are for learning and performance outcomes, efficiency, and impacts on learner motivation and engagement across different training and education contexts. In addition, researchers should also explore the potential benefits of employing the combination of adaptive training and personalized learning approaches.

References

1. Arroyo, I., Woolf, B.P., Burelson, W., Muldner, K., Rai, D., Tai, M.: A multimedia adaptive tutoring system for mathematics that addresses cognition, metacognition and affect. Int. J. Artif. Intell. Educ. **24**(4), 387–426 (2014). https://doi.org/10.1007/s40593-014-0023-y
2. Barto, J., Daly, T., LaFleur, A., Steinhauser, N.: Blending adaptive learning into military formal school courses. In: Proceedings of the Interservice/Industry Training, Simulation, and Education Conference. National Training Systems Association, Orlando (2020)
3. Billings, D.R.: Efficacy of adaptive feedback strategies in simulation-based training. Mil. Psychol. **24**(2), 114–133 (2012)
4. Bloom, B.S.: The 2 sigma problem: the search for methods of group instruction as effective as one-to-one tutoring. Educ. Res. **13**(6), 4–16 (1984)
5. Bond, A.J.H., Phillips, J.K., Steinhauser, N.B., Stensrud, B.: Revolutionizing formal school learning with adaptive training. In: Proceedings of the Interservice/Industry Training, Simulation, and Education Conference, Orlando. National Training Systems Association (2019)
6. Campbell, G.E.: Adaptive, intelligent training systems: just how "smart" are they? In: Campbell, G.E. (ed.) Adaptive Training Systems. Symposium conducted at the Naval Air Systems Command Fellows Lecture Series, Orlando (2014)
7. Dzikovska, M., Steinhauser, N., Farrow, E., Moore, J., Campbell, G.: BEETLE II: deep natural language understanding and automatic feedback generation for intelligent tutoring in basic electricity and electronics. Int. J. Artif. Intell. Educ. **24**(3), 284–332 (2014). https://doi.org/10.1007/s40593-014-0017-9
8. D'Mello, S., Graesser, A.: Automatic detection of learner's affect from gross body language. Appl. Artif. Intell. **23**(2), 123–150 (2009)
9. Graesser, A.C., Lu, S., Jackson, G.T., et al.: AutoTutor: a tutor with dialogue in natural language. Behav. Res. Meth. Instrum. Comput. **36**, 180–192 (2004). https://doi.org/10.3758/BF03195563
10. Johnson, C.I., Marraffino, M.D., Whitmer, D.E., Bailey, S.K.T.: Developing an adaptive trainer for joint terminal attack controllers. In: Sottilare, R.A., Schwarz, J. (eds.) HCII 2019. LNCS, vol. 11597, pp. 314–326. Springer, Cham (2019). https://doi.org/10.1007/978-3-030-22341-0_25

11. Koedinger, K.R., Anderson, J.R., Hadley, W.H., Mark, M.A.: Intelligent tutoring goes to school in the big city. Int. J. Artif. Intell. Educ. **8**(1), 30–43 (1997)
12. Kulik, J.A., Fletcher, J.D.: Effectiveness of intelligent tutoring systems: a meta-analytic review. Rev. Educ. Res. **86**(1), 42–78 (2016)
13. Landsberg, C.R., Mercado, A.D., Van Buskirk, W.L., Lineberry, M., Steinhauser, N.: Evaluation of an adaptive training system for submarine periscope operations. In: 56th International Proceedings on Human Factors and Ergonomics, Los Angeles, vol. 56, no. 1, pp. 2422–2426. SAGE Publications (2012)
14. Landsberg, C.R., Van Buskirk, W.L., Astwood, R.S., Mercado, A.D., Aakre, A.J.: Adaptive training considerations for simulation-based training. Special report No 2010-001, NAWCTSD. Naval Air Warfare Center Training Systems Division, Orlando (2010)
15. Lane, H.C., VanLehn, K.: Teaching the tacit knowledge of programming to novices with natural language tutoring. Comput. Sci. Educ. **15**, 183–201 (2005)
16. Lee, J., Park, O.: Adaptive instructional systems. In: Spector, J.M., Merrill, D., van Merriënboer, J., Driscoll, M. (eds.) Handbook of Research on Educational Communications and Technology, 3rd edn., pp. 469–484. Lawrence Erlbaum Associates, New York (2008)
17. Lusardi, A., Mitchell, O.S.: The Importance of Financial Literacy: Opening a New Field (No. w31145). National Bureau of Economic Research (2023)
18. Ma, W., Adesope, O.O., Nesbit, J.C., Liu, Q.: Intelligent tutoring systems and learning outcomes: a meta-analysis. J. Educ. Psychol. **106**(4), 901–918 (2014)
19. Marraffino, M.D., Johnson, C.I., Whitmer, D.E., Steinhauser, N.B., Clement, A.: Advise when ready for game plan: adaptive training for JTACs. In: Proceedings of the Interservice/Industry Training, Simulation, and Education Conference, Orlando. National Training Systems Association (2019)
20. Marraffino, M.D., Schroeder, B.L., Fraulini, N.W., Van Buskirk, W.L., Johnson, C.I.: Adapting training in real time: an empirical test of adaptive difficulty schedules. Mil. Psychol. **33**(3), 136–151 (2021)
21. Mettler, E., Kellman, P.J.: Adaptive response-time-based category sequencing in perceptual learning. Vis. Res. **99**, 111–123 (2014)
22. Office of Educational Technology: Reimagining the role of technology in education: 2017 national education technology plan update U.S. Department of Education Washington, DC (2017)
23. Park, O., Lee, J.: Adaptive instructional systems. In: Jonassen, D. (ed.) Handbook of Research for Educational Communications and Technology, pp. 651–684. MacMillan Publishers, New York (2003)
24. Reiser, B.J., Anderson, J.R., Farrell, R.G.: Dynamic student modelling in an intelligent tutor for LISP programming. In: Joshi, A.K. (ed.) Proceedings of the Ninth International Joint Conference on Artificial Intelligence, San Francisco, pp. 8–13. Morgan Kaufmann (1985)
25. Research and Markets. https://www.researchandmarkets.com/reports/5451259/global-adaptive-learning-market-2023-2028-by. Accessed 23 Jun 2023
26. Romero, C., Ventura, S., Gibaja, E.L., Hervas, C., Romero, F.: Web-based adaptive training simulator system for cardiac life support. Artif. Intell. Med. **38**(1), 67–78 (2006)
27. Serge, S.R., Priest, H.A., Durlach, P.J., Johnson, C.I.: The effects of static and adaptive performance feedback in game-based training. Comput. Hum. Behav. **29**(3), 1150–1158 (2013)
28. Shute, V.J., Zapata-Rivera, D.: Adaptive technologies. In: Spector, J.M., Merrill, D., van Merriënboer, J., Driscoll, M. (eds.) Handbook of Research on Educational Communications and Technology, 3rd edn., pp. 277–294. Lawrence Erlbaum Associates, New York (2008)
29. Spain, R., Rowe, J., Smith, A., et al.: A reinforcement learning approach to adaptive remediation in online training. J. Defense Model. Simul. **19**(2), 173–193 (2022)

30. Steenbergen-Hu, S., Cooper, H.: A meta-analysis of the effectiveness of intelligent tutoring systems on college students' academic learning. J. Educ. Psychol. **106**(2), 331–347 (2014)
31. Stottler, R.H., Vinkavich, M.: Tactical Action Officer intelligent tutoring system (TAO ITS). Defense Technical Information Center (DTIC) (2006)
32. Vanderwaetere, M., Desmet, P., Clarebout, G.: The contribution of learner characteristics in the development of computer-based adaptive learning environments. Comput. Hum. Behav. **27**, 118–130 (2011)
33. VanLehn, K.: The relative effectiveness of human tutoring, intelligent tutoring systems, and other tutoring systems. Educ. Psychol. **46**(4), 197–221 (2011)
34. Van Buskirk, W.L., Fraulini, N.W., Schroeder, B.L., Johnson, C.I., Marraffino, M.D.: Application of theory to the development of an adaptive training system for a submarine electronic warfare task. In: Sottilare, R.A., Schwarz, J. (eds.) HCII 2019. LNCS, vol. 11597, pp. 352–362. Springer, Cham (2019). https://doi.org/10.1007/978-3-030-22341-0_28
35. Vygotsky, L.S.: Mind in Society: The Development of Higher Psychological Processes. Harvard University Press, Cambridge (1978)
36. Wickens, C.D., Hutchins, S., Carolan, T., Cumming, J.: Effectiveness of part-task training and increasing-difficulty training strategies: a meta-analysis approach. Hum. Factors **55**(2), 461–470 (2013)

Effect of Visual Support Information and Participant's Personality on Training in Virtual Environments

Daiji Kobayashi[1]([⊠]) [iD], Ryusei Fukuda[2], Seiji Kikuchi[2], and Shinji Miyake[2]

[1] Chitose Institute of Science and Technology, Hokkaido, Japan
d-kobaya@photon.chitose.ac.jp
[2] Graduate School of Chitose Institute of Science and Technology, Hokkaido, Japan
{m2230290,m2210080}@photon.chitose.ac.jp

Abstract. In recent years, augmented reality and virtual reality have emerged as powerful technologies for education and training. The basic concept of augmented reality involves overlaying additional information on real world. In contrast, training using virtual reality technology is aimed at avoiding harm in real environments, or enhancing user engagement in immersive virtual environments. In this study, we observed participants' performances during iterative training in three types of virtual environments with different content supporting manipulation. Rod tracking was used as the training task, in line with a previous study. Twenty-eight healthy students (21.8 ± 1.2 yrs.) voluntarily participated in this study. The participants' performances were quantified via the number of contacts with the sides of the slit by the rod. Subjective fatigue, stress, and sense of embodiment are assessed by a questionnaire survey. The experimental results suggested that visual support information in training virtual environments enhanced the sense of self-location and body ownership. Further, the participants' personalities were classified as Type A or Type B based on their performance in the training session. Consequently, important information about designing the virtual environment for training and experimental tasks were obtained.

Keywords: Training environment · visual support information · Type A and Type B personalities

1 Introduction

Virtual reality (VR) as a human-computer interface is commonly used for simulator training. Recent virtual environments (VEs) displayed on high-resolution head-mounted displays (HMDs) provide elaborate VEs with a sense of immersion and reality to users. Concerning acquisition of skills for manipulation in virtual training environments, it has been demonstrated previously that artificial haptic feedback decreases the sense of embodiment (SoE) and interferes with the acquisition of manual skills [1]. Recent advanced HMD and haptic devices are able to present more realistic VEs. Gisler et al. (2020) suggested that high immersive virtual training environments are appropriate for better

P. Zaphiris et al. (Eds.): HCII 2023, LNCS 14060, pp. 128–138, 2023.
https://doi.org/10.1007/978-3-031-48060-7_10

performance [2]. Further, designing visual support information for learning skills has been implemented previously in augmented reality (AR) [3]. In practice, for enhancing situation awareness (SA) promoting skill learning, AR presents additional objects on the three-dimensional space for comprehending situations or human-computer interaction [4].

Concerning training for decision making task using a personal computer (PC), Kozlowski et al. (2001) discussed training goals and goal orientation traits considering multiple factors of training outcome [5]. Further, it is believed that recent immersive environments created by VR technology enable learning not only cognitive skills, but also manipulation skills. Although 'ISO/DIS 9241-820: Ergonomics of human-system interaction—Part 820: Ergonomic guidance on interactions in immersive environments including AR and VR is currently under development [6]. However, concrete design guidelines for virtual training environments are rarely discussed. It is possible to design or modify virtual training environments from the aspect of enhancing goal orientation without careful consideration of the trainee's characteristics, such as cognitive mechanism, personality, or motivation. This study aims to evaluate the potential harm from training in VE experimentally from the viewpoint of presenting information affording proper manipulation. In this regard, we focused on the method of presenting information for supporting manipulation task execution by trainees, referred to as visual support information (VSI).

2 Methods

2.1 Experimental Task for Training

The training task in VE and testing in the real world was performed repeatedly by the participants. The task goal was clearly described, and the participants were able to recognize the performance level each trial. Further, training in the VE was designed based on the real test environment to ensure consistent training-testing performance. A rod-tracking-task (RTT) was used in this study for training, and the SoE was in the virtual and physical environments was evaluated, as reported in a previous study [7]. When executing the RTT, the participants were required to grasp a rod with their right hand and attempt to move the rod between the ends of a curved slit in a panel, without contacting the sides of the slit. The panel was installed in front of the participants, and rotated anticlockwise 45° with respect to the participant, as shown in Fig. 1.

In this regard, successful execution of the RTT requires a certain level of skill, and the task must interest participants to some extent. The training VE for the RTT was displayed in an HMD (HTC Vive Pro Eye), and controlled by our software running Unity on a PC (Lenovo Legion T730) with Microsoft Windows 11 Pro operating system. The rod operated by the participants comprised a stick and a tracker (HTC Vive Tracker 3.0). To present haptic feedback, a vibrating device was attached on the back of right hand. The vibrating device contained a vibrating motor controlled by the PC via a USB I/O terminal (Contec AIO-160802AY-USB). Further, a hand avatar was presented in the VE to increase the sense of immersion. The hand avatar was controlled by the participant's hands as recorded by the PC via a motion sensor (Leap Motion) attached on the HMD.

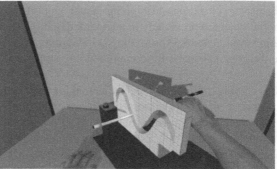

Fig. 1. A participant wearing HMD executing the RTT in the virtual environment, as shown in the left panel. The HMD shows the training VE in which the participant executes the RTT, as shown in the right panel.

To test the result of training in the virtual environment, a physical RTT system was constructed. The signal recording contact between the rod and the slit edges was sent to the PC via another USB I/O terminal, and contact was notified by a red LED indicator for the participants, as shown in Fig. 2.

Fig. 2. Experimental scene of a participant executing the RTT in the real world.

2.2 Training Environments

Considering the aim of this study, two types of training VEs presenting VSI as well as a type without VSI were created. A VSI presenting a blue line indicating the desired direction of the rod was applied in our previous study; however, the effectiveness of this approach was unclear [7]. Another type of training VE used was an unphysical scenario in which the participant was able to see the rod through the transparent parts of the slit. Normally, the rod through the slit was invisible in the physical environment, and therefore, the VE was also designed in accordance with the real world. However, it is possible to modify the training VE using the unphysical VSI if the training environments can be designed considering only the aspect of exposing the rod inside the slit. The VE type without VSI was also created for comparing the effectiveness of the two environments.

These virtual training environments are shown in Fig. 3. Further, the physical RTT system appropriated as a training environment in real. Consequently, we developed and used four training environments, i.e., three VEs and the real environment. Further, the training VEs are required to provide some level of SoE for successful training; therefore, the SoE comprising the sense of body ownership (SoBO), sense of agency (SoA), and sense of self-location (SoSL) were assessed by the participants using an SoE questionnaire. The SoE sores were averaged for each VE according to our previous study [7].

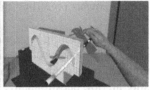

Fig. 3. Three types of training VEs: VE without additional VSI (Left side), VE with additional VE (center), and VE with unphysical VE (right side). The additional VSI indicates the proper direction of the rod by a blue line, and the

2.3 Participants and Their Characteristics

Participants were sixteen healthy male and twelve female student volunteers ranging from 20 to 26 years of age (mean = 21.8, SD = 1.2). They had no prior experience executing the RTT, but had experience using other HMDs such as for playing VR games. Thus, the participants were not RTT professionals or highly motivated individuals. Therefore, it was expected that their personalities could be classified (as Type A, Type B or other) based on their performance in the training task. Regarding the nature of Type A and Type B, Friedman and Rosenman (1974) discussed that Type B individuals may be equally or even more ambitious than Type A individuals, but the ambition associated with Type B individuals is characterized by confidence and satisfaction, whereas the ambition associated with the Type A behavior pattern is dominated by anxiety and anger [8]. Further, Ward and Eisler (1987) showed that not only are Type A subjects likely to set goals in excess of their performance potential, but also are generally less satisfied with their performance and evaluate it less favorably than Type B subjects [9]. Therefore, we evaluated the participants' type of personality in advance using the conventional Type A questionnaire for Japanese adults standardized by Yamazaki et al. (1992) [10].

The participants' informed consents were obtained before the experiment, and we divided the participants into four groups randomly; however, each group comprised three females and four males. The groups were assigned the different training environments, i.e., real, virtual without VSI, virtual with additional VSI, and virtual with unphysical VSI.

2.4 Procedure

After the questionnaire survey on the participants' personal characteristics, subjective fatigue was assessed using the subjective fatigue questionnaire (SFQ) before the experiment. Then, we explained the RRT, instructed them to conduct a few trials in the assigned training environment, and asked to execute the RTT without contacting the sides of the slit as far as possible fifteen times repeatedly, with a five-minute rest every five trials. Therefore, the participants assigned the virtual environments wore the HMDs for approximately an hour until they finished training. During the training session, we interviewed the participants regarding their subjective opinions during the rest between each five trials.

After the training session, the participants' subjective mental workload was assessed using the National Aeronautics Space Administration Task Load Index (NASA-TLX), and then, participants were assessed in terms of subjective fatigue using SFQ and SoE using an SoE questionnaire. Furthermore, the training was assessed by three test trials using the physical RTT system in the test session.

The performance in the training and test sessions were measured by the number of contacts with the sides of the slit by the rod; however, the participants' performances in the test sessions were measured by the average number of contacts over three times. The performance of the participants trained in the same environment were compared via the average number of contacts in the test. NASA-TLX scores were compared between the conditions using a paired t-test. Further, the averaged SFQ scores including the scores at the pre- and the post-sessions were compared for the different conditions.

3 Results

3.1 Characteristics of the Participants

From the investigation using the Type A questionnaire for Japanese, all twenty-eight participants included one of Type A individual, ten of Type B individuals, and the other. Table 1 shows the assigned training environments for Type A and Type B participants. The characteristics of the participants' performance for both Type A and Type B are discussed.

Table 1. Number of participants recognized as Type A and Type B.

Personality	Real	VR	VR with additional VSI	VR with unphysical VSI
Type A	0	0	1	0
Type B	3	3	1	3

3.2 Performance

Figure 4 shows the change in performances with the training environment over fifteen iterations and test performance. Additionally, the participants in each training environment were seven individuals, and the error bars indicate the standard errors (SE).

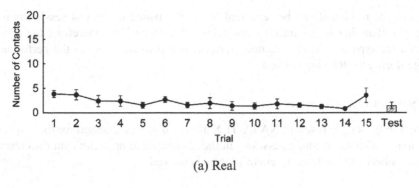

(a) Real

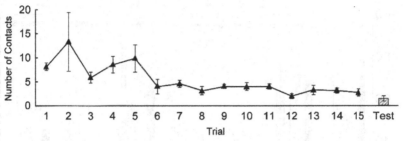

(b) VE without additional VSI

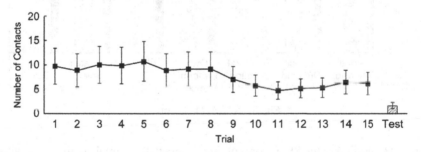

(c) VE with additional VSI

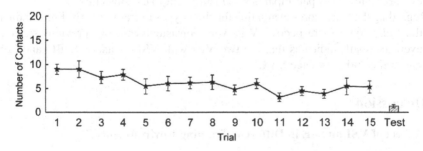

(d) VE with unphysical VSI

Fig. 4. Changes in performance in respective training environments.

From the results, it can be seen that the performance in the test session is more successful than that in the training regardless of training VEs; therefore, the relation between the type of VSI and training performance is not clear from the performance change during the training session.

3.3 Subjective Assessment

Figure 5 indicates the result of NASA-TLX averaged scores assessed for the respective participants after the training sessions. In the results, there no significant difference in the scores between the training environments is noticed.

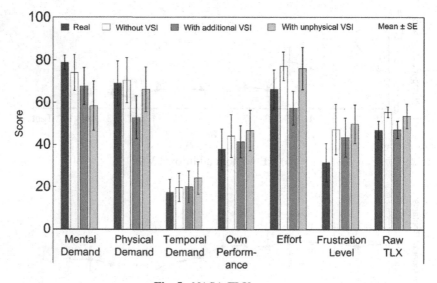

Fig. 5. NASA-TLX scores.

Figure 6 shows that the SFQ scores of drowsiness in the virtual environment without VSI was less than the scores in the virtual environment with additional VSI ($p < .1$). However, the number of participants was insufficient to establish this.

Regarding the SoE scores evaluating the three types of training VEs, Fig. 7 indicates that the SoE scores of respective VEs were consistent with our previous study [7]. However, the result indicates that the two VEs with VSI enhanced SoBO and SoSL, whereas VSI could weakened SoA.

4   Discussions

4.1   Effect of VSI on SoE in Different Training Environments

Considering the SoE provided by the different training VEs, Fig. 7 indicates that the characteristics of VE without VSI are different from the other VEs with VSI. For instance, the participants trained in the VE with VSI were exhibited enhanced SoSL and SoBO

(max score = 25)

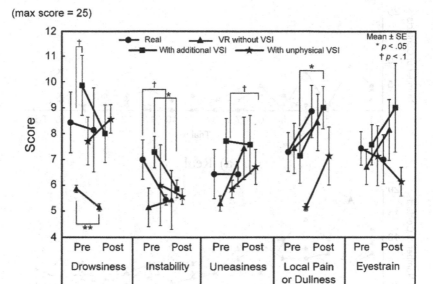

Fig. 6. SFQ scores.

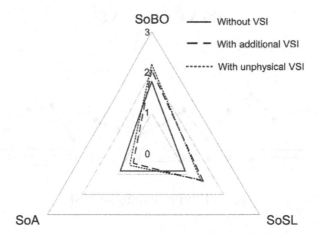

Fig. 7. SoE scores evaluating the three VEs.

than those for the VE without VSI; therefore, it is assumed that the VSI improved training VE. Although the standard errors in the number of contacts in the VE with additional VSI were higher than those in the VE with the unphysical VSI, the relationship between the characteristics of VSI and performance during training is not clear.

4.2 Effect of Participant's Characteristics on Performance During Training

The participants recruited for this study included ten of twenty-eight Type B individuals and one Type A individual. Therefore, we focused on the Type B participants'

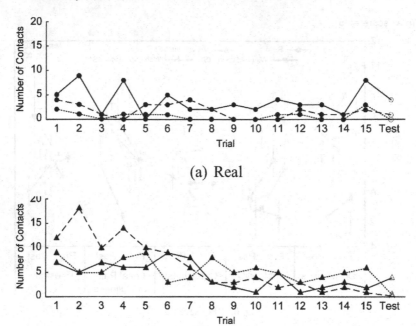

(a) Real

(b) VE without VSI

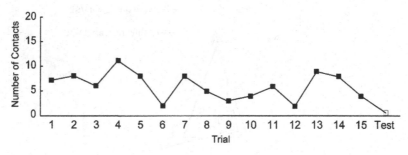

(c) VE with additional VSI

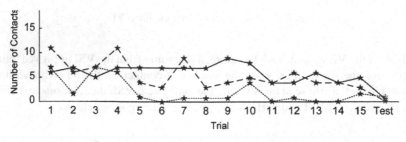

(d) VE with unphysical VSI

Fig. 8. Change of performance during training session by Type B participants.

performance during the training session. From the results, the performance in the real environment was identified as more successful than that in the other virtual environments, except for the last trial. In this regard, participants including individuals with Type B characteristics indicated that they were inattentive at the last trial. Figure 8(a) indicates the trend indicating the fifteenth performance was less successful than the fourteenth performance. As described before, Freedman and Rosenman (1974) noted that the ambition associated with Type B individuals is characterized by confidence and satisfaction. In the performance results shown in Fig. 4, it can be considered that training in real was easier than training in the other virtual environments, and manipulation skills were obtained in the early trials. Therefore, the Type B participants were satisfied with their performance, and had weak incentive to improve their performance toward the last trials.

5 Conclusions

In this study, the relationship between performances during training and VSI as well as the participants' Type B characteristics were considered. The number of participants were twenty-eight, and they were divided into four groups. Consequently, we are unable to obtain any definitive knowledge from statistical analysis. For instance, we could not obtain information on the subjective fatigue and stress from the results. However, several indicators concerning the design of VE for training were observed as follows. First, it is possible that the VSI applied in this study affected the trainees' SoSL and SoBO regardless of different design characteristics. Therefore, the design characteristics should be considered in future studies. Second, this study suggests that there is a potential for impact of the participant's personality (Type A and Type B) on their performance during training. Therefore, it is required the participants' personalities need to be considered when designing experimental VEs, and user engagement in the VEs in case of training tasks should be enhanced.

References

1. Kobayashi, D., et al.: Effect of artificial haptic characteristics on virtual reality performance. In: Yamamoto, S., Mori, H. (eds) HCII 2019, LNCS, vol. 11570, pp. 24–35. Springer Nature, Switzerland (2019). https://doi.org/10.1007/978-3-030-22649-7_3
2. Gisler, J., Hirt, C., Kunz, A., Holzwarth, V.: Designing Virtual Training Environments: Does Immersion increase Task Performance? International Conference on Cyberworlds, pp. 125–128 (2020)
3. Sun, L., Osman, H.A., Lang, J.: An augmented reality online assistance platform for repair tasks. ACM Trans. Multimed. Comput. Commun. Appl. 17(2), 1–23 (2021)
4. Bell, B., Höllerer, T.: An annotated situation-awareness aid for augmented reality. In: UIST 2002: Proceedings of the 15th Annual ACM symposium on User Interface Software and Technology, pp. 213–216 (2002)
5. Kozlowski, S.W.J., Gully, S.G., Brown, K.G., Salas, E., Smith, E.M., Nason, E.R.: Effects of training goals and goal orientation traits on multidimensional training outcomes and performance adaptability. Organ. Behav. Hum. Decis. Process. 85(1), 1–31 (2001)

6. ISO/DIS 9241-820: Ergonomics of human-system interaction—Part 820: Ergonomic guidance on interactions in immersive environments including augmented reality (2023)
7. Kobayashi, D., Ito, Y., Nikaido, R., Suzuki, H., Harada, T.: Virtual environment assessment for tasks based on sense of embodiment. In: Stephandis, C. et al. (eds.) HCII 2020, LNCS, vol. 12428, pp. 368–382. Springer Nature, Switzerland (2020). https://doi.org/10.1007/978-3-030-59990-4_28
8. Friedman, M., Rosenman, R.H.: Type A Behavior and Your Heart. Knopf, New York (1974)
9. Ward, C.H., Eisle, R.M.: Type A behavior, achievement striving, and a dyes functional self-evaluation system. J. Pers. Soc. Psychol. **53**(2), 318–326 (1987)
10. Yamasaki, K., Tanaka, Y., Miyata, Y.: A Type A questionnaire for Japanese adults (KG'S Daily Life Questionnaire): its standardization and methods of application. Type A **3**(1), 33–45 (1992)

Comics-Based Online Course as a Learning Resource for Encouraging Students' Speaking Activity Through Intensive Independent Learning

Marina S. Kogan(✉) [iD], Anna V. Gavrilova [iD], Natalia E. Anosova [iD], and Ekaterina D. Petrikova

St. Petersburg Polytechnic University, Polytechnicheskaya, 29, 19525 St. Petersburg, Russia
kogan_ms@spbstu.ru

Abstract. The reasons for the reluctance of junior students of technical universities to speak out in foreign language classes are diverse and difficult to identify in each case. The transition to online learning caused by the Covid19 pandemic exacerbated this trend. Today, one of the important tasks is to search for non-standard solutions and strong incentives that could encourage students to actively participate in discussions, make the "silent ones" speak. Using comics as an additional educational resource could be one of such solutions. Although there is a number of works discussing the use of comics in teaching, the prospects for their use in a foreign language course at university have not been studied thoroughly. The necessary prerequisites for using comics in the educational process are students' interest in them and teachers' awareness of their didactic potential. As part of the preliminary stage of the study, the interest of 1st–2nd year students in comics and the lack of experience of using them as an educational resource among SPbPU EFL teachers were revealed through a questionnaire. After creating an open online course on the *Stepik* platform based on the popular comics *Ava's Demon* and *Ghost Blade*, aimed at developing productive speech skills, including tasks for audio recording of speaking tasks, its effectiveness was assessed as part of intensive independent work of the students from the "risk group" due to their poor performance in the course of foreign language in the spring semester of 2020/2021 academic year. The results collected by analyzing the learning outcomes of the online course and monitoring the work of students, as well as surveying students feedback after completion of the course, and observing the work of students in the classroom after the end of the course confirmed its effectiveness in developing the speaking skills of "silent" students. The fact that there has been a growth in a number of users who registered on the *Stepik* platform – mainly young adults – proves the increased interest in learning English with the help of comics. Further research steps are outlined.

Keywords: Reluctance · Speaking activities · EFL classes · Engineering students · Comics · Comics-based online course · Learning resource

P. Zaphiris et al. (Eds.): HCII 2023, LNCS 14060, pp. 139–153, 2023.
https://doi.org/10.1007/978-3-031-48060-7_11

1 Introduction

The problem of motivating undergraduate students to be more active in the classes that are not related to the core of their major has been discussed by many authors. In particular, a number of authors mentioned the problems with EFL teaching in the countries where this discipline is compulsory for students of all majors. For example, A. Bolton [1] pointed out that there was a low level of students' knowledge of foreign language and the resulting problems in various types of communication. EFL teachers use modern computer technologies as a tool in solving many methodological problems. An overview of the most promising areas of research within the framework of CALL for 40 years is given in the article [2].

The lack of students' motivation can be manifested in the high level of truancy, untimely completion of homework, reluctance to speak in a foreign language in the classroom. In the context of the dominant communicative approach to teaching foreign languages, the students' behavior of keeping silent in the classroom is a big problem for teachers in assessing their knowledge. The most typical reasons for such behavior discussed in literature [3, 4] are the reluctance to speak due to some reason (e.g., the lack of interest in the topic, bad mood, focus on other priorities, etc.) and struggling with the hesitation to speak due to various reasons, with the most typical one being a sort of psychological barrier or lack of confidence in own speaking skills. Thus, Savaşç found that the reasons given by silent students in interviews differed from those given by them and their classmates when filling out a questionnaire devoted to the study of the same problem [4: 2684]. According to the outstanding Russian researcher E.I.Passov, the reason may be the lack of attention paid in high school to the development of students' ability to speak clearly and express their thoughts cohesively. According to the researcher, modern system of education, focused on the final assessment, contributes to the unconscious automatic memorizing of ready-made knowledge, rather than its critical comprehension [5].

So called "silent" students and students not paying proper attention to their University foreign language classes fail to complete their portfolio assignments and obtain admission to the exam session by the end of an academic year as they find it difficult to study the learning materials independently. It is obvious that independent study of teaching material in large volumes within a short time period cannot contribute to the development of communication skills in a foreign language, nor can it increase the motivation to study English for special purposes in the future. The situation with these students became even worse in spring of 2021, during the pandemic.

The transition to online learning caused by the Covid-19 pandemic in the spring of 2020 and the anti-Covid-19 measures in the fall of 2020 led to the following situation: the spring semester of 2020/2021 academic year was the first full semester of off-line classes for 1st year students after the autumn semester at university and the previous spring semester of their last high school year. Though many institutions of higher education (HE) managed aptly to organize online classes in different disciplines including English language classes [6, 7], others failed to do so, which resulted in students' dissatisfaction in online learning amid the COVID-19 [8]. Researchers from Harvard University concluded that online instruction was a primary driver of widening achievement gaps in secondary schools across all states in the USA, with high-poverty schools being leaders in this anti-achievement trend [9]. At the same time, students developed the habit of learning online. It is this circumstance that we decided to use in an attempt to increase the motivation of students to learn English by creating a comics-based online course.

2 Background

2.1 The Role of Comics in FL Teaching: A Brief Review of the Literature

Many researchers of the comics genre agree that the first comic artist who produced comics as we know them today was a Swiss teacher, author, painter, cartoonist, and caricaturist of the XIX century Rodolphe Töpffer (as Wikipedia refers to him) [10: 67]. Töpffer applied a new technique for teaching grammar and reading by creating sets (panels, series) of pictures with funny captions that formed complete plots. Comic books have long been treated as a "low genre". However, coverage of serious and even tragic topics by comics authors gradually changed the prevailing stereotype. These works are devoted to Holocaust (Pulitzer-prize winning graphic novel *Maus* designed by A. Spiegelman in 1986), siege of Leningrad (*Survilo* by Olga Lavrentyeva, 2019), racial discrimination/genocide [11]; there are websites with a collection of comics based on classic works[1], business[2], science [12], etc.

With the development of multimedia technologies, new comic's forms appear, for example, animated comics. Individual panels are expanded into a full shot while sound effects, voice acting, and animation are added to the original artwork. Text boxes, speech bubbles and the onomatopoeia are typically removed to feature more of the original artwork being animated. Motion comics are often released as short serials covering a story.

Recently, there has been a growing enthusiasm across a number of diverse fields and disciplines, including education, that comics might actually offer multiple opportunities for sophisticated literary engagement across all educational levels, and for readers of all abilities, ages, and persuasions [13]. The author cites research on the use of comics in history classes, creative writing, and ESL in high school; business education, and negotiation skills development at university level [14]. The use of comics in the development of children's reading skills in their native language in the light of the 'decline' of reading trend in America was supported by a well-known specialist in this field S. Krashen [15].

However, Lewkowich [13] notes that there can be polarized attitudes towards the use of comics in the classroom expressed by both teachers and students. These attitudes may range from excitement and happiness to worry, unease, and hesitation to use these texts as teaching aids.

In a review article [16] the authors analyze the experience of using comics and graphic novels in the ESL classroom, which was reflected in 25 articles published in peer-reviewed international and national (Indonesian) journals for 10 years (2012 - 2021). The authors show that comics can be most successfully used in secondary school education for improving vocabulary and grammar, reading and writing skills. The problems concern

---

[1] https://www.classicalcomics.com/.

[2] https://www.litres.ru/serii-knig/biznes-V-komiksah/.

the need to carefully choose the suitable topic corresponding to the student's level of proficiency, interest, or readiness. The lack of the comic strips for teaching a particular grammar aspect or vocabulary item, poor coverage of benefits of using comic strips in language learning in specialist literature might lead to the development of new procedures in using comic strips in the language classroom. A comprehensive overview of possible tasks/activities when using graphic novels as a learning resource is described by Lewis [17].

The study [18], not included in the review [16] can be an example of the creative use of comics in the ESL classroom in the absence of strict guidelines. As part of four-week quasi-experimental study, first-year students from an English Language Teaching Department of a state university in Turkey studied 40 most frequent and useful figurative idioms from the Michigan Academic English Spoken Corpus (MICASE) using graphic novel based on them. At the end of the experiment the participants in the experimental group performed significantly better on the post-test, thus demonstrating the efficiency of the graphic novel in teaching academic vocabulary. The interesting point is that there was no available graphic novel based on the MICASE idioms. It was the authors who first made up a story around the selected idioms, wrote a script, converted the script to a graphic novel with the use of computer software[3], and, finally, used the graphic novel throughout the study [18: 98]. Another important point about this research for our study is that it is one of the very few studies devoted to using graphic novels at University level while the majority research in the area is conducted with secondary school learners. Another valuable resource in academic English for (young) adult learners is Magoosh Comics developed by D. Recine on some topics for TOEFL and IELTS tests preparation (e.g., hard TOEFL words, prefixes in TOEFL vocabulary, Common Mistakes with Next, This and Last) available at Magoosh Blog – TOEFL Test[4]. The author consistently developed the main postulate of his Master thesis: "Comics aren't just for fun anymore" [19].

A longitudinal exploratory study by Calafato and Gudim, that lasted for the whole academic year [20], investigated ways of the use of comics as a pedagogical resource in order to increase 7-th Grade Moscow school pupils' willingness to communicate in Russian, their second language. The researchers conclude that "use of comics increased their desire to interact through Russian while also boosting their self-confidence and language skills" [20: 281]. They describe the teacher's approach to using comics as the combination of 'language-focused, reader-response, art critique, and visual story-telling approaches' thus highlighting how teachers can benefit from the lack of a strict procedure to follow when integrating comic strips into second language teaching methodology.

Before choosing the way to use comics for the purpose of developing communication skills among 1st year SPbPU students, we decided to conduct a preliminary survey to determine the degree of students' awareness about comics, their level of interest and their willingness to use comics to develop communication skills.

---

[3] Www.storyboardthat.com
[4] https://magoosh.com/toefl/author/davidr/.

2.2 Survey of SPbPU Junior Students About Their Attitude Towards Using Comics in Learning at the Preliminary Stage of the Experiment

The Questionnaire consisted of 20 multiple-choice questions and open-ended questions in Russian. The purpose of the survey was to find out the attitude of students towards comics; frequency of reading/watching comics of different genres; the language in which students read comics (in their native language or in English); whether they discuss the content of comics with friends; whether they think that reading comics in English would help them in learning the language; what aspects of English could be improved by reading comics; what format is preferable for using English-language comics for learning - individually or in the classroom.

53 students majoring in Physics and Engineering aged 18–19 took part in the survey. 66% of them rated their language level as intermediate, 19% as advanced, 15% - pre-intermediate. 20% of respondents have certificates confirming the level of the language.

The survey showed that although the majority of students do not regularly read comics (only in Russian – 43%, only in English – 8.6%; in both languages – 30% of students) and do not discuss them with friends (74%), more than half of the respondents gave examples of their favorite comics and films based on comics. The top five favorite genres were science fiction, superheroes, classic fantasy, school/student life, funny everyday situations. Of the major comic book universes, Star Wars, Marvel, and DC Comics were most frequently cited by respondents. Only two legendary comic book authors – Stan Lee and Neil Gaiman – received more points than the answer *I don't know any author from the list*, which was chosen by 22% of respondents. More than half of the respondents agreed with the key statements for our experiment: "I am interested in reading comics in English", "Discussion of favorite/interesting comics in English is good for improving my English speaking skills", and "I would be more interested in learning English if the FL course included using comics." Almost 80% of the respondents believe that the use of comics can be productive when studying English at university, arguing their answer in the field for a free answer by saying that it will make classes more interesting, more enjoyable, and allow you to master slang and idiomatic expressions from the speech of comic book characters (the studies show that comic book characters use idiomatic speech much more frequently than on the average [18]), expand vocabulary, guess the meaning of unfamiliar words from pictures, etc.

2.3 Survey of Teachers at the Preliminary Stage of the Experiment

The second survey was conducted among teachers of foreign languages at Peter the Great St. Petersburg Polytechnic University in order to determine the relevance of creating an online course. The questionnaire consisted of 15 questions. The main questions were the following: what is the percentage of students who prefer to keep silent during English classes; what is the reason for their silence, what pedagogical techniques can be used to motivate them to speak in class; whether comics could be an effective tool for increasing motivation to learn a foreign language. The survey involved 8 teachers at the Department of Foreign Languages of SPbPU aged 26 to 60 years with work experience from 5 to 30 years, working with undergraduate students. All teachers noted that the command of English among students within the groups differed significantly. 80% of teachers noted that there are "silent" students in their groups. According to their estimates, the number of such students is on average 10–20%. According to teachers, from 5% to 30% of students experience obvious psychological difficulties with speaking in the foreign language, and, in general, students experience greater difficulties with oral answers than with written ones.

The majority of respondents use the following methods to encourage students to talk: communicative tasks (6 responses); "small talk" (6 responses); a story about something that the student is fond of (personality, film, book) (7 responses); work in pairs/groups (8 responses). They consider teaching students phrases to politely enter into a conversation less effective (3 responses); increase time for speaking practice at the expense of other activities (3 responses); using interactive electronic resources that provoke conversation in a game format (2 responses). None of the respondents used comics as a didactic resource in their teaching practice. When asked whether comics could increase students' engagement in class, the majority of the teachers found it difficult to answer.

The results of the survey confirmed the need to develop an online resource based on comics for using it in the General English course.

3 Creating an Online Course Based on Comics

3.1 Pedagogical Goals and Means of Their Implementation

The online course was developed as a learning resource in addition to the main textbook "New Language Leader: Intermediate Course book[5]" for 1st year engineering students of SPbPU. When creating the course, an attempt was made to use all speech skills: reading, writing, listening/watching, speaking, revising grammar. Most tasks were assessed automatically, the others required the teacher's assessment. The main attention was paid to the development of speaking skills through working with comics; a variety of exercises were developed for this purpose. The introduction of material in modules 2 – 4 of the course was preceded by a glossary with key words and expressions for understanding the video/text.

For the stage of 'while' and 'after' watching/reading comics, the following types of written tasks were proposed:

– choose and write out key words (using the rewind and pause function, if necessary);
– write about your first impressions of the comic, mention the most interesting moment, in the comments section under the video;
– try to guess and write what will happen next in the story;
– compare what you have read with your expectations;
– share your assumptions about the behavior/ decisions made by the characters in the comments section.

The tasks offered to students after reading the comics included grammatical and communicative parts, involving both oral and written answers. For the grammar part, the authors' texts were written on the plot of the comic so that students could see how

---

[5] Cotton, D., Falvey, D. Kent, S. New Language Leader: Intermediate: Coursebook. Pearson Education Limited, Edinburg (2015).

the grammatical structures studied corresponded to what was happening in the story and how they could be used to retell it.

Grammar tasks were aimed at revising the most difficult grammar structures from the main textbook: Present Perfect Simple, Present Perfect Continuous tenses, Conditional sentences of types 1 and 2. For lexical and grammar tasks, digital forms of standard tasks were used: gap filling with the correct word or grammar form, synonym matching, multiple choice questions.

The lessons consist of steps, in the form of a web page filled with text and media elements. This page may include one of the exercises designed according to the templates provided by *Stepik*. Available templates allow you to create tasks for filling in the gaps, multiple choice tasks, matching values tasks, open clause texts, and others.

Any step containing tasks made using the platform tools is designated by the *Stepik* platform as a "test". The course designer can set how many points a student is awarded for passing the test, whether the student can go further without completing the exercise, how many attempts are allowed to do the task, and whether students may access other learners' answers after submitting their own. The online course that we designed contains 4 modules, 17 lessons and 35 tests, with each module containing from 8 to 16 steps.

Tasks for the development of speaking skills included self-recording speaking tasks. We have not conducted a specific study to find out the reasons why some students prefer to keep silent during English classes. We have developed a system of exercises in such a way as to gradually train students for speaking. With the conscientious completion of each step of the online course, the student acquires the necessary vocabulary and a set of strictures for using in the final task of modules 2–4. In our opinion, this approach reduces the psychological burden when speaking in a foreign language and creates a sense of readiness, competence and control over the situation when creating a monologue on a given topic.

3.2 Comics Selection Criteria

When choosing comics for online course materials, we used the following criteria: the popularity of the comic, its availability and open access, the fact that copyright does not belong to the publisher (the name of the comics is not registered as a trademark); its target audience is young adults, without taboo themes; colorful visual presentation; useful vocabulary and grammar structures corresponding to the curriculum of the course, correspondence of the genre to the interests of students identified during the preliminary survey.

In accordance with the criteria above, we chose two comics: *Ava's Demon* and *GhostBlade*. Both comics have millions of online readers aged between 15 and 30 and correspond to the genres that were mentioned as the most interesting during the preliminary students' survey: science fiction, classic fantasy, heroes with supernatural powers. *Ava's Demon*[6] is ongoing science fiction and fantasy created by Michelle Czajkowski, multimedia web comic about a girl named Ava and the demon haunting her with whom she teams up on a quest for revenge, while fighting her own inner demons along the

---

[6] https://avas-demon.fandom.com/wiki/Ava%27s_Demon#cite_note-8.

way. Many of its episodes have been animated. For our course we borrowed the animated pieces from the YouTube collection[7]. *GhostBlade*[8] is a fantasy comic series that takes place in another world named Neraland. The series set in an older age without any firearms or modern technology is designed by a modern Hong Kongese artist Wang Ling known by his pseudonym WLOP. The pieces for the course were selected from Wang Ling's official gallery on the Deviant Art website[9]. *GhostBlade* is a standard comic panel needed to be scrolled down while reading in the online course.

3.3 Choosing a Platform for Creating an Online Course

We chose *Stepik*[10] as the platform for the online course. The choice of the platform is determined by the following factors: the popularity of the platform in Russia (more than 7 million registered users), the possibility of free placement of the course; the possibility of hosting experimental courses and modules designed by novice teachers and researchers, including courses that are designed as part of Master thesis and PhD dissertations (in contrast to the leading Russian National educational platform *Open education*[11] policy which adopts MOOCs developed only by 12 leading Russian universities), ease of use and navigation; wide functionality, including tools for various exercises and tests; platform mobility, the possibility to use it on any device without downloading additional applications; ease of registration for students; availability of detailed statistics; attractive aesthetics of the platform.

LMS *Stepik* offers a material organization system as follows: the course is divided into modules (sections), each of which has a title and description. Inside the module, "lessons" are designed with individual names. The titles of the lessons and modules make up the general content of the course and are visible when viewing the content page. A cover image can be attached to each lesson. Our course is illustrated with images from the selected comics.

4 Research Questions

1. Is there an interest in comics among the target audience and what is the attitude of teachers towards the resource?
2. Does the individual study of an online course based on the comics help to remove the communication barrier in the classroom settings?
3. Is the designed course a useful resource for learning a foreign language?

---

[7] https://www.youtube.com/@angelinasalvadorini5281/featured.

[8] https://ghost-blade.fandom.com/wiki/Ghost_Blade_Wiki.

[9] https://www.deviantart.com/wlop.

[10] https://stepik.org/catalog.

[11] https://openedu.ru/.

5 Procedure

5.1 Participants

The core of the experimental group included 21 first year engineering students of SPbPU from two academic groups who failed continuous assessment during the spring semester of 2020/2021 academic year for different reasons (high absenteeism rate, staying passive and silent in the classroom; hereafter referred to as "students at risk" (of expulsion from university). They were assigned to the course on obligatory basis and completed it during the first week of May 2021. Another group of 12 students, their group mates, enrolled in the course as volunteers. All students enrolled in the course under their real names so the teacher could monitor their activity. Most of them had a command of English at A2-B1 level according to CERF.

5.2 Data Collection

In the course of the experiment three types of data were collected. They are the following:

- *Stepik* platform analytics about the students' achievements and the results of oral tasks assessed by the teacher through the students' recordings.
- The end-course Questionnaire which was filled out by the experiment participants after the online course completion. It was made up in Russian in electronic format using Google Forms. The questionnaire consisted of 16 questions: 10 on a 5-point Likert scale, with the degree of agreement, where 1 – "completely disagree", 5 – "absolutely agree"; 3 multiple choice questions and 3 questions with a free answer.
- The observation of the classroom session followed right after the online course completion partially devoted to discussion of the students' impressions about the online course.

6 Results and Discussion

6.1 Course Analytics and Audio Self-Recording Creating Task Assessment

The students of the experimental group successfully coped with most of the course assignments, which were automatically assessed, scoring from 225 to 451 points. At the same time, all students of the 'risk group', for whom passing the course with a score of at least 70% of the maximum score was mandatory to obtain admission to the exam, scored at least 300 points.

Let us take a closer look at the assessment of students' self-recorded answers to speaking tasks. For the fact that they were uploaded, students automatically received a certain number of points (25 points each for completing the final oral assignment for modules 2–4 and 60 for the final assignment for the course). In addition to uploading answers to the course, they had to send audio files by e-mail or links to them to the teacher if online tools were used for recording, such as *Speakpipe* voice recorder[12]. Speaking tasks in each module were different. They are presented in Table 1.

---

[12] https://www.speakpipe.com/voice-recorder.

Table 1. Speaking tasks in the online course by modules.

Contents of the module	Speaking task
Module 1 - introductory	—
Module 2 Ava's Demon	Record your own version of the voice over of one scene from the comic
Module 3 GhostBlade	Retel a story using relevant grammar patterns and phrases
Module 4 Comics comparison	Compare two comics in the format of an argumentative statement based on lexical expressions and abstracts prepared beforehand
Final task	Express your opinion about the course in the format of a 3-min monologue

Although all students in the group submitted an assignment for review, listening to the recordings showed that only half of them completed the assignments correctly and conscientiously. The rest referred to technical difficulties with recording or replaced the oral task with a written one. Some deviated from the topic. In some cases, it was impossible to hear the speech in the audio recording. For these students, the automatically assigned scores were recalculated downwards.

There were errors, inaccuracies and silences in the speech of students who sent completed assignments, however, students were actively looking for ways to solve speech difficulties, tried to imitate intonations in order to convey the character of the characters and the tone of the dialogues, and actively use the vocabulary of the lesson. Some students were very self-critical, accompanying the audio file with the following comment: "I listened to my recording and laughed at my typical Russian accent, which I had laughed at before, watching other people's videos". The authors' idea is that by listening to the recording of their own speech, students will pay more attention to pronunciation, the aspect which is not given enough attention in FL courses for engineers.

In the final assignment, many students made or wrote positive and detailed comments about the course itself, emphasizing that the course was more effective compared to standard textbooks and they wanted to work more with this kind of material. Several people mentioned that the course changed their attitude towards comics, which they were not previously interested in, and they would like to continue reading comics [in English] after taking the course. For example: *Very good course, I like it! Thank you for your work. Here is the work on the course! Such a high-quality selection of material and a very interesting presentation.* There were no negative comments.

In addition to automatically scoring for uploading an audio file, LSM *Stepik* counts a "random set of letters and other symbols" for a correct answer, as a result of which some students did not complete the task that required a detailed written answer. Quite indicative is the correspondence of the students of the experimental group during the course. Some complained about the failure to understand the system of tenses in the English language despite many years of effort, and asked to recommend simulators to deal with this problem. There were several comments about the fact that there was a lot of new difficult vocabulary, some asked their counterparts for the answers, but judging by the fact that their final result was far from 100%, they completed the tasks on their own. Meanwhile, there were also boastful reports like: *I'm in shock, at the first attempt* [have done the tasks correctly]; *Wow, it's amazing. I did it at the first attempt!* or *at the second attempt.* The glossary at the beginning of the module was also appreciated by students: *Many thanks. It was abundantly clear, especially after such a widely words consideration.* (original quotation without editing).

6.2   End-Course Questionnaire

21 students people took part in the survey. The results of the survey showed that all participants in the experiment assessed the proposed course as an effective tool in their studies (Score on the Likert scale – 4.7; there are no scores below 4 points). The statement "the course helped improve my English speaking skills" scored 4.6 points. 66% of the respondents said that using comics had a positive effect on their motivation to complete online course assignments.

60% of students noted that after completing the course they would like to continue reading comics in English. At the same time, students had doubts whether they wanted to continue reading exactly those comics that they analyzed during the course (average score 3.6 points). The statement "I am going to tell my teacher, friends or pen pals about the course in English" scored 4.3 points. This indicates the great potential of comics for the development of speaking skills, provided that they are used as a pedagogical resource or medium in a foreign language course. It was an interesting finding taking into account that in the preliminary survey, we found out that the majority of students who read comics had no desire to discuss them with friends.

66% of students supported the idea to use more comics in foreign language classes.

The complexity of the course was rated as medium (3.2 points on a 5-point scale). The willingness to share the online course with friends and acquaintances who study English was 4.7 points. All respondents agreed that this online course, in their opinion, is a useful additional resource for studying English.

Vocabulary, grammar, reading and speaking were mentioned as the most useful aspects of the course. Among the most interesting tasks, the respondents quoted reading comics (77%), followed by watching videos, choosing vocabulary and translating idiomatic phrases into English, all of which with equal marks (59%). Retelling turned out to be the most interesting self-recording speaking task, although with a significant lag behind the tasks on working with vocabulary.

The simplest tasks were making conditional sentences based on comics and reading comics. The most difficult are self-recording tasks, among which an argumentative statement with a persuasive speech is the most challenging one (as stated by 68% of respondents). It is followed in terms of difficulty by the task of retelling the episode (54.5%) and dubbing the comic book (50%) were mentioned as less difficult ones.

Among the reasons why recording an audio file turned out to be a difficult task for students, the following were mentioned: the difficulty of formulating thoughts in English; a small amount of previous conversational practice; increased level of students' self-criticism. For some students it took a lot of time and effort to make a satisfactory record; they had problems with poor quality of the microphone available; difficulties in making their arguments; difficulties in conveying emotions in English; pronunciation difficulties.

Students spent from 3 to 8 h to complete the course, within the period of 2–7 days.

6.3 Observation for 'Students at Risk' Activities in the Classroom

After the experiment the teacher conducted a classroom session summing up the results of the online course with the two groups (28 and 25 people) which participated in experimental training. The course designer was present at these sessions as an observer, recording the activity of 'students at risk'. 20 min of the total session were allotted for discussion.

The teacher asked in English the following questions, suggesting the first three for the all-class discussion, Question 4 – for pair work and Question 5 as a question for concluding discussion:

- What are your overall impressions about the course? Did you like it?
- How did you like the comics used in the course?
- Do you think this course was useful for your English skills? How?
- What parts were the most engaging, and what parts were the most challenging to you? (pair work with making lists and comparing them, and nominating a speaker to report the results to the class)
- Would you like to have more classes based on comics in future?

Students enthusiastically shared their positive opinions, noting that some tasks were more difficult and pointed out the need for a voice recorder. In general, the course was appreciated highly by the students. The observer noted that all students from the 'risk group' participated in group discussion and pair work. The teacher noted the positive impact of the course: students were more active and talkative in class, discussed their experiences with interest, they were less shy about expressing their opinions, including those who are usually silent or reluctant to speak out in class. The teacher's observations are consistent with the results of the final survey, in which some respondents noted the positive impact of the course on their learning outcomes in the course of a foreign language and a removal of communication barrier while speaking English. A month after the end of the online course, 'students at risk' successfully passed the exam in the summer examination session performing well in speaking tasks related to the topics of the course textbook, which confirms the positive impact of the designed online course on the development of speaking skills.

6.4 Interest in the Online Course After the Experiment

In addition to the final questionnaire of the participants in the experiment, the effectiveness of the designed online resource for learning English based on comics is the interest in the online course of the users registered on the *Stepik* platform. As soon as the course was launched on the *Stepik* platform[13,] platform users began to show interest in it, and within the first month 162 course learners besides the SPbPU experimental group

---

[13] https://stepik.org/course/94976/info.

signed up for the course. By the time of writing this paper the total number of registered learners exceeded 6 000. The analysis of the course statistics showed that the majority of learners did not go beyond the first introductory module without even starting the tasks of Module 2. By the end of 2021, 2156 learners enrolled in the course; 34 students (1.6%) completed the course, 533 people (25.3%) completed at least 75% of the tasks; in 2022, 3613 new users signed up for the course; 862 people (24.5%) completed at least 75% of the tasks, 28 people (0.8%) completed the course. During this time, the course was not moderated or updated. It is possible that the lack of feedback from the course moderator and the lack of organized mutual checking of audio recordings and written answers by participants (a common practice in many MOOC courses) led to a decrease in the motivation of enrolled participants to complete all tasks. However, the analysis of the written responses shows that the active learners who completed the course also were conscientious in completing the tasks and discussing each other's answers.

Users' star rating of the course, which represents user satisfaction with a particular MOOC [21], is 4.8. On the home page of the course, 20 participants left their feedback about it (in Russian). Interestingly, though looking as a small number it is close to the figure obtained by the researchers who investigated learner satisfaction with the MOOCs: in their sample of 249 randomly selected MOOCs there were reviews from 6391 users [21], which means that, on average, a MOOC course enjoys about 25,6 reviews. The reasons for low communication activities of learners in MOOC courses have been studied in MOOC literature but the discussion of this phenomenon goes beyond the scope of this paper.

All learner reviews are positive. The main criticism is that the course is short. The main thanks to the designers are for making the presentation of the material engaging, for the discovery of the fact that learning a language can be exciting. Some students, inspired by the course, are planning to continue reading comics or get acquainted with *Ava's Demon* and *GhostBlade* in full.

7 Conclusions and Further Work

In conclusion, it can be stated that all the research objectives of the study are fulfilled.

Our study showed that popular comics can be used for developing a learning resource for teaching a foreign language to undergraduate engineering students. The use of comics in the classroom on a regular basis is hardly possible for a number of reasons. First of all, the limitations relate to the unawareness of EFL teachers about the prospects and functional options of comics in teaching foreign languages, and the discrepancy between the topics of popular comics and the topics of basic English textbooks (in our case, Language Leader Intermediate). Since the topics of comics and textbooks differ a lot, the designed course based on comics can be used as a didactic resource for grammar revision and vocabulary acquisition necessary for communication skills, including the tasks on paraphrasing and summarising, making assumptions, arguing a point of view, etc. After developing these skills on the material of the comics, the student might be able to transfer thus required skills to new communication contexts.

The experiment showed that intensive independent work of students with the online popular comics-based course increases students' interest in the study of a foreign language, helps them to expand vocabulary, strengthens their knowledge of grammar structures and contributes to the removal of psychological barriers in communication in a foreign language. The limitations of this study were its short duration, limited number of participants and impossibility of further monitoring of students' progress in various aspects of learning a foreign language as the experiment was carried out at the end of the academic year.

Monitoring the activity of students in the online course by the teacher is a powerful incentive for students to complete all the tasks of the course while studying it independently. Technically, it would be more convenient to do this if MOOC platforms allowed the creation of closed user groups similar to the ones in social networks. However, this option is missing on the existing MOOC platforms, including *Stepik*.

Taking into account the interest in the designed online comics-based course shown by the students, it can be recommended to organize special seminars/master classes for university teachers on the didactic potential of comics in teaching a foreign language.

Acknowledgements. The authors would like to acknowledge colleagues: Olesya. Medvedeva, a young researcher and English language instructor for Peter the Great St. Petersburg University, PhD in Language Pedagogy, for valuables comments during the work on this paper, and Diana. Yusupova and Anna Boiko, IT engineers, for help in processing the online course statistics.

References

1. Boulton, A.: Testing the limits of data-driven learning: language proficiency and training. ReCALL **21**(1), 37–54 (2009). https://doi.org/10.1017/S0958344009000068
2. Lim, M.H., Aryadoust, V.: A scientometric review of research trends in computer-assisted language learning (1977–2020). Computer Assisted Language, 25p (2021). https://doi.org/10.1080/09588221.2021.1892768
3. Li, H., Lui, Y.: A brief study of reticence in ESL class. Theory Pract. Lang. Stud. **1**(8), 961–965 (2011). https://doi.org/10.4304/tpls.1.8.961-965
4. Savaşç, M.: Why are some students reluctant to use L2 in EFL speaking classes? An action research at tertiary level. Procedia. Soc. Behav. Sci. **116**, 2682–2686 (2014). https://doi.org/10.1016/j.sbspro.2014.01.635
5. Passov, E.I.: Tank modernizacii na nive obrazovanija [Tank of Modernization in the field of education]. GLOSSA-PRESS, Moscow (2008). (In Russian)
6. Brzezinska, M., Cromarty, E.: Emergency remote teaching in the university context: responding to social and emotional needs during a sudden transition online. In: Meiselwitz, G. (ed.) Social Computing and Social Media: Applications in Education and Commerce 2022, LNCS, vol. 13316202, pp. 30–47. Springer, Cham (2022). https://doi.org/10.1007/978-3-031-050 64-0_3
7. Windstein, E., Kogan, M.: Rapid response to the needs of ESL students of a technical university in the time of emergency covid-19 transfer to online classes: ITMO university case study. In: Zaphiris, P., Ioannou, A. (eds.) Learning and Collaboration Technologies: New Challenges and Learning Experiences 2021, LNSC, vol. 12784, pp. 547–567. Springer, Cham (2021). https://doi.org/10.1007/978-3-030-77889-7_38

8. Noori, A.Q.: Online learning experiences amid the COVID-19 pandemic: Students' Perspectives. Academia Letters, Article 4307 (2021)
9. Goldhaber, D., Kane, T., McEachin, A., Morton E., Patterson, T., Staiger, D.: The Consequences of Remote and Hybrid Instruction During the Pandemic. Research Report. Center for Education Policy Research, Harvard University, MA, Cambridge (2022)
10. Van Lente, F., Dunlavey, R.: Comic Book History of Comics. IDW Publishing, San Diego (2012)
11. Laurike in 't Veld The Representation of Genocide in Graphic Novels Erasmus University Rotterdam (2019). https://link.springer.com/book/10.1007/978-3-030-03626-3
12. Paschek, N.: Short science comics for a broad audience – an interview with Jessica Burton and Serge Haan from LUX:plorations. The Comics Grid: J. Comics Scholarship **12**(1), 8, 1–12 (2022). https://doi.org/10.16995/cg.6369
13. Lewkowich, D.: Talking to teachers about reading and teaching with comics: pedagogical manifestations of curiosity and humility. Int. J. Educ. Arts **20**(23) (2019). https://doi.org/10.26209/ijea20n23
14. Wallace, M.: Graphic novels: a brief history, their use in business education, and the potential for negotiation pedagogy. Manage. Depart. Facul. Public. **163** (2017). https://digitalcommons.unl.edu/managementfacpub/163
15. Krashen, S.D.: The decline 'of reading in America, poverty and access to books, and the use of comics in encouraging reading. Teachers College Record (2005). http://www.sdkrashen.com/content/articles/decline_of_reading.pdf
16. Wijaya, E.A., Suwastini, N.K., Adnyani, N.L., Adnyani, K.E.: Comic strips for language teaching: the benefits and challenges according to recent research. ETERNAL (English, Teaching, Learning, and Research Journal). **7**(1), 230–248 (2021). https://doi.org/10.24252/Eternal.V71.2021.A16
17. Lewis, S.: Using graphic novels and comics with ELT learners. In: Donaghy, K., Xerri, D. (eds.) The Image in English Language Teaching, pp. 165–177. Gutenberg Press, Malta (2017)
18. Başal, A., Aytan, T. Demir, İ.: Teaching vocabulary with graphic novels. English Lang Teach. **9**(9) (2016)
19. Recine, D.: Comics Aren't Just For Fun Anymore: The Practical Use of Comics by TESOL Professionals. Master of Arts in TESOL thesis. University of Wisconsin-River Falls (2013). https://minds.wisconsin.edu/handle/1793/65479
20. Calafato, R., Gudim, F.: Comics as a multimodal resource and students' willingness to communicate in Russian. J. Graphic Novels Comics **13**(2), 270–286 (2022). https://doi.org/10.1080/21504857.2021.1951788
21. Hew, K. F., Hu, X., Qiao C., Tang, Y.: What predicts student satisfaction with MOOCs: a gradient boosting trees supervised machine learning and sentiment analysis approach. Comput. Educ. **145**(103724) (2020). https://doi.org/10.1016/j.compedu.2019.103724

Learning Styles and On-Line Learning Analytics: An Analysis of Student Behaviour Based on the Honey and Mumford Model

Michael Lang[✉]🆔

J.E. Cairnes School of Business and Economics, University of Galway, Galway, Ireland
michael.lang@universityofgalway.ie

Abstract. This paper presents an analysis of student behaviour on a Learning Management System (LMS), as observed by means of learning analytics, and compares this against expected behaviour, as put forward by the Honey & Mumford Learning Styles Model (H&M LSM). The H&M Learning Styles Questionnaire (LSQ) was administered on-line to a class of 211 postgraduate students at an Irish university. A response rate of 25% was achieved, yielding 52 usable responses. Descriptive statistical analysis and hierarchical clustering was performed on the data, discovering ten clusters of learning styles, eight of which were distinct and could be quite clearly identified. The most common learning style found was 'Reflector' or variants thereof. Evidence of the existence of the 'Pragmatist', 'Activist' and 'Theorist' learning styles was also discovered. Overall, the study found sufficient evidence to suggest that the H&M LSM is a reasonable predictor of student behaviour on a LMS, notwithstanding its flaws and shortcomings.

Keywords: Learning styles · learning analytics · Learning Management Systems (LMS) · hierarchical cluster analysis

1 Introduction

The concept of learning styles can be very beneficial as it helps teachers tailor their methods to accommodate diverse learners and create a more inclusive and effective learning environment. It also promotes self-awareness among students, encouraging them to understand their personal strengths and weaknesses and adapt their own learning strategies accordingly.

This paper reports on an analysis of student behaviour on the Blackboard learning management system (LMS), using Honey & Mumford's Learning Styles Model (H&M LSM) as a theoretical foundation [1]. The H&M LSM identifies four distinct approaches – 'Activist', 'Theorist', 'Pragmatist' and 'Reflector' – and suggests that individuals will generally prefer one or perhaps a combination of two of these styles. Despite its popularity and widespread acceptance, some researchers have expressed concerns about the validity of this model. The research objective was therefore to explore if there is evidence for the H&M learning styles combinations and, if so, to assess how

P. Zaphiris et al. (Eds.): HCII 2023, LNCS 14060, pp. 154–166, 2023.
https://doi.org/10.1007/978-3-031-48060-7_12

those learning styles are manifest in different user behaviours on a LMS. Building on prior work in this area, the methodology involved testing for linkages between expressed learning style preferences and observed learning behaviour.

2   Background Literature

The H&M LSM is a popular framework, based on Kolb's experiential learning cycle [2], that attempts to classify individuals into learning styles based on their expressed preferences and approaches to learning. The four distinct styles within the H&M LSM are 'Activist', 'Reflector', 'Theorist', and 'Pragmatist'. It is proposed that learners tend to gravitate towards one of these styles or some combination of them.

Kolb's cycle has a horizontal axis representing what he terms the "processing continuum" (how learners go about executing a task) and a vertical axis representing the "perception continuum" (how learners think or feel about a task). The relationship between the H&M LSM and Kolb's model is illustrated in Fig. 1.

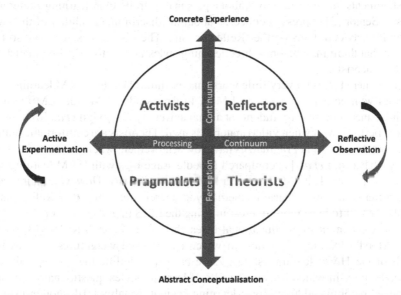

Fig. 1. H&M Learning Styles Model based on Kolb's Experiential Learning Cycle

"Activists" are characterised by a preference to engage in hands-on experiential learning. They have a tendency to be impulsive, enthusiastically getting stuck into tasks without much forethought or preparation. They like to try out new things and prefer dynamic, interactive 'learning by doing' trial-and-error approaches rather than passive observation.

In contrast, "reflectors" are much more contemplative and introspective, preferring to thoroughly analyse a situation and consider multiple viewpoints before taking action. They enjoy reading and listening and learn best when afforded the opportunity to absorb and process information in their own space and time.

"Theorists" are typically analytical by nature and inclined towards rational, methodical thinking. They strive to understand the underlying principles of a subject and enjoy organising information into coherent models and frameworks so as to grasp the logic behind concepts. Theorists learn best when provided with structured learning materials and opportunities to engage in critical thinking.

Finally, "pragmatists" are results-oriented learners. They are generally keen to apply their learning to 'real world' situations and seek out useful opportunities for experimentation and problem-solving. Pragmatists appreciate practical examples and learn best when given opportunities to work on problems that require them to directly apply their new skills and knowledge.

These four categories are not rigid or mutually exclusive. In practice, most individuals will exhibit some characteristics of all of them, while leaning towards a particular style or combination of styles, which may vary depending on the context or subject matter [3, 4].

The H&M LSM has been widely used for over 30 years but is not without its critics. Caple & Martin [5] raise issues about the coherence of the model and argue that some of the statements seem to be more about personality traits than learning preferences. Swailes & Senior [3] expressed concerns about the discriminant validity of the model, in particular between items on the 'Reflector' and 'Theorist' scales. They go so far as to suggest that there may be only three learning styles i.e. 'Activist', 'Pragmatist', and 'Reflector/Theorist'.

To date, there has been very little work that examines how the H&M learning styles correspond with actual behaviour in LMSs. In their study of Moodle LMS usage by first year business computing students at a Thai university, Sangvigit et al. [6] found that Reflectors perform well when video material is used, Theorists are comfortable with text material, but Activists and Pragmatists have low achievement when text material is used. Similarly, Baharudin et al. [7] compared Moodle usage logs with H&M learning styles amongst computer science students at a Malaysian university. However, their analysis did not differentiate by e-learning media type, merely reporting that Reflectors and Theorists seemed to have more interest in using the LMS than Activists or Pragmatists. Based on expert input from educational researchers in Lithuania, Krikun [8] presents a set of Moodle learning activities, to which apportioned weightings were assigned for each of the H&M learning styles. Zaric et al. [9] outline the conceptual design of a Moodle plug-in which uses the results of learning styles questionnaires to enable personalised recommendations for e-learning content. Maaliw [10], though using the Felder-Silverman learning style model rather than H&M, presents a feature mapping of learning styles to particular LMS learning behaviours and associated metrics captured by Moodle, which is then used to design an intelligent e-learning platform capable of flexibly adapting to individual preferences. Rasheed & Wahid [11] used machine learning analysis of behaviour on Moodle to detect learning styles. They observed that individual styles can change depending on the difficulty level of material and time factors, especially proximity to examination dates.

Despite these interesting contributions, there still remains a largely unfilled gap in the literature as regards the question of how well the H&M LSM can explain actual learner behaviour on a LMS.

3 Research Method

The H&M Learning Styles Questionnaire (LSQ) consists of 80 statements about behavioural tendencies, to which respondents give a binary 'Agree' (1) or 'Disagree' (0) response [12]. Each statement is associated with a particular learning style, thus yielding a raw overall score in the range of 0 to 20 for each of the four styles. A few examples are given in Table 1.

Table 1. Selection of sample statements and indicated learning style preference.

Statements	Learning style
"I believe that formal procedures and policies restrict people" *"I often find that actions based on feelings are as sound as those based on careful thought and analysis"* *"I thrive on the challenge of tackling something new and different"* *"In discussions I usually produce lots of spontaneous ideas"*	Activist
"I pay meticulous attention to detail before coming to a conclusion" *"I take pride in doing a thorough job"* *"I'm always interested to find out what people think"* *"I often get irritated by people who want to rush things"*	Reflector
"I get on best with logical, analytical people and less well with spontaneous, irrational people" *"I find it difficult to produce ideas on impulse"* *"I am keen on exploring the basic assumptions, principles and theories underpinning things and events"* *"I tend to be a perfectionist"*	Theorist
"What matters most is whether something works in practice" *"In meetings I put forward practical realistic ideas"* *"I do whatever is expedient to get the job done"* *"I think written reports should be short and to the point"*	Pragmatist

The questionnaire was implemented using an on-line survey built in Microsoft Forms. In the original paper-based LSQ provided by H&M, the order in which statements is presented is random, presumably to reduce the possibility of bias (as could occur if several statements pertaining to a particular learning style were presented in direct sequence). The on-line version of the instrument used in this study therefore employed random shuffling of statements so that each respondent saw things in a different order. The author performed a test/re-test reliability analysis of the on-line questionnaire by completing it on two separate dates. The responses were found to be 98% consistent with each other across 80 items, suggesting a very high level of reliability.

The survey was not anonymous, the principal reason being that students were promised they would receive a personalised profile of their individual learning style as an incentive to participate. Furthermore, it would not be possible to link the survey data to learning analytics data in the absence of identifiers. Participation was entirely voluntary and conditional on consenting for the data gathered to be used for the purpose of informing teaching practices, subject to the proviso that it would be anonymised, not exchanged with any other party, and stored and processed strictly in accordance with research ethics guidelines and data protection laws.

The link to the Microsoft Forms questionnaire was distributed by email to 211 students enrolled on a postgraduate module on 'Database Systems Development' at a leading AACSB-accredited business school in Ireland. After two follow-up reminders, a total of 52 responses (25% response rate) were received. The gender balance of respondents was female 40% versus male 60%, which was in line with the overall balance of the class. They were of six different nationalities but mainly Indian (63%), Irish (21%) and Chinese (8%). Respondents ranged in age from 21 to 50 years with a median of 25.

Interestingly, the time taken to complete the questionnaire had a wide range of values. Students who were subsequently identified as being 'Activists' or 'Pragmatists' typically spent substantially less time processing the items than did 'Reflectors' or 'Theorists'.

Following the recommended guidance on norms [12], respondents' total raw scores on the H&M LSQ were transformed into normalised values ranging from 1 (very low preference) to 5 (very strong preference). Each LSQ response was then manually inspected and classified into a prevalent learning style or combination of styles. For 12 of the 52 responses, no prevalent style or clear combination was apparent so they were classified as "indeterminate".

To statistically explore the natural groupings of H&M learning styles in the dataset, an approach similar to that used by Dyulicheva & Kosova [13] was followed. Hierarchical clustering algorithms were executed in SPSS version 27.0 using the centroid linkage method. Squared Euclidean distance was selected as the proximity measure to calculate the dissimilarity between participants. Inspection of the agglomeration schedule and dendrogram indicated that somewhere between 9 and 10 clusters was optimal. This analysis was very consistent with the clusters previously independently identified by the manual coding process (71% of responses were classified identically by the manual and automated processes; a further 15% were in partial agreement).

Additionally, analytics were extracted from the Blackboard LMS system which measured the extent of access by each student to various e-learning content sections, such as general course information, lecture materials, practical exercises and add-on resources, video recordings of lectures, links to the recommended textbook, course assignments, and formative quizzes. This data taken from the LMS system was then compared and correlated against the learning style clusters.

4   Results and Discussion

Similar to previous studies that used the H&M LSQ [3, 4], the majority of respondents did not exhibit any obviously dominant learning style but rather had various combinations of styles, as can be seen in Tables 2 and 3.

Tables 4 and 5 show the five LSQ statements that had the highest level of agreement and lowest level of agreement respectively. A mixture of H&M learning styles can be seen in both tables, but it must be asked if these are indeed learning styles or something else, such as disciplinary norms or cultural dispositions.

The majority of the students who responded to the LSQ were natives of countries with collectivist cultures [14], meaning that respect for other people's feelings and opinions

Table 2. Descriptive statistics for H&M learning styles (n = 52).

Learning style	Mean	Median	Std. Dev	Range	No. of items (out of 20) for which >70% agreed
Activist	9.87	10	3.02	3–17	3
Pragmatist	13.52	13.5	2.52	8–18	10
Reflector	15.75	16	2.38	6–19	14
Theorist	13.31	13	2.76	4–18	12

Table 3. Strength of H&M learning styles (n = 52).

Learning style	Very low	Low	Moderate	Strong	Very strong
Activist	1.9%	11.5%	50.0%	19.2%	17.3%
Pragmatist	3.8%	11.5%	50.0%	21.2%	13.5%
Reflector	1.9%	1.9%	19.2%	50.0%	26.9%
Theorist	3.8%	11.5%	40.4%	21.2%	23.1%

Table 4. Five LSQ statements with highest level of agreement.

Rank	Statement	Learning style	% Agree
1	*"I am keen to try things out to see if they work in practice"*	Pragmatist	96.2%
=2	*"I take pride in doing a thorough job"*	Reflector	94.2%
=2	*"It's best to think carefully before taking action"*	Reflector	94.2%
=2	*"In meetings I put forward practical realistic ideas"*	Pragmatist	94.2%
=5	*"I like to ponder many alternatives before making up my mind"*	Reflector	92.3%
=5	*"I am keen to reach answers via a logical approach"*	Theorist	92.3%
=5	*"I like people who approach things realistically rather than theoretically"*	Pragmatist	92.3%
=5	*"I think written reports should be short and to the point"*	Pragmatist	92.3%

is deeply ingrained within them. It was therefore not surprising that four of the five statements which received the lowest level of agreement pertained to interpersonal issues.

As regards the statements that received the highest level of agreement, they seem to be influenced by the disciplinary norms of respondents. The students were pursuing courses in areas such as business systems analysis, applications programming and data analytics, all of which place an emphasis on problem definition prior to the development of a solution. Thus, the students' acceptance of the importance of planning and systematic design strongly came through in the high incidence of 'Reflector' type behaviours. By the

Table 5. Five LSQ statements with lowest level of agreement.

Rank	Statement	Learning style	% Agree
1	*"People often find me insensitive to their feelings"*	Pragmatist	9.6%
2	*"Quiet, thoughtful people tend to make me feel uneasy"*	Activist	13.5%
3	*"I often act without considering the possible consequences"*	Activist	17.3%
4	*"I don't mind hurting people's feelings so long as the job gets done"*	Pragmatist	19.2%
5	*"In discussions with people I often find I am the most dispassionate and objective"*	Theorist	21.2%

same token, the applied and practical nature of the students' discipline revealed itself in the high incidence of 'Pragmatist' behaviour. Of relevance is that several of the statements that H&M regard as being characteristic of the 'Pragmatist' style are remarkably similar to principles of the Agile Manifesto [15], a popular software development philosophy which the students were exposed to (see Table 6).

Table 6. H&M LSQ statements compared to agile software development.

Agile principle/practice	H&M LSQ statement ('Pragmatist' style)
"Simplicity – the art of maximizing the amount of work not done – is essential"	*"I think written reports should be short and to the point"*
"Working software is the primary measure of progress"	*"What matters most is whether something works in practice"*
"We value responding to change over following a plan"	*"I accept and stick to laid down procedures and policies so long as I regard them as an efficient way of getting the job done"*
Use of techniques such as burndown charts, use cases, class diagrams and activity diagrams	*"I tend to be attracted to techniques such as network analysis, flow charts, branching programmes, contingency planning, etc."*
"Our highest priority is to satisfy the customer through early and continuous delivery of valuable software"	*"I do whatever is expedient to get the job done"*

The hierarchical cluster analysis revealed ten clusters, of which 'Reflector' and 'Reflector/Theorist' were the most substantial (see Fig. 2 and Table 7). All four learning styles, as well as several combinations thereof, were found. Clusters 2 and 7 had no observed dominant learning style, together accounting for about a quarter of all the students. Indeed, those two clusters were so close that they could be collapsed into one.

The order of popularity of the combined learning styles was consistent with empirical data from previous studies based on the H&M model [12], though surprisingly the

'Theorist/Pragmatist' combination was not observed. This might be due to possible issues with discriminant validity [3], as further suggested by a moderate correlation observed between the Theorist and Pragmatist normalised scores in this study (Spearman rs(52) = .48, p < .001). The 'Activist/Theorist' combination was not found either, but that was not surprising as those two learning styles are largely incompatible.

	Activist	Theorist	Pragmatist	Reflector
Activist	Cluster 10			
Theorist	(not found)	Cluster 8		
Pragmatist	Cluster 9	(not found)	Cluster 4	
Reflector	Cluster 5	Cluster 6	Cluster 3	Cluster 1

Fig. 2. Matrix of observed learning styles

Table 7. Interpretation of learning style clusters.

Cluster Number	% of Students	Rank	Observed dominant learning style(s)
1	42%	1	Reflector
2	12%	N/A	(Indeterminate)
3	6%	3	Reflector/Pragmatist
4	2%	5	Pragmatist
5	4%	4	Reflector/Activist
6	13%	2	Reflector/Theorist
7	12%	N/A	(Indeterminate)
8	6%	3	Theorist
9	2%	5	Activist/Pragmatist
10	2%	5	Activist

The next step of the analysis was to look at the actual learning behaviours exhibited by students in each of these clusters to see if they are consistent with that predicted by the H&M LSM. To do so, usage analytics for a module taken by all respondents ('Database Systems Development') were extracted from the Blackboard LMS. This module was selected because it contained a lot of e-learning content of various types, thus lending itself to being used in various different ways by learners. The module contained the following content sections:

- **Course information:** the outcomes, schedule, etc.) and persistent Microsoft Teams link to weekly on-line lecture.
- **Lecture materials:** copies of Powerpoint slide decks, some classroom working notes, supplementary readings, and links to a customised collection of relevant videos on LinkedIn Learning.

- **Lecture recordings:** video recordings of lectures and practical demonstrations, made available immediately after each week's class until after the examination (21 files, 13.5 h).
- **Practicals & resources:** a test bank of SQL exercises with solutions – which students were advised to work through as essential examination preparation – as well as links to other useful on-line tutorials hosted on external sites.
- **Textbook:** link to electronic copy of the recommended course textbook, which was prescribed as optional rather than mandatory (818 pages, PDF).
- **Course assignment:** the assignment specification, a video that clarified the requirements, and the on-line submission link.
- **Formative revision quiz:** link to Microsoft Forms quizzes to help students test their knowledge and prepare for the examination.

For each of the ten learning style clusters, Table 8 shows the mean number of times that students within that cluster accessed each content area on Blackboard LMS. Clusters 1, 3, 4, 6, 9 and 10 all exhibited substantial deviations from norms under one or more content areas.

Table 8. Observed learning behaviour of students on Blackboard LMS.

Learning Style: Cluster Number	LMS content area (mean number of times accessed):						
	Course information	Lecture materials	Lecture recordings	Practicals & resources	Textbook	Course assignment	Formative revision quiz
1	16.4	78.1 *	19.1	16.4	8.0	35.6	1.4
2	12.2	66.0	24.5	14.8	7.2	37.8	0.8
3	48.3 *	114.0 *	33.7	42.3 *	34.3 *	62.7 *	2.7 *
4	4.0 *	61.0	10.0	0.0 *	1.0 *	27.0	1.0
5	13.0	52.0	18.0	15.5	5.0	24.5	-
6	9.6	52.6	8.4 *	10.7 *	8.1	29.4	2.0
7	13.8	54.2	17.2	13.3	6.0	36.5	2.0
8	12.3	65.7	28.0	15.0	11.7	24.7	0.7
9	21.0	50.0	57.0 *	20.0 *	7.0	35.0	-
10	6.0 *	37.0 *	52.0 *	19.0	4.0	25.0	-

* Substantial deviations from norms observed

The radar charts presented in Figs. 3 and 4 are based on converted normalised scores on a scale of 1 = Very low, 2 = Low, 3 = Moderate, 4 = Strong, 5 = Very strong. The characteristics of each cluster are discussed below, with the exceptions of Clusters 2 and 7 which were of indeterminate style. Some of the learning style clusters were very small but are nevertheless included here as their LSQ response patterns were sufficiently different as to distinguish them from other clusters.

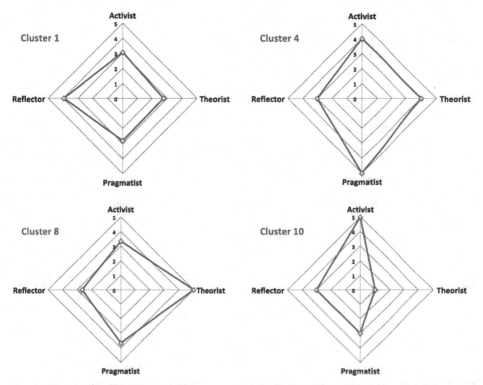

Fig. 3. The four basic learning styles as exemplified by Cluster 1 (Reflector), Cluster 4 (Pragmatist), Cluster 8 (Theorist) and Cluster 10 (Activist).

Cluster 1 (n = 22), exhibited a strong preference for the 'Reflector' learning style. The students in this cluster had a tendency to refer to Lecture Materials much more frequently than those in other clusters, consistent with their preference to read and to be prepared in advance for class.

Cluster 4 (n = 1), exhibited a very strong preference for the 'Pragmatist' learning style. Peculiarly though, this student accessed the Practicals & Resources section the least of all. That goes against the H&M predicted behaviour, but it may have been the case that this student accessed other materials outside of the Blackbord LMS.

Cluster 8 (n = 3), exhibited a very strong preference for the 'Theorist' learning style. No remarkable behaviour was exhibited by students in this cluster, but they accessed all of the content areas quite often, consistent with a desire to develop a solid grasp of fundamental subject area concepts.

Cluster 10 (n = 1), exhibited a very strong preference for the 'Activist' learning style. This student spent substantially less time than most others consuming the less exciting content in the Course Information and Lecture Materials content sections, but instead dived into the exercises in the Practicals section and watched back over the practical demonstrations in the Lecture Recordings section. This behaviour is consistent with the H&M LSM.

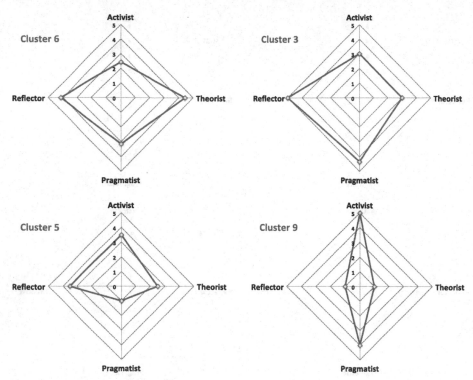

Fig. 4. Examples of combined learning styles observed: Cluster 6 (Reflector/Theorist), Cluster 3 (Reflector/Pragmatist), Cluster 5 (Reflector/Activist) and Cluster 9 (Activist/Pragmatist).

Moving on then to the clusters of combined learning styles, Cluster 6 (n = 7) exhibited a strong to very strong preference for the 'Reflector/Theorist' style. This cluster demonstrated a substantially less liking for Lecture Recordings and Practicals than other clusters, perhaps indicating their level of comfort and satisfaction with text materials provided in other content sections.

Cluster 3 (n = 3) exhibited a strong preference for the 'Reflector/Pragmatist' style. Across all but one of the content sections, this cluster had the highest number of content accesses, indicating their predilection to absorb all the material and then to put their newly acquired knowledge into practice.

Cluster 5 (n = 2) exhibited a strong prefence for the 'Reflector/Activist' style. No remarkable deviations in LMS behaviour were observed for this group, but the level of content access seems broadly consistent with expected behaviour for this learning style.

Finally, Cluster 9 (n = 1) exhibited a strong to very strong preference for the 'Activist/Pragmatist' style. Similar to the student in Cluster 10 ('Activist'), this person was inclined to make substantially higher use than average of the Practicals and Lecture Recordings section, suggesting a desire to get stuck in as quickly as possible to material, but not quite as quickly as an all-out 'Activist'. Notably, the two students in Clusters 9 and 10, who were outliers from the rest of the class as regards their LSQ responses, gravitated towards each other when forming self-selected groups for project work.

Hierarchical clustering of the standardised LMS learning analytics metrics also revealed ten distinct clusters with different patterns of behaviour observed. As the sample size was relatively small and fragmented, these differences between clusters were not found to be statistically significant. However, a cross-tabulation of the learning styles clusters against the LMS content access clusters revealed a significant causal relationship ($\lambda = .242$, p < .05) suggesting that different learning styles resulted in different usage behaviour of the LMS.

5 Conclusions and Further Work

This paper presented a preliminary analysis of the relationship between Honey & Mumford's Learning Styles Model (H&M LSM) and observed user behaviour on a Learning Management System (LMS). The findings revealed that observed behaviours were broadly in line with expected behaviours when comparing the results of students' responses on the Learning Styles Questionnaire (LSQ) with usage metrics extracted from Blackboard LMS for a particular module.

Although the results are promising, and the methodology is useful, this study has several limitations. Firstly, the sample size was quite small, although several previous studies based on the H&M LSM also had similar class sizes. It would be better to replicate this on a larger class or to gather data from several different classes over the course of a few academic semesters. Secondly, the H&M LSM has inherent weaknesses, as again found in this study, so it may be better to set it aside and replace it with an alternative model, or else to complement it with another (and triangulate the findings). Thirdly, the learning analytics data extracted from the Blackboard LMS for this study was quite primitive. A criticism that can be levelled at most learning management systems is that it is quite difficult to extract meaningful analytics data in a format that can be easily parsed. Fourthly, this study looked only at a single module. It is quite possible, even probable, that students might display different learning styles on different modules, depending on the nature of the subject material and their prior knowledge of it. It would therefore be better to collect data across several different modules. Fifthly, this study did not consider issues which may have affected learning styles such as age, gender, national culture or computer efficacy. There is much scope, then, for future follow-on work.

The next stage of this research will be to delve in greater depth into these preliminary findings to seek explanations of the apparent associations observed. Qualitative data obtained from student feedback and learning journals will be used to shed further light on interpretation of the quantitative findings.

References

1. Honey, P., Mumford, A.: Using Your Learning Styles. Chartered Institute of Personnel and Development, UK (1986)
2. Kolb, D.A.: Experiential Learning: Experience as the Source of Learning and Development, vol. 1. Prentice-Hall, Englewood Cliffs, NJ (1984)

3. Swailes, S., Senior, B.: The dimensionality of Honey and Mumford's learning styles questionnaire. Int. J. Sel. Assess. **7**(1), 1–11 (1999)
4. Lesmes-Anel, J., Robinson, G., Moody, S.: Learning preferences and learning styles: a study of Wessex general practice registrars. Br. J. Gen. Pract. **51**(468), 559–564 (2001)
5. Caple, J., Martin, P.: Reflections of two pragmatists: a critique of honey and mumford's learning styles. Ind. Commer. Train. **26**(1), 16–20 (1994)
6. Sangvigit, P., Mungsing, S., Theeraroungchaisri, A.: Correlation of Honey & Mumford learning styles and online learning media preference. Int. J. Comput. Technol. Appl. **3**(3), 1312–1317 (2012)
7. Baharudin, A.F., Sahabudin, N.A., Kamaludin, A.: Behavioral tracking in e-learning by using learning styles approach. Indonesian J. Electric. Eng. Comput. Sci. **8**(1), 17–26 (2017)
8. Krikun, I.: Applying learning analytics methods to enhance learning quality and effectiveness in virtual learning environments. In: 5th IEEE Workshop on Advances in Information, Electronic and Electrical Engineering, pp. 1–6 (2017)
9. Zaric, N., Roepke, R., Schroeder, U.: Concept for linking learning analytics and learning styles in e-learning environment. In: 10th International Conference on Educational and New Learning Technologies, pp. 4822–4829. Palma, Spain, July 2–4 (2018)
10. Maaliw, R.R.: A personalized virtual learning environment using multiple modeling techniques. In: 2021 IEEE 12th Annual Ubiquitous Computing, Electronics & Mobile Communication Conference, pp. 0008–0015 (2021)
11. Rasheed, F., Wahid, A.: Learning style detection in E-learning systems using machine learning techniques. Expert Syst. Appl. **174**, 114774 (2021)
12. Learning Styles Questionnaire. https://www.ilfm.org.uk/cms/document/ILFM_Learning_S tyles_Resource_TK_09Oct17_Ver1.0.pdf. Aaccessed 23 June 2023
13. Dyulicheva, Y.Y., Kosova, Y.A.: The students group detection based on the learning styles and clustering algorithms. In: 2nd International Scientific and Practical Conference on Digital Economy (ISCDE), pp. 106–111. Atlantis Press (2020)
14. Hofstede, G.: Culture's Consequences: Comparing Values, Behaviors, Institutions, and Organizations Across Nations. Sage Publications, Thousand Oaks, CA (2001)
15. The Agile Manifesto. https://agilemanifesto.org/

Research on Immersive Scenario Design in Museum Education

Qing Liu[1,2,3]([envelope]), Gaofeng Mi[1], and Oleksandra Shmelova-Nesterenko[3]

[1] College of Art and Design, Shaanxi University of Science and Technology, Xi'an 710021, Shaanxi, China
mollyliu0408@gmail.com
[2] College of Arts and Communications, Nanjing University of Aeronautics and Astronautics, Jincheng College, Nanjing 210000, Jiangsu, China
[3] Faculty of Design, Kyiv National University of Technologies and Design, Kyiv 01011, Ukraine

Abstract. In the current museum boom, the social impact of knowledge dissemination through museum visits is becoming increasingly evident, and the educational function of museums has received widespread attention and support. The innovation of digital technology provides technical support for the modern transformation of museum resources, enhancing the sensory and interactive experience of visitors through immersive scenario experiences to achieve educational goals in a scenario-based manner and enhance the effectiveness of knowledge transmission. This article focuses on analyzing excellent cases of museum education in China, which have successfully incorporated immersive scenario design into their programs. The article provides a detailed analysis of the practical methods used in these programs and identifies two combined methods for designing educational activities in museums. By showcasing the successful implementation of immersive scenario design in museum education, this article underscores the value and potential of this approach for enhancing the educational impact of museums in the modern era and suggests future developments in museum educational activities.

Keywords: Museum · Educational Activities · Scene Design · Cultural Heritage

1 Introduction

Museum education is a form of educational exchange activity between museums and their visitors, and it represents an informal educational approach. Through various exhibitions and programs offered within museums, museum education provides visitors with opportunities to learn, educate themselves, and experience culture related to history, culture, art, natural sciences, and other subjects. As a form of social education, museum education offers high-quality resources and plays a direct role in cultural heritage preservation, while cultivating visitors' civic awareness and social responsibility. With the innovation and development of technology, museum education has evolved beyond the simple one-way output mode of cultural relic lectures, and through new technologies and media, it attracts a wider audience, especially younger generations, to enter museums and meet the cultural understanding and knowledge needs of diverse age groups. The notion of

P. Zaphiris et al. (Eds.): HCII 2023, LNCS 14060, pp. 167–175, 2023.
https://doi.org/10.1007/978-3-031-48060-7_13

immersion as a phenomenon was first introduced by psychologist Mihaly Csikszentmi-halyi in the 1960s, who conceptualized the idea of flow [1]. In a series of systematic studies conducted, immersion has been regarded as a positive emotional experience. Immersive experiences, to some extent, share similarities with flow experiences, both involving the individual's complete absorption in a particular environment, leading to a state of self-forgetfulness [2]. Immersive experience design, while taking into account the audience's sensory experiences, creates a contextualized learning environment and medium by considering users' emotional and behavioral experiences, thereby enhancing the effectiveness and value of museum education.

2 Implementation Strategies for Situated Learning Theory

The theory of situated learning is a psychological theory of human learning that emphasizes the influence of learning environments and contextual factors on the learning process. (Situated learning theory (SLT), first presented by Jean Lave and Eti-enne Wenger (1991), explains the process and development of learning when individuals have the opportunity to participate in a community of practice. In such a community, new learners reach the level of the expert as they have more opportunities to practice within the context of learning. In this light, learning is unintentional; this unintentional nature of learning is what the authors call Legitimate Peripheral Participation (LPP) [3]. In addition to the support of technological means, education cannot do without the guidance of educational theory. The integration of immersive experience design and the theory of situated learning is one of the important ways to achieve the scenification of museum education. Situated learning emphasizes learning strategies that include: firstly, providing authentic learning environments that enable learners to engage in expert-like thinking and practice; secondly, providing diverse roles and perspectives, through social interaction and collaboration, to form a community of practice for learning[4].Based on the integration of these two principles, the following discussion will focus on the specific case of realistic and practical scenario designs.

3 Narrative Scenario Designs Rooted in Reality

The museum, as a cultural narrative subject, combines cultural cognition and immer-sive experience through narrative media, narrative space, narrative story, and narrative identity, in order to better develop, inherit, and disseminate culture [5]. According to the situational learning theory, people are more likely to accept external knowledge input and achieve dual understanding and acceptance in both consciousness and emotion by learning in conjunction with real-life situations. This allows them to actively think and integrate themselves into real-life situations. Therefore, narrative and situational design in museum education can immerse visitors in a contextualized learning experience. This can be achieved through the design of narrative stories, the creation of space, the inte-gration of technology in media, and the guidance of identity to provide an immersive and contextualized learning experience for the audience (Fig. 1).

One example of situational narrative design utilizing virtual technology is the educa-tional scenario design of the Grand Canal Museum in Yangzhou, China. Located in the

Fig. 1. The Sand Spaceship Physical Experience Digital Multimedia Exhibition

Three Bays Scenic Area of the Yangzhou Canal, the Grand Canal Museum in Yangzhou features a multidimensional exhibition design showcasing the Grand Canal, a world cultural heritage site in China. The *Boats and Oars on the Canal* exhibition is a highly distinctive showcase within the museum, which leverages virtual reality technology to create a completely immersive digital environment, placing visitors in a realistic exhibition environment. By combining physical and digital experiences, the exhibition provides visitors with a multimedia interactive display that allows them to deeply experience the theme of canal boats and oars in the Grand Canal. The exhibition includes multimedia displays showcasing the evolution and different types of canal boats and oars, as well as related historical stories. It also showcases how canal boats and oars have contributed to the integration of northern and southern Chinese cultures and the past and present good life. The second part of the exhibition features a physical experience and digital multimedia showcase of the *Sha Fei Ship*, which not only showcases the experience of the ship, but also extends to the historical and modern eras of the Grand Canal. The exhibition features a restored Kangxi-era Sha Fei ship, measuring 20 m in length, and offers visitors the opportunity to enter the cabin for an immersive experience. The entire exhibition uses an immersive experience approach, allowing visitors to experience the surprise and emotion brought about by the display techniques, which range from narrow to spacious and from real to virtual. The exhibition also features a documentary on the construction process, emphasizing the value of boat and oar culture and the importance of boat and oar protection and inheritance in the Grand Canal cultural heritage. The wall is adorned with construction drawings of the Sha Fei ship, allowing visitors to appreciate the charm of intangible cultural heritage. By allowing visitors to perform a live demonstration on the physical ship and using the integration of visual, audio, and sensory effects, along with a logical narrative design, the exhibition evokes visitors' associations and feelings based on real-life situations (Fig. 2).

Fig. 2. The *Terracotta Warriors*: Performance Still Photos

Another example is the theatrical narrative situational design, such as the art museum drama and public education activities at the Nanjing University of the Arts in China. *The Terracotta Warriors*: Performance + Workshop is an art museum activity based on dance drama and physical experience, planned by Nanjing University of the Arts in 2018. The activity consists of two parts: the performance of the work and interactive workshops. The performance is based on the form of ancient Chinese dancing figurines, presenting Han Dynasty dancing figurines in the form of solo, duet, and trio performances in the museum theater. Through the real interpretation of human body movements, the audience is immersed in a realistic context and the past and present are theatrically connected. In the interactive workshop, the visual image of the actor's body movements allows the audience to guess the meaning of the movements, and the audience recites ancient poetry while the actor performs random body movements. With the dual role of theater and interaction, the audience is brought into a more realistic situation, pondering the birth and meaning of cultural relics.

The development of virtualization technology and the integration of cross-media elements such as traditional opera and dance have enriched the realism of museum education scenarios, making it easier for visitors to feel immersed and resonate with the content. However, whether it is the presentation of virtualization technology or the creation of a theatrical environment, it must not deviate from the factual logic based on cultural subjects and should be consistent with people's experience in real-life scenarios. Through narrative design, familiar learning scenarios can be created to enhance the visitor's engagement and learning experience.

4   Experiential Situational Design Involving Real Practice

Based on the principle of interaction and collaboration, learning through experience is an important concept in the situational learning theory. It involves a transformation of experience from conscious understanding of knowledge to sensory perception of action. Situated cognition theory holds that knowledge is effective only when it is acquired and used in real life situations. It emphasizes the interaction between knowledge and situation. Learners can construct and improve their knowledge system in real learning situations through autonomous or cooperative learning [6]. David Howes, an anthropologist, conducted extensive research on the typical five senses and the diversity of perceptual experiences in his book *The Varieties of Sensory Experience*. His research has shown that human perceptual experiences are not limited to the five senses, but rather consist of multiple sensory modalities In particular, his studies have demonstrated that direct experiential engagement and tactile exploration of objects provide better cognitive, social, and therapeutic benefits, supporting their value in perception of object attributes [7]. This practical experiential approach is currently abundant in the artistic education of cultural heritage and can be divided into two types: traditional resource integration and script killing interpretation.

4.1   Traditional Resource Integration

The Nanjing Folk Customs Museum in China is an important showcase of Nanjing's folk and intangible cultural heritage. Located in the historic Gan family courtyard, which is a national key protected ancient building complex, the museum hosts many related public educational activities based on local customs. One such example is the 2023 Lantern Festival folk education event (Fig. 3).

Fig. 3. Display Photos of Folk Education Activities

The activity design begins by introducing folk art related to the Year of the Rabbit through the Spring Festival exhibition *Hundred Rabbits Racing for Spring*, which stimulates visual cognitive interest. Then, the origin and customs of the Lantern Festival are introduced to impart relevant folk knowledge. Through the dual effect of visual and conscious cognition, the event then incorporates hands-on practice led by the intangible cultural heritage inheritor of Qinhuai Lantern Art, allowing children to engage in creative practice. Finally, participants have the opportunity to make their own lanterns, completing the sensory experience of the museum's public education activity. Cognitive and motor actions occur simultaneously, with the motivational stimuli of earlier learning providing the groundwork for practical actions. Through hands-on practice and interaction, and through the tactile materials and experience of lantern-making, the museum provides an immersive and experiential education setting for real-world practice.

The implementation of this type of folk culture and education activities is relatively easy, with the key challenge lying in the correlation and connection of existing traditional resources in museums. When designing these activities, the liveliness and intangibility of folk activities are taken into consideration, and elements such as festival customs, folk arts and crafts, and hands-on experiences are integrated in a comprehensive and situational manner. This allows the audience to immerse themselves in the educational atmosphere through interaction and practice, and to deeply experience the activity through a sensory experience involving all five senses, thereby providing a reference for the dissemination of folk knowledge in museums.

4.2 The Murder Mystery Game Interpretation

As an interactive and practical game form, the Murder Mystery Game can provide a deeper cultural experience and educational opportunity. In order to create a more immersive experience for players, the game utilizes a narrative approach, leading participants from fragmented information reception to systematic presentation. By conducting Murder Mystery Game activities in cultural venues such as museums, participants can gain a deeper understanding of the history and cultural significance behind cultural artifacts through gameplay. Additionally, participants' awareness and cognition of cultural heritage protection are increased (Fig. 4).

Fig. 4. Photos of Museum Murder Mystery Scripted Activity

In 2022, the Luoyang Museum launched a popular interactive game called *Mystery Guest: Cultural Relics Protection Program* in the form of a murder mystery game, which received widespread attention. The game incorporated the popular trend of museum overnight stays, allowing players to enjoy cultural education through the fun of the game. The story is set more than 1000 years in the future, and players take on roles and face various challenges, such as recognizing precious objects and restoring the location of treasure. Players must also trace historical context, understand ancient technology and art, and engage in intellectual competition with the mysterious guests hidden within the game, ultimately decrypting and solving puzzles to complete the game. The game takes place in a real exhibition hall, where players can not only learn about cultural relics, but also interact with non-player characters and experience the history carried by the relics in an immersive way. After the activity, the staff will lead the audience into the exhibition hall to review the game through explanation, allowing them to gain a deeper understanding of the related cultural relics and history. What the audience loved the most was that the key clues in *Mysterious Guest: Cultural Relics Protection Plan* came from the museum's collection of precious cultural relics, such as the Stone Pi Xie, White Jade Cup, Three-Color Black Glaze Horse, and Gold Threaded Nanmu Pagoda. These cultural relics became the team leaders and through telling their own stories, allowed the audience to feel the weight of history. This event focuses on parent-child study projects, weakening the logical reasoning part, and allowing parents and children to solve puzzles and compete in a relaxed and pleasant atmosphere, learning about history and appreciating the charm of culture and art. The overnight stay at the museum allows the audience to immerse themselves in the atmosphere of history, extending this immersive experience.

Compared to the traditional resource-integrated hands-on experiential teaching approach, the scenario-based teaching activities of murder mystery games place more emphasis on the audience's active exploration process. The process is practiced and actualized, increasing the dual experience of thinking and action, in order to achieve the educational goal of strengthening cognition.

5 Conclusion

In conclusion, with the new development of museum functions, educational activities around museum resources, space, and media are becoming increasingly diverse and important places for the public to acquire knowledge. In order to better achieve the educational transformation of museum resources, integrating new technologies is necessary, but it still cannot do without the initial educational goals and educational subjects. By integrating the methods of situational learning theory into immersive experience design, the user's interactive experience and educational goals can be effectively achieved. The examples listed above have linked museum culture, audiences, technology, and drama through narrative design by means of practical and interactive situational design, enriching museum education media and cross-disciplinary collaboration. This study hopes to provide reference value for future museum education.

Based on the analysis of the above case study, the following recommendations are provided for the subsequent design of museum educational activities:

Firstly, it is recommended to broaden the scope of educational targets. As museum resources are cultural dissemination resources aimed at the entire society and all humanity, educational targets should not be limited to the normal population. Consideration should also be given to social special groups, such as the visually or hearing impaired.

Innovative technological means should be used to open up new channels of knowledge and education for special groups. The advancement of technology can be used to promote equal access to museum resources for all individuals regardless of their abilities. This can include the development of audio and tactile exhibits, as well as online resources that can be accessed through assistive technologies such as screen readers or captioning. By expanding the range of educational targets, museums can fulfill their mission of providing equal access to cultural resources and promote the inclusivity of all members of society.

Secondly, it is recommended to encourage the involvement of external educational institutions in the redesign of museum educational activities. Currently, most museum public education activities are planned and organized by the museum's own departments. However, with the increasing functionality and interactivity of museum exhibition design, other educational institutions should also utilize the interactive characteristics of museum exhibits to develop educational activities. This can help to achieve wider social dissemination of museum education. For instance, schools, universities, and community organizations can collaborate with museums to develop educational programs that are tailored to their respective needs and objectives. These programs can leverage the resources and expertise of both the museums and the external institutions to provide more engaging and effective educational experiences for the participants. Additionally, such collaborations can broaden the reach of museum education to communities that may not have easy access to museums or their resources. By involving external educational institutions in the redesign of museum educational activities, museums can expand their impact on society and foster greater community engagement with cultural resources. This can help to promote the cultural and educational development of society as a whole.

Thirdly, it is recommended to balance traditional methods with technological innovations. Due to regional differences, some museums may face budget constraints and be unable to implement advanced virtual technologies. Therefore, it is necessary to pursue a dual-path approach that combines traditional methods of organizing activities with modern virtual technology applications to develop museum education. The focus should not solely be on the pursuit and innovation of high-tech technologies. Instead, a balance must be struck to achieve immersive educational experiences for all regions. In many cases, traditional methods such as guided tours, lectures, and interactive workshops are still effective in engaging visitors and conveying educational content. Therefore, it is important to leverage the strengths of both traditional methods and new technologies to create diverse and effective educational experiences. For instance, virtual tours and interactive exhibits can supplement traditional methods of museum education to provide visitors with more engaging and immersive experiences. By pursuing a balanced approach to museum education that incorporates both traditional methods and new technologies, museums can provide educational experiences that cater to the diverse needs of visitors across different regions. This can help to promote greater accessibility to museum resources and improve the overall quality of cultural education.

References

1. Andria, G., Georg, V.: Complexity: Design Strategies and Worldviews. Huazhong University of Science and Technology Press, Wuhan (2011)
2. Huiyu, H.: Research on Contextual Co-Creation Design in the Display of Cultural Heritage Museums. Jiangnan University (2022)
3. Joy, E., Mary, R.: Theoretical Models for Teaching and Research. Washington State University, Washington(2020)
4. Cuibai, L.: The development and application of western contextual learning theory. Res. Electro-Chem. Educ. **06**(09), 20–24 (2006)
5. Hong, W., Suren, L.: Immersion and narrative: a study on the design of museum cultural immersion experience under new media image technology. Art 100, **34**(04), 161–169 (2018)
6. Xiaojun, Z., Xupeng, L., Ju, W., Changxiu, S.: Augmented Reality (AR) learning application based on the perspective of situational learning: high efficiency study of combination of virtual and real. Psychology **11**(9), 1340–1348 (2020)
7. Hong, Y.: Research on Digitization of Intangible Cultural Heritage. Social Science Literature Publishing House, Beijing, China (2014)

Acceptance and User Needs of Coaching Chatbots: An Empirical Analysis of a StudiCoachBot's Conversation Histories

Vanessa Mai[✉] ⓘ, Alexander Bauer ⓘ, Christian Deggelmann ⓘ, and Anja Richert ⓘ

TH Köln/University of Applied Sciences, Cologne, Germany
{vanessa.mai,alexander_christoph.bauer,
christian_michael.deggelmann,anja.richert}@th-koeln.de

Abstract. As technology advances, AI-based coaching continues to offer new opportunities in supporting humans. The StudiCoachBot of TH Koeln/University of Applied Sciences is a coaching chatbot, that is designed to support students with exam anxiety through low-threshold self-reflection. It is an intent-based AI-supported chatbot and is developed in the Conversational AI framework Rasa. This paper gives insights into how iterative development of coaching chatbots can be a key factor for successful chatbot design in terms of acceptance and user needs. Our study consists of two parts: In the first part, we present the iterative development of our coaching chatbot, consisting of user testings with several hundred test users. In the second part, we present the results from our field test after the chatbot release. We collected and evaluated conversation histories and questionnaires from users for a period of 10 weeks. Our results include the evaluation of 242 conversations and 24 questionnaires. On the one hand, the results provide information about access numbers and rates as well as chatbot coaching topics accessed by users. On the other hand, the data shows high acceptance rates and that users can build a relationship in chatbot coaching (measured via working alliance). However, users perceived naturalness of the conversation only moderate. This is understandable, as our intent-based chatbot only allows us to react flexibly to a limited extent to free user input. In a next iteration, we will therefore improve the conversation with the help of large language models to make it more natural.

Keywords: AI-based Coaching · Conversational AI · Working Alliance · Acceptance · Social Presence

1 Introduction

Due to their recent widespread applications, generative AI and chatbots have gained great importance in higher education [1, 2]. However, the focus is mainly on digital assistants that provide organizational or professional support to students. The use of digital assistants as a tool to support students' self-reflection processes is mostly new in universities and offers a wide range of applications. Chatbots can help a broad range of students in their everyday university life, not only in solving technical problems. AI-based technologies can support self-reflection processes on work and learning strategies,

P. Zaphiris et al. (Eds.): HCII 2023, LNCS 14060, pp. 176–190, 2023.
https://doi.org/10.1007/978-3-031-48060-7_14

and thus accompany students in different areas of their studies and university life [3]. To apply this approach, we developed an intent-based coaching chatbot called StudiCoach-Bot at the Cologne Cobots Lab of TH Köln/University of Applied Sciences [4]. We develop it as part of a co-creational project at the TH Köln in an interdisciplinary team of students, teachers and coaches from the fields of psychology, mechanical engineering, communication science and computer science. The StudiCoachBot is designed to stimulate low-threshold reflection processes among students. The use case is exam anxiety. The goal is for students to self-reflect on their anxiety to get an awareness and develop their own way of dealing with it. In April 2023, we deployed the StudiCoachBot via a webseite and pop-up widget[1], so that it is publicly available to students of all disciplines and ages.

An essential factor for successful chatbot development is the early involvement of test users [5], which we systematically evaluated for the further development of our chatbot prototype. In this paper, we (1) therefore provide insights into the development process and present the results from our user tests with several hundred users with different feedback methods. In addition, (2) we present first results from our field test starting with the deployment of the StudiCoachBot in April. We analysed the conversation paths of the users: How many students use the bot and how often is it accessed? We also implemented a short questionnaire via a feedback form at the end of the conversation with the StudiCoachBot to get feedback about acceptance and working alliance. The working alliance is considered to be one of the key effectiveness factors in coaching [6, 7].

The goal of our field study is to obtain information about user needs for coaching chatbots in university context and to further develop the StudiCoachBot in a user-centric way. The results also allow us to draw conclusions about the acceptance of and relationship-building in chatbot coaching at universities.

2 Coaching Chatbots at Universities: Concept & Development Process of the StudiCoachBot at TH Koeln

2.1 Dialog and Technical Design

The interaction with a chatbot cannot replace human-to-human coaching, but chatbots offer a valuable addition to the process [3, 8]. The concept of the StudiCoachBot is based on established process steps from coaching literature and offers different conversation paths [9]. Students can choose between the five topics "Recognizing Strengths", "Exploring Goals", "Understanding Signs", "Discovering Methods" and "Further Information" as displayed in Fig. 1. They are structured as separate conversation topics. Structurally, the topics are similar, with the exception of the "Discovering Methods". As visualized, the chapter consists of four further subsections. As the structure is different, we also analyse it separately in Sect. 3.

Self-reflection processes are stimulated via open-ended questions and combined with information on the topic of exam anxiety. Students work on the topics one after the other or individually. The coaching is framed by onboarding and final reflection. The concept

---

[1] The StudiCoachBot is available via www.th-koeln.de/studicoachbot.

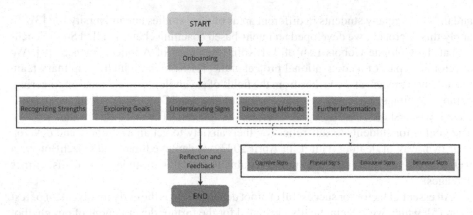

Fig. 1. Overall structure of the StudiCoachBot with topics/conversation paths

of the chatbot is based on a mixture of button-based (click-based) responses and free text input. Previous studies have shown that a "mixed" coachbot, which allows interaction via clicking as well as via free writing seems to be helpful [10].

We are developing our StudiCoachBot in the Conversational AI Rasa, which enables both rule-based chatbot processes and the addition of AI-based components that make the conversation with the bot natural language [11].

2.2 Development Process: Interdisciplinary User Testing with Different Feedback Methods

We develop our StudiCoachBot in an interdisciplinary co-creation process between students and teachers. For an overview of different phases/processes of chatbot development see e.g. [12]. A key factor for successful chatbot development is the early involvement of test users [5]. We decided to let three different user groups interact with our Studi-CoachBot at three different points in time and to get feedback from them: technology experts, coaching and university experts, as well as conversation designers and chatbot experts.

One challenge in chatbot testing is managing the expectations of the test users. Especially in the wake of the current discussion about chatGPT, many users expect a heavily AI-based chatbot when they participate in a user test. This leads to test users wanting to explore the limits of the chatbot, rather than interacting with it in terms of its use case. However, our StudiCoachBot is an intent-based chatbot with AI support. It is not yet designed to interact away from the use case and the prepared conversations. Therefore, it is enormously important to brief test users clearly in advance.

Online Workshop with Technology Experts. In December 2022, we held a 45-min workshop with 20 technology experts. The experts are part of an interdisciplinary team working in the field of social robotics at TH Koeln. It consists of mechanical engineers, computer scientists, social and communication scientists and psychologists. What they all have in common is that they work on the development and research of sociotechnical systems (chatbots, robots, machines for Industry 4.0) and thus have experience with early prototypes and technical realization conditions.

Participation in the workshop was voluntary. At the beginning, we sent participants a link to the StudiCoachBot and asked them to chat with it for five minutes. We pointed out that this is an early prototype that has not yet the final front-end. We then moved into an open discussion with participants based on guiding questions: What did you like about the StudiCoachBot? What did you miss? What (improvement) suggestions do you have? We noted down the feedback and discussion contributions and incorporated them into our prototype as feedback.

Feedback from Coaching and University Experts. In a second iteration and after incorporating feedback from the online workshop with the technology experts, we selected 10 coaching and higher education experts and asked for user feedback. These were individuals with extensive experience in higher education in either higher education didactics and/or student advising. Our expectation was that these individuals would be less concerned with technical implementation/feasibility, but would provide feedback on the content and language design of the StudiCoachBot. We contacted the individuals via email and sent them a link to our prototype. They could return their feedback either in writing via email or by phone. As in the first iteration, we asked only open-ended guiding questions and asked for overall impressions as well as positive and critical aspects. All selected experts gave us detailed written feedback and in some cases sent us screenshots of interactions with the coachbot for better understanding. We incorporated this feedback to survey further experts in a third step.

Online Peer Coaching with Conversation Designers and Chatbot Experts. For the third iteration, we involved two experts who are themselves active coaching chatbot designers and conversation designers. We sent both people our StudiCoachBot in advance via link so that they had enough time to chat with it and test it. Afterwards, two conversations of one hour each took place with one person and one conversation of 30 min each with the other person. We were coached very intensively and received feedback on the following aspects:

- Use case and onboarding: Does the StudiCoachBot makes tasks and limits clear and operates a clear expectation management?
- Conversation design: Is the flow of the conversation natural? This includes both linguistic and strategic aspects in the interaction script or conversation flow of the coachbot.
- Technical hurdles: At what points does the technology reach its limits and how can we deal with them?

2.3 Results of the Development Process

In the following, we summarize the three iterations and present the feedback we received under two aspects: Feedback on the technical aspects and feedback on the conversation design. In doing so, we present both positive and critical feedback and describe how we handled it.

Technical Aspects. Intent-based chatbots – like our StudiCoachBot, which we are developing in Conversational AI Rasa – rely on a large amount of training data and thus a comparatively long training time [11]. That means, we rely on a large number of conversations with test users during development, including failed conversations during the testing phase, through which the chatbot learns: if the bot is unable to understand the intent of the user, the conversation will not continue in the right way. However, we can then add these intents to the example lists of corresponding intents. This continuously improves the understanding and thus the performance of the StudiCoachBot. Therefore, each testing iteratively helps to optimize.

Overall, our StudiCoachBot worked technically robust in all three iterations. This means that users did not receive unexpected responses at most points and the bot did not unexpectedly "jump" into the planned conversation flow. One problem, however, was name recognition. To make the conversation with the StudiCoachBot more personal, we decided to ask users for their name at the beginning of the conversation. When they do, the bot picks up the name at various points in the conversation to address the user directly. However, so far the bot does not recognize every name even though it has been trained on a database containing 30.000 names. When user introduce themselves a phrase, sometimes the bot is not able to understand the name, even if the name is in the database. This then leads to the opposite effect: users whose names are not recognized are irritated and do not feel addressed. Our solution is, first, to constantly expand the name database with new names. Second, the bot now asks users to use a phrase to introduce themselves. Some users also didn't want to use their real name for introduction. They started using fictional names, which weren't in the database. To prevent this, we added a button, which allows people to stay anonymous.

Another important feedback we received, which only became clear in the second and third iterations, is that some users cannot join the conversation. Our Conversational AI that we work with is designed so that the initial input comes from the user. In the first phase, we assumed that it would be intuitive for the user to start with a "hello" or greeting, and we communicated this in the help text on the left side of the chat window. However, this wasn't always as intuitive as intended, and if the user didn't start with a greeting (but instead asked, e.g. "How can you help me?"), the bot didn't recognize or misunderstood the input and started at the wrong point in the conversation. We solved this via a widget. Our StudiCoachBot is embedded in a web page. When users accesses the web page, a chat window automatically opens where they can interact with the bot. Here it is possible that the first input comes from the bot, in which it introduces itself and asks the users for their name. This enables the desired entry into the conversation (see Fig. 2).

Conversation Design. The conversation design describes the flow of the chatbot inter-action. It is a key element in making a conversation feel natural and intuitive. To date, there are few systematic compilations and research on what aspects make up a suc-cessful conversation design [e.g. 13, 14]. However, chatbot developers agree that good conversation design starts with onboarding: Here it is important that the bot makes it clear in its first statements what its goals, tasks and limitations are [e.g. 8, 14]. Another essential element is a credible chatbot personality that runs throughout the conversation [e.g. 13]. We designed our StudiCoachBot to be a coaching expert with experience in

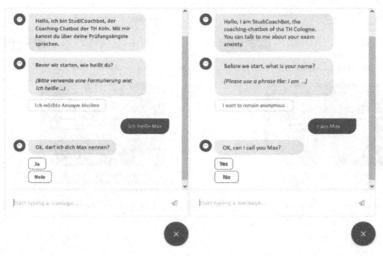

Fig. 2. Screenshot of a chat with the StudiCoachBot prototype via widget (left: original chat, right: English translation). A chat window opens automatically in which the StudiCoachBot greets the user with an onboarding message.

exam anxiety and coaching, while interacting with users at eye level and helping them help themselves. In addition, a chatbot should have a catchy name with high recognition value. We received positive feedback on all three aspects (clear onboarding and expectation management, credible chatbot personality, and memorable name) in all three iterations. Conversation design also includes linguistic and structural/strategic aspects. At the strategic level, we integrated the following elements for our StudiCoachBot (see Fig. 3 for an example):

- The bot alternates between button-based and writing-based interaction ("clicking vs. writing").
- The bot alternates between open-ended systemic coaching questions for self-reflection and presentations of information about exam anxiety.
- The bot shares information both in text form and via illustrations.

We have received feedback that the switch between button-based and writing-based interaction works well and leads to clear user guidance. We were already able to show this in an exploratory study [10]. It is also helpful for users that the coachbot alternates textual information with images. Regarding the relationship between information delivery and self-reflection, users reported that information has a strong overhang compared to open-ended questions that encourage self-reflection. At some points in the chat with the coachbot, users then wondered how it differs from an interactive website or what the added value of a chatbot is compared to other digital offerings.

This was very important feedback for us, whereupon we integrated further topics into the StudiCoachbot that are more strongly designed for self-reflection. The topic

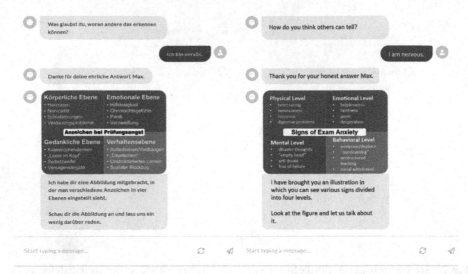

Fig. 3. Screenshot from a chat with the StudiCoachBot prototype (left: original chat, right: English translation). Here you can see different strategic elements in the conversation design: The bot alternates open coaching questions with information. Information is conveyed via text and as images.

"Recognizing strengths", e.g. only emerged after the last iteration. This is about appreciating and focusing on one's own strengths and resources in dealing with exam anxiety. Here, the coachbot uses resource-oriented questions to support users in perceiving and harnessing their own strengths [15]. Until the third iteration, the topic "Exploring goals" was also geared more towards conveying information. The focus here was more on describing situations in which exam anxiety occurs and less on helping users develop a future-oriented way of dealing with their anxiety.

On the language level, we received a lot of helpful feedback in all iterations, which led us to make several revisions to the language of the bot. We certainly underestimated how difficult it is to develop a conversational flow that feels natural and personal. In many places, the coachbot's statements were too long and sounded too "academic" and unnatural. One tip helped us revise the conversation scripts: We role-played reading chat histories to each other to get a feel for the bot's proper behavior in oral communication. In the process, we also revised various aspects of our conversation design such as the integration of different dislcosure behaviors of the bot, see e.g. [4].

3 Empirical Analysis of Acceptance and User Needs

Including different user groups at different points in time is a must in chatbot development. For our StudiCoachBot prototype, we were able to implement valuable feedback on technical aspects as well as on linguistic and structural-strategic aspects of the conversation design. This allowed us to release our bot in a version that we believe will be helpful to users. We accompanied the bot's deployment with a field study, and present the design and results below.

3.1   Target Group and Test Conditions

For our field study, we evaluate both the users' conversation histories and the results of an accompanying survey. Since our website and the bot are freely accessible, we analysed all the data we have collected since our release in April 2023. Users can access the bot via the official website of the TH Koeln/University of Applied Sciences. We implemted the bot via a pop-up widget. The bot was distributed via the faculty's email distribution list, social media channels of the departments and institutes of the university, flyers at a german-wide digital education fair, direct advertising at the study information day of the university and in direct contact with students.

The target group of our field study is primarily students with exam anxiety or nervousness before exams. However, pupils or other groups of people also have access to the bot. Our data analysis is based on the conversation histories, i.e. the user chats with our bot. We point out on our website that we use them anonymously for further development and research of the bot. We automatically statistically analyse the data but also manually examine it individually.

In addition, we implemented a survey in the chat with the bot and announced it on the website. Participation in the survey is voluntary and happens anonymously. It consists of a short questionnaire that ask about the overall impression of the bot, the level of exam anxiety, acceptance and working alliance. Comments are also possible via free text. In addition, we ask for demographic information such as age, profession, and field of study.

During the interaction with the bot and the field study, we value the privacy of the users. Providing the name is optional when interacting with the chatbot. Also, users receive information on data protection during onboarding with the bot. We also make transparent, which data we use for which purposes and who has access to it.

3.2   Data Collection and Evaluation: Conversation Histories and Survey

We evaluated the conversation histories with respect to the following questions: How many students use the bot and how often is it accessed? What topics are students working on and in what order? We also wanted to know when and how participants end the conversation and whether they reveal their name. In general, we looked for hints that allow us to draw conclusions about user behaviour and user-friendliness in order to optimise our bot. The conversation histories are analysed in a qualitative and quantitative way. On the one hand, we looked at data on important aspects of the conversation, such as usage figures or the conversation paths chosen, and analysed it statistically. On the other hand, we evaluated the conversations qualitatively. This involved examining the conversation progressions individually, checking the technical functionality, and correcting any dark figures in the statistical analysis.

As part of the field test, we embedded a survey to get feedback beyond the conversation histories. The survey consists of a questionnaire with 15 items. We asked for the overall impression of the StudiCoachBot in order to examine the acceptance of the chatbot. To investigate technology acceptance, relevant technology acceptance models such as the TAM (Technology Acceptance Model) or UTAUT (Unified Theory of Acceptance and Use of Technology) can be used [16]. Furthermore, we examined the working alliance since this is considered being a key factor in coaching for establishing a relationship and thus for a successful coaching [6, 7]. For the working alliance items, we used the subscales bonding and tasks from the Working Alliance Inventory (WAI-SR) [17]. We also measured social presence [18] by asking if the interaction with the chatbot felt natural. To see if the user who interacted with our StudiCoachBot actually suffer from exam anxiety we ask about the users exam anxiety ("On a scale from 1 to 10, how strong is your exam anxiety?"). For all other items, we uses a five-point Likert scale. At the end of the questionnaire, we collected demographic data such as age, profession, and field of study. Also, users could leave feedback via a free text entry.

3.3 Results

Sample Description. Our results are based on 242 conversation histories and 24 completed questionnaires. Out of the participants who took part in the survey (9,9%), the age ranges from 22 to 47 years. The average age is 28 years. 20 participants stated that they were studying, of which nine were studying for a bachelor's degree and 11 for a master's degree. Three participants are neither pupils nor students or apprentices. On a scale from 1 to 10, participants reported an average exam anxiety of M = 5.21.

Evaluation of the Conversation Histories. Since the public release of the StudiCoach-Bot (17th April 2023) until the 25th June 2023, there have been a total of 1628 visits to the project website. The integrated chat widget was used a total of 242 times, or by around 15% of the website visitors. Of those, 171 chose to remain anonymous or writing a fictitious name and 71 used a real name.

The onboarding was completed 159 times. The main topics were accessed 147 times, consisting of accesses to the topics "Recognizing Strengths", "Exploring Goals", "Understanding Signs" and "Further Information" and 69 accesses to the "Discovering Methods" block. It is important to note that one person can access one or more topics depending on the conversation length and willingness of the user. Among all completed onboarding accesses, 129 accesses were interested in further optional information on data protection and 26 accesses chose the option for even more detailed information on data protection. The offboarding was fully completed in 42 cases, of which 24 participated in the linked survey at the end of the conversation.

For our chatbot development, it is important to be able to understand which conversation paths are used by the users in order to be able to respond better to their needs in the future. The following Table 1 shows the results of the conversation path analysis. For the main topics "Recognizing Strengths", "Exploring Goals", "Understanding Signs" and "Further Information" we examined how often these paths were started and whether the users completed the paths ("finished"), dropped out or errors occurred. The block "Discovering Methods" is analysed in the next paragraph, as it has a slightly different structure than the other main topics.

A total of 147 accesses were made to the topics shown in Table 1, of which most interactions (70) were with the block "Recognizing Strengths". This topic was completed a total of 23 times, i.e. approx. 33% of all accesses related to this section. User dropped out in 41 cases and technical errors occurred six times. What is noticeable in this section is a relatively high dropout rate of about 58% in relation to the total number of accesses and in comparison to the other blocks. The "Understanding Signs" section was the second

Table 1. Results of the StudiCoachBot's conversation histories (N = 147)

	Recognizing Strengths	Understanding Signs	Exploring Goals	Further Information
started	70 (100 %)	39 (100 %)	28 (100 %)	10 (100 %)
finished	23 (33 %)	17 (44 %)	10 (36 %)	8 (80 %)
dropped out	41 (58 %)	14 (36 %)	14 (50 %)	2 (20 %)
error	6 (9 %)	8 (21 %)	2 (7 %)	0 (0 %)

most frequently accessed section, being accessed 39 times. It is completed 17 times, i.e. 44% of all accesses to this topic. Users dropped out of the conversation in 14 cases and technical errors occurred eight times in the course of the conversation. The relatively high error rate of 21% in relation to all accesses in this section should be emphasised. Demand is slightly lower for "Exploring Goals", with 28 accesses. There, the topic was finished a total of 10 times, which corresponds to 36% of the total number of accesses to this topic, and 14 times user dropped out during the conversation. Errors occurred twice. At this point, the high exit rate of 50% of all accesses to this section should be mentioned. The "Further Information" topic was accessed the least, 10 times. This topic was completed eight times (80%) and exited twice. No errors occurred at this point. At 80%, the completion rate is significantly higher than in the other topics.

The "Discovering Methods" topic was accessed a total of 69 times in the above-mentioned period. Table 2 shows the access rates for the individual sub-paths of the methods topic.

Table 2. Results of the StudiCoachBot's conversation histories. ("Discovering Methods", N = 69)

	Cognitive signs	Physical signs	Emotional signs	Behavioural signs
started	21 (100 %)	16 (100 %)	16 (100 %)	16 (100 %)
finished	7 (33 %)	9 (56 %)	11 (69 %)	10 (63 %)
cancelled	11 (52 %)	7 (44 %)	5 (31 %)	5 (31 %)
error	3 (14 %)	0 (0 %)	0 (0 %)	1 (6 %)

In Table 2, it can be seen that most conversations within the "Discovering Methods" topic are made in the subcategory "Cognitive Signs". This topic is completed a total of seven times and is most frequently dropped out with 52% (11 times). The error rate is also highest here with 14% (three errors). The other three subcategories are called up equally often with 16 calls each. The subcategory "Physical Signs" is completed nine times and user dropped out seven times. No errors occurred here. The topic "Emotional Signs" is completed most often (69%, 11 times). This topic is only cancelled five times. Last but not least the subcategory "Behavioural Signs" is completed a total of 10 times (63%).

Evaluation of the Survey. 24 participants completed the questionnaire, with one person not completing the questionnaire in full. All questions regarding acceptance, working alliance and social presence were answered on a five-point Likert scale (one = does not apply at all, five = applies completely). As can be seen in Table 3, the category acceptance consisted of one item and was rated on average with $M = 3.54$ (SD $= 0.96$). The working alliance was rated by 23 participants with an average of $M = 3.63$ (SD $= 0.94$). The subscale bonding within the working alliance was rated with $M = 4.00$ (SD $= 0.83$) and the subscale tasks with $M = 3.26$ (SD $= 1.05$). The only average rating below three is found in the social presence item with $M = 2.43$ (SD $= 1.01$).

Table 3. Statistical Analysis of Questionnaire Results (N = 24)

Group of Variables	Number of Items	Mean	Standard Deviation	Min	Max	N
Acceptance	1	3.54	0.96	2	5	24
Working Alliance	7	3.63	0.94	1	5	23
Working Alliance Bonding	4	4.00	0.83	1	5	23
Working Alliance Task	3	3.26	1.05	1	5	23
Social Presence	1	2.43	1.01	1	5	23

The participants had the opportunity to submit further comments about the chatbot via a free text field at the end of the survey. 14 out of 24 participants took the opportunity to fill in the free text field. Since the response rate was quite low, the following analysis is more explorative than representative. We can only present tendencies. We translated the quotations from German.

During the analysis, it quickly became apparent that some participants expect generative models such as ChatGPT when they think of chatbots. They expect the bot to be able to answer all conceivable questions: "You still need to work on this. If I enter something that the bot doesn't expect, I end up with the wrong answer. That doesn't feel good. [...]" The opinions regarding digital chatbot coaching in general also vary: "I think that anxiety can't really be alleviated by digital assistants, but only by personal interactions." "I really liked that I was encouraged to think about my anxiety through the exercises and follow-up questions of the chatbot. The 'help for self-help' was really well conveyed by it! [...]" Some participants would like the bot to be able to respond individually to all answers and statements: "[...] Unfortunately, there is still no real conversation because the StudiCoachBot does not really respond to the individual answers. It seems more like working through the individual points." "Of course, the bot couldn't react super individually to my answers, which was perhaps a bit of a shame. I would find it exciting if the bot could respond more specifically to answers in the future. [...]" However, the StudiCoachBot was also evaluated positively: "I found the chatbot very human and I was able to take away a lot."

3.4 Discussion

Acceptance and User Needs. From the results, we can draw conclusions about acceptance and user needs on various levels. Looking at the conversation histories, we see that of the 242 users who opened the chatbot widget on the website, 159 (66%) completed the onboarding. It seems, as if users are interested in our chatbot and the use case and that they accept the coachbot concept. The questionnaire results also show that the users accept the chatbot. An acceptance rate of $M = 3.54$ is above average. Also, the free text comments support the assumption that chatbot concept and onboarding are helpful as "help for self help". This is in line with research, that states that acceptance in (coaching) chatbots relies on a consistent concept as well as bot persona and must be based on a clear expectation management [8, 19].

The topic "Recognising Strengths" is the most frequently interacted path with. It is the one, that the bot recommends at the end of the onboarding. Presumably, a large number of people start with this topic. However, this topic also has a high dropout rate, with 58%. In this part of the bot, users are directed to an external link where they can work on an exercise about their own strengths. 63% of all dropouts occur during this exercise. It is possible that users, after being redirected to another tab, do not return to the chatbot to continue the conversation. We can see from this, that there are obviously critical points where the dropout rate increases. Although we conducted numerous user tests before the release (see Sect. 2), we could not identify this critical point in advance. Chatbot development therefore needs to be a continuous and iterative process [5, 13, 14].

We also see a high dropout rate in the "Exploring Goals" topic, where only half of all users completed the path. This path requires a high willingness of the users to reflect and engage in the chatbot coaching. It may be that only a few users are willing to do this or don't trust the technology to reveal something personal in the chatbot coaching. However, we can conclude from the questionnaire results that the participants do build trust in the chatbot and establish a working alliance. An average rating of 4.00 in the bonding subscale of the working alliance inventory is clearly above average. Compared to a previous study [4], which we conducted with a StudiCoachBot prototype, acceptance rates ($M = 3.54$ vs. $M = 3.37$) and especially working alliance rates ($M = 3.63$ vs. $M = 2.94$) are significantly higher in this field test. Higher values are due to the continuous optimisation of the StudiCoachBot (see Sect. 2). Since the last study, the productivity of the chatbot system has improved and we fulfilled the performance expectations of the users better – a key factor for chatbot acceptance [19, 20]. Also, our findings on the working alliance are in line with other studies, that state that it is possible to establish a working alliance (for the health domain [21]) or a bonding [22] in human-machine interaction.

However, in the evaluation of the questionnaire, it also became clear that the naturalness of the conversation is not yet satisfactory for the users. Users comment on this in the free text fields. In addition, the question on social presence, which is aimed at the naturalness of the conversation, was rated the lowest of all questions with an average of $M = 2.43$, which is moderate. Users also comment on this fact in the free text fields. One factor for the naturalness of conversations is the flexibility of the conversation process [12]. There is probably still a lot of potential for optimisation here.

Technical Aspects. Due to the number of hits on our chatbot since the release, we can make continuous improvements on a technical level. We collected a lot conversation data and used it to improve the model's language understanding. The interactions we evaluated, revealed some weaknesses. The robustness against unexpected answers needs to be improved, but also the language needs to be revised in some places to make the answers to questions more predictable. However, so far, we could already improve the technical robustness – also a key factor for acceptance in chatbot interaction [16]. The planned optimisations will continue to be tested and implemented in an iterative process.

3.5 Limitations, Design Implications and Future Research

Our field test has limitations. First of all, we released our bot at a time when it was not exam time at our university. We cannot say how representative our data is, how many users "seriously" chatted with the chatbot and how many only clicked on the bot out of curiosity. In addition, less than 10% of the users completed the questionnaire. Nevertheless, we assume that our data shows first tendencies. Of course, we will continue to evaluate both the conversation histories and the survey results.

Second, the coaching conversations with the chatbot were quite short and lasted a couple of minutes on average. It is possible that the short time users spent talking to the chatbot is not enough to establish a clear and measurable working alliance. In a next study, this should be considered.

Our chatbot needs to be further optimised in terms of technical and conversation design. The questionnaire made it clear that users' needs are not fully satisfied with the current state of the chatbot in terms of the naturalness of the conversation. Therefore, we would like to investigate whether the conversation with the bot can be made more natural through the use of large language models. For example, the coaching technique paraphrasing [15] can be used to give more individual attention to the user's statements.

4   Conclusion

In our paper we wanted to show that an iterative development of coaching chatbots with early user testings is a key factor for the successful design in terms of acceptance and user needs. Our study consisted of two parts: In the first part we presented the iterative development of our StudiCoachBot, consisting of user testings with several hundert test user from different fields. In the second part we presented the results from our field test after the StudiCoachBot release. We collected and evaluated conversation histories and feedbacks from users for a period of 10 weeks and evaluated both quantitatively and qualitatively. Compared to the results of a previous study on the StudiCoachBot [4], measurable improvements were achieved in the areas of acceptance and working alliance. The analysis of the conversation histories also provides valuable insights for the further technical and conversational design of the StudiCoachBot.

Research on acceptance and user needs will go on with our StudiCoachBot: We will improve the conversation to make it more natural, e.g. by optimising the phrasing of the questions and answers. Another focus will be the implementation of generative AI. Large language models offer many possibilities to increase the naturalness of the conversation. This will make it possible to respond more individually to the user.

References

1. Brown, M., et al.: 2020 EDUCAUSE Horizon Report. Teaching and Learning Edition, EDUCAUSE, Louisville (2020)
2. Nagarhalli, T.P., Vaze, V., Rana, N.K.: A review of current trends in the development of chatbot systems. In: 2020 6th International Conference on Advanced Computing and Communication Systems (ICACCS), pp. 706–710 (2020). https://doi.org/10.1109/ICACCS48705.2020.9074420
3. Kanatouri, S.: The Digital Coach, 1st edn. Routledge, London (2020)
4. Mai, V., Bauer, A., Deggelmann, C., Neef, C., Richert, A.: AI-based coaching: impact of a Chatbot's disclosure behavior on the working alliance and acceptance. In: HCI International 2022 – Late Breaking Papers: Interacting with extended Reality and Artificial Intelligence. Lecture Notes in Computer Science, vol. 13518, pp. 391–406. Springer, Cham (2022). https://doi.org/10.1007/978-3-031-21707-4_28
5. Potts, C., et al.: Toolkit for the Co-Creation of Health-Based Chatbots. 1st edn. Ulster University (2022)
6. Graßmann, C., Schölmerich, F., Schermuly, C.C.: The relationship between working alliance and client outcomes in coaching: a meta-analysis. Hum. Relations **73**(1), 35–58 (2019)
7. Lindart, M.: Was Coaching wirksam macht: Wirkfaktoren von Coachingprozessen im Fokus. Springer (2016). https://doi.org/10.1007/978-3-658-11761-0
8. Terblanche, N.: A design framework to create Artificial Intelligence Coaches. Int. J. Evidence Based Coach. Mentoring **18**(2), 152–165 (2020)
9. Berninger-Schäfer, E.: Online-Coaching. 1st edn. Springer Wiesbaden, Karlsruhe (2018). https://doi.org/10.1007/978-3-658-10128-2
10. Mai, V., Neef, C., Richert, A.: "Clicking vs. Writing": the impact of a Chatbot's interaction method on the working alliance in AI-based coaching. Coach. Theorie Praxis **8**(1), pp. 1–17 (2022). https://doi.org/10.1365/s40896-021-00063-3
11. Hussain, S., Ameri Sianaki, O., Ababneh, N.: A survey on conversational agents/chatbots classification and design techniques. Artificial Intelligence and Network Applications. Adv. Intell. Syst. Comput. **927**, 946–956 (2019)
12. Mai, V., Rutschmann, R.: Chatbots im Coaching. Potenziale und Einsatzmöglichkeiten von digitalen Coaching-Begleitern und Assistenten. Organisationsberatung, Supervision, Coaching, vol. 30, pp. 45–57 (2023). https://doi.org/10.1007/s11613-022-00801-3
13. Diederich, S., Brendel, A.B., Morana, S., Kolbe, L.: On the design of and interaction with conversational agents: an organizing and assessing review of human-computer interaction research. J. Assoc. Inf. Syst. **23**(1), 96–138 (2022)
14. Kohne, A., Kleinmanns, P., Rolf, C., Beck, M.: Chatbots: Conversation Design, 1st edn. Springer Vieweg, Wiesbaden (2020)
15. Schlippe, A., Schweitzer, J.: Lehrbuch der systemischen Therapie und Beratung I. Das Grundlagenwissen. Vandenhoeck & Ruprecht (2016)
16. Venkatesh, V., Morris, M.G., Davis, G.B., Davis, F.D.: User acceptance of information technology: toward a unified view. MIS Quar. **3**(27), pp. 425–478 (2003)
17. Wilmers, F., et al.: Die deutschsprachige Version des Working Alliance Inventory – Short revised (WAI-SR) – Ein schulenübergreifendes, ökonomisches und empirisch validiertes Instrument zur Erfassung der therapeutischen Allianz In: Klinische Diagnostik und Evaluation, vol. 1(3), pp. 343–358. Vandenhoeck & Ruprecht, Göttingen (2008).
18. Laban, G., Araujo, T.: Working together with conversational agents: the relationship of perceived cooperation with service performance evaluations. In: International Workshop on Chatbot Research and Design. Springer, pp. 215–228 (2019)

19. Terblanche, N.: Factors that influence users' adoption of being coached by an Artificial Intelligence Coach. Philosophy Coach. Int. J. **5**(2), 61–70 (2020)
20. Brandtzaeg, P.B., Følstad, A.: Why people use chatbots. In: Kompatsiaris, I., et al. (eds.) INSCI 2017. LNCS, vol. 10673, pp. 377–392. Springer, Cham (2017). https://doi.org/10. 1007/978-3-319-70284-1_30
21. Hauser-Ulrich, S., Künzli, H., Meier-Peterhans, D., Kowatsch, T.: A smartphone-based health care chatbot to promote selfmanagement of chronic pain (SELMA): pilot randomized controlled trial. JMIR mHealth uHealth **8**(4), e15806, 452–474 (2020). https://doi.org/10.2196/ 15806
22. Gratch, J., Wang, N., Gerten, J., Fast, E., Duffy, R.: Creating rapport with virtual agents. In: International Conference on Intelligent Virtual Agents. IVA 2007 LNCS, vol. 4722, pp. 125–138. Springer, Berlin, Heidelberg (2007).https://doi.org/10.1007/978-3-540-74997-4_12

Training Comic Dialog in VR to Improve Presentation Skills

Dohjin Miyamoto[1]($\boxtimes$), Akira Ishida[2], Natsuo Kanai[3], Riku Fukaya[4],
Saya Washikawa[1], Sota Tanaka[5], Hongil Yang[5], Tomohiro Tanikawa[1],
Michitaka Hirose[1], and Tomohiro Amemiya[1] (iD)

[1] The University of Tokyo, 7-3-1 Hongo, Bunkyo-ku, Tokyo 113-8656, Japan
{miyamoto,amemiya}@vr.u-tokyo.ac.jp
[2] Yoshimoto Kogyo Co., Ltd, Osaka 542-0075, Japan
[3] Natsu-Project, Inc., Tokyo, Japan
[4] Meiji University, Tokyo, Japan
[5] Yoshimoto Kogyo Holdings Co., Ltd., Osaka 542-0075, Japan

Abstract. Manzai is traditional style of comedy in Japanese culture, in which two comedians—a straight man *tsukkomi* and a funny man *boke*—engage in humorous conversation to make the audience laugh. We developed a VR application that simulates Manzai using first-person VR to improve the public speaking skills and gain confidence while exchanging opinions. This system was created based on body movements and conversations recorded in advance by motion capture and the user's performance was evaluated in terms of multiple factors. In this system, the user dons the avatar of a human tsukkomi of a famous Japanese comic duo and performs Manzai with the VR image of his boke partner. The Manzai performance is evaluated based on several axes and presented to the user after the completion of Manzai. The evaluation axes include measurements of pauses, movements, and smoothness, and the index is the degree of deviation from the movements of a professional comic actor, which serves as the ground truth. These factors are also important when exchanging opinions and speaking in front of an audience. We aim to enhance the user experience and abilities by enabling the users to objectively control these factors.

Keywords: Communication · Avatar · First-person perspective · Metaverse

1 Introduction

People often encounter situations where they are required to speak in public to exchange opinions, such as at a company meeting or during a meal with a group of friends. In these situations, it is easy to make mistakes due to nervousness while responding to comments, inability to proceed well, or lack of comic timing to liven up the situation. Considering these limitations, it is difficult to gain experience through practice and develop public speaking skills through experience.

Comedians constantly experience similar situations, yet they perform well. In particular, in the popular Japanese entertainment culture known as *Manzai*, two people, a

P. Zaphiris et al. (Eds.): HCII 2023, LNCS 14060, pp. 191–202, 2023.
https://doi.org/10.1007/978-3-031-48060-7_15

funny man *boke* and a straight man *tsukkomi*, stand on stage and engage in a comical conversation to make the audience laugh. Generally, a boke talks about strange things, while a tsukkomi points out fun things and talks about them. The tsukkomi and boke argue with each other, sometimes denying the other's opinions and reinforcing the setting of the strange world created by the other. There are many forms in which the tsukkomi is not bothered by the boke's unreasonableness but instead asserts their ideas positively and confidently. In Manzai, explaining a situation to the audience and communicating with one's partner are necessary.

In this light, we developed a Manzai VR system based on the idea that simulating the experience of a Manzai comedian, i.e., playing a role of a tsukkomi in Manzai, can help users gain confidence necessary to speak in front of an audience, enhance public speaking skills, and develop the ability to respond, which is important for Q&A sessions, and improve other skills needed during dialog presentation.

2 Related Works

In Japan, there has been plenty of research on Manzai. It is used to analyze conversations and study non-verbal language's effects [5, 12]. Sakata focused on the verbal and physical communications of Manzai performers by analyzing motion capture data and video and found that performers used physical and bodily movements and joint attention as clever techniques to stimulate laughter [7]. Okamoto et al., revealed that there is an "open communication" structure in Manzai dialogue because the gaze is toward each partner while their bodies are more likely to face the audience [13].

Several Manzai robots have been developed that automatically create Manzai scripts from Internet articles based on keywords [3] or that were connected through a network [2]. These studies used two robots playing the role of boke and tsukkomi.

Systems have also been developed that allow users to experience the role of a Manzai performer. The arcade game in which a user plays the role of tsukkomi during Manzai was released by Namco Inc. in 2002[1]. An omnidirectional video in which a viewer stands on a stage as a member of Manzai performers during Manzai has been published on YouTube[2]. An interactive system of Manzai VR using an omnidirectional video has been prototyped[3]. However, these systems differ from our system in that the main purpose of them is not to train dialog presentations as in our study, and they also employ omnidirectional video for the latter two cases.

In a general conversation, it is reported that generating whole-body motions such as nodding, blinking, and the actions of the head, arms and waist related to speech input enhances communication between humans, robots, and virtual avatars [1, 6]. This indicates that it is important to show the whole body when training dialog presentations.

Thanks to low-cost, high-quality VR devices such as Meta Quest 2, VR systems have been used for education and training. A customer service training VR system has

---

[1] https://ja.wikipedia.org/wiki/%E3%81%A4%E3%81%A3%E3%81%93%E3%81%BF%E9%A4%8A%E6%88%90%E3%82%AE%E3%83%97%E3%82%B9_%E3%83%8A%E3%82%A4%E3%82%B9%E2%98%85%E3%83%84%E3%83%83%E3%82%B3%E3%83%9F

[2] https://www.youtube.com/watch?v=KQ_lAVTmP2k.

[3] https://www.moguravr.com/manzai-vr/

been developed in which the user acts as an airport staff member and interacts with a visiting customer avatar [8]. In university classes, the change in the teacher's avatar influences the active participation of students in online learning [4, 11]. Thus, findings that experiences in VR can be used in the physical world are accumulating, and it is expected that VR is an effective tool for training dialog presentations.

3   Implementation

When practicing dialog presentation in daily life, one may fail because of nervousness when the other party is an actual person, leading to embarrassment and making one even more uncomfortable; however, these concerns are resolved with VR. In addition, if the framework practices comic dialog rather than the presentation itself, it is possible for those who have difficulty with dialog presentation to have fun while gaining a successful experience.

We designed this system such that this kind of experience will enhance the "ability to conduct dialog presentation," which is important in meetings and in casual conversations with colleagues as well as when conversing with friends. This system also strengthens public speaking skills, allowing to express one's own opinion even if sometimes denied or in a disagreement and gaining an upper hand.

3.1   Selection of Comedians

There are various types of Manzai, and randomly choosing a comedian for this study is unacceptable. The basic format of Manzai is that a standing microphone is placed between a boke and tsukkomi, which is used by the two performers to talk without moving too far away from each other. However, many types of Manzai, such as the trio Manzai and Manzai where performers move around the stage do not fit into our chosen format.

We asked NON STYLE, a well-known comedic duo in Japan, to participate in this study. NON STYLE has Akira Ishida as the boke and Yusuke Inoue as the tsukkomi. NON STYLE was the winner of the 2008 M-1 Grand Prix, the most prestigious Manzai award in Japan. In addition, Ishida, the boke, is a leading man in Manzai education who teaches young comedians through a comedian training course. We believed that Ishida would be the most suitable comedian for this study as this would allow us to gain his knowledge of the evaluation axes of Manzai and create Manzai suitable for VR.

3.2   Comic Script

We created an original Manzai script suitable for experiencing in a VR space. Professional comedians perform well only after repeated experience and practice. Therefore, to enable amateur users to speak while reading texts without difficulty, Ishida created a new comic script instead of existing comic scripts.

In addition, rather than focusing on making Manzai interesting from the audience's point of view, we designed the program with the objective of improving the dialog presentation skills. We also designed the script in a way that is not often considered in ordinary Manzai, such as not using the personal aspects of the comedian himself as subject matter and minimizing negative lines to avoid inducing negative feelings among users.

3.3 Motion Capture and Shooting Avatar

The movements of a Manzai were recorded from NON STYLE while performing the comic dialog (Fig. 1). We recorded the two performers simultaneously rather than separately, considering the sensitive nature of comic performances. This is because the important elements, such as pauses and movements, cannot be accurately reproduced if shot separately and then combined in the data. Motion capture suits with 37 markers were provided for each participant. In addition, 18 cameras (OptiTrack Flex 13), pin microphones, and a wireless communication system (transmitter WX-TB841, receiver WX-RJ800A, and mixer SS-444) were used.

Additionally, NON STYLE avatars were filmed with them wearing costumes used in the theater (Fig. 2). The still images were captured using 80 cameras (Raspberry Pi + Raspberry Pi camera module) at the VR Center, the University of Tokyo. After 3D modeling using Reality Capture (Epic Games, Inc.), the 3D model was shaped using Blender and Mixamo (Adobe Systems, Inc.). Rigging was added, and the 3D model was processed so that the avatar could move.

Fig. 1. Motion capturing while performing the comic dialog by comedic duo NON STYLE.

3.4 Application System

We developed a VR system that recreates a Manzai performance in a VR space, which can be experienced using an HMD (PICO 4, PICO). The VR system is composed of the HMD, two hand controllers, a headset microphone, and a VR-ready PC (Alienware m15

Fig. 2. Photographing to create a photo-real avatar.

R4, Dell; Windows 10, NVIDIA GeForece RTX 3070). The HMD was connected to the PC via Streaming Assistant[4]. It allows the user to manipulate the direction and position of the head and hands of the avatar playing the role of the tsukkomi according to their own head position and hand movements. Furthermore, through the headset microphone, the user can speak the lines of the Manzai, providing the experience of performing as the tsukkomi role.

Our system was developed using the VR Editable Scenario System: VRESS [8], which enables building VR systems with low code. VRESS was originally developed for the implementation of customer service training VR systems [9]. In this research, we modified the environment to a Manzai theater, and the user's avatars were transformed to the Manzai performers.

In VRESS, to allow users of the system, not just VR specialists, to flexibly modify scenarios and other elements, we based it on the Diarogue System [10] and made it possible to rearrange nodes using a GUI and edit scenarios. To realize the interaction of Manzai, we first used the voices and obtained data of the motion capture system for the avatar playing the boke role. We placed the motions and voices of the two people on one timeline and segmented them by dialogue (Fig. 3).

Next, we used one node for each segmented line, proceeding with triggers such as voice recognition and Timeline events. By doing so, when the system recognizes the user's voice and judges that the tsukkomi should have spoken, it moves to the next node, and the avatar playing the boke role reproduces the motion and voice associated with the node. Since Manzai includes unique intonations and expressions, we applied the Levenshtein distance to judge similarity and used it as a trigger to proceed to the next node. We harnessed the capabilities of the Web Speech API on Chrome to discern user speech, which was subsequently relayed to the main program via socket communication.

---

[4] https://www.picoxr.com/global/software/pico-link.

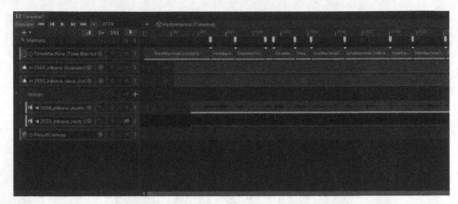

Fig. 3. Motion and voice of two people were placed on a single timeline, and segmentation was performed for each dialogue.

3.5 Procedure

The following is a description of how the user experiences the system. When the user wears the HMD, they see the theater from the first-person perspective of Inoue's avatar. The user has a 360° view of their surroundings, and the audience is in front of them (Fig. 4). On the right side, Ishida's avatar can be observed next to a standing microphone.

The comic script was shown in the view of the user. When reading a line displayed in the gray frame at the bottom of the screen, the system recognized it; after a beat, Ishida's avatar responds with a line. Another line was displayed, and when it was read, Ishida's avatar responded again, and the exchange was repeated. The comic script was constant and did not change interactively.

The performance carries on for approximately 3 min, and after the last line, evaluation of the comic performance is displayed on the screen. The evaluation is based on the three evaluation axes of pauses, smoothness, and movement, each of which is scored out of 100 points. The system scores the user for each line of the comic dialog, which is added at the end of the session. This concludes the experience.

3.6 Performance Index

We selected the evaluation axes for players performing VR Manzai to improve the user's dialog delivery. For this, we observed the comic performances of aspiring students in a comedian training course, investigated the differences between professional and amateur comic performances, and established three evaluation axes—pauses, smoothness, and movement. Although various other evaluation axes were extracted, this study focused on these three axes to evaluate user performance.

In a dialog between a boke and tsukkomi, pauses represent the timing of a response to the other person's line and have an important meaning [2]. The basic structure of Manzai that generates laughter is based on the following flow. The audience intuitively understands the dialog of the boke and then tries to verbalize it in their minds to create tsukkomi. The audience's sympathy is elicited, and laughter is triggered when the tsukkomi actor points out something funny at the slight timing between the intuitive

Fig. 4. A participant while playing a role of tsukkomi in VR Manzai.

understanding and verbalization of the line. A difference of a few tenths of a second can considerably affect the laughter obtained from the audience. If the tsukkomi is too fast, the audience will not recognize the boke. If the pause is too slow, the audience's own tsukkomi takes precedence, and they are left to finish the play in their minds. Pause is also important in dialog presentation. For the audience to understand, the speaker must speak not one-sidedly but with a sense of understanding, and the same ability is necessary for the audience to hear the conversation between the speaker and audience.

Smoothness is the ability to speak clearly and audibly to the audience. Comic dialog performed at the level of "listen carefully, and you will understand" or "somehow you will understand" will not generate laughter because the audience cannot understand the meaning instantly. When speaking in front of an audience that does not share the same context, speech must differ from how we speak in everyday life and be uttered more clearly and intelligibly, or the audience will often fail to understand the meaning. There is a considerable difference in the perception of whether words are being heard between speakers and listeners, and it is important to notice this difference through actual experience. Hence, this point is important in dialog presentations and comic dialog.

Movement refers to eye contact and body movement. It is difficult to attract the audience's attention if performing Manzai while standing on a stick. In addition, it is important to make the audience imagine fun situations; therefore, using the sense of sight and hearing can make it easier to understand the content of the conversation. For example, who is this line being spoken to and what shape is the blur pointing at in that space? Therefore, instead of constantly looking down while presenting, the presenter should look carefully at the partner and audience, sometimes using body language, pointing to the part they want the audience to see, and using various movements.

4   User Study

4.1   Method

The proposed system was opened for public use at the University of Tokyo's May Festival, held in May 2023. A total of 203 people experienced the system. Note that this is the number of participants who completed the experimental consent form and those who agreed to experience the system and left before filling the questionnaire.

In the demo, the flow of the experience was designed as follows. First, the participants were informed about the study's overview; next, we distributed a script of the comic performance they were about to experience. This script included lines to be read by the user, lines to be said by their avatar partner, and points to be aware of when saying the lines (e.g., how to move and loudness of voice).

In addition, we showed them a video introducing the objective of the study and NON STYLE's actual recording of Manzai using motion capture. The actual video played was almost the same as what the participants were about to experience. However, the participants were expected to be confused by the unfamiliar experience when they suddenly put on the head-mounted display and the Manzai performance began; therefore, it was considered essential for them to understand the content of the Manzai performance itself. Therefore, we encouraged them to practice the dialog in advance by speaking aloud along with the video.

Next, the user was fitted with the HMD and the voice headset. After activating the system, the user is prompted to look around the VR space and confirm that the Ishida avatar is on the right side. We also explained that the gray frame at the bottom of the screen displays the dialog. We explained that the dialog would begin when they started reading the lines aloud and asked the user to start the experience at any time. After approximately 3 min of the experience, the HMD and headsets were removed. Subsequently, we asked participants to complete a questionnaire at their discretion.

4.2   Result

A total of 146 participants (85 males, 60 females, and 1 non-response) completed the survey. Sixty-three participants were in their teens, 51 in their 20s, 4 in their 30s, 17 in their 40s, 9 in their 50s, and 2 in their 60s. When asked about their VR experiences in a multiple-choice format, the following responses were obtained: 1 "use it every day," 10 "use it often," 15 "use it occasionally," 68 "have experienced it several times," and 52 "have never experienced it."

The dialog in this experience is in Kansai dialect, often spoken in NON STYLE's hometowns. Therefore, we asked the users whether they spoke Kansai dialect. Twenty-nine participants spoke Kansai dialect, while the remaining 117 did not.

The following responses were received for the question: "Would you like to use such a system in the future?".

"Want to use it to improve my skills" (81 respondents).

"Want to introduce the system in the workplace" (17 respondents)

"Don't particularly want to use it." (32 respondents)

The choice also included an open-ended "other" response, and various responses were received. Some responses were as follows:

"If it were a little more sophisticated, I could use it for speaking practice."

"I want to do it again because it's fun."

"It was fun and I would like to do it again."

"I enjoyed it as a pastime. I enjoyed it very much as entertainment. Also, I felt that learning the pauses of a comedian like NON STYLE might be helpful in learning how to speak at a good tempo."

"I want to use it for fun."

Various responses were received to the following open-ended question: "Please describe any difficulties you experienced with this VR experience." Examples of the responses are shown in Table 1 under three broad categories.

Table 1. Feedback from participants.

Categories	Examples
Problems with poor reactions	"Ishida's reaction was slow." "The reaction of the system was slow." "I had to say the same line many times because he did not react." "Ad-libbing did not work."
Timing difficulties	"Timing of comic dialog was difficult." "Difficulty in timing when to start talking." "It was difficult to find the right timing to make a comment." "Timing is difficult if you are not used to it."
Difficulty in reading subtitles	"Subtitles were too low and difficult to read." "The subtitles were too small." "Subtitles were difficult to read."

5 Discussion

The system garnered positive reviews from those who had the opportunity to experience it firsthand. A specific inquiry, "Would you consider using this system in the future?" was met with a resounding affirmation from 57.4% of respondents (a clear majority), who indicated their interest in utilizing the system to enhance their capabilities. This response implies a considerable level of user satisfaction. However, problems relating to reaction, timing, and subtitling were also mentioned. Their causes and suggestions for future improvements are discussed below.

1. Poor response

A user commented that grasping the timing of speech utterances was difficult. The system uses a format that recognizes a string of speech and proceeds with the following line if it judges that the speech is somewhat accurate. Conversely, if the system judges the speech as inaccurate, it does not proceed, and the system hangs in a loop. However, because many participants wore masks, the sound entering the microphone seemed to be muffled, and there were frequent cases in which the speech was not recognized as accurate, making it difficult to get out of the loop. Therefore, in future, we aim to modify the format such that the lines will proceed without looping, even if the speech is inaccurate.

2. Timing difficulties

A participant commented that it was difficult to grasp the timing of the utterances. The system responds to the user's utterance after a beat and returns the avatar line of their partner. This was because it takes time for the system to recognize the string of characters uttered, determine whether it is correct, wait for a decision, and return the line. This is one reason it was difficult to decide on the timing. Therefore, in future, a one-stop system that proceeds continuously will be developed in parallel.

3. Difficulty reading subtitles

One user commented that the subtitles were difficult to read. In this system, the next line to be spoken by the user is displayed at the center of the screen. If the letters are enlarged for readability, the other person's avatar will not be visible. It would be ideal to have participants memorize all the lines in advance, but this may not be possible in situations such as this demonstration. Therefore, in future, we will develop a system that can be structured such that participants can practice slowly by reading dialogs carefully without rushing, as a "pre-practice," to recognize their part and repeat the experience as an actual performance.

In this study, we have not yet conducted an experiment to demonstrate whether the system improves the ability to present dialogs. We plan to test this hypothesis in our future studies. If this system can be improved and its effectiveness in enhancing the ability to give a presentation through dialogue is proven, it could be used for training at various companies or facilities, where many people who want to improve their presentation ability through dialogue are enrolled. We intend to investigate the possibilities of this system in the future. For example, some companies have set up courses to develop presentation and discussion skills during the training phase for new employees. Universities have active learning-type classes and opportunities to present graduation theses. Even in nursing homes, there are programs to develop interactive skills, which tend to decline, to maintain cognitive function.

6 Conclusion

Aiming to improve the ability to exchange opinions and enhance public speaking skills, we developed a VR system that enables users to experience the traditional style of comedy in Japanese culture called Manzai from a first-person perspective. We recorded a professional comedian duo's Manzai using motion capture, created realistic avatars for the performers, and developed an application that allowed users to wear head-mounted displays to experience Manzai performances. The system allowed users to present a predetermined line to which their partner's avatar responded. After approximately 3 min of comic dialog, the user was evaluated on the basis of three evaluation axes: pauses, smoothness, and movement. We received questionnaires from 146 users who experienced this system. Regarding the acceptance of the system, 81 users responded positively to using the system to improve speaking skills, while 17 users were willing to introduce this system at their workplace. Regarding difficulties with the VR experience, users identified poor response and difficulty in timing and reading subtitles. Accordingly, we aim to improve this system by improving the abovementioned three factors and will verify whether the experience improves participants' dialog delivery skills.

Acknowledgment. This research was conducted in collaboration with The University of Tokyo and Yoshimoto Kogyo Co., Ltd. We would like to thank Yusuke Inoue of NON STYLE, Akihiko Okamoto, Miyabi Haneda, and the members of the VR Center and FANY of Yoshimoto Kogyo Holdings Co., Ltd. for their cooperation in this study. Yusuke Kurita assisted on motion capture and avatar creation. Shogo Nishigaki and Saori Miki assisted in managing this study.

The demonstration at the May Festival was organized with the cooperation of Yusuke Koseki, Haruma Tasaki, and Ryo Onishi. We received the cooperation of Dr. Maiko Kodama to evaluate performance from a management perspective. We express our sincere gratitude to all those who played a role in the success of this project.

References

1. Lam, K.Y., Yang, L., Alhilal, A., Lee, L.H., Tyson, G., Hui, P.: Human-avatar interaction in metaverse: framework for full-body interaction. In: Proceedings of the 4th ACM International Conference on Multimedia in Asia, Article 10, pp. 1–7 (2022)
2. Hayashi, K., Kanda, T., Miyashita, T., Ishiguro, H., Hagita, N.: ROBOT MANZAI: robot conversation as a passive-social medium. Int. J. Hum.Rob. **5**(1), 67–86 (2008)
3. Umetani, T., Mashimo, R., Nadamoto, A., Kitamura, T., Nakayama, H.: Manzai robots: entertainment robots based on auto-created manzai scripts from web news articles. J. Robot. Mechatron. **26**(5), 662–664 (2014)
4. Amemiya, T., Aoyama, K., Ito, K.: Effect of face appearance of a teacher avatar on active participation during online live class. In: Proceedings of HCI International 2022: Human Interface and the Management of Information: Applications in Complex Technological Environments, pp. 99–110 (2022)
5. Okamoto, M., Nakano, Y.I., Nishida, T.: Toward enhancing user involvement via empathy channel in human-computer interface design. In: Bolc, L., et al. (eds.) Lecture Notes in Computer Science, vol. 3490, pp. 111–121. Springer-Verlag, Intelligent Media Technology for Communicative Intelligence (2005)

6. Watanabe, T., Okubo, M., Nakashige, M., Danbara, R.: InterActor: speech-driven embodied interactive actor. Int. J. Hum. Comput. Interact. **17**(1), 43–60 (2004)
7. Sakata, M.: Quantification of multimodal interactions as open communication in Manzai Duo-Comic Acts. In: Proceedings 2017 International Conference on Culture and Computing (Culture and Computing), pp. 65–66 (2017)
8. Tanikawa, T., et al.: Case study of low-code vr platform for training and evaluating employee's service skills. In: Proceedings of HCII 2023 (2023)
9. Tanikawa, T., Ban, Y., Aoyama, K., Shinbori, E., Komatsubara, S., Hirose, M.: Service VR training system: VR simulator of man-to-man service with mental/emotional sensing and intervention. In: Proceedings of IDW 2019, pp. 993–994 (2019)
10. https://www.pixelcrushers.com/dialogue_system/manual2x/html/index.html
11. Mizuho, T., Amemiya, T., Narumi, T., Kuzuoka, H.: Virtual omnibus lecture: investigating the effects of varying lecturer avatars as environmental context on audience memory. In: Proceedings of Augmented Humans International Conference 2023, pp. 55–65 (2023)
12. Zhang, H., Shoda, H., Aoyagi, S., Yamamoto. M.: A study on the back and forth Manzai of Milkboy by focusing on embodied motions and actions for liven-up. In: Rauterberg, M., Fui-Hoon Nah, F., Siau, K., Krömker, H., Wei, J., Salvendy, G. (eds.) HCI International 2022 – Late Breaking Papers: HCI for Today's Community and Economy. HCII 2022. LNCS, vol. 13520. Springer, Cham. https://doi.org/10.1007/978-3-031-18158-0_6
13. Okamoto, M., Ohba, M., Enomoto, M., Iida, H.: Multimodal analysis of Manzai dialogue toward constructing a dialogue-based instructional agent model. J. Japan Soc. Fuzzy Theory Intell. Inform. **20**(4), 526–539 (2008) (in Japanese)

How to Design a Successful Training Application with Used Mobile Augmented Reality

Liana Møsbæk and Thomas Bjørner(✉) ⓘD

Department of Architecture, Design and Media Technology, Aalborg University, A.C. Meyersvænge 15, 2450 Copenhagen, SV, Denmark
tbj@create.aau.dk

Abstract. Augmented Reality (AR) has been found useful and with strong affordances in education and training due to its potential to make the learning process easier, decrease the time for training, and increase motivation. Research has already highlighted the importance of UX when designing and developing mobile augmented reality. In this study we propose a framework within a UX perspective to design and implement a mobile augmented reality application. The framework is inspired by Donald Norman's six UX design principles. We used the framework to design and develop an AR mobile application for training field engineers in service and maintenance of a medical analyzer in the medical industry. Sixteen field engineers participated in the study. The evaluation of the developed AR application was inspired by the technology acceptance model, including items in ease of use, user satisfaction, usefulness, supplemented with items in visual interface, and learnability. The findings revealed that all the field engineers expressed positive feedback in terms of being able to see, train, and practice on the medical analyzer via the mobile augmented reality. A reason for the positive evaluation, could be due the high degree of effort to include the users at a very early stage and throughout the entire design process. Further, much effort was made to design the AR application based upon an explicit understanding of the users, tasks, and environments. However, future work is needed to create significant evidence of and insight into the training and learning outcomes of AR.

Keywords: Augmented Reality · UX design · design principles · training · technology acceptance · medical industry

1 Introduction

The accelerated evolution of augmented reality (AR) has brought forth new possibilities for developing innovative applications and has diversified the modalities of interacting with them. AR has become a fast-growing interactive technology for improved training and learning within various applications [1–4]. AR blends real-world and digital information [5] with a live view of a real-world environment whose elements are augmented by computer-generated content, such as sound or graphics [6]. This combination of the real world and virtual world has been applied for a wide variety of functions, especially in education and health care. AR can display a physical environment that encompasses

© The Author(s), under exclusive license to Springer Nature Switzerland AG 2023
P. Zaphiris et al. (Eds.): HCII 2023, LNCS 14060, pp. 203–216, 2023.
https://doi.org/10.1007/978-3-031-48060-7_16

learners with virtual interactive information, which could enhance learners' perspective and sense in real-time interaction [6–9]. However, when designing AR applications, important user aspects sometimes are overlooked [8–11]. One of the major challenges when designing AR technologies is to match the users' motivation, attention, and interest with perceived usefulness, learnability, and user satisfaction within a very specific context. This study is applied research with the following research question: How can a mobile AR application be designed and developed for training of Radiometer's field engineers in service and maintenance of AQT90FLEX medical analyzer? The mobile AR application is defined as a minimum viable product (MVP) for training experience for the field engineers at Radiometer to perform maintenance on the AQT90FLEX, an immunoassay analyzer. The AQT90FLEX analyzer is based on the quantitative determination of time resolved fluorescence to estimate the concentrations of clinically relevant markers on whole-blood and plasma specimens to which a suitable anticoagulant has been added. It is intended for use in the medical industry, such as in point-of-care and laboratory settings. Radiometer is a Danish multinational company that develops, manufactures, and markets solutions within healthcare, especially blood sampling and other diagnostic tools. The company has more than 3,200 employees and direct representation in more than 32 countries. The need from the company was improved online training for their field engineers making service and maintenance of AQT90FLEX. The training should lead to an increase in the quality of the training with visual representation of guidelines for service and maintenance of the analyzer.

2 Related Works

A prevalent and significant number of use cases of AR technology is encountered in education and training across various subject areas in both a formal and informal context. AR has been found useful and with strong affordances in healthcare education and training [5, 9] due to its potential to make the learning process easier [7], decrease the time for training [12], provide trainers an outlet for assessment, and increase success rates [13]. Research has shown AR is cost-effective training in which everyone can practice real-world tasks [14], reduces human errors [15–17], provides feedback and navigation, provides remote assessment and training [7], and increased motivation [16]. Research has already highlighted the importance of considering the user experience (UX) when designing and developing mobile augmented reality [8–11]. However, examples in the literature of a UX methodology used within an applied AR training for internationally widespread field engineers are limited. The novelty in this study is the target group of geographically spread field engineers, for which the AR application needs to have highly accurate design details within a highly specific and complex training context. In the literature, UX is used as well as defined quite differently, with no coherent taxonomy. However, there is a common understand that UX approaches emphasize the importance of the users of the technology, rather than designing the technology itself [34]. Using TAM (Technology Acceptance Model) [18, 19] as in evaluation of AR tools for industrial applications is already performed by other scholars [20], as the foundation from TAM can provide perceived ease of use and perceived usefulness of behavioral intention to use AR. Due to hardware and software advances AR has been used more and more frequently, also in industrial training contexts, including used HMD's (Head-Mounted Displays), wearable smart glasses (e.g., Microsoft Hololens 2), and mobile devices such as smartphones or tablets. One of the most important takes from the past research in the context of service and maintenance, is the necessity for developing a mobile AR application. Service and maintenance are inherent as mobile and needs flexibility and requirements [20].

3 Principles for Designing in AR

It is already described how engagement and motivation are important factors during training in AR [16, 20, 21]. However, there is less focus on how-to set-up principles that form a successful mobile augmented reality training system that engage the users. We would therefor like to propose (and emphasize) important principles for the user engagement in a mobile AR training system. A previous suggested design framework is the mobile augmented reality education (MARE) [7]. The MARE is a general framework with focus on the design development and learning but is not focusing on neither the users nor the technology. Other influential foundations are the PCK (Pedagogical Content Knowledge) and the TPACK (technological pedagogical and content knowledge) framework [23] but is not focused on AR training. Recently, there are presented conceptual frameworks within learning analytics from theoretical and pedagogical perspectives on Augmented Reality [24, 25]. However, the previous frameworks mainly provide a theoretical perspective, but do not include examples to the applied use of the theory. Our proposed framework with principles for training in AR (Fig. 1) consists of five main components (A-E), namely A: Foundation, B: Design, C: Prototype and implementation, D: Evaluation, and E. Disengagement/reengagement. All elements act as a part of a continues cycle process that can be adjusted over the time according to the present needs. The basic tenet in the framework is that the designers go through a dynamic progression of different elements (A E). At all stages, there is the possibility of carrying over knowledge and practice, in ways that the designer may or may not have intended. However, the elements in each of the stages are crucial, as it currently affects the outcomes and the impact of the AR training. A well-designed process provides a better likelihood for a successful AR training system.

A. Foundation
1. Needs, users, and context: Before starting the design of an AR application for online training, it is important to consider the needs, the users, and the context. An identification and analysis of the needs is very important, which can answer the question of what the relevance of using the AR training is. The users can be identified in terms of age, culture, social influence, geography, and other demographic variables. Further, the users can be identified by psychographic variables (e.g., Personality, values, attitudes, interests, hobbies, or lifestyles) or behavioral variables (e.g., usage rate, brand/product loyalty, or user status - potential user, first time user, regular user, rare user). Contextual factors are dynamic constructs that surround the used technology, taking both time and space into account, or in short where (working place and time is the technology going to be used.

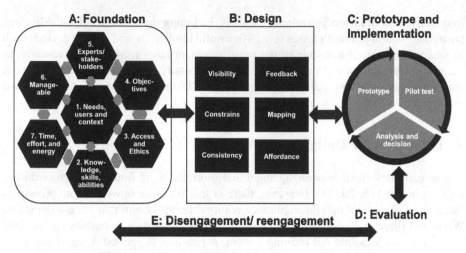

Fig. 1. A framework with principles for training in AR

2. Knowledge, skills, abilities: The success in raising training, awareness, and learning depends on users' knowledge, skills, and abilities. Knowledge is the awareness or familiarity gained by experience, including both different experiences with AR and other similar technologies. Skills is the ability to use the knowledge effectively and readily in execution or performance. A good briefing (matched accordingly to the users' knowledge, skills, and abilities) is important to have the users understand the system's purpose, framework, and controls, which can be included as an introduction or tutorial. There could also be differences in users' cognitive abilities, skills, attitudes, and competences for using the AR training, which is needed to be considered in the foundation.

3. Access and ethics: Ethical guidelines must be followed, but specific access requirements and ethical issues within an AR's foundation are also related to the users' context. Such ethical considerations are even more relevant regarding an AR context with target groups of patients, children, or other vulnerable groups, for sensitive topics, but also considerations if it is safe to use the AR equipment during e.g., field work with complex machines. The ethical issues also includes GDPR (General Data Protection Regulation) with important components of e.g., data storage, general provisions, rights of the data subject, and duties of data controllers or processors.

4. Objectives: The objectives (desired result) are very important to define in collaboration with the stakeholders to create a useful AR training system. The objectives must be very clearly defined as within metrics and indicators, as to explore the results and improve the training or learning.

5. Experts/stakeholders: Experts and other stakeholders are crucial to ensure that the right information is provided in the training. Collaboration with experts can also provide a framework to add relevance and knowledge to the AR content. It can include an analysis of the characteristics of the key stakeholders, their role in the process, the actions that execute, and their relationship to the users and context, the AR content, and learning objectives.

6. Manageable: An AR training system needs to be considered in terms of manageability. AR training systems are often to be developed within a specific timeframe and with limited resources. It is important to be realistic about the scope and scale of the training program, but also to have a manageable research question and/or specific goals that can be tackled and evaluated without promising too much.

7. Time, effort, energy: It must not be neglected that the users starting point comes with many different variables. One important factor is the users' motivation to start using the AR training and spend their time, effort, and energy on it. Hence, users' intentions to interact with the AR training are crucial.

B. Design

There are many different approaches in terms of specific design elements in AR. We are inspired by Donald Norman's six UX design principles [22] including visibility, feedback, constrains, mapping, consistency, and affordance. We will in the design and implementation section explain these principles in further details and link the principles to the specific and applied design and implementation made for the AR application. After the design the next step is prototyping and implementation, which is already well described within the context of training and mobile AR solutions [3, 4, 9, 21], most often within an iterative process that includes pilot testing and analysis.

C. Prototyping and Implementation

Prototyping and design are already well described within the context of immersive training and mobile AR solutions [21, 26], most often within an iterative process that includes pilot testing and analysis. A more difficult phase is evaluation and assessment [21, 26, 27]. Training is a complex construct, making it difficult to measure whether an AR training app is effective at achieving its intended learning goals.

D. Disengagement/Reengagement:

Our inspiration for including disengagement/reengagement in our framework comes from O'Brien and Toms [28] in a context of human–computer interaction. O'Brien and Toms [28] critically deconstruct and demonstrate various definitions of engagement and suggest that we look at engagement as a process comprised of four stages: a point of engagement, a period of sustained engagement, disengagement, and reengagement. Furthermore, they suggest various attributes of engagement that pertain to the user, the system, and user–system interaction. Disengagement (the lack of motivation to use the AR training again) and reengagement (motivation to use again) involve complex elements of motivation. At this stage the user has already tried the new system, and by that the experience will not be the same; however, there remain elements of both intrinsic and extrinsic motivation at training. The strength of reengagement contributes to the intensity of the motivational force experience. Reengagement is not dependent on the pleasantness of the previous experience, because the usefulness can intensify the attractiveness of using it again. The lack of motivation to use the AR training again can instead stem from aspects like interrupted smoothness and availability [28] because of updates, downloads, bugs, or computer incompatibility. Also, interruptions or distractions in the users (this case the field workers') environment can provide challenges for using the AR training again.

4   Methods

4.1   Participants

All the participants were from the Technical Service Department at Radiometer. The participants were from countries where Radiometer commercializes the AQT90FLEX analyzer. There were 12 participants from Europe, and 4 from Australia. As part of the foundation (Fig. 1), a 20-item questionnaire that included 15 open ended questions was developed with the purpose of identifying user characteristics. The questionnaire included demographic information, work experience, tool set skills, AQT90FLEX training experience, and preferred learning styles.

All participants gave informed consent, and they were informed that they could withdraw from the study at any time. In addition, all participants were provided with anonymized ID numbers. We applied special considerations when recruiting participants across countries, in accordance with the international code of conduct and ethical approval from Radiometer.

4.2   Iterative Design- and Prototyping

The prototype development was within an iterative process, and it included pilot testing, conducted with field engineers in Denmark (n = 6). The prototyping and pilot testing included usability testing with interviews and co-creation sessions. Seven field engineers were interviewed in depth to identify the possible features of and use cases for the AR training. As part of the pilot testing, three co-creation sessions were conducted [32] with two groups (Group A had 3 participants, Group B had 5 participants), lasting 90 min each. Based on the interviews and co-creation, there were outlined personas, application features, and design considerations.

4.3   Evaluation and Data Analysis

The final evaluation of the AR-application was conducted using a questionnaire (n = 16) and interviews (n = 7). The participants received a questionnaire for the assessment of the ease of use, visual interface, user satisfaction, learning outcome/usefulness of the AR application, and the application's learnability. The questionnaire was inspired by the technology acceptance model (TAM) [18, 19]. The questionnaire was followed by interviews with seven field engineers to gain further in-depth insights into their AR experience. Researchers analyzed the questionnaires using cumulative frequency. They analyzed the interviews using traditional coding [33] and content analysis. The interviews were transcribed verbatim to be organized and prepared for data analysis. Researchers then categorized and interpreted each interview statement by following an interpretation and content analysis of positive, neutral, and negative statements within each of the categorized themes.

5 Design and Implementation

The AR application was built for both Android and iOS. For recognizing and tracking objects, we used the Vuforia AR engine for Unity3D. Vuforia uses computer vision technology to recognize and track planar images and 3D objects in real time. The AR application (Fig. 2) consisted of troubleshooting, hands-on library, and how-it-works features, as well as a video module.

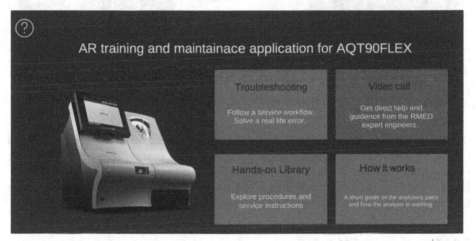

Fig. 2. The AR training and maintenance application for AQT90FLEX

The troubleshooting consisted of three steps: (a) retrieving and saving a service dump file, (b) determining the error code from the ACT90FLEX analyzer, and (c) inserting the code in the AR application. After inserting the detected error code, the application displayed the reason an error might occur as well as the service action needed. In this paper, we will follow error code 1267 as an example, accompanied by a service action involving a needle wash procedure. Error code 1267 has 12 steps, each of which is an activity the field engineer should follow in solving the error. The design and implementation of the AR application was followed by the principles made for "AR Design" in Fig. 1.

5.1 Visibility and Feedback

Visibility is about the users need to know what the options are and know straight away how to access them [22]. The AR application was developed to have the most import elements in sight when the field engineer was performing the training sessions. This could be with e.g., the screwdriver (Fig. 3), asking the engineer to reassemble the analyze (Fig. 3).

Feedback is the principle of making it clear to the field engineers what action has been taken and what has been accomplished [22]. Therefore, we made it clear at which step the field engineers were at now, and what to do next. This was implemented in

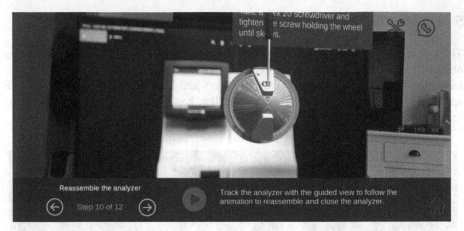

Fig. 3. Most important elements in sight, well-known icons, and clear indications of steps

the AR application as "Step X of Y" in the lower-left corner of the screen (Fig. 3) and providing leftwards and rightwards arrows to indicate a moving step back or forward. Further, there was text of what to now, and what to next (within the specific step) (Fig. 3). Each of the steps can be individually played, and there is no dependency or need to wait for the animations to be finished before going to the next step.

5.2 Constrains and Mapping

Constrains is about limiting the range of interaction possibilities for the field engineers to simplify the interface and guide them to the appropriate action. The constraints are clarifying, since they make it clear what can be done. An example of one of the constrains is the input of the error code; which also provided a systematic procedure, process, and identification. Mapping is about having a clear relationship between controls and the interactions and behavior [22]. This was implemented in the AR application by clear icons, e.g., the leftwards and rightwards arrows (Fig. 3), and the "house" in the lower right corner for main/home menu (Fig. 3). Further, there was implemented well-known icons for troubleshooting and help support call in the upper right corner (Fig. 3).

5.3 Consistency and Affordance

Consistency is about to restrict a particular form of user interaction with an interface [22]. The consistency was implemented by having similar operations and similar elements for achieving similar tasks in the AR application. Different error codes followed the same overall stepwise procedure, and within the same design. This could potentially be very important, as this AR application was new, and not used and tried out before. Affordance refers to an attribute of an object that allows people to know how to use it. Besides the implemented well known icons in the mapping, we also provided a "how it works" (Fig. 2), a tutorial accessible from the front page. This was implemented to get the field engineers high affordances within this new technology development. Further, for improved affordances in the high complex tasks, we included in some of the steps (in the AR representation of the training activities) further information and helpful media elements (Fig. 4), including e.g., videos, text box instructions, 3D models, figures, tables, and pictures.

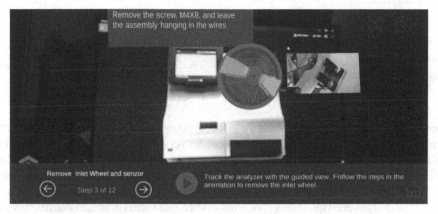

Fig. 4. Included video or other representations in the AR training.

6 Findings

6.1 A Subsection Sample

The AR training application was positively evaluated. In particular, the usefulness and user satisfaction were perceived as high, both from the questionnaire results (Table 1) and the interviews (Fig. 5). The usefulness items in the questionnaire covered questions concerning perceived enhanced skill level of performing the tasks as well as whether the AR training application was a valuable training tool and whether the AR training could improve the skills transfer between experience and everyday work tasks. The usefulness had a mean of 4.3 (SD = .50) from the questionnaire (Table 1), and the user satisfaction had a mean of 3.8 (SD = .90) (Table 1). The user satisfaction covered questions such as, "I enjoy the time I spend using the AR training application," "I am satisfied with how the activities are presented by the AR training application," and "I would recommend this AR training application to my colleagues."

It is interesting that despite the positive usefulness and user satisfaction ratings, the learnability was evaluated with the lowest score (M = 3.6, SD = .48; Table 1). The learnability was evaluated positively, but it also appeared difficult to ask the right questions within the learnability because the learnability comes with many individual preferences and specific context, which might be difficult to cover and answer in a questionnaire. In the interviews the participants suggested improvements concerning the learnability, such as "It takes too long to learn the functions in the AR training application," "The AR training disrupted the way I normally like to arrange my learning/work," "There is not enough information provided on the screen," and "The AR application presents the

Table 1. Questionnaire results for the user engagement and learnability.

Items	Range	Mean	SD
Ease of use	2.83–4.83	3.63	.55451
Visual interface	3.00–5.00	3.78	.55277
User satisfaction	2.00–5.00	3.81	.89925
Usefulness	4.00–5.00	4.33	.50000
Learnability	3.00–4.50	3.58	.46771
Average		3.83	.595

information clearly and understandably". The wording "too long to learn," "disruption," "normally," and "enough information" might be very differently perceived as well as used/interacted with in various contexts. The ease of use item (M = 3.6, SD = .55) mainly covered questions concerning usability: understandable and ease to use buttons, icons, menus, settings, instructions, and error/mistake codes. The visual interface item (M = 3.8, SD = .55) covered questions concerning perceived visual interface consistency and the aesthetics of the interface.

The positive results concerning the usefulness and user satisfaction items were validated by the interviews (Fig. 5).

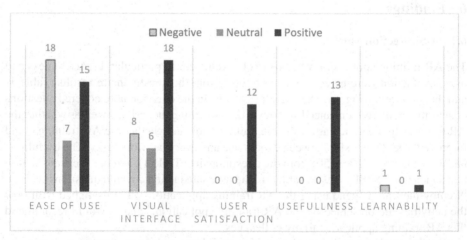

Fig. 5. Content analysis displayed from the interviews.

The ease of use came with mixed attitudes and was the category with the highest number of negative coded statements. However, the ease of use is with a more complex picture when looking into the four coded subthemes in this category. For example, is the subtheme "user flow" with 14 positive remarks, 2 neutral, and 2 negative. The subtheme 'AQT recognition' and "content" came with 8 negative statements, and only 1 positive comment.

7   Limitations

The main limitation of this study is the imperfect study design with a small sample size, lack of randomization, missing proper baselines, and the lack of control groups. In that regard, we had difficulties reporting the specific learning and training effects of the designed AR application. However, an imperfect study design is a very common limitation in many other AR training studies [1–4, 15]. Future work is needed to create significant evidence of and insight into the training and learning outcomes of AR. The exact methods of interaction with the field engineers were difficult to describe in detail due to being within an iterative design process within a very context-specific AR application. Therefore, even though we followed a rather systematic methodology, it is difficult to repeat the study. Thus, we should be careful about concluding the cause of any effect was due to the AR technology. Further, as within many other experimental technology studies, we also need to consider the novelty effect. Many AR studies (including this one) are not longitudinal enough to exclude these novelty effects.

Many scholars across disciplines have used the Technology Acceptance Model (TAM) in many different contexts [29, 30]. In spite that the TAM model [18, 19] was useful in this study, there are some limitations towards the model, which should be considered. One limitation of the TAM is the variable of user behavior, which is evaluated through subjective means like behavioral intention and interpersonal influence [31]. We mitigated this limitation and critique towards the TAM model by including not only TAM-questions in the questionnaire, and especially by used interviews. The interviews provided lots of further beneficial insights and complexity – in contrast to the simplicity of the TAM model. The insights from the interviews included (as it appears from the quotes) also some subjective reflections towards (engineering) norms and personality traits. Another limitation in the TAM is the missing external variables like age, education, and skills, which was mitigated by asking for exactly those variables. However, with sixteen field engineers included in the study, one should be very careful of making statistical analysis on these external variables.

8   Conclusion

The AR training application was positively evaluated with an average mean score of 3.83. The most positively evaluated items was within the usefulness ($M = 4.33$), user satisfaction ($M = 3.81$), and visual interface ($M = 3.78$). From the questionnaire and interviews it can be concluded that the learnability ($M = 3.58$) and ease of use ($M = 3.63$) can be improved. It appears from the interviews that within the ease of use it is mainly the content and AQT recognition that comes with negative remarks, whereas the user flow is evaluated positively. With the developed AR training application in this study, all the field engineers expressed positive feedback in terms of being able to see, train, and practice on the AQT90FLEX analyzer. A reason for the positive evaluation of the AR training application, especially within the usefulness and user satisfaction items, could be due the high degree of effort to include the users (i.e., field engineers) at a very early stage and throughout the entire design process. Further, much effort was made to design the AR application based upon an explicit understanding of the users, tasks, and environments. It is important to motivate the field engineers to use this AR training system on a more regular basis or as part of everyday work life. A crucial element in this motivation could be to continue the co-design of the AR training system with design input from the field engineers. In this specific context, AR can supply two significant advantages. First, the AR solution is capable of recognizing images immediately through the camera on a mobile device by focusing on the service and maintenance of AQT90FLEX. Second, the AR solution is capable of immediately projecting information concerning the service and maintenance of AQT90FLEX to provide visual help and guidance concerning the most important aspects. Potentially, the AR solution could even decrease the costs associated with the training; especially the travelling costs, as the field engineers are spread worldwide.

References

1. Babichenko, D., et al.: SterileAR: Exploration of augmented reality and computer vision approaches for real-time feedback in sterile compounding training. In: Proceedings of 6th International Conference of the Immersive Learning Research Network, pp. 62–69. IEEE (2020)
2. Campisi, C.A., Li, E.H., Jimenez, D.E., Milanaik, R.L.: Augmented reality in medical education and training: from physicians to patients. In: Geroimenko, V. (ed.) Augmented Reality in Education. SSCC, pp. 111–138. Springer, Cham (2020). https://doi.org/10.1007/978-3-030-42156-4_7
3. Endsley, T.C., Sprehn, K.A., Brill, R.M., Ryan, K.J., Vincent, E.C., Martin, J.M.: Augmented reality design heuristics: designing for dynamic interactions. Proc. Hum. Fact. Ergon. Soc. Annu. Meet. **61**(1), 2100–2104 (2017)
4. Horst, R., Fenchel, D., Retz, R., Rau, L., Retz, W., Dörner, R.: Integration of game engine based mobile augmented reality into a learning management system for online continuing medical education. In: Reussner, R.H., Koziolek, A., Heinrich, R. (eds.) INFORMATIK 2020, pp. 955–962. Gesellschaft für Informatik, Bonn (2021)
5. Kipper, G., Rampolla, J.: Augmented reality: an emerging technologies to guide AR. Elsevier, Waltham (2013)
6. Yuen, S.C.-Y., Yaoyuneyong, G., Johnson, E.: Augmented reality: an overview and five directions for AR in education. J. Educ. Technol. Develop. Exchange **4**(1), 119–140 (2011)
7. Zhu, E., Lilienthal, A., Shluzas, L.A., Masiello, I., Zary, N.: Design of mobile augmented reality in health care education: a theory-driven framework. JMIR Med. Educ. **1**(22), e4443 (2015)
8. Bitkina, O.V., Kim, H.K., Park, J.: Usability and user experience of medical devices: an overview of the current state, analysis methodologies, and future challenges. Int. J. Ind. Ergon. **76**, 102932 (2020)
9. Dirin, A., Laine, T.: User experience in mobile augmented reality: emotions, challenges. Opportun. Best Pract. Comput. **7**(2), 33 (2018)
10. Branaghan, R.J., O'Brian, J.S., Hildebrand, E.A., Foster, L.B.: Home healthcare. In: Humanizing Healthcare – Human Factors for Medical Device Design, pp. 367–383. Springer, Cham (2021). https://doi.org/10.1007/978-3-030-64433-8_15
11. Sommerauer, P., Müller, O.: Augmented reality in informal learning environments: a field experiment in a mathematics exhibition. Comput. Educ. **79**, 59–68 (2014)
12. Farrell, W.A.: Learning becomes doing: applying augmented and virtual reality to improve performance. Perform. Improv. **57**(4), 19–28 (2018)
13. Herron, J.: Augmented reality in medical education and training. J. Electron. Resour. Med. Lib. **13**(2), 51–55 (2016)

14. Kamphuis, C., Barsom, E., Schijven, M., Christoph, N.: Augmented reality in medical education? Perspect. Med. Educ. **3**(4), 300–311 (2014)
15. Escalada-Hernández, P., Soto Ruiz, N., San Martín-Rodríguez, L.: Design and evaluation of a prototype of augmented reality applied to medical devices. Int. J. Med. Informatics **128**, 87–92 (2019)
16. Akçayır, M., Akçayır, G.: Advantages and challenges associated with augmented reality for education: a systematic review of the literature. Educ. Res. Rev. **20**, 1–11 (2017)
17. Herbert, B., Wigley, G., Ens, B., Billinghurst, M.: Cognitive load considerations for augmented reality in network security training. Comput. Graph. **102**, 566–591 (2022)
18. Davis, F.D.: User acceptance of information technology: system characteristics, user perceptions and behavioral impacts. Int. J. Man Mach. Stud. **38**(3), 475–487 (1993)
19. Venkatesh, V., Speier, C., Morris, M.G.: User acceptance enablers in individual decision making about technology: toward an integrated model. Decis. Sci. **33**(2), 297–316 (2002)
20. Jetter, J., Eimecke, J., Rese, A.: Augmented reality tools for industrial applications: what are potential key performance indicators and who benefits? Comput. Hum. Behav. **87**, 18–33 (2018)
21. Ip, H.H.S., et al.: Design and evaluate immersive learning experience for massive open online courses (MOOCs). IEEE Trans. Learn. Technol. **12**(4), 503–515 (2019)
22. Norman, D.A.: The Design of Everyday Things. Doubleday, New York (1990)
23. Zou, D., Huang, X., Kohnke, L., Chen, X., Cheng, G., Xie, H.: A bibliometric analysis of the trends and research topics of empirical research on TPACK. Educ. Inf. Technol. **27**(8), 10585–10609 (2022)
24. Kazanidis, I., Pellas, N., Christopoulos, A.: A learning analytics conceptual framework for augmented reality-supported educational case studies. Multim. Technol. Interact. **5**(3), 9 (2021)
25. Doerner, R., Horst, R.: Overcoming challenges when teaching hands-on courses about virtual reality and augmented reality: methods, techniques and best practice. Graph. Vis. Comput. **6**, 200037 (2022)
26. Scaravetti, D., François, R.: Implementation of augmented reality in a mechanical engineering training context. Computers **10**(12), 163 (2021)
27. Zhang, J., Xia, X., Liu, R., Li, N.: Enhancing human indoor cognitive map development and wayfinding performance with immersive augmented reality-based navigation systems. Adv. Eng. Inform. **50**, 101432 (2021)
28. O'Brien, H.L., Toms, E.G.: What is user engagement? A conceptual framework for defining user engagement with technology. J. Am. Soc. Inform. Sci. Technol. **59**(6), 938–955 (2008)
29. Marangunić, N., Granić, A.: Technology acceptance model: a literature review from 1986 to 2013. Univ. Access Inf. Soc. **14**(1), 81–95 (2014)
30. Bjørner, T.: The advantages of and barriers to being smart in a smart city: the perceptions of project managers within a smart city cluster project in Greater Copenhagen. Cities **114**, 103187 (2021)
31. Malatji, W.R., Eck, R.V., Zuva, T.: Understanding the usage, modifications, limitations and criticisms of technology acceptance model (TAM). Adv. Sci. Technol. Eng. Syst. J. **5**(6), 113–117 (2020)
32. Jones, P.: Contexts of co-creation: designing with system stakeholders. In: Jones, P., Kijima, K. (eds.) Systemic Design. TSS, vol. 8, pp. 3–52. Springer, Tokyo (2018). https://doi.org/10.1007/978-4-431-55639-8_1

33. Bjørner, T.: Data analysis and findings. In: Bjørner, T. (ed.) Qualitative Methods for Consumer Research: The Value of the Qualitative Approach in Theory and Practice. Hans Reitzel, Copenhagen (2015)
34. Korsgaard, D., Bjørner, T., Sørensen, P.K., Bruun-Pedersen, J.R.: Older adults eating together in a virtual living room: opportunities and limitations of eating in augmented virtuality. In: Proceedings of the 31st European Conference on Cognitive Ergonomics, pp. 168–176. ACM, Belfast (2019)

A Study on Qualitative Comparison of Mental Maps Between Elementary School Students and Adults

Makoto Oka[✉], Yasushi Komura, and Hirohiko Mori

Tokyo City University, 1-28-1, Tamadutumi, Setagayaku, Tokyo, Japan
moka@tcu.ac.jp

Abstract. Japan is prone to frequent natural disasters, such as earthquakes and floods. To prepare for these unpredictable events, individuals must take responsibility for their own safety and well-being. Therefore, disaster education is implemented in elementary schools, often involving the use of hazard maps for learning. However, during actual disasters, individuals may not have access to maps and must rely on their memory to evacuate to safety. In such situations, people depend on their cognitive maps to guide their actions. However, cognitive maps of children are considered less developed compared to those of adults. Understanding the developmental process of cognitive maps in elementary school students is crucial as it can provide valuable information for creating effective hazard maps. Therefore, it is essential to elucidate the developmental process of cognitive maps in elementary school students.

In this study, we surveyed cognitive maps of fifth-grade elementary school students to investigate the development of their cognitive maps. The results revealed that compared to adults, these students displayed lower rates of remembering important landmarks and lacked specific details in their maps. However, we also observed the initiation of global memory, as evidenced by their awareness of the relationship between the surveyed area and its surroundings.

Keywords: disaster education · cognitive map · children

1 Background

Natural disasters, such as earthquakes, typhoons, and floods, are increasing in frequency and impact worldwide. Japan is also prone to natural disasters, particularly periodic occurrences of massive earthquakes. As a result, disaster preparedness education is being implemented in elementary schools. Representative examples include evacuation drills and hazard map creation. Evacuation drills enable elementary school students to learn how to respond in the event of a disaster. However, to prepare for unpredictable disasters, it is essential for students not only to learn how to respond at school but also to understand evacuation procedures and coping strategies while commuting or at home. One class involves creating hazard maps that identify dangerous areas in their own community. Through this exercise, elementary school students explore their neighborhoods,

P. Zaphiris et al. (Eds.): HCII 2023, LNCS 14060, pp. 217–227, 2023.
https://doi.org/10.1007/978-3-031-48060-7_17

identify hazardous locations during disasters, and map them out, aiming to understand the potential danger spots and evacuation sites in their community. The objective is to equip them with the knowledge to protect themselves during disasters, particularly when parents or guardians may not be available to assist them.

However, during actual disasters, students may not have access to maps and might need to rely on their memory to evacuate safely. The mental representation of the environment stored in one's mind is referred to as a cognitive map or image map. Cognitive maps represent an individual's psychological mapping of the world. Unlike objective and accurate survey maps like Google Maps (referred to as survey maps hereafter), cognitive maps are subjective and vary among individuals.

Compared to adults, elementary school children have underdeveloped cognitive maps. Understanding the developmental process of cognitive maps in elementary school children is crucial for acquiring the necessary information for creating hazard maps. Therefore, it is imperative to investigate the developmental process of cognitive maps in elementary school children.

2 Related Work

2.1 Cognitive Maps

In analyzing cognitive maps, a significant challenge lies in understanding how to study psychological maps. Directly studying cognitive maps is exceedingly difficult, and one must indirectly comprehend their nature through spatial representations expressed by some means. There are several methods for representing cognitive maps on a two-dimensional plane. One notable approach is the map drawing method, where participants are asked to draw a map of a specific area without referring to a survey map. This externalization method involves drawing on a blank sheet of paper or on a pre-drawn map with landmarks such as rivers or city halls.

Hart et al. [1] argue that it is essential to distinguish between the development of cognitive maps and the development of expressive abilities. Especially in children, there might be cases where cognitive maps are sufficiently developed, but their ability to represent them on paper is limited, leading to the misjudgment of cognitive maps as underdeveloped. In Japanese elementary schools, map-related education typically begins in the third grade. The subjects of this study are fifth-grade elementary school students, and both their cognitive maps and expressive abilities are in the process of development, but it is expected that many of them possess sufficient expressive abilities for analysis.

Siegel [2] states that acquiring accurate cognitive maps covering extensive areas is challenging in large cities. Due to the vast spatial extent of large cities, it becomes difficult to create a single cognitive map, leading to certain distortions when compared to survey maps. Some studies focus on these distortions in cognitive map research, such as phenomena like the rectilinearization effect. However, in this study, we deal with cognitive maps of a narrow area around the participants' homes, so distortions will not be considered.

2.2 Analysis of Cognitive Maps

In conducting urban analysis, Lynch [3] defined five elements—Paths, Edges, Districts, Nodes, and Landmarks. Paths represent linear features such as roads or railways, Edges are linear features like coastlines, Nodes are the points where Paths intersect, Districts are areas bounded by Paths or Edges, and Landmarks refer to prominent buildings or topographical features. Similar perspectives are often employed when analyzing cognitive maps.

Shemyakin [4] categorized cognitive maps based on their focus on routes: a map centered on routes is called a "route map," and a map encompassing both routes and their surroundings is referred to as a "survey map." A route map mainly includes routes and landmarks along those routes. Unlike an overview map, a route does not depict the overall structure, but it is cognitively perceived as a scene along the path, with no explicit relationships between landmarks. A survey map is a state where multiple route maps are interrelated. Thus, cognitive maps can evolve from route maps to survey maps.

Iwamoto [5] classified the drawing range based on landmark density, which decreases as one moves farther from home, creating three zones: Zone 1 with high landmark density, Zone 2 with relatively coarse landmark density, and Zone 3 with low and fragmented landmark descriptions. Mental maps with only fragmented information, even within the vicinity of one's home, are excluded from the analysis. Based on hand-drawn maps including depictions of homes and schools by elementary school students, Iwamoto conducted a detailed analysis, introducing four types: Route Map Type I, Survey Map Type IV, and two intermediate types. If the area around one's home is a survey map, but they cannot draw the route to their school, it is categorized as Intermediate Type II. Hand-drawn maps combining Route Map Type I and Intermediate Type II are classified as Intermediate Type III. The study revealed an increase in Type IV maps as age advances.

Previous studies have analyzed hand-drawn maps based on drawing range and the number of landmark descriptions. Montello [6] argued that these changes should not be seen merely as quantitative developments but also as qualitative advancements in cognitive maps, occurring concurrently.

We also believe that drawing a landmark at an intersection where a left turn is made differs in meaning from drawing the same landmark along a straight route. For instance, even if the same landmark is drawn at an intersection, the meaning attributed to that landmark by the mapmaker may vary depending on whether it represents a left turn or a straight path. Rather than focusing on the extent of the drawing area or the accuracy of landmark positioning, we will conduct our analysis based on the characteristics of the drawn landmarks.

3 Research Objective

The ability to evacuate independently during disasters is considered crucial for children, and cognitive maps are believed to play a significant role in this capacity. In this study, we aim to support Montello's argument and divide the development of cognitive maps into quantitative development, which represents the spread of cognitive maps, and qualitative development, which signifies changes in the composition and positioning of mental map elements. Our primary focus is to elucidate the developmental process of qualitative development in cognitive maps.

4 Research Method

The analysis of cognitive maps will be conducted using hand-drawn maps obtained through the map drawing method. Even among elementary school students attending the same school, the locations of their homes vary. As suggested by Iwamoto's classification, cognitive maps around their homes are expected to develop early. Hand-drawn maps reflect both detailed aspects of cognitive maps and less-detailed parts. Whether landmarks are drawn at specific intersections depends on whether the participants reside in the vicinity or use those intersections as routes. Therefore, a simple aggregation of the number of drawn elements, such as landmarks, in hand-drawn maps would be meaningless. It is natural to expect differences in whether specific landmarks are drawn based on whether they are present near their homes or along their routes. Ignoring these differences and merely comparing the number of drawings would not yield a suitable analysis.

We have previously conducted experiments to obtain cognitive maps from elementary school students. Among them, one experiment involved drawing the route from their homes to the "Aiji Elementary School" as a hand-drawn map. However, the collected data had limited information since participants only drew the routes, making the analysis challenging. Specifically, when two points are specified, the resulting hand-drawn maps often form linear route maps connecting those two points. To address this, we decided to specify three points to ensure that a certain drawing range is covered. For the convenience of the experiment, the specified points must be landmarks known to all participants. Around "Aiji Elementary School," there are four railway lines, and within a 1 km radius, there are five stations: Iidabashi Station, Ichigaya Station, Ushigome-Kagurazaka Station, Ushigome-Yanagimachi Station, and Kagurazaka Station. Based on previous experiments, we expect that all participants are familiar with these stations. Therefore, we chose to draw maps of the area surrounding the three specified points: their homes, Kagurazaka Station, and Ushigome-Kagurazaka Station.

Furthermore, when hand-drawn maps take the form of survey maps, it becomes challenging to distinguish between routes primarily used and those not used, and the mapmaker's interpretation of each intersection as either a right or left turn or a straight path remains unclear. This hinders the analysis based on landmark characteristics. To address this, we introduce written directions to accompany the hand-drawn maps. The written directions require participants to describe in words the route between the specified multiple points, as if explaining it to a third party. Combining the hand-drawn maps with the written directions allows us to understand the utilized routes and intersections, enabling the estimation of the intended meaning behind drawing landmarks. Consequently, we can classify landmarks based on this meaning and conduct the analysis. However, due to the difficulty of precise intention estimation, we categorized landmarks based on whether they are broadly located along routes or not, whether they are at intersections or on straight roads. Specifically, we divided intersections into five categories: right turn, left turn, straight, or crossroads.

Additionally, when discussing qualitative development, even if differences in characteristics in the drawn content are detected, it may not be possible to determine which aspect is more developed. To address this, we will collect hand-drawn maps and written directions from adults and define the adult cognitive maps as being developed. We will conduct an analysis based on these data.

4.1 Experimental Method

Participants were given three tasks in the experiment. Task 1 involved drawing a hand-drawn map on a single A4 sheet of paper, including three specified points: their homes, Kagurazaka Station, and Ushigome-Kagurazaka Station. In Task 2, participants were asked to describe the route between Station 1 and Station 2 in writing, and in Task 3, they were requested to describe the route between their homes and Station 1. The allocation of Station 1 and Station 2 was considered arbitrary, as either could represent Kagurazaka Station or Ushigome-Kagurazaka Station. For all tasks, participants were explicitly instructed to include landmark information in their drawings. In Tasks 2 and 3, it was emphasized that they should not use pictures or diagrams. The tasks were performed in the following order: Task 1, Task 2, and Task 3. Participants were instructed not to modify completed tasks once they started the next task. Moreover, they were directed not to consult or cooperate with others and not to refer to survey maps such as Google Maps while working on the tasks.

4.2 Participants

We requested the cooperation of 69 fifth-grade students from two classes at Aiji Elementary School, located in the central area of Tokyo's Shinjuku Ward, along with their parents. A letter of request from the teachers was distributed to the parents, and subsequently, the tasks were collected.

We collected 68 hand-drawn maps from the elementary school students and 69 sets of written directions. Some entries were excluded due to missing or illegible names, or content that deviated from the instructions. For our analysis, which required both hand-drawn maps and written directions, we considered 62 sets of complete data as the analysis sample. From the parents, we collected 25 hand-drawn maps and 25 sets of written directions. Entries with content that deviated from the instructions were excluded, leaving us with 24 sets of data for analysis.

5 Results and Discussion

Based on Iwamoto's classification of drawing density [5], 12 elementary school students whose homes were classified as Zone 3 were excluded from further analysis. For the remaining 50 participants, the results of Iwamoto's hand-drawn map classification are presented in Table 1. Despite being fifth-grade students who had learned maps in third grade, many of them exhibited characteristics of Type I maps. This observation may suggest a possible connection to Tani's argument [7]. According to Tani, during the developmental process, there may be a decline in the quality of cognitive maps as individuals restructure the relationships between previously learned landmarks. Fifth-grade students may correspond to a phase of decline during the process of map reconstruction.

Table 1. Classification of hand-drawn maps using drawing density (Iwamoto's classification)

Type	Number of Persons
Type 1	14
Type 2	2
Type 3	8
Type 4	25

Throughout the analysis, hand-drawn map areas were extensive, while route descriptions were limited to the path only. Entries that appeared in both hand-drawn maps and route descriptions were classified as "within the route," while those solely present in hand-drawn maps were classified as "outside the route." Based on the characteristics of the locations, these were further divided into three categories within the route: right/left-turn intersections, straight-path intersections, and straight roads; and two categories outside the route: intersections and straight roads. We designated them as Class 1 (within the route, right/left-turn intersection), Class 2 (within the route, straight-path intersection), Class 3 (within the route, straight road), Class 4 (outside the route, intersection), and Class 5 (outside the route, straight road). We conducted the analysis by replacing the meaning of landmarks drawn by participants according to these five classifications.

It is important to note that one intersection can be considered within the route by some individuals and outside the route by others. If a majority of individuals perceive it as outside the route, the number of participants drawing it will be low. Therefore, a simple aggregation without considering this distinction may not allow for a meaningful analysis, as it may not be clear whether important landmarks are not being drawn or if they are actually outside the route. To address this, we investigated the drawing count only for individuals who perceived the intersection as within the route and expressed it as a ratio. Similarly, we determined the ratio of areas drawn as outside the route to the total drawn area. This approach enables us to conduct an analysis that considers the difference in sample size due to residential location variability.

Table 2 presents the landmark drawing rates for each location characteristic category among adults. We will use these adult drawing rates as criteria for developmental judgment.

Table 2. Landmark Drawing Rates by Location Characteristics (Adult Results)

Location Characteristics			Landmark drawing rate [%]
Inside route	Right and left turn intersections	class 1	46.7 (56.8)
	Straight-through intersections	class 2	18.1
	Straight road	class 3	13.1
Outside route	Intersections	class 4	11.9
	Straight road	class 5	23.0

5.1 Characteristics of Adults

Landmark Drawing Rate Within the Route

From Table 2, it is evident that Class 1 (indicating a tendency to draw landmarks at right/left-turn intersections within the route) has a drawing rate of 46.7%. One of the nearest intersections to the station is frequently drawn, but landmarks are not described. This indicates the absence of identifiable landmarks at this intersection. Excluding this intersection, the result for Class 1 increases to 56.8% (shown in parentheses). Therefore, for one out of the two right/left-turn intersections within the route, landmarks are not drawn.

The drawing rate for Class 2 (indicating a tendency to draw landmarks at straight-path intersections within the route) is 18.1%. In cases where the purpose is to represent the number of intersections passed, only the intersections are drawn without including landmarks. For instance, when expressing the instruction "Turn left at the third intersection," participants may draw landmarks only at the third left-turn intersection, leaving out the intermediate straight-path intersections. Thus, not all intersections have landmarks drawn. The lower drawing rate for Class 2, which is less than one-third of Class 1's rate, can be explained by the intention to depict the number of intersections passed, leading to a lower landmark drawing rate.

Considering these aspects, it becomes evident that over half of the right/left-turn intersections have landmarks drawn, while the low drawing rate for straight-path intersections is due to their function in indicating the number of intersections passed.

Certain intersections are equipped with individual nameplates displaying the intersection names. These nameplates are often installed by local municipalities at major intersections, signifying their importance. In the study area, there are three intersections with named nameplates. When considering only these three intersections, the landmark drawing rate for Class 1 reaches 83.3%. This finding indicates that adults draw landmarks at a higher rate for important intersections, such as those with nameplates. The drawing rate for intersection nameplates is 50.0%, and the combined drawing rate for either landmarks or intersection nameplates is 95.2%. This high drawing rate suggests that when dealing with significant intersections, adults utilize appropriate means to identify locations, not limited to landmarks alone.

Landmark Drawing Rate Outside the Route

Turning to Class 4 (indicating a tendency to draw "Aijitsu Elementary School" outside the route), some instances of drawing "Aijitsu Elementary School" were observed. This can be attributed to the fact that the study was conducted with parents of elementary school students attending Aijitsu Elementary School.

The drawing rate for Class 5 (indicating a tendency to draw landmarks on straight roads outside the route) is 23.0%. Landmarks outside the route do not directly provide useful information. However, several large facilities with significant public land areas are present in these areas, and it was confirmed that some participants included these landmarks in their drawings even though they were outside the route. It is presumed that these landmarks were added to serve as reference points when aligning the cognitive map with reality.

Additionally, outside the route, landmarks and place names are sometimes written on the edge of the hand-drawn map. These notations indicate "extend beyond" and each hand-drawn map contains an average of 1.83 such notations. It is considered that these notations serve the same purpose as landmarks in Class 5. They are effective for aligning the map's orientation with the cognitive map and are likely to have been added by the participants.

5.2 Characteristics of Elementary School Students

Landmark Drawing Rate Within the Route

From Table 3, it can be observed that Class 1 (indicating a tendency to draw landmarks at intersections within the route) has a drawing rate of 10.7%. Many intersections lack landmarks, suggesting a low awareness of these locations as points of right/left turns in their cognitive maps. None of the elementary school students drew intersection nameplates, indicating a lack of specific location information at intersections.

The drawing rate for Class 2 is 5.9%, which is half of Class 1's rate. The lower drawing rate for Class 2, which is already considered less important than Class 1, suggests a further decline in landmark depiction.

On the other hand, instances were observed where landmarks were drawn on the straight road sections before or after the intersections. This could be attributed to the students depicting memorable elements from scenes along the route or simply drawing landmarks they remember.

With a scarcity of landmarks at most intersections, it is likely that the elementary school students fall into the second category as proposed by Iwamoto, where drawing density becomes relatively coarse. As a result, their hand-drawn maps may be challenging to interpret as navigational aids.

Landmark Drawing Rate Outside the Route

From Table 3, it is evident that Class 4 (indicating a tendency to draw "Aijitsu Elementary School" outside the route) exhibits some instances of drawing "Aijitsu Elementary School." This can be attributed to the fact that the study was conducted with elementary school students attending Aijitsu Elementary School.

The drawing rate for Class 5 (indicating a tendency to draw landmarks on straight roads outside the route) is 33.5%. This rate is four times higher than the drawing rate for straight road sections within the route and 1.5 times higher than that of adults. While it was assumed that adults would draw representative landmarks, elementary school students are adding landmarks of lower importance and visibility. Similar to Sect. 5.2.1, it is possible that they are drawing landmarks they remember.

Regarding notations representing "extend beyond," there were 0.86 notations per hand-drawn map. This number is lower compared to adults. Iwamoto et al. [5] mentioned that as children move further away from their homes in concentric circles, the landmark drawing rate decreases. The scarcity of notations representing "extend beyond" may be related to the students' limited knowledge and memory about areas outside the drawing range of their hand-drawn maps. It is likely that elementary school students are less conscious of the spatial relationship between the drawing area around their homes and the area outside the drawing range.

Table 3. Landmark Drawing Rates by Location Characteristics (Child Results)

Location Characteristics			Landmark drawing rate [%]
Inside route	Right and left turn intersections	class 1	10.7
	Straight-through intersections	class 2	5.9
	Straight road	class 3	8.1
Outside route	Intersections	class 4	5.1
	Straight road	class 5	33.5

5.3 Comparison Between Elementary School Students and Adults

The comparison between adults and children is conducted from Class 1 to Class 5 in sequence. Due to the minimal difference between adults and elementary school students for Class 3 and Class 4, these will be omitted from the analysis.

Comparison of Class 1 and Class 2

Class 1 represents intersections with landmarks within the route, indicating significant locations on the map. The depiction of these points is considered crucial for analyzing cognitive maps. Comparing the landmark drawing rates for these important locations, adults have a rate of 56.8%, while elementary school students have a rate of 10.7%, showing a difference of over 5 times. It is likely that elementary school students are less conscious of landmarks, even at critical intersections. However, when limited to instances where landmarks are drawn, there is no difference in the landmarks they draw. Whether or not landmarks are drawn in Class 1 could serve as an indicator of cognitive map development.

Focusing on the three intersections with particularly significant intersection nameplates within Class 1, considering intersection nameplates as map elements, the drawing rate for adults reaches 95.2%. However, none of the elementary school students drew intersection nameplates. This suggests that while adults are more likely to draw landmarks at important intersections, elementary school students may not be aware of the varying significance of different intersections and perceive all intersections as equal.

From the difference in drawing rates between Class 2 and Class 1 among adults, it is inferred that Class 2 carries a different meaning from Class 1. The disparity suggests that adults intentionally added intersections to represent the number of intersections they pass through without landmarks, indicating a clear intention not to include landmarks there. On the other hand, elementary school students have no landmarks in either Class 1 or Class 2, implying that their cognitive maps are underdeveloped, and they may not remember or consider landmarks as important.

Elementary school students need to be encouraged to not only focus on the route but also pay attention to the presence and characteristics of landmarks. In times of disasters, buildings may collapse, roads may be impassable, and landscapes may drastically change. Being aware of landmarks becomes crucial in determining one's current location.

Moreover, it is important to provide information that helps elementary school students recognize landmarks that are prone to collapsing or catching fire during disasters.

Comparison of Class 5

Class 5 represents straight roads outside the route, which are typically considered less important areas. The drawing rate for adults is 23.0%, and for elementary school students, it is 33.5%, showing no significant difference. However, examining the content of their drawings reveals a significant difference. Adults tend to draw landmarks with higher recognition, such as public facilities or large-scale establishments. In contrast, no consistent trend is observed in the landmarks drawn by elementary school students. While adults draw landmarks, even in less important areas, elementary school students draw landmarks they are familiar with, irrespective of their recognition level.

Landmarks with large areas are likely to retain their landmark function even during disasters. Recognizing these landmarks becomes important. In Class 5, landmarks written outside the drawing range of hand-drawn maps are presumed to represent "extend beyond." Adults draw an average of 1.83 instances of "extend beyond" per person, while elementary school students draw an average of 0.86 instances, less than half. Among the 50 elementary school students, 22 draw landmarks representing "extend beyond," and the average number of these drawings among the 22 students is 1.95. The remaining 28 students did not draw any landmarks representing "extend beyond." This suggests that the cognitive maps of elementary school students who draw landmarks representing "extend beyond" are closer to those of adults in terms of development, while those who do not draw any landmarks of this type likely have less developed cognitive maps. The presence or absence of landmarks representing "extend beyond" can serve as an indicator of the cognitive map development of elementary school students.

6 Conclusion

In disaster-prone Japan, disaster education is crucial, especially for elementary school students. Understanding the cognitive maps, which are the psychological maps of elementary school students, is essential for providing effective disaster education. In this study, hand-drawn maps were collected using the map-drawing method to gather cognitive maps. To establish criteria for cognitive map development, cognitive maps of adults, who are parents of elementary school students, were also collected. The analysis focused on qualitative rather than quantitative development of the collected cognitive maps. Additionally, adult data was used as a reference to compare and analyze the cognitive maps of elementary school students.

Quantitative analysis of landmark drawing frequencies in a specific area, which could be affected by different residential locations, was deemed less suitable for useful analysis. Instead, for qualitative analysis, the elements of mental maps and the meanings behind their depiction were considered. To understand the intention behind the depicted landmarks, participants were asked to describe the directions (routes) between two points. Based on these descriptions, the routes between the two points were classified and analyzed.

The comparison between adults and elementary school students revealed that the latter had a lower rate of drawing landmarks at intersections, even within the route.

Moreover, no intersection nameplates were drawn, indicating that elementary school students were not familiar with specific place names. As they also did not draw landmarks at straight intersections within the route, many intersections lacked landmark descriptions. Consequently, it was found that elementary school students struggled to identify specific intersections, indicating that the ability to appropriately draw landmarks at intersections within the route can serve as an indicator of cognitive map development.

Regarding locations outside the route, differences between adults and elementary school students became evident. While adults drew landmarks with higher recognition, elementary school students drew landmarks they personally knew, irrespective of recognition level. Furthermore, in regard to drawing landmarks outside the map area, a dichotomy was observed in elementary school students, where they either drew landmarks representing "extend beyond" or did not. The ability to draw landmarks with high recognition outside the route or the ability to draw landmarks representing "extend beyond" can serve as indicators of cognitive map development.

These findings reinforce existing research. Initially, cognitive maps are generated around one's home, followed by cognitive maps of the route between home and school, leading to the development of route-map-type cognitive maps. Then, landmarks within the route are drawn, initially without regard to their importance in the drawing's context. Gradually, appropriate landmarks increase. Finally, it was found that elementary school students eventually draw landmarks at important intersections, such as those requiring right or left turns. Furthermore, the development progresses from route maps to survey maps, and this progression can be assessed by the landmarks drawn outside the route.

Going forward, utilizing the insights gained from this study on cognitive map development, it is essential to create educational materials for disaster education.

References

1. Hart, R.A., Moore, G.T.: The development of spatial cognition: a review. In: Downs, R.M., Stea, D. (eds.) Image and Environment, pp. 246–288. Aldine, Chicago (1973)
2. Siegel, A.W., White, S.H.: The development of spatial representations of large-scale environments. Adv. Child Dev. Behav. **10**, 9–55 (1975)
3. Lynch, K.: The Image of the City. The M.I.T. Press (1960)
4. Shemyakin, F.N., et al.: General problems of orientation in space and space representation. Psychol. Sci. USSR **1**, 184–225 (1962)
5. Iwamoto, H.: The imaginary environment of "community" in a children's mind. Assoc. Jpn. Geograph. **54**(3), 127–141 (1981) in Japanese
6. Montello, D.R.: A new framework for understanding the acquisition of spatial knowledge in largescale environment. In: Golledge, R.G., Egemhofer, M.J. (eds.) Spatial and Temporal Reasoning in Geograohic Information Systems, pp. 143–154 (1998)
7. Tani, N.: A transromation of image map from route-map type to survey-map type. Jpn J. Educ. Psychol. **23**(3), 192–201 (1890)

Extended Reality in Aviation Training: The Commercial Single Pilot Operations Case

Konstantinos Pechlivanis[1]([⊠]) [iD], Dimitrios Ziakkas[2], and Abner Del Cid Flores[2]

[1] Faculty of Engineering, Environment and Computing, Coventry University, Coventry CV1 5FB, UK
pechlivank@coventry.ac.uk

[2] School of Aviation and Transportation Technology, Purdue University, West Lafayette, IN 47907, USA

Abstract. Single pilot operations (SiPO) of cargo aircraft are expected by the end of the 2020s, and commercial airline passenger flights around 2030. More sophisticated interfaces and state-of-the-art system autonomy will be required for both general configurations, the future single-pilot airliners (i.e., the replacement of the second pilot with much-increased levels of onboard automation/autonomy (an aircraft-centric approach) and also the displacement of the second pilot to the ground with on-demand availability (a distributed air/ground sociotechnical system). The challenge of training the potential commercial single pilot has been emphasized in the recent literature. The apprenticeship-style training employed for current multi-crew operations (MCO) would cease to exist. A radical training redesign would be required to serve either pilots' transition from MCO to SiPO or a direct introduction to single pilot operations. The training design and delivery for the future single pilot will focus on ensuring safety.

In the last decades, simulators have facilitated high-risk industries such as aviation to provide appropriate safety-related training in situations where conventional methods are inapplicable or when hazards or expenses make conventional training impractical. New efforts and technology generate emerging opportunities to enhance the efficacy of training. Extended reality (XR) (i.e., Virtual (VR), Augmented (AR), and Mixed Reality (MR)) is recognized for its vast educational potential by immersing the user in a nonexistent environment or activity.

XR has already been used as a training device in various domains, offering the opportunity to develop skills such as problem-solving and decision-making under stress without exposing trainees or others to unacceptable risks. Aviation training organizations (ATO) consider XR applications as affordable, versatile, and time-efficient training methods. Currently, XR-based training is supplementary to the overall training due to regulatory non-admittance by authorities. However, the benefits of XR training enhance conventional methods of instruction. Even in low-resolution XR, elements of the natural world cannot be recreated in a classroom.

XR augments training of sociotechnical systems that do not yet exist or are not yet safe for humans and thus cannot be adequately prepared for in situ, for example, commercial SiPO. XR allows training in locations and events with no safe and realistic parallels. Additionally, such simulations can be rapidly and efficiently updated as new information becomes available, unlike other full-fidelity-built environments, which are considerably less shapeable.

P. Zaphiris et al. (Eds.): HCII 2023, LNCS 14060, pp. 228–239, 2023.
https://doi.org/10.1007/978-3-031-48060-7_18

Significant potential exists for XR-based procedural training to transform the aviation training industry completely. Purdue SATT implements immersive technologies in aviation training and explores the feasibility eMCO/SiPO. Therefore, the purpose of this study was to conduct a review of the current applications of XR in cognitive skill training and to make suggestions regarding potential areas for the implementation of XR scenario-based training (SBT) for both technical and non-technical skill development in the future commercial SiPO in order to address identified hazards and challenges.

Keywords: Immersive technologies · Extended Reality (XR) · SiPO · Aviation Training

1 The Extended Reality (XR) in Aviation

Since World War II aviation training has pioneered immersive learning methods. Well-established full-flight simulators are far off the wooden Link Trainers, but the goal always remains: how to provide realistic training to pilots in the safest and most efficient way. Towards that goal, technological development brought extended reality (XR) technologies to the modern educational scene. XR is an umbrella term for any combination of human and computer-generated graphics interaction that alters reality by adding digital elements to the physical or real-world environment to any extent and includes, but is not limited to, augmented reality (AR), mixed reality (MR) and virtual reality (VR). In brief: Augmented Reality (AR) refers to virtual objects and imaginations being placed in the real world. In the virtual reality (VR) concept, the users are placed into an entirely virtual environment where they can interact only in the virtual world. Mixed reality (MR) is a combination of both AR and VR, where one can simultaneously interact with the digital and the real world.

Any existing or emerging technologies that alter reality by blending the digital and the physical world or by creating an entirely virtual environment are considered XR. XR-related applications serve a broad spectrum of industries and growing up significantly in popularity. This increasing trend resulted from the overall technology development worldwide, ease of access to the technology due to novel and more robust communications networks, and the cost of acquisition of the technology itself [1].

Extended reality is utilized in education and training and constitutes a paradigm shift in terms of traditional instructional methodologies in use. XR resources are highly recognized for enhancing instruction and learning experiences in different environments outside of typical classrooms, such as flight training [2]. The real power behind XR technologies lies in their perceived capability to provide a solid foundation for incorporating new learning environments and experiences. Another advantage exists in its inherent ability to create unique communities of inquiry and practice (Ryoo & Winkelmann, 2021).

USAF experimental training in aviation virtual reality provides excellent and relevant insights [3]. The Air Force discovered that "experimental virtual reality fighter pilot training is performing best for pupils who desire to fly the ser-most vice's advanced stealth platforms" (USAF, 2021). The US Army has found that Aviator Training Next (ATN) uses low-cost, low-fidelity commercial-off-the-shelf virtual reality (VR) technologies to educate pilots [4] effectively. Boeing has tested numerous use cases in this arena, including building, repairing, and maintaining commercial and military airplanes and pilot training for vehicle and device operations [5]. Alaska Airlines recently adopted virtual reality for training. Purdue university implements immersive technologies through its technology pyramid (Fig. 1).

Fig. 1. Purdue technology pyramid (Ziakkas, 2022).

CAE Trax Academy also embraced COTS (commercial off-the-shelf) VR technology into their unique learner training ecosystem. XR-based training is utilized as a training aid and complements the overall training [6]. However, recent improvements in XR technology have dramatically reduced training expenses compared to other systems. Due to a reduction in full-motion simulator time, remote learning and practicing basic piloting abilities may lower training expenditures for new pilots by 70% [5].

Modern aviation changed commercial pilot skills from sensory and motor to cognitive and decision-making [7]. XR uses in training could meet the dynamic demands of pilot training, especially in extended multi-crew or single-pilot commercial operations.

2 Purdue XR Training Development for eMCO/SiPO

Rapid workplace developments make training evaluation and assessment more challenging than ever. As scientific and technical breakthroughs impact enterprises and industries, employee skilling, reskilling, and upskilling become more critical for survival. VR, AR, and MR offer employees and organizations new learning and development options. XR-based simulated training can be evaluated (Value to training) in reaction, learning, behaviors, and results using Kirkpatrick's four-level evaluation process. Purdue SATT proposes a data triangulation approach (Quantitative – Qualitative – biometrics) using Kirckpatrick's Four Levels of Evaluation [8].

XR-based simulated training evaluation requires Level I participant reaction because the incentive to interact and presence distinguish VR learning from traditional training methodologies. Thus, XR-based training simulations quantify learners' emotional arousal and engagement to assess training effectiveness. The triangulation of the after-the-fact quantitative approach (e.g., engagement survey), qualitative approach (e.g., open-ended self-reflection protocol and structured interview), and real-time biometric approach (e.g., GSR, HRV, and eye-tracking) to evaluate and assess XR-based simulated training leads to a better understanding of learners' reactions to and experiences with stimuli. Level II training evaluation measures actual learning or how much learners learn. Knowledge exams measure learning by comparing before-and-after test scores. Level III training evaluation evaluates the workplace application of training information. Qualitative and biometric methods measure behavioral changes. Onsite observations and supervisor performance evaluations are qualitative methods for evaluating expected behavioral changes after training. Business consequences of training outcomes are evaluated at Level IV. Purdue VR analysts collect and evaluate training data from all stakeholders and provide financial outcomes and impacts to the global aviation ecosystem decision-makers. Triangulating these three data sources can help the customer - organizations analyze and document training program financial implications.

Training should adapt to new development and learning contexts as technology transforms training, evaluation, and assessments. XR is an applied interdisciplinary topic and comprehending new training evaluation and assessment skills in light of technological breakthroughs like biometrics is crucial to its advancement. Efficient data collection -Machine Learning applications will open new avenues for organizational training and development evaluation and assessment. Moreover, Purdue is aware of GDPR – data policies for worldwide research – training – operations.

Creating specialized training for immersive technologies and different ways of operations (i.e., eMCO – SiPO -Advanced Air Mobility, AAM) is a top priority on the CARE scientific research agenda. Based on the most common SiPO ConOps configurations [9, 10], the emphasis is on improving these single pilot resource management (SRM) competencies to reduce the identified risks [11] and partially replace the need for the demand that is solely apprenticeship-style. Adopting XR as a fundamental part of the SiPO flight training procedure can be a useful tool in improving the pilots' ability to manage their workload and make decisions, as well as to maintain current levels of system safety.

The more immersive the task performance, the more engaged the neurophysiological subsystems become. For this reason, regulating operational settings in AR/VR/MR/XR was vital to prevent cybersickness. This was especially important in the learning process, which may require hours of human activity. Purdue follows the "ADDIE" ICAO model (Analyze, Design, Develop, Implement, and Evaluate), to thoroughly analyze training needs (Competency Based Training Assessment-CBTA) and describe a training specification and certification in response to changes in technology. The research project team, following the risk framework results and the human factors analysis, will provide answers to questions regarding the purpose of the XR training, the tasks associated with the purpose, the operational environment, the technical, testing, certification regulatory (i.e., FAA 14 CFR Part 60 Flight Simulation Training Device Initial and Qualification and Use; and ICAO 9625 Manual of Criteria for the Qualification of Flight Simulation Training Devices (FSTDs) and organizational requirements, (Competency-based Training and Assessment, CBTA).

Figures 2 and 3 show the difference in distance perception between a curved screen typically used in traditional flight simulators and VR goggles. Three targets marked by red, green, and blue X's are represented at the same distance on a curved screen, while they in VR appear to be at their correct distance from the observer. Another essential lesson every pilot must learn is to perform a proper lookout.

Fig. 2. Perceived distance of three targets (red, green, blue) seen on a curved screen (Color figure online)

Fig. 3. Perceived distance of three targets (red, green, blue) seen through VR goggles (Color figure online)

Lookout must be performed to monitor traffic and when performing a landing circuit. Traditional flight simulators rarely have a field of vision of more than 180° (Fig. 4), severely limiting the possibility of performing a proper lookout. In these simulators, pilots who train must often resort to alternative methods of reference, such as timing their turns, because they cannot use the lookout procedures they would use in real aircraft. VR goggles allow the student pilot to look in any direction (Fig. 5). This means the student can practice lookouts the same way he or she would in the real aircraft.

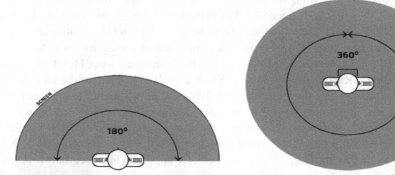

Fig. 4. Field of view on a curved screen   **Fig. 5.** Field of view with VR goggles

The limitations of the sensation of touch in VR are clear. Let us consider the extensively used touch controllers which deliver life-like hand presence and enable fundamental interactions in the VR environment. These touch controllers try to simulate the touch sense, blocking natural interaction via the fingertips. Moreover, when it comes to naturally doing things, nothing can compete with the human hand. As a result, the pilot trainees cannot interact naturally as they would in the real cockpit, significantly affecting the muscle memory required and the overall learning outcome. Pilots must get familiar with cockpit setups and memorize several flows when learning how to operate a new aircraft. Airlines and operators are always looking to become more effective and efficient. Costs associated with the actual cockpit simulators are a significant obstacle to overcome. The cockpit of traditional simulators is typically constructed with certified aircraft parts identical to those used in the actual aircraft; as a result, the cost of these simulators can be extremely high.

Consequently, pilots are turning to more interactive ways of learning, such as VR (virtual reality), for cockpit procedural training. Such solutions save airlines & operators thousands of $ USA by partially or even completely replacing the need for fixed-base simulators, suitable for the initial stages of a pilot's conversion training. However, although Virtual Reality Pilot Training has been so popular recently because it enables pilots to interact via vision and auditory senses, it could not provide the same level of immersion in touch sense. This is because the current state-of-the-art solution, the VR touch controllers, blocked the natural and intuitive interaction via users' fingers (Fig. 6). The identified problem is that touch sense requires integration with the human hand, which is a complex system, as it has 16 joints which provide 27° of freedom to perform every possible movement and motion with the fingers and wrist. The current VR touch controller only models a single joint and provides just 6° of freedom.

Fig. 6. Interaction with controllers

Purdue SATT, VRPilot, and Magos focused on implementing a solution that can simulate the touch sensation inside a virtual cockpit allowing a broader adoption of immersive technologies in the aerospace sector. The Purdue research team uses the Magos Virtual Reality Pilot Training (MVRPT), a combination of software (VRflow provided by VRpilot) and hardware (Magos Gloves provided by the Magos team) components. It works towards all the above-mentioned innovative features, such as depth perception, 360° vision, and touch sensation. It aims to completely revolutionize the current state-of-the-art pilot training solutions and create a new industrial value chain around aerospace and advanced manufacturing by developing a long-term, internationally competitive solution that combines different competencies and innovative solutions (Fig. 7).

MVRPT enables remote (home-based) procedural training in which the trainee can engage in a digital cockpit leveraging the VRflow platform using their fingertips while wearing Magos gloves. This allows the trainee to interact in the same manner as they would in a physical simulator with reduced cost of training and significant return of investment (ROI) for the training organizations. Due to VR-assisted learning, pilots

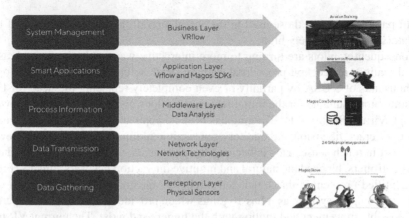

Fig. 7. MVRPT architecture

can remember the emergency checklist more effectively, requiring less retraining and resulting in better pilots. Following Edgar Dale's Cone of Experience and Purdue Virtual Reality Research Laboratory technology pyramid (Fig. 1), students recall 10% of what they read but 90% of what they do. This demonstrates the validity of the adage "you learn by doing."

3 The eMCO/SiPO Concepts in Commercial Jets

The aviation industry is moving toward further evolutionary de-crewing of commercial jets due to the anticipated pilot shortage [12] and the all-time aim of reducing manning costs [13, 14]. Both of these factors are driving the industry. Additional benefits may include the adaptability of the schedule and the possibility of financial gain from the sale of discounted tickets to satisfy customer demand [9]. Single pilot operations (SiPO) are projected to take place very soon, according to the vehicle roadmap published by the Aerospace Technology Institute [15]. It is anticipated that personnel reductions will be implemented gradually, utilizing a spiral approach to both technological and procedural development. This seems to ensure both the viability and acceptability of the changes [16]. Extended multi-crew operations (eMCO) and cargo SiPO should ensure a smooth and risk-controlled transition to SiPO passenger flights in order to meet the requirements of the FAA [15].

However, as with previous crew reductions [17], SiPO should be proven to be as safe as multi-crew operations (MCO) [18]. The transition to SiPO assumes that the current level of system safety is maintained [17, 19, 20]. Contrary to popular belief, multi-crew aircraft may not be a panacea for flight safety [18, 21, 22]. This viewpoint was shared by SMEs and former military pilots [11]. Enabling technology could enable more airliners to de-crew [17, 22] and compensate for human factors deficiencies, ensuring equal or even higher levels of safety. Transitioning to SiPO necessitates a structured risk management (RM) approach to ensure accurate hazard identification, risk assessment, mitigation, and acceptance (ICAO, 2018).

Researchers concentrated on human factors and challenges associated with the SiPO concept [12, 14]. Pechlivanis & Harris [11] maintained that the main identified hazards were SRM-related. High WL levels, insufficient training, a lack of pilot self-assessment regarding physical and mental preparedness to assume duties, a lack of self-discipline, insufficient SA levels, and poor DM choices were all associated with these.

According to Neis et al. [10], two basic design philosophies, aircraft-centric or distributed systems, could dictate the future of SiPO ConOps. In the first, automation will replace the second pilot, while in the latter, the second pilot will be relocated to the ground. Nonetheless, technological enablers are expected to take on some or all of the pilot-not-flying tasks [23]. Increased autonomy in cockpit real estate and the absence of a second pilot onboard would necessitate redistributing tasks between liveware and hardware, while training requirements would need to be redefined. The future single pilot training design will play a catalytic role [14, 24], and XR could improve the required soft skills. Purdue considered using XR based on the need to mitigate risks and facilitate training for a nonexistent system. Moreover, the Purdue SATT team focuses on the importance of behavioral biometrics in XR and SiPO, as pilot incapacitation remains one of the main threats in the transition from multi-crew to eMCO/SiPO.

4 Behavioral Biometrics in XR and SiPO

Behavioral biometrics tracks emotional state changes over time. Biometric techniques are suggested for XR-based behavioral change research; GSR, HRV, and fEMG may detect emotional valence and arousal. Eye tracking also shows virtual environment focus and attention. GSR measures sweat gland-induced skin conductance variations. There is ample evidence that autonomic nervous system alterations like sweat glands are linked to emotional arousal [25, 26]. Because of its properties, GSR is utilized in VR training to measure stress and immersion. HRV measures heart rate variation. HRV, like GSR, is autonomic. The sympathetic nervous system (SNS) activates and raises the heart rate in response to physiological stressors. In contrast, the parasympathetic nervous system (PSNS) lowers heart rate in calm people [27]. Thus, ECG and GSR measurements indicate emotional arousal. Numerous studies show that higher HRV helps people manage negative emotions, while lower HRV makes it more challenging [27–29]. When faced with scary events in an immersive virtual environment, people with higher HRV had better emotional regulation [30]. Other research has examined HRV and cognition [31]. Higher HRV improves cognitive and attentional performance [32].

GSR and HRV can indicate emotional arousal but not valence (e.g., positive and negative emotions). A camera can record and classify emotions, and VR headsets block facial expression webcams. This situation requires a more sensitive and versatile tool. fEMG can be inserted in the VR headset to assess facial emotional response, and it is increasingly used in VR studies to acquire quantitative emotional data [33, 34]. Electrodes on two key face skin areas record fEMG facial muscle activity in response to diverse emotions.

XR-based simulated training with an eye-tracking function calculates the subject's gaze in a virtual world. It shows where trainees look during the session, helping to identify a person's or group's interests [35]. Researchers generate diverse physical

Table 1. Technical Requirements

a) Existing VR controllers	b) Other Haptic gloves
Touch controllers allow a tactile presence in VR. By holding the devices, the users can establish contact with VR objects. However, the present solutions do not provide life-like interaction in the VR environment	*The haptic gloves can recreate a tactile presence in VR and allow a basic interaction with objects. The current state-of-the-art sensors can be used for low-fidelity training or recreative purposes. The critical limits of existing haptic gloves are:*
Finger tracking: touch controllers only track one joint of the hand (wrist) and cannot realistically replicate the finger movement in VR	Finger tracking: no existing solution can track the 16 joints of the human hand. This results in a very simplistic and inaccurate representation of the hand and movement in the digital world. It also affects the haptic & force feedback – since there is a delay in the feedback sent by the glove to the user when entering into contact with a surface
Ability to move: touch controllers only allow 6 degrees of freedom	Wearability: current fabric gloves limit hand movement (e.g., aluminum box in SenseGlove). The user can only perform certain degrees of freedom but not all of them. The gloves are often complex to put in the hand and to take out. Additionally, fabric soaks up sweat and other dirt. Fabric-based gloves are difficult to clean and raise hygiene concerns
Awkward user experience: holding touch controllers does not replicate natural hand and finger movements and affects the whole user experience	Solution features (Ability to change or intentionally degrade key system parameters (e.g., resolution, the field of view, latency, etc.) for testing purposes. Interface for emulating environmental parameters (i.e., weather) and sensors/displays (i.e., Enhanced Vision Systems, Heads-Up-Displays, Night Vision Goggles, etc.) within the virtual/augmented environment.)

and gaze behaviors in social encounters by monitoring eye-tracking gaze locations and constructing XR avatar areas of interest.

It is becoming increasingly common for augmented, virtual, mixed, and extended realities to focus on technological advancements without focusing on the risks of the implementation of immersive technologies in aviation training and transition to emco/SiPO.

The following comparison tables (Tables 1 and 2) summarize the technical requirements - Risks - Mitigation Strategies:

Table 2. Associate risks and mitigation controls

Risks	Mitigations
#R1: Delays on hardware (Magos) development and optimization. An extended lead time of material components. Longer development time than expected (Probability: H, Impact: M)	As mitigation actions the following are considered (each #Mx action corresponds to risk #Rx):
#R2: Delays in the integration between Magos-VRflow or other subsystems due to technical reasons. This could be the case if more time is needed to integrate all h/w and s/w sub-components. (P: L, I: H)	#M1: This risk is highly possible due to the COVID-19 impact to the worldwide logistics and production sector. However, with great planning and management we may fine tune all orders and in case any critical problem, we may use a previous version of the delayed elements (electronics, 3D printer material, sensors, raw material)
#R3: Delays due to technical reasons (technical problems – fails - bugs). (P: L, I: M)	#M2: Magos and VRflow are already integrated project and some optimization might be required but the teams are already working remotely in a very efficient way. It will be a low effort task
#R4: Operational-travel-dissemination restrictions due to pandemic: a) difficulties for each team separately to conduct technical operations and b) travel difficulties. (P: M, I: H)	#M3: With the proper management such an event will be avoided. In case it occurs, the teams, using proper management, shall adapt the work plan in order to solve the issue
	#M4. The current situation shows that due to the vaccination program as well as the measures, this risk can be avoided. In the unlikely case however, that #R4 takes place, the situation shall be assessed and as a mitigation plan full remote operation

5 Conclusions

It is becoming increasingly common for XR technologies to be integrated into all aspects of human daily life and activities. It is essential to remember that the artificial environment is not natural for humans and that the influence this has on a person's mental and physiological processes has not been adequately researched. Personal (internal, inherent in humans; physiological; mental; health); technological (technical means, ergonomic); operational (adaptation, the degree of control, head movements, general visual flow, linear and rotational acceleration, speed of self-movement, brightness level, section); these are some of the factors that can influence a student's cybersickness in XR. Other factors that can influence a student's cybersickness include: (the illusion of self-movement, duration, and cognitive workload).

The following are outlined from the Purdue research case study considering the integration of XR in aviation training and supporting the transition to eMCO-SiPO:

- The viability aspects depend on the inclusive framework and the decided technology change.

- Technology roadmap and related research focus on SiPOs and the concept of the artificial (or cognitive) implementation in cockpit design concerning operational reliability.
- Moreover, a conclusive accuracy threshold analysis for biometrics XR-SiPO implementation in aviation operations is lacking
- XR application functional utility research presents limited analysis literature.
- Finally, A Systems Theoretic Early Concept Analysis (STECA) is recommended as a follow-up, focusing on a safety-guided design- hazard identification approach.

References

1. Wohlgenannt, I., Simons, A., Stieglitz, S.: Virtual reality. Bus. Inf. Syst. Eng. **62**(5), 455–461 (2020). https://doi.org/10.1007/s12599-020-00658-9
2. Ryoo, J., Winkelmann, K.: Introduction. In: Ryoo, J., Winkelmann, K. (eds.) Innovative Learning Environments in STEM Higher Education: Opportunities, Challenges, and Looking Forward, pp. 1–16. Springer, Cham (2021). https://doi.org/10.1007/978-3-030-58948-6_1
3. USAF. The Air Force's Virtual Reality Fighter Training is Working Best for 5th Generation Pilots (2021)
4. Armyaviation. Training Army Aviators...Today and Tomorrow, vol. 69 (2020)
5. Laughlin, B.: XR drives aerospace excellence at boeing. Manuf. Eng. **82** (2018)
6. Careless, J.: VR sims gaining traction in pilot training. Aerosp. Tech Rev. (2022)
7. Mosier, K.L., Fischer, U.M.: Judgment and decision making by individuals and teams: issues, models, and applications. Rev. Hum. Factors Ergon. **6**(1), 198–256 (2010). https://doi.org/10.1518/155723410X12849346788822
8. Kirkpatrick, D.L., Kirkpatrick, J.D.: Evaluating Training Programs, 3rd edn. Berrett-Koehler Publishers, Inc. (2006)
9. Comerford, D., et al.: NASA's Single Pilot Operations Technical Interchange Meeting: Proceedings and Findings (NASA/CP-2013-216513) (2013)
10. Neis, S.M., Klingauf, U., Schiefele, J.: Classification and Review of Conceptual Frameworks for Commercial Single Pilot Operations (2018). https://doi.org/10.1109/DASC.2018.8569680
11. Pechlivanis, K., Harris, D.: Single Pilot Concept of Operations: Hazard Identification and Mitigation Measures [Manuscript Sumbitted for Publication]. Faculty of Engineering, Environment and Computing, Coventry University, UK (2022)
12. Myers, P.L., Starr, A.W.: Single pilot operations in commercial cockpits: background, challenges, and options. J. Intell. Robot. Syst. **102**(19) (2021). https://doi.org/10.1007/s10846-021-01371-9
13. Harris, D.: Estimating the required number of Harbour Pilots to support airline operations of a single pilot commercial aircraft at a UK regional airport. Aeronaut. J. 1–13 (2022). https://doi.org/10.1017/aer.2022.10
14. Schmid, D., Stanton, N.A.: Considering single-piloted airliners for different flight durations: an issue of fatigue management. In: International Conference on Applied Human Factors and Ergonomics, pp. 683–694 (2019)
15. ATI. Accelerating Ambition: Technology Strategy 2019 (2019)
16. Matessa, M., Strybel, T.Z., Vu, K.L., Battiste, V., Schnell, T.: Concept of Operations for RCO/SPO (2017)
17. McLucas, J.L., Drinkwater, I.F., Leaf, H.W.: Report of the President's Task Force on Aircraft Crew Complement (1981)

18. Moehle, R., Clauss, J.: Wearable technologies as a path to single-pilot part 121 operations. SAE Int. J. Aerosp. **8**, 81–88 (2015). https://doi.org/10.4271/2015-01-2440
19. EASA. European Plan for Aviation Safety (EPAS) 2020–2024 (2019)
20. Boy, G.A.: Requirements for single pilot operations in commercial aviation: a first high-level cognitive function analysis. In: Boulanger, F., Korb, D., Morel, G., Roussel, J.-C. (eds.) Complex Systems Design and Management, pp. 227–234. Springer, Cham (2015)
21. Gilbert, G.: Accident Analysis: Single-Pilot Versus Two-Pilot - Is There a Safety Advantage? (2015). https://www.ainonline.com/aviation-news/business-aviation/2015-06-05/acc ident-analysis-single-pilot-versus-two-pilot-there-safety-advantage. Accessed 07 Apr 2022
22. Harris, D.: A human-centred design agenda for the development of single crew operated commercial aircraft. Aircr. Eng. Aerosp. Technol. **79**(5), 518–526 (2007)
23. Vito, V.D., et al.: Flight management enabling technologies for single pilot operations in Small Air Transport vehicles in the COAST project (2021)
24. Li, W.C., Harris, D.: A systems approach to training aeronautical decision making: from identifying training needs to verifying training solutions. Aeronaut. J. (2007). https://doi.org/10.1017/S0001924000004516
25. Kreibig, S.D.: Autonomic nervous system activity in emotion: a review. Biol. Psychol. **84** (2010). https://doi.org/10.1016/j.biopsycho.2010.03.010
26. Tarnowski, P., Kołodziej, M., Majkowski, A., Rak, R.J.: Combined analysis of GSR and EEG signals for emotion recognition (2018)
27. Appelhans, B.M., Luecken, L.J.: Heart rate variability as an index of regulated emotional responding. Rev. Gen. Psychol. **10**(3), 229–240 (2006). https://doi.org/10.1037/1089-2680.10.3.229
28. Geisler, F.C.M., Vennewald, N., Kubiak, T., Weber, H.: The impact of heart rate variability on subjective well-being is mediated by emotion regulation. Pers. Individ. Dif. **49** (2010)
29. Williams, D.P., Cash, C., Rankin, C., Bernardi, A., Koenig, J., Thayer, J.F.: Resting heart rate variability predicts self-reported difficulties in emotion regulation: a focus on different facets of emotion regulation. Front. Psychol. (2015)
30. Hildebrandt, L.K., McCall, C., Engen, H.G., Singer, T.: Cognitive flexibility, heart rate variability, and resilience predict fine-grained regulation of arousal during prolonged threat. Psychophysiology **53**(6) (2016). https://doi.org/10.1111/psyp.12632
31. Park, G., Van Bavel, J.J., Vasey, M.W., Thayer, J.F.: Cardiac vagal tone predicts inhibited attention to fearful faces. Emotion (2012). https://doi.org/10.1037/a0028528
32. Johnsen, B.H., et al.: Attentional and physiological characteristics of patients with dental anxiety. J. Anxiety Disord. **17**(1) (2003). https://doi.org/10.1016/S0887-6185(02)00178-0
33. McGhee, J.T., et al.: Towards a novel biometric facial input for emotion recognition and assistive technology for virtual reality. Int. J. Child Heal. Hum. Dev. (2018)
34. Yoo, W., Lee, D.R., Cha, Y.J., You, S.H.: Augmented effects of EMG biofeedback interfaced with virtual reality on neuromuscu-lar control and movement coordination during reaching in children with cerebral palsy. NeuroRehabilitation (2017)
35. Clay, V., König, P., König, S.U.: Eye tracking in virtual reality. J. Eye Mov. Res. **12** (2019). https://doi.org/10.16910/jemr.12.1.3

Exploring the Use of Metaverse
for Collaborative Learning in Higher Education:
A Scoping Review

Abhishek Sharma[1]([✉]) [iD], Lakshmi Sharma[2], and Joanna Krezel[1]

[1] Victoria University, Melbourne, Australia
{abhishek.sharma,joanna.krezel}@vu.edu.au
[2] Amity University, Noida, India

Abstract. Student engagement in higher education is strongly associated with positive learning outcomes; however, not all learning methods are equally engaging or stimulating. Recent technological developments hold the potential to make learning more exciting and attractive, especially through the use of Virtual Reality (VR) and Augmented Reality (AR) technologies. These two technologies, blending the real and virtual worlds, create a digital space called the 'Metaverse'. In the Metaverse, people can interact in a virtual environment with lifelike avatars, providing an immersive learning experience. Several studies have explored the potential of Metaverse technology as a learning tool, highlighting its ability to make learning more engaging, interactive, and interesting. Other advantages of Metaverse include the visualisation of learning materials and allowing teachers to innovate learning processes. This research extensively reviews the literature from designated databases such as Scopus, ProQuest, and Google Scholar to explore the possibilities, effectiveness, and advantages of using Metaverse and AR/VR technologies to facilitate collaborative learning in higher education sectors. Finally, the paper concludes by acknowledging the limitations of using Metaverse and AR/VR technologies, such as the costs associated with their implementation and the skills required in the industry.

Keywords: Metaverse · Virtual Reality · Augmented Reality · Collaborative Learning · Higher Education

1 Introduction

With the rapid growth of technology, advanced technologies such as augmented reality (AR), virtual reality (VR) and Metaverse have gained immense attention within its application in enhancing the collaborative experiences of students within the higher education institutions (Now 2023, Wood 2022, Kshetri et al., 2022). Furthermore, some reports indicate that investment in the Metaverse is increasing and is expected to reach more than 13 trillion by 2030, with a user base of approximately 5 billion (Morris 2022). Moreover, this growth is also visible within the educational technology market which currently stands at approximately $106 billion in 2021 and is expected to skyrocket to

P. Zaphiris et al. (Eds.): HCII 2023, LNCS 14060, pp. 240–251, 2023.
https://doi.org/10.1007/978-3-031-48060-7_19

more than \$300 billion by 2028 (Kshetri et al., 2022, Wood 2022). Many higher education institutions (HEIs) have partnered with businesses to provide immersive experiences to students in order to increase student engagement and collaborative experiences (VictoryXR, 2023, Kshetri et al., 2022, Koenig 2022). In addition, the use of these revolutionary technologies will not only improve collaborative and student engagement experiences but will also serve as a key enabler towards outcome-based performance of students at higher education institutions (Wood 2022, Kshetri et al., 2022, VictoryXR, 2023, Kefford 2022).

The term "metaverse" is a fusion of the prefix "meta," which means "beyond," and the word "universe," which refers to a parallel or virtual environment associated to the physical world (Hwang and Chien, 2022, Tlili et al., 2022, Mystakidis 2022). The metaverse is defined as not only combining the physical and virtual worlds, but also as a continuation of the physical entities within the virtual world. Additionally, recent discussions by Hwang and Chien (2022) highlights the fact that there is a distinction between Metaverse and AR, VR technologies. Furthermore, key characteristics that distinguish Metaverse from traditional notions of AR and VR are terms such as "shared," "persistent," and "decentralised" (Hwang and Chien, 2022, Tlili et al., 2022).

While AR and VR are well-known terms, their applications are visible in a variety of lifestyle sectors. Precisely, augmented reality enhances the user's perception by incorporating real-world experiences such as sound, images, and video, whereas virtual reality is thought to create visual experiences by completely replacing the real world with a virtual environment (Kye et al., 2021, Tlili et al., 2022). More specifically, examples of AR technology include virtual dressing rooms, Nintendo Pokemon Go, and Snapchat Filters, whereas examples of VR technologies include VR headsets and VR virtual meetings. Further, from the point of view of Metaverse, Tlili et al. (2022) stated that revolutionary technologies such as AR or VR along with artificial intelligence (AI) could play a crucial part within the establishment of the Metaverse. As a result, Metaverse is believed to offer the possibility of immersion experience, collaborations, and interaction that aids in the development of social experience allowing for the emergence of "parallel world[s]" (Hwang and Chien, 2022).

Several literature reviews exist that explain Metaverse and its relationship with consumer behaviour, 3D virtual contexts, and gaming interactions (Shen et al. 2021, Park and Kim 2022, Jovanović and Milosavljević, 2022). However, there are few studies that show how Metaverse can improve the teaching and learning experience in higher education sectors (Salloum et al. 2023, Kye et al. 2021, Tlili et al. 2022). As a result, in order to fill a gap in the existing literature, this study focuses on conducting a scoping review across several databases such as Proquest, Google Scholar, and Scopus to determine how different Metaverse attributes can be beneficial in facilitating collaborative learning in higher education sectors.

2 Background

The introduction of immersive technologies such as augmented reality and virtual reality has expanded the ways in which Metaverse can be used in higher education sectors. Metaverse has been visualized as the next space where people can meet and socially interact, necessitating higher education to be proactive in leveraging it for teaching and learning objectives. It is also suggested that the 3D digital virtual environment would enhance the interaction and communication via avatars, which would reflect the physical presence. According to Kye et al. (2021) and Tlili et al. (2022), Metaverse is composed are four forms of technology: Augmented Reality (AR), Lifelogging, Mirror Worlds, and Virtual Worlds (See Fig. 1). Precisely, augmented reality is said to fuse new visual experiences for individuals by superimposing digital technologies, while simulation technology is said to substitute physical interactions and experiences with virtual interactions and experiences. Additionally, the technology in the external world concentrates on the users' external environment by presenting information about the surroundings and how to control them, whereas the technology in the intimate world concentrates on individual behaviour by generating avatars or digital profiles in which users have controls in the digital space. Furthermore, as shown in Fig. 1, the integration of axes generates several types of Metaverse. In relation to the above explanation, examples of these different types of Metaverse are Pokemon Go (i.e., Augmented reality), smart watches, AR technology in FB (i.e., Lifelogging), Google Earth (i.e., Mirror worlds), and avatars (i.e., Virtual worlds).

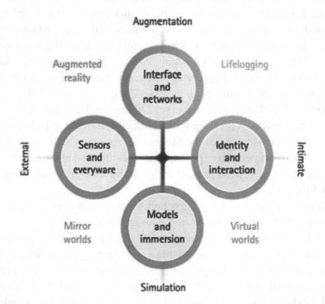

Fig. 1. Types of Metaverse. Source- (Tlili et al., 2022, Kye et al., 2021)

The revolution of AR, VR, and Metaverse technologies has resulted in creative disruptive changes across multiple sectors. Furthermore, while some studies do provide evidence that the implementation of Metaverse technologies has benefited student interaction, a brief review of how Metaverse could facilitate collaborative learning in higher education sectors has not yet been explored (Siyaev and Jo, 2021.b, Salloum et al., 2023,

Hwang and Chien, 2022, Tlili et al., 2022). As a result, the current study focuses on discussion the role of Metaverse in enhancing collaborative learning and providing answers to the following research question:

(a) Determine the potential implications of Metaverse in allowing students to have collaborative and interactive learning experiences in higher education institutions.
(b) Proposing ideas for Metaverse-based teaching and training programmes that provide students with real-world case study experience in higher education institutions.
(c) Determine the challenges and limitations of Metaverse-based teaching and learning implementations in higher education institutions.

In addition, the following sections showcase the search strategy that was used to conduct an extensive review search across various databases to gather studies demonstrating the role of Metaverse in enhancing collaborative learning in higher education sectors.

3 Methodology

To meet the above-mentioned objectives, an extensive literature review search is conducted upon designated databases such as Scopus, ProQuest and Google Scholar. Several keywords shown in Table 1 below were selected to conduct this review.

Table 1. Keyword and Search Results from Designated Databases

Keywords	ProQuest	Scopus	Google Scholar
("Metaverse") AND (("augmented reality") or ("virtual reality")) AND ("collaborative learning") AND ("Higher education")	44	-	-
TITLE-ABS-KEY ("Metaverse") AND (("augmented reality") or ("virtual reality")) AND ("collaborative learning") AND ("Higher education") AND (LIMIT-TO (DOCTYPE,"ar")) AND (LIMIT-TO (PUBYEAR,2023) OR LIMIT-TO (PUBYEAR,2022) OR LIMIT-TO (PUBYEAR,2020))	-	18	-
("Metaverse") AND (("augmented reality") or ("virtual reality")) AND ("collaborative learning") AND ("Higher education")	-	-	234

4   Implementation of Metaverse in Higher Education Institutions

4.1   Metaverse and Interactive Learning Experiences

In the domain of education, Metaverse has an array of applications that have been developed to improve student engagement in areas of learning that are collaborative, interactive, and problem-based. Furthermore, studies show that Metaverse and its applications are widely visible in a variety of learning scenarios, including game-based learning, problem-based learning, collaborative learning, blended learning, and immersive individual learning. To these discussions, Siyaev and Jo (2021.a) and Siyaev and Jo (2021.b) stated that immersive experiences can be improved with the integration of advanced technologies (i.e., voice recognition and eye-ball tracking technologies) to the teaching & learning conducted within the higher education institutions. Furthermore, the incorporation of several technologies into higher education teaching, such as the Hololens2 smart glasses and wearable devices, is an important instrument where student engagement and learning experiences can be tracked through the use of eye ball tracking/blinking movements. For instance, Siyaev and Jo (2021.a) stated that aircraft maintenance and recognition of outdated aircrafts models can be easily visualised through the use of HoloLens2 where by students can interact through a collaborative space and understand through use of technology such as Neuro-Symbolic AI (See Fig. 2).

Fig. 2. Usage of HoloLens2 in Aircraft Maintenance Metaverse. Source- Siyaev and Jo (2021a)

Additionally, the use of these technologies will be useful to students in virtual worlds where students would interact and receive feedbacks and guidance through virtual teaching systems. With the virtuality and immersive experiences in education, Metaverse is seen add more enhanced experiences for students within STEM, architectural and business fields. In addition, technology, and learning environments like Second Life, in which students learn by interacting with digital representations of themselves called "avatars," can be easily represented through applications like Pocket Metaverse iPhone for Second Life and Mobile grid client Second Life. These programmes allow users to communicate and collaborate inside a virtual environment.

On these notions, several universities have adopted immersive technologies that have been infused within the teaching and learning processes in order to increase collaborative experiences among students (Kshetri et al., 2022, Kefford, 2022, Fourtané 2022). For instance, INSEAD, the world's top management school, has significantly depended on digital transformation techniques and has integrated virtual reality in case-based teaching approaches, allowing students to virtually tour wet markets in Singapore and juice bars in Zanzibar (INSEAD, 2023, Kefford, 2022). Moreover, several other universities (such as the University of Chicago and the University of Pennsylvania) have bridged the gaps in the adoption of virtual interactions for staff and students within the university (Truong 2020, Chicago 2023, Kshetri et al., 2022).

As a result, higher education institutions are constantly striving to increase student engagement and create a more interesting, collaborative environment for student learning. Furthermore, the preceding discussion demonstrates how Metaverse provides a wide range of benefits in this context of collaborative learning in higher education institutions. The table below shows how various Metaverse applications have been implemented in the domains of higher education institutions (Table 2).

4.2   Metaverse-Based Teaching and Training in Higher Education Institutions

Although the concept of the Metaverse is relatively new, several higher education institutions have adopted the implementation of AR, VR, and Metaverse technologies. The learning and teaching opportunities vary depending on the technology (AR, VR, Metaverse) and how it is implemented in a discipline (Siyaev and Jo, 2021.b, Gsaxner et al., 2023, Kefford, 2022, Truong, 2020, Mystakidis, 2022). While the business and architectural fields have focused on providing immersive learning and teaching experiences, several higher education institutions in the medical fields have used equipment such as HoloLens to provide students with real-life scenarios on anatomy and identify the state of healthy or damaged body parts of a human body (Gsaxner et al., 2023, Vergel et al., 2020). Furthermore, one of the remarkable steps towards the implementation of technological advancements is depicted by the University of Pennsylvania, which designed a virtual space called Levine Hall, which is a virtual building that can accommodate 200 virtual users at a time and has six floors of computer science department where laboratories and classrooms can be easily located. Furthermore, during regular office hours, students and employees can engage via avatars and set up video conversations when they are near virtual rooms (Lee 2022). Moreover, Kemp and Livingstone (2006) envisioned Second Life as a virtual learning system for creating interactive and collaborative learning experiences for students. In addition, Salloum et al. (2023) empirically tested the intention to adopt Metaverse in higher education institutions and discovered that the use of innovative technology has a positive influence on students' learning experiences (Fig. 3).

Further, technological advancements have skyrocketed in recent years, and their application to various sectors comes with its own set of challenges and limitations. As a result, the next section showcases the challenges and limitations of Metaverse-based teaching and learning implementations in higher education institutions.

Table 2. Key Literatures on the Implementation of AR/VR and Metaverse in Higher Education Institutions

Domain	Implementation of AR/VR/Metaverse	Related Literatures
Higher Education Sector	Simulation of Virtual Laboratory Environments	Figols Pedrosa et al. (2023), Gan et al. (2023), Kennedy et al. (2023), Son et al. (2023), Vergel et al. (2020), Gsaxner et al. (2023), Guaya et al. (2023), Zhu et al. (2023), Sáiz-Manzanares et al. (2022), Pregowska et al. (2022), Dreimane and Daniela (2021), Joshi and Pramod (2023), Wang et al. (2022)
	Simulation of Immersive Language Environments	Pinto et al. (2019), Symonenko et al. (2020), DeWitt et al. (2022), Wu et al. (2023), Yuan et al. (2023), Joshi and Pramod (2023), Wang et al. (2022)
	Simulation of Business and Management Environments	Gupta and Bhaskar (2023), Yang and Goh (2022), Kshetri et al. (2022), Cunha et al. (2023), Joshi and Pramod (2023)
	Developing Virtual 3D Models for Building, Construction, Architecture, and Design	Ghanem (2022), Safikhani et al. (2022), Lucas and Gajjar (2022), Diao and Shih (2019), AbuKhousa et al. (2023), Wang et al. (2022)
	Gamification and the Introduction of Game-like Elements Such as Challenges or Rewards that increase motivation and knowledge retention	Ahmad et al. (2022), Jovanović and Milosavljević (2022), Kumar et al. (2023), Bühler et al. (2022), Çelik and Yangın Ersanlı (2022), Rincón-Flores et al. (2020), Jarnac de Freitas and Mira da Silva (2020), Joshi and Pramod (2023), Wang et al. (2022)
	Virtual Laboratory Environment for Hands-on Learning Experiences and the Exploration of Scientific Concepts	Mystakidis (2022), Sırakaya and Alsancak Sırakaya (2022), Kim and Irizarry (2021), Abdinejad et al. (2021)

(*continued*)

Table 2. (*continued*)

Domain	Implementation of AR/VR/Metaverse	Related Literatures
	3D Models That Allow Students to Explore Detailed Structures, and Visualise and Understand Complex Processes and Concepts	Weeks et al. (2021), Dreimane and Daniela (2021), Diao and Shih (2019)
	Use of the AR-Enabled Devices (e.g., tablets and smartphones) to Expand Learning Material from Static to Interactive to Enhance Problem-Solving and Critical-Thinking Skills	Marcel (2019), Raith et al. (2022), Kumar et al. (2021)

Fig. 3. Implementation of Second Life as a Virtual Collaborative Learning Space in Higher Education Institutions. Source- Kemp and Livingstone (2006)

5 Challenges and Limitations of Metaverse-Based Teaching and Learning Implementations in Higher Education Institutions

The decline in traditional teaching and learning experiences is very much apparent in the higher education sector. Furthermore, the rise of flexible, collaborative, and technologically rich advancements has resulted in the rise of Metaversity. Metaverse provides numerous benefits to students' collaborative and immersive experiences in higher education institutions, but some of the major challenges and barriers to its widespread adoption in higher education institutions are as follows:

(a) Higher financial costs (i.e., $20,000-$100,000) that is required for higher education institutions to set-up technological rich campuses that is expected to give rise to Metaversities (D'Agostino 2022, Kshetri et al., 2022).
(b) Higher costs associated with training faculty and administration in delivering Metaverse related teaching and learning (Kshetri et al., 2022).
(c) Higher risk of privacy, data security, and safety concerns are associated with the implementation of Metaverse-related teaching and learning in higher education institutions (Wang et al., 2022, Stanoevska-Slabeva 2022, Kshetri et al., 2022).
(d) The lack of existing infrastructure and advanced communication channels prevents widespread implementation of Metaverse-related teaching and learning in higher education institutions (Inceoglu and Ciloglugil, 2022, Kshetri et al., 2022).
(e) Challenges in developing effective curriculum and assessments for Metaverse-related teaching and learning in higher education institutions (Jeong et al. 2022, Kshetri et al., 2022).

6   Conclusion and Implications

Metaverse, either through the VR or AR application, holds an enormous potential to increase levels of engagement and create a more interesting higher education teaching and learning environment while delivering financial savings (Noghabaei, Heydarian, Balali and Han 2020); however, the successful adoption and use of these technologies are dependent on the skills of the teaching personnel. These skills are not only restricted to the design of the teaching content, assessment and activities that need to carefully manoeuvre the desired levels of engagement, time limitations and the specific characteristics of the content but also include fluency in using the technologies themselves. While there appears to be little doubt that the Metaverse classroom gained its permanent place in higher education, the focus of higher education institutions remains predominantly on the application of the technology itself rather than on the development and improvement of the skills of educators. The first step appears to be the inclusion of these technologies as educational tools in the development of relevant pedagogy.

The implementation of Metaverse within the higher education sector is thought to not only bridge traditional classroom-based concepts, but also to build digital-based platforms for students that are immersive, interactive, and personalized to each individual's needs. Furthermore, this review is expected to inform teachers and industry about the skill sets needed to help build the technological foundations of Metaverse in higher education sectors.

References

Abdinejad, M., Talaie, B., Qorbani, H.S., Dalili, S.: Student perceptions using augmented reality and 3d visualization technologies in chemistry education. J. Sci. Educ. Technol. **30**, 87–96 (2021)

Abukhousa, E., El-Tahawy, M.S., Atif, Y.: Envisioning architecture of metaverse intensive learning experience (MiLEx): Career readiness in the 21st century and collective intelligence development scenario. Future Internet **15**, 53 (2023)

Ahmad, I., Sharma, S., Singh, R., Gehlot, A., Priyadarshi, N., Twala, B.: MOOC 5.0: A roadmap to the future of learning. Sustainability **14**, 11199 (2022)

Bühler, M.M., Jelinek, T., Nübel, K.: Training and preparing tomorrow's workforce for the fourth industrial revolution. Education Sciences **12**, 782 (2022)

Çelik, F., Yangın Ersanlı, C.: The use of augmented reality in a gamified CLIL lesson and students' achievements and attitudes: a quasi-experimental study. Smart Learning Environments **9**, 30 (2022)

CHICAGO, U. O.:. Visit UChicago's Online Gather Campus. University of Chicago (2023)

Cunha, C.R., Martins, C., Mendonça, V.: Using extended reality in experiential learning for hospitality management education. Procedia Computer Science **219**, 634–641 (2023)

D'Agostino, S.: College in the Metaverse Is Here. Is Higher Ed Ready? : Inside Higher Ed (2022)

Dewitt, D., Chan, S.F., Loban, R.: Virtual reality for developing intercultural communication competence in Mandarin as a Foreign language. Education Tech. Research Dev. **70**, 615–638 (2022)

Diao, P.-H., Shih, N.-J.: Trends and research issues of augmented reality studies in architectural and civil engineering education—a review of academic journal publications. Appl. Sci. **9**, 1840 (2019)

Dreimane, S., Daniela, L.: Educational potential of augmented reality mobile applications for learning the anatomy of the human body. Technol. Knowl. Learn. **26**, 763–788 (2021)

Figols Pedrosa, M., Barra Perez, A., Vidal-Alaball, J., Miro-Catalina, Q., Forcada Arcarons, A.: Use of virtual reality compared to the role-playing methodology in basic life support training: a two-arm pilot community-based randomised trial. BMC Medical Education **23**, 1-8 (2023)

Fourtané, S.: Metaverse: The University Becomes the Metaversity. *Fierce Education* (2022)

Gan, W., et al.: Researching the application of virtual reality in medical education: one-year follow-up of a randomized trial. BMC Med. Educ. **23**, 3 (2023)

Ghanem, S.Y: Implementing virtual reality-building information modeling in the construction management curriculum. J. Inf. Technol. Constr. **27**, 48-69 (2022)

Gsaxner, C., Li, J., Pepe, A., Jin, Y., Kleesiek, J., Schmalstieg, D., Egger, J.:. The HoloLens in medicine: a systematic review and taxonomy. Medical Image Analysis, 102757 (2023)

Guaya, D., Meneses, M.Á., Jaramillo-Fierro, X., Valarezo, E.: Augmented reality: an emergent technology for students' learning motivation for chemical engineering laboratories during the COVID-19 pandemic. Sustainability **15**, 5175 (2023)

Gupta, K.P., Bhaskar, P.: Teachers' intention to adopt virtual reality technology in management education. Int. J. Learn. Chang. **15**, 28–50 (2023)

Hwang, G.-J., Chien, S.-Y.: Definition, roles, and potential research issues of the metaverse in education: an artificial intelligence perspective. Computers and Education: Artificial Intelligence **3**, 100082 (2022)

Inceoglu, M.M., Ciloglugil, B.: Use of Metaverse in education. Computational Science and Its Applications–ICCSA 2022 Workshops: Malaga, Spain, July 4–7, 2022, Proceedings, Part I, 2022. Springer, 171–184

INSEAD. VR Immersive Learning Initiative (2023)

Jarnac de Freitas, M., Mira da Silva, M.: Systematic literature review about gamification in MOOCs. Open Learning: The Journal of Open, Distance and e-Learning, 1–23 (2020)

Jeong, Y., Choi, S., Ryu, J.: Work-in-progress—design of LMS for the shared campus in metaverse learning environment. In 2022 8th International Conference of the Immersive Learning Research Network (iLRN), pp. 1–3 (2022)

Joshi, S., Pramod, P.: A collaborative metaverse based a-la-carte framework for tertiary education (CO-MATE). *Heliyon,* 9 (2023)

Jovanović, A., Milosavljević, A.: VoRtex Metaverse platform for gamified collaborative learning. Electronics **11**, 317 (2022)

Kefford, M.: Artificial Intelligence To Virtual Reality: How Business Schools Teach Online MBAs. *Business Because* (2022)

Kemp, J., Livingstone, D.: Putting a Second Life "metaverse" skin on learning management systems. Proceedings of the Second Life education workshop at the Second Life community convention. The University of Paisley CA, San Francisco (2006)

Kennedy, G.A., Pedram, S., Sanzone, S.: Improving safety outcomes through medical error reduction via virtual reality-based clinical skills training. Saf. Sci. **165**, 106200 (2023)

Kim, J., Irizarry, J.: Evaluating the use of augmented reality technology to improve construction management student's spatial skills. Int. J. Constr. Educ. Res. **17**, 99–116 (2021)

Koenig, R.: With Money From Facebook, 10 Colleges Turn Their Campuses into 'Metaversities. Edsurge (2022)

Kshetri, N., Rojas-Torres, D., Grambo, M.: The metaverse and higher education institutions. IT Professional **24**, 69–73 (2022)

Kumar, A., Mantri, A., Dutta, R.: Development of an augmented reality-based scaffold to improve the learning experience of engineering students in embedded system course. Comput. Appl. Eng. Educ. **29**, 244–257 (2021)

Kumar, A., et al.: Gamified learning and assessment using ARCS with next-generation AIoMT integrated 3D animation and virtual reality simulation. Electronics **12**, 835 (2023)

Kye, B., Han, N., Kim, E., Park, Y., Jo, S.: Educational applications of metaverse: possibilities and limitations. Journal of educational evaluation for health professions, 18 (2021)

Lee, I.: Penn students use digital platform Gather to imitate in-person office hours. *The Daily Pennsylvanian* (2022)

Lucas, J., Gajjar, D.: Influence of virtual reality on student learning in undergraduate construction education. Int. J. Constr. Educ. Res. **18**, 374–387 (2022)

Marcel, F.: Mobile augmented reality learning objects in higher education. Research in Learning Technology, **27** (2019)

Morris, C.: Citi says metaverse economy could be worth $13 trillion by 2030. *Fortune* (2022)

Mystakidis, S.: Metaverse. Encyclopedia **2**, 486-497 (2022)

Now, T.: Education technology to see massive growth with Metaverse and AI: APAC CEO of Global University Systems. *Times Now* (2023)

Park, S.-M., Kim, Y.-G.: A metaverse: taxonomy, components, applications, and open challenges. IEEE access **10**, 4209–4251 (2022)

Pinto, D., Peixoto, B., Krassmann, A., Melo, M., Cabral, L., Bessa, M.: Virtual reality in education: Learning a foreign language. New Knowledge in Information Systems and Technologies: **3**, Springer, pp. 589–597 (2019)

Pregowska, A., Osial, M., Dolega-Dolegowski, D., Kolecki, R., Proniewska, K.: Information and communication technologies combined with mixed reality as supporting tools in medical education. Electronics **11**, 3778 (2022)

Raith, A., Kamp, C., Stoiber, C., Jakl, A., Wagner, M.: Augmented reality in radiology for education and training—A design study. Healthcare, MDPI, **672** (2022)

Rincón-Flores, E.G., Mena, J., Montoya, M.S.R.: Gamification: a new key for enhancing engagement in MOOCs on energy? International Journal on Interactive Design and Manufacturing (IJIDeM) **14**, 1379–1393 (2020)

Safikhani, S., Keller, S., Schweiger, G., Pirker, J.: Immersive virtual reality for extending the potential of building information modeling in architecture, engineering, and construction sector: systematic review. International Journal of Digital Earth **15**, 503–526 (2022)

Sáiz-Manzanares, M.C., Carrillo, C., Llamazares, M.D.C.E., Arribas, S.R., Gómez, D.S.: Nursing students' perceived satisfaction with flipped learning experiences: a mixed-methods study. Sustainability **14**, 16074 (2022)

Salloum, S., Al Marzouqi, A., Alderbashi, K.Y., Shwedeh, F., Aburayya, A., Al Saidat, M.R., Al-Maroof, R.S.: Sustainability model for the continuous intention to use metaverse technology in higher education: a case study from Oman. Sustainability, **15**, 5257 (2023)

Shen, B., Tan, W., Guo, J., Zhao, L., Qin, P.: How to promote user purchase in metaverse? a systematic literature review on consumer behavior research and virtual commerce application design. Appl. Sci. **11**, 11087 (2021)

SıRAKAYA, M., SıRAKAYA, A.L.S.A.N.C.A.K., D.: Augmented reality in STEM education: a systematic review. Interact. Learn. Environ. **30**, 1556–1569 (2022)

Siyaev, A., Jo, G.-S.: Neuro-symbolic speech understanding in aircraft maintenance metaverse. IEEE Access **9**, 154484–154499 (2021)

Siyaev, A., Jo, G.-S.: Towards aircraft maintenance metaverse using speech interactions with virtual objects in mixed reality. Sensors **21**, 2066 (2021)

Son, Y., Kang, H.S., de Gagne, J.C.: Nursing students' experience of using holopatient during the coronavirus disease 2019 pandemic: a qualitative descriptive study. Clin. Simul. Nurs. **80**, 9–16 (2023)

Stanoevska-Slabeva, K.: Opportunities and challenges of metaverse for education: a literature review. EDULEARN22 Proceedings, 10401–10410 (2022)

Symonenko, S.V., Zaitseva, N.V., Osadchyi, V.V., Osadcha, K.P., Shmeltser, E.O.: Virtual reality in foreign language training at higher educational institutions. CEUR Workshop: proceedings 2nd International Workshop on Augmented Reality in Education, 22 March 2019,. Kryvyi Rih, 37–49 (2020)

Tlili, A., et al.: Is Metaverse in education a blessing or a curse: a combined content and bibliometric analysis. Smart Learning Environments **9**, 1–31 (2022)

Truong, V.: Beyond Zoom: Virtual Gathering Spaces for the Holidays and Beyond. Extreme Tech (2020)

Vergel, R.S., Tena, P.M., Yrurzum, S.C., Cruz-Neira, C.: A comparative evaluation of a virtual reality table and a HoloLens-based augmented reality system for anatomy training. IEEE Transactions on Human-Machine Systems **50**, 337–348 (2020)

Victoryxr: Our Partnership with Meta-VictoryXR & Meta. VictoryXR (2023)

Wang, M., Yu, H., Bell, Z., Chu, X.: Constructing an Edu-metaverse ecosystem: a new and innovative framework. IEEE Trans. Learn. Technol. **15**, 685–696 (2022)

Weeks, J.K., et al.: Harnessing augmented reality and CT to teach first-year medical students head and neck anatomy. Acad. Radiol. **28**, 871–876 (2021)

Wood, L.: Global Education Technology (EdTech) Market Report 2022–2027: Virtual Classroom Infrastructure Market will Reach $58.9 Billion. *PR Newswire* (2022)

Wu, J.G., Zhang, D., Lee, S.M.: Into the Brave New Metaverse: Envisaging Future Language Teaching and Learning. IEEE Transactions on Learning Technologies (2023)

Yang, F., Goh, Y.M.: VR and MR technology for safety management education: an authentic learning approach. Saf. Sci. **148**, 105645 (2022)

Yuan, J., Liu, Y., Han, X., Li, A., Zhao, L.: Educational metaverse: an exploration and practice of VR wisdom teaching model in Chinese Open University English course. Interactive Technology and Smart Educationi (2023)

Zhu, K., Cao, J., Chen, G., He, Q., Zhang, P.: A general construction method of virtual simulation experiment platform based on bibliometrics and analytic hierarchy process. Education Sciences **13**, 80 (2023)

A Systematic Review of User Experience in Motivation and Education

Harini Srivatsan, Komal Chhajer[(✉)], and Vincent G. Duffy

Purdue University, West Lafayette, IN 47906, USA
{hsrivats,kchhaje}@purdue.edu

Abstract. This study aims to explore the topic of motivation and education in the context of user experience. A systematic review is employed to cover trends, analyze literature, comprehensively understand the topic, and explain the purpose and future scope of user experience in motivation and education. For this, metadata was generated from Harzing's Publish or Perish via Scopus. This data was analyzed using MAXQDA's Wordcloud, VOS Viewer for visualization, BibExcel, and Citespace for an in-depth understanding of trends and clusters, and Mendeley for hosting and formatting references. The review shows that user experience can be crucial in building engagement and critical thinking skills. This review briefly explores the economic viability of involving a better user experience in motivation and education. This review demonstrates the potential of data analysis tools in bibliometric synthesis and describes the future of user experience in Motivation and Education. The review and discussion identify the following factors influencing user experience in motivation and education: Information and Communication Technology, User Centric Interfaces, and Gamification for Education. Further, Augmented Reality in the context of education has been identified in the scope of future work.

Keywords: Motivation · Education · User Experience · Scopus · Mendeley · MAXQDA · BibExcel · VosViewer · Citespace

1 Introduction

Education is pivotal in shaping the career and personal growth of individuals. Motivation helps individuals engage in academic pursuits, enabling them to contribute to society (Baguley et al., [1]). User experience can be a powerful tool in shaping motivation, focus, and academic retention in students. Factors that drive the importance of this topic are the need for adaptability to an increasingly digital world, the shift to remote learning since the Covid-19 Pandemic, and the need for motivation and education to counter technology and social media that threaten the human attention span (Deci et al., [2]). User experience in this context is relevant to human factors and industrial engineering as it is built to optimize learning techniques, design education systems based on user preferences, and grow motivation efficiently and productively.

Outside of industrial engineering, computer scientists are deploying Natural Language Processing models and virtual reality experiences to apply user experience to motivation and education. Funding initiatives in experiential Edutech, empowering institutions to leverage interactive technology in the classroom, and being inclusive of diverse student needs and behaviors in the learning process are fundamental to improving motivation and education (Thompson et al., [3]). HFE has encouraged memory and attention retention research, and HCI has developed adaptive learning systems to support this cause. Given below in Fig. 1 is the distribution of works in this topic by country, analyzed by Scopus. The prevalence of user experience, motivation, and education in the top five countries could be due to their investment in education, and the persistence of virtual tools in these countries. The United States has the largest number of works in this area. Virtual classrooms and innovation in educational technology are fields of interest in the United States.

Documents by country or territory

Compare the document counts for up to 15 countries/territories.

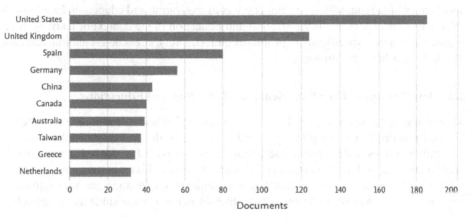

Fig. 1. Number of publications in the searched topic, sorted by Country (via Scopus)

2   Purpose of Study

This study highlights the scope and methods by which user experience applies to motivation and education. Infrastructure, activities, well-rounded curriculum, ethical teaching practices, and personal attention to student groups strongly influence their motivation to succeed (Maiorescu et al., [4]). This study thus attempts to observe user experience research that addresses these challenges. Tools that export or analyze research metadata, such as Harzing's Publish or Perish, CiteSpace, VOSViewer, BibExcel, and MAXQDA are used to introspect on the persistence of relevant research that would aid the systematic review. The uniqueness of the topic can also be discovered concerning an article. The topic suggests how user experience design elements can shed light on the learning outcomes that are desired in an educational environment. One relevant article to demonstrate this point is Halverson et al. ([5]) which evaluates learning outcomes in a blended learning environment using a cognitive framework developed by the research. Another example in the literature that the uniqueness of the topic can compare is Chapter 11, "Stress and Safety" in David L. Goetsch's "Occupational Safety and Health for Technologists, Engineers and Managers", page 248 ([6]). This chapter is concerned with the behavioral aspects of safety and the cognitive aspects that shape it. It models theories to understand human decisions regarding safety. In contrast, this review is concerned with the behavioral and cognitive aspects of education and motivation.

2.1 Justification of Topic Concerning Course Reading

The topic, "User Experience in Motivation and Education" is relevant to the 33rd chapter "Ergonomics" in Roger L. Brauer's "Safety and Health for Engineers", Page 593 [7]. The chapter covers human capability analysis, elements that contribute to comfort and are related to user experience, anthropometry which is related to gathering data on human abilities, people-machine interfaces which are relevant to using technology in education, and factors of fatigue, which one can connect to motivation and education. Ergonomics relates to User experience in Motivation and Education in the context of learning environments designed specifically to promote comfort, safety, stress de-escalation, and ease of use for teachers and students.

2.2 Applications of User Experience in Motivation and Education

Motivation builds engagement. Education is retained when served in a comprehensible and practical form. Employing User Experience in the context of Motivation and Education ensures that the non-value-adding cognitive load of students decreases, while crucial concepts and their interrelationships are absorbed. This empowers education professionals to pursue creative and interactive elements in education and motivates user experience professionals to leverage cognitive science to engage students [8] actively.

3   Research Methodology

3.1 Data Collection

Identifying search sources and analyzing publication trends is a valid method of reviewing and contextualizing literature [9]. Metadata was generated by entering the keywords into the following databases. Table 1 shows the number of works yielded. Web of Science offered the highest number of results. Scopus data was extracted as a CSV file. WoS data, which included author, source title, source, abstract, and references, was extracted as a Txt file. Harzing's Publish or Perish data was extracted in the format called WoS.

3.2 Measure of Engagement

Using Vicinitas.io, it is possible to see the engagement on a topic on Twitter. The keywords searched were "user experience education". This resulted in 73 posts from the past ten days and 131 in the engagement category, and the analysis on Vicinitas is given below in Fig. 2. The graphs suggest an upward increasing trend on the topic.

Table 1. The search of keywords in various databases

Database	Keywords used	The number of works yielded
Scopus	"user experience" AND "motivation" AND "education"	973
Web of Science	"user experience" AND "motivation" AND "education"	1358
Harzing's Publish or Perish	"user experience" AND "motivation" AND "education"	1000

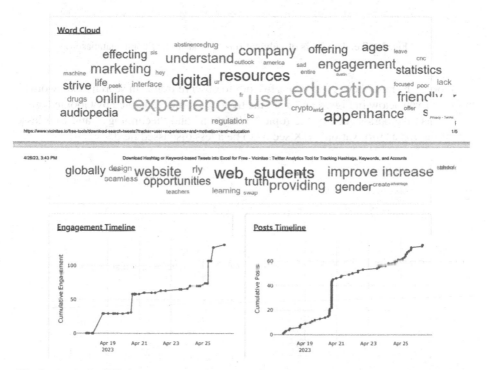

Fig. 2. Analysis of Twitter engagement on the topic "user experience education" in Vicinitas

3.3 Trend Analysis

The 973 document results from Scopus were analyzed for trends in research on the topic of user experience in motivation and education. The analysis captured the number of publications by year in Fig. 3. Publications from 1990 to 2022 were considered to analyze the topic in the context of the personal computers era.

The trend analysis shows that interest in the topic has been increasing annually since 2006, with a noted upward trend from 2012, and the current highest in 2021–22 at 110 works. This suggests that user experience in the context of motivation and education has gained research interest in the past 10 years.

Documents by year

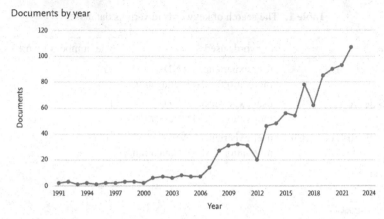

Fig. 3. Trend analysis of publications by year in the Scopus database

Google Ngram Viewer is a powerful tool to observe trends in searched keywords in books. Given below in Figs. 4 and 5 are the trend diagrams generated by Google Ngram. It suggests the persistence of the topic "education" and "technology" and to a lesser extent the topic "motivation". UX seems to be a less discussed field.

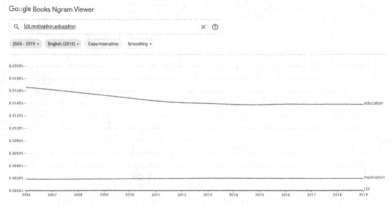

Fig. 4. Trend Analysis in Google Ngram Viewer- "UX"

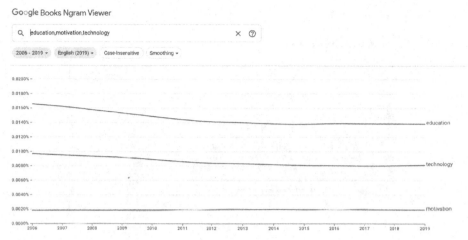

Fig. 5. Trend Analysis in Google Ngram Viewer- "Technology"

4 Results

4.1 Co-citation Analysis

Articles that are mutually cited in another article are co-cited. Co-cited articles often have common ground. This process empowers researchers to map the structure of a scientific field. Research gaps can also be identified. For co-citation analysis, the Scopus CSV file of 973 articles was uploaded on VOS Viewer. Citations of 5 and above were selected. This resulted in 10 references of which 4 formed clusters as given in Fig. 6.

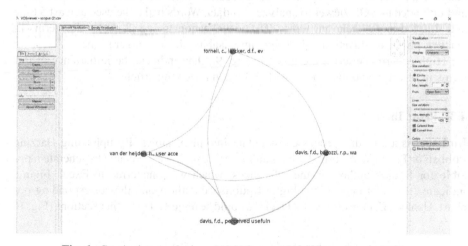

Fig. 6. Co-citation Analysis on VOSViewer ("VOSViewer", n.d., [16])

Of these 4 articles, works by Davis F.D. are explored in the Discussion section. Other relevant citations that could support discussion are obtained from VOSViewer as shown in Fig. 7.

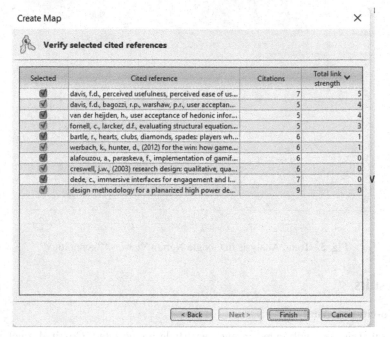

Fig. 7. Co-citation Articles table on VOSViewer

4.2 Content Analysis

Harzing's Publish or Perish yielded 1000 results, which were saved in the WoS format and uploaded to VOSViewer to analyze text data. Words had to be used at least 5 times, and this led to 194 relevant terms. The visualization in Fig. 8 shows that terms like teacher, physical education, e-learning, and usability have a larger scope.

High occurrence terms are given in Fig. 9. They indicate the importance of these terms in research and must be considered when reviewing articles.

4.3 Pivot Table

BibExcel is a tool that processes metadata into pivot tables. By uploading Harzing's Publish or Perish WoS format metadata into BibExcel, we were able to generate a pivot table for leading authors in the references, which we transferred to Excel. Figure 9 indicates the pivot table of the highest published authors and the corresponding pivot chart. Ushioda E, Fonseca D, and Deci EL could be reviewed in further sections (Fig. 10).

4.4 Cluster Analysis

CiteSpace is used to obtain labeled clusters during co-citation analysis. CiteSpace also offers a citation burst diagram that indicates periods of persistence of articles. It is important to have a larger database of works to ensure that the co-citation analysis can

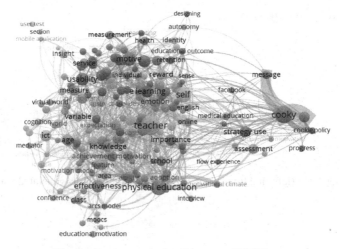

Fig. 8. Content analysis of terms on VOSViewer

Selected	Term	Occurrences	Relevance ∨
☑	educational motivation	7	4.33
☑	user test	5	2.87
☑	location	6	2.47
☑	high school	5	2.33
☑	educational game design	6	1.95
☑	vocational education	9	1.89
☑	marketing	6	1.86
☑	virtual world	7	1.77
☑	immersion	6	1.76
☑	motivational affordance	8	1.64
☑	motivation factor	9	1.60
☑	educational software	6	1.59
☑	moocs	8	1.57
☑	individual difference	5	1.52
☑	variance	6	1.51
☑	cookie policy	6	1.50
☑	cookie setting	6	1.50
☑	flow	7	1.49
☑	motivational design	6	1.49
☑	domain	11	1.47

Create Map ✕ / Verify selected terms / < Back   Next >   Finish   Cancel

Fig. 9. Content analysis keywords on VOSViewer

consider a larger number of clusters over a broad range of topics. In this review, the Web of Science search resulted in 1358 works, which were exported into three text files, which are stored in one folder and uploaded to CiteSpace. Co-citation analysis was conducted and clusters were named using keywords as a basis, as shown in Fig. 11. These clusters inform us of subtopics and articles associated with those subtopics in our interested area.

Leading Authors	Sum of Number of Publications
Ushioda E	8
Fonseca D	7
Deci EL	6
Ryan RM	5
Deterding S	5
Hamari J	5
Grand Total	**36**

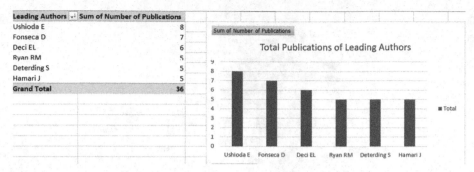

Fig. 10. Pivot Table (left) and Pivot chart (right) for leading authors generated via BibExcel

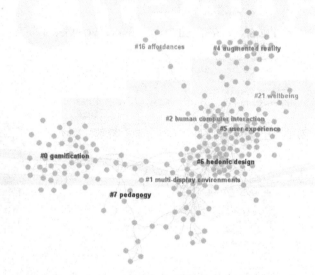

Fig. 11. Named clusters by keywords using CiteSpace ("CiteSpace", n.d., [17])

Citation Burst is given in Fig. 12, with 11 references. This assures us of the relevance of our topic in recent research.

Citations Burst History

Top 11 References with the Strongest Citation Bursts

References	Year	Strength	Begin	End	2013 - 2023
Deterding S., 2011, P 15 INT AC MINDTREK, V0, PP11, DOI 10.1145/2181037.2181040, 10.1145/2181037.2181040, DOI	2011	4.94	**2013**	2016	
McGonigal J., 2011, REALITY IS BROKEN WH, V1, P0	2011	3.15	**2014**	2016	
Dominguez A, 2013, COMPUT EDUC, V63, P380, DOI 10.1016/j.compedu.2012.12.020, DOI	2013	4.51	**2015**	2018	
Hamari J, 2014, P ANN HICSS, V0, PP3025, DOI 10.1109/HICSS.2014.377, DOI	2014	3.62	**2015**	2019	
Jordan K, 2014, INT REV RES OPEN DIS, V15, P0, DOI 10.19173/irrodl.v15i1.1651, DOI	2014	2.87	**2015**	2016	
Hanus MD, 2015, COMPUT EDUC, V80, P152, DOI 10.1016/j.compedu.2014.08.019, DOI	2015	4.41	**2018**	2020	
Seaborn K, 2015, INT J HUM-COMPUT ST, V74, P14, DOI 10.1016/j.ijhcs.2014.09.006, DOI	2015	3.95	**2018**	2019	
Hamari J, 2016, COMPUT HUM BEHAV, V54, P170, DOI 10.1016/j.chb.2015.07.045, DOI	2016	2.96	**2018**	2021	
Deterding S, 2015, HUM-COMPUT INTERACT, V30, P294, DOI 10.1080/07370024.2014.993471, DOI	2015	3.68	**2019**	2020	
Koivisto J, 2019, INT J INFORM MANAGE, V45, P191, DOI 10.1016/j.ijinfomgt.2018.10.013, DOI	2019	4.77	**2020**	2023	
Akcayir M, 2017, EDUC RES REV-NETH, V20, P1, DOI 10.1016/j.edurev.2016.11.002, DOI	2017	3.07	**2021**	2023	

Fig. 12. Citation Burst references using CiteSpace

4.5 Word Cloud Content Analysis

Based on database search and co-citation analyses, relevant references were downloaded. Upon uploading them to MAXQDA, we generate a Wordcloud depicting frequently used words in our references. This helps us decide on keywords in existing and future systematic reviews, as shown in Fig. 13.

Fig. 13. Wordcloud using MAXQDA

Commonly occurring words were education, research, learning, engagement, motivation, school, and students. This may lead one to infer that user experience should enhance the practical aspects of learning. This lexical search could be reviewed further.

5 Discussion

Information technology is vital to applying user experience in motivation and education, according to many of the works listed by VOSViewer. Davis F.D. ([10]) describes perceived usefulness versus perceived ease of use in the use of technology. Their work establishes the following findings: perceived usefulness is a better predictor for system usage than perceived ease of use. This implies that technology whose benefits and accessibility are clear to the users- in our topic, teachers and students- are more likely to enhance the experience of education and engagement. Articles downloaded from Scite.ai also indicate the same. Perceived usefulness is an extension of intention; In a study by Sharma L. et al. ([11]), an exploratory-descriptive approach and questionnaire were used to gauge teachers' intention to use technology in their educational practices. Their values, perceived ease of use, and influence over peers and students have positively correlated with their intention to use technology. Many studies have pondered the relationship between Information and Communication Technologies (ICT) and motivation in education. A work by Igna Cornel ([12]) explains that the use of Information and Communication

Technologies in education is associated with faster comprehension, diverse skill development, and quick data transfer. Information and Communication Technologies allow for a more interactive and enjoyable learning experience, increasing motivation in students. This study specifically covered the correlation between motivation and the use of Information and Communication technologies in primary school pupils.

Interfaces are another factor of user experience that paves the way for motivation and education across diverse learning groups. Another high-quality work taken from the most cited references in this topic according to VOSviewer, Dede C. ([13]), talks about immersive interfaces and how they can build digital fluency in children. Immersive interfaces are involvement-inducing interfaces that allow the user to let go of expectations of realism. This is achieved by engaging the senses and interactions of users. According to the work, immersive interfaces can enhance education in three ways. Immersive interfaces can enable multiple perspectives, can induce situated learning experiences even when immersive to a lesser degree, and can also allow seamless transfer of learning. When students are engaged in a highly visual learning environment, it tends to have a positive impact on their knowledge retention and transfer. User experience tools that can be used to improve motivation and education also include user testing and focus groups. Inclusivity is also a key factor in designing interfaces that are accessible to children from minority groups or disabilities. Perceiving their representation in the media and interfaces that host their education creates relatability and informs all students from different demographics of ethical and empathetic elements. The ability to choose one's assignments and goals can also increase autonomy and independent thinking.

An intersectional set between technology and interfaces is the use of gamification in education. The process of adding game elements to an educational experience increases interaction and motivation to pursue academic goals in students. The teacher's perspective on gamification must also be considered. Aini et al. ([14]) expand on lecturers' negligence in providing suitable test scores in gamified learning environments. The study tests the validity of a Viewboard. The reliability of the Viewboard is measured in the study and it concludes that gamification can motivate student behavior but can, in addition, improve lecturer assessment, increasing accountability and satisfaction levels. One study on gamification in education which also serves as a methods article for this review, whose methodology this review has followed, is Parreno et al.([15]). The paper explores the use of games in building student motivation to learn. The systematic review analyzes 193 articles that are highly cited, and sorts by leading authors, important keywords, and explores trends. Through the use of bibliometric analysis, lexical analysis, and social network trends, the study arrives at four themes: acceptance, social interaction, the effectiveness of games, and motivational engagement.

It may insightful to explore the top 10 keywords generated by VOSViewer, in the context of user experience in motivation and education. Educational motivation refers to the drive to learn in an educational setting. Understanding how to design educational experiences that enhance motivation is important for improving existing educational practices. User testing is the process of evaluating a product or service by testing it with representative groups. It is used in the design of immersive interfaces and other educational technology products to ensure they are effectively engaging. High school in this topic's context can be about designing incrementally challenging and accessible experiences for youths going through a transformation from childhood to adulthood. "Educational game design" is another keyword, related to design factors in games that can achieve learning outcomes. Vocational education is an unexpected keyword and indicative of a subset of education. Designing user experiences for vocational education would involve considering more practical and visual aspects that could support trade schools and reduce physical resource costs. Marketing in the context of this topic implies the importance of creating and marketing educational interfaces to promote growth in the education sector. A virtual world is a computer-generated virtual environment that can link several virtual environments and engage users in an interactive experience. Simulating realistic scenarios can improve practical thinking and critical thinking skills. The dangers of overindulgence in virtual environments and the potential negative impact it has on learning must be explored. Immersion, the act of total engagement, can improve deep motivation and focus in students. Finally, motivational affordance refers to factors that inspire behavior, and in this topic's context, these factors are central to the user experiences designed for educational motivation.

6 Conclusion

The review and subsequent discussion identify the following factors influencing user experience in motivation and education: Information and Communication Technology for accessible user experiences, knowledge transfer, and measurement of motivation; User Centric Interfaces, either immersive or visually appealing in other ways, to actively build student engagement in learning processes; and the potential of Gamification in designing educational environments which contribute to student motivation, support decision making, and analytical thinking, and improve focus and retention of coursework topics.

This systematic review utilizes a list of 10 ways to analyze the topic, "user experience in motivation and education": 1) It examines the purpose, which is to observe the user experience design factors which shape motivation and education. 2) It covers literature in the introduction and discussion sections. 3) It offers justification and uniqueness of the topic, forming the theoretical basis. 4) It touches upon the application, namely, to empower students to retain classroom resources through user experience. 5) It contributes analysis of keywords and trends in this topic. 6) It extensively covers the methodology, from data collection to analysis through a variety of bibliometric tools. 7) It builds on the trends from current discussions in media and research on the given topic. 8) The results are presented as a summary of two outcomes: technology is essential to the user experience, and the human element of a guide or teacher is equally crucial to motivation, discipline, and education. 9) The conclusions are drawn based on the literature reviewed. 10) Future work, mentioned in the following section, includes exploring the technologies that can contribute to motivation and education.

7 Future Work

The review covers works that relate Information and Communication Technologies, User Interface design factors, and the use of Gamification to user experience in motivation and education. However, the specific tools used to design and host a virtual classroom could be explored further in future work.

To scour emerging research to establish future work in this study, a keyword search was done on the National Science Foundation's funded awards section. This led to a display of 3000 results. For this review, a proposal on the use of augmented reality for real-time collaboration and problem-solving in STEM curricula has been voted for funding by the NSF ([18]). The screenshot of the selected work on the NSF website is given below in Fig. 14.

Fig. 14. A screenshot of a funded work on AR in education, hosted on nsf.gov

This work is interested in developing an augmented reality tool that is collaborative, to promote Next Generation Science Standards in Science, Technology, Engineering, and Mathematics (STEM). The work would give special attention to troubleshooting, an often neglected aspect of marge classrooms. The author hopes to reduce the cost of formal education through AR platforms, which can be used in formal and informal learning. The freedom of the research is limited by the technical requirements, including diverse device integration,3D space recognition, and user interfaces for both teachers and students. There is scope in exploring the use of Augmented Reality in motivation and education ([19, 20]). Immersive interfaces can also be further explored for cautious user experience design, as an excessively immersive experience can hamper education ([21, 22]). Gamification and its' advantages and disadvantages to instructors is an interesting subtopic ([23]). The features of user experience in virtual classrooms is a vast topic in itself ([24, 25]) and the rapid innovation in the forms of technology used in virtual classroom settings since the Covid-19 pandemic ([26]) can also be analyzed in future work.

References

1. Baguley, M.M., Kerby, M.C., Findlay, Y.S.: Meanings and Motivation in Education Research (n.d.). http://ebookcentral.proquest.com/lib/purdue/detail.action?docID=2028292
2. Deci, E., Vallerand, R., Pelletier, L., Ryan, R.: Motivation and education: the self-determination perspective. Educational Psychologist 26(3), 325–346 (1991)
3. Thompson, J., Fraser, S., Archambault, I., Beauregard, N., Dupéré, V., Frohlich, K.: Schooling, interrupted: a critical account of motivation and education during the first wave of the COVID-19 pandemic in Quebec. J. Teaching and Learning 15(2), 60–80 (2021)
4. Maiorescu, I., Sabou, G.C., Bucur, M., Zota, R.D.: Sustainability barriers and motivations in higher education – a students' perspective. Amfiteatru economic 22(54), 362–375 (2020)
5. Halverson, L.R., Graham, C.R.: Learner engagement in blended learning environments: a conceptual framework. Online learning (Newburyport, Mass.) 23(2) (2019)
6. Goetsch, D.L.: Occupational Safety and Health for Technologists, Engineers, and Managers. Ninth edition. Pearson, NY, NY, p. 248 (2019)
7. Brauer, R.L.: Safety and Health for Engineers. Third edition. Wiley, Hoboken, NJ, p. 593 (2016)
8. Metcalfe, J., Kornell, N.: Principles of cognitive science in education: the effects of generation, errors, and feedback. Psychonomic Bulletin; Review 14(2), 225–229 (2007). https://doi.org/10.3758/BF03194056
9. Guo, F., Ye, G., Hudders, L., Lv, W., Li, M., Duffy, V.G.: Product placement in mass media: a review and bibliometric analysis. J. Advert. 48(2), 215–231 (2019)
10. Davis, F.D.: Perceived usefulness, perceived ease of use, and user acceptance of information technology. MIS Q. 13(3), 319–340 (1989)
11. Sharma, L., Srivastava, M.: Teachers' motivation to adopt technology in higher education. J. Applied Research in Higher Educ. 12(4), 673–692 (2020)
12. Igna, C.: Pupils motivation in education based on information and communication technologies: pupils motivation in education based on information and communication technologies. Educația-plus 17(1), 51–59 (2017)
13. Dede, C.: Immersive interfaces for engagement and learning. Science (American Association for the Advancement of Science) 323(5910), 66–69 (2009)
14. Aini, Q., Hariguna, T., Putra, P.O.H., Rahardja, U.: Understanding how gamification influences behaviour in education. Int. J. Advanced Trends in Computer Science and Eng. 8(1), 269–274 (2019)
15. Martí-Parreño, J., Méndez-Ibáñez, E., Alonso-Arroyo, A.: The use of gamification in education: a bibliometric and text mining analysis. J. Computer-Assisted Learning 32(6), 663–676 (2016)
16. Thompson, A.: A STEM Curriculum Platform using Augmented Reality for Real-Time Collaboration and Problem-Solving. NSF.gov: https://www.nsf.gov/awardsearch/showAward?AWD_ID=1913637&HistoricalAwards=false
17. "VOSviewer" (n.d.). https://www.vosviewer.com/
18. "CiteSpace" (n.d.). http://cluster.cis.drexel.edu/~cchen/citespace/
19. Bower, M., Howe, C., McCredie, N., Robinson, A., Grover, D.: Augmented reality in education - cases, places and potentials. Educ. Media Int. 51(1), 1–15 (2014)
20. Wu, H.-K., Lee, S.-Y., Chang, H.-Y., Liang, J.-C.: Current status, opportunities, and challenges of augmented reality in education. Comput. Educ. 62, 41–49 (2013)
21. Grenfell, J.: The best of all worlds: immersive interfaces for art education in virtual and real world teaching and learning environments. Australian Art Education 35(1/2), 38–53 (2013)
22. Setozaki, N., Ikemi, N., Kitamura, F.: Development of immersive VR learning equipment for peace education with tangible user interface. Japan Journal of Educational Technology 45(Suppl.), 49–52 (2021)

23. Dicheva, D., Dichev, C., Agre, G., Angelova, G.: Gamification in education: a systematic mapping study. Educ. Technol. Soc. **18**(3), 75–88 (2015)
24. van Roy, R., Zaman, B.: Need-supporting gamification in education: an assessment of motivational effects over time. Computers and Education **127,** 283–297 (2018)
25. Bautista, N.U., Boone, W.J.: Exploring the impact of TeachMETM lab virtual classroom teaching simulation on early childhood education majors' self-efficacy beliefs. J. Science Teacher Educ. **26**(3), 237–262 (2015)
26. Sprenger, D.A., Schwaninger, A.: Technology acceptance of four digital learning technologies (classroom response system, classroom chat, e-lectures, and mobile virtual reality) after three months' usage. Int. J. Educ. Technol. High. Educ. **18**(1), 1–17 (2021)

Case Study of Low-Code VR Platform for Training and Evaluating Employee's Service Skills

Tomohiro Tanikawa[1]($\boxtimes$), Riku Fukaya[2], Takenori Hara[3], Haruka Maeda[3], Shigeru Komatsubara[3], Kazuma Aoyama[1], Tomohiro Amemiya[1], and Michitaka Hirose[1]

[1] The University of Tokyo, 7-3-1 Hongo, Bunkyo-Ku, Tokyo 113-8656, Japan
tani@cyber.t.u-tokyo.ac.jp
[2] Meiji University, Tokyo, Japan
[3] Dai Nippon Printing Co., Ltd., Tokyo, Japan

Abstract. For service industry, quality of customer service skills and customer satisfaction are very important topic. However, it is difficult to learn and master this kind of service skill without on-the-job-training (OJT). Thus, we propose a service VR simulator in which the user can train man-to-man service by using VR technologies. Through interviews and preliminary experiments with various service companies, we found that a customer service training VR system is effective for training service skills. However, the work content of each industry is very different, and the contents to be trained are also diverse, so the development cost and difficulty of operation and customization were raised as problems. Therefore, we proposed and implemented a VR platform that enables low-code development with little need for programming. In addition, we developed several business training VR systems using the proposed platform and conducted interviews.

Keywords: VR Training System · Low-code platform · Avatar · Service industry

1 Introduction

For service industry, quality of customer service skills and customer satisfaction are very important topic. However, it is difficult to learn and master this kind of service skill without on-the-job-training (OJT). In this research, we proposed a service VR simulator in which user can train man-to-man service by using VR technologies. In fact, through interviews with various service companies and preliminary experiments, we found that a customer service training VR system is effective for training service skills. However, the cost of development and the difficulty of operation and customization of each system were identified as problems because of the wide variety of business activities in each industry and the wide variety of contents to be trained.

The creation of high-quality VR content requires specialized skills such as three-dimensional and spatial design and modeling techniques, knowledge and skills in game engine and programming such as motion and physical simulation. Therefore, in order

© The Author(s), under exclusive license to Springer Nature Switzerland AG 2023
P. Zaphiris et al. (Eds.): HCII 2023, LNCS 14060, pp. 267–279, 2023.
https://doi.org/10.1007/978-3-031-48060-7_21

to create VR content production, it is necessary to gather human resources with the various skills mentioned above and build them over time. In addition, when modifying existing VR content or updating hardware or game engines, the same specialized skills are required, which results in costly and time-consuming requests to the developer for modifications, which hinders the introduction of VR systems.

Therefore, as in the case of web application development, we considered that a platform that enables VR content creation and modification using a method called "low code," which modularizes necessary functions and enables content creation using GUI, would be effective. In this platform, VR parts (3D models, motion, sound, etc.) and templates are prepared in advance, and by combining them on the GUI with mouse operations, application development and modification become possible (Fig. 1). In this case, the application requires almost no programming skills or knowledge, thus lowering the technical hurdle and making it possible for anyone to easily develop the application. This paper reports a concrete implementation of the proposed method and its effects.

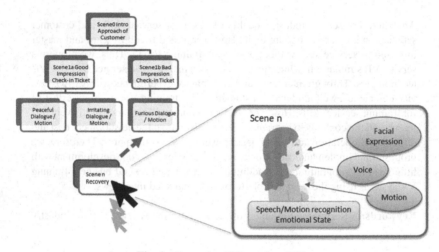

Fig. 1. Scenario editing using GUI.

2 System Design

2.1 Customer Service Training VR System

In this research, we are constructing a system including hardware and software for training service industry workers using VR technology, including HMDs. The simulator is based on a scenario in which the trainee is working as a staff member of a company, and is trained to perform customer service tasks on an autonomously operating customer avatar. In order to conduct effective training in service skills, the psychological state of the trainee during the experience is estimated and service skills are assessed.

A simulator that utilizes VR technology for job training requires an environment/avatar model, a verbal interaction module, a nonverbal interaction module, and an evaluation module. This is because the service industry requires both verbal and non-verbal skills, and because role-play training with an AI as a teacher can remove temporal and spatial constraints by using an autonomous avatar as the opponent. Among the environment and avatar models, the environment model can realize training in which both customer service and procedural tasks are performed in parallel in a work environment unique to each company. Furthermore, the Avatar model aims for a Proteus effect, in which the appearance of the Avatar is changed, leading to a change in self-perception, which in turn enhances one's own training performance.

The evaluation module should be developed with an eye to assessing training proficiency, but the evaluation of non-verbal interaction performance, in particular, varies from company to company, making a uniform evaluation difficult. Therefore, it is essential to construct a recording system that allows a skilled teacher to review video records of training and logs of movement and interaction in the system after training and give feedback. The evaluation module also includes an evaluation of the trainee's psychological state, such as stress, etc. The avatar equipped with AI changes its next response based on the trainee's response skill and psychological state, such as stress level, etc. This allows the trainee to respond appropriately. This allows the trainee to learn the appropriate response in an appropriate stress environment.

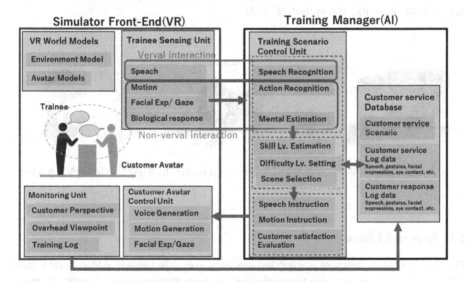

Fig. 2. System diagram of service VR training system

2.2   Low-Code Development

For the production of high-quality VR content, specialized skills such as three-dimensional and spatial design and modeling techniques, motion and physical simulation game engine and programming knowledge and skills are required. Therefore, to produce VR content, it will take time to gather human resources with the various skills mentioned above. In addition, when modifying already existing VR content or responding to updates in hardware or game engines, the same specialized skills are required, and this requires cost and time, such as requesting modifications from the developer, which currently hinders the introduction of VR systems.

Therefore, as in the case of web application development, a platform has been proposed that enables VR content production and modification using a method called low code (a method that does not require the creation of programming source code necessary for system development and allows content production using a graphical user interface (GUI)) as well as modularizing the necessary functions. A platform that enables VR content creation and modification using a method called low code (a method that does not require the creation of programming source code necessary for system development and allows content creation using a GUI (graphical user interface)) has been proposed. In this platform, VR parts (3D models, motion, audio, etc.) and templates are prepared in advance, and by combining them on the GUI with mouse operations, application development and modification become possible (Fig. 2). In this case, since almost no programming skills or knowledge are required, the technical hurdle is lowered and anyone can easily develop the application. Furthermore, since the programming process can be made labor-saving, it can also be used by employees involved in operations in the field departments and by information system-related developers who cannot program but wish to customize the system (Fig. 3).

Fig. 3. Transition of development and management entities by using Low-code VR platform.

2.3 Expected Effects

The low-code development is expected not only to enable users to edit scenarios themselves with no code, but also to enable content development (scenario implementation + 3DCG production) basically within the company that provides vocational training. In the conventional VR system development method, the development company handles everything from planning to scenario implementation, program development, 3DCG, audio, motion data, and other components, and is also involved in the operation of the system. In the proposed method, however, scenario implementation can be done by users themselves using a scenario editing platform, programs can be realized by customizing existing programs, and users can create 3DCG, voice, and motion data or create them by social outsourcing. The proposed method enables users to create 3DCG, voice, and motion data, or by social outsourcing (Fig. 4).

In addition, users themselves can edit scenarios and create 3DCGs, making it possible to update contents (scenario implementation + 3DCG creation) while checking the effects of job training. Therefore, unlike the conventional development method in which a development company revises the content after receiving feedback once it has been delivered, this system allows for a flexible development system in which only the 3DCG production is outsourced and the scenario is edited by the users. This enables a reduction in development costs and production time, and more flexible updating of the VR system, which is expected to improve the effectiveness of training.

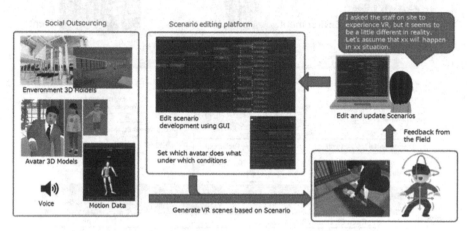

Fig. 4. Development pipeline with Low-code VR platform.

3 Implementation

3.1 VRESS: VR Editable Scenario System

In this study, we implemented the system as a "VR Editable Scenario System: VRESS," which can be built in low code. The overall structure of the platform is shown in the figure. The VR system is a composite of space, people, and things, and was designed so that each can be handled as separately as possible. The training space and human models are prepared as 3DCG models, and the system is configured to manage events and human behavior based on scenarios.

The core part of this platform is a scenario editing platform that enables scenario creation by modularizing scenes with human models, motions such as gestures, speech, facial expressions, and conditional branching, and arranging and integrating each scene using a GUI. A VR scene is an assortment of various elements such as environment information (environment 3D model, lighting, material information), human information (human 3D model, skeleton, motion information, facial expression information, voice), and event information (what happens when you do what (interpersonal), physical simulation). In conventional platforms, all of these elements are registered one by one in unity and implemented by writing scripts, making it difficult to grasp the entire picture even for minor scenario modifications in operation. Therefore, it was difficult for anyone other than the developer to modify the scenario, resulting in a time-consuming situation where the developer had to modify the scenario. On the other hand, the low-code platform allows scenario editing through a GUI, which facilitates on-the-spot modification (Fig. 5).

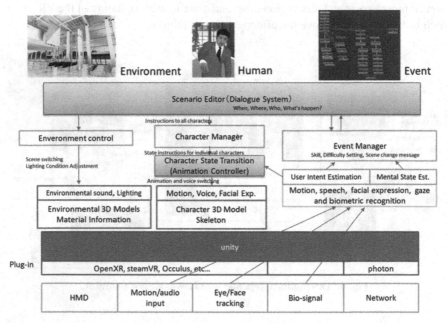

Fig. 5. Overview of Proposed Low-code VR Platform "VRESS".

3.2 Scenario Editor

The scenario editor, which can be edited via GUI, was implemented by customizing the Dialogue System [3]. As shown in the figure, when the project is opened, there is a scenario editor area with individual scenes that have been segmented in advance and are connected to each other as nodes. Each scene contains information on which characters to move and what to say, as well as information on how the stress value and the customer satisfaction level are changed (Fig. 6).

The scenario editor has the ability to freely load and run pre-saved scenarios and to create new ones(Fig. 7(left)). Nodes can be added by right-clicking in the editor, and scenarios can be extended by linking to existing nodes. In the same way, the scenario can be modified intuitively by deleting and re-linking nodes. As shown in Fig. 7(right), each node can specify which character performs which action, generates which sound, etc., and by writing simple scripts for judging events and changing states, it is possible to change the parameters representing the character's state and to perform conditional branching.

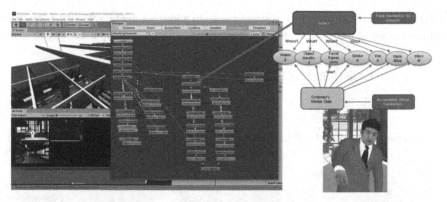

Fig. 6. Relationship between Scenario Editing Platform and VR Scenes.

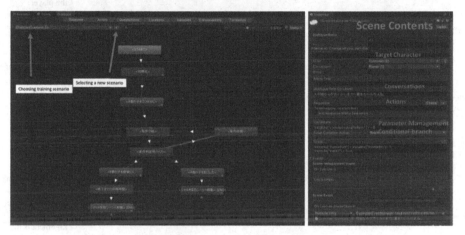

Fig. 7. (left) Scenario Editing Platform (right) Inspector of each node.

3.3   Character State Descriptions and Transitions

In the scenario editor, functions for scenarios that cannot be realized in the standard Dialogue System have been developed and added. A customer service training VR system commonly requires functions to handle both verbal and non-verbal interactions. For verbal interaction, we implemented a function that performs speech recognition using the Web Speech API via Websocket and determines whether the user has given the expected response. For nonverbal interactions, we implemented a function that recognizes eye gaze and movement in unity, senses biometric signals and estimates stress state in an external program, receives them in unity via UDP communication, sets the difficulty level, and determines whether to proceed with the scene or not. The functions added as project-specific functions are grouped under the Character Manager. For example, in the case of a training system for a nursery school, various behaviors of infants have not been added to the existing platform, so they have been added as shown in the table below and can be called from the scenario editing screen. In addition, the infant's states can be set to transition using unity's Animation Controller functionality (Table 1).

Table 1. Table of Dedicated functions for the Childcare project

Function Name	Parameters	Return Value	Example	Description
ChildrenManager/CheckInnerAreaFromPlayer	Double, Double	Bool	CheckInnerAreaFromPlayer(3, 10) = = true	Returns true if there is a baby with the first argument number within a distance closer than the second argument from the player (caretaker)
ChildrenManager/ReadyToFinish		Bool	ReadyToFinish() = = true	Returns true if all babies are not LyingFaceDown (prone), Coughing (coughing), Vomiting (nausea), or Seizure
ChildrenManager/CheckSleepState	String, Double	Bool	CheckSleepState("DeepSleep", 1) = = true	Specify the baby's state as a string and return true if the baby numbered in the second argument is in that state
ScenarioUtilFunctions/TimeOutedSeconds	Double	Bool	TimeOutedSeconds(90) = = true	True when the time specified in the first argument has elapsed. Assumes the role of a timer
SpeechRecognizer/CheckSpeech	String	Bool	CheckSpeech("Thank you") = = true	Returns true if the string of the first argument is recognized as the most recent one by the speech recognition function. The speech recognition function must be enabled

4 Case Studies

Through interviews and preliminary demonstrations with various service companies, we asked four companies that had expressed interest to cooperate in participating in the demonstration experiment, and based on the interviews, we implemented and experienced the VR training system.

4.1 Low-Code Deveropment of VR Training System

The following three screens show the implementation of VR training systems developed simultaneously using this platform for completely different industries, such as retail, passenger, and daycare, respectively. Each has a scenario editing screen on the left, where scenarios for each industry are edited. The development started with a VR system for nursery schools, but it was possible to implement three different VR systems in three months for four companies in three different industries, and to actually conduct reviews from the companies. The system was designed for a single person to create the scenes and implement the system.

The specific schedule was that planning for the VR training system for nursery schools began in June 2022, and full-scale implementation began in September. The VR training system for nursery schools was previewed on 12/21/2022 and a demonstration was conducted on 2/24/2023. The VR training system for the retail industry had two companies participating, and demonstration tests were conducted on 2023/2/14 and 2023/2/17, respectively. The VR training system for the passenger industry was demonstrated on 2023/2/20. Thus, the completion dates of the VR training systems for three completely different industries were concentrated within a two-week period, which meant that development had to be conducted simultaneously.

VR Training System for Daycare Centers
In this VR training system, a baby is checked during a nap, and the baby performs random behaviors such as falling asleep, stopping breathing, getting up, crying, spitting up, etc. The trainee experiences a failure scene if he or she cannot detect the behaviors such as falling asleep, stopping breathing, spitting up, etc.

As shown on the screen, it is possible to record and replay the experience from the viewpoint of the surveillance camera at the same time as from the viewpoint of the person who experienced it, allowing the user to look back and check for problems. In addition, a biometric signal sensor attached to the HMD allows the user to check the stress level during the experience (Fig. 8).

VR Training System for the Passenger Industry
In this VR training system, you will become a hotel staff member and train to handle check-in problems. The following three scenarios can be switched to experience the system. The scenarios are switched using the scenario editor function. This one likewise

Fig. 8. Screenshot of VR training system implementation for nursery school.

shows the staff's subjective viewpoint and the surveillance camera images, allowing for recording and replaying.

  (i) Scenarios that could have been handled well
 (ii) Different scenario from the reserved room, if the room is available.
(iii) Different scenario from the reserved room, if there is no room (Fig. 9).

Fig. 9. Screenshot of VR training system implementation for passenger industry.

VR training system for retail industry.

In this VR training system, you become a staff member of a supermarket and deal with a problem where a receipt does not come out of the self-checkout. Three different scenarios can be experienced by switching between them.

(i) Scenarios that could have been handled well
(ii) Poor language and angry scenario.
(iii) A scenario in which the order of response is wrong and you get angry (Figs. 10 and 11).

Fig. 10. Screenshot of VR training system implementation for retail industry.

4.2 Feedback from Companies

Experiences and interviews were conducted by two or three frontline staff and manager-level employees from each company. It was more powerful than expected. Positive feedback was obtained, including that it was good because there is a big difference between having the experience and not having it. This was an evaluation that did not differ between the VR training system using the low-code development platform and the earlier VR training system, and it is considered that there was no decrease in quality due to the use of the proposed platform. In addition, we were able to obtain more specific feedback because we were able to build a VR training system customized for the industry. In addition, the ability to easily change scenarios and replace 3D models via GUI was commented as very attractive for actual implementation and operation.

Fig. 11. (top) VR training system experience by companies. (bottom) Replay from each perspective during the VR training system experience.

5 Conclusion

Although a VR training system is effective, the work content of each industry is very different, and the contents to be trained vary widely, making the cost of development, operation, and customization difficult. Therefore, we proposed and implemented a VR platform that enables low-code development with little need for programming.

The VR system by low-code not only shifts the development and management to the field, but also makes it possible to improve development efficiency by distributing and consolidating various tasks such as modeling, scenario creation, and integration into the VR system to personnel with specialized skills at the development stage. The creator of a VR system can order 3D models of the environment and people that will be the components of the VR system, as well as voice and motion data, through a crowdsourcing site, and create the data by recruiting people who specialize in 3DCG modeling, people who specialize in voice (such as narrators) or who specialize in choreography (such as in theater), and so on. By recruiting and creating data through crowdsourcing sites, it is possible to place orders with professionals in each field and concentrate on the creation and adjustment of the VR scene. In addition, by ordering to crowdsourcing, the time and training cost for the VR system itself can be reduced, and the efficiency and cost reduction effects were demonstrated in the parallel creation of VR education and training systems for four companies in three industries using this platform.

Acknowledgement. This work was supported by Council for Science, Technology and Innovation, "Cross-ministerial Strategic Innovation Promotion Program (SIP), Big-data and AI-enabled Cyberspace Technologies". (funding agency: NEDO).

References

1. Tanikawa, T., Shiozaki, K., Ban, Y., Aoyama, K., Hirose, M.: Semi-automatic reply avatar for VR training system with adapted scenario to trainee's status. Proceedings of HCII 2021 (2021)
2. Tanikawa, T., Ban, Y., Aoyama, K., Shinbori, K., Komatsubara, S., Hirose, M.: Service VR training system: VR simulator of man-to-man service. In: Proceedings of IDW'19, pp. 993–994 (2019)
3. https://www.pixelcrushers.com/dialogue_system/manual2x/html/index.html

Mining and Analysis of Search Interests Related to Online Learning Platforms from Different Countries Since the Beginning of COVID-19

Nirmalya Thakur$^{(\boxtimes)}$, Karam Khanna, Shuqi Cui, Nazif Azizi, and Zihui Liu

Department of Computer Science, Emory University, Atlanta, GA 30322, USA
{nirmalya.thakur,karam.khanna,nicole.cui,mohammad.nazif.azizi,
chloe.liu2}@emory.edu

Abstract. The interdisciplinary work at the intersections of Big Data, Data Mining, and Data Analysis presented in this paper, focuses on the mining and analysis of web behavior on Google related to different online learning platforms from different countries, since the beginning of COVID-19. This paper makes multiple scientific contributions to these fields. First, a comprehensive review of about 150 recent works was conducted to identify a list of 101 online learning platforms that were used in different parts of the world during COVID-19. Second, using Google Trends, the search interests related to these online learning platforms emerging from all 38 OECD countries for 133 weeks between March 11, 2020, and October 1, 2022, were mined, and a database was developed. Third, K-means clustering was run on this database 10,000 times to identify clusters based on search interests. Fourth, a recursive algorithm was developed and run on this database to identify the list of online learning platforms that recorded very high search interests, the specific countries from which these platforms recorded such interests, and the associated queries on Google related to these platforms that contributed to the high search interests. These results, along with the original database, were published as a dataset on IEEE Dataport. Finally, two comprehensive comparative studies are presented that compare the findings of this paper with about 150 prior works in this field to uphold its novelty and significance.

Keywords: Big Data · Data Mining · Data Analysis · COVID-19 · Google Trends

1 Introduction

After the initial outbreak in December 2019 in Wuhan, China [1], the severe acute respiratory syndrome coronavirus-2 (SARS-CoV-2, 2019-nCoV) that causes COVID-19 in humans [2] soon spread to other parts of the world and on March 11, 2020, the World Health Organization (WHO) declared COVID-19 an emergency [3]. At the time of writing this paper, there have been a total of 684,906,699 cases and 6,837,598 deaths worldwide on account of COVID-19 [4]. After the initial outbreak, the virus rampaged unopposed across different countries, infecting and leading to the demise of

P. Zaphiris et al. (Eds.): HCII 2023, LNCS 14060, pp. 280–307, 2023.
https://doi.org/10.1007/978-3-031-48060-7_22

people the likes of which the world had not witnessed in centuries. As an attempt to mitigate the spread of the virus, several countries across the world went on partial to complete lockdowns [5]. Such lockdowns affected the educational sector immensely. Universities, colleges, and schools across the world were left searching for solutions to best deliver course content online, engage learners, and conduct assessments during the lockdowns. During this time, online learning was considered a feasible solution. Online learning platforms are applications (web-based or software) that are used for designing, delivering, managing, monitoring, and accessing courses online [6]. This switch to online learning took place in more than 100 countries [7] and led to an incredible increase in the need to familiarize, utilize, and adopt online learning platforms by educators, students, administrators, and staff at universities, colleges, and schools across the world [8]. These needs transformed into the generation of Big Data on the internet by these specific user groups as they explored solutions.

In today's Internet of Everything era [9], Google is the most popular search engine and processes about 1.2 trillion search queries annually [10]. Google Trends is the most widely used tool for mining and analysis of web behavior on Google [11]. In the last few years, the use of Google Trends to mine and analyze web behavior related to virus outbreaks has been of keen interest to researchers, as can be seen from the works related to Google Trends that focused on the analysis of web behavior related to Middle East Respiratory Syndrome [12], Ebola [13], measles [14], Swine flu [15], Lyme disease [16], urinary tract infection [17], asthma [18], and MPox [19], just to name a few. While there exist several works that focused on the analysis of web behavior in the context of online learning during COVID-19, those works have several limitations (discussed in Sect. 2). The interdisciplinary work proposed in this paper at the intersections of Big Data, Data Mining, Data Analysis, and Machine Learning aims to address these limitations by mining and analyzing web behavior data that emerged from all 38 members of the Organization for Economic Cooperation and Development (OECD) [20] for 133 weeks between March 11, 2020, and October 1, 2022. The web behavior data in this context included the search interests and related information associated with 101 online learning platforms. The OECD member countries were selected for this study as OECD members had a high degree of influence on policy, socioeconomic reforms, preparedness, and the response of the global education sector during COVID-19. The rest of this paper is organized as follows. A review of recent works in this field is presented in Sect. 2. Section 3 presents the methodology that was followed for this work. The results are discussed in Sect. 4, which is followed by conclusions and references.

2 Literature Review

The COVID-19 pandemic exposed and exacerbated existing disparities in students' access to resources associated with online learning, the most prominent of which were digital resources [21–23] and internet connectivity [24–26]. Prior works in this field have shown that various factors, such as socioeconomic circumstances [27–29], individual perceptions [30–35], culture and society [36], geographic regions [37–39], individual readiness [40], attitudes [41, 42], and mindset [43, 44] influenced the success of online learning [45–47]. Furthermore, the above-mentioned factors had diverse effects on the experience [48–52], well-being [53–55], self-regulation [56], and sleep quality [57] of students who participated in online learning. The objective of the work by Prosen et al. [58] was to develop and test a tool for evaluating the experience of students during online learning. The authors analyzed the data from 342 students using the 3EScale. Alfayumi-Zeadna et al. [59] performed a comprehensive study to analyze the mental health of students during online learning. The authors collected data from 420 students who were enrolled in schools in Israel. The methodology focused on the participants completing questionnaires, and the mental health status of the participants was analyzed by using the DASS-21 scale. The results showed that severe symptoms of depression, anxiety, and stress were reported by 49.3%, 45.2%, and 54% of the students, respectively. Badiuzzaman et al. [60] reported that although the majority of the students in Bangladesh had access to the necessary technologies for online learning, only 32.5% of them could attend online classes in a seamless manner. The work of Spitzer et al. [61] showed that the academic performance of K-12 students improved after switching to online learning. Stoehr et al. [62] aimed to analyze the attitudes of students toward online learning. 3286 medical students from 12 different countries participated in this study. The findings showed that the majority of students were satisfied with the quality and quantity of online courses. A similar study was performed by Konukman et al. [63]. However, this study focused on the perceptions of educators toward online learning. Qiao et al. [64] performed a comprehensive study to comment on the adoption of online learning before and after the COVID-19 pandemic. The work done by Choi et al. [65] involved several focus group interviews associated with online learning. The interviews were conducted in South Korea and Malaysia. In this work, the authors also provided recommendations for the improvement of online classes and blended learning. In the work done by Mullen et al. [66], the authors conducted 23 interviews associated with online learning in Australia and Ireland and identified 5 themes central to the shared experiences and perspectives of educators and students. Birkelund et al.'s work [67] reported that there was no evidence of any major learning slides in students in Denmark, 14 months into the pandemic. Slack et al. [68] used a mixed-methodological approach to analyze the data collected from 10 focus group interviews associated with online learning. The findings of this work indicated that some students felt a higher level of effort was required for online learning. The study also reported that other students valued the flexibility of online learning.

Recent works in this field have investigated how the degree of digital literacy [69] and approaches of acceptance for online learning technologies [70] have resulted in causing barriers [71, 72] towards online learning. Studies in this field show the relationships between varied perspectives from students [72–81] with productivity [82], engagement [83–86], and satisfaction [87–92] in the context of online learning. The findings from review papers in this field have shown that understanding students' experiences and engagement in online education is essential for ensuring their academic success and mental well-being [93–95]. Such works have also identified various factors that influence students' engagement in online learning [96–99]. Competence and motivation are critical factors for students' engagement in online education. Studies have shown that students who perceive themselves as competent are more likely to get involved in the process, as are those who are more self-motivated. Effective time management strategies can also help students cope with the demands of online learning. In addition to motivation and time management, self-regulation and discipline have been identified to play a crucial role in students performing effective time management in online learning [100–103].

The work by Galkienė et al. [104] was conducted in three Baltic countries (Lithuania, Latvia, and Estonia) and involved 1432 educators. The results of the study showed that self-regulatory collaborative learning had a sustainable and strong impact on the performance of students. Prasetyanto et al. [105] investigated the intention of undergraduate students to engage in online learning. The study focused on using different types of questionnaires and included 906 students. The findings of the study showed that teaching quality and time management were found to influence students' intention to spend more time associated with online learning. Martínez-García et al. [105] compared the levels of student satisfaction towards learning in face-to-face and forced online learning scenarios. The findings of this study showed that students learning in a face-to-face format expressed a higher level of satisfaction. Resch et al. [106] analyzed the effects of COVID-19 on the social and academic integration of students by using Tinto's integration theory. The study included a total of 640 students in Austria. The work by Papouli et al. [107] investigated the views of students in the social work major towards the utilization of digital technologies during the COVID-19 lockdown. The study used questionnaires and included 550 students.

In contrast to the public perception that gaming may be a harmful component in students' academic performance [108, 109], gamification emerged as a prominent trend during the pandemic to simulate and enhance student engagement and motivation toward online learning. Studies have focused on the development of game-based learning activities, applications, and models [110–113] with an aim to improve the effectiveness of online learning [114–120]. Researchers also investigated the quality and effectiveness of virtual university services, including different learning management systems (LMS) associated with online learning [121, 122], to understand the perceptions of students towards the same. Studies in this field also commented that understanding the perspectives of students towards various technologies and platforms associated with online learning was crucial during the transition from in-person learning to online learning [123–127]. In addition to focusing on various LMS, researchers in this field also investigated the effectiveness of various online communication platforms such as Zoom, Microsoft Teams, WebEx, SIPEJAR, Moodle, Padlet, and Google Meets, just to name a few, to promote active learning, seamless communication, engagement, and skill development associated with online learning [128–141]. Venkat et al. [142] focused on studying and addressing the underrepresentation of women in STEM disciplines during COVID-19. The objective of the work done by Lottin et al. [143] was to identify effective strategies for online learning to reduce fatigue and increase the retention of students. Vinodha et al. [144] studied various platforms that were utilized during online learning to identify possibilities of cyberattacks on those platforms. Furthermore, the authors proposed a framework to fight such cyberattacks. Maniar et al. [145] developed an automated proctoring system associated with online learning during COVID-19. The system used computer vision techniques and comprised features such as eye gaze tracking, mouth open or close detection, object identification, head posture estimation, and face detection. The objective of the work done by Sasikumar et al. [146] was to analyze student learning during video conferences. Munemo et al. [147] reported some of the challenges faced by students during online learning in their paper. Rahman et al.'s work [148] focused on sharing the experience and approach of teaching a programming course in a completely virtual manner during the pandemic. Butko et al. [149] presented the results of utilizing various online learning platforms such as Google Classroom, Microsoft 365, and VES at universities in Ukraine from 2020 to 2022. The feasibility and applications of project-based online learning techniques were investigated and explored by Edy et al. [150]. Zagirniak et al.'s work [151] aimed to study the dynamics of academic achievement of the Ukrainian Generation Z during the transition to online learning during COVID-19. The findings of this study indicated that Generation Z showed higher academic performance in online learning environments as compared to in-person forms of learning. Chierichetti et al. [152] presented the findings of a university-wide study that aimed to investigate the impact of COVID-19 on student learning, student achievement, and faculty issues. Yahuarcani et al. [153] discussed the university-wide implementation of virtual technologies to support learning and education at the National University of the Peruvian Amazon (UNAP). The UNE 66181:2008 standard was utilized in this study. The relevance and effectiveness of online classes for students in the power engineering major were reported by the work of Merzlikina et al. [154]. Dahnoun et al. [155] discussed the importance of innovation in the context of online teaching by educators. The work of Djeki et al. [156] outlined the vulnerabilities in different technologies associated with online learning and the impact cyberattacks would have on the same. The authors utilized the classification of the most common web application vulnerabilities presented by the Open Web Application Security Project (OWASP) and Common Weakness Enumeration (CWE) in their work. Lara et al. [157] reported the experiences of teaching programming in a virtual manner during COVID-19. The work reported that the major challenges associated with online learning were the lack of connection in terms of geographical locations and the lack of adaptation to virtual education. Nazar et al. [158] explored various attacks on online learning platforms [159–170], such as Zoom, Google Meet, Microsoft Teams, and Cisco Webex, to determine the degree of security offered by each of these platforms. Furthermore, the authors also analyzed the encryption features to assess the levels of confidentiality, integrity, and availability offered by these online learning platforms.

To summarize, while there have been several works published in the last few years related to the analysis of web behavior in the context of COVID-19, those works have multiple limitations. First, many studies did not focus on interests related to online learning platforms from several countries. Second, several works focused on search interests involving only a very limited number of online learning platforms. Finally, these works did not identify specific online learning platforms that recorded a high search interest during different timelines associated with the COVID-19 outbreak. The work presented in this paper aims to address these limitations and research gaps.

3 Methodology

This section presents the methodology that was followed for this research work. The primary tool that was used for data collection was Google Trends [171]. Google Trends is a website developed by Google, and it was initially released on May 11, 2006 [172].

This platform allows mining and analysis of Big Data related to web behavior on Google. Its features include Trending Searches, Year in Search, and Explore, just to name a few, with the objective of allowing the user to gain a comprehensive understanding of the interest associated with specific keyword(s) on Google. Google Trends also provides the patterns of regional and global variations in search interests. Google Trends has several benefits over traditional techniques of collecting data via surveys. These benefits include (1) no costs associated with mining and studying the necessary data, whereas surveys are sometimes associated with expenses related to survey development and participant recruitment; (2) the ability to study and analyze data from different regions of the world simply by visiting the Google Trends website, whereas traditional surveys may struggle to have representation from all geographic regions of the world; and (3) the results of data mining or data analysis on web behavior data are provided immediately by Google Trends whereas in surveys participants need to be provided a sufficient amount of time to complete the same. Google Trends uses a scale of 0 to 100 to assess search interests connected to a topic based on web behavior on Google relating to that topic. A search interest score of 100 on Google Trends reflects the highest interest, while a search interest score of 0 represents the lowest interest associated with that topic during a specific timeline. To perform the data mining involving online learning platforms that have been used in different parts of the world, a collection of such platforms had to be prepared first. This list was prepared by reviewing the prior works in this field (Sect. 2). The different online learning platforms those works focused on were identified, compiled, and the duplicates were removed to develop this collection that comprised 101 online learning platforms. The names of all 101 online learning platforms are presented in Table 1.

Table 1. Names of 101 online learning platforms which were used for Data Mining.

Names of Online Learning Platforms
Google Classroom, Pear Deck, Flipgrid, Edmodo, Canva, Zoom, Blackboard, ClassDojo, Microsoft Teams, NearPod, Hapara, Explain Everything Whiteboard, Bloomz, Khan Academy, Seesaw, Kahoot!, Habyts, CK-12, Brainpop Jr, Newsela, Mystery Science, Prodigy, Abcmouse.Com, Xtramath, Quizlet, Gizmos, Icivics, Duolingo, Storytime Online, PBS Kids, Edulastic, Quiziz, Bookflix, Screencastify, Webex, Loom, Schoology, Powerschool, I-Ready, IXL, Moodle, Coursera, Thinkific, Easy Class, CodeAcademy, Learntopia, Memrise, CodeSpark, Gradescope, ProctorU, Prairie Learn, Proctorio, Kaltura, LMS Docebo, Adobe Captivate Prime, SAP Litmos LMS, TalentLMS, iSpring Learn, Neo LMS, Articulate 360, Abcya, Teach TCI, Raz Kids, Akeba, Think Central, Quia, Age Of Learning, Bamboo Learning, Beast Academy, Boclips, Emathinstruction, Everfi, Explain Everything, Fact Monster, Labxchange, Learning.Com, Mathnook, Pebblego, Phet Interactive Simulations, Science Buddies, Smartlab, Studycat, Skyward, Castle Learning, Eboard, Eduplanet, Pearson, Study Island, Discovery Education, Kami, Carnegie Learning, Talking Points, Padlet, Biz Kids, Varsity Tutors, Sheppard Software, Thatquiz, Topmarks, Usa Learns, Zinc Learning Labs, Go Math!

Thereafter, the search interests related to all these 101 online learning platforms for 133 weeks between March 11, 2020, and October 1, 2022, for all 38 OECD countries were mined. Here, March 11, 2020, was selected as the start date for the data collection as the World Health Organization declared COVID-19 as a pandemic on March 11, 2020 [3]. October 1, 2022, was the most recent date at the time of data mining. Figure 1 shows a comparison between the search interests associated with Zoom (blue) and Microsoft Teams (red) in the United States during this timeline. As can be seen from Fig. 1, there was a higher level of interest associated with Zoom as compared to Microsoft Teams in the United States during this timeline. Figures 2 and 3 show the specific cities in the United States where high levels of search interests associated with these two platforms were recorded. This process was repeated for the remaining 99 online learning platforms during this timeline to develop a dataset. Here, for the paucity of space, the images are presented for only two platforms – Zoom and Microsoft Teams.

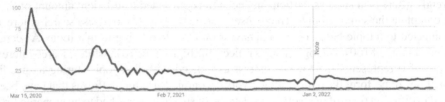

Fig. 1. A comparison between the search interests associated with Zoom (blue) and Microsoft Teams (red) between March 11, 2020, and October 1, 2022, for the USA

Fig. 2. Representation of specific cities in the USA where high levels of interest were recorded towards Zoom between March 11, 2020, and October 1, 2022

For this data mining task associated with these 101 online learning platforms, a program was written in Python 3.10 installed on a computer with a Microsoft Windows 10 Pro operating system (Version 10.0.19043 Build 19043) comprising Intel(R) Core (TM) i7-7600U CPU @ 2.80 GHz, 2904 MHz, 2 Core(s) and 4 Logical Processor(s). The program connected with the Google Trends API and followed the rate limits of this API for the data mining task. The workflow diagram of Fig. 4 shows the approach by which this database was developed. To speed up data acquisition, the process was parallelized, with 10 runners, shown in the far left of the diagram. The rest of the process was built so that the 10 runners could run concurrently to avoid slow API calls. Each runner initially received a country value to work on. Each runner had an offset value, so it started at different parts of the dataset to avoid repetitions. Once a country was allocated, the runner read the CSV file corresponding to that country and loaded it into

Fig. 3. Representation of specific cities in the USA where high levels of interest were recorded towards Microsoft Teams between March 11, 2020, and October 1, 2022

memory as a data frame. Next, the runner went through its list of platforms and picked the next platform that was not already present in the data frame. This allowed the runners to pick up where they left off in the event of any issues. Once a platform and country combination was selected, the runner made an API request to get the search interest data from Google Trends for the given platform and country during the time period of focus. The data that was obtained was an array of the search interest values for each week over the timeframe of focus. Once the API request was returned, the runner updated the data frame in memory for the country with the new data. Next, it wrote the data frame to a CSV file and updated the CSV file in memory. In this manner, each runner worked over each combination of platform and country until all the data was written into CSV files. The final step was to write the data in each CSV for each country into the final PostgreSQL database.

The result of running the 10 runners was a database with search interest data for each combination of weeks, platforms, and countries covered in this study. During this data mining task involving 101 online learning platforms, it was observed that 4 platforms - Adobe Captivate Prime, CK 12, Phet Interactive Simulations, and Prairie Learn did not record significant interest for several weeks in a majority of the countries. So, these platforms were not considered for the analysis, which is discussed in Sect. 4. After developing this dataset on PostgreSQL, the data visualization of the search interests associated with the 97 online learning platforms for 133 weeks between March 11, 2020, and October 1, 2022, showed distinct patterns. Therefore, K-means clustering was run on this database 10,000 times to identify clusters based on search interests. K-means clustering is a vector quantization approach derived from signal processing that tries to split n observations into k clusters, with each observation belonging to the cluster with the nearest mean (cluster centers or cluster centroid), which serves as the cluster's prototype. The K-means clustering was performed to identify a cluster of high search interests and its centroid. After this data was obtained, a recursive algorithm was developed and run on this database to identify the list of platforms that recorded search interests equal to or greater than the value of this centroid, the specific countries from which these platforms recorded such interests, and the associated queries on Google related to these platforms that contributed to this high search interest. The step-by-step methodology that was followed in this regard is shown in Fig. 5. The results are discussed in Sect. 4.

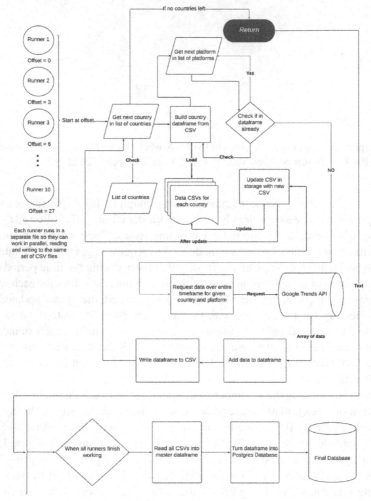

Fig. 4. A workflow diagram that represents the process that was followed for data mining and dataset development

4   Results

This section presents the results of this work. The data mining process that involved mining the search interests of all the 101 online learning platforms for all 38 OECD countries for 133 weeks between March 11, 2020, and October 1, 2022, involved the development of multiple algorithms, which worked both in a parallel capacity as well as in a sequential manner. For the paucity of space, the pseudocode of a couple of major

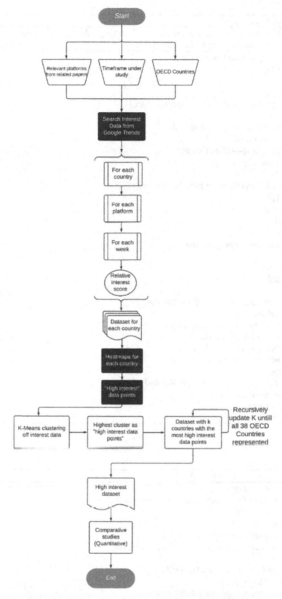

Fig. 5. A flowchart to represent the overall methodology.

algorithms is presented next. Algorithms 1 and 2 present the pseudocode that represents the methodology that was followed for building new data in the dataset and for converting the master dictionary to CSV files, respectively.

Algorithm 1: to build new data
Local Variables: df, to store the data while reading and creating a data frame. Keywords, to build random keywords and total to count the total keywords.

function creates a new data builder(geo)
        empty_list = []
        open the file
            for line in file
            append that file into the empty_list(no space)
        if it is a file, do:
            local variable: df, then read ◄——file
        else: create Data Frame
            write CSV file ◄—— Data Frame
        key Words: create keywords
        total: count keys
        skipped, added, valueCount = initialize to zero
        empty_list: []
        ignore warnings
        open file as f
            for line in f
            append ◄—— empty_list(strip)
        for i= 1 to 3
        for keyword in keywords:
            if keyword ≠ in files column
                try:
                    create a query and put the columns
                    listCout += 1
                    check the current value in query
                    write to the CSV file
                    decrement the total by 1
                    increment to the added by 1
                except:
                    print: geo, keyword, total, skipped and added
                    increment skipped by 1
                    continue
            else: total = total - 1

Algorithm 2: convert masterDict to CSV files

OecdCode: get_oecd_code
      Master Dictionary: for weeks, platforms, interests, and geo
      For code in oecdCodes
         df: get the data frame
         dic: week, platform, interest, and geo
         for column name and columnDate in df(iteritems)
         i = 0
         for interestValue in columnData value
             dict(week): append
             dict(platform): append columName
             dict(interest): append interestValue
             dict(Geo): append code(upper)
             masterDict: append week(i)
            masterDict: append platform(columnName)
             masterDict: append Interest(InterestValue)
            masterDict: append Geo(code(upper))
             increment i by one
      write: to dic to csv
      write: to masterDict to csv

The working of these algorithms was analyzed to compute the time complexity of the entire process. It was observed to be $O(n^2)$. After the data mining process was performed, the search interests associated with different platforms for 133 weeks between March 11, 2020, and October 1, 2022, for each country, were analyzed using heatmaps. To perform this analysis, the platforms were assigned index numbers. These index numbers were assigned to the online learning platforms in the order in which they were listed in Table 1, i.e., Google Classroom was assigned P0, Pear Deck was assigned P1, and so on. For the paucity of space, the heatmap of two countries – the United States and Australia are presented in Figs. 6 and 7, respectively. As can be seen from these images, the generated heat maps had three primary features, which were week, platforms, and interest values. In all these images, the Y-axis represents the weeks, the X-axis represents the platforms, and the interest values are marked by varying the intensity of the color. For the clustering process, the K-means clustering algorithm was developed and implemented in RapidMiner [173]. The K-means algorithm [174] was run 10,000 times on this dataset with the value of k as 5, Bregman Divergences as the measure types, Squared Euclidean Distance as the divergence, and 100 as the value of the maximum optimization steps. The application of K-means resulted in each search interest value being assigned a certain cluster. The representation of these clusters with their centroid values as well as the number and fraction of the total number of observations that belonged to each of them are presented in Table 2. As can be seen from Table 2, the centroid value of cluster_3 was the highest.

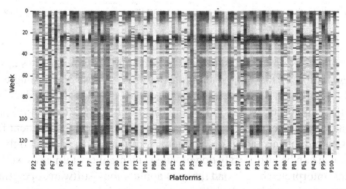

Fig. 6. A heatmap-based representation to demonstrate the search interests for different online learning platforms in the United States.

This centroid value of 88.42 was used to identify those learning platforms which had a high level of search interest associated with them during this timeline. Specifically, a recursive algorithm was developed and run on this database to identify the list of platforms that recorded search interests equal to or greater than 88.42 each week, the specific countries from which these platforms recorded such interests, and the associated queries on Google related to these platforms that contributed to this high search interest. These results, along with the original database developed in PostgreSQL, were published as dataset in IEEE Dataport, available at https://dx.doi.org/10.21227/x56b-8n27, to allow replication of these results as well as for the investigation of any research questions in

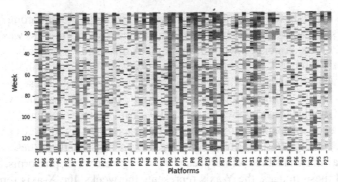

Fig. 7. A heatmap-based representation to demonstrate the search interests for different online learning platforms in Australia.

Table 2. Characteristics of the clusters after running K-means on the dataset 10,000 times

Cluster Name	Number of Observations	Percentage of Observations	Centroid Value
cluster_0	145933	0.572756	0.677133
cluster_1	19821	0.077793	61.70546
cluster_2	33742	0.13243	40.66389
cluster_3	8478	0.033274	88.41991
cluster_4	46817	0.183747	21.78098

this field for which a similar dataset might be necessary. Figure 8 shows a word cloud-based representation of the online learning platforms whose search interests reached or crossed 88.42 from at least one country in at least one week. This dataset complies with the FAIR (Findability, Accessibility, Interoperability, and Reusability) principles of scientific data management [175]. The dataset has a unique and permanent DOI, which makes it easily findable and accessible online. Additionally, the dataset only consists of CSV files, which can be effortlessly downloaded any number of times as well as opened, processed, and interpreted by a broad range of applications, software, operating systems, and frameworks, ensuring its reusability and interoperability.

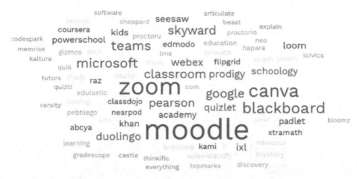

Fig. 8. A word cloud-based representation of the online learning platforms whose search interests reached or crossed 88.42 from at least one country in at least one week.

Next, two comprehensive comparative studies were performed to compare the contributions of this paper with prior works in this field (reviewed in Sect. 2) to uphold its novelty. The first comparative study focused on comparing this paper with previous works in this field in terms of the number of online learning platforms which were studied or analyzed in those works. Figure 9 shows this comparative study where this paper was compared with 63 prior works (reviewed in Sect. 2) in this field which focused on at least one online learning platform. As can be seen from this Figure, this is the first work in this field where the data associated with 97 online learning platforms was studied and analyzed. The second comparative study, shown in Fig. 10, focused on comparing this paper with previous works in this field in terms of the number of countries that were represented in the studies. For this comparative study, this paper was compared with 85 prior works (reviewed in Sect. 2) in this field which focused on the mining or analysis of data associated with online learning from at least one country. As can be seen from this Figure, this is the first work in this field where the data associated with online learning from 38 OECD countries was studied and analyzed.

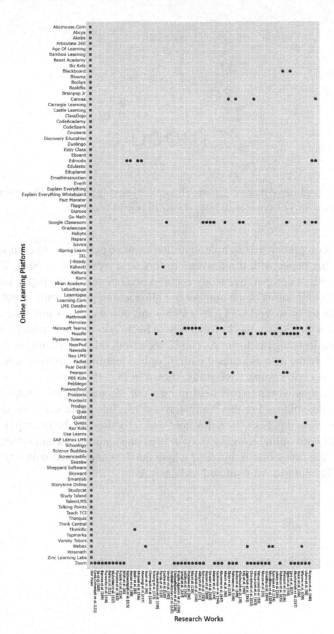

Fig. 9. Comparison of this work with 63 prior works in this field in terms of the number of online learning platforms

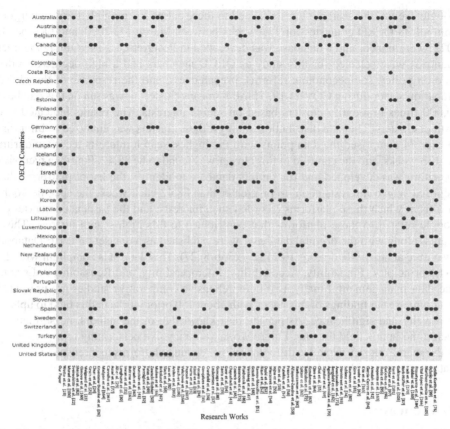

Fig. 10. Comparison of this work with 85 prior works in this field, which focused on the mining or analysis of data associated with online learning from at least one country.

5 Conclusion and Future Work

Mining and analysis of web behavior by using Google Trends, especially the web behavior associated with virus outbreaks such as Middle East Respiratory Syndrome, Ebola, measles, Swine flu, Lyme disease, COVID-19, and MPox, just to name a few, has been of keen interest to researchers from various disciplines in the last few years. The existing works that focused on the analysis of web behavior in the context of COVID-19 have multiple limitations, such as lack of focus on different online learning platforms, focusing on web behavior data from a very limited number of countries, and lack of analysis to identify any specific online learning platforms that consistently experienced a high level of interest from the general public as evidenced by web behavior data. The interdisciplinary work of this paper at the intersections of Big Data, Data Mining, Data Analysis, and Machine Learning addresses these limitations and makes multiple scientific contributions to these fields. First, a comprehensive review of about 150 papers related to online learning during COVID-19 was conducted to identify a list of 101 online learning platforms that were used in different parts of the world during COVID-19. Second, using

Google Trends, the search interests related to these online learning platforms emerging from all 38 OCED countries for 133 weeks between March 11, 2020, and October 1, 2022, were mined, and a database was developed in PostgreSQL. The OECD member countries were selected for this study as OECD members had a high degree of influence on policy, socioeconomic reforms, preparedness, and the response of the global education sector during COVID-19. Third, K-means clustering was run on this database 10,000 times to identify clusters based on search interests. The results indicated five distinct clusters. The data distribution amongst these clusters was analyzed to infer that Cluster #4 comprised the data points with the highest search interests recorded during the 133 weeks, and the centroid of this cluster was found to be 88.42. Fourth, a recursive algorithm was developed and run on this database to identify the list of platforms that recorded search interests equal to or greater than 88.42 each week, the specific countries from which these platforms recorded such interests, and the associated queries on Google related to these platforms that contributed to this high search interest. These results, along with the original database, were published as a dataset on IEEE Dataport (available at https://dx.doi.org/10.21227/x56b-8n27). This dataset is compliant with the FAIR principles (Findability, Accessibility, Interoperability, and Reusability) of scientific data management. Finally, two comprehensive comparative studies are presented that compare the findings of this paper with about 150 prior works in this field to uphold its novelty and significance. As per the best knowledge of the authors, no similar has been done in this field thus far. Future work would involve performing topic modeling on the search queries related to different online learning platforms to infer specific topics that were associated with high search interests.

References

1. Fauci, A.S., Lane, H.C., Redfield, R.R.: Covid-19 - navigating the uncharted. N. Engl. J. Med. **382**, 1268–1269 (2020)
2. Ksiazek, T.G., et al.: SARS working group: a novel coronavirus associated with severe acute respiratory syndrome. N. Engl. J. Med. **348**, 1953–1966 (2003)
3. Cucinotta, D., Vanelli, M.: WHO declares COVID-19 a pandemic. Acta Biomed. **91**, 157–160 (2020)
4. COVID - Coronavirus statistics – worldometer. https://www.worldometers.info/corona virus/. Accessed 21 June 2023
5. Allen, D.W.: Covid-19 lockdown cost/benefits: a critical assessment of the literature. Int. J. Econ. Bus. **29**, 1–32 (2022)
6. Kumar, V., Sharma, D.: E-learning theories, components, and cloud computing-based learning platforms. Int. J. Web-based Learn. Teach. Technol. **16**, 1–16 (2021)
7. Muñoz-Najar, A., Gilberto, A., Hasan, A., Cobo, C., Azevedo, J.P., Akmal, M.: Remote Learning During COVID-19: Lessons from Today, Principles for Tomorrow. World Bank (2021)
8. Simamora, R.M., De Fretes, D., Purba, E.D., Pasaribu, D.: Practices, challenges, and prospects of online learning during covid-19 pandemic in higher education: lecturer perspectives. Stud. Learn. Teach. **1**, 185–208 (2020)
9. Miraz, M.H., Ali, M., Excell, P.S., Picking, R.: A review on internet of things (IoT), internet of everything (IoE) and internet of nano things (IoNT). In: 2015 Internet Technologies and Applications (ITA). pp. 219–224. IEEE

10. Google search statistics. https://www.internetlivestats.com/google-search-statistics/. Accessed 21 June 2023
11. Mavragani, A., Ochoa, G., Tsagarakis, K.P.: Assessing the methods, tools, and statistical approaches in Google Trends research: systematic review. J. Med. Internet Res. **20**, e270 (2018). https://doi.org/10.2196/jmir.9366
12. Poletto, C., Boëlle, P.-Y., Colizza, V.: Risk of MERS importation and onward transmission: a systematic review and analysis of cases reported to WHO. BMC Infect. Dis. **16**, 448 (2016)
13. Hossain, L., Kam, D., Kong, F., Wigand, R.T., Bossomaier, T.: Social media in Ebola outbreak. Epidemiol. Infect. **144**, 2136–2143 (2016). https://doi.org/10.1017/S0950268816000039X
14. Mavragani, A., Ochoa, G.: The internet and the anti-vaccine movement: Tracking the 2017 EU measles outbreak. Big Data Cogn. Comput. **2**, 2 (2018). https://doi.org/10.3390/bdcc2010002
15. Bentley, R.A., Ormerod, P.: Social versus independent interest in "bird flu" and "swine flu." PLoS Curr. **1** (2009)
16. Seifter, A., Schwarzwalder, A., Geis, K., Aucott, J.: The utility of "google trends" for epidemiological research: lyme disease as an example. Geospat. Health **4**, 135–137 (2010). https://doi.org/10.4081/gh.2010.195
17. Rossignol, L., Pelat, C., Lambert, B., Flahault, A., Chartier-Kastler, E., Hanslik, T.: A method to assess seasonality of urinary tract infections based on medication sales and google trends. PLoS ONE **8**, e76020 (2013)
18. Mavragani, A., Sampri, A., Sypsa, K., Tsagarakis, K.P.: Integrating smart health in the US health care system: Infodemiology study of asthma monitoring in the Google era. JMIR Public Health Surveill. **4**, e24 (2018)
19. Martins-Filho, P.R., de Souza Araújo, A.A., Quintans-Júnior, L.J.: Global online public interest in monkeypox compared with COVID-19: Google trends in 2022. J. Travel Med. **29** (2022). https://doi.org/10.1093/jtm/taac104
20. https://www.oecd.org/about/members-and-partners/. Accessed 21 June 2023
21. Fuchs, K.: Students' perceptions concerning emergency remote teaching during COVID-19: a case study between higher education institutions in Thailand and Finland. Perspect. Glob. Dev. Technol. **20**, 278–288 (2021)
22. Sveinsdóttir, H., et al.: Predictors of university nursing students burnout at the time of the COVID-19 pandemic: a cross-sectional study. Nurse Educ. Today **106**, 105070 (2021). https://doi.org/10.1016/j.nedt.2021.105070
23. Melgaard, J., Monir, R., Lasrado, L.A., Fagerstrøm, A.: Academic procrastination and online learning during the COVID-19 pandemic. Procedia Comput. Sci. **196**, 117–124 (2022). https://doi.org/10.1016/j.procs.2021.11.080
24. Churi, P., Mistry, K., Asad, M.M., Dhiman, G., Soni, M., Kose, U.: Online learning in COVID-19 pandemic: an empirical study of Indian and Turkish higher education institutions. World J. Eng. **19**, 58–71 (2022)
25. Kirsch, C., Engel de Abreu, P.M.J., Neumann, S., Wealer, C.: Practices and experiences of distant education during the COVID-19 pandemic: The perspectives of six- to sixteen-year-olds from three high-income countries. Int. J. Educ. Res. Open. **2**, 100049 (2021). https://doi.org/10.1016/j.ijedro.2021.100049
26. Duenke, J., Suksatan, W.: The competence of university students and factors related to learning motivation during the covid-19 pandemic: a cross-sectional study in Finland and Austria. Malays. J. Publ. Health Med. **22**, 137–144 (2022)
27. COVID-19 pandemijos iššūkių valdymas Lietuvos ir Slovėnijos bendrojo ugdymo sistemoje: mokyklų vadovų požiūris. Pedagogika. **143**, 5–22 (2021)

28. Wotto, M.: The future high education distance learning in Canada, the United States, and France: insights from before COVID-19 secondary data analysis. J. Educ. Technol. Syst. **49**, 262–281 (2020)

29. Ali, I., Narayan, A.K., Sharma, U.: Adapting to COVID-19 disruptions: student engagement in online learning of accounting. Acc. Res. J. **34**, 261–269 (2021). https://doi.org/10.1108/arj-09-2020-0293

30. Longhurst, G.J., Stone, D.M., Dulohery, K., Scully, D., Campbell, T., Smith, C.F.: Strength, weakness, opportunity, threat (SWOT) analysis of the adaptations to anatomical education in the United Kingdom and Republic of Ireland in response to the Covid-19 pandemic. Anat. Sci. Educ. **13**, 301–311 (2020). https://doi.org/10.1002/ase.1967

31. Imran, A.S., Daudpota, S.M., Kastrati, Z., Batra, R.: Cross-cultural polarity and emotion detection using sentiment analysis and deep learning on COVID-19 related tweets. IEEE Access. **8**, 181074–181090 (2020)

32. Parmigiani, D., Benigno, V., Giusto, M., Silvaggio, C., Sperandio, S.: E-inclusion: online special education in Italy during the Covid-19 pandemic. Technol. Pedagog. Educ. **30**, 111–124 (2021). https://doi.org/10.1080/1475939x.2020.1856714

33. Küsel, J., Martin, F., Markic, S.: University students' readiness for using digital media and Online Learning—comparison between Germany and the USA. Educ. Sci. (Basel). **10**, 313 (2020)

34. Ferraro, F.V., Ambra, F.I., Aruta, L., Iavarone, M.L.: Distance learning in the COVID-19 era: Perceptions in southern Italy. Educ. Sci. (Basel). **10**, 355 (2020). https://doi.org/10.3390/educsci10120355

35. Gonçalves, S.P., Sousa, M.J., Pereira, F.S.: Distance learning perceptions from higher education students—the case of Portugal. Educ. Sci. (Basel). **10**, 374 (2020). https://doi.org/10.3390/educsci10120374

36. Cranfield, D.J., Tick, A., Venter, I.M., Blignaut, R.J., Renaud, K.: Higher education students' perceptions of online learning during COVID-19—a comparative study. Educ. Sci. (Basel). **11**, 403 (2021)

37. Loukomies, A., Juuti, K.: Primary students' experiences of remote learning during COVID-19 school closures: a case study of Finland. Educ. Sci. (Basel). **11**, 560 (2021). https://doi.org/10.3390/educsci11090560

38. Guncaga, J., Lopuchova, J., Ferdianova, V., Zacek, M., Ashimov, Y.: Survey on online learning at universities of Slovakia, Czech Republic and Kazakhstan during the COVID-19 pandemic. Educ. Sci. (Basel). **12**, 458 (2022)

39. Tørris, C., Gjølstad, E., et al.: Students' experiences with online teaching and learning in Norway: a qualitative study into nutrition education one year after the COVID-19 lockdown. Educ. Sci. **12**, 670 (2022)

40. Dorsah, P.: Pre-service teachers' readiness for emergency remote learning in the wake of COVID-19. Eur. J. STEM Educ. **6**, 01 (2021). https://doi.org/10.20897/ejsteme/9557

41. Duroisin, N., Beauset, R., Tanghe, C.: Education and digital inequalities during COVID-19 confinement: from the perspective of teachers in the French speaking Community of Belgium. Eur. J. Educ. **56**, 515–535 (2021)

42. Almaiah, M., et al.: Explaining the factors affecting students' attitudes to using online learning (Madrasati platform) during COVID-19. Electronics (Basel). **11**, 973 (2022)

43. Chrysafiadi, K., Virvou, M., Tsihrintzis, G.A.: A fuzzy-based evaluation of E-learning acceptance and effectiveness by computer science students in Greece in the period of COVID-19. Electronics (Basel). **12**, 428 (2023)

44. Burns, D., Dagnall, N., Holt, M.: Assessing the impact of the COVID-19 pandemic on student well-being at universities in the United Kingdom: A conceptual analysis. Front. Educ. **5** (2020)

45. De Coninck, D., Matthijs, K., Van Lancker, W.: Distance learning and school-related stress among Belgian adolescents during the COVID-19 pandemic. Front. Educ. **7** (2022). https://doi.org/10.3389/feduc.2022.836123
46. Plakhotnik, M.S., et al.: The perceived impact of COVID-19 on student well-being and the mediating role of the university support: evidence from France, Germany, Russia, and the UK. Front. Psychol. **12**, 642689 (2021)
47. Versteeg, M., Kappe, R.: Resilience and higher education support as protective factors for student academic stress and depression during Covid-19 in the Netherlands. Front. Public Health **9**, 737223 (2021)
48. Gosak, L., Fijačko, N., Chabrera, C., Cabrera, E., Štiglic, G.: Perception of the online learning environment of nursing students in Slovenia: Validation of the DREEM questionnaire. Healthcare (Basel). **9**, 998 (2021)
49. Yates, A., Starkey, A., Egerton, B., Flueggen, F.: High School Students' Experience of Online Learning during Covid-19: the Influence of Technology and Pedagogy (2020). https://doi.org/10.26686/wgtn.13315877
50. Zawacki-Richter, O.: The current state and impact of Covid-19 on digital higher education in Germany. Hum. Behav. Emerg. Technol. **3**, 218–226 (2021). https://doi.org/10.1002/hbe2.238
51. Ramos-Morcillo, A.J., Leal-Costa, C., Moral-García, J.E., Ruzafa-Martínez, M.: Experiences of nursing students during the abrupt change from face-to-face to e-learning education during the first month of confinement due to COVID-19 in Spain. Int. J. Environ. Res. Public Health **17**, 5519 (2020). https://doi.org/10.3390/ijerph17155519
52. Rizun, M., Strzelecki, A.: Students' acceptance of the COVID-19 impact on shifting higher education to distance learning in Poland. Int. J. Environ. Res. Public Health **17**, 6468 (2020). https://doi.org/10.3390/ijerph17186468
53. Dodd, R.H., Dadaczynski, K., Okan, O., McCaffery, K.J., Pickles, K.: Psychological well-being and academic experience of university students in Australia during COVID-19. Int. J. Environ. Res. Public Health **18**, 866 (2021)
54. Wieczorek, T., et al.: Class of 2020 in Poland: students' mental health during the COVID-19 outbreak in an academic setting. Int. J. Environ. Res. Public Health **18**, 2884 (2021). https://doi.org/10.3390/ijerph18062884
55. Jojoa, M., Lazaro, E., Garcia-Zapirain, B., Gonzalez, M.J., Urizar, E.: The impact of COVID 19 on university staff and students from iberoamerica: online learning and teaching experience. Int. J. Environ. Res. Public Health **18**, 5820 (2021)
56. Kim, S.-Y., Kim, S.-J., Lee, S.-H.: Effects of online learning on nursing students in South Korea during COVID-19. Int. J. Environ. Res. Public Health **18**, 8506 (2021). https://doi.org/10.3390/ijerph18168506
57. Puteikis, K., Mameniškytė, A., Mameniškienė, R.: Sleep quality, mental health and learning among high school students after reopening schools during the COVID-19 pandemic: results of a cross-sectional online survey. Int. J. Environ. Res. Public Health **19**, 2553 (2022). https://doi.org/10.3390/ijerph19052553
58. Prosen, M., Karnjuš, I., Ličen, S.: Evaluation of E-learning experience among health and allied health professions students during the COVID-19 pandemic in Slovenia: an instrument development and validation study. Int. J. Environ. Res. Public Health **19**, 4777 (2022). https://doi.org/10.3390/ijerph19084777
59. Zeadna, S., Gnaim-Abu Touma, L., Weinreich, M., O'Rourke, N.: COVID-19 and mental health of minority Arab higher-education students in Israel: social, economic, and academic factors. Int. J. Environ. Res. Public Health **19**, 13466 (2022)
60. Badiuzzaman, M., Rafiquzzaman, M., Rabby, M.I.I., Rahman, M.M.: The latent digital divide and its drivers in E-learning among Bangladeshi students during the COVID-19 pandemic. Information (Basel). **12**, 287 (2021)

61. Spitzer, M., Musslick, S.: Academic Performance of K-12 Students in an Online-Learning Environment for Mathematics Increased during the Shutdown of Schools in Wake of the Covid-19 Pandemic (2020)
62. Stoehr, F., et al.: How COVID-19 kick-started online learning in medical education-the DigiMed study. PLoS ONE **16**, e0257394 (2021)
63. Konukman, F., Filiz, B., Ünlü, H.: Teachers' perceptions of teaching physical education using online learning during the COVID-19: a quantitative study in Turkey. PLoS ONE **17**, e0269377 (2022)
64. Qiao, P., Zhu, X., Guo, Y., Sun, Y., Qin, C.: The development and adoption of online learning in pre- and post-COVID-19: combination of technological system evolution theory and Unified Theory of Acceptance and use of technology. J. Risk Fin. Manag. **14**, 162 (2021). https://doi.org/10.3390/jrfm14040162
65. Choi, J.-J., Robb, C.A., Mifli, M., Zainuddin, Z.: University students' perception to online class delivery methods during the COVID-19 pandemic: a focus on hospitality education in Korea and Malaysia. J. Hosp. Leis. Sport Tour. Educ. **29**, 100336 (2021). https://doi.org/10.1016/j.jhlste.2021.100336
66. Mullen, C., Pettigrew, J., Cronin, A., Rylands, L., Shearman, D.: Mathematics is different: student and tutor perspectives from Ireland and Australia on online support during COVID-19. Teach. Math. Appl. Int. J. IMA. **40**, 332–355 (2021)
67. Birkelund, J.F., Karlson, K.B.: No Evidence of a Major Learning Slide 14 Months into the COVID-19 Pandemic in Denmark
68. Slack, H.R., Priestley, M.: Online learning and assessment during the Covid-19 pandemic: exploring the impact on undergraduate student well-being. Assess. Eval. High. Educ. 1–17 (2022)
69. Tejedor, S., Cervi, L., Pérez-Escoda, A., Jumbo, F.T.: Digital literacy and higher education during COVID-19 lockdown: Spain, Italy, and Ecuador. Publications. **8**, 48 (2020). https://doi.org/10.3390/publications8040048
70. Aguilera-Hermida, A.P., Quiroga-Garza, A., Gómez-Mendoza, S., Del Río Villanueva, C.A., Avolio Alecchi, B., Avci, D.: Comparison of students' use and acceptance of emergency online learning due to COVID-19 in the USA, Mexico, Peru, and Turkey. Educ. Inf. Technol. **26**, 6823–6845 (2021)
71. Anastasakis, M., Triantafyllou, G., Petridis, K.: Undergraduates' barriers to online learning during the pandemic in Greece. Technol. Knowl. Learn. (2021). https://doi.org/10.1007/s10758-021-09584-5
72. Baticulon, R.E., et al.: Barriers to Online Learning in the Time of COVID-19: A National Survey of Medical Students in the Philippines (2020). https://doi.org/10.1101/2020.07.16.20155747
73. Morais, N.S., Raposo, R.: Blended-Learning in contexts conditioned by the pandemic: the perceptions of higher education students. In: 2021 International Symposium on Computers in Education (SIIE), pp. 1–6. IEEE (2021)
74. Schlenz, M.A., Schmidt, A., Wöstmann, B., Krämer, N., Schulz-Weidner, N.: Students' and lecturers' perspective on the implementation of online learning in dental education due to SARS-CoV-2 (COVID-19): a cross-sectional study. BMC Med. Educ. **20**, 354 (2020). https://doi.org/10.1186/s12909-020-02266-3
75. Baranova, S., Nīmante, D., Kalniņa, D., Oļesika, A.: Students' perspective on remote on-line teaching and learning at the university of Latvia in the first and second COVID-19 period. Sustainability. **13**, 11890 (2021)
76. Teidla-Kunitsõn, G., Põlda, H., Sisask, M.: Construction of learning during the inevitable distance learning period: a critical perspective of the experiences of young people in Estonia. Sustainability. **15**, 494 (2022)

77. Environmental education using distance learning during COVID-19 lockdown in Israel. Perspect. Educ. **39** (2021)
78. Khachouch, M.K., et al.: E-learning techniques and technologies analysis for a moroccan virtual university perspective. In: 2020 IEEE 2nd International Conference on Electronics, Control, Optimization and Computer Science (ICECOCS), pp. 1–5. IEEE (2020)
79. Atalan, A.: Is the lockdown important to prevent the COVID-19 pandemic? effects on psychology, environment and economy-perspective. Ann. Med. Surg. (Lond.) **56**, 38–42 (2020)
80. Baumann, C., et al.: Effect of the COVID-19 outbreak and lockdown on mental health among post-secondary students in the Grand Est region of France: Results of the PIMS-Cov19 study (2021). https://doi.org/10.21203/rs.3.rs-534261/v1
81. Gore, J., Fray, L., Miller, A., Harris, J., Taggart, W.: The impact of COVID-19 on student learning in New South Wales primary schools: an empirical study. Aust. Educ. Res. **48**, 605–637 (2021)
82. Shirish, A., Chandra, S., Srivastava, S.C.: Switching to online learning during COVID-19: theorizing the role of IT mindfulness and techno eustress for facilitating productivity and creativity in student learning. Int. J. Inf. Manage. **61** (2021)
83. Bedir, A., Desai, R., Kulkarni, N., Wallet, K., Wells, R., Smith, M.: Assessing student learning of systems thinking concepts in an online education module. In: Systems and Information Engineering Design Symposium, pp. 1–6. IEEE (2020)
84. García-Castro, V., O'Reilly, J.: Foreign language anxiety and online engagement during the COVID-19 pandemic: a comparison between EMI and FMI university students. Engl. Teach. Learn. **46**, 273–291 (2022)
85. Rifah, L., Zunaidah, A., Sari, C.C.: Developing ESP-based CLIL to increase students' engagement in higher education. In: 2022 8th International Conference on Education and Technology (ICET), pp. 147–152. IEEE (2022)
86. Maxim, B.R., Limbaugh, T., Yackley, J.J.: Student engagement in an online software engineering course. In: 2021 IEEE Frontiers in Education Conference (FIE), pp. 1–9. IEEE (2021)
87. Bork-Hüffer, T., et al.: University students' perception, evaluation, and spaces of distance learning during the COVID-19 pandemic in Austria: what can we learn for post-pandemic educational futures? Sustainability. **13**, 7595 (2021)
88. Tasnim Wan Hussin, W.N., Harun, J., Shukor, N.A.: Students' perception on using edmodo as collaborative problem-based learning platform. In: IEEE International Conference on Engineering, Technology & Education, pp. 01–06. IEEE (2021)
89. Basri, N.R.H., Mohktar, M.S., Abdullah, JCPG, Aspanut, Z.: A survey of student's perception on conducting online learning in the home environment during movement control order (MCO). In: 2021 2nd SEA-STEM International Conference (SEA-STEM), pp. 88–90. IEEE (2021)
90. Pratama, RY, Aji, BH, Putra, H.G., Sari, R.: Analysis of effective online learning media during covid-19 pandemic (study of student's and teacher's perception). In: 2022 International Conference on Information Management and Technology (ICIMTech), pp. 550–553. IEEE (2022)
91. Yahuarcani, I.O., et al.: Perception of the quality of virtual educational services during the COVID-19 pandemic at the National University of the Peruvian Amazon (UNAP). In: 2021 4th International Conference on Inclusive Technology and Education (CONTIE), pp. 96–101. IEEE (2021)
92. Lau, E.Y.H., Li, J.-B., Lee, K.: Online learning and parent satisfaction during COVID-19: child competence in independent learning as a moderator. Early Educ. Dev. **32**, 830–842 (2021)

93. Stanistreet, P., Elfert, M., Atchoarena, D.: Education in the age of COVID-19: implications for the future. Int. Rev. Educ. **67**, 1–8 (2021). https://doi.org/10.1007/s11159-021-09904-y

94. Gaur, U., Majumder, M.A.A., Sa, B., Sarkar, S., Williams, A., Singh, K.: Challenges and opportunities of preclinical medical education: COVID-19 crisis and beyond. SN Compr. Clin. Med. **2**, 1992–1997 (2020)

95. Ikeda, M., Yamaguchi, S.: Online learning during school closure due to COVID-19. Jpn. Econ. Rev. **72**, 471–507 (2021)

96. DeCoito, I., Estaiteyeh, M.: Online teaching during the COVID-19 pandemic: exploring science/STEM teachers' curriculum and assessment practices in Canada. Discip Interdscip Sci Educ Res. **4** (2022)

97. Akhtar, M.H., Ramkumar, J.: Primary Health Center: Can it be made mobile for efficient healthcare services for hard to reach population? A state-of-the-art review. Discov Health Systems **2** (2023)

98. Utami, A.D.W., Arif, S., Satrio, P.U.D.: Understanding usability and user experience cloud-based learning management system from teacher review. In: 2021 7th International Conference on Electrical, Electronics and Information Engineering (ICEEIE). IEEE (2021)

99. Ochnio, L., Rokicki, T., Czech, K., Koszela, G., Hamulczuk, M., Perkowska, A.: Were the higher education institutions prepared for the challenge of online learning? students' satisfaction survey in the aftermath of the COVID-19 pandemic outbreak. Sustainability. **14**, 11813 (2022). https://doi.org/10.3390/su141911813

100. Hassan, R., Murad, D.F., Wahi, W., Wijanarko, B.D., Asmak Ismail, N.H., Awwad, S.A.B.: Online learning experience assessment survey during the covid-19 pandemic. In: 2022 International Conference on Information Management and Technology (ICIMTech), pp. 133–138. IEEE (2022)

101. Ferri, F., Grifoni, P., Guzzo, T.: Online learning and emergency remote teaching: opportunities and challenges in emergency situations. Societies (Basel). **10**, 86 (2020). https://doi.org/10.3390/soc10040086

102. Arslan, A., Haapanen, L., Tarba, S.: Prosocial skills development in children and social value creation during COVID -19. Strateg. Change. **30**, 109–115 (2021). https://doi.org/10.1002/jsc.2394

103. Galkienė, A., Monkevičienė, O., Kaminskienė, L., Krikštolaitis, R., Käsper, M., Ivanova, I.: Modeling the sustainable educational process for pupils from vulnerable groups in critical situations: COVID-19 context in Lithuania, Latvia, and Estonia. Sustainability. **14**, 1748 (2022). https://doi.org/10.3390/su14031748

104. Prasetyanto, D., Rizki, M., Sunitiyoso, Y.: Online learning participation intention after COVID-19 pandemic in Indonesia: do students still make trips for online class? Sustainability **14**, 1982 (2022)

105. Martínez-García, R., Fraile-Fernández, F.J., Búrdalo-Salcedo, G., Castañón-García, A.M., Fernández-Raga, M., Palencia, C.: Satisfaction level of engineering students in face-to-face and online modalities under COVID-19—case: school of engineering of the university of León. Spain. Sustainability **14**, 6269 (2022)

106. Resch, K., Alnahdi, G., Schwab, S.: Exploring the effects of the COVID-19 emergency remote education on students' social and academic integration in higher education in Austria. High. Educ. Res. Dev. **42**, 215–229 (2023)

107. Papouli, E., Chatzifotiou, S., Tsairidis, C.: The use of digital technology at home during the COVID-19 outbreak: views of social work students in Greece. Soc. Work. Educ. **39**, 1107–1115 (2020)

108. Sa, S., Cruz, M.L.: Using a valid game-based learning activity to practice communication competencies online. In: 2021 4th International Conference of the Portuguese Society for Engineering Education (CISPEE), pp. 1–6. IEEE

109. Barrera G, M.I., Benalcazar Ch., D., San Lucas S, DC: Gamification in the teaching of prevention measures for Covid-19. In: 2022 IEEE Global Engineering Education Conference (EDUCON), pp. 1512–1516. IEEE (2022)
110. Purwanto, E.S., Danielson, Flawrenxius, K., Anderson, B., Sari, A.C.: Students experience testing in the implementation of the "gather town" meeting platform as an alternative learning media other than zoom cloud meeting application. In: 2022 4th International Conference on Cybernetics and Intelligent System (ICORIS), pp. 1–8. IEEE
111. Bello, K.A., Maladzhi, R.W., Kanakana-Katumba, M.G., Bolaji, B.O.: Disruptive technologies in engineering education: a case study. In: IEEE IFEES World Engineering Education Forum - Global Engineering Deans Council. IEEE (2022)
112. Muheidat, F., Tawalbeh, L.: ZOOM sandwich: an adaptable model for distance learning. In: 2020 International Conference on Computational Science and Computational Intelligence (CSCI), pp. 1004–1008. IEEE (2020)
113. Fonseca, N.G., Macedo, L., Mendes, A.J.: The importance of using the CodeInsights monitoring tool to support teaching programming in the context of a pandemic. In: 2021 IEEE Frontiers in Education Conference (FIE)
114. Fulzele, R., Jain, R., Fulzele, V., Kaur, A.: A new paradigm of learning: Evaluation of higher education students' preferences for online meeting platform. In: 2021 International Conference on Computational Performance Evaluation (ComPE), pp. 662–666. IEEE (2021)
115. Ratnaningsih, S., Miswan, Hady, Y., Sari Dewi, R., Fahriany, Zuhdi, M.: The effectiveness of using edmodo-based E-learning in the blended learning process to increase student motivation and learning outcomes. In: 2020 8th International Conference on Cyber and IT Service Management (CITSM), pp. 1–5. IEEE (2020)
116. Mrayed, S.M.: Using Edmodo online application as a supplement to enhance student level of performance and critical thinking in the learning process of Thermodynamic course. In: 2020 Sixth International Conference on e-Learning (econf), pp. 390–394. IEEE (2020)
117. Nursisda Mawangi, P.A., Yoto, Pramudhita, A.N.: Life-based E-learning models in mechatronics. In: 2020 4th International Conference on Vocational Education and Training (ICOVET), pp. 195–198. IEEE (2020)
118. Alexandrescu, A., Butnaru, G.: An architecture of identity management and thirdparty integration for online teaching in a university. In: 2020 24th International Conference on System Theory, Control and Computing, pp. 850–855. IEEE (2020)
119. Panda, S., Chowdhury, N.A., Deshmukh, A.: TEDxEdisonHighSchool: a template for virtual TEDx conferences. In: 2021 IEEE Integrated STEM Education Conference (ISEC), p. 226. IEEE (2021)
120. de Souza Castro, V., Ronaldo Bezerra Oliveira, S.: An analysis of application the kahoot! Tool in a gamified approach to face-to-face and emergency remote teaching and learning of software engineering. In: 2022 IEEE Frontiers in Education Conference (FIE), pp. 1–8. IEEE (2022)
121. Cook-Chennault, K., Cummings, D., Anthony, M., Balar, T., Izzell, L., Boone, S., Watson, C.: What informal learning programs teach us about adaptation to contactless and remote learning environments. In: 2021 IEEE Frontiers in Education Conference (FIE), pp. 1–8. IEEE (2021)
122. Ruberg, P., Ellervee, P., Tammemae, K., Reinsalu, U., Rahni, A., Robal, T.: Surviving the unforeseen – teaching IT and engineering students during COVID-19 outbreak. In: 2022 IEEE Frontiers in Education Conference (FIE)
123. Wijayati, R.D., Nuryana, Z., Pranolo, A., Ma'Arif, A., Sularso, Suyadi: Higher education response to the COVID-19: Do students feel comfortable studying with distance learning? In: 2022 XII International Conference on Virtual Campus (JICV), pp. 1–6. IEEE (2022)

124. Ay, S., Karabatak, S., Karabatak, M.: The relationship between teacher candidates' technology usage and online learning readiness. In: 2022 10th International Symposium on Digital Forensics and Security. IEEE (2022)
125. Andrade-Arenas, L., Nunez, D.L., Sotomayor-Beltran, C.: Leveraging digital tools for a better virtual teaching-learning process in a private university of Lima. In: 2021 IEEE World Conference on Engineering Education, pp. 1–5. IEEE (2021)
126. Trujillo-Aguilera, F.D., Blazquez-Parra, E.B., De La Paz-Morgado, J.: Adapting power electronics to the flipped classroom for internationalisation. In: 2021 XI International Conference on Virtual Campus, pp. 1–4. IEEE (2021)
127. Ismail, H., Khafaji, H., Fasla, H., Younis, A.R., Harous, S.: A cognitive style-based usability evaluation of zoom and teams for online lecturing activities. In: 2021 IEEE Global Engineering Education Conference, pp. 1565–1570. IEEE (2021)
128. Choquehuanca, E.G., Aguilar-Calero, E., Saldana-Manche, W., Iraola-Real, I.: Evaluation of virtual performance of teachers of the professional career of initial education of a private university in Lima - Peru. In: 2021 IEEE Sciences and Humanities International Research Conference (SHIRCON), pp. 1–4. IEEE (2021)
129. Ma, X., Azemi, A., Buechler, D.: Integrating Microsoft teams to promote active learning in online lecture and lab courses. In: 2021 IEEE Frontiers in Education Conference (FIE), pp. 1–9. IEEE (2021)
130. Prestiadi, D., Wiyono, B.B., Mustabsyiroh, N.: Analysis of online learning media at SIPEJAR as a learning management system (LMS) during the covid-19 pandemic in improving student performance. In: 2021 7th International Conference on Education and Technology (ICET), pp. 74–80. IEEE (2021)
131. Nur Hidayat, W., Suswanto, H., Wijaya Kristanto, C., Pramudya Wardhani, A., Hamdan, A., Kartika Sari, R.: The effectiveness of interactive digital evaluation training for improving teacher skills in the covid-19 pandemic period. In: 4th International Conference on Vocational Education and Training (ICOVET), pp. 310–314. IEEE (2020)
132. Rohman, M., Suyono, Wiyono, A., Baskoro, F.: Combination of moodle online learning application (vilearning UNESA) and Google classroom to improve the quality of online learning. In: 2021 Fourth International Conference on Vocational Education and Electrical Engineering (ICVEE), pp. 1–6. IEEE (2021)
133. Djojo, B.W., Hafizh, W., Gui, A., Shaharudin, M.S., Made Karmawan, I.G., Suryanto: Analysist acceptance of video conference at zoom application using technology acceptance model. In: 2021 8th International Conference on Information Technology, Computer and Electrical Engineering (ICITACEE), pp. 18–23. IEEE (2021)
134. Spernjak, A.: Using ICT to teach effectively at COVID-19. In: 2021 44th International Convention on Information, Communication and Electronic Technology (MIPRO), pp. 617–620. IEEE (2021)
135. Juhary, J.: Padlet for remote learning: Lessons learned. In: 2021 Universitas Riau International Conference on Education Technology (URICET), pp. 291–296. IEEE (2021)
136. Pilakasiri, A., Nivatwongs, S., Ratanathummawat, S.: Preparedness of blended education prior to SARS-COV-2 pandemic via Google classroom for the fifth year medical students, otolaryngology rotation. In: 2022 International Conference on Digital Government Technology and Innovation (DGTi-CON), pp. 71–75. IEEE (2022)
137. Abushamleh, H., Jusoh, S.: Usability evaluation of distance education tools used in Jordanian universities. In: 2021 Innovation and New Trends in Engineering, Science and Technology Education Conference, pp. 1–5. IEEE (2021)
138. Wiyono, B.B., Hadi, S., Imron, A., Indreswari, H.: Use of information technology in online learning process applied by the lecturers based on the education and rank level. In: 2021 10th International Conference on Educational and Information Technology (ICEIT), pp. 144–149. IEEE (2021)

139. Jacques, S., Ouahabi, A., Lequeu, T.: Synchronous E-learning in higher education during the COVID-19 pandemic. In: 2021 IEEE Global Engineering Education Conference (EDUCON), pp. 1102–1109. IEEE (2021)

140. Reynoso, M.M., Bibangco, E.J.P., Dormido, J.M.D.: Usability of cloud-based learning management systems among the selected higher education institutions in Negros occidental: a comparative analysis. In: 2022 IEEE 7th International Conference on Information Technology and Digital Applications (ICITDA), pp. 1–9. IEEE (2022)

141. Lewis, D.: What scientists have learnt from COVID lockdowns. Nature **609**, 236–239 (2022)

142. Venkat, V., Kunadharaju, I.: Edison high school WiSTEM | FOCUS: addressing female underrepresentation in STEM. In: 2021 IEEE Integrated STEM Education Conference (ISEC), p. 221. IEEE (2021)

143. Lottin, J., et al.: Reduce academic fatigue and enhance retention for the determined ones (TDOs) in online learning. In: Sustainable Leadership and Academic Excellence International Conference (SLAE), pp. 1–5. IEEE (2021)

144. Vinodha, Deshmukh, V.M., Rath, S.: Secured online learning in COVID-19 pandemic using deep learning methods. In: IEEE International Conference on Mobile Networks and Wireless Communications, pp. 1–5. IEEE (2021)

145. Maniar, S., Sukhani, K., Shah, K., Dhage, S.: Automated proctoring system using computer vision techniques. In: 2021 International Conference on System, Computation, Automation and Networking (ICSCAN), pp. 1–6. IEEE

146. Sasikumar, S., Prabha, S., Reddy Chandra, N.B., Suravarapu, D., Goda, RK: Students live behavior monitoring in online classes. In: 2022 6th International Conference on Intelligent Computing and Control Systems, pp. 1749–1755. IEEE (2022)

147. Munemo, R.T., Gundidza, P.: Online learning a rude wake-up call on inclusive education in Zimbabwean university context. In: 3rd International Multidisciplinary Information Technology and Engineering Conference, pp. 1–7. IEEE (2021)

148. Rahman, M.M., Morgan, R.P.: A remote instructional approach with interactive and collaborative learning to teach an introductory programming course during COVID-19 pandemic. In: 2021 International Conference on Computational Science and Computational Intelligence (CSCI), pp. 940–946. IEEE (2021)

149. Butko, L., Vasylenko, D., Fedorenko, S., Dobryden, O., Martynyshyn, Y.: Summarizing the experience of using educational online platforms in Ukrainian universities. In: 2022 IEEE 4th International Conference on Modern Electrical and Energy System (MEES), pp. 1–5. IEEE (2022)

150. Edy, D.L., Widiyanti, Basuki: Revisiting the impact of project-based learning on online learning in vocational education: Analysis of learning in pandemic covid-19. In: 2020 4th International Conference on Vocational Education and Training (ICOVET), pp. 378–381. IEEE (2020)

151. Zagirniak, D., Sizova, K., Bilous, R., Soshenko, S., Herasymenko, L., Shmeleva, A.: Academic performance' dynamics of generation Z representatives (electrical engineering students and other specialties) during the transition to E-learning in covid-19 crisis. In: IEEE International Conference on Modern Electrical and Energy Systems, pp. 1–4. IEEE (2021)

152. Chierichetti, M., Backer, P.R.: Student Experiences after the move to fully online instruction: A case study of one large public institution. In: 2021 IEEE Frontiers in Education Conference (FIE), pp. 1–9. IEEE (2021)

153. Yahuarcani, I.O., et al.: Study of the quality of virtual university services at the National University of the Peruvian Amazon, during the COVID-19 pandemic. In: IEEE World Conference on Engineering Education, pp. 1–5. IEEE (2021)

154. Merzlikina, E.I., Dolbikova, N.S., Kuznetsova, A.V., Farafonov, G.V.: Automation and measurement classes for power engineering students in the online-mode. In: 2021 44th International Convention on Information, Communication and Electronic Technology (MIPRO), pp. 1576–1580. IEEE (2021)
155. Dahnoun, N.: Pedagogy for engineering and digital pedagogy. In: 2020 9th Mediterranean Conference on Embedded Computing (MECO), p. 1. IEEE (2020)
156. Djeki, E., Degila, J., Bondiombouy, C., Alhassan, M.H.: Security issues in digital learning spaces. In: 2021 IEEE International Conference on Computing (ICOCO), pp. 71–77. IEEE (2021)
157. Lara, E., Garcia, J., Minero, JJ: Teaching programming experiences in times of COVID-19 in the state of Zacatecas. In: 2021 10th International Conference On Software Process Improvement, pp. 98–104. IEEE (2021)
158. Nazar, N., Darvishi, I., Yeboah-Ofori, A.: Cyber threat analysis on online learning and its mitigation techniques amid covid-19. In: 2022 IEEE International Smart Cities Conference (ISC2), pp. 1–7. IEEE (2022)
159. Stewart, R., Metz, C.: SCTP: new transport protocol for TCP/IP. IEEE Internet Comput. **5**, 64–69 (2001)
160. Klimova, B.: An insight into online foreign language learning and teaching in the era of COVID-19 pandemic. Procedia Comput. Sci. **192**, 1787–1794 (2021). https://doi.org/10.1016/j.procs.2021.08.183
161. Butrime, E.: Virtual learning environments and learning change in modern higher education during the covid-19 Coronavirus pandemic: Attitudes of university teachers. In: Advances in Intelligent Systems and Computing, pp. 222–231. Springer International Publishing, Cham (2021)
162. Bergdahl, N., Nouri, J.: Covid-19 and crisis-prompted distance education in Sweden. Technol. Knowl. Learn. **26** (2021)
163. Rapanta, C., Botturi, L., Goodyear, P., Guàrdia, L., Koole, M.: Balancing technology, pedagogy and the new normal: Post-pandemic challenges for higher education. Postdigit Sci Educ. **3**, 715–742 (2021)
164. Ermenc, K.S., Kalin, J., Mažgon, J.: How to run an empty school: The experience of Slovenian school heads during the COVID-19 pandemic. SAGE Open **11**, 215824402110321 (2021)
165. Nishimura, Y., et al.: Impact of the COVID-19 pandemic on the psychological distress of medical students in japan: Cross-sectional survey study. J. Med. Internet
166. López-Valenciano, A., Suárez-Iglesias, D., Sanchez-Lastra, M.A., Ayán, C.: Impact of COVID-19 pandemic on university students' physical activity levels: an early systematic review. Front. Psychol. **11**, 624567 (2020)
167. Carvalho, P.M.M., Moreira, M.M., de Oliveira, M.N.A., Landim, J.M.M., Neto, M.L.R.: The psychiatric impact of the novel coronavirus outbreak. Psychiatry Res. **286**, 112902 (2020)
168. Velichová, Ľ., Orbánová, D., Kúbeková, A.: The COVID-19 pandemic: Unique opportunity to develop online learning. TEM J. 1633–1639 (2020). https://doi.org/10.18421/tem94-40
169. Babbar, M., Gupta, T.: Response of educational institutions to COVID-19 pandemic: an inter-country comparison. Pol. Futur. Educ. **20**, 469–491 (2022). https://doi.org/10.1177/14782103211021937
170. Hadi, M.O.: Cross Sectional Study Comparing the Quality of Life, Academic Stress, Ethnic Identification and Alcohol Use of Norwegian and International Students and Examining the Relationship between these Variables. https://oda.oslomet.no/oda-xmlui/bitstream/handle/10642/7068/Hadi.pdf?sequence=2. Accessed 24 June 2023
171. Google Trends. https://trends.google.com/trends/. Accessed 24 June 2023

172. Jun, S.-P., Yoo, H.S., Choi, S.: Ten years of research change using Google Trends: From the perspective of big data utilizations and applications. Technol. Forecast. Soc. Change. **130**, 69–87 (2018)
173. Mierswa, I., Wurst, M., Klinkenberg, R., Scholz, M., Euler, T.: YALE: Rapid prototyping for complex data mining tasks. In: Proceedings of the 12th ACM SIGKDD international conference on Knowledge discovery and data mining. ACM, New York, NY, USA (2006)
174. Likas, A., Vlassis, N., Verbeek, J.: The global k-means clustering algorithm. Pattern Recognit. **36**, 451–461 (2003). https://doi.org/10.1016/s0031-3203(02)00060-2
175. Wilkinson, M.D., et al.: The FAIR Guiding Principles for scientific data management and stewardship. Sci. Data. **3**, 160018 (2016)

The Application of KANO Model in the Design of Children's Interactive Educational Products

Xiaomeng Wang[✉], Ting Yang, Yue Zhang, and Shan Xu

Guangxi Normal University, Guilin 541006, China
18763278583@163.com

Abstract. The common design elements are extracted from the existing children's interactive products, and the KANO model is applied to analyze the users' design needs and make innovative designs according to the users' requirements for the products. From the perspective of design thinking and consumer preference, we meticulously classify the design principles and attributes of consumer preference, and use the KANO model to quantitatively and qualitatively analyze the valid recall samples. Based on the preliminary research and KANO model analysis, relevant strategies about children's interactive product design are proposed. The common design elements are extracted from the existing children's interactive products, and the KANO model is used to obtain the design elements of users' needs for children's interactive toys and accurately locate their design elements in order to design products that meet users' needs and experience expectations. Through the application of KANO model, a new idea is proposed for the innovative design of children's interactive products, which helps designers to make comprehensive design decisions and improve the competitiveness of product design.

Keywords: KANO model · Interaction · Education · Children's products · User needs

1 Introduction

Children's cameras have become a popular product in the camera market in recent years. However, many children's cameras simply record photos or videos and lack interactive and educational designs. In order to deeply explore a wider range of consumers' perceived needs for children's educational camera products, this paper uses questionnaire design and KANO model data analysis to obtain consumers' ideas about product needs. Therefore, through the application of KANO model, from the perspective of children users and combined with user research and demand analysis, an intelligent interactive camera product for children's animal science education is designed, aiming to provide a more fun and educational camera experience for children. The camera's function can identify the animals taken, while introducing animal-related information through voice broadcast, and the camera is connected to parents' cell phones, so that parents can observe the content taken by their children in real time through their cell phones to ensure the safety of their children.

2 Definition

2.1 KANO Model Theory

The KANO model is a qualitative analysis model of "functionality" and "satisfaction", which was originally proposed by Professor Noriaki Kano of the Tokyo Institute of Technology in Japan and has become a widely used product design method. By understanding the different types of user needs for a product, it can help designers to design product functions to better meet the needs and expectations of users [1]. The basic requirements are the foundation of product design. The basic needs are the basis of product design and must be satisfied; the desired needs are those that can provide the competitiveness and value of the upgraded product, and at the same time enhance the user's experience; the excited needs refer to some surprising experiences that the user gets when using the product beyond expectations, these experiences add uniqueness to the product and can also bring a strong sense of satisfaction to the user. In the real application, KANO model is often combined with user research, through questionnaires, user interviews, user experience testing and other methods to obtain the user's reaction and evaluation of the product. By analyzing these responses and evaluations, we can determine the basic needs, expectations and surprises of the product, and design products that better meet the needs and expectations of users. The product can be designed to better meet users' needs and expectations [2].

2.2 Brief Description of Interaction Design Concept

The creation of interaction as a behavior is closely related to people. The interaction design concept of children's educational products includes putting user experience first, designing according to user orientation, providing timely and accurate feedback, interesting interaction process, simple operation process and healthy safety. In the design process, designers should pay attention to the cognitive characteristics and learning ability of children and adopt appropriate visual elements and operation methods to improve the ease of use, comprehensibility, and attractiveness of the products, and also need to strengthen the safety and security mechanisms to avoid problems such as undesirable content and leakage of privacy information to ensure the healthy growth of children. In the process of interaction design of children's educational products, tests and evaluations need to be conducted to detect whether the product design meets the cognitive characteristics and learning ability of children, and to obtain timely feedback and evaluation results through questionnaire analysis and user surveys to optimize the product design [3]. At the same time, it is necessary to focus on user feedback and needs to continuously improve and update the products. From the perspective of interactive product design, the integration of interaction design concepts in children's educational products is to give children a better experience, and the design of children's interactive educational products must be planned in an integrated manner in terms of function, interaction form, form and connotation, making the entertainment and education coexist and allowing the product itself to be enhanced in terms of interactivity, connotation and intuitiveness [4].

2.3 Relevance of Kano Model to Children's Interactive Educational Products

The KANO model and children's interactive education products are closely related. By applying the KANO model, we can better meet the needs of children's interactive education products and improve the quality and user satisfaction of the products. First of all, the basic requirements in the KANO model may include the ease of use of the product, clear operation interface, good safety and security mechanism, etc. These basic requirements can be considered as the basic features of the product, the lack of which will lead to users' dissatisfaction and complaints. Secondly, expectation needs are users' expectation and anticipation of the product. Visual design, abundant content, etc., can be considered as competitive features of the product, and the lack of these features will lead to less choice of the product and make users doubtful. Finally, excitement needs include innovative interaction methods and personalized learning experiences of the product, which are motivating features of the product that can increase user satisfaction and loyalty, and promote the promotion and development of the product [5].

Therefore, designers can determine the basic, desired, and excited needs of the product according to the classification of the KANO model, and also use market research methods, such as questionnaires and user tests, to evaluate the relationship between product features and user needs, and improve and optimize the product based on the evaluation results to meet the relationship between user needs and product features to provide product competitiveness and user satisfaction.

3 User Needs Analysis

3.1 Targeting People and Demand Gathering

This design takes the theory of interaction design as the starting point, uses the KANO model to distinguish the demand attributes, mainly for children's education products for innovative design, the user orientation design to 6–12 years old children as the main user group, this age of children's inner world is rich and wonderful, has a very strong imagination, full of curiosity about things, with a certain dependence on psychology, lively and active, eager to get praise. By studying the consumer psychology and needs and desires of the target users, we can provide the basis and reference for the style formation of product design and product design optimization. Children in this period have the characteristics of consumer intuitive psychology, children's emotions and interest in products often originate from the influence of product characteristics, they are easily attracted by toys with simple structure, bright colors and strong interactivity [6]. And because young children know little about products and consumer use experience, they are less concerned about product brands and quality and will buy based on intuition. They also have consumer curiosity and consumer dependence, and children are naive, childish, and have fairy-tale imaginations, and these characteristics are more evident in their purchasing behavior.

Combining the needs of each level of users into children's education products, the user portrait in Fig. 1 is shown. User profile construction is the process of converging similar user needs. Combining user needs with design goals establishes the right user model to fulfill user needs, which is then incorporated into the actual product design development. The intention to use the educational product is derived by talking to the users and organizing the user information data [7].

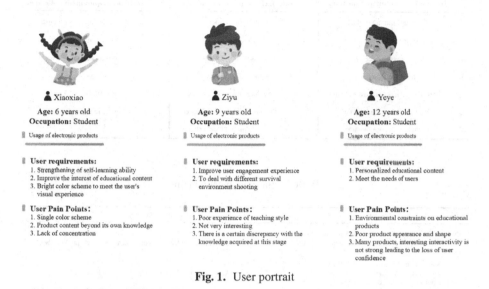

Fig. 1. User portrait

3.2   KANO Questionnaire Design

Through the above analysis of child users and educational interactive products, the questionnaire is now designed according to the five different categories of the Kano model, namely, needs that must be satisfied, needs that are expected to be satisfied, needs that are not apparently concerned but will increase satisfaction, needs that are not thought of but are still useful and needs that are unnecessary but still provide value. Based on the user needs information in Table 1, the two-factor questionnaire design of the KANO model was conducted for the users. Some parts of the research questionnaire are presented in Table 2 [8].

In the specific questionnaire design, appropriate adjustments and additions can be made according to the actual situation of the product. When designing the questionnaire, attention should be paid to the simplicity and clarity of the heavy questions, and try to avoid complex or ambiguous questions. At the same time, it should also consider all aspects of the product as comprehensively as possible, and issue from the perspective of user needs, questionnaire design and survey to facilitate a better understanding of user needs and preferences, to improve the competitiveness of the product and market share.

3.3   Analysis of the Results of the KANO Mode

The KANO questionnaire was designed to locate user needs as a function point, and each questionnaire set one positive and one negative, and set the satisfaction level as very satisfied, deserved, indifferent, barely accepted, and very dissatisfied, and then the

Table.1. Organize user demand information

No.	Interface requirement indicators	No.	Interface requirement indicators	No.	Interface requirement indicators
X_1	Clear interaction interface	X_8	Operation History	X_{15}	Reasonable price of products
X_2	Easy and simple to operate	X_9	Moderate jump speed	X_{16}	Enough storage space
X_3	Highly recognizable screen	X_{10}	Color matching coordination	X_{17}	Waterproof and functional
X_4	Minimalist appearance	X_{11}	Sound safety and security	X_{18}	Easy maintenance
X_5	Personalized function customization	X_{12}	Science education function	X_{19}	Bluetooth Quick Connect
X_6	High animal recognition rate	X_{13}	Gesture interaction experience	X_{20}	Device reminder function
X_7	Language prompt function	X_{14}	Strong sense of product interest		

Table 2. Sample questionnaire

Question	Satisfaction
Positive question: What would you say if the children's interactive educational camera had a clear interactive interface?	Enjoyed it As it should be Doesn't matter Reluctantly accept Very dislike
Reverse question: What is your evaluation if the children's interactive educational camera does not have the function of clear interactive interface?	Enjoyed it As it should be Doesn't matter Reluctantly accept Very dislike

questionnaire survey was conducted on users. The total number of questionnaires was 101, and 101 valid questionnaires were obtained after the questionnaires were collected. Then, the statistical data of the questionnaires were referred to the Kano evaluation model to obtain the relationship between user needs and the quality characteristics of children's interactive education products.

Where Mi indicates the number of the ith demand selected as basic demand, Oi indicates the number of the ith demand selected as expectation demand, Ai indicates the number of the ith demand selected as excitement demand, Ii indicates the number of the ith demand selected as undifferentiated demand, Ri indicates the number of the ith demand selected as reverse demand, Qi indicates the number of the ith demand selected as problem demand, and Xi denotes the attribute categorization of the ith demand. The attribute categorization Xi is the largest one among Mi, Oi, Ai, Ii, Ri, and Qi, for example, if Mi is the largest, then Xi is M, which means the requirement is a basic requirement (Table 3).

The obtained data are first organized with reference to the Kano evaluation table, and then the maximum value is taken for individual demand attributes to determine the type of demand to which they belong. The product quality characteristics are determined by the highest quantitative value in the statistics of the interactive demand attributes [9]. The relative satisfaction Si (Eq. 1) and relative dissatisfaction (DSi) were obtained and calculated as follows:

$$SI_i = (A_i + O_i)/(A_i + O_i + M_i + I_i) \qquad (1)$$

Table 3. Results of the questionnaire research

Function / Service	Demand	Ai%	Oi%	Mi%	Ii%	Ri%	Qi%	Classification Result
X_1	Clear interaction interface	5	46	8	33	3	5	O
X_2	Easy and simple to operate	5	8	7	26	5	4	M
X_3	Highly recognizable screen	42	10	1	7	38	2	A
X_4	Minimalist appearance	8	2	54	31	5	0	M
X_5	Personalized function customization	2	45	8	23	20	2	O
X_6	High animal recognition rate	8	0	7	45	39	1	I
X_7	Language prompt function	50	7	9	28	5	1	A
X_8	Operation History	4	4	3	49	39	1	I
X_9	Moderate jump speed	4	63	8	2	4	19	O
X_{10}	Color matching coordination	8	54	8	21	5	4	O
X_{11}	Sound safety and security	8	9	56	19	7	1	M
X_{12}	Science education function	16	34	8	20	12	8	O
X_{13}	Gesture interaction experience	46	1	5	26	12	10	A
X_{14}	Strong sense of product interest	3	38	5	40	13	1	O
X_{15}	Reasonable price of products	4	0	6	6	28	2	I
X_{16}	Enough storage space	5	4	60	12	5	5	M
X_{17}	Waterproof and functional	6	3	56	4	3	1	M
X_{18}	Easy maintenance	8	2	8	45	37	0	I
X_{19}	Bluetooth Quick Connect	46	3	7	34	8	2	A
X_{20}	Device reminder function	5	4	6	47	36	2	I

$$DI_i = (M_i + O_i)/(A_i + O_i + M_i + I_i) \tag{2}$$

The Kano model questionnaire was distributed, and by calculating the data in the recovered questionnaires, the requirements were categorized, and finally the final analysis results were obtained by calculating the user satisfaction. It can be seen that the interactive interface is clear, personalized function customization, moderate jump speed, color coordination, and strong sense of product fun belong to the desired demand, convenient and simple operation, simple appearance, sound security, large enough storage space, and strong waterproof function belong to the basic essential demand, high animal recognition rate, operation history record, reasonable product price, easy maintenance, and equipment reminder function belong to the undifferentiated demand The rest belong to the excited demand. For these needs, the later product model design is focused [10].

4 Design Principles of Interactive Educational Products for Children

4.1 Exploratory Principle

Children will actively explore to learn and recognize new things. The product should be able to be experienced by children right from the hand, encourage children to explore and discover on their own, and provide opportunities for independent learning in order to foster children's creativity and spirit of exploration. Clear and concise interaction, simple visual hierarchy, and positive guiding feedback are the prerequisites to ensure that children are allowed to explore freely, diversify learning content, customize learning content and learning styles to children's personalities and interests, challenge children's learning interests and intellectual levels, and allow children to choose their own learning content and learning styles; therefore, the exploratory principle makes the product more innovative and personalized [11].

4.2 Interesting Principle

In the design of children's interactive products, focus on increasing the fun and attractiveness of the products to enhance children's learning interest and motivation. Children are naturally fond of playing and transforming the learning process into a game, and they like to learn in a game rather than a monotonous way of learning. Therefore, it is very important to focus on the principle of fun in the design of interactive products for children. For example, voice interaction, virtual reality, etc., by photographing animals, the camera can voice broadcast information about the animals and the sounds they make, which can make children feel that the product is very novel and interesting, thus increasing children's interest and motivation in learning. In short, focusing on the principle of fun can make children's interactive products more attractive and competitive, so that children can have more fun and sense of achievement in the learning process and improve their learning motivation [12].

4.3 Security Principle

The principle of security means that in the design of children's interactive products, attention should be paid to ensuring the security of the products and the privacy of users, ensuring that children are not exposed to undesirable content when using the products, and avoiding adverse effects on children. In order to ensure the safety and reasonableness of children's use of the product, parental monitoring functions can be provided to allow parents to monitor and manage children's use behavior; filtering undesirable content, limiting children's online activities, limiting children's use time, etc., to ensure that children are exposed to safe and harmless content when using the next product. The product is more secure and reliable in order to protect children's safety and privacy and promote the long-term development and promotion of the product [13].

4.4 The Principle of Both Educational and Entertaining

Balance the relationship between education and entertainment, so that the product is both interesting and has learning functions to meet children's learning and entertainment needs. The products allow children to learn in games through interesting interactive forms or elements such as music and video, thus improving the learning effect; they also allow children to learn in various ways such as listening, watching and touching, enhancing the diversity and flexibility of learning. In today's market, products that are both educational and entertaining can better attract children's attention and interest, as well as meet parents' expectations for children's learning, and have higher market competitiveness and commercial value.

4.5 Emotional Principle

In the actual product design, the emotionality principle should run through the whole design process, from demand research, user research to product design, all should focus on the influence and embodiment of emotionality. First, in the demand research and user research stage, understand children's feelings and expressions in order to design products that meet children's emotions. Second, in product design, emotions should be expressed in a variety of ways, such as bright, rich colors and sound effects, to enhance the emotional expression of the product. In the user interface design, a simple, intuitive and easy-to-use design is used so that children can operate the products independently and easily and can have a pleasant emotional experience. Emotional design can also develop children's emotional competence and emotional intelligence, help children better understand and express their emotions, and promote their healthy growth [14].

5   Children's Interactive Educational Product Design Practice

Based on the quantitative and qualitative user research, the user needs are further analyzed with the help of KANO model. Through questionnaire design and KANO attribute analysis, the product's function points are divided so as to determine the attributes of the product's function points, followed by calculating the satisfaction and dissatisfaction coefficients of each function point with the help of Kano satisfaction coefficient formula, and calculating the user needs can be divided into four categories: expectation-based needs, basic needs, undifferentiated needs, and excitement-based needs [15].

5.1 Analysis of Functional Requirements

Desired needs include a clear interactive interface, personalized function customization, moderate jump speed, color coordination, strong sense of product fun five functional needs, part of the camera color matching and personality customization performance is not strong, the color should choose bright colors, according to the characteristics, taking into account the age group using the product, breaking the stereotypical impression of the previous product to people black and white gray color scheme. Basic needs include convenient and simple operation, simple appearance, sound safety and security, storage space is large enough, waterproof functional five needs, operation, a clear division of the area is necessary. Children are under-aged, have low awareness of safety using the Internet, and are vulnerable to bad information, so in order to create a green and healthy Internet environment, it is extremely important to strengthen children's Internet education and management [16]. In the undifferentiated demand there are five functional needs of high animal recognition rate, operation history record, reasonable product price, easy maintenance, and equipment reminder function, and some products have less satisfaction in terms of charging, and the process of connecting the product to the charging device often bends leading to wire damage and weak security, after which the product design should take this into account, and the charging interface can be adopted with concave hidden design, and the charging interface Directly connected to the internal product, reducing the opportunity for children to contact the charging interface, the remaining five points belong to the excitement of the demand. Traditional cameras have complicated operating interfaces that are not suitable for children, and their lenses are easily damaged on wet or rainy days and need careful protection. Some children's cameras were selected for comparison and their advantages and disadvantages were analyzed, as shown in Table 4.

5.2 Design Description

The design of the children's educational interactive camera, compared with the traditional camera, more lightweight and easy to operate, suitable for children aged 6–12 years old, its price is moderate with drop-proof, waterproof features, soft colors and a variety of colors for parents to choose, but also independent customization of the camera's corresponding function keys, convenient for children to use. When children use the camera to photograph animals, the camera will broadcast information about the photographed animals and simulate animal sounds, and children deepen their perception of different animals through visual and auditory senses by using and playing with the camera on a daily basis, and the camera has a touch screen function to zoom in and observe the details of micro and small animals [17]. It is a breakthrough from the traditional books with a single text-based learning method and is more interesting and interactive. The time children spend using the camera instead of playing mobile games protects their eyesight while guiding them from the virtual online game world to real life, allowing them to

Table. 4. Comparative analysis of children's cameras

Competitive products	Price	Advantage and disadvantage analysis
Platypus simulation camera	¥40	**Advantages:** High brightness and high saturation color matching and cartoon image for children's interests. **Disadvantages:** It is only a toy in the shape of a camera, and does not have the camera function. This kind of camera is widely used in children's cameras in China.
Little tikes camera	¥1000	**Pros:** Fantastic styling, beautiful packaging, safe materials, powerful zoom function, can be filmed underwater. **Disadvantages:** High price, low pixel, modeling is too abstract, which makes it difficult to recognize the camera.
Nikon S560	¥780	**Pros:** Nikon VR optical shock absorption system, configuration, built-in CCO image sensor and 5x Nikkor optical zoom lens. **Disadvantages:** The styling is too adult, and the metal body makes children feel distant
Pentax WG-10	¥1400	**Pros:** Race-car design, dust and cold resistance, waterproof and anti-fall. **Disadvantages:** Although children aged 9-12 years old are mature, they still pursue new, special and strange consumer psychology. The current model is only suitable for some children who love racing cars.

keep an eye on the life around them to recognize the diversity of species and understand how to better live in harmony with natural creatures. Parents can use the cell phone to associate with the interactive camera to understand their children's learning trends, which can be used as a daily communication topic to focus on the physical and mental growth of children and make the parent-child relationship more harmonious (Figs. 2 and 3).

5.3 Design Display

Fig. 2. Design display

Fig. 3. Design display

6 Conclusion

This paper provides a comprehensive and in-depth analysis and discussion of children's interactive educational product design by exploring in depth the KANO model theory, interaction design principles, and the relevance of the KANO model to children's interactive educational products. In the product design and development process, the characteristics and needs of children should be fully considered, and design principles and concepts consistent with pedagogy and other related disciplines should be adopted to improve the safety, reliability, emotion and entertainment of the product, so as to achieve the improvement of user satisfaction and market competitiveness of the product. In the actual product design and development of children's interactive education products, the design principles and concepts proposed in this paper can be combined with the analysis and application of the KANO model to design children's interactive education products that are more high-quality, efficient, convenient, safe, emotional and entertaining according to the characteristics and needs of children, so as to improve the market competitiveness and user satisfaction of the products and promote the healthy growth and learning development of children.

Funding. Innovation Project of GuangxiGraduate Education, "Innovative design of children's educational AIDS under the concept of STEAM education" (Serial number: XYCSR2023014).

References

1. Jia, H., Haoqi, H., Bomin, L.: User demand analysis of reading room tables and chairs for preschool children based on service design concept. Packaging Eng. **43**(22), 134–142 (2022)
2. Xiangyuan, Z., Xijie, W.: A study on user requirements of 3D printers for children based on KANO model. Art and Design (Theory) **2**(11), 96–98 (2020)
3. Bijuan, L.: Humanized design of children's products. Packaging Eng. **01**(2006), 213–214+217
4. Hailong, Z., Bo, Z.: Research on the design of leisure and entertainment products for the elderly based on user experience. Design **35**(05), 126–128 (2022)
5. Xiaoying, L., Iridium Yiyao, D.: Children's interactive toy design based on KANO model and associative sensory experience. Design **35**(03), 60–63 (2022)
6. Jianhua, L., Lei, Z., Rong, G.: Interaction design related concepts in classroom teaching. Design **33**(17), 131–133 (2020)

7. Yang, L., Kan, W.: Research on intelligent interaction design method based on GDD-Kano model. Hunan Packaging **37**(02), 53–56+69 (2022)
8. Han, Z., Xiaoping, Z.: Research on children's educational product design based on user experience. Industrial Design **09**, 47–49 (2022)
9. Bingchen, Z., et al.: Research on the interaction design of intervention APP based on ASD children's needs analysis. Packaging Eng. **43**(18), 122–135 (2022)
10. Ling, Y., Yushi, D.: KANO demand-driven human-computer interaction design for public transportation facilities. Design **35**(10), 16–19 (2022)
11. Jun, W., Zhou, Y.: Research on the design of elementary school art playthings based on STEAM education concept. Fine Arts Education Res. **01**, 139–141 (2023)
12. Liping, L., Awei, Z.: Research on the design of toy cars for preschool children based on experience design. Design **36**(08), 116–119 (2023)
13. Han, J., Zijun, Z., Menglei, R.: Design of an intelligent vegetable growing device for children based on cognitive motivation analysis. Packaging Engineering **43**(10), 177–182+189 (2022)
14. Nan, H.: Exploration of children's product design based on the concept of emotional design. Art Education **02**, 232–235 (2022)
15. Junfeng, Z.: Research on the Design of Stroller Based on the Concept of Sustainable Design. Guangdong University of Technology,MA thesis (2020)
16. Ying, X.: Research on interactive products for children's online safety education. Technol Innov Innov. **15**, 89–91 (2019)
17. Huang, J.: Design principles and sensory experience of children's interactive e-books. Popular Literature and Arts **23**, 84–85 (2019)

Gamification Design of a Carbon Neutral Science App for Children Based on the Octagon Behavior Analysis Model

Yushan Wang[✉]

College of Art Design and Media, East China University of Science and Technology,
130 Meilong Road, Xuhui District, Shanghai 200237, People's Republic of China
2282214261@qq.com

Abstract. As a product of the combination of science education and the information age, popular science apps for children are playing an increasingly important role, and popular science games have gradually become a new way to disseminate scientific knowledge. Gamification can stimulate children's desire to explore, curiosity. From the perspective of gamification driving forces, this paper explores the triggering of eight core driving forces for different types of player user behaviors, and combines the status quo and user characteristics of children's science popularization apps to obtain the game driving mechanism for four types of player users, and then through children's science popularization The user journey analysis of similar APPs, according to the user's usage process habits, builds a gamification driving model for children's popular science APPs. And use this to guide the gamification design of children's popular science APP with the theme of carbon neutrality, and finally evaluate the design plan. Introducing gamification design into the field of children's science popularization can actively guide user behavior, provide children with an entertaining way of learning, and promote their interest in and understanding of science.

Keywords: Gamification · Science popularization · Octagon Behavior Analysis · Driving force

1 Overview of "Gamification" and "Octagonal Behavior Analysis" Theory

"Gamification" is a design approach that uses gamification thinking and elements and applies them to non-game scenarios to motivate users to interact [1]. "Gamification" was first proposed by Nick Pelling in 2002, and gradually emerged in 2010. It has been widely used as a strategy to improve the experience of Internet products [2].

Scholars have slightly different understandings of "gamification". Kevin Werbach believes that gamification refers to a design method that applies game elements and game design techniques in non-game situations. The implementation of gamification includes combining game elements and game design techniques. Game design techniques are incorporated into non-game contexts [3]. In gamification design, Kevin Werbach of the

University of Pennsylvania proposed an incentive system called "PEL" (Point, Badge, Leaderboard), which is common in many applications and platforms. The incentive system can effectively increase user stickiness, increase user activity and online time by using elements such as points, medals, and leaderboards [4]. In recent years, Octalysis (octalysis behavior analysis method) proposed by Yu-kai Zhou, a behavioral expert, has become one of the important research methods widely used in the field of game design and interaction design.

Yu-kai Zhou concluded that all human behaviors can be traced back to one or more core driving forces. Using behavioral motivation as a starting point, he proposed a gamification design framework called "Octagonal Behavior Analysis," which is based on eight core drivers (see Fig. 1). The eight core driving forces include: (1) Meaning: Epic meaning and sense of mission, which refers to the significance that players give to the goals they pursue or the roles they play beyond the things themselves. (2) Accomplishment: progress and sense of accomplishment, which refers to the inner motivation for players to complete things; (3) Empowerment: creativity and feedback, which refers to driving players to invest in the creative process and constantly try new things. (4) Ownership: ownership and Sense of possession, which means that players feel entitled to own or control something and are motivated. (5) Social Influence: social influence and relevance: refers to the mutual relationship between players and other players. (6) Scarcity: scarcity and desire, refers to the player's desire because they cannot obtain something immediately. (7) Unpredictability: unknownness and curiosity, which means that unknown things will always attract attention and stimulate players' curiosity to explore. (8) Avoidance: non-destructive With avoidance, it means that the player does not want bad things to happen.

Fig. 1. Octalysis

2 Analysis of the Current Situation of Children's Popular Science APP

2.1 Development Status

China has proposed science education goals called the "2049 Plan", which aims to make China a country where all citizens are scientifically literate by 2049. The field of science popularization for children is currently in a stage of rapid development. The advancement of science and technology and the importance of popular science education have gradually been recognized by people. More and more parents have begun to pay attention to the cultivation of children's exploration of scientific knowledge. In children's popular science knowledge education, design plays an important role in the form and content of popular science knowledge, and can stimulate children's interest and yearning for scientific knowledge [5]. Gamification design can stimulate learners' interest in learning. Educational games on mobile terminals have been widely used in children's learning, but they are rarely used in the field of science popularization. The inevitable trend. At present, children's science popularization mobile apps on the market can be roughly divided into three types: one is science popularization apps with the theme of picture book stories; application. Among them, popular science applications that focus on gameplay and interaction, embed scientific knowledge into them through gamification design, and provide a variety of rich scenes, interesting games and challenges. Let children learn scientific principles and concepts during play, encourage children to actively participate, and understand scientific knowledge through exploration and practice. This interactive participation method can greatly improve children's learning motivation and interest.

2.2 Problem and Needs Analysis

At present, the quality of popular science education applications for children is uneven, and some of them copy foreign popular science picture books and interactive experiences mechanically, and there are the following problems:

(1) Lack of interest and interactivity: science popularization education products in some developed countries pay more attention to stories and logic, use rich colors, and have better interaction with users, exploratory understanding, parents and children are entertaining Learning from it in a fun way can attract users to use repeatedly, such as Swift Playgrounds, children can use Swift code to control characters, and learn programming concepts through the main task of adventure in the 3D game world.

(2) It is difficult to establish a connection with real life: Some popular science education applications on the market often abstract scientific knowledge, fragment the knowledge content, and the correlation between knowledge points is not strong, and does not constitute a complete knowledge system, which is difficult for children to understand. At the same time, the boring subject knowledge is out of touch with children's actual life experience, the degree of social participation is low, and it is difficult to establish the connection between knowledge and practice, which makes children have a poor sense of harvest and experience in popular science education, and cannot apply the scientific knowledge they have learned to in real life.

(3) Lack of timely feedback and perfect incentive mechanism: The lack of positive feedback and reward mechanism in the learning process makes it difficult to stimulate children's learning motivation and interest.

To summarize, popular science education applications suffer from issues such as a lack of interest and interaction, disconnection from real-life scenarios, and a dearth of real-time feedback and incentive mechanisms. Therefore, there is a need for innovative approaches to science education that offer enjoyable, interactive, and personalized learning experiences.

3 Analysis of Driving Forces of Users' Behavior of Children's Science Popularization APP

3.1 Types of Users of Children's Popular Science APP

In the book "Hearts, Clubs, Diamonds, Spades: MUD Game Player Classification," Richard Bartle proposed a concept for classifying game players into four types: (1) Achievers, whose main goal is to upgrade their roles; (2) Explorers, who enjoy uncovering all the links in the game, understanding its mechanics and levels, without necessarily focusing on the outcome of game challenges; (3) Socializers, who view the game as a platform for interacting with other players and forming partnerships; and (4) Killers, who have a strong desire to dominate the game, earn the respect of others, and derive inner satisfaction from it. For the four types of players, Yu-kai Chou combined the Octalysis Behavior Analysis Framework to provide corresponding interpretations. For achievers, achievement and scarcity are the main driving forces, which are also influenced by secondary driving forces such as empowerment and a sense of ownership. The primary driver that affects Seekers is the unpredictability, with achievement and scarcity being secondary drivers. Socializers are primarily driven by networking, with empowerment, the unpredictability, and possession serving as secondary drivers. Impact killers are driven by achievement and social Influence as primary drivers, while empowerment, loss, and ownership act as secondary drivers [6]. Yanli Wei and her team utilized the octagonal behavior analysis method, in conjunction with learners' initiative and behavioral interaction, to classify learners into four distinct types corresponding to game player profiles. These four types encompass competitive learners, goal-oriented learners, exploratory learners, and interactive learners [2].

Piaget, an expert in child psychology, proposed that children's cognitive development follows a sequence of four stages. Among these stages, the concrete operational stage occurs between 7 and 12 years old, during which children's thinking begins to display a certain level of variability. They can use specific objects or images to classify and comprehend logical relationships. Additionally, they can perform group operations on specific items. However, at this stage, they do not yet possess the ability to construct a complete cognitive system [7]. Erikson's theory of personality development proposes that children aged 7–12 face a psychological conflict between diligence and inferiority [8]. During this stage, children are influenced by educational and parental factors as they actively work to resolve the conflict between diligence and inferiority. Successfully resolving this conflict leads children to develop a sense of diligence, enabling them to face setbacks in their future studies and lives with an active mindset. However, if the conflict remains unresolved, children may develop a sense of inferiority during this stage.

Science popularization essentially involves the process of cognitive learning. By combining the cognitive characteristics of children aged 7–12 with the four types of learners mentioned above, the needs of children's science popularization users can be summarized into the following four categories:

(1) Interactive users: They are willing to share knowledge and communicate with others.
(2) Achievement-oriented users: They seek a sense of accomplishment and progress, with the aim of obtaining scarce rewards.
(3) Exploratory users: They are driven by curiosity towards new things and unknown areas, and are willing to engage in various experiences.
(4) Challenge-seeking users: They are eager to compare and compete with other users in pursuit of victory."

3.2 Behavioral Drivers of Children's Science Popularization Users

According to the octagonal behavior analysis method, four distinct user motivations for popularizing science among children can be summarized, with each motivation being driven by a core factor. Children aged 7–12 are in the early stages of cognitive development, characterized by their enthusiasm and curiosity to explore the world and acquire new knowledge. They possess a strong desire to learn, satisfy their curiosity, and seek recognition and appreciation from others by gaining new knowledge. Therefore, by analyzing the core needs of different types of users in children's science popularization, it is possible to guide and educate them effectively, fulfilling their objectives.

When using science popularization apps, achievement-oriented users expect to accomplish their goals, improve their abilities, and eagerly overcome all checkpoints. Child users, on the other hand, are interested in learning and understanding every aspect of the app. They enjoy exploring new fields, mastering unknown knowledge, and engaging with different scenes and adventure levels. These aspects attract such users. Interactive child users are willing to communicate with others about their experiences and achievements while using the product. For child users, whether it's their friends, parents, teachers, or peers, social interaction facilitated by using the product is a driving force. Competitive children are more inclined to compare and compete with others, and their main pursuit is to achieve what others haven't. Finally, the game driving force mechanism for 4 types of learners is obtained (see Fig. 2).

4 Construction of Gamification-Driven Model for Children's Popular Science APP

4.1 Journey Analysis of Children's Popular Science APP Users

Yu-Kai Chou proposed that the player's journey can be divided into four stages using the octagonal behavior analysis method. The gamification design, which brings about a good user experience, runs throughout the entire user journey, with the eight core driving forces playing different roles. The player's user journey includes: Discovery (the reasons why

Types of popular science users for children		Motivational elements		Game drive
Interactive user	→	Interaction, Emotion	→	Accomplishment, Social Influence, Empowerment
Achiever	→	Progress, Goal	→	Ownership, Social, Influence
Explorer	→	Unknown, Curious	→	Accomplishment, Unpredictability
Challenging user	→	Challenge, Competition	→	Accomplishment, Empowerment, Ownership

Fig. 2. Four game driving forces of children's science popularization users

the user wants to experience the product), Onboarding (the initial learning of gameplay mechanics and tools), Shaping (the repetitive daily actions the user performs to achieve the goal), and Ending (how the experience fosters user loyalty) [9].

At different stages of the user experience with a product, the priority of the user's core driving force varies [7]. The user's behavior is influenced by the main core driving force, while the secondary core driving force provides assistance and guidance. In the discovery stage, the primary driving force for children using a popular science app is curiosity, stemming from the unknown, which motivates them to explore the product. Additionally, children may be influenced by parents, teachers, and classmates, making social interaction and achievement the secondary driving forces. During the entry stage, newcomers are guided smoothly into using the popular science product. They experience a sense of accomplishment as they gain access to or unlock rare content, which they then share and discuss with friends. Achievement becomes the primary driving force at this stage, while social interaction, the unknown, and scarcity also influence user behavior. In the shaping stage, users have acquired proficiency in using the product and possess knowledge or features that other users lack or may not understand. Here, the main driving forces are social interaction and scarcity, motivating users to explore unfinished tasks and acquire unique elements that differentiate them from others. Loss, possession, and achievement also impact user behavior. Users develop a heightened sense of ownership towards the product and start considering potential losses. In the final stage, the core driving force for users is the fear of loss. As they discontinue using the product, they experience a sense of loss and concern about losing their existing achievements. Social interaction, ownership, and achievements continue to affect user behavior during this stage. Maintaining social circles, reminders of social relationships, exploring the unknown, and the sense of accomplishment from achieving most goals can somewhat prolong the decline period of the product's life cycle.

The user journey of children when using a popular science app includes three stages: front, middle, and back. These three stages correspond to the four stages of the player's journey.

4.2 The Gamification Driving Model of Children's Popular Science APP

In the gamification-driven design process of popular science apps for children aged 7–12, a method is proposed based on the psychological and behavioral characteristics of children and their user journey. This method consists of three stages: discovery, introduction, shaping, and finalization. In each stage, users are driven by different primary and secondary motivations, and the core factors that influence their actions also vary. Gamification driving model of children's popular science APP (see Fig. 3).

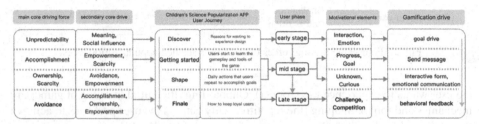

Fig. 3. Gamification driving model of children's popular science APP

(1) Target motivation. In the early stages of children using popular science apps, users are unfamiliar with the product. Children aged 7–12 have a strong desire for knowledge and are full of curiosity about things. To attract them to use the app, it is important to stimulate their curiosity and motivation to learn. Product names, icons, and slogans can pique children's interest, but it is more important to understand their learning goals and motivations in order to ignite their desire and enthusiasm for learning.

(2) Information transfer. Children's popular science apps transmit scientific knowledge and information through their product functions and content. The presentation of information should be concise, lively, and interesting to capture children's attention and cultivate their interest in learning. Simultaneously, the transmission of information needs to be comprehensible and interactive, enabling children to easily acquire and understand knowledge.

(3) Share feelings. Children have a strong need for emotional communication and interaction. Popular science apps can establish emotional connections and interactions with children through role-playing, interactive games, captivating animations, and engaging sound effects. Encouragement, praise, and reward mechanisms can enhance children's positive emotions and active participation, fostering their love and enthusiasm for science learning.

(4) Interactive form. Diverse interaction methods are the key to popular science apps for children. They provide a rich interactive experience by stimulating their senses through images, sounds, touch, and motion. Interactive games, experimental simulations, interesting Q&A sessions, and exploration tasks are some of the interactive forms that can spark children's curiosity, engage their sense of participation, and nurture their desire to explore. This way, children can have fun while learning.

(5) Behavioral feedback. In the later stages of children's science app learning, providing timely behavioral feedback to children is crucial. This can be achieved through

reward systems, level upgrades, medals, badges, and other means. Additionally, offering personalized learning suggestions and recommendations can help children perceive their own progress and accomplishments, thereby stimulating their motivation and boosting their self-confidence.

5 Design of Children's Carbon Neutral Knowledge Science Popularization APP Based on Octagonal Behavior Driving Force Analysis Model

In September 2020, China made a solemn commitment to 'peak its carbon dioxide emissions by 2030 and achieve carbon neutrality by 2060.' This paper applies a gamification-driven model of a children's science popularization app and uses carbon neutrality knowledge popularization as an example for practical design (see Fig. 4). "Carbon Baby" is an environmentally friendly leisure experience game designed for children aged 7–12, aiming to popularize the concept of carbon neutrality. Through engaging games, the process of carbon emissions and carbon absorption is personified as the activities of adorable carbon babies. The game provides various scenes where players can experience carbon emissions and carbon absorption firsthand, allowing them to understand the concepts and processes involved. By guiding children step by step, the game fosters an understanding of carbon neutrality, promotes awareness of reducing carbon emissions, encourages recording of carbon reduction behaviors in a personalized diary, generates visually appealing summary postcards, and rewards players. These elements aim to guide children towards developing eco-friendly and low-carbon living habits.

In popular science games, learning content refers to the synthesis of system knowledge and skills that users need to master, while game content serves as the means and path to achieve learning goals [10]. Carbon neutrality knowledge can be complex and difficult to understand, involving concepts such as ecological balance and human behavior. When the majority of children delve deeper into carbon neutrality theory, they may lose interest in experiential products due to the perceived dullness of fundamental concepts. However, the primary objective of promoting carbon neutrality knowledge among children is to foster a broader understanding of the impact of human behavior on the environment and cultivate awareness of low-carbon environmental protection. Therefore, popular science materials focus on providing children with a level of understanding about how carbon neutrality achieves balance and the process of carbon emissions through engaging products.

(1) Target motivation. The Carbon Baby APP allows children to receive knowledge about carbon neutralization in a relaxed and immersive atmosphere through fun games, and allows children to complete activities related to carbon neutrality in the game, save wild animals, and develop a low-carbon life in real life behavior habits. The logo of APP is made of green carbon treasure, which represents the amount of carbon dioxide that can be absorbed. After entering the game, the forest residents and the red panda game image will guide users to understand the game world and game levels. Interesting game tasks and real-time feedback stimulate users' thirst for knowledge and enthusiasm, and drive users to explore the unknown of the application.

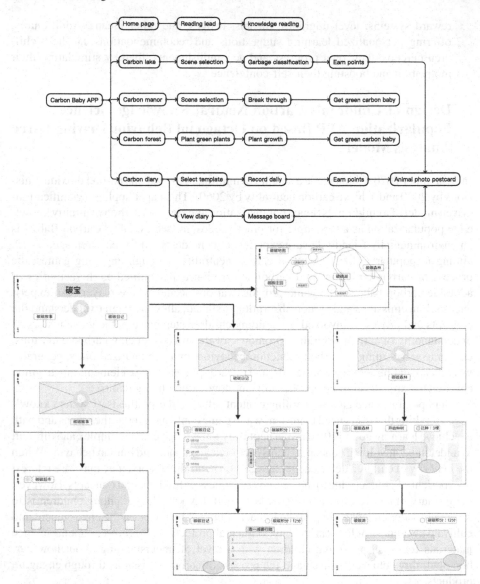

Fig. 4. Carbon Baby APP information architecture and partial prototype design

(2) Information transfer. It is meaningful for users to clarify their own behaviors. There-fore, at the entry stage, unlocking the problems of the Carbon Supermarket and dis-playing the progress of the user's task completion can enhance user retention rates. By providing guidance through reading guides and rewarding user points, active user engagement can be generated, encouraging them to learn more about low-carbon knowledge.

Fig. 5. Carbon Baby APP visual design scheme

(3) Share feelings. The Carbon Supermarket popularizes knowledge about life-related carbon emissions through animation and sound effects, establishing an emotional connection and interaction with children. Upon achieving carbon balance, players can receive postcards featuring small animals and share them with friends through social platforms. In the carbon forest, they can interact with other players and leave messages. The social driving force is applied to cultivate children's positive emotions and increase user participation.

(4) Interactive form. In the Carbon Baby APP, children primarily engage in gesture-based interactions and interact with game characters using their fingertips and on-screen buttons to perform actions. With visual and auditory guidance, users can plant trees and rescue wildlife in the 'Carbon Forest' section, capturing photos with wild animals to create personalized postcards. They also have the option to print these postcards as souvenirs, leveraging the drive for scarcity and achievement.

(5) Behavioral feedback. In the carbon diary section, children can apply the carbon emission reduction knowledge learned in the game to real life and record the carbon emission reduction actions completed by the user in the form of a diary. Children are rewarded with points through the points system, which can be exchanged for postcards featuring rare animals. The point exchange function extends the product's lifecycle and utilizes the driving forces of ownership, curiosity, and loss. Additionally, users can view other people's carbon footprints, leave messages, interact, and share with friends, thus applying social motivators.

The output and completed design scheme for the aforementioned children's carbon-neutral knowledge popular science app, driven by gamification (see Fig. 5). The objective of the app's design is to help children comprehend carbon-neutral knowledge, foster their understanding of low-carbon and environmentally friendly lifestyles, and inspire their curiosity and desire for exploration. Moreover, it aims to encourage children to practice low-carbon and environmentally conscious behaviors in their daily lives. The design scheme visualizes the process of carbon emission reduction and absorption, utilizing anthropomorphic carbon babies as a representation of the total amount of carbon absorbed. The scheme comprises four components: the Carbon Forest, Supermarket, Lake, and Diary. It includes virtual concepts such as images, a collection book, a diary, points redemption, answer rewards, and design functions. Through story-based game tasks, children can engage with the app, enjoy the educational aspect of carbon neutrality, and experience the fun of popular science games.

6 Design Verification

After the production of the Carbon Baby APP, ten school-age children were invited to be divided into two groups, A and B, to carry out science popularization using traditional methods of pictures and texts, as well as the Carbon Treasure APP for promoting carbon neutral knowledge. The testing process required children to complete the tasks independently and took 30 min. Finally, interviews were conducted with the children to analyze their learning and cognitive effects on carbon neutrality knowledge acquired through the two methods.

Children using the Carbon Baby APP have shown longer learning durations and a greater willingness to engage with it repeatedly. On the other hand, children utilizing the traditional picture-text science popularization method find it difficult to read all the content continuously, and most of them are unwilling to revisit the initial section. A comparison between the two methods reveals that the gamified APP interaction approach successfully captivates children, encouraging them to explore independently. Additionally, the inclusion of a comprehensive feedback mechanism fosters a willingness to learn and motivates repeated usage of the APP, thereby improving user retention rates. Moreover, the graphic and text recognition objectives are more clearly defined within a shorter time frame, providing a certain advantage in terms of efficiency.

Secondly, children who use the Carbon Baby APP for exploration can gain a more comprehensive and three-dimensional understanding of the dynamic process of carbon neutrality. This, in turn, can increase their willingness to protect the environment through low-carbon practices within their capacity, foster awareness of carbon neutrality, and translate theoretical knowledge into actionable behavior.

Based on the communication between children and parents using the app, most users prefer the gamified form of science popularization. They find it more engaging than traditional methods due to its use of vibrant visuals. Moreover, they appreciate the inclusion of content on carbon neutrality and popular science knowledge, as the levels are logically designed. Some users are able to progress through the levels quickly and express a desire for an expanded manor scene and a greater variety of rare animal species. This would allow them to explore more interactive science content.

7 Conclusion

With the advancement of science and technology, the digitalization of children's science education is an inevitable trend. It can address the shortcomings of traditional science education and provide a more engaging and interactive learning experience. Furthermore, real-time feedback and a reward mechanism can enhance children's motivation and interest in learning, satisfying their thirst for knowledge. This paper proposes a gamification-driven design model for children's science education applications, with a focus on designing a children's science education app based on the analysis of octagonal behavior. The aim is to provide design ideas for similar products.

References

1. Luo, J., Zhang, J.: Research on gamification design in the tmall double 11 "star show cat" activity - based on the octagonal behavior analysis framework. Radio TV J. (12) 139–141 (2021)
2. Wei, Y., Zhou, X., Liu, Y.: Research on gamification driver design of learning APP based on octagonal behavior analysis method. Packag. Eng. **42**(08), 148–155 (2021)
3. Wu, X., Xin, X.: Gamification design application for persuading users to change their behavior. Packag. Eng. **38**(20), 194–198 (2017)
4. Luo, W.: Gamification design framework - research on the application of octagonal behavior analysis in social apps. West Leather **41**(4), 133 (2019)
5. Zhang, F., Li, J.: The development path of science popularization education for children and adolescents based on design driven. Tianjin Sci. Technol. **48**(06), 50–52+56 (2021)
6. Chang, J.H., Zhang, H.X.: Analyzing online game-players: from materialism and motivation to attitude. Cyber-Psychol. Behav. **11**(6), 711–714 (2008)
7. Piaget, E.: Child Psychology (1980)
8. Yu, J.: Reflections on introducing Ericsson's personality development theory into moral education and school management. J. Yunnan Open Univ. (02), 31–35 (1996)
9. Ji, Y.: Research on gamification driver design of social e-commerce based on octagonal analysis method. West Leather **42**(21), 47–48+52 (2020)
10. Qian, F.: Research and Design of Hanfu Popular Science Games Based on Gamification Theory. Beijing University of Posts and Telecommunications (2021)

Research on the Influence of Artificial Intelligence Interactive Function on Youth Sports Training – Taking Tiantian Skipping Rope App as an Example

Luming Wang[1], Yin Cui[2(✉)], Xibin Gong[2], and Fei Liu[3]

[1] Honam University, Gwangju 62399, Korea
[2] Beijing Institute of Technology, Beijing 100081, China
cuiyin360@163.com
[3] Foreign Language School Affiliated to Beijing Foreign Studies University Beijing, Beijing 100085, China

Abstract. This study aims to explore the teaching effect of sports training app integrated with artificial intelligence interactive function as a teaching aid for teenagers. In this study, we compared the learning interest, learning attitude, learning behavior and willingness to continue learning of 123 children aged 7–12 years in the course of physical training. The subjects were divided into two groups: the experimental group used artificial intelligence interactive app to assist physical education, and the control group used traditional teaching methods for physical training and learning. The results showed that there is no significant difference in the influence of gender on AI interactive sports learning interest, learning attitude, learning behavior and willingness to continue learning.

Keywords: AI interaction · Learning interest · Learning willingness · Learning behavior · Willingness to continue learning · Physical education

1 Introduction

The teaching of "physical education" is different from that of other subjects. The modern physical education pays attention to the appropriate and efficient coordination of theoretical learning and sports training. It requires teachers to flexibly arrange the course content and adopt effective physical education teaching methods according to the general requirements and implementation principles of modern school physical education. In the past, primary and secondary schools in the stage of compulsory education paid less attention to physical education. On April 21, 2022, the Ministry of Education of China issued the Curriculum Standards of Physical Education and Health for Compulsory Education (2022 version), and the new curriculum standards will officially come into effect in the autumn semester of 2022. Among them, "Physical education and health" accounts for 10%–11% of the total class hours, surpassing foreign language to become the third major subject in primary and primary schools [1]. According to the new curriculum standard plan, "Physical education and health" accounts for 10%–11% of the total class hours, surpassing foreign language (6%–8%), chemistry and biology, science (8%–10%), and becoming the third major subject in primary and primary stages after Chinese and mathematics. This shows the importance of physical education in primary and secondary school education.

In the post-epidemic era, "artificial intelligence + physical education" has completely subverted the traditional teaching model, mainly changing the structure of educational resources, teaching feedback and evaluation mechanism, and becoming an intelligent teaching method. Through the artificial intelligence platform, teachers and learners are accurately connected, so as to form a multi-level, wide-ranging and multi-element new "artificial intelligence + physical education" teaching system1. Most education resources and teaching are based on digitalization, and more emphasis is placed on the diversity and re-optimization of resources [2]. It is worth our attention that "artificial intelligence + physical education" is built on a lot of artificial intelligence equipment and big data processing center to complete, it cannot be separated from the technical support and environment structure, but the teaching service it provides is intelligent, novel and advanced [3].

Therefore, this study explores the effect of using artificial intelligence interactive app to assist PE teaching. The purpose of this study is to examine its influence on the learning attitude, learning interest, learning behavior and willingness to continue learning in physical education teaching of students of different genders. In traditional PE teaching, it is difficult for teachers to pay attention to the learning situation of each student, and it is difficult for students to continue learning outside the PE curriculum. In traditional teaching, teachers' incentives are also limited. The integration of artificial intelligence in PE teaching enables students to have a more personalized experience. This study provides a reference for the application of artificial intelligence interactive function in sports fitness and teaching software.

2 Literature Review

2.1 Current Status of Sports Fitness Apps

As people pay more attention to their own health status and have a stronger and stronger need for fitness, the rapid development of research, design and development of various sports and fitness apps has been greatly promoted. Under the background of mobile Internet era, the emerging fitness market has entered a stage of rapid development, and the fitness market gradually tends to be centralized and diversified. The competition pattern of the fitness market has basically formed [4]. Through the statistical analysis of the data of the top 100 sports and exercise apps downloaded from each APP store, the results show that the content of the apps has a serious degree of homogeneity, single function, more service functions are focused on women, the accuracy of the collected sports and exercise data is relatively poor, and the business model is backward, and the corresponding solutions are put forward. For example, establish a sound supervision platform, scientific and balanced content, improve services and expand functions, and innovate operation and management mode [5]. By investigating the experience and feeling of white collar women in Zhengzhou who use sports and fitness apps and whether it affects their own sports and exercise, it is concluded that this group mainly uses fitness apps such as slim body shaping, running, local exercise and brisk walking, and most of the white collar women are satisfied with the functions and services provided by fitness apps [6]. However, 60.96% of white-collar women believed that the use of such software had no impact on their own sports awareness [7]. There are few studies on the application of fitness apps in primary and secondary school students.

2.2 The Application of Artificial Intelligence Technology in Sports

With the advent of artificial intelligence, coaches and athletes no longer rely solely on empirical theory, but use more scientific methods to train. The modern application of AI technology in physical education combines many related disciplines, especially new concepts and theories established with the development of information technology [8]. They penetrate each other and form an appropriate basic theoretical system, which promotes the sustainable development of AI in the field of sports training. It is mainly applied in the following aspects: the guidance and training of athletes in training [9]; Grab the performance of the athletes; Adjust skills and tactics based on the data obtained; And applying artificial intelligence to ensure athletes' safety and other fields [10].

2.3 Application of Intelligent Interactive Technology

Intelligent Interaction, also known as Human-Computer interaction, is a process in which humans and computers exchange specific information in a special way to complete specific targets and tasks [11]. Human-computer interaction mainly studies the relationship between human cognitive pattern, information processing process and human-computer interaction behavior, and studies how to design, implement and evaluate computing systems according to users' tasks and activities [12]. Intelligent interaction can achieve cognitive enhancement. Combining machine learning technology with intelligent interaction, wearable sensor devices can be used to improve the understanding of the intuitive perception of the external environment. Portable multi-channel biosensors can be used to study how multi-sensory stimuli induce different brain cognitive activities in real environments, and to measure and record the effects of different environments on brain activity in real time. Interactive devices can also be used to improve human cognition and processing efficiency of complex information and help reduce the risk measurement of trial and error costs [13]. The combination of intelligent interaction and software can enhance user experience through specific design. For example, in intelligent interactive art, intelligent media can enhance the appeal of artistic works and interact with audiences by sending feedback signals through output devices, so as to eliminate the "gap" between artworks and audiences more effectively, so that the audience can be integrated into artistic works [14]. Different from traditional media, intelligent media is not only an extension of human senses and bodies, but also an expansion of intelligence, which provides favorable conditions for the audience to participate in the creation [15].

2.4 Learning Interest

Interest has been studied to be linked to motivation. Hidi and Renninger describe interest as "the mental state of a tendency to engage or re-engage with a particular class of object, event, or idea over time" [16]. Interest can play an important role in guiding certain goals that a student chooses to pursue or helping the student pursue them (Hui & Bao, 2013). However, Hidi and Renninger argue that interest is a long-term change in state of mind; In the short term, Hong, Hwang, Liu, Lin, and Chen (2016a, 2016b) hypothesize that interest can be viewed as a temporary change in mental state, based on Mehrabian's (1994) theory. Emotional states are divided into three levels: valence (i.e., pleasure), arousal (i.e., energy), and dominance [17], and emotional states of gameplay interest are divided into three levels: like, enjoyment, and participation [18]. In addition, topic interests are content specific and related to deeply personal interests [19].

2.5 Learning Attitude

Hsu (2010) argues that learning attitude represents learning attitude, which is shaped by environment rather than innate heredity and is a phenomenon rather than an essence, therefore it is variable. In school education, students can be cultivated to establish a positive attitude through appropriate guidance. From the perspective of learning, students' attitude towards people and the process of learning activities involving things and events, such as teachers, teaching materials, facilities and environment, will have a profound impact on students' learning behavior. In addition, the learning behavior will also affect the effect of students' learning. Some studies speculate that in the technology acceptance model (TAM) and the expectation - confirmation model (ECM) [], Attitude as a direct determinant of ongoing willingness is similar to satisfaction [20]. Despite this, many researchers still treat attitude and satisfaction as conceptually independent variables [21]. In addition, attitude is an emotional response to a specific behavior that can improve the accuracy of intent to predict behavior, rather than satisfaction based on past experience.

2.6 Continuous Learning Intention

Continuous learning intention refers to the learner's willingness to participate or participate in learning in the future. The definition of willingness to continue learning is derived from a previous study [22], and the same idea is applied to AI learning intent assessment applications [23] and MOOCs [24]. In this study, regarding the willingness to learn continuously in sports training, reference is made to the concept of continuous willingness in the field of information systems. Continuous willingness first appeared directly as a concept in the expectation confirmation theory proposed by Bhattacharya. Expectation confirmation theory has been widely used in the literature on consumer behavior to study consumer satisfaction, repurchase intention, and branding. The predictive power of the theory has been demonstrated in the context of various product buybacks and service continuity, including automotive buybacks, camera buybacks, restaurant services, and business specialty services. Oliver proposed the following process for consumers to achieve buyback intention in the ECT framework. First, consumers form initial expectations for a specific product or service before purchasing based on previous experience or recommendations from others. Second, they accept and use the product or service. After a period of initial consumption, they form a perception of whether it is useful or not. Third, they compare their perception of whether a particular product or service is useful with their original expectations to determine the extent to which their expectations are confirmed. Fourth, they form satisfaction based on the level of substantiation and expectation. Finally, satisfied consumers form buyback intentions, while dissatisfied users stop their subsequent use [21]".

2.7 Behavioral Intention

By combing relevant literature, it is found that scholars have a unified definition of the concept of behavioral intention. The concept originates from psychology and can also be called behavioral inclination and intention or behavioral will. Fishhein and Ajzen (1975) first proposed this concept. They believed that clear intention should be generated before action and expression, which is the decision-making and thinking before the expression of behavior, and can predict the intention of behavior, while the intention of behavior is the most important factor in predicting behavior, and it is the thinking goal and behavior trend generated by the subject before taking a certain action. It is the connection between the subject's attitude and behavior [25]. Henry Jenkins (1992) believed that behavioral intention is the degree of autonomy when one participates in a specific task. Ajzen and Fishbein (1980) believed that people would be influenced by their behavioral intention before taking a certain behavior, which would lead to changes in time, place and way. For example, the stronger the degree of an individual's behavioral intention for a certain activity, the greater the probability of taking action, excluding the interference of special environment.

3 Research Design and Method

In this study, the app "Jumping Rope every day" is used as an intelligent interactive sports fitness platform. The innovative AI interactive counting eliminates the need for extra hardware and allows people to do sports lightly. The mobile phone is aimed at the human body, and the elements on the screen are interactive training points. Real-time automatic recording of training results, statistical growth data, together to achieve daily exercise goals [26]. As this study combines theory and demonstration, taking primary and middle school students as the main object, using structural equation for data analysis, to develop a study on the impact of artificial intelligence interactive function on youth sports training.

3.1 Research Methods

Literature Research Method. By searching the keywords "artificial intelligence", "sports training", "primary and secondary school students" and so on, this study investigated the background of artificial intelligence and youth sports training respectively, and summarized the current research status of the influence of interactive function of artificial intelligence on youth sports training through literature analysis. By further sorting out the relevant literature, this study summarized the relevant important theories and practical methods, which provided the theoretical basis and method guidance for the follow-up questionnaire design and data analysis.

Questionnaire Survey Method. Based on the analysis of relevant literature before the research, the questionnaire design of the study on the influence of artificial intelligence interactive function on youth sports training was carried out. Questions were set respectively for artificial intelligence interactive function and youth sports training. Secondly, dimension classification of the questions was carried out, simple validity test was conducted by combining online and offline methods, and the questionnaire was modified and improved. After passing the simple validity test, the questionnaire is formally issued, so as to obtain the questionnaire data for follow-up data analysis.

Statistical Analysis. In this study, the collected sample data were processed and analyzed by using Excel, SPSS and other software.

After screening the collected questionnaires, this study first conducted a descriptive analysis of the obtained data, and then normalized the obtained data through APH weight calculation to derive the total value of the measure. Further combined with the quantitative data, it conducted multiple linear regression analysis and one-way analysis of variance, and finally got the main conclusion of the study.

3.2 Questionnaire Design

The questions of the questionnaire are designed according to the topic of this paper and related literature. The latent variables, coding, items and source information are shown in Table 1:

Table 1. Measurement scale

Latent variables	Coding	Project	Source information
Learning Attitude	LA1	It is a good way to use artificial intelligence to assist students in sports learning	Hsu(2010)
	LA2	The approach of using artificial intelligence to aid students' physical education learning appeals to me	
	LA3	Using AI as an aid for sports learning is an enjoyable experience	

(continued)

Table 1. (*continued*)

Latent variables	Coding	Project	Source information
Continuance Intention	CI1	I plan to continue using AI as an aid for sports learning in the future	Yen Hsu, Jiangjie Chen, Chao Gu, Weilong Wu (2021)
	CI2	I plan to often use artificial intelligence as an auxiliary tool for sports learning in my daily life	
	CI3	In general, I intend to continue to use AI as an aid for sports learning on a regular basis	
Behavioral Intention	BI1	I like using AI as an aid for sports learning	Venkatesh et al., (2012)
	BI2	I will actively use artificial intelligence as an auxiliary tool for sports learning	
	BI3	I would recommend using artificial intelligence as an aid for sports learning to those around me	
	BI4	I am confident in using AI as an auxiliary tool for sports learning	
Learning Interest	LI1	Sports learning with the help of AI will make the training process more enjoyable	Hong, Hwang, Liu, Ho, Chen, (2014)
	LI2	I am so impressed by this innovative approach to learning that I am interested in learning more sports learning methods	
	LI3	Using artificial intelligence as an auxiliary tool to learn sports stimulates my motivation to learn sports	

4   Data Collection and Analysis

This study mainly distributed online questionnaires to primary and middle school students (including primary school students and junior high school students). A total of 130 samples were collected within 48 h. After deleting 7 invalid samples, the remaining samples were 123, with an effective rate of 94.61%. Therefore, there are a total of 15 questionnaire questions and 123 valid samples in this study. Data statistics are carried out according to valid samples, and the results are shown in Table 2.

Table 2. Basic information of the interviewees

Sample	Categories	Quantity	Percentage (%)
Gender	male	54	43.90
	female	69	56.10
Grade	First grade	15	12.20
	Second grade	56	45.53
	Third grade	10	8.13
	Fourth grade	2	1.62
	Fifth grade	4	3.25
	Sixth grade	6	4.87
	Seventh grade	1	0.82
	Eighth grade	4	3.25
	Ninth grade	24	19.51
	First grade	1	0.82

According to the data in the table above, the number of female samples in this study is higher than that of male. Primary school students and middle school students have a larger number of samples.

4.1 Reliability and Validity Analysis

Reliability Analysis. SPSS software was used to test the reliability of the questionnaire, and the obtained Cronbach's α coefficient value was 0.918 (Table 3), and the reliability coefficient value of the research data was higher than 0.9, which comprehensively indicated that the reliability of the data was of high quality and could be used for further analysis.

Table 3. Reliability analysis

Cronbach's α coefficient	Number of terms	Number of samples
0.918	15	123

Validity Analysis. SPSS software was used to test the validity of the questionnaire, and the obtained KMO value was 0.938 (greater than 0.7), the Bartlett sphericity test Chi-square distribution value was 2639.047, and the significance level value was 0.000***(Table 4) showed significance at the level, indicating that the questionnaire could be judged to be reasonable with high validity.

Table 4. Validity analysis

KMO test and Bartlett test		
KMO values		0.938
Bartlett test for sphericity	Approximate chi-square	2639.047
	df	105
	P	0.000 * * *

Note: ***, ** and * represent significance levels of 1%, 5% and 10% respectively

4.2 Weight Analysis

SPSS software was used to test the weight of the questionnaire, and the CI value was 0.000 (Table 5), and the RI value was 1.590. Therefore, the calculated CR value was 0.000 < 0.1, which means that the judgment matrix of this study met the consistency test, and the calculated weight was consistent.

Table 5. Summary of consistency test results

Maximum feature root	CI value	RI value	CR value	Consistency test results
15.000	0.000	1.590	0.000	Through

4.3 Multiple Linear Regression Analysis

This part analyzes and studies the linear relationship between the independent variable and the dependent variable by constructing the regression equation, and uses multiple independent variables to estimate the dependent variable, so as to explain and predict the value of the dependent variable.

Wherein, the independent variable -- learning attitude is set as X, and the dependent variable -- learning behavior is set as Y.

SPSS software was used to conduct multiple linear regression analysis on the independent variable and learning behavior (Y), and the obtained prediction model information was shown in Table 6, Table 7 and Table 8.

Based on the data in the above table, the following analysis results can be obtained:

1. As can be seen in Table 6, the adjusted R square is 0.747, indicating that the independent variable can explain the variance change of the dependent variable to 74.7%.

Table 6. Model summary1

R	R square	R squared after adjustment	Error in standard estimation	D-W
0.869	0.755	0.747	0.539	2.282

Table 7. ANOVA tables2

	Sum of Squares	Degrees of freedom	Mean square	F	P
Return	110.150	4	27.538	90.971	0.000
Residual	35.719	118	0.303		
Total	145.870	122			

2. As can be seen from Table 7, it is found that the model passes the F test (F = 90.971, p = 0.000 < 0.05) when the model is tested, which means that the construction of the model is meaningful.
3. As shown in Table 8, P values of information application ability and information classification ability are less than 0.05, indicating that this independent variable has a significant and positive impact on learning behavior.
4. Based on the above analysis results, the multiple linear regression equation of the influence of learning attitude (X) on learning behavior (Y) can be written as follows:

$$Y = 0.532 + 0.420 - 0.070 + 0.361$$

4.4 One Way Analysis of Variance

SPSS software was used to conduct one-way analysis of variance between basic information, independent variables and dependent variables, and the summary analysis results showed whether there were differences between different basic information and variables.

Gender Differences in Independent Variables. First, verify the variance homogeneity test of gender on variable sports learning. In the test results, the significance P values are all greater than 0.05, showing no significance at the level, which means that the volatility of gender and sample data is consistent without difference. Therefore, the data meet the homogeneity of variance, and one-way analysis of variance can be conducted, as shown in Table 9.

After the homogeneity test of variance, one-way analysis of variance was conducted, and the results showed that all P values were > 0.05, so the statistical result was not significant, indicating that there was no significant difference between genders in sports learning. The specific situation is shown in Table 10.

Differences in Independent Variables between Grades. Multiple post-hoc comparisons were made on the significant differences between different grades in "using artificial intelligence to assist students' physical education learning is a good method",

Table 8. Regression coefficients3

Model		Unstandardized coefficient		Standardized coefficient	t	P
		B	Standard error	Beta		
1	Constant	0.532	0.201		2.643	0.009 * *
	I like to use artificial intelligence as an aid for sports learning	0.448	0.136	0.420	3.292	0.001 * *
	I will actively use artificial intelligence as an auxiliary tool for sports learning	0.189	0.162	0.182	1.172	0.244
	I would recommend the use of artificial intelligence as an aid for sports learning to those around me	0.073	0.129	0.070	0.566	0.572
	I am confident in using artificial intelligence as an auxiliary tool for sports learning	0.351	0.144	0.361	2.445	0.016 *

and the specific differences between variables were analyzed, with the results shown in Table 11.

According to the above results, samples from different grades do not show significant differences in "using artificial intelligence to assist (skipping rope every day) students' physical education learning is a good way".

Table 9. Test of homogeneity of variance

	Gender		F	P
	Male (n = 54)	Female (n = 69)		
It is a good way to use artificial intelligence to assist students in sports learning	1.06	1.12	0.001	0.980
The method of using artificial intelligence to aid students' physical education learning attracts me	1.10	1.17	0.350	0.555
Using AI as an aid for sports learning is an enjoyable experience	1.07	1.11	0.051	0.822

Table 10. Results of analysis of variance

Variable names	Variable value	Sample size	Average	Standard deviation	F	P
It is a good way to use artificial intelligence to assist students in sports learning	male	54	1.96	1.06	0.002	0.968
	female	69	1.97	1.12		
	Total	123	1.97	1.09		
The approach of using artificial intelligence to aid students' physical education learning attracted me	male	54	2.07	1.10	0.083	0.774
	female	69	2.01	1.17		
	Total	123	2.04	1.13		
Learning sports using AI as an aid is an enjoyable experience	male	54	2.06	1.07	0.078	0.780
	female	69	2.00	1.11		
	Total	123	2.02	1.09		

Table 11. Results of multiple post hoc comparisons4

	Item	Sample size	Average	Standard deviation	F	P
It is a good way to use artificial intelligence to assist students in sports learning	Grade 1	15	1.87	1.30	0.152	0.998
	Second grade	56	2.04	1.12		
	Third grade	10	2.00	0.77		
	Fourth grade	2	1.50	0.71		
	Fifth grade	4	2.00	1.41		
	Sixth grade	6	1.83	0.75		
	Seventh grade	1	2.00	null		
	Eighth grade	4	2.25	1.50		
	Ninth grade	24	2.00	1.13		
	Freshman year	1	1.96	null		
	Total	123	1.96	1.09		

5 Conclusion

The main purpose of this study is to explore the influence of artificial intelligence interactive function on youth sports training. The collected questionnaires are used as research samples to conduct quantitative research and analysis on the influence of artificial intelligence interactive function on youth sports training.

In the study, learning attitude as the independent variable, the use of artificial intelligence to assist students in sports learning is a good method. The method of using artificial intelligence to assist students' sports learning attracts me, and the use of artificial intelligence as an auxiliary tool for sports learning is a pleasant experience to measure; As the dependent variable, youth sports learning is measured from three aspects: learning behavior intention, learning behavior and learning interest. After multiple regression analysis and one-way analysis of variance on the collected data, it can be seen that there is still some space for exploration on the influence of artificial intelligence interactive function on youth sports learning. It is believed that in the future, researches on the relationship between artificial intelligence interactive function and youth sports learning will be more abundant.

References

1. https://mp.weixin.qq.com/s?__biz=MjM5MTMxNzUyMg==&mid=2651061802&idx=1&sn=6f8e98ef9a1d9321277168dd09b0dde5&chksm=bd4035578a37bc41d2466fc8705b43e405d3254ebd679766c3d09f38b7a1f32d8bc0a1bfb8b0&scene=27
2. Yonghe, W., Bowen, L., Xiaoling, M.: Build an "artificial intelligence + education" ecosystem. J. Dist. Educ. **35**(05), 27–39 (2017)
3. Yuanbo, L.: Design and practice of artificial intelligence in physical education teaching system. Mechanical design **38**(6), 165166 (2021)

4. Hongcheng, C., Qingguo, C.: Research on continuous use intention of mobile fit-ness app users. J. Capital Univ. Phys. Educ. **32**(01), 75–81+96 (2020)
5. Ruoxi, W., Qingjun, W.: The development status, problems and countermeasures of sports fitness APP. J. Shandong Univ. Phys. Educ. **004**, 18–22 (2015)
6. Jossa-Bastidas, O., et al.: Predicting physical exercise adherence in fitness apps using a deep learning approach. Int. J. Environ. Res. Public Health **18**(20), 10769 (2021)
7. Yeqiao, W.: Research on brand communication strategies and effects of fitness apps. Guangxi University (2017)
8. Muntaner-Mas, A., et al.: Smartphone app (2kmFIT-App) for measuring cardi-orespiratory fitness: validity and reliability study. JMIR mHealth and uHealth 9.1 e14864,(2021)
9. Jiang, L.C., Sun, M., Huang, G.:Uncovering the heterogeneity in fitness app use: a latent class analysis of Chinese users. Int. J. Environ. Res. Public Health **19**(17) 10679 (2022)
10. Rospo, G., et al.: Cardiorespiratory improvements achieved by American college of sports medicine's exercise prescription implemented on a mobile app. JMIR mHealth and uHealth **4**(2), e5518 (2016)
11. Weibo, F.: Analysis and Integration of Urban Recreation Space. Chong-qing University, Chongqing (2007)
12. Dingwei, Z., Liesheng, C.: Design and research of intelligent interaction in fresh fruit and vegetable packaging. Packaging Eng. 1–8 (2021)
13. Jing, C., Tingguan, H., Di, C.: Yu interactive landscape experience enhancement design. (Small. Landscape Archit. **6**(02), 30–41 (2018)
14. Wenfeng, W., Rong, Z.: Application of intelligent technology in interactive painting design and its creation mechanism research. Packag. Eng.. Eng. **43**(S1), 89–95 (2022)
15. Wu, Z., Ji, D., Yu, K., et al.: AI Creativity and the Human-AI Co-Creation Model. Remin Publish, Beijing (2021)
16. Renninger, K.A., Hidi, S.E.: Interest development, self-related information processing, and practice. Theor. Pract. **61**(1), 23–34 (2022)
17. Mehrabian, A.: Individual differences in achieving tendency: review of evidence bearing on a questionnaire measure. Curr. Psychol.. Psychol. **13**, 351–364 (1994)
18. Yu, Z.: The effects of the superstar learning system on learning interest, attitudes, and academic achievements. Multimedia Tools Appl. **82**, 17947–17962 (2022)
19. Zhou, W., et al.: Deep learning modeling for top-n recommendation with interests exploring. IEEE Access **6**, 51440–51455 (2018)
20. Bhattacherjee, A.: Understanding information systems continuance: an expectationcon-firmation model. MIS Q. **25**, 351–370 (2001)
21. Oliver, R.L.: A cognitive model of the antecedents and consequences of satisfaction decisions. J. Mark. Res. **17**(4), 460–469 (1980)
22. Wu, C.-H., Liu, C.-H., Huang, Y.-M.: The exploration of continuous learning intention in STEAM education through attitude, motivation, and cognitive load. Int. J. STEM Educ. **9**(1), 1–22 (2022)
23. Chai, C.S., et al.: Modeling Chinese secondary school students' behavioral intentions to learn artificial intelligence with the theory of planned behavior and self-determination theory. Sustainability **15**(1), 605 (2022)
24. de Jong, P.G.M., et al.: Development and application of a massive open online course to deliver innovative transplant education. Transplant Immunol. **66**, 101339 (2021)
25. Fishhein, A.: Taking and information handling in consumer behavior. Boston-Graduate School of Business Administration, Harward University, pp. 176–210 (1975)
26. https://baike.baidu.com/item/天天跳绳/58496102?fr=aladdin
27. Smith, T.F., Waterman, M.S.: Identification of common molecular subsequences. J. Mol. Biol. **147**, 195–197 (1981)

AMbER - Adaptive Instructional Systems as a Use Case for the Holistic Assessment Platform

Thomas E. F. Witte$^{(\boxtimes)}$ [ID], Torsten Gfesser [ID], and Jessica Schwarz [ID]

Fraunhofer FKIE, Fraunhoferstr. 20, 53343 Wachtberg, Germany
`{thomas.witte,torsten.gfesser,`
`jessica.schwarz}@fkie.fraunhofer.de`

Abstract. Adaptive instructional systems support learner and teacher to determine which learning material would be best at a specific time to reach the learner's goals. The learner's current state, personality traits, and learning history are important data for a system and a teacher to support the learning process. For a beneficial use of an adaptive instructional system, the effectiveness, efficiency, and the satisfaction of the user must be tracked and evaluated to optimize the learning outcome. The human factors analysis platform AMbER uses objective and subjective measures to evaluate the user state, the efficiency, and effectiveness of the learning process. The modular architecture of the assessment platform AMbER leads to highly flexible dashboards, that can be adapted to the specific requirements of the use case. Assessing adaptive instructional systems is one of many possible scenarios to make use of AMbER. An adaptive instructional system scenario is used as an example, to showcase the benefits of the assessment platform.

Keywords: Adaptive instructional systems · evaluation · learning management system · holistic assessment · artificial intelligence · affective computing · iteration by design

1 Introduction

Advances in Artificial Intelligence (AI) offer new opportunities to design learning systems that provide individualized support to the learner and the teacher [1]. An example is the implementation of AI for adaptive instructional systems (AIS). An AIS adapts the learning content or method according to the needs of the learner to reach a specific learning goal [2]. Hereby, AI functionalities often classify the data provided by the instructional system and provide feedback for the user of the system. However, major challenges must be solved for a widespread integration in curricula. One of these is to perform a robust evaluation of an AIS to improve the quality of adaptation to rise the efficiency and effectiveness of the AIS [3].

A proposed solution is to use a design assistance system, which incorporates iterative evaluations over the whole lifecycle of a system [4]. The concept, called *Iteration by Design*, is based on the premise of combining subjective and objective offline data (e.g.

© The Author(s), under exclusive license to Springer Nature Switzerland AG 2023
P. Zaphiris et al. (Eds.): HCII 2023, LNCS 14060, pp. 346–356, 2023.
https://doi.org/10.1007/978-3-031-48060-7_26

questionnaires, usability tests) and online data (e.g. log data analysis), to give the system's design team feedback for further improvements of the system's design. Feedback of the assistance system can be, for example, a classification of user workflows, suggestions of design improvements regarding usage of functionalities, or suggestions of design improvements regarding the human machine interface. Figure 1 gives an overview of the concept.

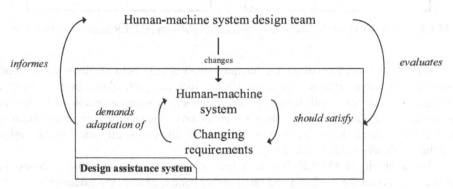

Fig. 1. Overview of the Concept *Iteration by Design,* reproduced [4].

A design team of, for example, an AIS gets informed by the design assistance system, which evaluates the AIS semi automatically. If necessary, the design team will then reiterate the system design to improve the quality of the system. Especially for systems with a long lifecycle, requirements of the system can change over time. So, the system must change as well from time to time to counteract the system-requirements gap. However, the design assistance system itself needs to be supervised as well, because not all decisions of an evaluation process can be automated, yet. An example is the use of inference statistical methods. It depends on the characteristics of the raw data which method is most appropriate. Also, some outcomes can be ambiguous in their meaning and still needs to be interpreted by a human. In summary, the design concept *Iteration by Design* combines the strength of automation by using its repetitive precision and unobtrusive data retention, with the strength of a human design team, by incorporating the flexibility and creativity of humans.

2   Analysis of Mobile Ergonomic Records (AMbER)

To apply the described concept *Iteration by Design* in practice, it needs to be operationalized with all its constructs. The human factors analysis platform *Analysis of Mobile Ergonomic Records (AMbER)* was created for this purpose. AMbER is meant for two main areas of use in the context of AIS. First, as a tool for user state analysis, that gives real time feedback to the adaptation management component of the AIS. Second, as a tool for human-machine system evaluations to support design decisions regarding the AIS (see Fig. 2).

AMbER is primarily a modular software, which attempts to derive information about the user's state and interaction workflow by recording and analyzing user interactions,

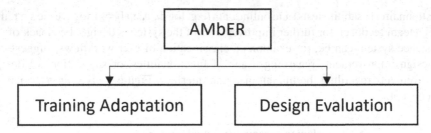

Fig. 2. Areas of use for the human factors analysis platform AMbER in the context of AIS.

e.g. mouse clicks, duration of interaction and temporal links between these interactions, together with further information from devices such as eye tracking, biosensors, or a webcam. The software with which the user interacts is interchangeable. The derived information of the interaction can then be matched with the original design intentions of the human-machine design team to evaluate the effectiveness, efficiency of the design and the user's satisfaction with the system.

The modularity of AMbER allows to selectively capture the metrics that are necessary for the analysis on the one hand and on the other hand it ensures the extensibility of the system through further modules. The general data flow within AMbER is shown in Fig. 3.

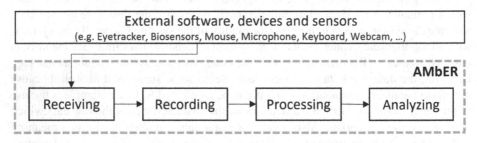

Fig. 3. General data flow of AMbER.

First, AMbER receives objective, and subjective data. These can be, for example, physiological, behavioral, or performance data, but also video, and audio streams. Then, AMbER records and preprocesses the received data. Finally, AMbER semi automatically analyzes the data to provide feedback to a technical system, like an AIS, or a design team of human machine systems.

Figure 4 shows a screenshot where AMbER is used for a human interface design evaluation of an air surveillance task. This configuration of AMbER contains the modules Screen Capture, Webcam Capture, BioHarness, and two modules for creating and displaying individual markers. The Screen Capture module displays the subject's screen in real time. Likewise, the Webcam Capture module displays the subject in front of the PC. The BioHarness Module is connected via Bluetooth to the Zephyr™ BioHarness device, which is worn by the subject and displays the subject's heart rate, heart rate variability, and body tilt. Via the Marker Generator module, an individual marker can be stored during the experiment in order to log special features (e.g. errors, observations, etc.) during the experiment. The created markers are displayed in the module below.

With its current modules, AMbER can receive and collect data from the following devices and sensors: Tobii ProFusion Eyetracker, Zephyr™ BioHarness, gamepads and joysticks, mouse, microphone, keyboard, and webcam. These devices and sensors provide raw data that is received and stored by AMbER. Subsequently, the data is processed and sometimes combined into new metrics. For example, the delivered image from the webcam is used for multiple purposes. Single webcam images are used to determine how many users are recognizable in the image, whether their faces are recognizable, where their faces are located in three-dimensional space related to the position of the webcam, and which emotions the faces exhibit within the webcam image. These metrics can then be used within the analysis functions in AMbER, for example, to infer the user's satisfaction based on the emotions.

3   Benefits of Multifactorial, Multidimensional Assessments of User States in Adaptive Instructional Systems

AIS usually assess the learner's performance to adjust the process and content of the learning program. However, there may be different reasons why learning outcomes differ between individuals and, also, within an individual from one time to another. Apart from individual characteristics such as skill level and experience, various adverse mental states of learners, such as inattention, negative emotional states (e.g. frustration), or high workload can considerably deteriorate learning performance. As proposed by Fuchs & Schwarz mitigating these states in an effective way requires different types of adaptation [5]. Still, addressing these factors within an AIS is challenging as it requires a continuous assessment of these states in real-time.

Our approach is to use our Human Factors Analysis Platform AMbER to collect on-task measures of learner performance as well as the learner's current mental state that can be used by an AIS to provide tailored feedback and adapt the learning content accordingly during the learning process.

The Human Factors Analysis platform AMbER takes up an approach of a multidimensional assessment of mental states proposed by Schwarz, Fuchs & Flemisch [6] that was technically implemented for adaptive system design as the Real time Assessment of Multidimensional User State (RASMUS, see [7]). The authors consider user state as a multidimensional construct by distinguishing six user state dimensions that can considerably affect operator performance: mental workload, engagement or motivation, situation awareness, attention (including vigilance), fatigue and emotional states (including stress).

The assessment of these states takes place in a multifactorial way. Physiological and behavioral data are combined with individual characteristics and environmental factors including task volume and complexity. This enables the technical system (e.g. an AIS) to not only react to different kinds of user states but also to address potential causes for critical user states. Hence, the multifactorial assessment enables the adaptive system to mitigate critical user states more effectively. During human-computer interaction, physiological activities of humans can be observed, processed, and interpreted by the

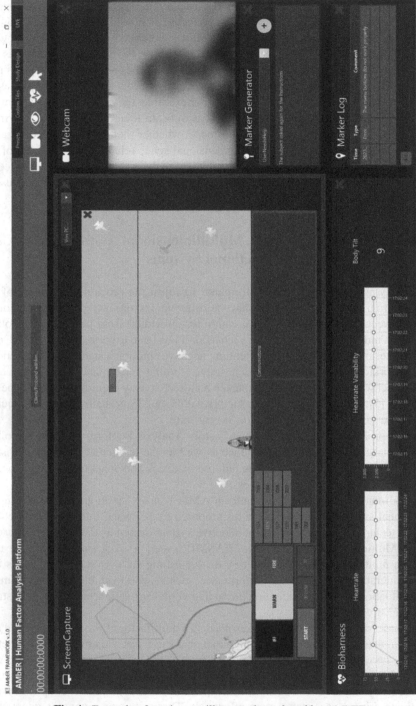

Fig. 4. Example of an air surveillance task, analyzed by AMbER.

computer via devices and sensors such as eye trackers or biosensors to infer underlying psychological processes.

Figures 5 and 6 show a possible step towards the operationalization of a design assistant system for AIS with the integration of user state analysis. Figure 5 addresses the first use case of AMbER named training adaptation (cf. Fig. 2). It details the workflow of the human machine system consisting of the user and the AIS. The real time user state analysis component RASMUS collects data on the user and analyzes the mental state of the user in real-time. RASMUS diagnostics are then used to decide whether there is a demand for adaptation of the training. If a demand for adaptation has been detected the adaptation management component ADAM (see [5]) selects and configures an appropriate adaptation strategy that causes changes in the system state. Figure 6 details the second use case of AMbER. It shows the interaction concept in which the human-machine system design team provides and changes the system design based on AMbER's design evaluations.

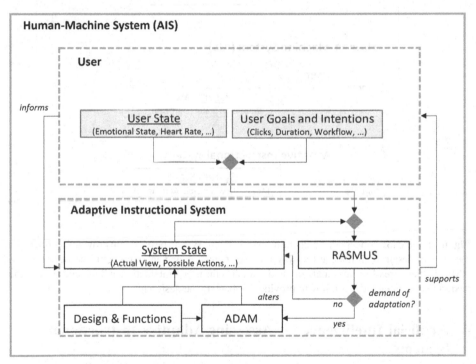

Fig. 5. A prototypical adaptive instructional system with the use of real time user state analysis RASMUS and the adaptation management component ADAM.

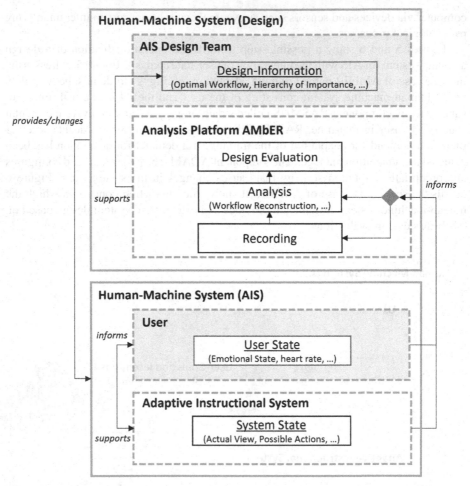

Fig. 6. Interaction concept in which the human-machine system design team provides and changes the system design to influence the way the user perceives and interacts with the design itself. AMbER therefore observes, analyzes, and evaluates the user's interaction and matches it with the design team's intended workflow to provide feedback to the design team.

4 Artificial Intelligence for Assessing Adaptive Instructional Systems

Progress in the research area of *Artificial Intelligence (AI)* makes AI suitable for the use of AIS. In the presented concept, different data, such as eye tracking information, heart rates, mouse interactions, and others, are collected over a period of time. These psychophysiological data are time series data due to the temporal recording. Also, the individual data points are often related to each other. For example, the build-up and decay of an emotion over time is a possible feature to better identify emotions compared to a static single image [8]. Thus, a time series provides not only static information of the individual data points, but also additional temporal information defined by the differences between the data points.

Each individual modality in human-computer interaction yields a univariate time series defined by $\{X_{1:n}\} = \{X_1; t = 1, 2, \ldots n\}$. Synchronized with each other, multiple univariate time series $\{X1:n\}$ form a multivariate time series $\{X_{1:n;1:k}\} = \{X_{1;1}; t = 1, 2, \ldots n; k = 1, 2, \ldots n\}$ over t time points and k modalities.

Semi automated, computer-aided analysis of multiple time series is particularly challenging, because it requires domain knowledge about each individual modality and well-prepared, synchronized data. The algorithms for analysis can be divided into statistical analysis models and models that make use of artificial intelligence [9]. The statistical analysis models are well suited for linear long-term data but have problems with non-linear and dynamic dependencies between multiple variables. In artificial intelligence models, artificial neural networks have emerged in processing multiple time series, because they can handle non-linearity and corresponding uncertainties in the data well. Psychophysiological data are often non-linear, which is why artificial neural networks are also a way to capture the state of a user. This can be done by analyzing inputs, behaviors, and interactions.

Multivariate time series analyses can reveal possible relationships between modalities. This allows statements about the variance explanatory proportion of individual modalities, as well as their content overlap, emergent properties, and interaction. A frequently encountered feature of human multimodal interaction is a high redundancy between modalities, as Chen has shown [10]. The information content of one modality overlaps with that of other modalities. For example, facial expressions as well as the tone of voice partly indicate the emotional state of a person [11]. Besides redundancy, the interaction of several modalities often leads to a complementary effect. In the example, since neither facial expression in detail nor pitch alone can unambiguously infer the emotional state, the interaction of both modalities better clarifies the actual emotional state. In general, an often-made assumption is, that the more information is available, the more accurate inferences can be made (see [12, 13]). However, the practical, everyday processing of large amounts of information comes up against natural and technical boundaries for humans and computers. Regarding the steady expansion of these technical limits, computers are increasingly able to process multimodal amounts of information efficiently and in near real time. In addition, developments in machine learning techniques, such as deep neural networks, have greatly fueled re-search around multimodal data over the past decade. So, despite the advances of technology and theory, the integration of more modalities and raw data should still be led by thriftiness due to the limitations [14].

4.1 Metric Extraction

Our analysis platform AMbER combines various data streams from a wide range of devices and sensors, which record different user states. The resulting time series can be processed into individual metrics, for example through classification algorithms. Using these metrics, AMbER can perform targeted analyses. For example, AMbER can capture the webcam image at 30 Hz, process each frame, and generate metrics such as emotion through neural network classification. The information about emotions represents a processed metric, which together with the time course over the other processed images provides an overview of the emotional course. Based on the progression of emotions, the user's mood can in turn be inferred. In summary, the perceived emotion at a specific time t, the course of emotions over a period of time defined by the timespan $t_{n:m}$, or the derived mood can each be used as a value for further analysis.

4.2 Workflow Reconstruction

By actively recording the software, being evaluated, and the user's input on the interface, AMbER attempts to reconstruct the user's individual workflow. This is made possible by the temporal sequence of inputs such as mouse clicks on certain interface elements. If the user clicks on a certain button A at a time t0, which changes the interface, and the user then clicks on another button B at a subsequent time, t1 for example, AMbER reconstructs the workflow based on a graph representation. A graph representation is a way of visually representing relationships between objects or entities. It consists of nodes, which represent the objects, and edges, which represent the connections or relationships between the objects (see [15, 16]). Both buttons would be represented as nodes, which are connected by their temporal interaction sequence with a directed edge from element A to B. The connection itself is weighted by a factor $w_{A:B}$ which can be between zero and 100%. The basic concept is shown in Fig. 7.

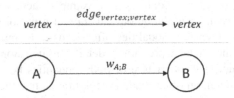

Fig. 7. General graph representation of the user's workflow, where (A) and (B) represent different interface elements, like two buttons.

Through a reinforcement learning algorithm, the weighting of the connection of two elements is adjusted with each interaction that takes place in the context of one of the two elements. The factor $w_{A:B}$ of the edge of two elements A and B becomes smaller if the user interacts with another element, for example C, instead of B after interacting with element A. This would result in an additional connection A to C, which would initially be weighted equally as the connection from A to B. If the user now predominantly interacts with element C after element A, then the $w_{A:B}$ would be increasingly devalued and the weighting $w_{A:C}$ would be increasingly upgraded, as shown in Fig. 8. The sum of all weights w starting from one element, like A, is always 100%.

The reconstructed workflows of a single user can then be aggregated by taking all connections and interactions into the graph representation and weighting them accordingly so that the sum of the weights of outgoing edges always remains 100%. In the same way, the reconstructed workflows of all users can be aggregated to obtain the average workflow of all users. The aggregated, as well as the non-aggregated, workflows can then

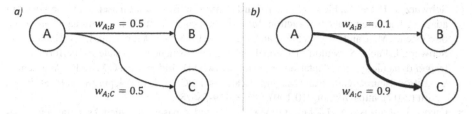

Fig. 8. Weighted interaction connections. In a) there is an equal interaction connection from A to B and C. In b) there is an unequal interaction connection, whereas C is the more likely interaction that follows A.

be compared with the originally conceived UX workflow stated by the human-machine design team to initialize improvements.

5 Conclusion and Future Developments

AMbER is the attempt to operationalize the design concept *Iteration by Design* [4]. The modular software architecture provides flexibility to use the analysis platform for a wide variety of domains. It supports design teams to evaluate different design solutions of human-machine-systems as adaptive instructional systems. The incorporated user state analysis RASMUS further offers real-time assessments of user states that can trigger adaptations with an AIS.

Future developments are aimed at integrating more modules for different sensors, like light sensors and for the analysis and visualization of recorded data.

References

1. Altun, D., et al.: Lessons learned from creating, implementing and evaluating assisted e-learning incorporating adaptivity, recommendations and learning analytics. In: Sottilare, R.A., Schwarz, J. (eds.) Adaptive Instructional Systems, pp. 257–270. Springer, Cham (2022)
2. Kelley, C.R.: What is adaptive training? Hum. Fact. J. Hum. Fact. Ergon. Soc. **11**, 547–556 (1969). https://doi.org/10.1177/001872086901100602
3. Rerhaye, L., Altun, D., Krauss, C., Müller, C.: Evaluation methods for an AI-supported learning management system: quantifying and qualifying added values for teaching and learning. In: Sottilare, R.A., Schwarz, J. (eds.) Adaptive Instructional Systems, pp. 394–411. Springer, Cham (2021)
4. Witte, T.E.F., Hasbach, J., Schwarz, J., Nitsch, V.: Towards iteration by design: an interaction design concept for safety critical systems. In: Sottilare, R.A., Schwarz, J. (eds.) Adaptive Instructional Systems. LNCS, vol. 12214, pp. 228–241. Springer, Cham (2020). https://doi.org/10.1007/978-3-030-50788-6_17
5. Fuchs, S., Schwarz, J.: Towards a dynamic selection and configuration of adaptation strategies in augmented cognition. In: Schmorrow, D.D., Fidopiastis, C.M. (eds.) Augmented Cognition. Enhancing Cognition and Behavior in Complex Human Environments. LNCS, vol. 10285, pp. 101–115. Springer, Cham (2017). https://doi.org/10.1007/978-3-319-58625-0_7

6. Schwarz, J., Fuchs, S., Flemisch, F.: Towards a more holistic view on user state assessment in adaptive human-computer interaction. In: Proceedings of the IEEE International Conference on Systems, Man, and Cybernetics, San Diego, CA, USA, 5–8 October, pp. 1228–1234 (2014)

7. Schwarz, J., Fuchs, S.: Multidimensional real-time assessment of user state and performance to trigger dynamic system adaptation. In: Schmorrow, D.D., Fidopiastis, C.M. (eds.) Augmented Cognition. Neurocognition and Machine Learning. LNCS, vol. 10284, pp. 383–398. Springer, Cham (2017). https://doi.org/10.1007/978-3-319-58628-1_30

8. Ouzar, Y., Bousefsaf, F., Djeldjli, D., Maaoui, C.: Video-based multimodal spontaneous emotion recognition using facial expressions and physiological signals. In: 2022 IEEE/CVF Conference on Computer Vision and Pattern Recognition Workshops (CVPRW), pp. 2459–2468. IEEE (2022)

9. Sarker, I.H.: Machine learning: algorithms, real-world applications and research directions. SN Comput. Sci. 2(3), 1–21 (2021). https://doi.org/10.1007/s42979-021-00592-x

10. Chen, L.S.H.: Joint processing of audio-visual information for the recognition of emotional expressions in human-computer interaction. University of Illinois at Urbana-Champaign (2020)

11. Schirmer, A., Adolphs, R.: Emotion perception from face, voice, and touch: comparisons and convergence. Trends Cogn. Sci. 21, 216–228 (2017). https://doi.org/10.1016/j.tics.2017.01.001

12. Lu, J.T.: Causal network inference from gene transcriptional time series response to glucocorticoids (2019). https://doi.org/10.1101/587170

13. Moreno-Fernández, M.M., Matute, H.: Biased sampling and causal estimation of health-related information: laboratory-based experimental research. J. Med. Internet Res. 7(22), e17502 (2020). https://doi.org/10.2196/17502

14. Escolano, F.: Graph-Based Representations in Pattern Recognition: 6th IAPR-TC-15 International Workshop, GbRPR 2007, Alicante, Spain, June 2007, Proceedings, pp. 11–13. Springer, Germany (2007)

15. Jaimes, A., Sebe, N.: Multimodal human–computer interaction: a survey. Comput. Vis. Image Underst. 108, 116–134 (2007). https://doi.org/10.1016/j.cviu.2006.10.019

16. Seng, K.P., Ang, L., Liew, A.W.-C., Gao, J.: Multimodal information processing and big data analytics in a digital world. In: Multimodal Analytics for Next-Generation Big Data Technologies and Applications, pp. 3–9. Springer, Cham (2019)

Research on the Interaction Design of Teaching Aid Products Based on the Concept of Modularity

Shan Xu[✉], Yue Zhang, Ting Yang, and Xiaomeng Wang

Guangxi Normal University, Guilin 541006, China
1148346814@qq.com

Abstract. This thesis gives analyses and summary on the requirements of teaching aids for primary school classrooms from different aspects through understanding the different physiological and psychological characteristics and needs of primary school students. Considering the current situation that "multiple uses of one room" is common for early childhood education centers in China, it is concluded that we should apply interactive modularity to analyse and innovate the design of existing teaching aids for classroom teaching, so the designs can not only meet the needs of primary school students' visual and tactile sensory development, but also promote their mental and physical development in a coordinated and healthy manner. At the same time, the proposal tidying-up is also beneficial for primary school students to develop a good self-management and tidying-up habit. On this basis, the modular concept can be scientifically distilled into separate modules and unit blocks, maintaining the integrity of the product, but also decomposing it and maintaining the independence of the modular design concept. Interactive modularity aids product design is conducive to students cognitive development. The reorganization of interactive modularity provides a good interactive experience for students to give full play to their inquisitive spirit, enabling their hands-on, exploratory and divergent thinking skills to be effectively developed. Therefore, the concept of interactive modular product design is the inevitable result of meeting the future market demand for intelligent classrooms.

Keywords: Interaction Design · Modularity · Teaching Aid · Innovative Design

1 Introduction

With the rapid development of technology, high-tech products through design have been applied to serve the mass in recent years, and because of the increasing number of children in China for the three-child policy, teaching aids for children become more and more important. Therefore, lots of teaching aids have entered the classroom, and changed the traditional teaching aids, bringing more innovative interactive experience design. However, In the current market, most of the teaching aids have the same shortcomings, such as single function, outdated shape and lack of innovative service design. At present, in order to solve the problems on the market and to meet the needs of users, it is necessary to carry out product innovation, and at the same time add emotional service design and interesting design, and take effective digital innovation and modelling innovation, keeping pace with the development of the era. On this basis, a teaching aid product that combines the concept of modularity and interaction is designed, with deliberately ideological guidance and transmission for the children, cultivates students' thinking and hands-on skills early, so that the students can not only gain some extra-curricular knowledge but also have a better interactive experience when using the modular teaching aid product.

2 Definition

Interaction design, or communicative interaction, is the behaviour and design domain that defines the designer-making system, the content and structure of communication between two or more interacting individuals that work together to achieve an interactive experience. The goals of interaction design can be analyzed on two levels: 'usability' and 'user experience'. In order to help children use interactive modular teaching aids and to maximize the meaning of teaching aids, more time is supposed to be spent on helping users understand and use the aids. The design of the visual pages, tactile pages and assemblies is suitable to set up the connection between the aids and users behaviour. The elements in the shape of the teaching aids and the layout of the interface, such as the colors, the various messages conveyed, the elements of composition, etc., are all able to convey the interactive information that assists the teaching aids to the user and enhance the user initial experience.

In fact, compared to traditional design disciplines, interaction design is an emerging discipline that integrates the knowledge of several disciplines and can be said to be a product of the Internet era and the age of intelligence. Interaction design adheres to the concept of "human-oriented" and uses various high-technology tools to improve the user experience from different aspects.

The so-called block-based design is simply the combination of various parts of a product to form a subsystem with specific functions, and the subsystem is common to other elements of the product to form a new system combination, with different functions or the same functions and different performance of the product portfolio, is the same or similar modules in the product identification, classification, definition, specification, to establish a common module. On this basis, generic modular combinations and variants are made to design interactive modular teaching aids that can quickly meet users' diverse and high quality needs at low cost [1].

3 Trends in Teaching Aid Products

Firstly, this thesis has researched and analysed a wide range of traditional and modern classroom teaching aids. Traditional teaching aids are one of the most important teaching aids, which are not only teaching aids but also carrying a certain cultural deposits. With the rapid development of science and technology in the new era, traditional teaching aids have been subjected to a huge impact and have gradually fallen out of favour, thus losing the mainstream market for teaching aids. But what is certain is the educational significance of traditional teaching aids in spreading culture, and in the new era of constantly advocating that Made in China should be transformed into Intelligengtly Made in China, traditional teaching aids should keep up with the times and be updated. Most of the teaching aids currently on the market have a single function and fail to truly integrate the technology of the new era with the cultural meaning of traditional teaching aids, which is a problem that needs to be solved. It is necessary to innovate the design of traditional teaching aids, add interactive modularity and emotional design, and take effective digital innovation and modelling innovation, keeping pace with the development of the times. The current social development trend shows that children will occupy an important position in the future society and children's products will be expanded and developed in the future. The advancement of technology also determines the shape of products, children can no longer be satisfied with a single product form, the future development trend of children's teaching aids must be multi-functional, innovative and intelligent [2]. The design of "modular teaching aids" is combined with fun, simplicity, learning and interactivity, and innovative design elements are extracted according to different combinations of modular teaching aids and different modules for animal, plant and geometric shapes. First of all, it visually attracts children and allows them to think and assemble new horizons through visual, tactile and auditory use of the modular teaching aids. Children can have fun thinking and learning in the process and at the same time develop their hands-on skills. Interactive modular aids are more attractive to children (see Fig. 1).

4   Significance of the Interactive Innovation Design of Modular Teaching Aids

This design focuses on the theme of "interactive modular teaching aid product design". Through the innovation of the teaching aid shape, the most direct and simple way of interaction is used to enhance children's love for teaching aids, and also to develop children's ability to assemble, put together and store them, so that children can learn more and have fun while interacting with the teaching aids. Secondly, through their own activities, children can observe and explore the design of the modular surroundings and practice the interaction design. In this process, children are guided through the visual symbolism of the teaching aids to solve problems, develop logical thinking, stimulate divergent thinking and creativity through tactile, visual and auditory factors, and learn more about modular assembly while gaining a better interactive experience [3]. The focus of this design is to emphasise the innovative, interesting and interactive nature of the teaching aids and to have a certain emotional design, i.e. to meet the functional needs and at the same time provide an amount of companionship for the children's growth. The modular storage design is planned in such a way that children can develop good storage practices from an early age and optimise the use of classroom space. This is the meaning of the innovative design of the "interactive modular teaching aids" (see Fig. 2).

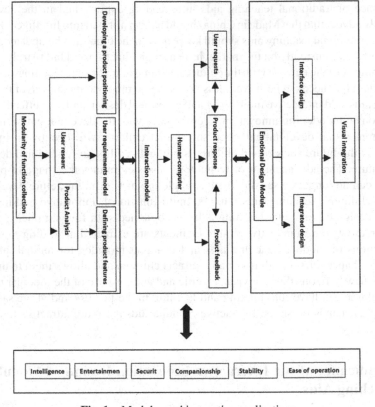

Fig. 1. Modular and innovative applications

5 Principles of Interactive Innovation Design for Modular Teaching Aids

5.1 Safety Principle

4–8 years old children are in the most energetic period, the surrounding environment and things are always full of curiosity, especially the shape of a novel and unique bright color and interactive function of intelligent products can quickly attract their attention, and stimulate their thinking and curiosity. Children lack the ability to judge the safety of things around them and lack the awareness and ability to protect themselves [4]. Children use products in a more rudimentary way for practical operation and do not have the patience to learn and use complex functions. Therefore, product operation and functionality must be designed in moderation to ensure that overly complex use does not result in children losing interest. In addition, children's products must first and foremost meet the most basic requirements in terms of structural and material safety. In terms of ergonomics and user experience, the design must be comfortable and easy to use.

Ergonomic data is used in the design of the structure, the physical characteristics of children of all ages are accurately analyzed and children's teaching aids are analyzed in

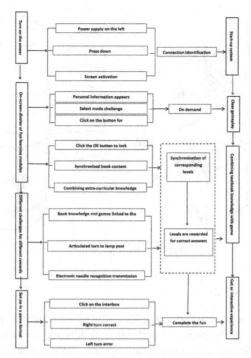

Fig. 2. Flow chart of the use of modular teaching aids

terms of size and height, while scientific divisions and rational planning are carried out [5]. When children use teaching aids, they need to consider whether the height at which they access things is appropriate for the child and whether it is the most comfortable and safe height for the child, so that the design of the teaching aids is rationalized, safe and practical (Fig. 3).

5.2 The Educative Principle

The development and design of interactive modular teaching aids is based on the principle of the educational nature of children. The most prominent aspect of the teaching aids is the subtle cultivation of children's independent learning. Children's teaching tasks and extended knowledge outside the classroom are integrated into the teaching aids, teaching modes, interactive modes and play modes are cleverly combined with modularity and appearance of shapes and colors, the development and design of teaching aids focusing on children's sensory training, tactile abilities, cognitive abilities, social skills and logical thinking skills are explored, and theory and practice are integrated into the interactive modular teaching aids. In the process of transforming interactive modular teaching aids, the attributes and importance of the teaching aid products are reflected in the knowledge structures and learning abilities as well as the physical, psychological, emotional and attitudinal aspects that are important in promoting children's language, intellectual, emotional, thinking and social development [6].

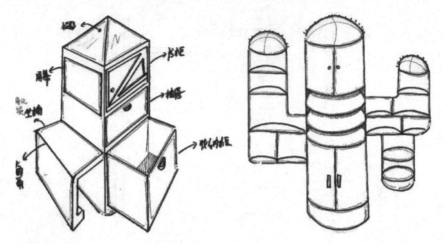

Fig. 3. . Design sketch

5.3   The Interest Principle

Early children's products design often reflect a focus on function, while neglecting the form and playfulness of the product, with most children's products reflecting a singularity of function. Interactive modular teaching aids, on the other hand, should present a clever combination of learning content and game form, not only as a fun-filled way of learning using games as a medium, but also as an important vehicle for ability shaping and development, no longer simply fun in the sense of fun [7]. Therefore, the design of interactive modular teaching aids should be based on the children's educational curriculum, choosing appropriate types of games to explore the rewarding pathways of the different modules and ensuring that the form of the game matches the curriculum knowledge effectively. Intellectually creating a game environment, clarify game rules, organise game content and game situations, using games as clues to advance curriculum content, and using games to develop knowledge of people and objects, communication between people, and interaction between people and society, and to fully emphasise the interactive narrative approach of games rather than the games themselves, ultimately activating children's learning and training through gamified learning experiences. Interactive modular teaching aids are based on the idea that children can learn, train, participate and enjoy independently [8]. Not only objects, but also games, stories and educational content. In the experience of constantly trying and reaping the joy, children build up a certain level of self-confidence, and develop the ability to think independently and solve problems, allowing themselves to learn while having fun and highlighting the greatest advantages of interactive modular teaching aids.

5.4   The Participation Principle

The company of family and friends in the process of children's growth is indispensable. In the process of interacting with assistive teaching aids with the participation of small partners are in mutual assistance to further the process of interactive modular exploration and learning. If children's assistive teaching aids are simply operated without interaction or communication, children will lose some of their sense of participation and experience in the process [9]. For example, in assistive teaching aids, children can assemble and store them and interact with them, so that they can observe, touch and assemble them carefully. The interactive and collaborative part of the design of the aids can greatly increase children's interest in the aids, as well as developing their ability to work with a team (Fig. 4).

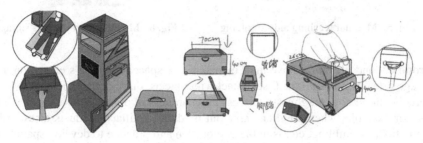

Fig. 4. . Design sketch

6 Innovative Design Practice for Teaching Aid Product Interaction

6.1 Design Introduction

The "Fun Learning House" is an interactive modular teaching aid, which is scientifically divided according to the human-computer relationship, designed with the most convenient, direct and interesting interactive modules, and precisely produced the modular internal structure and articulated combination shape of the product, expanding the storage space of the product to achieve the maximum modularity to meet the users The interactive modular teaching aids are more effective in bringing children's needs to life [10]. Interactive modular teaching aids can bring more pleasure and knowledge to children and stimulate their potential. In the face of traditional single children's products, children are more willing to choose smart products that are new, vibrant and colourful and can bring convenience to their life. Therefore, children's pursuit of intelligent products is a major trend in design philosophy [11]. The screen to the left of the teaching aid records children's individual learning, borrowing and answering data. The "Fun Learning House" allows you to compete with your friends in a game format to gain knowledge inside and outside the classroom, consolidate knowledge in the classroom and gain knowledge outside the classroom through small interactions, increasing the sense of interaction between friendships (see Fig. 5–6).

6.2 Application of Innovative Design Principles for Teaching Aid Product Interaction in Practice

Modular DAY Design Approach. Spatial cognitive ability is a relatively important ability in children's growth and development. Children themselves are in a huge spatial

Fig. 5. Modular teaching aids unfolding   **Fig. 6.** Modular teaching aids storage

environment and all things have their own sense of space. Children's education at an early age often begins with the first contact with objects, through the touch of the hands to perceive the shape, roughness, softness and hardness of objects and other character-istics, for example, when children carry out modular auxiliary products disassembly, combination, assembling, etc. is in the exploration and practice to develop spatial cog-nitive ability, through the hand, eye, brain and other movements and thinking, to form a relatively comprehensive cognition of things [12]. When direct contact between the body and teaching aids brings a rich tactile sensation to the child, the child will have a phys-iological or psychological effect based on tactile perception and the generalized effect of touch, enriching the child's understanding of the world and the perception of things in this process of constant contact. The children next tactile experience will combine with existing memories to jointly influence feedback, and create a more accurate tactile sensory experience as tactile memories accumulate and connections between imagery continue to be refined.

Children have an advantage in perceiving colour as they grow up. Children typically learn about things through colour, shape and sound. Creating a positive environment can stimulate children's education while developing their imagination, perception and choices. Colour is most likely to develop one's imagination, enrich one's imagination and stimulate the production of emotions. A well-coloured environment is key to children's artistic creativity. When designing for colour, attention should be paid to the educational properties of colour. Children at this stage are most attracted to natural elements and more refreshing shades [13], so the overall palette is dominated by red, yellow, blue and green colours that can attract children's attention (Figs. 7 and 8).

Modular Interactive Experience Mode. Mainly for children (4–8) years old, some interactive experience designs are supposed to be added to the children's modular inter-active teaching aids when the designer consider the functionality of the product (see Fig. 9–10), like some interactive reward forms with game-play, such as adding some dra-matic elements. For example, characters, stories, collecting, planting, etc., and designing levels to motivate children to participate. It is important to inspire children's minds and expand their interest while meeting their spiritual and 'material' needs. After the satis-faction of being rewarded, the development of their interest and the expansion of their knowledge is a very important added value of our interface. At the same time, the modu-larity of the different interactive combinations has to be unlocked with different answers in order to be used accordingly, the symbols on the left screen will guide children in their

Fig. 7. Stowing the box portable   **Fig. 8.** Screen

actions, children can play in single or double mode for entertainment, the challenges vary depending on the needs of the child, when the challenge is completed the screen will send out a prompt page to pass the level and also receive the corresponding reward, if the answer is wrong, the corresponding failure page will appear. The rewards set, such as the use of a storage cart for passing the first level and the best position to watch the video for passing the second level, reduce the potential for children to become utilitarian compared to physical rewards such as toys and pocket money. Due to the age, the range of things available to children has become more and more varied and the way in which their sense of achievement is met must keep pace with the times. Therefore, compared to simple formal rewards, such as posting small red flowers, our reward mechanism is richer in both varied and visual aspects, and is more able to attract children to complete tasks, for them to adhere to this behaviour of punching cards to complete tasks in the long term, cultivate their perseverance, and tap into children's exploratory abilities and contribute to the development of their minds, and at the same time it can achieve the purpose of teaching and learning while having fun [14].

Fig. 9. Projection   **Fig. 10.** 360°projection

Modular Material Perception Analysis. The choice of materials and the design of children's products should not only be in line with children's development, but also follow sustainable design trends [15]. The use of cheap, poor quality materials not only threatens the health and safety of children, but also causes environmental pollution. In the choice of materials, children's products should be reasonable and safe, with priority given to the use of green, non-toxic materials. At present, green materials are expensive in the market and consumers feel that children grow up too quickly and some products are "discarded" after a few years or else they are omitted because children's cognitive abilities continue to strengthen and become resistant to certain products, resulting in a waste of resources. The materials used in children's products must be safe in terms of composition and the materials chosen should be non-toxic. Also, children's products should pay attention to the physical properties of the materials when choosing them, and we should pay attention to their quality, density, odour, colour and thermal conductivity. However, the choice of materials in the design of children's products does not have to be "perfect"; reasonable, suitable and safe materials are preferred, and the products are green and non-toxic, simple and practical for maximum affinity.

6.3   The Ultimate Practical Significance of Modular Teaching Aid Product Design

The "Fun Learning House" teaching aids combine intelligence, skills, fun and other aspects.

In the appearance of the geometric shape and plant and animal shape for organic combination to give a unique and novel shape, color selection will be based on the needs of users, as children are more sensitive to color changes [16], so the choice of bright colors will enhance the children's sensitivity to the appearance of color at the same time gradually exercise their aesthetic ability and color matching ability. In terms of combination, "Fun Learning House" uses the principle of modularity to combine the parts of the product to form a specific functional combination, and the parts are disassembled into different sub-combinations to form a new system, which improves children's hands-on assembly and splicing ability. In terms of interaction, children can operate according to the interactive interface in the screen, open the game breakthrough mode and answer questions according to the corresponding questions in the screen, so as to gain new knowledge in the fun interactive experience, it increases children's love for teaching aids, and improve children's interest in learning, so that they can implicitly gain knowledge in the game (Figs. 11 and 12).

Fig. 11. Reading scenario

Fig. 12. Viewing scenario

7 Conclusion

In summary, children's modular products must follow the laws of children's cognition and development, combine and integrate games and teaching materials with each other in conducting modular interactive experiences, and focus on fun and interactivity. Besides, they should meet the educational learning needs of children, parents and teachers, and promote children's spatial literacy. Children's multi-level needs are progressive and simultaneous, and in order to accurately identify children's needs, it is necessary to specifically analyse children's characteristics at different stages and in different environments, as well as to emphasise a more specific and in-depth understanding of children's needs at different levels when designing different functions and types of products. The modular teaching aids are designed to promote children's growth and enhance their exploration and imagination, cognitive, perceptual and thinking skills as well as their hands-on abilities. The choice of shapes, colors, components and interactions of the modular teaching aids have been designed to better serve the needs of children. The "Learning House" is targeted at children aged 4–8 years. It is designed to maximize the meaning of interactive modular teaching aids, and combine theory and practice, teaching materials and games. Most importantly, it improves children's hands-on assembly and storage skills, that is to say, they may have fun while learning and gain knowledge while entertaining, which creates them a safe and interesting modular aid.

Funding.   Innovation Project of Guangxi Graduate Education, "Innovative Design of children's Educational AIDS Under the Concept of STEAM Education" (Serial Number: XYCSR2023014).

References

1. Bijuan, L.: A study of children's product design based on modular design approach. Mech. Des. **31**(7), 3 (2014)
2. Zizhu, C.: On the innovation and development of children's product design. J. Tonghua Normal College **39**(4), 4 (2018)
3. Yanqun, W., et al.: Research on the product design of interactive children's play and teaching aids based on interest guidance. Packag. Eng. (2018)
4. Chang, Y.: Research on children's product design based on children's need levels. Art Des. Theory Edn. **10**, 3 (2015)
5. Bijuan, L.: Humanized design of children's products. Packag. Eng. **27**(1), 3 (2006)
6. Talking about the influence of color on children's physiology and psychology in product design. Western Leather **40**(8), 1 (2018)
7. Tingting, Q., Diying, S., Xin, L.: Combined innovative design and engineering analysis of children's furniture. J. Eng. Des. **18**(4), 4 (2011)
8. Bingjie, Z.: Knowledge visualization-based interaction design for early childhood education products. Autom. Instrum. **008**, 000(2022)
9. Meng, L., Yunpeng, J.: Research on the interaction design of children's games in smart home scenarios. Packag. Eng. **43**(16), 68–75 (2022)
10. Yi, C., Zensheng, L.: Product design opportunities for early education products for preschool children based on physical interaction. Design **19**, 3 (2018)
11. Yudong, F., Lin, Y.: Design of educational furniture for preschool children based on transplantation design method. Design **33**(21), 3 (2020)

12. Ling, C.: Research on the product design of interactive children's play and teaching aids based on interest guidance. Sci. Technol. Wind **13**, 2(2021)
13. Weibin, D., Yichun, W.: Color science in children's product design. In: Popular Literature and Arts: Academic Edition 2, p. 1 (2017)
14. Xiaohong, X., Yunyi, L.: A study on digital-assisted children's interface design for developing self-control. Art Technol. **4**, 2 (2019)
15. Ying-Xi, C.: Product development for younger children from a sustainable perspective. In: Popular Literature and Arts: A Study of Science Education 016 (2021)
16. Xinyi, Y.: Exploring the emotional elements of color in children's product design. In: Popular Literature and Art: Academic Edition 13, p. 1 (2016)

Design of Educational Interactive Teaching Aids for Children Based on the Art of Chinese Character Structure

Ting Yang, Xiaomeng Wang, Shan Xu, Yue Zhang, and Yun Liang[✉]

School of Design, Guangxi Normal University, Guilin 541006, China
liangyun0730@me.com

Abstract. In order to address the problem of children's interest in learning to read and recognise Chinese characters, which is caused by the boring teaching and the uniform practice of writing, the theory of interactive teaching aids is proposed, which takes into account the diversity of educational methods and the flexibility of teaching methods. By incorporating interactive, experiential and educational features into children's interactive educational aids, we use questionnaires and surveys to understand the current educational market for children's educational interactive products related to Chinese characters, and analyse and optimise them, so that we can develop and integrate our thinking and adopt an interactive design for children that is consistent with the teaching of Chinese characters. The design of a teaching aid with an interactive experience and a novel learning method is proposed for children aged 3–6. The starting point is to dismantle the Chinese character strokes and pinyin, to make learning Chinese characters fun, to allow children to learn the art of Chinese character culture through product interaction, to receive a lot of information about Chinese character strokes, colours and space, to subvert the traditional Chinese character teaching and to enhance children's hands-on and logical thinking skills.

Keywords: The art of Chinese character structure · interactive design · educational · children's products · Chinese character culture

1 Introduction

Chinese characters are a long-standing Chinese treasure handed down from five thousand years of Chinese culture, and are the result of the ancient Chinese ancestors' understanding and thinking about everyday matters. It is one of the carriers of culture, recording the historical trajectory of cultural development; it is also a symbolic system for recording and transmitting language, becoming a unique tool for human thinking and communication [1]. Created spontaneously by our ancestors, Chinese characters reflect the development of the Chinese nation from ancient times to the present day. Chinese cultural literacy teaching aids should be designed in such a way that children can experience the beauty and rhythm of Chinese characters in the process of learning their shapes, meanings and sounds [2]. Nowadays, with the rapid development of the economy, people are

P. Zaphiris et al. (Eds.): HCII 2023, LNCS 14060, pp. 369–381, 2023.
https://doi.org/10.1007/978-3-031-48060-7_28

paying more and more attention to the interaction behaviour between users and products. With the development of interaction technology, interaction forms have become rich and diversified [3], and the study of the application of children's educational aids and interaction design has certain practical significance. The five elements of interaction design are: the person, the action, the tool or medium, the purpose and the scene [4].

The importance of combining fun with teaching is emphasised by the Chinese tradition of education, as mentioned in the book "The Book of Modern Thinking", where it is said that "if you do not see the fun in teaching, you will not enjoy learning"[5]. Innovative learning methods stimulate children's interest in learning and make literacy teaching fun in a relaxed and enjoyable learning context, so that students can learn and play while they play. With the full implementation of China's two-child policy and three-child policy, there will be more and more educational problems to be solved by identifying problems, solving them from a design perspective, and conducting in-depth problem solving with an innovative approach.

2 The Relationship Between Interaction Design and Children's Literacy Teaching Aids

2.1 The Significance of Behavioural Analysis in Interaction Design for Children's Teaching Aids

Interaction design is the analysis of the psychological and behavioural characteristics of the user to enhance the interaction between the user and the product in the design of the product, which is very important in the design of the product [6] and is the key to a good or bad product design.

With the complexity of products and the variety of ways to use them, interaction design has gradually come into the public eye. The link between "products" and "people" is getting stronger and stronger. People use various products to satisfy their needs in life, and the value of the product is reflected in the interaction between people and the product [1]. Behavioural analysis in interaction design can generate appropriate and reasonable behavioural and emotional connections between products and users, pay attention to the physiological and behavioural characteristics of users, integrate interaction design concepts into the design of children's teaching aids, improve product functions, innovate product usage, make products provide better services to users, reduce user cognitive friction, and increase product functionality and efficiency. Therefore, the application of interaction design behavioural analysis in children's educational tools will enable designers to better identify the pain points of children's educational tools in the design process and find solutions and solutions quickly and efficiently, so that they can accurately capture the specific needs of users and thus better design children's educational toys.

2.2 Methods and Steps for the Use of Interaction Design in Children's Teaching Aids

The research methodologies used in the study were questionnaires and market research. Firstly, in the early stages of the design process, the designer investigates the user's behaviour towards the subject or learning scenario of the tool, records the learning behaviour of the target user and the problems that arise, and then summarises and analyses the pain points and target users. As the object of interaction design is dynamic user behaviour [7]. On this basis, the design is based on the learning behaviour of the target user as the main object of study, so that the teaching aids are fundamentally for and understood by children. While conducting the research and analysis of the existing teaching aids on the market in terms of function, colour, discipline, usage and material, the common features were summarised (Table 1). Interaction refers to a dialogue between a person and a machine using a certain language. In educational games a certain interaction is used to complete the process of information exchange between the child and the learning system [8]. There are many different types of interactive teaching aids in today's educational market, depending on the nature of the education, and the variety of colours, types of aids, sizes, materials and interaction methods used can make a difference in the way the aids are placed on the market. Through this variation, children use different teaching aids to understand more quickly what they are trying to communicate, to understand the meaning of the pictures or videos, and to induce independent learning behaviour through the use of the aids.

The target information is extracted and integrated to optimise the design. During the design process, the target users are invited to experience and comment on the design, increasing the interactivity between the teaching aid and the interactive design, and arriving at a design that best meets the consumer's psychological expectations. In the later stages of the design process, the design is optimised and improved based on the feedback received from the initial market launch and the issues that have arisen, resulting in a final draft design and research report.

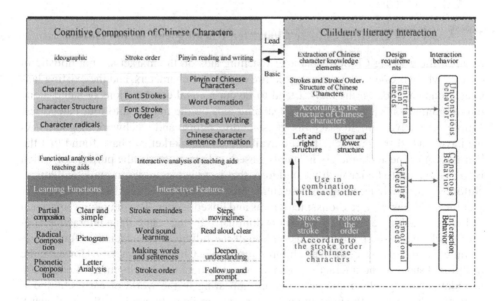

Table 1. Analysis of the functions, colours, interaction methods and material extraction of the composition of text teaching aids on the market

Functional expressions	Color Analysis	Types of teaching aids	Material Analysis
• Basic expressions • Word meaning type • Contact Scene Type • Radical type	• high saturation type • wood color type • Monochromatic • light color type • dark color type	• Hand-eye coordination: educational hands-on, object recognition and knowledge • Academic puzzle type: intersection of disciplines, knowledge interpolation • Hands-on exercise type: puzzle interaction, hands-on coordination • coloring type: color initiation, picture recognition and drawing	• Plastic material: small volume of material, color diversity, versatile shape, less production costs • pure wood: with a long time, eye protection, close to nature • paper material: low cost, easy to observe

3 Analysis and Relevance of the Current Situation of Educational Teaching Aids for Children Under the Structure of Chinese Characters

3.1 Analysis of Existing Chinese Character Teaching Aids on the Market

Most of the existing Chinese character teaching aids on the market are not holistic in design, which is due to the special structure of Chinese characters, and the existing language teaching aids on the market tend to favour manual combinations or stand-alone interaction, classifying the language teaching aids on the market into four categories: simple interactive, simple assembly, press-and-recognise and patchwork magnetic. As we have studied the products that are available on the market, we have found that the learning of Chinese characters is mainly based on literacy cards, the purpose of which is to communicate better with the children, that is, to use graphics to guide and attract children's interest in learning Chinese characters. They are categorised according to their graphic style: basic expressions, pictograms and linked scenes. The interactive approach of literacy teaching aids on the market is dominated by the stand-alone interactive approach, which is rather monotonous, although the bilingual pronunciation function is complete and can correct the way children pronounce Chinese characters. However, the traditional stand-alone interactive method does not meet the development of education in today's society, electronic products are appearing in the world of early childhood education, how to use the interaction of electronic products to combine children's early childhood education is a difficult point to overcome in this design. Therefore, we need to analyse in depth the external assistance and intervention required in children's literacy and integrate interaction with electronic screens into children's language teaching aids, so that flexible electronics can be used to assist children's Chinese learning.

3.2 The Significance of Innovative Design of Children's Teaching Aids Under the Art of Chinese Characters

Chinese characters are a pictorial style used by ancient ancestors to express and record the representational characteristics of things, and among the teaching aids for learning Chinese characters, pattern recognition is particularly important. Graphic patterns are an important component of literacy products. Graphic patterns have accompanied the development of human civilisation since ancient times, and they convey the message that the product needs to convey. In the choice of design elements, the choice of graphics can have a direct impact on children's moods. Therefore, when designing literacy cards, cute or simple cartoon images made up of colours that are more approachable to children are often used to aid cognition (Fig. 1).

Fig. 1. Electronic screen interaction page design

As a teaching aid, the Chinese character teaching aids are based on a summary of the key points needed in teaching Chinese characters, and the analysis of the literacy cards often requires knowledge of pinyin, radicals, strokes, phonetic sequence and structure. The Chinese character teaching aids are designed by taking the strokes of Chinese characters that have certain rules, dismantling the strokes of Chinese characters so that they can be assembled, rotating and changing them or modularising them for storage. By visualising the strokes of the characters in an interactive way, and breaking them down in steps to help children learn to master them, and by adding interest to the product with interactive pictures, children can put together and combine the strokes of the characters themselves, thus creating a new cultural experience. The design of the teaching aids overturns the traditional way of teaching language and writing, taking the dismantling of Chinese strokes and pinyin as the starting point to make teaching fun, increase children's hands-on and logical thinking skills, and incorporate knowledge of Chinese characters into play, allowing children to learn and be enlightened through play [9].

Chinese characters have evolved over thousands of years of history, gradually changing in form to strokes and in principle from representational, ideographic to morphosyntactic [10]. The Chinese character stroke is the smallest constituent unit of a Chinese character. The ancient script had no concept of strokes, and from the Li script onwards the flat, straight strokes gradually developed. In 1988, the State Language Commission and the Press and Publication Department published the "Modern Chinese Character List", which specifies five basic strokes (Table 2), namely: four single strokes: horizontal, vertical, apostrophe and dot; and one compound stroke: fold. The horizontal stroke includes the cross and the tilde: the dot includes the point and the press: the folding stroke can be subdivided into eight categories of 25 types according to the stroke forms they contain: horizontal, vertical, skew, dot, fold, tilde, bend and hook. The Chinese character teaching aids are aimed at children from 3–6 who are in contact with Chinese characters and therefore have certain requirements on the user's ability to think and work with them. The design of the teaching aids must be in line with the children's thinking logic and cognitive level, and the teaching aids must be within the children's acceptable range.

After the above analysis, a more specific and detailed understanding of the product under study has been achieved, which will facilitate the subsequent design work and make the designed product more acceptable to the market and achieve the optimal solution for the design.

Table 2. Illustrations of the five basic strokes of Chinese characters

Five basic strokes	
Single Stroke	**Stroke variants**
横 一	平横：工、平、天、干 提横：拉、场、理、地
竖 丨	短竖：师、临、坚、归 长竖：干、丰、中、车
撇 丿	卧撇：千、舌、兼、乔 竖撇：月、川、头、周 长撇：刀、无、勿、为 短撇：面、白、舟、北
点 丶	短点：商、母、兴、邑 长点：双、头 挑点：河、求、冷、凉 左点：办、刃、心、必
Start-up system	
折 ㄱ	横勾、横折、平捺、斜捺、竖提、竖折、坚弯、竖勾、坚折折、竖折、 竖折折勾、竖弯勾、横折提、横撇、横撇弯勾、横折折撇、横折折折、 横折折折勾、横折勾、斜捺、平捺

4 Design of Educational and Interactive Teaching Aids for Children

4.1 Design Concepts for Interactive Teaching Aids Under the Art of Chinese Characters

There are so many strokes in Chinese characters, especially complex ones, that children may not know which one to start with, and they may not be familiar with the strokes and may write them in short or long lengths. If there are too many strokes, there will be a voice prompting the children to reduce the chance of misspelling, and additional cards will be added to those characters that have a high error rate and appear frequently to facilitate the children's understanding of the strokes and to aid teaching. Children learn Chinese characters by playing with the teaching aids, which improves learning efficiency and increases children's ability to learn independently.

4.2 Target User Research Analysis

The target user of this design is now positioned at children aged 3–6 years who are learning the initial development of Chinese characters. The target customers are educational institutions who want to make a profit, teachers who want to improve the efficiency of their classes and parents who want to help their children learn. It can also be for people who are interested in educational teaching aids for children, with the use of scenarios mainly at home and in educational settings.

According to relevant data, the average of 10–20 toys among children will probably be 5 educational-based products, and statistically speaking, the long-term development of the educational toy market is very optimistic.

In the market research, a sample of 60 families with children aged 3–6 years old around them found that 86.67% of people observed that children around them had toys about educational puzzles and only 13.33% found that children around them did not have educational puzzles. A pie chart comparing the two is shown in Fig. 2. As China's economy grows, the income of Chinese residents increases, and with it, the investment in education expands. With this increase in income, parents will be able to afford to invest in education, which will lead to an increase in demand for educational products for children. In the survey, 86.67% of people chose to buy educational toys for their children when their financial situation allows them to do so, while only 3.33% of people would not choose to buy educational toys for their children. See Fig. 3 for a pie chart comparing the two.

The design is focused on serving parents, school teachers and educational institutions for children aged 3–6 years old, who are at the beginning of learning Chinese characters. This is why a product designed to teach Chinese characters is essential for children to learn Chinese characters. The Chinese characters that children need to master in their first grade Chinese language textbooks are extracted in (Fig. 4).

Through user surveys and analysis of the strengths and weaknesses of children's educational teaching aids already on the market, the information was planned and summarised to create a modular design of teaching aids for Chinese characters required by first grade children in China and to extend the innovative interactive design with animations to enable children to acquire knowledge of Chinese characters in an innovative way

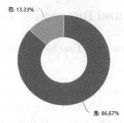

Fig. 2. Comparative analysis of Chinese parents' priorities for their children's education (left)

Fig. 3. Analysis of whether parents would buy educational toys for their children if they could afford it (right)

一、二、三、十、木、禾、上、下、土、个、八、入、大、天、人、火、文、六、七、儿、九、无、口、日、中、了、子、门、月、不、开、四、五、目、耳、头、米、见、日、田、电、也、长、山、出、飞、马、鸟、云、公、车、牛、羊、小、少、巾、牙、尺、毛、卜、又、心、风、力、手、水、广、升、足、走、方、半、巴、业、本、平、书、自、己、东、西、回、片、皮、生、里、果、几、用、鱼、今、正、雨、两、瓜、衣、来、年、左、右、万、百、丁、齐、冬、说、友、话、春、朋、高、你、绿、们、花、红、草、爷、亲、节、的、岁、行、古、处、声、知、多、忙、洗、真、认、父、扫、母、爸、写、全、完、关、家、看、笑、着、兴、画、金、妈、合、奶、放、午、收、女、气、太、早、去、亮、和、李、语、秀、千、香、听、远、唱、定、连、向、以、更、后、意、主、总、先、起、干、明、赶、净、同、专、工、才、级、队、蚂、蚁、前、房、空、网、诗、黄、林、闭、童、立、是、我、朵、叶、美、机、她、过、他、时、送、让、吗、往、吧、得、虫、很、河、借、姐、呢、呀、哪、进、凉、怕、量、跟、最、圆、脸、因、阳、为、光、可、法、石、找、办、许、别、那、到、都、吓、叫、再、做、象、点、像、照、沙、海、桥、军、竹、苗、井、面、乡、忘、想、念、王、这、从、进、边、道、贝、男、原、爱、虾、跑、吹、乐、地、老、快、师、短、淡、对、热、冷、情、拉、活、把、种、给、吃、练、学、习、非、苦、常、问、伴、例、共、伙、汽、分、要、没、孩、位、选、北、湖、南、秋、江、只、帮、星、请、雪、就、球、跳、玩、桃、树、刚、三、座、各、带、坐、急、名、发、成、动、晚、新、有、么、在、变、什、条

Fig. 4. Chinese characters required for recognition by Chinese primary school students in Grade 1

and to exercise children's hands-on skills and increase their interest in learning Chinese language.

4.3 Strategies for Implementing the Interactive Design of Chinese Character Teaching Aids

The focus of the design is to visualise the strokes of the characters to be learnt in Year 1 and to break them down in steps to help children learn the structure of Chinese characters. The Chinese characters are taught by combining a hexagonal display with six hexahedrons of the same size and volume (Fig. 5).

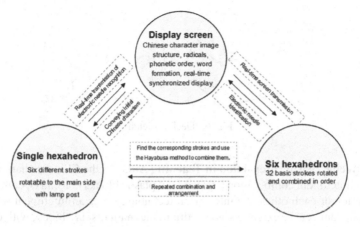

Fig. 5. Implementation development path

The 32 types of Chinese character strokes are located on six equal hexahedral surfaces according to the different stroke categories, and a display screen is set up in front to connect with them, so that the learning and interaction of Chinese character strokes can be carried out through an intelligent sensing system. Six hexahedra of equal size and volume can be combined backwards and forwards using the Hayabusa structure. 32 types of Chinese strokes are located on different sides of the hexahedra according to their different stroke categories, and an electronic screen is set up to combine with each hexahedron. When the power is switched on and the Chinese character appears on the electronic screen, the child needs to put the six individual hexahedra together in the order of the Chinese character strokes appearing on the electronic screen, the strokes are turned to the correct strokes by turning the hexahedra, each hexahedron has an electronic pin on the correct side and the main body is connected, using the electronic pin for identification, the electronic screen shows the correct strokes in writing simultaneously. The design sketch implementation is shown in Fig. 6. The electronic screen will synchronise the images of the Chinese characters displayed to help children understand the characters and add interest to the product by interacting with the pictures, allowing children to put together and combine the strokes of the Chinese characters themselves, thus creating a new cultural experience. The design of the teaching aids overturns the traditional language and script teaching process by deconstructing the strokes and pinyin of Chinese characters to make teaching fun and increase children's hands-on and logical thinking skills.

Therefore, in the process of this design, it is necessary to fully and completely understand the Chinese character strokes, stroke order and pinyin, to integrate children's logical thinking and knowledge system in the design, to protect children's safety and meet their needs in the product, to enhance users' interest in learning while learning Chinese character culture, to let users understand the beauty of Chinese character culture through this product, to fall in love with Chinese culture in the process of reading and recognising characters, and to develop a sense of national pride and self-confidence.

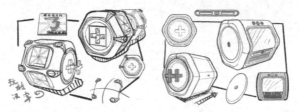

Fig. 6. Design sketch

The Specific Use of Interaction in Teaching Aids. As the Chinese character teaching aids are intelligent combination toys made of plastic blocks that can be combined and stacked on top of each other, the interaction technology uses an intelligent recognition unit that can connect six extended hexahedra to the main display block, with electronic pins in each for recognition, connected by the Hayabusa structure. The main display block has a power supply, a loudspeaker and an intelligent recognition system with buttons for adjusting the sound level and for resetting and determining the displayed Chinese characters, which can be identified and illuminated according to the sequential direction of the Hayabusa structure formed by each extended hexahedron and displayed on the main display block with a voice announcement. The variety of options for audio input and graphic output systems allows for a diverse and rich content format. The design process of the audio-visual interactive platform guides children through the real-time input of audio information and the dynamic feedback of visual effects [11]. It is simple to play and easy for children to understand and use. See Fig. 7 for a rendering of the product design.

Fig. 7. Design rendering

Designing the Flow of Use. The product can be used in four steps: turning on the power, displaying the Chinese character on the electronic screen, finding the hexahedron where the corresponding stroke is located and using the Hayabusa structure to assemble it (Fig. 9). If the name corresponding to a Chinese character stroke is repeated on the same hexahedron, press the reset button at the bottom of the electronic screen to reuse the same hexahedron once the previous stroke has been rotated and assembled (Fig. 8).

Turn on the power: First, turn on the switch below the electronic display to the right to access the intelligent identification unit, then the corresponding Chinese characters already stored in the system will appear on the electronic screen.

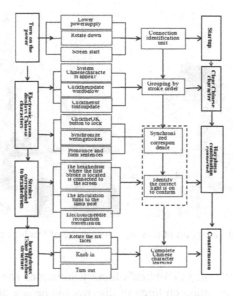

Fig. 8. Flow chart of product use

Electronic screen displaying Chinese characters: After turning the product on and off, the Chinese characters from the product's word bank will appear randomly on the electronic screen to use the product. You can also press the button at the bottom of the screen to update and refresh the word bank. You can deepen your understanding and knowledge of the Chinese characters through the process of repeated learning, and the essence of cognitive play is the consolidation nature of the activity through repeated practice [12].

Finding the hexahedron where the corresponding stroke is located: when the Chinese character appears on the electronic screen, the child is required to find the hexahedron where the first stroke in the sequence of Chinese strokes is located among the six hexahedrons of the same shape and volume and of different colours, and the hexahedron where the electronic screen is located is connected by a combination of falcon mou, after which the child turns the corresponding stroke to stop the position with the lamp post, and when the corresponding stroke is turned, the electronic needle receives the When the child turns the corresponding stroke, the electronic needle receives the correct stroke and transmits the information to the electronic screen, which displays the stroke simultaneously, and the light on the column lights up to indicate that the child has made the correct combination and can proceed to the next stroke.

4.4 Summarize

In today's rapidly advancing economic times, people's needs for products are gradually changing from being satisfied with the shape of the product and the single function of the product to emphasising the experience they get from the product. The design of the children's educational aids is based on the structure of Chinese characters, which is the

Fig. 9. Diagram of scenarios for the use of teaching aids

most basic and essential part of children's literary initiation. The main purpose of the design is to teach and entertain children to discover the beauty of Chinese characters. The interactive design is integrated into the design of the children's educational aids, focusing on children's pain points in learning Chinese characters and increasing the scientific and practicality of the design. The design will provide new ideas for future educational tools for children.

Funding. Innovation Project of Guangxi Graduate Education, "Innovative design of children's educational AIDS under the concept of STEAM education" (Serial number: XYCSR2023014).

2023 The Pearl River - West River Economic Belt Development Research Institute Project, "Innovative Research on the Design of Red Cultural Resources in the Xiangjiang Campaign under the Background of Cultural and Tourism Integration" (Serial number: ZX2023028).

References

1. Rong, H., Zhiyu, H., Ping, L.: Research on interaction design strategies based on user scenarios. Design **35**(04), 106–109 (2022)
2. Jingwen, H.: How to infuse cultural implications in primary school literacy teaching. Lang. Teach. Newsletter **12**, 84–86 (2021)
3. Zhaowei, S.: Creative luminaire design based on interactive experience. Qingdao University, MA thesis (2020)
4. Xiangyang, X.: Interaction design: from physical logic to behavioral logic. Decoration **01**, 58–62 (2015)
5. Fei, Y.: Teaching for fun. China Academy of Art, MA thesis (2018)
6. Yanling, Z., Ting, L.: Behavior analysis in interaction design for community public facilities. Packag. Eng. **42**(04), 256–262 (2021)
7. Zhao, Z., Wu, C., Liu, C.: Research on application of behavioral analysis of interaction design to product design. Packag. Eng. **33**(06), 73–77 (2012)
8. BingXue, L., XiangLong, P., JieLong, W.: Research on the redesign of traditional folk toys based on the concept of interaction. Design **35**(17), 26–28 (2022)

9. Zhou, X., XinYuan, Y.: Interactive design of characters in educational games for preschool children. Packag. Eng. **43**(06), 243–251 (2022)
10. Hong, H., Zhoufeng, Z., Yuxin, J.: Research on the design of teaching AIDS for school-age children from the perspective of multi-modal interaction. Design **34**(11), 88–91 (2021)
11. Xiaoying, L., Yaping, Y.: A study on children's audio-visual interaction design based on multi-modal sensory experience. J. Graph. **43**(04), 736–744 (2022)
12. Hong, H., Zhoufeng, Z., Yuxin, J.: A study on the design of teaching AIDS for school-age children from the perspective of multi-modal interaction. Design **34**(11), 88–91 (2021)

Research on the Interactive Design of Children's Educational Products of Weaving and Embroidering under Intangible Cultural Heritage Perspective

Yue Zhang[✉], Shan Xu, Xiaomeng Wang, Ting Yang, and Feng He

Guangxi Normal University, Guilin 541006, China
798862630@qq.com

Abstract. The development of weaving and embroidery intangible cultural heritage handicraft industry has lagged in recent years. Under the impact of Internet, how to stimulate children's interest in learning embroidery crafts, thus promoting the inheritance of embroidery intangible cultural heritage is the focus of this paper. This paper focuses on the application of children's embroidery gamified interactive design in children's education, which makes it easier for children to grasp the knowledge of embroidery through gamified interaction, so that today's intangible cultural heritage skills can be inherited and popularized. Secondly, we analyze the psychological characteristics of children from the point of view of teaching for fun, and use gamified interaction to guide children to know more about the intangible cultural heritage of embroidery. Finally, we analyze the design relationship between embroidery skills and product interaction from the perspective of a large number of actual cases.

Keywords: Children's education · Embroidery · Experience · Digital gamification interaction · Heritage

1 Introduction

China faces a number of challenges on the road to the preservation and transmission of intangible cultural heritage. Weaving and embroidering skills are an indispensable part of this subject, and Chinese ethnic groups have a culture of weaving and embroidering skills. However, due to the complexity of the traditional skill process and the mismatch with the production value of handmade products, many key techniques are facing the phenomenon of loss of transmission. Many regions are even experiencing a shortage of resources for aesthetic educators, which results in a lack of cultural identity in childhood. In recent years under the globalization pattern, local traditional handicraft techniques must be more protected and inherited to better maintain the cultural ecology of the region. How to adapt the intangible cultural heritage of embroidery to the new times, acquire new economic and cultural values, return to the public with more vitality, and especially stimulate the interest of this generation of "digital natives" which have been receiving the Internet since birth, has become a new problem for the preservation and inheritance of intangible cultural heritage.

© The Author(s), under exclusive license to Springer Nature Switzerland AG 2023
P. Zaphiris et al. (Eds.): HCII 2023, LNCS 14060, pp. 382–391, 2023.
https://doi.org/10.1007/978-3-031-48060-7_29

Under the influence of the Internet, gamified interactive experience design is becoming a hot topic as a composite, interactive art form. It combines the potential of new technologies, interactive media and emotional narratives to stimulate the interest of the young "digital indigenous" generation in traditional culture, promote cultural dissemination and cultural confidence, and stimulate the interest of "indigenous" people in the art of embroidery, thus promoting the art of embroidery [1]. The use of virtual technology is therefore a good way to present the traditional culture in a better way. Therefore, using virtual technology to better present and inherit traditional folk crafts, and using educational game design to deeply integrate traditional culture and games are good ways to spread culture and build cultural confidence.

2 Product Design Theory of Children's Educational Interaction in Weaving and Embroiderin from the Perspective of Intangible Cultural Heritage

2.1 The Importance of Weaving and Embroidering Crafts for Children's Education

Cultural Perspective. Traditional Chinese weaving and embroidering techniques can be divided into four major parts: embroidery techniques represented by Su embroidery, Xiang embroidery, Shu embroidery, Guangdong embroidery and embroidery of ethnic minorities; weaving techniques represented by silk weaving, cotton and linen weaving and cloud brocade weaving; printing and dyeing techniques represented by blue printing cloth, batik and tie-dye of ethnic minorities; costumes of ethnic minorities such as Inner Mongolia, Miao and Nei Lian Sheng thousand-layer sole cloth shoes making techniques, etc. In this century, due to the rapid development of Internet technology, electronic information technology has stimulated the daily life of young people, which has made the traditional method of passing on skills from teacher to apprentice unable to cope with the transmission of intangible cultural heritage [2]. According to the above situations, two opposing phenomena emerge; firstly, the inheritance of this intangible cultural heritage is dependent on the development of economic society, and today's inheritors are not able to meet people's consumption needs; secondly, the cultural connotation of intangible cultural heritage is constantly changing with the development of the times, and this feature is out of touch with the modern young population [3]. Therefore, it is difficult for Chinese children nowadays to truly understand the connotation of intangible cultural heritage, which requires the combination of traditional culture and education, so that intangible cultural heritage of weaving and embroidering can meet the learning and cognitive habits of children nowadays.

Aesthetic Education Perspective. In August 2021, the Office of the State Council of the Central Committee of the Communist Party of China issued "the Opinions on Further Strengthening the Protection of Intangible Cultural Heritage", which proposed to incorporate intangible cultural heritage into the national education system, to establish and improve the curriculum and teaching materials of non-material intangible cultural heritage, to publish popular reading materials, and to offer majors in non-material intangible cultural heritage at universities, secondary schools, and colleges [4]. Education and intangible cultural heritage have a complementary composition. Intangible cultural heritage can make the educated better understand the value of intangible heritage through the means of education, and also make the educated enhance the cultural confidence of their own nation. Secondly, intangible cultural heritage of weaving and embroidering is an important part of China's excellent national culture, and it is an important treasure for pattern design course teaching reform, which varies in color scheme, composition rules, craft means and cultural connotation to make embroidery intangible cultural heritage has strong aesthetic value. Finally, embroidery ICH requires craftspeople to incorporate creative thinking in its expression, the characteristic allows children to gain numerous training in thinking, and also enhance the way children explore their thinking paths.

Therefore, the entry of intangible cultural heritage of weaving and embroidering into children's education is an essential part, which can enhance children's cultural confidence and make them grow up better (Fig. 1. Advantages of children's education in embroidery intangible cultural heritage crafts).

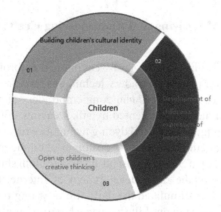

Fig. 1. Advantages of children's education in embroidery intangible cultural heritage crafts.

Logical Construction. Gamification is an inescapable design element in the education of children. Since the intangible cultural heritage of weaving and embroidering belongs to the intangible cultural heritage items of craftsmanship category, the huge manual labor system and complex visual patterns of this type of intangible cultural heritage combined with the special characteristics of children require that when designing such gamified interactive products, in addition to strengthening the visual behavior guidance, the operation experience of the finished product should be restored through the interactive way [5]. Following Nielsen's 10 usability principles as the basis for design, the design of educational interactive products for children's intangible cultural heritage such as embroidery should not only focus on children's behavior, but also on the psychological activities behind children's behavior. Therefore, many educational products on the market refer to the game: leaderboards, points, and medals. Combined with the 8 core drivers proposed in the book "Gamification in Action". I found that when the "class time" in education is replaced by "levels"; every correct answer will have a certain number of points in return, and the points can be aggregated by ranking, and the high ranking will have the reward mechanism of medals. Therefore, when gamification is used as an incentive mechanism, it creates motivation and enhances the coping ability of users, which can stimulate children to have an immersive experience and effectively guide them to make purposeful behavioral transformations.

Fig. 2. Five factors that make gamification more interesting than work

2.2 Advantages of Gamification Interactive Design Concept in Intangible Cultural Heritage Handicraft Heritage of Weaving and Embroidering

The Development Advantage of Internet 5G. Based on the development of the Internet and the development and popularization of 5G integrated media, gamification products have gradually become popular. Digital games are games designed and developed using digital technology and run on digital devices. This concept was first proposed by game scholar jesper juul in 2003. In 1984, Charles Currante in the book "the game of Work" summarized five factors that interest generated by gamification is superior to work: 1. Clear goals 2. a sound scoring system 3. Timely feedback 4. a high degree of freedom of personal play 5. (coach) continuous guidance [6] (Fig. 2. Five factors that make gamification more interesting than work).

Advantages of Gamified Fun Experience. In addition to the advantages of entertainment, socialization, and virtualization, digital gamification also has the advantages of plurality, cross-media, interactivity, and compatibility that traditional games do not have. These advantages greatly enhance the immersive experience and interest of child players, thus enhancing their intention to play and deeply attracting the child community to join in the embroidery activities [6]. Secondly, the process of "playing the game" is a spontaneous problem-solving activity in which the designer's creative mechanism, the process of structuring the dynamic model in the game, and the final visual presentation appear to the target users through a reverse process, as shown in Fig. 3. The gamification framework, which is also Marc LeBlanc's MDA design framework proposed for game design [7].

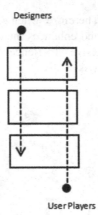

Fig. 3. The gamification framework

Sustainability Advantage. Take the games "King of Glory" and "Yin Yang Shi" for example, which are popular among children today, most of the characters in this type of games originate from traditional Chinese culture, and on an auditory level, this type of game uses traditional Chinese music to match the transformation of situational kinetic effects, and this type of communication allows children to relax and feel the charm of traditional culture at the same time. Secondly, in the Horizon Report from 2011 to 2019, game-based learning was predicted five and four times respectively as a technology that would be adopted in and for basic and higher education; in April 2018, the latest report released by the Organization for Economic Cooperation and Development proposed six pedagogies that are different from traditional ones and would profoundly change the future direction of education, including game-based learning methods [8]. It can be seen that game-based learning is becoming more and more common and significant in the field of education.

3   Status and Shortcomings of Educational Interactive Products of Gamified Children's Embroidery Intangible Cultural Heritage

According to a large number of research findings, there are many differences in how gamified children's intangible cultural heritage educational interactive products treat the inheritance of intangible cultural heritage. Some of the products adhere too much to traditional culture in the path of inheriting intangible cultural heritage, and make the appearance of the products disconnected from reality. Some products go beyond the framework of intangible cultural heritage, losing the meaning of the products and making it difficult for children to understand the deeper meaning of traditional culture. Letting the intangible cultural heritage "live" state and creating a cultural function of the game is a major trend. Some media have sorted out the cooperation cases between video games and intangible cultural heritage in recent years, and summarized their forms into three categories: firstly, "in-game expression", secondly, "out-game expression" at the sales level, and the last is "functional games of intangible cultural heritage".

(1) The "in-game expression" is mainly reflected in the emergence of many study and learning experience products, which are service products based on study and learning activities of intangible cultural heritage and intangible cultural heritage handicraft activities. Children learn intangible cultural heritage mainly through intangible cultural heritage reserves or in museums. The types mainly include watching ICH movies, visiting ICH exhibitions, experiencing ICH projects and making ICH goods. To keep pace with the development of the times, many new technologies and media are utilized in the research process. For example, 3D scanning and reconstruction technologies are able to restore and construct ICH items and their production scenes in a very realistic way. VR and AR technologies are able to combine multiple senses, such as audio and visual, so that children can gain a certain degree of first-hand experience of ICH, thus reducing the distance between them and ICH. However, this category requires a specific environment and children need a designated time as well as place to be able to learn about ICH [10].

(2) The "out-game expression" is mostly at the level of product sales, usually at the elementary school level, where children engage in a parent-child interaction in which parents and children learn the knowledge and skills of intangible culture together and make traditional cultural works with individual characteristics. In the process of acquiring knowledge, the relationship between parents and children is enhanced, the child's social interaction skills are improved, and the child gains satisfaction and joy. However, most of the experiential products of intangible cultural heritage are still in a more traditional educational mode, the use of digital technology is still rusty and rigid, and there is no clear concept in the design of the content, which lacks some creativity. In addition, such activities are time-consuming and expensive, making it difficult for parents to give their children long-term support in their consumption process.

(3) After the explosion of "functional games of intangible cultural heritage" in China's functional game market in 2018, as these interactive game products themselves are products of intangible cultural heritage, they all integrate the traditional culture of intangible cultural heritage into the game's "story", "design" and "aesthetics" of the games. For example, Tencent's Nishan Shaman, the game was a reference to the traditional Chinese Manchu culture, the folk literature Biography of Nishan Shaman, from its inception period. Later, the gamified children's ICH educational interactive products appeared in the form of ICH mini-games, which also exploded with very good social benefits. I am the inheritor of intangible cultural heritage" is a public welfare mini-game launched by the social media department of People's Daily, which combines poverty alleviation with intangible cultural heritage and strengthens the protection of intangible cultural heritage by understanding the various ways of poverty alleviation of intangible cultural heritage. With the development of interactive product design technology, educational interactive products that gamify children's intangible cultural heritage are also being innovated. For example, Changsha University of Technology has developed an AR game on Meishan Nuo culture, "Nuo God Battle". The game takes Meishan Nuo culture as the main, combined with the zeitgeist of fighting the epidemic. Players walk outdoors to count the way to accumulate the energy to defeat the enemy in the game, and go on trips to defeat the virus that randomly appears.

4 Product Design Principles and Case Studies of Education Interactive Products of Children's Embroidery Intangible Cultural Heritage

4.1 Principle of Environmental Relevance

In the design and development of educational interactive products for gamified children's intangible cultural heritage of embroidery, attention should be paid to the professional techniques and the explanation of professional terms, and try to use language texts that can be easily understood by children. When a child user receives information and encounters words that are difficult for him or her to understand, it will cause him or her to reject the product. Under normal circumstances, child users should be able to understand the meaning expressed by the instruction without outside help. The applet YALELA Yelula is an original video fusion digital interactive product that incorporates the four famous jinx courses as well as a gamified experience craft bar. The product uses the main visual image of the little monster that children love, and dresses the image in the costumes of the four famous brocades of China. The program allows children to learn about the four famous brocades in a playful and easy way.

"Costumes of the Qing Dynasty" is an app showcasing the traditional costumes of the Palace Museum, which selects several collections of Qing Dynasty costumes and painted accessories from the Palace Museum collection and presents them in a three-dimensional way. Among them, it visually classifies the dresses according to the occasions of wearing them, introducing the six categories of dresses of the emperors of Qin Dynasty such as: dress, auspicious dress, regular dress, casual dress and military dress. By clicking on the corresponding area, the user player can learn the explanation of the part and the way of handicraft production and can also see the high resolution picture of the costume pattern. In this way, the cultural content can also be conveyed in a straightforward manner, allowing children users to experience the cultural connotations more intuitively.

4.2 User-Controllable Principle

In the design of gamified children's embroidery educational interactive products, children's curiosity should be protected and children should be actively encouraged to explore the products, and the game mechanism should be set up to allow children to make mistakes and help them correct them during the game. Since children lack precise hand control and rigorous reasoning ability in the process of growing up, it is necessary to expand the scope of children's hand operation in the game operation design. For example, in the mini-game "Soga", children only need to press and hold the screen to move up, down, left and right. For children who are a little younger, the control in operation is not smooth enough, so it is easier to set aside a larger operation space for different age groups to reach their goals. Therefore, it is necessary to strengthen the reversibility of the design in the design of the gamified children's embroidery non-heritage educational interactive products, encourage children to explore, allow children to correct the exit and expand the scope of operation at any time.

4.3 Motivating and Challenging Principles

After meeting the above principles, we should pay attention to the incentive strategy and the establishment of appropriate challenge mode. Appropriate challenges can stimulate children's sense of accomplishment, and after completing the project challenges, the incentive mechanism can be appropriately added, which will give children a certain sense of satisfaction after obtaining certain incentives, and thus can better guide children to go through the next operation. Take the short video "Jitterbug", which now occupies a large share of the market, for example, the R&D team uses a 15-s full-frequency immersion video, with a simple sliding up and down to switch the interaction, all in the first time to the user feedback. But in this process the user never knows what the next video is and what kind of surprise it will bring. Incorporating this sense of unknown challenge is more likely to lead child users into the process of mind-flow experience. The American psychologist Mihaly Histzantemiha suggested that entering a mindstream state when a person devotes his or her attention completely to an activity creates a strong sense of immersion in the user [2]. At the same time how immersion is obtained in a mind-flow experience is determined by the challenges and skills brought to the user by the interactive product, both of which check and balance each other. In the relationship between the two, too much skill or challenge in one aspect will make the user bored and anxious, and the real state of achieving a balance of mind flow should be a balance of skill and challenge [9], as shown in Fig. 4–2.7 below.

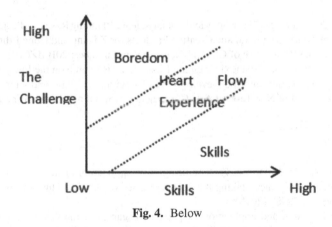

Fig. 4. Below

"Logical Huayao" is a gamified intangible cultural heritage educational game for children, which mainly combines the Huayao flower picking craft in Longhuai County, Hunan Province, China. The game deeply integrates the positioning of the yarn counting in Huayao, as well as the basic techniques in Huayao and game elements, extracting the folklore and the characteristics of the Huayao handicraft, and incorporating the patterns and composition of the craft and the elements of the culture into the game. The design of the interactive game follows the behavior of children in their developmental stages and the current environmental context of learning mathematics, and it chooses appropriate technologies and interaction methods to express the overall architecture of the product.

First of all, the game's mechanics follow the principle of variability, classifying different symmetrical shapes, making the process of change from easy to difficult through the exponential radiation of patterns, and using mathematical geometry to understand Hwayao patterns. In the game, the R&D team also added a "creation" aspect, where children players can create new stories and upload them by choosing the color of the canvas and the size of the canvas, and invite their friends to play the levels they create together [1]. This format creates a good environment for children to learn about intangible cultural heritage and enhances their interest.

5 Conclusion

This paper examines the design of an interactive child-centered educational game in the context of intangible cultural heritage. This type of educational activity for children requires a thorough examination of the environment from the child's perspective. It is important to consider not only the inheritance and transmission of culture, but also the ability of traditional culture to be used by children. Secondly, the integration of games and culture cannot just be superficial, but should start from the main vision of the game, then to the game mechanics and storyline, and finally to the aesthetics of the game. In different contexts, different technological approaches are used to integrate cultural products to provide children with a good learning environment for intangible cultural heritage.

Funding:. 1. 2020 Guangxi Philosophy and Social Science Planning Research Project, "Research on the Design of Tourism Cultural and Creative Products for Zhuang and Dong Ethnic Minorities in Guangxi from the Perspective of Cultural Genes" (Serial number: 20BMZ016).

2. Innovation Project of Guangxi Graduate Education, "Research on the Integration of Graduate Curriculum Education into the Development of Regional Cultural and Creative Industries under the Background of New Liberal Arts Construction" (Serial number: XJCY2023030).

References

1. Yuanyuan, Y., Tie, J., Doduo, Z.: The design and application of traditional culture in children's educational games - taking the design practice of "Logical Huayao" as an example.". Decoration. **12**, 78–81 (2018)
2. Xuan, F.: Research and application of persuasive games in the design of children's non-heritage education products. MA thesis, Hunan University (2020)
3. Doduo, Z.: Designing for Development: Rural Craft Revitalization from the Perspective of Capability Approach. Public Art .05 (2020)
4. Pingting, L.: The promotion and protection of intangible cultural heritage in Fujian Provincial Library. Henan Libr. J. **42**(02), 82–85 (2022)
5. Yingqing, X., La, T.: Digital transmission and dissemination of Chinese culture under the perspective of immersive narrative. Packag. Eng. **44**(02) (2023)
6. Ye, Q.: A study on the foreign communication path of non-foreign heritage ip with digital games as a carrier. New Med. Res. **8**, 23 (2022)
7. Doduo, Z., Pengri, L.: Research on gamified tourism experience design for cultural sustainability. Packag. Eng. **41**, 14 (2020)

8. Doduo, Z., et al.: Two-line aesthetic education: making excellent national cultural heritage succeeding generations. Hunan Educ. Version A.**09**, 36–37 (2020)
9. Yarong, D.: Research on the design of Guanxiang cultural narrative for children's virtual community platform. MA thesis, Guangdong University of Technology (2020)
10. Chu, L.: Research on the design of somatic interactive display resources for non-genetic heritage education. MA thesis, University of Science and Technology Suzhou (2019)

U+X: A Participatory Interaction Design Pattern for Improving Communication Skills in Preschoolers

Aijia Zhang[1], Runqing Lin[1], Caihong He[2], and Guanghui Huang[1,3(✉)]

[1] Faculty of Humanities and Arts, Macau University of Science and Technology, Avenida Wai Long, Taipa, Macau 999078, China
ghhuang1@must.edu.mo
[2] Guangzhou Wanqu Cooperative Institute of Design, Guangzhou, Guangdong, China
[3] Zhuhai M.U.S.T. Science and Technology Research Institute, Zhuhai, Guangdong, China

Abstract. Communication problems seriously affect the social interaction and normal life of preschoolers. Digital books are increasingly used by families as a learning and cognitive enhancement tool for children because of their lower cost and side effects than traditional therapies. However, the interactive format, the effectiveness of complementary therapies, and the negative effects of electronic devices are still huge obstacles to the current work. This paper proposes a U+X participatory interaction design pattern and uses it to develop a digital book application that incorporates relevant stakeholders. A paired experimental design conducted with 60 preschoolers examined the effect of the U+X on enhancing preschoolers' communication skills. The collected scale questionnaires were analyzed by paired samples t-test. The results show that the U+X design pattern has a positive effect on promoting preschoolers' language skills and communication behaviors. In response, this paper presents suggestions for including users in the interaction design process. In a participatory context, it provides new ways to improve the communication problems of preschoolers by stimulating children's creativity, enhancing family connections, and encouraging children's self-expression.

Keywords: Participatory design · Interaction design · Preschoolers · Communication skills · Digital books

1 Introduction

Communication issues commonly arise during the preschool years in children and encompass difficulties in verbal fluency, expression, and behavioral refusal to communicate [1]. These problems ultimately threaten children's familial relationships and overall quality of life [2]. Current therapeutic interventions for children with communication and language delays primarily rely on educational training and psychological support approaches [1]. Despite the many therapeutic theories and derived methods implemented, particular environments and unfamiliar therapists are still disturbing, especially for young and shy children [3]. Therefore, it is necessary to develop effective methods to enhance communication skills in preschoolers.

P. Zaphiris et al. (Eds.): HCII 2023, LNCS 14060, pp. 392–410, 2023.
https://doi.org/10.1007/978-3-031-48060-7_30

Historically, paper books have been utilized to aid preschoolers in learning text and comprehending written content [4]. With the integration of new technology, digital books have emerged as a medium to connect children with others and society. The combination of text and images not only contributes to the development of children's literacy skills [5] but also facilitates the improvement of their social skills. This is because reading requires preschoolers to interact with peers, parents, and teachers [6]. Through the mediation of others and communication during reading, preschoolers enhance their understanding of content and their perception of the world [7, 8]. Additionally, reading digital books is a safe and accessible activity that does not require any specialized skills or training.

Despite the positive effects of digital books on the physical and mental development of preschoolers, several obstacles hinder progress, such as the interactive format [9, 10], the effectiveness of complementary therapies [11], and the negative impact of electronic devices [12]. Designing digital books that meet the needs of contemporary preschoolers and parents is a complex task. On the one hand, using vision and hearing to help preschoolers actively communicate and express themselves is a necessary work that needs more experience and knowledge. On the other hand, the presence of game-like interactive features may divert preschoolers' attention and impede their comprehension of the story. Parents' concerns about eye safety and electronic addiction must also be considered.

Therefore, this paper aims to explore a user-centered design pattern that creates digital book applications supporting preschoolers' active participation. We propose the U+X participatory interaction design pattern, with a technical focus on involving users in the interaction design process. To this end, we have developed Babbling, a collaborative digital book application for stakeholders, and validated the effectiveness of U+X through a paired experimental design involving 60 preschoolers. Based on the experimental results, we discuss the beneficial effects of U+X in three areas: stimulating preschoolers' creativity, enhancing family connections, and encouraging preschoolers' self-expression. Specifically, this paper aims to address the following questions:

(1) What role do design elements such as text, images, sound, and interactive features play in the preschoolers' reading process?
(2) How to leverage the initiative of preschoolers in the interaction process and provide solutions for improving their communication skills?

The main contributions of this paper are twofold:

(1) We propose the U+X participatory interaction design pattern, which aims to facilitate participatory interaction among preschool children, adults, and the social environment. Its goal is to promote the development of children's verbal representation and self-expression skills. While this paper focuses on applying U+X in digital book design, the principles and methods of this design pattern are also adaptable to other areas of narrative-based interaction design, such as game design.
(2) We consolidate empirical knowledge on how preschoolers can utilize U+X to express themselves and improve their language and social communication skills. This knowledge includes preferences for design elements, the effectiveness of interaction mechanisms, and methods for facilitating social interaction. Through the

analysis and experimental validation of relevant case studies, this paper provides valuable references for designers and researchers.

2 Related Works

2.1 Communication Problems in Preschoolers

Montessori discovered preschoolers aged 3–6 years go through a sensitive period for language, order, senses, interest in subtle things, movement, social norms, writing, and reading [13]. Neglecting this critical period of life by parents or other adults significantly increases the risk of serious harm to children's growth and development [14]. The factors such as family environment, parents' education level, congenital disorders, and teachers' teaching experience [14, 15] can contribute to communication problems in preschool children.

Educational training and psychological assistance methods are currently relied upon to treat and intervene in children with symptoms such as poor communication and lagging language [1]. Parents and caregivers can interact with preschoolers in a supportive and positive way through clear dialogue and provide them with opportunities to practice expressing themselves [14, 15]. In addition, providing books and toys that encourage communication, such as board games and puppets, also helps children learn and practice communication skills [16–18]. Non-educational interventions are emerging as essential to help rapport and increase children's communication [19].

2.2 Design of Digital Books

Based on traditional paper books, digital books provide interactive features for preschoolers' independent learning in a distance learning context [20]. Reading digital books contributes to preschool children's cognitive development and social integration [21], especially for children with underdeveloped attention regulation. This is due to the ability of digital books to respond to the touch of preschoolers. This interaction encourages them to be curious about perceiving new things and stories and helps them to perform simultaneous narratives of visual and verbal information [22–24].

Many digital book applications are on the market with sophisticated presentation and technology. They focus on developing children's literacy and cognitive skills, allowing them to receive and learn more vocabulary [25, 26]. However, there is little experience and knowledge on how to get children to actively "output" rather than passively "input," i.e., to enhance children's active expression and communication skills. The focus on digital books is not on the differences in form or medium but on the contribution that digital improvements can make. It means that the primary issue at hand is how to optimize the form of the digital book design to be of practical help to its primary audience, the preschoolers.

2.3 Using Participatory Design to Enhance Preschoolers' Communication Skills

The participatory design originated from the Nordic democratization movement in the 1970s and 1980s and was developed into a practical design approach by American companies [27]. Multi-user participatory design defines requirements wholly and accurately

[28], optimizes user interfaces [29], delivers on user promises [30], and is an innovation over traditional product-centric design approaches. The user plays the role of a significant participant in the design in several design phases, such as requirements analysis, concept generation, prototyping, evaluation, and improvement [31]. It not only enhances user experience and motivation, but for designers, it also provides insight into user expectations, challenges, and usage contexts to meet their needs better.

In educational tools and game design, user-friendly interfaces and manipulation for preschool children have been created and studied. Researchers have designed educational games that are interactive and fun based on children's interests and needs in order to stimulate creativity and a sense of cooperation. Children's emotional cognition is developed through role-playing, situational simulation, and collaborative tasks. With the assistance of technologies such as physiological sensors [32], eye-tracking [33], and electroencephalography [34], participatory design reconfigures the way users, technology, and products are integrated. It stimulates engagement and emotional expression in children with special communication needs, such as those with ASD, by enabling integration with perceptual interaction and communication.

Previous research has illustrated the advantages and value of introducing users into the design process. These findings support our decision to use participatory design as the primary design approach for enhancing communication skills in preschoolers. However, how to effectively include preschoolers in the design process to increase their willingness to participate is a pressing issue. At the same time, studies often lack follow-up experiments and evaluations to understand the effects of products on preschoolers' communication skills. Therefore, we aim to explore a design model that focuses on user needs and creates a digital book application that promotes preschoolers' active participation. Based on this, we incorporated a paired experimental design to evaluate the potential impact of the developed app on preschoolers' communication skills. It ensures the scientific validity of the study.

3 Methods

The research process consisted of design, development, and experimentation. Figure 1 illustrates the research process and the participation of relevant stakeholders throughout the research cycle. In the design phase, extensive interviews were conducted with parents and teachers of preschoolers to establish the groundwork for the conceptual design and prototype development of the U+X. Subsequently, in the development phase, a collaborative digital book application called Babbling was created for stakeholders using the U+X approach. Finally, in the experimental phase, the efficacy and feasibility of U+X were evaluated through a paired experimental design.

3.1 The Design Phase

To analyze preschoolers' needs and design objectives, we conducted a preliminary study using observation and in-depth interviews. In the first phase, we observed three families using the digital book application face-to-face, focusing on child behavior, parent

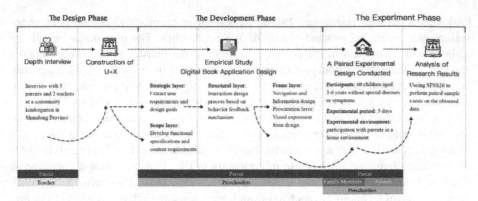

Fig. 1. The research process.

behavior, and communication during the reading process. In the second phase, we conducted face-to-face interviews lasting approximately 40–60 min with three preschoolers, three parents, and two teachers, explicitly discussing their experiences with existing digital book applications available in the market. This process served as an initial stage to observe user behavior, identify potential user needs, and inform the subsequent development of U+X.

3.2 The Development Phase

Jesse James Garrett introduced a model framework for user experience in Elements of User Experience - User-Centered Product Design [35]. This framework comprises five levels: strategic, scope, structure, framework, and surface. It outlines the product design process and tasks, progressing from high-level considerations to more concrete elements, and provides a standardized approach for constructing the framework. As digital books encompass functional and information-based aspects, U+X combines principles from both types of product design.

At the strategic and scope level, U+X identified the critical needs of preschool children. Moreover, the design objectives, functional specifications, and content requirements were determined based on this. In the structural layer, U+X incorporated mechanisms for preschoolers' behavior feedback into the interaction design process, balancing playfulness with a focus on enhancing preschoolers' sense of realistic control. In the framework and surface layers, U+X designed interfaces, navigation information, and other visual elements based on the interests and preferences of preschoolers.

3.3 The Experiment Phase

(1) Participants

The paired experimental design was conducted from January 15, 2023, to January 19, 2023, involving a sample of 60 preschool children (34 females, 26 males) with no specific diseases or symptoms. The participants were selected from a community kindergarten in

Shandong Province, aged between 3 and 6 years. The experiment took place in a home setting, with the children participating alongside their parents.

(2) **Experiment Process**

Prior to the experiment, we conducted an assessment of the participants' language skills and communication behaviors. The participants were required to complete a demographic information questionnaire and an assessment scale questionnaire. During the experiment, the participants used the Babbling digital book application for 30 min daily, accompanied by their parents, for five days. It was recommended that each child read in a relatively quiet environment. On the evening of the fifth day, the participants were again administered the scale questionnaire.

(3) **Questionnaire Design and Result Evaluation**

The questionnaire utilized in the study consisted of three parts. The first part was a demographic questionnaire that collected information regarding gender, age, daily reading habits, and proficiency with electronic devices. The second part involved a language proficiency assessment based on the Chinese Preschool Language Scale (CPLS), developed by the Hong Kong University of Education and Beijing Language and Culture University. This scale incorporates language development and cognitive characteristics specific to Chinese children aged 3–6 years and serves as a screening tool for identifying abnormal language development in preschoolers. The third part of the questionnaire was the Communication Behavior Assessment, which was based on the parent questionnaire in the Rutter Children's Behavior Questionnaire (RCCQ). The RCCQ, developed by Rutter in 1967, is widely used in epidemiological studies to assess behavioral problems in school-age children, providing valuable insights into emotional disorders and delinquent behavior [36].

The questionnaire employed a three-level scoring system; a score of 0 denoted disagreement or the absence of the condition, a score of 1 indicated fair or mild symptoms, and a score of 2 represented strong agreement or severe symptoms. Preschool children's language skills were assessed on a scale ranging from a maximum score of 16 to a minimum score of 10. Scores equal to or exceeding the threshold were indicative of good language skills. Communication behaviors of preschoolers were evaluated using a scale with a maximum score of 30, and a threshold score of 10 was used to categorize the absence of behavior problems. The parents were responsible for providing the relevant data, assessing their child's condition, and completing the questionnaire.

(4) **Experiment Process**

The data obtained from the study were analyzed using SPSS (version 26). Frequency and percentage distributions were used to represent qualitative data, while quantitative data were described using means and standard deviations. To examine the significance of differences in preschoolers' language skills and communication behaviors before and after using Babbling, paired-sample t-tests were conducted. The specific analysis steps were as follows:

Firstly, the null hypothesis is stated as follows.

Null Hypothesis H$_0$: The mean language skills of preschoolers before and after using Babbling are equal, indicating no significant difference.

Alternative Hypothesis H$_1$: The mean language skills of preschoolers before and after using Babbling are not equal, indicating a significant difference. Expressed as:

$$H_0 : \mu_1 - \mu_2 = 0, \; H_1 : \mu_1 - \mu_2 \neq 0 \tag{1}$$

Here, μ_1 represents the mean language skills of preschoolers before using Babbling, and μ_2 represents the mean language skills of preschoolers after using Babbling.

The Null Hypothesis H$_2$: The mean communication behaviors of preschoolers before and after using Babbling are equal, indicating no significant difference.

Alternative Hypothesis H$_3$: The mean communication behaviors of preschoolers before and after using Babbling are not equal, indicating a significant difference. Expressed as:

$$H_2 : \mu_3 - \mu_4 = 0, \; H_3 : \mu_3 - \mu_4 \neq 0 \tag{2}$$

Here, μ_3 represents the mean communication behaviors of preschoolers before using Babbling, and μ_4 represents the mean communication behaviors of preschoolers after using Babbling.

Secondly, calculate the observed test statistic value t and the corresponding two-tailed probability *p*-value. The formula for calculating t is (3), where the degrees of freedom are calculated as (4).

$$t = \frac{\overline{X} - \mu}{\sqrt{\frac{S^2}{n}}} \tag{3}$$

$$df = n - 1 \tag{4}$$

Finally, make a decision based on the p-value. We set a significance level of $\alpha = 0.05$ and compared it with the p-value. If $p < \alpha$ ($\alpha = 0.05$), the null hypothesis is rejected, indicating a significant difference in preschoolers' language skills or communication behaviors before and after using Babbling. Conversely, if $p > \alpha$ ($\alpha = 0.05$), the null hypothesis is not rejected. It indicated no significant difference in preschoolers' language skills or communication behaviors before and after using Babbling.

4   The Practical Application of U+X

4.1   The Concept of U+X

U+X comes from the new form of economic and social development "Internet+" created by Internet technology. "Internet+" uses the information advantage of the Internet platform to optimize and upgrade traditional industries, thereby motivating them to adapt to new developments [37]. It is not just a combination of the two but a new form of economic development using IT and platforms [38]. Similarly, the central word in U+X is the user. The meaning of U+X is users can be involved in every design phase. It is based on user needs and takes full advantage of user heterogeneity and flexibility. In this way, a new form of application development is formed that is more personalized and active.

4.2   The Features of U+X

U+X can be divided into two levels. On the one hand, the symmetrical design [39] and the counterpointed triad technique [40] have shown advantages in the process of digital book design in previous studies. Based on this, the focus of U+X is on the "+", which means that users can add and combine any element. Specifically, U+X introduces the user's concepts into a combination of images, audio, and stories, thus creating a scenario in which the user can interact with design elements (Fig. 2).

On the other hand, the deeper meaning of U+X is to put the user at the heart of the design process. While increasing user engagement and satisfaction, it works to improve the user experience and quality of life. Incorporating preschoolers, adults, and their environment into the interaction design content creates more opportunities for preschoolers to communicate with each other and to facilitate effective communication with adults. Increased participation by preschoolers means that adults can more accurately understand and address the practical problems they have in communicating. At the same time, an enjoyable participatory atmosphere can increase preschoolers' sense of engagement with the product and provide their quality of life.

Fig. 2. Symmetrical design (left), the counterpointed triad technique (center), and U+X (right).

4.3   The Practical Application of U+X

We used U+X to develop a collaborative stakeholder digital book application for preschoolers aged 3–6 called Babbling. The design framework of Babbling was constructed with three aspects that distinguish it from existing cases.

(1) Strategic and Scope Layers: Users + Stories
Text, visuals, and audio are usually presented to users in a fixed combination in traditional digital book applications. Users cannot recombine or use these elements to create new story meanings. In contrast, U+X takes the "user" as an essential element and organically combines it with images, audio, and story to create a textless book system (Fig. 3). This design model removes text constraints and gives preschoolers greater freedom and creativity. It allows preschoolers to fully use their imagination to interpret the meaning of book stories and gives them new narrative meaning by expressing their perspectives. In addition, incomprehensible and uncertain contexts can stimulate preschoolers' curiosity. When preschoolers are confronted with the content of a book without texts, they are forced to rely on other elements, such as images, sounds, and context, to understand the story. This challenging context encourages children to think and explore actively. At the

same time, it creates opportunities for social communication between preschoolers and adults. Preschoolers may seek help from adults or share their perspectives as they try to understand and interpret story content, thus facilitating interaction and communication with adults.

Fig. 3. The story interface of Babbling.

(2) Structural Layer: User + Audio
Existing digital book applications are often accompanied by gamified interactive features that can lead to varying degrees of harm from preschoolers' immersion in electronics. Unusually, U+X explores a design approach that weakens electronics. This approach reduces how preschoolers use electronics without restricting their reading. On the one hand, each page in Babbling is an interaction point that provides feedback on preschoolers' behavior (Fig. 4). When preschoolers interact with the interface, it can capture their needs and respond in real-time. This behavior-feedback mechanism is increasing preschoolers' sense of control over reality. On the other hand, the combination of user and audio guides preschoolers to think about the pictures and encourages them to ask questions. It not only reduces the interactive function of play but also transforms the reward of preschool children completing reading into the encouragement of adults in reality. For example, when a preschooler completes a reading task in Babbling, the audio will say, "You're awesome! Let Mommy and Daddy give you a hug." It encourages adults to interact with preschoolers to increase their interest in reading.

(3) Framework Layer and Presentation Layer: User + Image
Content such as character images, colors, and scenes are often pre-designed in digital book applications. It limits the ability of preschoolers to make choices based on their visual preferences. U+X differs from traditional design approaches by focusing on user engagement and supporting users' immediate choices. In Babbling, preschoolers can independently select their favorite character images, colors, scenes, and other design

Fig. 4. The interactive interface of Babbling.

elements and randomly generate story images based on these components (Fig. 5). This design approach has two advantages.

First, 3–6 years old is a critical period when preschoolers are sensitive to visual stimuli. The flat cartoon images and vivid colors enhance preschoolers' ability to discriminate between graphics and colors in free choice. Second, the combination of non-deterministic design elements empowers preschoolers to make choices, enhancing their motivation and willingness to participate in reading. By introducing user participation, U+X provides preschoolers with greater autonomy and creativity. Preschoolers can choose based on their interests and preferences and have a more positive and exciting reading experience with personalized story images. This design pattern promotes the development of preschoolers' perceptual and decision-making skills and fosters their aesthetic awareness and creative thinking. It also provides a way for children to actively participate in reading actively, increasing their level of interaction and engagement with digital books.

Fig. 5. Babbling supports children's autonomous selection interface.

5 Results

5.1 Demographics

Among the participants were 34 females (56.7%) and 26 males (43.3%). The average age was 4.92 years (Table 1). Nearly all preschool children (93.3%) had previous experience using electronic devices such as smartphones or iPads. Furthermore, as an integral part of their daily routine, most parents fostered their children's interest in reading storybooks, with over half of the families utilizing digital book applications.

Table 1. Comparison of demography characteristics of participants.

Options	Quantity	Percentage (%)	Average
Female	34	56.7	/
Male	26	43.3	
3 years old	6	10	4.92
4 years old	13	21.7	
5 years old	21	35	
6 years old	20	33.3	
Have the habit of reading storybooks	53	88.3	/
No habit of reading storybooks	7	11.7	
Have used electronic devices	56	93.3	/
Have not used an electronic device	4	6.7	
Used book-related applications	41	68.3	/
No previous use of book-related applications	19	31.7	
Total	60	100	/

5.2 Analysis of the Scale Questionnaire for Language Skills

Table 2 shows the paired sample statistics. The mean pre-test language proficiency score was 8.68, and the mean post-test score was 10.98. The post-test mean was 2.3 points higher than the pre-test mean. This indicates increased participants' language skills scores after five days of using Babbling. To further compare whether the two scores reached a statistically significant level of difference, a paired-sample t-test was performed.

The correlation between the pre-and post-experimental language proficiency scores was 0.696, with a significant p-value of 0.000 (Table 3). It is less than 0.05 at the significance level, so the original hypothesis is rejected. It indicates a significant correlation between the pre-and post-experimental language proficiency scores for the paired samples t-test. Therefore, the above data can be applied to the paired sample t-test.

Table 2. Paired sample statistics for language skills assessment.

Pairing 1	Average	Quantity	Standard Deviation	Standard Error
Language skills score before the experiment	8.68	60	2.079	.268
Language skills score after the experiment	10.98	60	1.882	.243

Table 3. Paired sample correlation in language skills assessment.

Pairing 1	Quantity	Correlation	Significance (p)
Pre experiment language skills score & post experiment language skills score	60	.696	.000

Table 4 shows that the t-value of the paired t-test between the pre-and post-experimental language skills scores was -11.46, with a significant p-value of 0.000 (<0.05). Therefore, the original hypothesis is rejected. A significant difference between the pre-experimental and post-experimental scores of language skills exists.

Table 4. Paired sample statistics for language skills assessment.

Pairing 1	Paired Differences					t	df	Sig.
	$\overline{X}$	SD	SE	CI (95%)				
				Lower Limit	Upper Limit			
Pre experiment - post experiment language skills score	−2.300	1.555	.201	−2.702	−1.898	−11.460	59	.000

5.3 Analysis of the Communication Behavior Scale Questionnaire

The mean pre-experiment communication behavior score was 10.85, and the mean post-experiment score was 8.5 (Table 5). The post-experiment mean was 2.35 points lower than the pre-experiment mean. It indicates that the participants' communication behavior problems improved after five days of using Babbling.

The correlation between pre- and post-experimental communication behavior scores was 0.815, with a significant p-value of 0.000 (<0.05), thus rejecting the original hypothesis (Table 6). It indicates a significant correlation between the pre-and post-experimental

Table 5. Paired sample statistics for communication behavior assessment.

Pairing 2	Average	Quantity	Standard Deviation	Standard Error
Communication behavior score before the experiment	10.85	60	2.711	.350
Communication behavior score after the experiment	8.50	60	2.151	.278

Table 6. Paired sample correlation in communication behavior assessment.

Pairing 2	Quantity	Correlation	Significance *(p)*
Pre experiment communication behavior score & post experiment communication behavior score	60	.815	.000

scores of language skills for the paired samples t-test. Therefore, the above data can be applied to the paired sample t-test.

The t-value of the paired t-test between the pre-experimental and post-experimental communication behavior scores was 11.585, with a significant *p*-value of 0.000 (<0.05). Therefore, the original hypothesis was rejected. A significant difference was considered between the pre-experimental communication behavior scores and the post-experimental scores (Table 7).

Table 7. Paired sample statistics for communication behavior assessment.

Pairing 2	Paired Differences					t	df	Sig.
	$\overline{X}$	SD	SE	CI (95%)				
				Lower Limit	Upper Limit			
Pre experiment - post experiment communication behavior score	2.350	1.571	.203	1.944	2.756	11.585	59	.000

6 Discussions

The results of the study support the hypothesis that digital books designed with U+X have the effect of influencing children's communication skills. Based on the findings, we discuss the advantages of introducing preschoolers into the interaction design process. We propose recommendations for designing for the initiative of preschoolers, which can provide solutions for improving their communication skills.

6.1 Considering Including Preschoolers in the Interaction Design Process to Stimulate Their Creativity

U+X values user autonomy, so it provides preschoolers with available design tools and materials in the design process. Specifically, it stimulates creativity in the reading process by providing preschoolers with diverse graphics, colors, shapes, and other elements and story content that can be freely combined and adjusted.

Observations of the preschoolers during the experiment showed that without textual guidance, the preschoolers could describe the story content of the digital books with the assistance of images and audio. Moreover, they were more likely to express their own opinions. Since preschoolers have different understandings of shapes, patterns, and degrees of change [41], the absence of textual allows preschoolers' imagination to flourish [42, 43], thus increasing their willingness to communicate actively. Such a design tool encourages preschoolers to make their own choices. Participating in the interaction design process allows them to express their thoughts and ideas freely, thus creating a unique and personalized interaction experience that stimulates and develops their creativity.

6.2 Considering Amplifying Interpersonal Interactions to Enhance Family Connections

It is known from previous research that the interactive features of electronics are highly appealing to preschoolers, but that excessive use of images or animations may distract them from the narrative content. U+X, therefore, extends the previous design approach. We used human-machine interactions as an entry point to amplify human-human interactions. Considering preschoolers' developmental characteristics and cognitive abilities, we designed an easy-to-understand interaction and interface based on preschoolers' cognitive levels, attention span, and manipulative skills. It enables preschoolers to participate and express their creativity easily. Supporting self-expression is one of the most interesting parts of the interactive experience because it emphasizes user autonomy.

Building on this, the audio will guide parents to give children interactions such as hugs and kisses when preschoolers complete reading tasks, building self-confidence and a sense of accomplishment for children. This collaborative and participatory process enhances the connection between families by bringing parents, educators, and other relevant stakeholders into the interaction design process. It provides preschoolers with the opportunity to interact with adults and other children as a way to develop their social skills and cooperation.

6.3 Considering Encouraging Preschoolers' Self-expression Through Adult Support

Preschoolers' discussion after using Babbling is a way to promote their social interaction. Communication with adults not only helps preschoolers better understand the meaning of stories but also provides positive support [44]. The absence of texts affects children's self-confidence to a certain extent, as they like to ask their parents, "Is this right?" and expect approval and more knowledge from adults. For example, the parents of 5-year-old

Jimmy talked about the process of children gradually losing control of their emotions (Fig. 6):

In the beginning, my child was very interested in reading books on the phone. After three or four days, he could not sit still anymore. The only way to calm him down is to stay with and guide him repeatedly.

The process of asking questions and asking for adult help deepens text learning and comprehension [7]. U+X lays the groundwork for adult intervention. Since context plays a vital role in communication [45], parental accompaniment can create a favorable reading atmosphere, facilitating the development of interest in reading and early reading awareness in preschool children [46]. The adult feedback establishes an environment that supports and respects preschoolers' voices. This environment allows preschoolers to experience the importance of their own opinions and contributions as they participate in the design of interactions. It helps enhance preschoolers' perceptions of their abilities and build their self-confidence. Thus, this study supports previous work emphasizing that adult support helps make children more engaged and expressive [17].

Fig. 6. The process of using Babbling with preschoolers.

6.4 Limitations

Many factors, including individual differences, home environment, and cultural background, can influence preschoolers' use of Babbling. We did not examine or control for these factors. In addition, although most preschoolers can use electronics relatively proficiently, this device is not regularly used in the home environment. This makes it challenging to develop a broad consensus on the study results. Higher sample size studies will overcome Some of these limitations in the future. In the future, long-term attention should be paid to individual differences and particular needs of preschoolers to provide individualized participatory interaction design solutions. In this way, the applicability of the study will be increased.

7 Conclusions

The development of digital technology has facilitated a shift in the function of design from monolithic to composite. It has also influenced the progression of users' needs for design from simplicity to complexity. We introduce a U+X participatory interaction design pattern that builds on existing designs and emphasizes putting the user at the center of the design process. It prioritizes enhancing user engagement and quality of life while ensuring user experience and satisfaction. The results of the study provide some evidence that digital books designed with U+X have the effect of improving preschoolers' language skills and communication behaviors. As a result, we have summarized our empirical knowledge of how preschoolers use U+X-designed digital books to express themselves and improve their language and communication skills. It provides a good reference for research on preschool children's user groups. Also, based on the results of this study, the use of U+X-designed digital books is an option for improving preschoolers' communication skills in kindergarten and home settings. This is a safe, inexpensive, and accessible strategy to supplement psychological assistance and offers a possibility to improve communication problems in preschool children.

Acknowledgments. This research was funded by the "Research on Digital Art and Cultural Industry Development" project of Guangzhou Wanqu Cooperative Institute of Design (9028). We would like to thank Associate Professor Huang Guanghui of Macau University of Science and Technology for her guidance on this paper. We would like to thank Guangzhou Wanqu Design Institute for their support. We would also like to thank all the families who participated in the research.

References

1. Jin, J.: Strategies for children with communication and learning disabilities. Chinese J. Child Health Care. **20**(10), 865–866 (2012)
2. Doove, B.M., Feron, F.J., Van Os, J., Drukker, M.: Preschool communication: Early identification of concerns about preschool language development and social participation. Front. Public Health **8**, 536–546 (2021)
3. Günay Bilaloğlu, R., Aktaş Arnas, Y.: Barriers to parental involvement in preschool education and problems encountered in process. Hacettepe University J. Educ. **34**(3), 804–823 (2019). https://doi.org/10.16986/HUJE.2018043536
4. Courage, M.L.: From print to digital: the medium is only part of the message. In: Kim, J.E., Hassinger-Das, B. (eds.) Reading in the Digital Age: Young Children's Experiences with E-books: International Studies with E-books in Diverse Contexts, pp. 23–43. Springer, Cham (2019). https://doi.org/10.1007/978-3-030-20077-0_3
5. Schryer, E., Sloat, E., Letourneau, N.: Effects of an animated book reading intervention on emergent literacy skill development: an early pilot study. J. Early Interv. **37**(2), 155–171 (2015). https://doi.org/10.1177/105381511559884
6. Coetzee, T., Moonsamy, S., Neille, J.: A shared reading intervention: changing perceptions of caregivers in a semi-rural township. South Afr. J. Commun. Disorders **70**(1), a948 (2023). https://doi.org/10.4102/sajcd.v70i1.948

7. Takacs, Z.K., Swart, E.K., Bus, A.G.: Can the computer replace the adult for storybook reading? A meta-analysis on the effects of multimedia stories as compared to sharing print stories with an adult. Front. Psychol. **5**, 1366 (2014). https://doi.org/10.3389/fpsyg.2014. 01366

8. Lin, J., Litkowski, E., Schmerold, K., et al.: Parent–educator communication linked to more frequent home learning activities for preschoolers. Child Youth Care Forum **48**, 757–772 (2019). https://doi.org/10.1007/s10566-019-09505-9

9. Munzer, T.G., Miller, A.L., Weeks, H.M., Kaciroti, N., Radesky, J.: Differences in parent-toddler interactions with electronic versus print books. Pediatrics **143**(4), e20182012 (2019). https://doi.org/10.1542/peds.2018-2012

10. Polyzou, S., Botsoglou, K., Zygouris, N.C., Stamoulis, G.: Interactive books for preschool children: from traditional interactive paper books to augmented reality books: listening to children's voices through mosaic approach. Education **3–13**, 1–12 (2022). https://doi.org/10. 1080/03004279.2021.2025131

11. Egert, F., Cordes, A.K., Hartig, F.: Can e-books foster child language? Meta-analysis on the effectiveness of e-book interventions in early childhood education and care. Educ. Res. Rev. **37**, e100472 (2022). https://doi.org/10.1016/j.edurev.2022.100472

12. Richter, A., Courage, M.L.: Comparing electronic and paper storybooks for preschoolers: attention, engagement, and recall. J. Appl. Dev. Psychol. **48**, 92–102 (2017). https://doi.org/ 10.1016/j.appdev.2017.01.002

13. Montessori, M.: The Montessori Method. Transaction Publishers, Somerset, New Jersey (2013)

14. Maleki, M., Chehrzad, M.M., KazemnezhadLeyli, E., Mardani, A., Vaismoradi, M.: Social skills in preschool children from teachers' perspectives. Children **6**(5), 64 (2019). https://doi. org/10.3390/children6050064

15. Hu, B.Y., Fan, X., Wu, Z., LoCasale-Crouch, J., Yang, N., Zhang, J.: Teacher-child interactions and children's cognitive and social skills in Chinese preschool classrooms. Child Youth Serv. Rev. **79**, 78–86 (2017). https://doi.org/10.1016/j.childyouth.2017.05.028

16. Craig-Unkefer, L.A., Kaiser, A.P.: Improving the social communication skills of at-risk preschool children in a play context. Top. Early Childhood Spec. Educ. **22**(1), 3–13 (2002). https://doi.org/10.1177/027112140202200101

17. Kaderavek, J.N., Pentimonti, J.M., Justice, L.M.: Children with communication impairments: caregivers' and teachers' shared book-reading quality and children's level of engagement. Child Lang. Teach. Therapy **30**(3), 289–302 (2014). https://doi.org/10.1177/026565901351 3812

18. Julien, H.M., Finestack, L.H., Reichle, J.: Requests for communication repair produced by typically developing preschool-age children. J. Speech Lang. Hear. Res. **62**(6), 1823–1838 (2019). https://doi.org/10.1044/2019_JSLHR-L-18-0402

19. Fängström, K., Salari, R., Eriksson, M., Sarkadi, A.: The computer-assisted interview In My Shoes can benefit shy preschool children's communication. PLoS ONE **12**(8), e0182978 (2017). https://doi.org/10.1371/journal.pone.0182978

20. Mashfufah, A., Nurkamto, J., Novenda, I.L.: Conceptual: digital book in the era of digital learning approaches (DLA). IOP Conf. Ser. Earth Environ. Sci. **243**(1), 012107 (2019). https:// doi.org/10.1088/1755-1315/243/1/012107

21. Dickinson, D.K., Morse, A.B.: Connecting Through Talk: Nurturing Children's Development with Language. Paul H. Brookes Publishing Co, Towson, Maryland (2019)

22. Sarı, B., Başal, H.A., Takacs, Z.K., Bus, A.G.: A randomized controlled trial to test efficacy of digital enhancements of storybooks in support of narrative comprehension and word learning. J. Exp. Child Psychol. **179**, 212–226 (2019). https://doi.org/10.1016/j.jecp.2018.11.006

23. Eng, C.M., Tomasic, A.S., Thiessen, E.D.: Contingent responsivity in E-books modeled from quality adult-child interactions: effects on children's learning and attention. Dev. Psychol. **56**(2), 285–297 (2020). https://doi.org/10.1037/dev0000869

24. Shamir, A., Korat, O., Fellah, R.: Promoting vocabulary, phonological awareness and concept about print among children at risk for learning disability: can e-books help? Read. Writ. **25**(1), 45–69 (2012). https://doi.org/10.1007/s11145-010-9247-x

25. Zhou, N., Yadav, A.: Effects of multimedia story reading and questioning on preschoolers' vocabulary learning, story comprehension and reading engagement. Educ. Tech. Res. Dev. **65**(6), 1523–1545 (2017). https://doi.org/10.1007/s11423-017-9533-2

26. Zipke, M.: The importance of flexibility of pronunciation in learning to decode: a training study in set for variability. First Lang. **36**(1), 71–86 (2016). https://doi.org/10.1177/014272 3716639495

27. Schuler, D., Namioka, A. (eds.): Participatory Design: Principles and Practices. CRC Press, Florida (1993)

28. Maiden, N.A., Rugg, G.: ACRE: selecting methods for requirements acquisition. Softw. Eng. J. **11**(3), 183–192 (1996)

29. Smith, A., Dunckley, L.: Prototype evaluation and redesign: structuring the design space through contextual techniques. Interact. Comput. **14**(6), 821–843 (2002). https://doi.org/10.1016/S0953-5438(02)00031-0

30. Markus, M.L., Mao, J.Y.: Participation in development and implementation-updating an old, tired concept for today's IS contexts. J. Assoc. Inf. Syst. **5**(11), 14 (2004). https://aisel.aisnet.org/jais/vol5/iss11/14

31. Aloizou, V., Rangoussi, M.: Mobile devices and e-learning in preschool education: design, development and evaluation of an educational intervention. In: ICERI2016 Proceedings, pp. 2981–2990 (2016). https://doi.org/10.21125/iceri.2016.1643

32. Xin-long, J., Chen, Y., Liu, J., Hu, L., Shen, J.: Wearable system to support proximity awareness for people with autism. J. Zhejiang Univ. (Eng. Sci.), 637–647 (2017). CNKI:SUN:ZDZC.0.2017-04-001

33. Noris, B., Nadel, J., Barker, M., Hadjikhani, N., Billard, A.: Investigating gaze of children with ASD in naturalistic settings. PLoS ONE **7**(9), e44144 (2012). https://doi.org/10.1371/journal.pone.0044144

34. Wolfson, S.: Diagnosing ASD with fractal analysis. Adv. Autism. **3** 47–56 (2017). https://doi.org/10.1108/AIA-03-2016-0007

35. Jesse, J.G.: The Elements of User Experience: User-centered Design for the Web and Beyond. China Machine Press, Beijing (2019)

36. Goodman, R.: A modified version of the Rutter parent questionnaire including extra items on children's strengths: a research note. J. Child Psychol. Psychiatr. **35**(8), 1483–1494 (1994). https://doi-org.libezproxy.must.edu.mo/https://doi.org/10.1111/j.1469-7610

37. Aijia, Z., Guanghui, H., Fangtian, Y.: Babbling: a digital book application to improve preschool children's social communication ability. Des. Stud. Intell. Eng. Proc. DSIE **2022**, 379–389 (2023). https://doi.org/10.3233/FAIA220731

38. Chuxin, H., Dan, W.: What does "Internet plus" mean— Deep understanding of "Internet plus." News Writing. **05**, 5–9 (2015)

39. Nikolajeva, M.: How Picturebooks Work. Routledge, New York (2013). https://doi.org/10.4324/9780203960615

40. Sargeant, B., Mueller, F.F.: How far is up? Bringing the counterpointed triad technique to digital storybook apps. In: Proceedings of the 2018 CHI Conference on Human Factors in Computing Systems, vol. 519, pp. 1–12 (2018). https://doi.org/10.1145/3173574.3174093

41. Liu, X.: The generation of children's meaning world and its enlightenment on modern children's education. J. Educ. Sci. Hunan Normal Univ. **19**(04), 42–48 (2020). https://doi.org/10.19503/j.cnki.1671-6124.2020.04.006

42. Lili, S.: The eye of innocence: another application of picture books in children's philosophy. Res. Educ. Dev. **41**(02), 50–57 (2021). https://doi.org/10.14121/j.cnki.1008-3855.2021. 02.010

43. Raluca, B.O., Bocoş, M.: Formative influence of preschoolers through art education. Proc. Soc. Behav. Sci. **76**, 71–76 (2013). https://doi.org/10.1016/j.sbspro.2013.04.076

44. Richter, A., Courage, M.L.: Comparing electronic and paper storybooks for preschoolers: attention, engagement, and recall. J. Appl. Dev. Psychol. **48**, 92–102 (2017). https://doi.org/ 10.1016/j.appdev.2017.01.002

45. Dan, L., Han, X., Xiao, S., Xu, F., Chen, X., Xu, S.: A review of the research on the application of auxiliary communication system to the intervention of communication skills in "nonverbal" autistic children. China Spec. Educ. **07**, 62–70+81 (2022)

46. Zhao, S.: Analysis of the influence of parents' accompanying reading style on children's early reading effect. New Century Libr. **07**, 43–46 (2015). https://doi.org/10.16810/j.cnki. 1672-514x.2015.07.010

eCommerce, Digital Marketing and eFinance

Underlying Factors of Technology Acceptance and User Experience of Machine Learning Functions in Accounting Software: A Qualitative Content Analysis

Cristina Cristofoli[1] and Torkil Clemmensen[2(✉)]

[1] Independent UX Researcher, Copenhagen, Denmark
[2] Copenhagen Business School, 2000 Frederiksberg, Denmark
cristinacristofoli@me.com

Abstract. This research examines which factors influence users' technology acceptance (TA) and user experience (UX) of machine learning (ML) functions in accounting software. Although the two methods are widely acknowledged, they are rarely understood in unity. This study analyses factors underlying UX and TA of ML function in accounting software. It contributes to the ongoing discussion in the Human-Computer Interaction (HCI) community about the relation between UX and TAM, and it does so with a focus on AI functions of software and within a business domain. Six hypotheses were established based on the three concepts of innovativeness, trust, and satisfaction to understand their influence on TA and UX. To evaluate the hypotheses and answer the research question, an accounting software (AS) was chosen as a case. A qualitative content analysis was done of user experts' perceptions of acceptance and experience with ML functions. The study concludes that innovativeness, trust, and satisfaction influence users' TA and UX of ML functions in AS confirming the six hypotheses The results are discussed in relation to the literature on UX, TAM, and accounting. The study questions the measurability of TAM and UX and suggests re-evaluating the use of these methods for products with artificial intelligence.

Keywords: User Experience · Artificial Intelligence · Machine Learning · Accounting · Technology Acceptance Model · Qualitative content analysis

1 [1]Introduction

The challenges of measuring users' choice and usage of IT are many-faceted. A common aim is to determine and answer how to design IT and what makes consumers choose and adopt a specific software [1]. Currently, there are predominantly two popular ways to answer these complex questions: user experience (UX) or technology acceptance (TA). UX is measured in various ways. Researchers have attempted to create definitions and

---

[1] Acronyms in this paper: AS: accounting software, TA: technology acceptance, UX: user experience, ML: machine learning; ERP: enterprise resource planning.

© The Author(s), under exclusive license to Springer Nature Switzerland AG 2023
P. Zaphiris et al. (Eds.): HCII 2023, LNCS 14060, pp. 413–433, 2023.
https://doi.org/10.1007/978-3-031-48060-7_31

frameworks to better grasp the aspects UX implies, e.g., [2–4]. Although no universal agreement exists, Merčun and Žumer [5] argues that generally researchers agree that a system's hedonic and pragmatic qualities shape the user experience. In contrast to the messy situation with the UX concept, TA is typically measured through the Technology Acceptance Model (TAM) [6] and its later development in a unified model of intention and use that says that performance expectancy, effort expectancy, social influence, and facilitating conditions shape behavioral intention and use behavior [7]. Thus the UX and TA concepts appear to conceptually overlap in unclear ways [1], which this study helps to unravel with the context of ML in accounting systems.

Moreover, a new wave of IT-user literature has emerged, pointing out the difficulties and issues occurring with designing for AI. The challenges span from designers' difficulties in comprehending the capabilities of AI to struggle with utilising existing UX design methods to collaborating with data scientists ([8–10]. Though there has been an increased focus on creating meaningful frameworks by both big companies such as Microsoft [11] and Google [12] as well as researchers [13], there is a lack of research on how AI experiences differ from regular user experiences [14]. However, it is of great importance to further study this interaction between UX and AI, whilst the more humans become reliant on technology, the less prepared they are to take control when it fails [15]. In this paper, we aim to get an in-depth view of users' experience and acceptance of AI understood as machine learning (ML) functions in software to create a stepping-stone for future studies in the interrelation between TA, UX and AI. A good example of ML's impact on the TA and UX is the accounting field, since in accounting software, ML functionalities are appearing at a rapid pace [16]. The field of accounting was chosen since accounting likewise has experienced a shift from manual work to nearly completely automated due to computers' evolution [17]. Thus, the software used in the accounting field has evolved significantly, and the use of AI within accounting is gaining more popularity, making it an interesting area to research. Furthermore, it is interesting to understand how this professional user group relates to the shift in accounting and the evolution of the software.

Our aim is to map out existing variables found in literature and understand why these influences the users' experiences and acceptance when utilising the ML functions in accounting software. To achieve a broad and detailed overview of users' experience and acceptance this research applies qualitative research interviews with real expert user informants, rather than future end-users of imagined AI applications. With this delimitation in mind, this research aims to answer the following research question: *Which factors affect the technology acceptance and user experience of the machine learning functions in accounting software?* We propose the following contributions:

Conceptually, we advance the theory on relation between UX and TA [1, 18] by identifying common underlying factors that allow us to establish a relationship between UX and TA. The factors explain the transition from initial technology acceptance to actual use of the IT product or system; the attributes of the end-users and their company shape both the TX and UX of the ML, but in varying degrees. This means that, compared to Hornbæk and Hertzum's [1] argument that for the entertainment domain UX and TAM largely focuses on individual-psychological variables and tasks, we argue that for business software the technology acceptance and user experiences are inseparable from the organisational work contexts. Furthermore, we help updating this discussion to the era of AI by analysing the use of ML functions in business software.

Empirically, we establish that the UX and TA indeed share underlying factors, meaning that these phenomena may not be alone in being expressions of employees' relation to their software in real work settings. For example, power relations and social relations can be added to acceptance and user experience as experience categories [19]. Additionally, we contribute to fill the void of studies of UX in professional work and business domains with accounting as an example.

To answer the research question, this paper will first discuss the current literature. Then the hypotheses are defined. This is followed by a methodology section that clarifies the research design and approach, and a content analysis of the proposed factors in the interview data. Finally, the discussion relates the findings and hypotheses to the HCI literature, followed by a conclusion that answers the research question.

2   Theoretical Background

2.1   Artificial Intelligence and Accounting

The amount of research done on AI and accounting field is limited, although there is significant potential due to its repetitive and error-prone tasks. Many tasks that accountants currently perform are cumbersome and could easily be replaced by AI, leaving the accountants with more important, valuable and strategic tasks [20–22]. The strength of AI is that it can perform repetitive tasks at high volumes and paces without experiencing fatigue. As many parts of an accountants' work are made up of repetitive tasks, it would be possible for accountants to reconsider every stage of their work processes [22].

Even though some companies have implemented AI functions in their AS, most still rely on outdated AS due to the managements' unwillingness to adopt new technologies [23]. The major obstacles to a digital transformation in accounting are due to resistance to change and organisational culture [21, 22]. However, the specific factors of resistance are still yet to be fully discovered in the accounting field. There are many discussions and perspectives to explore to fully understand the risks and opportunities that the technologies entail for the accounting field [24].

Furthermore, as accountants' jobs have changed over the past 20–30 years, resistance to change may result from their fear of their jobs being replaced and not seeing it as an opportunity to improve their skills and take on more valuable tasks [20]. However, studies of the fear of workplace automation among recruiters indicate an optimism about the opportunities that automation could bring them, rather than fear of e.g., replacement [25]. Resistance seems to stem from a lack of knowledge regarding AI, as it is viewed as a "black box", which can result in accountants being unwilling to use AI technologies [22]. Algorithm aversion is found to influence the behaviour of accountants, as they show less trust in advice generated from AI than humans [26]. This resistance could be based on concerns about capability and lack of knowledge regarding AI among accountants [26]. Criticism of this problem is emerging, with researchers blaming the universities for not preparing for the new types of technologies, as newly graduated accountants today are ill-equipped to perform tasks where technology skills are needed [20, 22]. This causes an issue, as the tendency to embrace technology directly influences the acceptance and usage of these technologies [20, 27].

2.2 Technology Acceptance of Accounting Software (AS)

The well-known Technology Acceptance Model (TAM) was developed to measure users' acceptance and actual use of new technologies [28]. In the TAM, perceived ease of use (PEOU) and perceived usefulness (PU) are two key factors that influence users' acceptance levels. Technology success depends on perceptions of these two variables, which can be used to measure intentions to use and actual usage [28]. Due to its parsimoniousness and broad applicability, the framework has been used extensively for assessing success and user acceptance [29, 30]. Its broad applicability is partly due to its ability to be revised and expanded with new external variables. Some of the best-known are TAM2 [29] and TAM3 [31] with new external factors to support social and individual influence on usage intentions such as experience, computer anxiety and image being used. Thus, many factors are considered when understanding users' acceptance and adoption of technology. AI-based systems, however, introduce new factors that affect adoption and trust, such as "creepiness" and emotional factors [14].

Multiple studies have evaluated the acceptance of AS based on TAM and external variables.[27, 32, 33] Among others, it has been discovered that users consider service quality and appealing alternatives when selecting AS, however previous experience with similar products does not influence their choice [32]. When it comes to attitude and usage, users' innovativeness, however, has been shown to have a significant impact on AS acceptance [20, 27]. In addition to innovativeness, factors such as user control, content richness, two-way communication, and perceived personalisation may influence the technology acceptance in the accounting field [27].

While the TAM is widely recognised for its utility in explaining external variables and technology acceptance, it has also been criticised. First, for being deterministic along with doubts regarding its actual predictive power [34–37]. Further, the advancement of technologies and society at large has raised doubts about whether TAM can still be used to understand the acceptance of todays' technologies [38]. Another critique regards how TAM only measures the initial acceptance, and not the continuance, which is necessary for software to be successful in the long-term [33]. Satisfaction is a more decisive measure method of continuance than PU and PEOU, as dissatisfaction is necessary for system discontinuance [33]. However, due to the increase in system use over time, the question is whether not all constructs in TAM are continually formed and reformed [1]. In addition to determining use, PU and PE are shaped by external variables, which means they are influenced by system use. As a result, the intention to use is shaped by the systems' usefulness and enjoyment at a particular time [1].

2.3 User Experience of Accounting Software

UX has, unlike TAM, no uniformly accepted model driving research in UX. This is due to several meanings assigned to the term UX [39]. UX is connected to many vague and changing concepts, such as experiential, emotional or aesthetic variables [40]. These concepts are included or excluded depending on the researchers' aim, making it challenging to form a proper unified definition [41]. Researchers have attempted to create definitions and frameworks to better grasp the aspects UX implies (e.g., [4, 41, 42]). However, no framework manages to create a universal definition. Although no universal agreement exists, generally, researchers agree that a system's hedonic and pragmatic qualities shape the user experience [43]. A system or a product's hedonic qualities capture the enjoyment and stimulation generated by its use. In contrast, pragmatic qualities refer to usability aspects such as perceived usefulness, efficiency, and ease of use. Product acceptance is influenced by the combination of pragmatic and hedonic values, as those are accountable for emotions evoked by the user [43].

AS is essential to all successful businesses as bookkeeping is an unavoidable task in all businesses. Researching the UX and usability of AS is essential to ensure successful utilisation and continuation of usage, since the primary reason for system failure and maintenance costs is poorly designed user interfaces [44]. Metrics to measure the UX of AS that ensure that the systems' design creates a proper UX may include several factors: Subjective satisfaction, consistency, attractiveness, familiarity, error tolerance, predictability, system terminology, feedback, help, control and freedom [44]. Although the evaluation metrics were confirmed to be influencing the user of the studied AS, the metrics have, however, not yet been tested on other types of AS [44]. Noteworthy, they have not been studied for AS using ML functions. Even a study that measured usability and satisfaction to discover how the user perceived a bookkeeping application with ML technology to scan receipts, did not specifically focus on them, making it less clear how ML specifically influenced these measures [45].

3 Hypothesis Development

TAM measures the initial intention to use, while UX measures the continued usage of a product. However, the literatures' focus regarding the interaction between AI and accounting seems to center around the initial TA rather than the UX and continued usage. Although different underlying factors have appeared throughout the literature, as indicated above, there is no clear understanding of which factors affect the interaction between AI and accounting. Thus, it is also unclear whether these factors are present only in the measure of TA, UX or both. However, three factors appear to be of central importance and mentioned repeatedly throughout the literature: **Satisfaction** (e.g., [1, 33, 44–46]), **Trust** (e.g., [1, 14, 22, 26, 47, 48]) and **Innovativeness** (e.g., [1, 20, 27]). Therefore, to understand which factors influence the acceptance and experience of ML functions in accounting, we chose to start by uncovering these three factors' impact on the UX and TA of ML functions in accounting.

3.1 Innovativeness

AI should be regarded as a complementation tool to human performance, which can manage tasks that are repetitive and prone to errors. These valuable properties are especially favourable for accounting, as many daily tasks are mundane. AI can relieve routine tasks leaving space for more valuable, creative, and strategic tasks for the accountants. However, the technology faces resistance in the accounting world. The specific factors that drive this resistance are still to be discovered; however, users' willingness or innovativeness has been acknowledged to influence the TA of accounting systems. Innovativeness is a dimension of technology readiness and is defined as a perceived affirmative metric contributing to the level of technology readiness rather than inhibiting it [20]. The innovativeness of users can be characterised by their willingness to try new products and affect their attitude towards using technologies [27]. While there was no recollection of innovativeness concerning UX, the importance of showing users that AI is a valuable tool was emphasised [49]. Hornbæk and Hertzum [1] highlighted that innovativeness was categorised as a user characteristic and was left out of their review of studies. Since the variable is affecting digitalisation in the accounting field, it is theorised that innovativeness is affecting UX the same way it is affecting the TA. We propose the following hypotheses:

H1: Innovativeness affects the TA of the ML functions in AS.
H2: Innovativeness affects the UX of the ML functions in AS.

3.2 Trust

Trust is an outcome of predictability, and explainability is needed to ensure trust is built when the systems' predictability cannot be controlled [14]. Trust is defined as a result of the characteristics of a relationship and context, which is the basis of an interaction between two individuals [47]. Trust is not a consideration when one part is not required to perform some function related to the other part's goals [47]. Trust between humans is influenced by reliability and honesty and breaks when being let down or betrayed [48]. The factors influencing trust between humans are the same as those that affect trust in technologies [48]. Trust is also affected by new factors which have appeared along with AI, such as "creepiness" and emotional factors, according to Kliman-Silver et al., (2020). However, no other literature has evaluated those factors. The accounting field shows that accountants are less trusting of AI, which stems from a lack of knowledge [22, 26]. Since it has been established that trust influences both the experiences and acceptance of AI and accounting, two hypotheses are created to better understand how trust influences the interaction with ML functions in accounting:

H3: Trust affects the TA of the ML functions in AS.
H4: Trust affects the UX of the ML functions in AS.

3.3 Satisfaction

Satisfaction is a metric that also covers the TA aspect. The amount of research done in the accounting field with a focus on UX is minimal; thus, there is a clear gap in the literature covering UX measurement metrics for accounting tools, especially with a focus on AI. However, satisfaction has been measured for the usage of accounting tools [44][45], and it has been argued that satisfaction influenced the continued usage of IT [46]. Thus, satisfaction is an outcome that covers the overall usage of a system. However, satisfaction has also been tested in relation to TAM, which was found to be a more substantial influence on the TA than both the PU and PEOU [33]. Hornbæk and

Hertzum (2017) state how satisfaction was defined differently throughout the mapped studies and was defined as a broad construct that is the gathering of an overall feeling or attitude relating to the factors influencing the situation. Satisfaction is an affect and should thus be measured through bipolar evaluation dimensions such as satisfied/dissatisfied and frustrated/content [33]. High levels of satisfaction are a pleasurable fulfilment, and high satisfaction can result in higher fulfilment in terms of pleasure and enjoyment [46]. Furthermore, satisfaction is based on the users' satisfaction with the interaction with a product and may be measured through ease of use and level of complexity [44]. Adopting the views of satisfaction as an outcome of interaction with a product is also in line with Hornbæk and Hertzums' [1] argument that satisfaction is a broad construct that ultimately is about the overall feelings towards a specific situation. To understand how satisfaction influences the interaction with ML functions in accounting, the definition leads to the following hypotheses:

H5: Satisfaction affects the TA of the ML functions in AS.

H6: Satisfaction affects the UX of the ML functions in AS.

An understanding of how the above concepts are related is represented in a conceptual framework (Fig. 1). With the hypotheses established, the next section will defend the approach and research design chosen to best answer the research question.

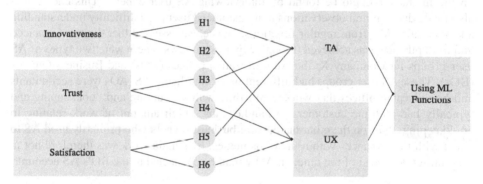

Fig. 1. Conceptual framework: Underlying factors for TA and UX of ML functions.

4   Methodology

This study aimed to understand TA and UX of ML functions in AS by studying what factors influences these phenomena. We applied non-probability purposive sampling in a case study approach with primary data consisting of a mono-method qualitative data collection to achieve this objective. The data collection technique was conducting semi-structured interviews and equivalent qualitative content analysis. The qualitative data was analysed by assessing participants' attributed verbal meanings and associate relationships that required categorising data into codes. The case study strategy was chosen as it enabled in-depth theorization of the experience of ML in accounting.

4.1 Case

A case with accounting software (AS) was chosen to study how TA and UX are affected by ML. The software chosen was owned by a company X, which provided cloud-based software, and at the time of writing this paper held the responsibility for some of Denmark's most utilised cloud solutions in the fields of ERP and accounting. The software was aimed at small to medium-sized companies and accountants and bookkeepers. The software offered packages that used ML to help customers book their income and expenses. The ML functions were designed to have a work-facilitating functionality; hence they were designed to facilitate work and not replace human interaction. The functions were designed to streamline bookkeeping and minimise decision-making. Thus, we chose Company X' AS as the case software, because it applied ML in various essential functions, and was from one of the leading cloud-based ASs providers in a typical European market. Therefore, purposive sampling pointed to AS in company X as an exemplary case of ML functions in AS.

The data collected through semi-structured interviews was done with employees who were AS user experts at Company X. This approach was chosen to ensure a holistic and nuanced view of users' interaction with the ML functions. Since ML may seem frightening and complex to users, we assessed that the most precise and detailed data on the interaction could be found by interviewing AS user experts. This choice was also made due to initial observations that customers' users had difficulty understanding and separating ML from regular functions. Hence, we assessed that the most nuanced and in-depth view was achieved through expert interviews. There were two types of AS user groups for Company X: the Administrative Offices (AOs) and Business Owners (BOs). These AS user groups had different ways of utilising AS. AOs were accountants and bookkeeping offices that worked full time with accounting and bookkeeping and typically had multiple customers to handle, thus a high amount of work relating to bookkeeping. BOs, on the other hand, were business owners who primarily used AS to assist with their finances within their businesses. BOs main work was therefore not in accounting, and most of the time, an AO would be connected to the BO's AS account.

4.2 Participants

Sampling and Descriptions of participants. Getting a nuanced understanding of how the factors influence the users' interaction with ML functions in accounting was achieved by obtaining a wide variety of participants through non-probability sampling. The aim was to capture the participants' (AS user experts) different perspectives on the researched topic, enabling a broadest possible view of potential patterns and relations between factors and TA/UX phenomena. The criteria were that participants were employees working within the case company and had deep and substantial interactions with client-side users either using or having rejected the ML functions. All eight participants were chosen prior to the data collection and were specifically chosen based on their position and daily tasks. See Fig. 2 for an overview of positions.

The participants consisted of two participants from the UX team (P4/*years in current position:2/years at Company X:2*; P5/3/3). This team optimised the UX and worked daily with parts of AS containing ML functions. Participants from the UX team were chosen, as their daily tasks consisted of understanding the users' behaviour on a qualitative level and solving their problems. Thus, providing perspective on users' experience with the ML functions. Two participants were from the Customer Insights team (P6/3/3; P7/1/5). They were chosen to acquire a more generalisable point of view. This team conducted research and analyses data based

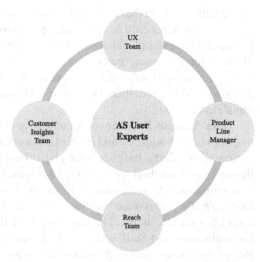

Fig. 2. Participant categories (AS user experts).

on the users, which was done both qualitatively and quantitatively. Additionally, three employees from the sales department Reach were chosen (P1/4/8; P2/2/2; P3/2/8). They had knowledge from contact and upgrade existing customers, as well as contact potential new customers. Further, this department was responsible for reaching out to customers with surveys. They had daily contact, thus experiencing direct user feedback. Lastly, a product line manager was chosen (P8/3/3), due to being responsible for the overall handling of the product and being in contact with multiple teams, including the teams for this study. This participant was chosen as they possessed insights from multiple sources, thus providing an overarching perspective.

4.3 Data Collection and Analysis

Data Collection. A semi-structured interview approach, 'expert interviews' [50], was chosen for the data collection method. Expert interviews are an information-gathering instrument in evaluation research, which is an argumentative, and discursive interviewing focused on a stakeholder problem [50], which in our case is how end-users accept and experience ML functions in accounting software. The data were collected cross-sectionally, meaning the interviews were conducted within single time point of four weeks. This time horizon allowed viewing the current state of ML's impact on users. The verbal data of the interviews were transcribed by the first author. The development of the interview protocol began with developing specific questions relating to the constructs which was done through a collection of previous and validated measurements [20, 27, 32, 46, 51–55], see also uploaded supplementary material. This collection was followed by a comparison and evaluation of similar or equal nature questions resulting in the most central questions being selected as a source for generating the interview questions. The protocol was constructed with a few preliminary questions to gain the participants' trust and confidence in answering the questions according to their reality. The preliminary questions were altered depending on the employee's position. The introduction was followed by a mid-section of questions connected to the relevant theories. The interview was terminated, with the researchers asking a few closing questions to ensure a soft exit to the interview. After each interview, the questions were reviewed and occasionally altered for clarity. For example, although the research objective was explained at the beginning of the interview, some participants had difficulties separating automation from ML; thus, the questions were altered from asking about 'automation' to asking about 'ML functions'. Most participants were native Danish speakers; thus, the interview guide was translated into Danish.

Data Analysis Procedure. A qualitative content analysis of the data was conducted to discover the frequency and content of topics across the interviews. With the deductive nature of this study, the data were coded based on pre-existing concepts derived from theory to evaluate their applicability to the research focus. Thus, the analysis' main focus was on the established concepts from TAM and UX and the factors derived from the literature. The codes were built based on concepts found through theory and were coded through a set of criteria. The concepts were defined into three types of codes: Trust, Innovativeness and Satisfaction, and the criteria were developed into a codebook from the measurements derived from existing theory. Codes were evaluated by the most coded categories and the content of these presented in the analysis sections.

5   Analysis – Underlying Factors for UX and TA

This content analysis aimed to understand how the three theoretically derived factors fit with the qualitative interview data collected to get an understanding of how the factors influence the TA and UX of ML functions in accounting. The following three sections present the analysis per factor, followed by a hypothesis overview.

5.1   Analysis 1 - Innovativeness

Innovativeness was measured by asking the participants questions regarding users' willingness to use the functions, to what degree they were actively seeking the functions and what level of intuitiveness the users have in using the ML functions in AS. Innovativeness was the prominent factor in the data, as this concept was coded 146 times compared to satisfaction and trust, respectively coded 95 and 96 times. Three participants mentioned innovativeness as the most significant factor for using the ML functions. When speaking with the participants, there were two significant types of user groups regarding their level of innovativeness. One user group is widely accepting of digitalisation and curious about ML functions, while another is very reluctant to use ML functions, even if they are currently using them. Most participants state that the main obstacle blocking users from using ML functions is due to the fact that they do not want to change the way they work or find it easier to continue their processes manually. Generally, the participants believe that two factors are causing the issue. Either users do not know that there is a smarter way of doing things, or the users have difficulty getting into how to start using the functions. Multiple participants state that they doubt anyone would object to being more efficient. It is emphasised that it is very much about how the user is experiencing the onboarding and taking the first step into a more digitised way of working. However, Participant 2 (P2, hereafter participants referred to as P) explained how some users accept taking a trial even though they are not willing and accepting of the functions: *"If they try it out, they may think it's difficult, not because it is difficult, but they may feel it's difficult because they don't really want to try and learn something new, but they may feel like they have to try it out. So they probably won't be very satisfied because they don't feel that it's very beneficial."* P2. After the trial period, the users have not changed their opinion regarding the functions, stating that they found it inconvenient. According to the participant, this is due to low innovativeness. The participants think it is primarily the existing BOs who are sceptical and unwilling to try the functions due to unfamiliarity. This user group is already using AS without ML functions, meaning it is a question of initial TA. The existing BOs are distancing themselves from ML and want to continue in their existing work habits. Participant 1 believes that approximately half of the existing BOs agree to try the AS packages with ML, and around half of them will upgrade their packages afterwards: *"There are definitely some people who would like to give it a chance and there are some people who just think, it's fine but I don't want to, I want to do what I'm used to. I think it's about 50/50."* P1. This shows that over half of all BOs choose not to convert to the AS packages with ML. Participants believe that the reason for the reluctance from this user group is due to their primary occupancy not being accounting; thus, they have less interest in the different functions as long as the accounting is done. Participant 2 believes that the resistance from the existing BOs is due to having been working manually in AS for many years and therefore having difficulties changing behaviour: *"It's about having a habit and routine in your head. "I do it this way and I've done it for 20 years, the whole time I've been running the business and I want to continue doing it that way." That's primarily what we come across. And then it's also difficult to change their mindset."* P2. Both Participant 2 and Participant 3 argue that newly gathered users are more aware of the automation, as they actively seek AS because it contains the ML functions: *"Now I am working on these conversions and they usually actively made a decision to switch over to us. So there it's like that. There's no need to come up with a big sales pitch, because they've already made the decision."* P2. However, as BOs for the most part have an AO connected, many participants believe that the BOs depend on how digital their AO is. Thus, the participants mention that generally, the less innovative user group is BOs; however, many AOs do not want to change how they are used to working. The participants believe that AOs influence BOs significantly, whether it being towards or away from automation. According to the participants, AOs are more innovative and want things smarter as they are working with AS constantly. Participant 7 mentions that AOs are doing much repetitive work and are keen to automate things to heighten efficiency: *"But I think I would put my head on the line and say that our AOs, especially the more digital ones, really want more automation. Their practice has moved towards them being more controllers than direct bookkeepers."* P7. Participant 8 explained how many of the AOs are using a specific automation extension on top of AS, which costs more than the whole system of AS; thus, the participant believes that the users are ready for more automated ways of working: *"We are looking at two systems very closely....We can see that they have good growth and wild growth, and the AOs are crazy about them and they just... They remove some of the manual processes."* P8. Although the AOs are perceived as the most innovative group by the participants, they state that there are, however, also "old school" AOs. This user group is regarded as stubborn and not willing to change how they work, which means they can still be physically bookkeeping things. The participants believe the reason is due to the AOs fearing being replaced entirely by the functions. Participant 8 also believes that these "old school" types of AOs which have had the same 10 clients for the past 20 years who are only doing repetitive tasks all day are difficult to change: *"But there are also a lot of accounting firms that have had the same 10 customers for the past 20 years, who just do the same thing. Bente who is 45 and has been doing the same thing all the time... She is just as hard to move as all the others."* P8. Though AOs are generally perceived as the most innovative user group, Participant 5 still believes that most AOs want to check their work through, as they are working for others and in a sensitive field. However, the participant believes it is mainly the "old school" AOs who want a high level of control over their work: *"A few accountants that I met, that were young, a few...they want full automation. "I don't care". But most of the accountants, since it's a critical job because they're working for other people as well, they want to check it first."* P5. Therefore, AOs are perceived as innovative because they want to work more efficiently; however, they still want to check the work done by the ML functions to ensure that it is correct. The participants generally state that at least half of the AOs are of the "old school" type; however, they see a shift that will change in the next couple of years. This shift is partly due to the "new school" of digital accountants that are very innovative and open to all new types of functions that will make their work more efficient, as they found a way to take a new and more advisory role of being an accountant. Participant 4 and Participant 6 believe that it is mainly the big AOs leading the field and are the most progressive types: *"Accounting firms, and those AOs who have large base of customers, in my perception, it's also them who are at the forefront of not having a need for manual handling....but in terms of the overall time savings you can get, if you are an AO who just sits and goes through the software every day, there is a lot of time to save."* P6. However, Participant 4 also thinks that these big AOs have higher requirements and that they find the functions in AS too simple, thus, will not use it: *"Where in comparison to those who were disappointed, it's those who are superusers in terms of automation and where we can't....They have too many demands or they have more demands than we can match."* P4. This shows that although AOs are perceived as the most innovative user group, a big part of this user group is not innovative and does not want to accept ML functions. However, the new wave of digital AOs are becoming a more extensive user group.

5.2 Analysis 2 - Trust

Trust is measured by asking the participants questions regarding users' familiarity, trust and confidence in using the ML functions in AS. It was found to be the second largest concept, with 96 codes out of 337 related to it. Two participants mentioned that trusting the ML functions was the most important factor. The participants do not believe that people are initially trusting ML blindly; thus, there is a period where the user has to understand how ML works and learn to trust it. This initial learning curve also concerns understanding that ML needs data input to work. Participant 8 states that when users do not understand that this is an ongoing process, they get impatient and perceive it as not working, thus stopping using it: *"So you have to train it [the ML], and maybe some people are trying it for the first time and don't know that it needs to be trained or don't understand the logic, then they just give up like, "OK, it didn't work the first 10 times. We'll forget it. It's not for us." P8.* Therefore, it is crucial to ensure that the initial encounters for the users are found easy and make the users feel comfortable using the ML functions, as they need to understand that the functions improve the longer they use them. If the users do not understand that ML evolves and becomes more valuable the more they use it, there may be a high risk of the users perceiving the functions as simply unfulfilling; thus, they stop using the functions. Although the participants state that all users want control and that this distrust is to be found in all users, it is primarily the BOs that do not trust the system and are reluctant to use it. Participants express that it is primarily found in the existing BOs already using AS without ML functions. Participant 1 and Participant 2 believe that existing BOs are generally nervous and unsure of how automation works, which makes them reluctant: *"The greater the consequences, the fear there is, irrational fear perhaps, the more… They are more afraid to use it, if that makes sense." P1. "Yes, I would actually say with the old customers or not the old, but the existing customers, they are often very reserved. And it can seem a bit scary for them."* P2. This shows that users not using the ML functions are not trusting and are generally insecure due to their lack of knowledge regarding ML. Thus, making it apparent that the level of ML knowledge influences trust, which affects the TA in the users. It is found that some BOs who use the AS packages with ML have low trust in the ML functions, even if they are not the ones handling the accounting. This is stated by Participant 4, who expresses that AOs stated that their customers – BOs – want to control everything before accepting it: *"Or at least that's what the customers have said, that "well the boss, the BO, he wants to see everything through" P4.* However, Participant 1 states that BOs generally trust their AOs blindly and do whatever they are told is best: *"Often there is also a blind trust on those who are in charge of the accounting or the bookkeeper and say if he or she wants it, and it makes sense, then just buy it." P1.* The BOs who have an AO connected, mainly rely on what the AO believes is best. This is emphasised by Participant 2, who explains how BOs are informed that they can do the accounting themselves with the ML functions, instead of using money on an accountant but still refuse: *"And there, it can be a bit difficult, because we really want to be able to go in and tell this customer, "you can actually do it yourself, save some money on the accountant" P2.* This could, however, also be due to the BOs not having a high interest in accounting, and thus trusting the AOs to do what is best instead of doing it themselves. Though there is a general belief that users have low trust in the ML functions, some participants mention that the users' age significantly influences their trust in AS among AOs and BOs. Participant 1 and Participant 2 believe that the older generation of BOs do not want automation because they are frightened of ML and do not entirely trust the functions: *""It should not do things for me, because I don't trust it 100%." There are definitely some of them, and especially the older they are, there may be some limit that makes it difficult" P1. "And we often talk to people who are older and have done it the old fashioned way. For them, it can definitely be a bit scary and they don't want to learn something new" P2.* When talking about the "old school" AOs, Participant 5 mentions the distrust being caused by not liking changes and needing a long time to build trust and confidence in the functions: *"They use it, but not everyone is happy. And again, there are users that need a long time to understand and trust, and say "Okay, I am confident that it works. ""* P5. Participant 1 expresses that the AOs seem to think they are better than the machine. The participant believes a part of this mindset is due to the AOs being scared of being replaced, as they think that the functions will automate everything, and they, therefore, are reluctant as they do not want to be replaced: *"Especially the "old school" bookkeepers may have that thought with "I need to sit and type because I know best. "Also because a lot of their work may also lie in the typing part, so if they lose that part, well, how do they make money?"* P1. This shows that the older generations of users have some issues with trusting the functions, which generally can be due to intimidation either due to new unknown technologies or fear of replacement. Though the older users are experiencing low trust, two participants specifically mention the younger or more digitised and larger AOs showing the most trust in the functions. Participant 6 believes that the big AOs are most comfortable around the functions, which is believed to be due to their high workload: *"Where a small BO who likes to use all these different functions, does not necessarily do it as often as if it is 100% of their workday. So, the big AOs are very comfortable because they sit with it every day and on many customers".* P6. It is therefore believed that the more experience with ML functions, the higher the trust. However, Participant 4 believes that many bigger AOs are using an automation extension, which has close to no errors due to human validation: *"There are a lot of people who use [XX software extension] and their scanner performs really well, but it's also because behind the scenes, there are people... They have a department in India that handles those documents. So if the scanner can't figure it out, there is someone behind it who looks at it manually. But you know.. It may be that the users know it, but they don't know which documents... But it always works, and that's why they also trust it, at least that's my clear perception."* P4. Therefore, the participant believes that a low error rate will make users trust, although they might or might not know it is validated through humans. In the extension of this, Participant 5 believes there is a growing threshold for errors, as users are beginning to accept and trust the functions despite the higher error rate. The participant believes this is due to being transparent regarding what caused the error: *"But if I showed them that several things, even if the machine failed, but I showed them the machine failed, and this field, this field, this field, "yeah, I'm not sure, as a machine, that those are correct, just check it". At least they see that the machine is trustworthy."* P5. This further indicates that errors influence the level of trust in the ML functions, which can be mediated through transparency.

5.3 Analysis 3 - Satisfaction

Satisfaction is measured by asking the participants questions regarding users' level of satisfaction with using the functions, how and if the functions met all the needs of the user and whether users expressed that the functions were complicated to use, making the experience less pleasing. Satisfaction was the least coded factor of innovativeness, trust and satisfaction, with 95 codes related to it, however only one code in difference from trust. Nonetheless, it was found that four variables were found concerning satisfaction. It is expressed that the level of satisfaction is at a reasonable level and that the level of satisfaction is significantly heightened once the user has overstepped the initial onboarding barrier and trained the ML to work well enough. The participants expressed that satisfaction is extensively linked to functionality performance. Multiple participants state that when the functions are working, the satisfaction is high, but when there are issues, users get incredibly frustrated. This is emphasised by Participant 7, who states that the overall Net Promoter Score (NPS) at the time of the interview was 46 and believes that a significant part is linked to performance: *"We have a lot on performance that doesn't always work P7"*. Although there are still issues with accuracy, Participant 5 argues that there are users who are satisfied as long as it saves them more time than doing it manually. The participants expressed that the users generally do not have issues with using the functions as it is designed to be as easy as possible and that there is ensured an as easy as possible adaptation. However, some of the older users are taking longer to understand how the functions work. Occasionally, some users do not know how to use a phone or application, making it additionally difficult to use the functions. However, Participant 1 believes users say this because they do not want to change their way of working: *"There are some who say, I can't figure out how to use an app...I am 80 years old, and I don't want such an app, I don't care, I just have a folder that stands on my office. It's more just because they are stubborn and work that way, and it works fine for them."* P1. This means that the less innovative users also have lower satisfaction as they do not want to change. This is also emphasised by Participant 2, who believes that if they are not open and innovative regarding the functions, then they will express dissatisfaction due to being opposed to the digitalisation of their work: *"So they probably won't be very satisfied because they don't feel that it's very beneficial."* P2. Another group of users state that they do not require ML functions. Many participants believe that everyone needs to make things smart, and they believe that it is instead a question of the users not seeing the value and is not understanding the ML functions. Often this is due to the users trying the ML functions in a trial period due to the performance of the functions not being satisfactory enough. This also depends on how high their expectations are when trying the ML functions for the first time, according to Participant 1 *"The only thing we sometimes loose on, is that they want to use [XX, an ML function], but it's just not good enough. So, they have some greater requirements"* P1. Participant 2 mentions that the BOs often use their business size as a reason for not receiving enough value and satisfaction for them. Participant 1 believes this is also linked to price sensitivity as the performance of the functions is not worth the price: *"So is it more like that, does it provide enough value and is it worth the money to move up a pack to get it? And it is, after all, more of a matter of an individual assessment."* P2. This behaviour is again linked to the low innovativeness that makes the users less willing to try the functions and, thus, get satisfaction. Some users express that the current ML functions meet all their needs, and more functions would be too much. This could be due to the users do not know what or how more ML functions could be helpful, which lowers the anticipated satisfaction level of using the functions. However, this is not relevant for all users, as Participant 8 states that some users pay four times more for an extension than their AS package: *"There are some who will pay 4 times as much for their system as for AS, so we have many who give 1000 DKK for AS, but gives 4000 DKK for another system which can only handle invoices, where you can handle it all in AS. It is pretty crazy to think you're paying more for one system than a complete accounting software."* P8. These types of users can, on the contrary, find the ML functions too austere for their needs. Participant 4 states that users use extensions instead of, functions in AS because it is not good enough yet: *"Right now, we may need such a large survey to uncover it, because those I have spoken to, who are a little more digital in this, are a little disappointed because it can't do what they want. So it's not quite good enough." P4.* These users are very into ML functions.

5.4 Hypothesis Overview

This section summarizes the analysis1–3 results in relation to the hypotheses, Table 1.

Table 1. Hypotheses, and their empirical status.

Hypothesis	Status	Evidence
H1: Innovativeness affects the TA of the ML functions in AS	Confirmed	Section 5.1
H2: Innovativeness affects the UX of the ML functions in AS	Confirmed	Section 5.1
H3: Trust affects the TA of the ML functions in AS	Confirmed	Section 5.2
H4: Trust affects the UX of the ML functions in AS	Confirmed	Section 5.2
H5: Satisfaction affects the TA of the ML functions in AS	Confirmed	Section 5.3
H6: Satisfaction affects the UX of the ML functions in AS	Confirmed	Section 5.3

6 Discussion

6.1 Factors Underlying UX and TAM

This research aimed to explore and explain underlying factors that affect the TA and UX of ML functions in AS. The results suggested that as expected trust, innovativeness and satisfaction influence both the TA and UX in AS. The three concepts holistically affected both the initial TA and further continued usage and UX. For example, innovativeness led to unachievable expectations, which again lead to lower trust and satisfaction. Thus, this study highlighted how the factors were intertwined in a complex matter. That the same factors are present in both the initial TA and further in the continued usage with the UX emphasise the overlap between the concepts. However, it can be discussed whether TAM even can embrace modern technology anymore [38]. The line between TA and plain technology adoption is becoming vague as technology is deeply immersed in everyone's everyday life. Most people in modern society are extensively acquainted with computers, an infinite amount of software and are, whether they are aware or not, interacting with AI daily. It can thus be questioned whether initial TA exists anymore and if TAM thus should be reiterated.

Further, it was questioned by Hornbæk and Hertzum [1] whether all constructs of TAM are continually reformed through the interaction with the product, which makes the issue a question of continuity of experiences that form the choice of using technology. As this study illustrates, the factors and complexities of users' feelings and experiences are formed based on multiple intertwining aspects that continue to be present throughout the usage. Although some factors are more present in the first encounter than in later usage and vice versa, the user continues to carry the experiences with them. Therefore, this study questions whether the TAM and UX methods should rather be viewed holistically. Neither of the two methods can fully embrace the complexities of user technology usage. Thus, whether initial and continued usage should be regarded as one whole rather than two separate methods and experiences should be considered. Apart from viewing usage as a holistic experience, the issues with measuring the experience of AI are further problematic and complex. The outputs that AI can generate are beyond the capabilities of regular experiences and thus create unique challenges. Although the findings of this study do not fit with Kliman-Silver et al. [14], who stated that AI creates new variables influencing the experience, this may be due to the limitations of this study. The possibility of new variables not yet related to either TAM or UX indicates the methods' further inadequacy in grasping the complexities of the usage of products with AI. Lastly, this study has shown how users' understanding and perception of AI differ significantly. These differences make it further challenging to create software and systems that embrace these different user groups' feelings towards AI.

6.2 TA and UX of ML Functions in Accounting Software

The low level of innovativeness and trust in ML functions was telling for the accounting work domain, given that AS at the time was the biggest cloud-based accounting system in Denmark. An interesting finding was how accountants had a great fear of being replaced, which resulted in significant opposition to using ML functions. The fear of replacement results aligned with Damerji and Salimis' (2021) theory that resistance to change is due to the fear of replacement. However, it somewhat contradicts the research by Eißer et al. (2020), who measured the replacement fear in recruiters. Although this research also discovered that there are both optimistic and sceptic AOs, the majority of current AOs are, in contrast to the recruiters in Eißer et al. (2020) study, sceptic and were found to be among the lowest trusting users in AS. The results indicate that the fear of replacement is more widespread in accounting than in other fields, such as recruiting. This could be due to the general organisational culture in accounting, which is also brought forward by multiple articles [21–23]. It could also be due to ML's capabilities of nearly completely replacing accountants, which might not be as comprehensive in fields such as recruiting.

6.3 Limitations

The sample size of this study was small and not representative. Apart from the general problem of generalisability of small sample sizes, the choice of participants further influenced this. The subjectivity of the participants might have resulted users having other experiences with the ML than what was perceived by the user expert participants in our study. They were however chosen with careful purposeful sampling to offer a complete picture of users' experience and acceptance of ML in accounting. Hence, this research provided valid results in the form of conducting research that ensured consistent and reliable outcomes by ensuring the dependability, credibility, and transferability. Furthermore, the case chosen for this study was based on its representativity and inclusion of ML functions, which should inspire further research.

7 Conclusion

This study aimed to understand which factors influence users' TA and UX of ML functions in AS. The central question for this research was: *Which factors affect the technology acceptance and user experience of the machine learning functions in accounting software?* The conclusion of this study is that innovativeness, trust and satisfaction influence users' TA and UX of ML functions in AS, signifying that the six hypotheses of the study are confirmed. Further, the results showed that all three concepts were present in both the initial and continued usage of technology, however, to a different degree. Innovativeness was found to be more present in the initial usage stage, while trust and satisfaction were more dominant in the continued usage. Lastly, the study questions the measurability of TAM and UX and concludes that using TAM and UX as measurement methods for AI should be reviewed. While the choice of conducting a qualitative case study limits the generalisability of the results, this approach provided the ability to understand how the users of AS perceived ML functions, and thus laid the foundation for further research on the topic. This study illustrates that research on users' experience with ML functions in accounting can be based on already existing concepts; however, it also raises the question of whether yet undiscovered concepts and variables specific to ML functions exist. Future research should thus explore whether there are still factors that have not been discovered within the TA and UX of ML functions in business software such as AS. In the future, researchers should explore whether viewing technology utilisation holistically is more effective than measuring it separately through TAM and UX. Specifically, it may be worth doing exploratory and inductive qualitive studies into performance, ML knowledge, control, and other possible variables related to the three underlying factors that were identified in this study.

References

1. Hornbæk, K., Hertzum, M.: Technology acceptance and user experience. ACM Trans. Comput. Human Interact. **24**, 1–30 (2017). https://doi.org/10.1145/3127358
2. Hassenzahl, M., Burmester, M., Koller, F.: AttrakDiff: Ein Fragebogen zur Messung wahrgenommener hedonischer und pragmatischer Qualität. In: Szwillus, G. and Ziegler, J. (eds.) Mensch & Computer 2003: Interaktion in Bewegung. pp. 187–196. Vieweg+Teubner Verlag, Wiesbaden (2003). https://doi.org/10.1007/978-3-322-80058-9_19
3. Law, E.L.-C., Roto, V., Hassenzahl, M., Vermeeren, A.P.O.S., Kort, J.: Understanding, scoping and defining user experience: a survey approach. In: Proceedings of the ACM SIGCHI Conference on Human Factors in Computing Systems, pp. 719–728. ACM (2009). https://doi.org/10.1145/1518701.1518813
4. van Schaik, P., Ling, J.: Modelling user experience with web sites: usability, hedonic value, beauty and goodness. Interact. Comput. **20**, 419–432 (2008). https://doi.org/10.1016/j.intcom.2008.03.001

5. Merčun, T., Žumer, M.: Exploring the influences on pragmatic and hedonic aspects of user experience (2017)
6. Davis, F.D.: A technology acceptance model for empirically testing new end-user information systems: theory and results. Doctoral Dissertation, Sloan School of Management, Massachusetts Institute of Technology. (1986)
7. Venkatesh, V., Morris, M.G., Davis, G.B., Davis, F.D.: User acceptance of information technology: toward a unified view. MIS Q. **27**, 425–478 (2003). https://doi.org/10.2307/300 36540
8. Carmona, K., Finley, E., Li, M.: The relationship between user experience and machine learning. SSRN Electron. J. (2018). https://doi.org/10.2139/ssrn.3173932
9. Dove, G., Halskov, K., Forlizzi, J., Zimmerman, J.: UX design innovation. In: Proceedings of the 2017 CHI Conference on Human Factors in Computing Systems, pp. 278–288. ACM, New York, NY, USA (2017). https://doi.org/10.1145/3025453.3025739
10. Yang, Q., Steinfeld, A., Rosé, C., Zimmerman, J.: Re-examining Whether, why, and how human-AI interaction is uniquely difficult to design. In: Proceedings of the 2020 CHI Conference on Human Factors in Computing Systems, pp. 1–13. ACM, New York, NY, USA (2020). https://doi.org/10.1145/3313831.3376301
11. Amershi, S., et al.: Guidelines for human-AI interaction. In: Proceedings of the 2019 CHI Conference on Human Factors in Computing Systems, pp. 1–13. ACM, New York, NY, USA (2019). https://doi.org/10.1145/3290605.3300233
12. People +AI Research. https://pair.withgoogle.com. Accessed 27 Sep 2022
13. Pu, P., Chen, L., Hu, R.: A user-centric evaluation framework for recommender systems. In: Proceedings of the fifth ACM Conference on Recommender Systems, pp. 157–164. ACM, New York, NY, USA (2011). https://doi.org/10.1145/2043932.2043962
14. Kliman-Silver, C., Siy, O., Awadalla, K., Lentz, A., Convertino, G., Churchill, E.: Adapting user experience research methods for AI-driven experiences. In: Extended Abstracts of the 2020 CHI Conference on Human Factors in Computing Systems, pp. 1–8. ACM, New York, NY, USA (2020). https://doi.org/10.1145/3334480.3375231
15. Guszcza, J.: Smarter Together: Why artificial intelligence needs human-centered design . (2018)
16. Nielsen, S.: Management accounting and the concepts of exploratory data analysis and unsupervised machine learning: a literature study and future directions. J. Account. Organ. Chang. **18**, 811–853 (2022). https://doi.org/10.1108/JAOC-08-2020-0107
17. How Did the Field of Accounting Evolve? https://www.investopedia.com/articles/08/accoun ting-history.asp. Accessed 11 Nov 2022
18. van Schaik, P., Ling, J.: An integrated model of interaction experience for information retrieval in a Web-based encyclopaedia. Interact. Comput. **23**, 18–32 (2011). https://doi.org/10.1016/ j.intcom.2010.07.002
19. Clemmensen, T., Hertzum, M., Abdelnour-Nocera, J.: Ordinary user experiences at work: a study of greenhouse growers. ACM Trans. Comput. Human Interact. **27**(3), 1–31 (2020). https://doi.org/10.1145/3386089
20. Damerji, H., Salimi, A.: Mediating effect of use perceptions on technology readiness and adoption of artificial intelligence in accounting. Acc. Educ. **30**, 107–130 (2021). https://doi. org/10.1080/09639284.2021.1872035
21. Gonçalves, M.J.A., da Silva, A.C.F., Ferreira, C.G.: The future of accounting: how will digital transformation impact the sector? Informatics. **9**, 19 (2022). https://doi.org/10.3390/inform atics9010019
22. Kommunuri, J.: Artificial intelligence and the changing landscape of accounting: a viewpoint. Pac. Account. Rev. **34**, 585–594 (2022). https://doi.org/10.1108/PAR-06-2021-0107

23. Petkov, R.: Artificial intelligence (AI) and the accounting function—a revisit and a new perspective for developing framework. J. Emerging Technol. Account. **17**, 99–105 (2020). https://doi.org/10.2308/jeta-52648

24. Wang, T.: The impact of emerging technologies on accounting curriculum and the accounting profession. Pac. Account. Rev. **34**, 526–535 (2022). https://doi.org/10.1108/PAR-05-2021-0074

25. Eißer, J., Torrini, M., Böhm, S.: Automation anxiety as a barrier to workplace automation. In: Proceedings of the 2020 on Computers and People Research Conference, pp. 47–51. ACM, New York, NY, USA (2020). https://doi.org/10.1145/3378539.3393866

26. Commerford, B.P., Dennis, S.A., Joe, J.R., Ulla, J.W.: Man versus machine: complex estimates and auditor reliance on artificial intelligence. J. Account. Res. **60**, 171–201 (2022). https://doi.org/10.1111/1475-679X.12407

27. Kumari, P.: How does interactivity impact user engagement over mobile bookkeeping applications? J. Glob. Inf. Manag. **30**, 1–16 (2021). https://doi.org/10.4018/JGIM.301270

28. Davis, F.D.: A technology acceptance model for empirically testing new end-user information systems: Theory and Results (1985)

29. Venkatesh, V., Davis, F.D.: A theoretical extension of the technology acceptance model: four longitudinal field studies. Manage. Sci. **46**, 186–204 (2000). https://doi.org/10.1287/mnsc.46.2.186.11926

30. Yousafzai, S.Y., Foxall, G.R., Pallister, J.G.: Technology acceptance: a meta-analysis of the TAM: part 2. J. Model. Manag. **2**, 281–304 (2007). https://doi.org/10.1108/17465660710834462

31. Venkatesh, V., Bala, H.: Technology acceptance model 3 and a research agenda on interventions. Decis. Sci. **39**, 273–315 (2008). https://doi.org/10.1111/j.1540-5915.2008.00192.x

32. Göğüş, Ç.G., Özer, G.: The roles of technology acceptance model antecedents and switching cost on accounting software use. J. Manage. Inf. Decis. Sci. **17**(1), 1 (2014)

33. Halilovic, S., Cicic, M.: Understanding determinants of information systems users' behaviour: a comparison of two models in the context of integrated accounting and budgeting software. Behav. Inf. Technol. **32**, 1280–1291 (2013). https://doi.org/10.1080/0144929X.2012.708784

34. Bagozzi, R.: The legacy of the technology acceptance model and a proposal for a paradigm shift. J. Assoc. Inf. Syst. **8**(4), 244–254 (2007). https://doi.org/10.17705/1jais.00122

35. Chuttur, M.: Overview of the Technology Acceptance Model: Origins, Developments and Future Directions. All Sprouts Content, 290 (2009)

36. Lee, Y., Kozar, K.A., Larsen, K.R.T.: The technology acceptance model: past, present, and future. Commun. Assoc. Inf. Syst. **12**, 1–12 (2003). https://doi.org/10.17705/1CAIS.01250

37. Legris, P., Ingham, J., Collerette, P.: Why do people use information technology? A critical review of the technology acceptance model. Inf. Manage. **40**, 191–204 (2003). https://doi.org/10.1016/S0378-7206(01)00143-4

38. Lowe, B., Dwivedi, Y., D'Alessandro, S.P.: Guest editorial. Eur. J. Mark. **53**, 1038–1050 (2019). https://doi.org/10.1108/EJM-06-2019-966

39. Forlizzi, J., Battarbee, K.: Understanding experience in interactive systems. In: Proceedings of the 5th Conference on Designing Interactive Systems: Processes, Practices, Methods, and Techniques. pp. 261–268. ACM, New York, NY, USA (2004). https://doi.org/10.1145/1013115.1013152

40. Hassenzahl, M., Tractinsky, N.: User experience - a research agenda. Behav. Inf. Technol. **25**, 91–97 (2006). https://doi.org/10.1080/01449290500330331

41. Law, E.L.-C., Roto, V., Hassenzahl, M., Vermeeren, A.P.O.S., Kort, J.: Understanding, scoping and defining user experience. In: Proceedings of the SIGCHI Conference on Human Factors in Computing Systems, pp. 719–728. ACM, New York, NY, USA (2009). https://doi.org/10.1145/1518701.1518813

42. Hassenzahl, M.: The thing and I: understanding the relationship between user and product (2003).https://doi.org/10.1007/1-4020-2967-5_4
43. Merčun, T., Žumer, M.: Exploring the influences on pragmatic and hedonic aspects of user experience (2017)
44. Mashapa, J., van Greunen, D.: User experience evaluation metrics for usable accounting tools. In: Proceedings of the 2010 Annual Research Conference of the South African Institute of Computer Scientists and Information Technologists, pp. 170–181. ACM, New York, NY, USA (2010). https://doi.org/10.1145/1899503.1899522
45. Garcia, M.B., Claour, J.P.: Mobile bookkeeper: personal financial management application with receipt scanner using optical character recognition. In: 2021 1st Conference on Online Teaching for Mobile Education (OT4ME), pp. 15–20. IEEE (2021). https://doi.org/10.1109/OT4ME53559.2021.9638794
46. Deng, L., Turner, D.E., Gehling, R., Prince, B.: User experience, satisfaction, and continual usage intention of IT. Eur. J. Inf. Syst. 19, 60–75 (2010). https://doi.org/10.1057/ejis.2009.50
47. Frison, A.-K., et al.: In UX we trust. In: Proceedings of the 2019 CHI Conference on Human Factors in Computing Systems. pp. 1–13. ACM, New York, NY, USA (2019). https://doi.org/10.1145/3290605.3300374
48. Parasuraman, R., Riley, V.: Humans and automation: use, misuse, disuse, abuse. Human Fact. J. Human Fact. Ergon. Soc. 39, 230–253 (1997). https://doi.org/10.1518/001872097778543886
49. Google Design: AI and Design: Putting People First: A discussion on how designers can harness and humanize AI's vast potential. https://design.google/library/ai-design-roundtable-discussion/. Accessed 15 Sep 2022
50. Trinczek, R.: How to interview managers? Methodical and methodological aspects of expert interviews as a qualitative method in empirical social research. In: Bogner, A., Littig, B., Menz, W. (eds.) Interviewing Experts, pp. 203–216. Palgrave Macmillan UK, London (2009). https://doi.org/10.1057/9780230244276_10
51. Doll, W.J., Torkzadeh, G.: The measurement of end-user computing satisfaction. MIS Q. 12, 259 (1988). https://doi.org/10.2307/248851
52. Elnagar, A., Alnazzawi, N., Afyouni, I., Shahin, I., Nassif, A.B., Salloum, S.A.: Prediction of the intention to use a smartwatch: a comparative approach using machine learning and partial least squares structural equation modeling. Inform. Med. Unlocked. 29, 100913 (2022). https://doi.org/10.1016/j.imu.2022.100913
53. Mashapa, J., van Greunen, D.: User experience evaluation metrics for usable accounting tools. In: Proceedings of the 2010 Annual Research Conference of the South African Institute of Computer Scientists and Information Technologists, pp. 170–181. ACM (2010). https://doi.org/10.1145/1899503.1899522
54. Yi, M.Y., Fiedler, K.D., Park, J.S.: Understanding the role of individual innovativeness in the acceptance of IT-based innovations: comparative analyses of models and measures. Decis. Sci. 37, 393–426 (2006). https://doi.org/10.1111/j.1540-5414.2006.00132.x
55. Jian, J.-Y., Bisantz, A.M., Drury, C.G.: Foundations for an empirically determined scale of trust in automated systems. Int. J. Cogn. Ergon. 4, 53–71 (2000). https://doi.org/10.1207/S15327566IJCE0401_04

E-Shopping and its Influence on Customer Satisfaction in Retail Stores. Peru Case

Madeleine Espino Carrasco[1]([envelope]) [ORCID], Danicsa Karina Espino Carrasco[2] [ORCID],
Luis Jhonny Dávila Valdera[3] [ORCID], Anny Katherine Dávila Valdera[4] [ORCID],
Lady Violeta Dávila Valdera[5] [ORCID], Mayury Jackeline Espino Carrasco[1] [ORCID],
Royer Vasquez Cachay[1] [ORCID], Ana Maria Alvites Gasco[6] [ORCID],
Ricardo Rafael Díaz Calderón[7] [ORCID], Enrique Santos Nauca Torres[7] [ORCID],
and Edson David Valdera Benavides[5] [ORCID]

[1] Señor de Sipan University, Pimentel, Peru
ecarrascomadele@crece.uss.edu.pe
[2] Cesar Vallejo University, Chulucanas, Peru
[3] Santo Toribio de Mogrovejo University, Chiclayo, Peru
[4] National University of San Marcos, Lima, Peru
[5] Pedro Ruiz Gallo National University, Lambayeque, Peru
[6] Particular de Chiclayo University, Pimentel, Peru
[7] Cesar Vallejo University, Pimentel, Peru

Abstract. The purpose of this research is to determine the influence of e-shopping on customer satisfaction in retail stores in a region of Peru, for which the model proposed by Nebojša, Milorad and Tanja (2019) who study the variables was used. e-shopping and customer satisfaction, in addition, the sample consisted of 384 people to whom a questionnaire was applied, applying a non-probabilistic snowball sampling, it is also an investigation with a quantitative approach, correlational type, non-experimental cutting design cross-sectional, in terms of the results, it was found that the e-shopping variable has a significant positive influence on customer satisfaction, so it is concluded that e-shopping is part of the purchase process that is constantly evaluated by the customer during the acquisition of a product through electronic commerce platforms through retail companies.

Keywords: e-shopping · customer satisfaction · availability of information

1 Introduction

The use of the internet has been generating consumer empowerment for more than a decade, physical stores are slowly closing due to the rise of e-commerce, compared to physical stores, online businesses offer convenience to customers, customers can simply sit at home, place their orders, pay with a credit card and wait until the products arrive at their home (Szegedi 2021).

Online shopping has increased significantly in the last two decades and has become a legitimate alternative to traditional shopping for consumers. Online shopping has also

P. Zaphiris et al. (Eds.): HCII 2023, LNCS 14060, pp. 434–443, 2023.
https://doi.org/10.1007/978-3-031-48060-7_32

gained momentum in developing countries due to factors such as quick access to product-related information, convenience of time, delays due to traffic jams, limited parking space, and most of all, the Pay-On-Delivery (POD) payment method (Tandon and Kiran 2019).

Park et al. (2020) argued that customer satisfaction is an important way for companies to build long-term relationships with consumers and that only few companies succeed without a stable relationship, furthermore, they consider customer satisfaction as a decisive factor that It affects the valuation of a business after the purchase of tangible and intangible brand assets, as well as customer retention.

Almost two years after the start of the pandemic, and that this will mark a before and after in digital commerce in Peru, electronic commerce continues to accelerate its steps in digital transformation, not only for Peruvian consumers, but also for companies. This reality was also reflected in the department of Lambayeque, where the main sector that has developed is retail through online transactions. This online shopping item has a retail channel where products from categories that are quite common in purchases such as household appliances, clothing, cosmetics, accessories and electronics are sold, growing 55% compared to 2020 (Chamber and of Electronic Commerce - CAPECE 2022).

In a region of Peru, consumers are adopting new ways of buying and consequently have had some experience that involves both the variables under study. This investigation will be carried out in this city applied to three well-known retail stores in the city, which have department stores as their characteristic.

This problem leads to the following research question: What is the influence of e-shopping on customer satisfaction in retail stores in Chiclayo 2022? With the general objective: Determine the influence of e-shopping on customer satisfaction in retail stores in the city of Chiclayo, 2022; and as specific objectives: Determine the influence of security, information availability, shipping, quality, price and time on customer satisfaction in retail stores in the city of Chiclayo, 2022.

2 Literature Review

As for the background, there is Bhandari (2021) who carried out his research on those factors that influenced the making of electronic purchases, resulting in a level of positive influence, in relation to the three factors such as: consumer vigilance, shopping experience and satisfaction. In the same way, Tandon and Kiran (2019) carried out an analysis on the quality of websites, as well as other drivers of online purchases and in this way to obtain an answer on the impact regarding customer satisfaction, they obtained positive results. in customer satisfaction, motivating those electronic retailers to make their purchases with complete confidence through the cash on delivery payment method. However, in the research by Das, Nath and Das (2017) presented the factors that directly affect customer satisfaction, their results revealed that online purchase intention and satisfaction depend on reliability, the budget to spend, the payment method, the quality of service of online stores, the quality of the product, the price, the speed of delivery of the product and the online shopping experience. In the article by Olasanmi (2019) they also inquired about those factors that influenced consumer satisfaction to boost the use of online shopping, resulting in the factors; level of knowledge, time, convenience, product quality and risk, are the ones that customers obtain the most benefits for which they make the decision to buy online.

Likewise, Jain and Sharama (2020) explored certain factors that determine the level of customer satisfaction, they obtained as a result that the development of strategies on their websites of online retailers for customer satisfaction will be useful. Similarly, Shah et al. (2020) examines the factors that affect customer satisfaction in online purchases, among their findings there is a significant positive influence between customer service, information quality, response time, transaction capacity, delivery, merchandise attributes, security/privacy, convenient payment method, and price on customer satisfaction in online shopping. In addition, Masyhuri (2022) analyzed the key factors of customer satisfaction for e-commerce companies, they came to the result that Amazon and eBay applied all the key factors, which have a significant impact on their performance and customer satisfaction. While, Rao et al. (2021) compared the purchase in a direct electronic store and in an indirect electronic store, for which they found that consumers feel more satisfied when they buy through a direct electronic store than in an indirect electronic store, while their perception and real experience are different, in addition, perceived risk, perceived uncertainty and price are some of those antecedents that play a significant role in affecting the degree of consumer satisfaction, resulting in retaining a consumer or outraging him.

The conceptual model developed in the research is the one proposed by Nebojša, Milorad and Tanja (2019), which is based on the development of the e-shopping variable (security, availability of information, shipping, quality, price and time), in addition to the variable customer satisfaction.

Regarding the e-shopping variable, it is mentioned that they are activities carried out online through the Internet that allow the exchange of goods and services through the web (Olasanmi 2019). Likewise, it contemplates six dimensions:

Security which is defined as the website's ability to protect consumers' personal data from unauthorized disclosure of information during electronic transactions (Guo et al. 2012). Users tend to buy a product from a supplier they trust or a brand name product they are familiar with (Chen and He 2003).

Shoppers expect online retailers to provide relevant and accurate product information (Smith 2006). Since online shoppers sometimes have the opportunity to touch and feel products before deciding to purchase, online retailers must provide information on this (Lim and Dubinsky 2004).

The quality of products and services in online commerce has a positive impact on customer satisfaction, defined as the consumer's judgment on the general excellence or superiority of a product (Lim and Dubinsky 2004). Service quality determines whether customers will develop strong and loyal relationships with online retailers by offering quality service that meets their expectations (Khristianto et al. 2012).

The delivery or service of entering presents presents the most critical factor to meet the expectations and satisfaction of the electronic client (Wolfinbarger and Gilly 2003). In the online environment, timely and reliable delivery plays a key role in meeting consumer expectations and generating satisfaction (Chakraborty et al. 2007).

Price is such a fundamental component in buyer satisfaction, because customers continually turn their attention to cost once they evaluate the price of the product and service (Cronin et al. 2000). Pricing directly impairs the perception of delivered cost and transaction usage has a particular bearing on the satisfaction of experienced online customers (Jiradilok et al. 2014).

Regarding time, analyzing the online catalog during online purchases saves time and reduces stress compared to classic purchases. Saving time does not show an element of motivation for customers to buy online, because it takes any time for the delivery of the goods. Morganosky and Cude (2000) mentioned that a time-saving item was named as the top item among customers who have already experienced e-shopping. Also, there is a difference between online customers and offline customers.

Customer satisfaction is the result of comparing expectations and experience (Khristianto et al. 2012). If the product or service provides customers with a high degree of enjoyment and satisfaction, then it is assumed that customer expectations are met (Lin 2014). Anderson and Srinivasa (2003) show that customer satisfaction with online businesses has a positive effect on customer loyalty. Satisfied customers tend to return to buy more in the future than dissatisfied customers.

3   Materials y Methods

The approach is quantitative, since the survey was used as a technique and the questionnaire as a tool, the information was analyzed through statistical analysis. The research was of the applied type, since it was characterized by the search for the application and use of the acquired knowledge, likewise the level was correlational and the cross-sectional non-experimental design. Regarding the sample, the finite formula was applied, which resulted in surveying 384 women and men between the ages of 25 and 39, and who have made at least one purchase in a retail store, for which a type of non-probabilistic snowball sampling.

For the development of the research, the questionnaire proposed by Nebojša, Milorad and Tanja (2019) was applied. The design of the questionnaire was developed in the Google Forms program, after that, the link was sent to the clients through WhatsApp, Facebook and Instagram, later the database was exported in Excel and then the data was transferred to the SPSS program v. 25, where the reliability of Cronbach's alpha was developed, obtaining a result of 0.832 for the e-shopping variable and 0.913 for the customer satisfaction variable. After that, the linear regression test was applied with the intention of responding to the general objective. Finally, the estimates of the correlation values were made using the Rho Spearman analysis (Tables 1, 2, and 3).

4   Results y Discussion

4.1   Demographic Analysis

The Rho Spearman is 0.721 indicating that the relationship of the e-shopping variable with the satisfaction variable is direct and its degree of influence is high from the customers of the retail stores in the city of Chiclayo. This suggests that because it is an

Table 1. Demographic

		Number of respondents	%
Gender	Male	225	58.6%
	Female	159	41.4%
Age	25 a 29	150	39.1%
	30 a 35	120	31.3%
	36 a 39	114	29.7%

Table 2. Network interaction

How often do you surf the internet during the day?	Less than 1 h	52	13.5%
	1 to 2 h	77	20.1%
	2 to 3 h	135	35.2%
	more than 4 h	120	31.3%
Which statement best describes the expenses you are willing to pay for the delivery of products sold online?	I always choose the product that has the free shipping option	198	51.6%
	I always choose the minimum shipping rate, because I think they give me the best price for both the product and the delivery	112	29.2%
	I am willing to pay any cost for the delivery of the product that makes the total price of my purchase the least	74	19.3%
What is the maximum shipping time you are willing to accept after purchasing online so that you do not get charged for shipping?	3 days	69	18.0%
	4 days	63	16.4%
	5 days	74	19.3%
	1 week	150	39.1%
	More than 1 week	28	7.3%

online system and offers many advantages over the traditional channel, people may feel more comfortable transacting through this medium, it also suggests that recently, as a result of everything that has happened in the world, it has become a very popular form and is used by many clients, these results compared with what was found by Bhandari (2021) and Shah et al. (2020), point out that there is a positive influence between e-shopping and satisfaction, being the transaction capacity the most influential through online purchases, therefore, e-shopping contributes in a favorable way to satisfaction the client's (Table 4).

The Rho Spearman coefficient is 0.452, indicating that the relationship of the shipping dimension with the satisfaction variable is direct and a positive influence of moderate

Table 3. Influence of E-Shopping on Customer Satisfaction in retail stores in the city of Chiclayo, 2022

			Customer satisfaction
Rho de Spearman	E-shopping	Correlation coefficient	0,721**
		Sig. (bilateral)	0.000
		N	384

**The correlation is significant at the 0.01 level (bilateral).

Table 4. Shipping Dimension

			Customer satisfaction
Rho de Spearman	Shipping	Correlation coefficient	0,452**
		Sig. (bilateral)	0.000
		N	384

**The correlation is significant at the 0.01 level (bilateral).

degree of the customers of the retail stores in the city of Chiclayo. This is due to the fact that the shipping dimension is part of one of the main processes within the online sales of these retailers, these results compared to what was found by Das, Nath & Das (2017) and Shah et al. (2020), indicate that the speed of delivery of the product or shipment influences the intention to purchase online and satisfaction, so the speed of the shipment contributes favorably to customer satisfaction (Table 5).

Table 5. Dimension Price

			Customer satisfaction
Rho de Spearman	Price	Correlation coefficient	0,533**
		Sig. (bilateral)	0.000
		N	384

**The correlation is significant at the 0.01 level (bilateral).

The Rho Spearman coefficient is 0.533, indicating that the relationship of the price dimension with the satisfaction variable is direct and its influence is moderate, of the customers of the retail stores in the city of Chiclayo. Customers visually analyze price as one of the key features on these retailers' platforms when making a purchase decision, and the offers and cards from these organizations make price even more sensitive, these findings compared to what Das found., Nath & Das (2017) and Rao et al. (2021), mention that price is a factor that directly affects consumer satisfaction, resulting in retaining a consumer or outraging him (Table 6).

Table 6. Quality Dimension

			Customer satisfaction
Rho de Spearman	Quality	Correlation coefficient	0,633**
		Sig. (bilateral)	0.000
		N	384

**The correlation is significant at the 0.01 level (bilateral).

The Rho Spearman coefficient is 0.633, indicating that the relationship of the quality dimension with the satisfaction variable is direct and its moderate influence of the customers of the retail stores in the city of Chiclayo. This indicates that consumers place a high value on quality in all respects and are extremely demanding in this regard, since they demand to be served in every possible way to be satisfied, it is clear that the efforts of the retail industry are not yet complete., these results are similar to what was found by Das, Nath & Das (2017) and Olasanmi (2019) who mention that product quality is an important factor for the user and has a significant influence on customer satisfaction (Table 7).

Table 7. Security Dimension

			Customer satisfaction
Rho de Spearman	Security	Correlation coefficient	0,385**
		Sig. (bilateral)	0.000
		N	384

**The correlation is significant at the 0.01 level (bilateral).

The Rho Spearman coefficient is 0.385, indicating that the relationship of the security dimension with the satisfaction variable is direct and its degree of influence is low from the customers of the retail stores in the city of Chiclayo. What has been discovered suggests that there is concern about the purchase system, which many people believe is not a safe channel because it is virtual. This result, being the lowest of all, responds to the insecurity on the web that is increasing every day, and that the levels of insecurity have also increased. These results are similar to what was found by Shah et al. (2020) and Masyhuri (2022) who state that security/privacy and the convenient payment method influence customer satisfaction in online purchases (Table 8).

The Rho Spearman coefficient is 0.637, indicating that the time dimension with the satisfaction variable is direct and its moderate influence of the customers of the retail stores in the city of Chiclayo. The results show that, in fact, the satisfaction of using an online channel lies in not having to physically visit the store; this is a significant benefit that is partially reflected in the result. However, since it is possible to carry out the task from home or the office instead of having to travel, convenience also plays an important role, these results compared to those of Olasanmi (2019) and Shah et al.

Table 8. Time Dimension

			Customer satisfaction
Rho de Spearman	Time	Correlation coefficient	0,637**
		Sig. (bilateral)	0.000
		N	384

**The correlation is significant at the 0.01 level (bilateral).

(2020), who point out that time is a factor that influences customer decision-making in online purchases (Table 9).

Table 9. Information Availability Dimension

			Customer satisfaction
Rho de Spearman	Information Availability	Correlation coefficient	0,741**
		Sig. (bilateral)	0.000
		N	384

**The correlation is significant at the 0.01 level (bilateral).

The Rho Spearman is 0.741, indicating that the relationship of the information availability dimension with the satisfaction variable is direct and the degree of influence is high in the customer of the retail stores in the city of Chiclayo. This is the result with the highest correlation value, due to the ease of access to the information and that it is possible to obtain it from any mobile device. This not only means that the customer has more and better options, but also that they can compare them with other options, something that could not be done in such a useful way in the physical channel. These results are related to what was found by Rita et al. (2019) and Masyhuri (2022) who point out that website design and ease of use are factors that affect the quality of electronic service in customer satisfaction.

5 Conclusions

There is a high positive influence between e-shopping and customer satisfaction, this is explained because e-shopping is part of the purchase process that is constantly evaluated by the customer during the purchase of a product through the platforms of the market. Electronic commerce through retail companies.

Shipping influences customer satisfaction in a moderately positive way, because it is a fundamental process since it covers the logistical aspect, given the circumstances of deliveries, customers are often in disagreement with the deadlines established by retail companies.

The price influences customer satisfaction in a moderately positive way, because for the customer the variety of prices depends on the standards offered by each retail company, influencing the offers, the use of credit cards so that the customer can be satisfied according to the need you have.

Quality influences customer satisfaction in a moderately positive way, since the choice of the product does not always meet expectations, affecting the experiences for a next purchase.

Security influences customer satisfaction in a low positive way, because customers, despite the fact that they are locally recognized retail companies, are concerned that their personal information is used for other purposes.

Time influences customer satisfaction in a moderately positive way, the reason is that there is a saving of time when making purchases, in addition each purchase can be made from any portable device and from anywhere.

Finally, the availability of information influences customer satisfaction in a moderately positive way, because each product has the necessary information for the customer to make comparisons to choose their purchase.

The research contributes in a positive way, enabling access to knowledge of e-shopping, through the review and analysis of key concepts of the subject, allowing the importance of the elements that make up this activity to be understood. In addition, it is important because it provides real and reliable information about virtual purchases and what factor is the most influential in customer satisfaction.

References

Anderson, R., Srinivasan, S.: E-Satisfaction and E-loyalty: a contingency framework. Psychol. Market. **20**(2), 123 (2003). https://www.scinapse.io/papers/2017624521

Bhandari, J.: Consumer behavior towards e-shopping in Pune City. UGC Care J. **44**(1), 7–13 (2021). https://mmimert.edu.in/images/ncss2021/2.pdf

Peruvian Chamber of Electronic Commerce – CAPECE: Electronic commerce in Peru moved US\$ 9,300 million in 2021. Gana Más digital magazine, Lima (2022). https://revistaganamas. com.pe/comercio-electronico-en-peru-movio-us-9300-millones-en-el-2021/

Chakraborty, G., Srivastava, P., Marshall, F.: Are drivers of customer satisfaction different for buyers/users from different functional areas? J. Bus. Indus. Market. **22**(1), 20–28 (2007). https://doi.org/10.1108/08858620710722798

Chen, R., He, F.: Examination of brand knowledge, perceived risk and consumers' intention to adopt an online retailer. Total Qual. Manage. Bus. Excell. **14**(6), 677 (2003). https://doi.org/10.1080/1478336032000053825

Das, S., Nath, T., Das, S.: Customer satisfaction on online shopping in Bangladesh. Dhaka Univ. J. Manage. **12**(1), 51–70 (2017)

Guo, X., Ling, K., Liu, M.: Evaluating factors influencing customer satisfaction towards online shopping in China. Asian Soc. Sci. **8**(13), 40–50 (2012). https://doi.org/10.5539/ass.v8n13p40

Jain, R., Sharama, S.: Determinants of customer satisfaction in online shopping Maharshi Dayanand. Univ. Res. J. **19**(1), 51–66 (2020). https://mdu.ac.in/UpFiles/UpPdfFiles/2021/Jun/2_06-17-2021_11-22-44_Chapter-5.pdf

Khristianto, W., Kertahadi, I., Suyadi, I.: The influence of information, system and service on customer satisfaction and loyalty in online shopping. Int. J. Acad. Res. **4**(2), 28–32 (2012). https://www.researchgate.net/publication/260719238_The_Influence_of_Inform ation_System_and_Service_on_Customer_Satisfaction_and_Loyalty_in_Online_Shopping_ of_Forum_Jual_Beli_KaskusUs_Malang_RegionInternational_Journal_of_Academic_Res earch_Vol2_No4_Mar

Lim, H., Dubinsky, A.: Consumers' perceptions of e-shopping characteristics: an expectancy-value approach. J. Serv. Market. **18**(6), 500–513 (2004). https://doi.org/10.1108/088760404 10561839

Lin, C.: Factors affecting online repurchase intention. Indus. Manage. Data Syst. **114**(4), 597–611 (2014). https://doi.org/10.1108/IMDS-10-2013-0432

Morganosky, M., Cude, B.: Consumer response to online grocery shopping. Int. J. Retail Distrib. Manage. **28**(1), 17–26 (2000). https://doi.org/10.1108/09590550010306737

Olasanmi, O.: Online shopping and customers' satisfaction in Lagos State, Nigeria. Am. J. Ind. Bus. Manag. **9**, 1446–1463 (2019). https://doi.org/10.4236/ajibm.2019.96095

Park, E., Chae, B., Kwon, J., Kim, W.H.: The effects of green restaurant attributes on customer satisfaction using the structural topic model on online customer reviews. Sustainability **12**, 2843 (2020). https://doi.org/10.3390/su12072843

Smith, A.: Collaborative commerce through web-based information integration technologies. Int. J. Innov. Learn. **4**(2), 127–144 (2006). https://doi.org/10.1504/IJIL.2007.011689

Szegedi, K.: Retail Trends 2021. Deloitte (2021). https://www2.deloitte.com/ch/en/pages/con sumer-business/articles/retail-trends.html

Jiradilok, T., Malisuwan, S., Madan, M., Sivaraks, J.: The impact of customer satisfaction on online purchasing: a case study analysis in Thailand. J. Econ. Bus. Manage. **2**(1), 5–11 (2014)

Tandon, U., Kiran, R.: Factors impacting customer satisfaction: an empirical investigation into online shopping in India. J. Inf. Technol. Case App. Res. **21**(1), 13–34 (2019). https://doi.org/ 10.1080/15228053.2019.1609779

Wolfinbarger, M., Gilly, M.: ETailQ: dimensionalizing, measuring and predicting eTail quality. J. Retail. **79**(3), 183–198 (2003). https://doi.org/10.1016/S0022-4359(03)00034-4

Effects of Luxury Hotel Guests' Feedback on Average Daily Rate (ADR), Revenue Per Available Room (RevPAR), and Goodwill – An Empirical Study in Pensacola

Shaniqka Green and Xuan Tran[✉]

University of West Florida, Pensacola, USA
sg143@students.uwf.edu

Abstract. Although hotel guests have controlled quick accessibility to force hoteliers instantly update their hotel room rates, little has focused on guest comments and average daily rate. The purpose of the paper is to examine the relationship between hotel average daily rate (ADR), revenue per available room (RevPAR), and goodwill and guests' motivation for location, rooms, value, cleanliness, service, and sleep quality.

The study has designed to use consumer motivation at the unconscious level to examine the relationship between hoteliers' price and guests' preference at the conscious level. Linguistic Inquiry and Word Count was used to retrieve the consumer motivation at the unconscious level. Structural Equation Modeling was conducted to examine the relationships among the exogenous variables including ADR, RevPAR, and goodwill and the endogenous variables including location, rooms, value, cleanliness, service, and sleep quality that were mediated by the unconscious motivation of hotel guests.

The results from the study revealed pertinent information about customer preferences. ADR would be associated with location, value and rooms. RevPAR would be associated with cleanliness and service. Finally, hotel goodwill would be associated with sleep quality.

Although the small sample size of 163 guest comments is the limitation of the study for generalization, the sample randomly selected for 13 years (2009–2022) has identified the different effects of ADR, RevPAR, and Goodwill on each of the 6 hotel criteria to contribute to hotel marketing strategies.

Keywords: Actor-network theory · Three-needs theory · average daily rate · revenue per available room · goodwill

1 Introduction

Failure to appropriately understanding the impact of hotel guests' feedback through mobile communication on hotel operations has created critical issues in the hotel industry. Trends within both the hotel and communication sector change frequently. On one hand, the industry 4.0 interconnection among hotel guests through guest comments has

© The Author(s), under exclusive license to Springer Nature Switzerland AG 2023
P. Zaphiris et al. (Eds.): HCII 2023, LNCS 14060, pp. 444–454, 2023.
https://doi.org/10.1007/978-3-031-48060-7_33

forced hoteliers instantly update their hotel room rates for their sustainability in hotel business. On the other hand, the industry 4.0 communication through guest comments has provided hoteliers information transparency to understand what hotel guests need or prefer to help them in their decision making. The reasons depend on customer preferences, modernization, and business predictions. The refinements have come a long way over a short period (McCabe, 2010). The following are significant impacts of technology in hotel guests' feedback through mobile communication on hotel operations listed as smart devices, robotics, big data, artificial intelligence, and green engineering.

Companies have gained the flexibility of managing properties from across the world. Firms can allot spaces at different times and conduct transactions without being physically present. Property managers can track complaints and monitor reviews with just a few swipes of a smart device (Shumakova, 2021). Robotics have wheeled its way into the hotel industry, moving from iconic movies to housekeeping duties thanks to the pandemic. Robots have been used to assist in waiting tables to alleviate the decline in employees. They have also been used to test and store guest temperatures. Popular hotels like the Beverly Hilton have deployed robots to sanitize hotel rooms. One such robot used was the Xenex LightStrike which was used to disinfect rooms and kill the coronavirus (Haskell, 2020). Automation paired with analytics has the capacity to produce personalization. High personalization in turn leads to an elevation in loyalty. However, to reach this point, hoteliers must consider a few features. These characteristics entail analytics, on-demand optimization, social listening tools, artificial intelligence, green engineering, and exclusivity (Escobar, 2022). Research revealed that almost half of millennials use their mobile services to make reservations. Over 700 billion people are expected to use smart devices to transact business by 2025. Many millennials prefer making memories over purchasing random items. Captured memories are then shared via social spaces to showcase affiliation (Net Affinity, 2022).

Big data has expanded even further than where it used to be, therefore awareness of customer preferences is more available. The quest to use them to an advantage is the next step. Guest profiles and social media reviews are informational diamond minds in the internet of things sensors. These components supply entities with pertinent details for guest retention. That is, tailoring customer experiences precede guest satisfaction, profits, loyalty, and word-of-mouth marketing. Customization paves the way for superior keepsakes in the form of memories. Processing the data retrieved empowers hoteliers to make changes that align with motives like power (Werner, 2023). Artificial Intelligence supports predictive analytics by transforming the customer service experience. It does this by guessing frequently asked questions and giving correct responses (Boston University, n.d.).

The analytical aspects of apps aid with storing customer favorites. Targeting with artificial intelligence can then be used to notify customers of similar proposals. Creating deals and discounts only available in mobile apps are great ways to generate business traffic. While the websites are good, apps are a touch away and carry more visibility. Their convenient nature also inspires quick purchases and more transactions. Mobile offers permit push notifications thus capturing attention. Allotting an expiration to the offers multiply the effects (Net Affinity, 2022).

Guest motivation interlinks with hotel performance. Therefore, implementing green technology, a motivating factor, prompts sales. The Kind Traveler Impact Tourism Survey 2022 revealed that almost all guests prefer hotels that make worthwhile impacts on society. The research also revealed that consumers are concerned about carbon footprint levels. Utilizing solar and other self-sustaining equipment engenders more revenues. Consumer interest in sustainability and corporate social responsibility has spiked over the years. Resource saving techniques such as low-pressure shower heads and sensor-controlled faucets increase favorability. The integration of virtual reality to host tours and make room selections saves travel time and lessens carbon emissions. The revolutionized auto industry requires the support of the accommodation industry. Therefore, auto-charging stations are a plus in the sustainability quest. Provisions of hybrid co-working, and meeting rooms are swiftly normalizing. Installing these spaces to facilitate "bleisure travel" will also support green operations (Morgan, 2022).

Since there have been a lot of changes affecting hotel operations, the study attempts to modeling them into one model of hoteliers' value and guests' expectation in hotel operations in the mobile communication. In terms of hoteliers' value, there are 3 exogenous variables: average daily rate, revenue per available room, and goodwill. The average daily room rate (ADR) is a tool for hoteliers to attract hotel guests because it is based on the number of rooms sold whereas revenue per available room (RevPAR) is used to measure the effectiveness of hoteliers when they run the hotel operations. The ADR is measured by dividing the annual room revenue by the number of room nights sold in a year whereas the RevPAR is measured by dividing the annual room revenue by the number of room nights available in a year.

Hotel goodwill is measured by the price premium the buyer willing to pay higher than the fair value. In sum, the two concepts ADR and Goodwill are related to the willingness of the hotel guests to pay at the daily price (ADR) or higher than the annual price (Goodwill) resulting in the daily revenue for the hoteliers (RevPAR). Therefore, the first two types of guests are related to friendliness (ADR) and long-term achievement (Goodwill) whereas the third type of guests as a business owner with power (RevPAR).

In terms of guests' expectation, there are two levels: unconscious motivation and conscious motivation. At the unconscious level, guest comments include writing texts that imply implicit motives (Winter, 1996). There are 3 types of implicit motives: achievement, power, and affiliation (McClelland, 1985). The achievement motive is an unconscious need for excellence, unique and long term impact (Chusmir & Azevedo, 1992). The power motive is an unconscious need for controlling other people (Winter, 1996). The affiliation motive is an unconscious need for friendliness (McClelland, 1985). The Linguistic Inquiry and Word Count (LIWC) by Pennebaker, Francis, and Booth (1999) is a software can measure the unconscious level of the 3 motives in a text message by identifying which words using related to the 3 motives. At the conscious level, hotel guests would prefer location, rooms, value, service, sleep quality, and cleanliness.

The purpose of the study is thus to examine the use the LIWC to measure the levels of the three motives from the guest comments in a Hilton hotel in Pensacola, Florida during the 14 year period (2009–2022). Then the three motives would be correlated with guests' preference for location, rooms, value, sleep quality, service, and sleep quality which were included in each guest comment from TripAdvisor website. Finally, the 3 exogenous variables ADR, RevPAR, and Goodwill would be added to the system of endogenous variables including achievement, affiliation, power, location, cleanliness, service, value, rooms, and sleep quality in a structure equation model to see the levels of correlations through coefficients.

The remaining of the paper includes the literature of the theory of actor-network, the goodwill theories, the 3-need theory of motivation to support for the hypotheses of the relationships among ADR, RevPAR, Goodwill, achievement, affiliation, power, location, rooms, service, sleep quality, cleanliness, and value. Next, the study has used Structure equation modeling (SEM) in the methodology to measure the correlation coefficients among the variables in a fit model to confirm the hypotheses. Finally, the study will discuss the practical applications of the study with concluding remarks.

2 Literature

2.1 Actor-Network Theory

"The Actor-Network Theory is defined as a set of concepts that categorizes social order on the basis of human and non-human factors" (Kobayashi, 2019). The human side of the ANT theory consists of motivational facets offset by psychological influences. These influences are created by social stimuli used to provoke decisions. The study has applied the Actor Network Theory (Latour, 2005, Tran, 2017) including human, non-human, and process to this study as guests' motivation, hoteliers' price, and guests' preference, respectively. The horizontal axis is the vector of non-human (price – average daily rate, revenue per available room, and goodwill). The vertical axis is the vector of human (motivation-achievement, affiliation, and power). The diagnose axis is the vector of process (preference-location, rooms, service, value, sleep quality, and cleanliness).

Customer motivation arises from personal preferences, societal clusters, environmental effects, uniqueness, trends, and other factors (Wang et al., 2020). Families select vacation packages based on the perception that there will be activities that suit each person. For example, a family unit of two adults and one child should have unique content in one advertisement. If the family views a brochure advertising dinner, relaxation, and fun they are likely to make a reservation because it meets individual needs (Cohen & Cohen, 2012). Choices also differ based on gender associations. Men's preferences are reliant on purchase intentions while women are convinced by social media, word-of-mouth, and interpretation (Tan, 2020). Therefore, persuasion takes into consideration online reviews.

2.2 Goodwill Theories

The International Financial Reporting Standards (IFRS) defines goodwill as being "an asset representing the future economic benefits arising from other assets acquired in a business that are not individually identified and separately recognized" (Ratiu et al., 2013). It is an interdisciplinary concept that spans across many fields and is of utmost importance. Research in various contexts of goodwill has been used to strengthen the knowledge within fields such as accounting and many others. (Amel-Zadeh et al., 2021).

Goodwill may be described as "the right that grows out of past efforts for profit to increase value or create an advantage" (Leake, 1921). One such right is the profits arising from marketing materials. Though relevant to an extent, tangible marketing materials play a part in helping to rake in revenues. Intangible marketing materials such as social media have also been immensely effective (DeMers, 2014). Social media promotes brands in real time. It revamped the marketing value chain by removing the middlemen usually involved in message communication.

Goodwill is also known as corporate reputation. Corporate reputation refers to the fact that reputation stems from branding. Branding is an intangible asset in every company and positively influences financial performance (Gamayuni, 2015). Though its significance is often underutilized, reputation generates substantial returns. Corporate reputation significantly impacts returns on assets. It largely influences firm performance in huge corporations (Satt & Chetioui, 2017).

Goodwill can be proven credible when share price rises in value. The asset positively affects the stock price. Goodwill has been poised to assist decision makers with daily functions. It contains the capabilities to generate excess profit consistently. In addition, extracting profits from different areas of goodwill, without third parties, allows further cost cutting to take place (Ji, 2020).

There are 3 goodwill theories: the Tobin's Q theory, the Super-Profit theory, and the Momentum theory as follows.

Tobin's Q Theory developed by James Tobin in 1969 is used to measure a firm's goodwill regardless of size. The concept presumes that a favorable relationship exists between firm value and material risk management (Carter et al., 2017). Proper management of a firm's intangible assets is fundamental to achieving its aims. One such asset is research and development (R&D). Material risk management increases a firm's future profits (Lev & Sogiannis, 1996). Physical capital responds slower to changes in demand and supply. As such, precedence should be given to nonphysical commodities found in goodwill. Nevertheless, both tangible and intangible investment work together to create successful results for companies (Peters & Taylor, 2017).

The Super-Profit Theory was coined the understanding of goodwill (Leake, 1921). The Super-Profit Theory reasons that "super-profit" is the amount by which increases in revenue value or other advantages exceed any economic expenditure incidental to its production. Superior profits can be gained by targeting numerous audiences. Social media utilization opens the windows for these revenues (Kumar & Mirchandani, 2012). Social media platforms have been one of the leading generators of returns on investments due to their interactive and convenient nature (Song, 2019). The convenience of mobile devices also assists with audience reach and targeting. Segmentation occurs as a result of "Big Data" collected from platforms such as Facebook, Instagram, TikTok, YouTube and many others. The insights provided by these platforms assist with identifying social interest essential to goodwill. Therefore, data can be mined and analyzed to target multiple groups (Liang & Zhu, 2017).

The momentum theory is a" marketing or promotional push purchased by businessmen" (Nelson, 1953). When goodwill is paid for, in this case, promotional content, branding receives a head start. The momentum theory states that goodwill considers customer lists, organization and development costs, trade names, secret processes, patents, copyrights, licenses, franchises, superior earning power, and going value. According to Nelson, this goodwill should not be written-off. Instead, it should sit with the other assets like equipment on the balance sheet. The theorist assumes that goodwill earned from marketing momentum is just as deserving as other assets (Ratiu & Tudor, 2013). However, the momentum disappears over time. That happens because the benefits derived slows down and eventually stops. As such, the non-tactile value provided by the theory should be replaced periodically. Investments in brands, trademarks, research and development and other areas should be made to relay the momentum (Sandner & Block, 2011).

2.3 McClelland's (1985) Theory of Motivation

The word "motivation" from Latin *movere*, which means "to move", describes the processes involved in starting, directing, and maintaining physical and psychological activities (Gerrig & Zimbardo, 2002). Motivation is often used by experimentalists, but personality theorists or clinicians think in terms of motives (McClelland, 1985). Motives are in both the conscious and unconscious levels. The unconscious motive is what an individual unconsciously feels like doing, whereas the conscious motives refer to what an individual consciously believe he should do in particular situation (Langens & McClelland, 1997). A guest in the hotel unconsciously comment how he or she felt in his/her feedback (Winter, 1996) whereas he/she should prefer location, value, cleanliness, service, rooms, or sleep quality consciously. There are 3 motivations: Achievement, Affiliation, and Power in human beings (McClelland, 1985). Achievement motivation is the human desire to exceed their normal performance (McClelland, 1985). At the unconscious level, a guest with a high achievement motive always wants to stay at the best valued hotel. According to the Tobin's Q theory and Momentum theory, the extra annual value of the hotel is measured by its goodwill through its best risk management and lists of customers and patents. At the conscious level, a guest with a high achievement would like to get the best sleep quality as the final goal. Therefore, the first hypothesis in this study is as follows.

Hypothesis 1: There would be significant relationships among hotel goodwill, guests' achievement, and guests' selection of sleep quality in the hotel.

Affiliation motivation is the human desire to make friends with other people (McClelland, 1985, Tran, Tran, & Tran, 2018). At the unconscious level, a guest with a high affiliation motive always wants to please others by willing to pay at the daily average hotel rate. The average daily rate (ADR) becomes a measurement of the guests' willingness to pay for a room in the hotel to reflect the unconscious level of affiliation of the hotel guest. At the conscious level, a guest with a high affiliation motive always prefers rooms, value, and location to make them happy during the stay. Due to its opposite expectation, this preference is different from the sleep quality of the guest with a high achievement. If the affiliation network focuses on people orientation; i.e., rooms, location, value, the achievement network will focus on task performance of hotel, i.e., sleep quality.

Hypothesis 2: There would be significant relationships among hotel average daily rate, guests' affiliation, and guests' selections of rooms, location, and value in the hotel.

Contrary to previous networks focusing on the open relationship, the power motivation and the later reward motivation are focusing on reserved relationship. Power motivation is the human desire to control over other people (Winter, 1996). At the unconscious level, a guest with a high power motive always wants to compete over the owner of the hotel. The daily revenue of an available room of the hotel owner is a measurement for the hotelier's effectiveness. The revenue per available room (RevPAR) thus reflects the power of the guest who wants to compete over the hotelier's productivity. At the conscious level, a guest with a high power motive always prefer to control over cleanliness and service, the two key responsibilities of hotel staff. Therefore, the third hypothesis in this study would be as follows.

Hypothesis 3: There would be significant relationships among revenue per available room, guests' power, and guests' selection of service and cleanliness in the hotel.

3   Methodology

Sample: The sample of the study include 163 comments on Hilton Gulf Front Pensacola Beach retrieved from TripAdvisor from 2009 to 2022. Linguistic Inquiry and Word Count (LIWC) was conducted to retrieve the three unconscious motives from hotel guests in addition to their conscious selections for location, rooms, value, cleanliness, service, and sleep quality.

The description for the sample in Fig. 1 indicates that variables are normalized with the sample size over 100. In addition, the Cronbach's alpha reliability Lamda was 0.75 to show that the sample includes reliable and valid variables to prepare for the fit model.

Descriptive Statistics					
	N	Minimum	Maximum	Mean	Std. Deviation
HiltonADR	163	146.00	664.00	253.8466	88.53475
HiltonGW	163	10033.00	11984.00	11119.4049	761.62515
HiltonRevPAR	163	78.00	1017.00	314.7853	164.52174
Location	163	2.00	5.00	4.3742	.87550
Rooms	163	1.00	5.00	3.6626	1.14515
Service	163	1.00	5.00	3.8160	1.25334
Value	163	1.00	5.00	3.5153	1.12412
Cleanliness	163	1.00	5.00	3.6994	1.11186
SleepQuality	163	1.00	5.00	3.7791	1.08880
Gaffiliation	163	.00	14.29	3.8191	2.88254
Gachieve	163	.00	5.71	1.2918	1.25267
Gpower	163	.00	8.96	2.6067	1.82823
Valid N (listwise)	163				

Fig. 1. Descriptive of ADR, RevPAR, Goodwill, Location, Rooms, Sleep Quality, Cleanliness, Servcie, and Cleanliness with reliability Cronbach's alpha of 0.75

Structure Equation Modeling (SEM) was used to fit the exogenous and endogenous variables in a model including ADR, RevPAR, Goodwill, achievement, affiliation, power, location, rooms, value, cleanliness, service, and sleep quality.

Figure 2 indicates the result of the well fit model with Chi-squared > 0.05, Root mean square error of approximation (RMSEA) = 0.08, Comparative Fit index (CFI) = 0.91, Parsimonious normed fit index (PNFI) = 0.6, Parsimonious Comparative Fit index (PCFI) = 0.05, Adjusted Goodness of fit (AGFI) = 0.81, and Minimum discrepancy function by degree of freedom divided (CMIN/df) = 5.

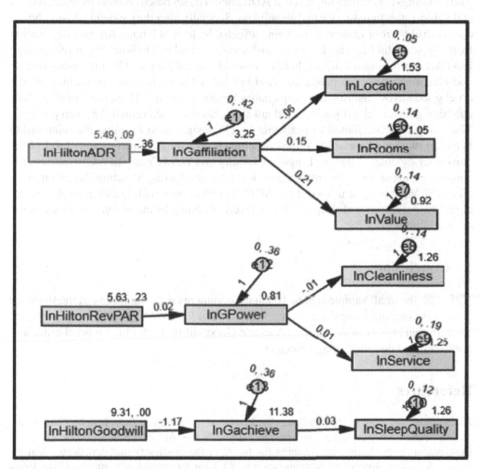

Fig. 2. Well-fit model of ADR, RevPAR, Goodwill, Location, Rooms, Cleanliness, Service, Sleep Quality, and Value.

4 Discussion

The hotel guests' controlling quick accessibility has forced hoteliers instantly update their hotel values. The study has built a model to examine the effectiveness of hoteliers' financial tools on what they offer. Using consumer motivation at the unconscious level to find the relationship between the hotel price and the guests' preference, the study has found 3 significant relationships: (1) ADR and location, rooms, and value. (2) RevPAR and service and cleanliness. And (3) Goodwill and sleep quality. The contribution of the study findings to hoteliers implies that ADR should be set based on hotel location, rooms, and value, rather than service and cleanliness. Specially after the pandemic, luxury hotels can control the room rate without being affected by lack of labour. Another implication from the study findings is cleanliness and service are related to hoteliers' profit through RevPAR. As the matter of fact, hoteliers would control the profit by increasing service and cleanliness after the pandemic. And last but not least, hoteliers could increase the hotel goodwill by ensuring the sleep quality for guests through Hampton's mission "satisfaction guaranteed"; if guests could not sleep, hotels would refund the room payment. The study has contributed to academia by (1) designing to examine the relationship between two set of variables at the conscious level using the unconscious level of the consumer variables. (2) using Linguistic Inquiry and Word Count (LIWC) to retrieve the consumer motivation at the unconscious level. (3) conducting Structural Equation Modeling (SEM) to build a fit model for ADR, RevPAR, goodwill, location, rooms, value, cleanliness, service, and sleep quality that were mediated by the unconscious motivation of hotel guests.

5 Conclusion

Although the small sample size of 163 guest comments is the limitation of the study for generalization, the sample randomly selected for 13 years (2009–2022) has identified the different effects of ADR, RevPAR, and Goodwill on each of the 6 hotel criteria to contribute to hotel marketing strategies.

References

Amel-Zadeh, A., Glaum, M., Sellhorn, T.: Empirical goodwill research: Insights, issues, and implications for standard setting and future research. Eur. Account. Rev. 1–32 (2021)

Boston University: Technology shaping the future of the hospitality industry. Boston University School of Hospitality Administration (n.d.). https://www.bu.edu/hospitality/2023/01/26/technology-trends-in-hospitality/

Carter, D.A., Rogers, D.A., Simkins, B.J., Treanor, S.D.: A review of the literature on commodity risk management. J. Commod. Mark. **8**, 1–17 (2017)

Cohen, E., Cohen, S.A.: Current sociological theories and issues in tourism. Ann. Tour. Res. **39**(4), 2177–2202 (2012)

Chusmir, L.H., Azevedo, A.: Motivation needs of sampled Fortune-500 CEOs: relations to organization outcomes. Percept. Mot. Skills **75**(2), 595–612 (1992)

DeMers, J.: The top 10 benefits of social media marketing. Forbes.com **11** (2014)

Escobar, M.: Hospitality tech in 2022: What does the future hold? Hospitality Tech (2022). https://hospitalitytech.com/hospitality-tech-2022-what-does-future-hold

Gamayuni, R.R.: The effect of intangible asset, financial performance, and financial policies on the firm value. Int. J. Sci. Technol. Res. **4**(1), 202–212 (2015)

Gerrig, J.R., Zimbardo, G.P.: Psychology and Life. Allyn and Bacon, Boston (2002)

Haskell, J.: Beverly hills hotels using coronavirus-fighting robots to keep guests safe (2020). Abc7.com. https://abc7.com/coronavirus-hotel-industry-beverly-hilton-waldorf-astoria-hillls/6286355/

Ji, H.: Financial analyses and corporate evaluation on sustainable ability to generate excess profit. Sustainability **12**(11), 4647 (2020)

Kobayashi, A.: International Encyclopedia of Human Geography. Elsevier, Amsterdam (2019)

Kumar, V., Mirchandani, R.: Increasing the ROI of social media marketing. MIT Sloan Manag. Rev. **54**(1), 55 (2012)

Langens, T., McClelland, D.C.: Implicit motives, explicit motives, and emotional well-being. Poster presented at the 105th convention of the American Psychological Association, Chicago (1997)

Leake, P.D.: Commercial goodwill: its history, value, and treatment in accounts. Sir J. Pitman & sons, Limited (1921)

Liang, H., Zhu, J.J.: Big data, collection of (social media, harvesting). In: The International Encyclopedia of Communication Research Methods, pp. 1–18 (2017)

Lev, B., Sougiannis, T.: The capitalization, amortization, and value-relevance of R&D. J. Account. Econ. **21**(1), 107–138 (1996)

McCabe, S.: Marketing communications in tourism and hospitality. Routledge, Milton Park (2010)

McClelland, D.C.: Human Motivation. Scott, Foresman and Company, Glenview (1985)

Morgan, B.: What is bleisure travel, and how is it transforming the hospitality industry? (2022). https://www.forbes.com/sites/blakemorgan/2022/06/27/what-is-bleisure-travel-and-how-is-it-transforming-the-hospitality-industry/?sh=70430abe7231

Nelson, R.H.: The momentum theory of goodwill. Account. Rev. **28**(4), 491–499 (1953)

Net Affinity. Approaching mobile in 2023 (2022). Hoteliers. https://www.4hoteliers.com/features/article/15577

Peenbaker, J., Francis, M., Booth, R.: Linguistic Inquiry and Word Count (1999). https://www.researchgate.net/publication/246699633_Linguistic_inquiry_and_word_count_LIWC

Peters, R.H., Taylor, L.A.: Intangible capital and the investment-q relation. J. Financ. Econ. **123**(2), 251–272 (2017). https://doi.org/10.1016/j.jfineco.2016.03.011

Ratiu, R.V., Tudor, A.T.: The theoretical foundation of goodwill-a chronological overview. Procedia Soc. Behav. Sci. **92**, 784–788 (2013)

Sandner, P.G., Block, J.: The market value of R&D, patents, and trademarks. Res. Policy **40**(7), 969–985 (2011)

Satt, H., Chetioui, Y.: Does goodwill improve firm performance? Evidence from the mena region. Risk Gov. Control Financ. Markets Inst. **7**(2), 108–115 (2017)

Shumakova, E.V.: Impact of digitalization on hotel industry development. In: Solovev, D.B., Savaley, V.V., Bekker, A.T., Petukhov, V.I. (eds.) Proceeding of the International Science and Technology Conference "FarEastCon 2020." SIST, vol. 227, pp. 587–595. Springer, Singapore (2021). https://doi.org/10.1007/978-981-16-0953-4_57

Song, T., Huang, J., Tan, Y., Yu, Y.: Using user-and marketer-generated content for box office revenue prediction: differences between microblogging and third-party platforms. Inf. Syst. Res. **30**(1), 191–203 (2019)

Tran, X.: Actor-network theory in tourism. In: Tourism and Opportunities for Economic Development in Asia, pp. 261–269 (2017). https://doi.org/10.4018/978-1-5225-2078-8.ch016

Tran, X., Tran, H., Tran, T.: Information communications technology (ICT) and tourism experience: can serotonin become a measurement for tourism experience? EReview Tourism Res. **9**, 20–24 (2018)

Tan, C.: The motivation of hotel reservations: from a gender perspective. Int. J. Organ. Innov. **13**(2) (2020)

Tobin, J.: A general equilibrium approach to monetary theory. J. Money Credit Bank. **1**(1), 15–29 (1969)

Wang, W., Ying, S., Mejia, C., Wang, Y., Qi, X., Chan, J.H.: Independent travelers' niche hotel booking motivations: the emergence of a hybrid cultural society. Int. J. Hosp. Manag. **89**, 102573 (2020)

Werner, H.: Top 10 hospitality technology trends for 2023 (2023). https://www.mitel.com/blog/top-10-communication-tech-trends-hospitality

Winter, D.G.: Personality: Analysis and Interpretation of Lives. McGraw-Hill, New York (1996)

The Influence Factors of the Characteristics of Live Broadcast E-commerce Anchors on Consumers' Intention to Recommend WOM: A S-O-R Perspective

Linwei Hu[✉], Chuanmin Mi, and Lili Liu

College of Economics and Management, Nanjing University of Aeronautics and Astronautics, Nanjing, China

hulinwei123@126.com, {cmmi,lilili85}@nuaa.edu.cn

Abstract. In the era of Marketing 4.0, recommendation has become a typical feature of marketing, the effectiveness of word-of-mouth (WOM) has exceeded the influence of traditional marketing methods such as advertising and published. However, little research attention has been devoted to understand the formation mechanism of customers' willingness to recommend WOM under the marketing model of live broadcast e-commerce. To fill this gap, we thus ground our research in the migration theory, more specifically, the SOR (stimulus-organism-reaction) model to enhance our understanding of the influence factors of the characteristics of anchors who plays a leading role in the live broadcast scene on customers' intention to recommend WOM. The results show that: (1) the influence factors of the characteristics of anchors including reliability, speciality and attractivity had positive impacts on Perceived Experience; (3) anchors' Interactivit don't have positive impacts on Perceived Experience (5) perceived experience had positive impacts on users' intention to recommend. Finally, the stimulate factors jointly explained 86.2% variance of perceived experience, which in turn explained 69.9% variance of users' intention to Recommend WOM.

Keywords: Live broadcast e-commerce · SOR model · Recommend WOM

1 Introduction

E-commerce platforms have changed their traditional marketing methods under the influence of the epidemic, such as promotion and advertising, and started to carry out online marketing with the new model of "live+", hoping to further expand market share through this business model. Live broadcast e-commerce is developing rapidly, while live broadcast consumers are increasing. Users are more likely to pay attention to and recommend the products recommended by the anchors and even the anchors and stores participating in the live broadcast after watching the commercial live broadcast of the e-commerce anchors. As of June 2021, the number of online live broadcast users in China has reached 638 million, a year-on-year increase of 75.39 million, accounting for 63.1% of the total

© The Author(s), under exclusive license to Springer Nature Switzerland AG 2023
P. Zaphiris et al. (Eds.): HCII 2023, LNCS 14060, pp. 455–464, 2023.
https://doi.org/10.1007/978-3-031-48060-7_34

Internet users. Among them, the number of live broadcast users of e-commerce was 384 million, an increase of 75.24 million, accounting for 38.0% of the total Internet users [1]. However, there are many difficulties behind the vigorous development of live broadcast e-commerce. The user conversion rate is low: a lot of consumers only watch but not buy [2]. Although the live broadcast with goods has a wide spread and good sales effect, the public praise of the live broadcast with goods shows a downward trend: moer consumers complain about the quality of the goods in the live broadcast room and the quality of after-sales service, etc. As a result, consumers do not trust or even accept the live shopping method [3].

Many empirical studies have not paid enough attention to the formation mechanism of customers' willingness to recommend word of mouth under the new marketing model of e-commerce live broadcast. Prior researches on customers' intention to recommend Word of mouth (WOM) is mostly based on offline stores and traditional social media (such as virtual brand communities, e-commerce trading platforms, etc.) [4–6], and demonstrates the driving factors affecting consumers' intention to recommend WOM from the aspects of product service quality, personal motivation and social situation [7]. Live broadcast e-commerce users whose recommendation behavior can bring more attention and benefits to the live broadcast are very important in the live broadcast scene. At the same time e-commerce anchors play a leading role in the live broadcast. Hence, we build a model on the basis of SOR (stimulus-organism-reaction) theory, focusing on the analysis of the characteristics of e-commerce anchors can influence customers' intention of word-of-mouth recommendation.

2 Theoretical Background

2.1 S-O-R Model

The basic principle of SOR (that is, "stimulus organism reaction") is an environmental psychology theory that uses "organism" as a medium to explain the internal psychology of the human body. The SOR model includes three elements: "stimulation", "organism" and "reaction", while "stimulation" refers to "influence on individuals" [8], including the influence of various external factors. The "organism" is the medium that a person in SOR mode reacts to the influence of the outside world. "Reaction" is the final action generated by the psychological state when people are stimulated [9] The SOR model was proposed by Belk and Russell. Donovan and Rossiter subsequently introduced the SOR model into the retail industry and analyzed customers' shopping behavior [10]. In the empirical analysis of the auction field, Chen [11] used "website environment and promotion activities" as the environmental incentive factors to explore the impact of users' impulse buying tendencies and standard evaluation values on consumers' impulse buying. Zhang confirmed the impact of customers' impulse buying behavior under the live broadcast of SOR mode.

2.2 Word of Mouth Recommendation Concept

Word of mouth (WOM for short) is an informal way of communication, which mainly comes from the company's potential, existing or former consumers. It generally refers to the subjective and objective evaluation of consumers on the enterprise and the products or services provided by the enterprise [12, 13], which usually affects the purchase decisions of other consumers. WOM can be divided into positive word of mouth and negative word of mouth. Positive word-of-mouth promotes the advantages and advantages of products or services, and can actively encourage people to pay attention to and buy a product or service. While negative word of mouth highlights the problems or shortcomings of products or services to prevent people from buying or consuming [14]. WOM recommendation intention refers to a positive WOM behavior intention based on positive WOM. Carroll and Ahuvia [15] suggest that WOM recommendation intention is the behavioral tendency of customers to actively recommend a product or brand to others or groups based on their own product experience and brand perception.

3   Research Model and Hypotheses

The research model is presented below in Fig. 1.

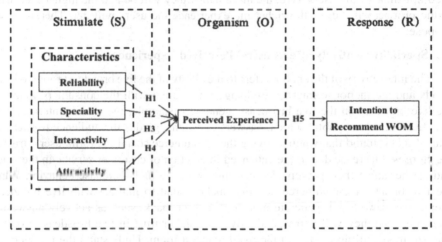

Fig. 1. Research Model

In the model, the stimulus factors include the characteristics of the anchor (reliability, speciality, interactivity, attractivity), the intermediate organism variable is the perception experience, and the result response is the user's intention to recommend word-of-mouth. Assumptions discussed in the following section.

3.1   S-->o

The reliability of the anchor refers to whether the anchor himself and the products he recommends are more authentic and trustworthy. When the reliability of e-commerce anchors is high, the perceived risk and product uncertainty of customers will decrease [16], which can promote customers to have a good feeling about the content of e-commerce live broadcasts, and even customers will have psychological dependence on the anchors or products they believe can be trusted. Secondly, from the perspective of information source of information transmission, when individuals recognize that the information source has high reliability, they will receive the information transmitted with a positive attitude [17]. When the reliability of the anchor and the product introduced is higher, users will be more willing to buy the product or stay and watch the live broadcast for many times, and the richer the user experience in the live broadcast room. Therefore, we propose:

H1. Reliability positively affects users' Perceived Experience

The professional nature of the anchor refers to the professional knowledge, skills and qualities of the anchor who brings goods in the live broadcast room, such as the understanding of the products he brings and whether he has some experience in using them. Han Xiaoyi [18] is studying that the live broadcast e-commerce delivery anchor can improve the trust and pleasure of live broadcast users by enhancing the professionalism of the delivered products. When the live broadcast e-commerce brings goods, the host introduces the products. The deeper the understanding, the more professional skills and accomplishments the users have, the more happy they will be and the higher their trust in the product will be, so the richer the experience the users will get. Therefore, we propose:

H2. Speciality positively affects users' Perceived Experience

The interactivity of the anchor refers to the ability of the live broadcast room to bring goods and the anchor to interact, exchange information with the consumers watching the live broadcast in the live broadcast scene. For example, the anchor interacts with the audience on the public screen, answers questions, guides the audience to speak or likes. Lu [19] found that when studying the e-commerce social platform, users' trust in the store will increase due to the enhanced interaction of customer service in the store, and further affect their perceived value, thus affecting their purchase behavior. When the live broadcast e-commerce delivery anchors tend to interact with live broadcast users, live viewers will generate more positive feedback, such as actively answering questions, and they will correspondingly have higher trust in live broadcast products and are more willing to stay in the live broadcast room. Understand the products, so as to improve the value perception of live broadcast products. The more attractive the live broadcast e-commerce delivery anchor is, that is, when the anchor brings better live viewing experience to live broadcast users through external conditions, the more happy the live broadcast users will be, the more time they will stay in the live broadcast room, and the more they will feel the live broadcast experience. Therefore, we propose:

H3. Interactivity positively affects users' Perceived Experience

The attraction of the anchor refers to the unique attraction and charm of the individual anchor in the live broadcast room, which can attract the consumers watching the live broadcast to stay. For example, the appearance, sense of humor, voice, eloquence, etc. displayed by the anchor during the live broadcast. In the research of social psychology, it is mentioned that people are more likely to be attracted by attractive people, such as personality, appearance, etc., which will bring higher pleasure [19]. Yang Qiang [20] divided it into three dimensions when studying the characteristics of the anchor's information source, and found that when the live broadcast e-commerce anchor has excellent appearance, sound and sense of humor, the internal curiosity of the live broadcast users is more easily aroused, and the sense of experience is stronger. Therefore, we propose:

H4. Attractivity positively affects users' Perceived Experience

3.2 O-->R

First, the theory of planned behavior emphasizes that the positive attitude of individuals is one of the important factors to promote their behavioral intentions [21]. It has been studied that when customers provide market information and knowledge to others, they will introduce their products and consumption experience. When customers get a good experience, they can awaken their behavior and willingness to recommend products to others [22]. Customers who feel happy with the live broadcast of e-commerce will have positive emotions, which makes it easy to choose to spread positive word of mouth information about the anchor or product. Customers' good perception experience can be seen as their positive attitude towards the content related to the live broadcast of e-commerce. Therefore, a good customer experience may further stimulate customers' willingness to recommend by word of mouth. Therefore, we propose:

H5. Perceived Experience positively affects users' Intention to Recommend

3.3 Data Collection

Data collection was carried out via wjx.cn, a Chinese online survey platform. The questionnaire consists of two parts: demographic information and measurement items of variables in the research model, including 27 questions. All items in the questionnaire were adopted from prior studies and measured with 7-likert scale ranging from 1 (strongly disagree) to 7 (strongly agree). A total of **151** valid responses were collected. Detailed demographic information was shown in Table 1:

3.4 Data Analyses and Results

There is a two-step method used to carry out the survey and analyze data [23]. Smart PLS 3.33 [24] and partial least squares structural equation model (PLS-SEM) [25] were used to verify the research model and corresponding hypotheses. First, reliability is evaluated by checking composite reliability and Cronbach's α values. Table 2 showed that composite reliability values of this study were all higher than the suggested value of 0.70 [26]. Besides, internal consistency was verified by Cronbach's α values, which were all greater than 0.893, thus exceeding the threshold of 0.70 recommended by Fornell and Larcker [27].

Discriminant validity of the measurement model is evaluated by comparing the square root of AVE with the correlation between the measurement items. The results in Table 3 showed that the AVE square root of each structure is greater than the correlation between any pair of corresponding structures. In summary, our measurement model has sufficient reliability, convergence validity and discriminant validity.

Table 1. Respondent demographics.

Measure	Item	Frequency	Percentage(%)
Gender	Male	72	47.7
	Female	79	52.3
	<18	0	0
	18-25	12	7.9
	26-30	36	23.8
Age	31-40	27	17.9
	41-50	34	22.5
	51-60	34	22.5
	>60	8	5.3
	Middle school or below	15	9.9
	High school	13	8.6
Education	College	48	31.8
	Bachelor	61	40.4
	Master and above	14	9.3
	≤2000	0	0
	2001-5000	39	25.8
Income	5001-8000	45	29.8
	8001-10000	50	33.1
	≥10000	17	11.3

We then tested the structural model and hypotheses. As shown in Fig. 2, The results showed that: (1) reliability had positive impacts on Perceived Experience ($\beta = 0.386$, t = 4.423); (2) speciality had positive impacts on perceived experience ($\beta = 0.335$, t = 4.337); (3) interactivit don't have positive impacts on perceived experience ($\beta = 0.063$, t = 0.697); (4) attractivity had positive impacts on perceived experience ($\beta = 0.328$, t = 4.444); (5) perceived experience had positive impacts on users' intention to recommend WOM ($\beta = 0.734$, t = 18.459). Finally, the stimulate factors jointly explained 86.2% variance of perceived experience, which in turn explained 69.9% variance of users' intention to Recommend WOM. Thus proving that the model had high degree of fifit and strong prediction ability.

Table 2. Individual item reliability

Measures	Item	Loading	CR	Cronbach alpha	AVE
Speciality	P1	0.876	0.927	0.894	0.760
	P2	0.882			
	P3	0.887			
	P4	0.840			
Interactivity	I1	0.818	0.922	0.894	0.702
	I2	0.824			
	I3	0.825			
	I4	0.856			
	I5	0.863			
Attractivity	A1	0.899	0.936	0.898	0.830
	A2	0.919			
	A3	0.916			
Reliability	R1	0.900	0.945	0.922	0.811
	R2	0.905			
	R3	0.902			
Perceived Experience	E1	0.897	0.935	0.895	0.826
	E2	0.923			
	E3	0.907			
	E4	0.911			
Intention to Recommend WOM	R1	0.909	0.934	0.894	0.825
	R2	0.917			
	R3	0.899			
	R4	0.903			

4 Contribution

Based on the conclusion of the data analysis, we can put forward substantive suggestions for the development of live broadcast e-commerce: when selecting the anchors in the live broadcast room, we can pay more attention to the professionalism, credibility and attractiveness of the anchors, and improve the user's sense of experience in the process of live broadcast operation, so as to improve the user's willingness to recommend by word

Table 3. Discriminant validity

	Speciality	Interactivity	Attractivity	Reliability	Perceived Experience	Intention to Recommend WOM
Speciality	**0.871**					
Interactivity	0.860	**0.838**				
Attractivity	0.865	0.837	**0.901**			
Reliability	0.757	0.793	0.760	**0.909**		
Perceived Experience	0.812	0.826	0.820	0.788	**0.856**	
Intention to Recommend WOM	0.815	0.828	0.816	0.778	0.826	**0.911**

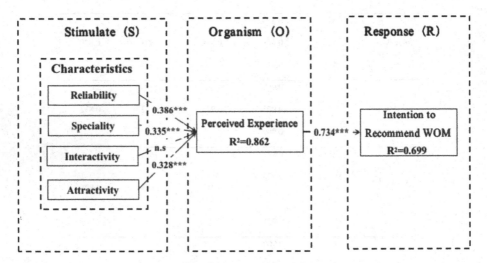

Fig. 2. Structural Model

of mouth and ultimately improve the live broadcast revenue. For e-commerce anchors, improve their professionalism, credibility and attractiveness of the live broadcast products to improve their competitiveness and bring better shopping experience to users in the live broadcast room.

This research has contributed to the emerging literature of user word-of-mouth recommendation in the context of live e-commerce through the following ways. First of all, there are few studies on user word-of-mouth recommendation in the live broadcast room, and there are also few studies on user recommendation from the perspective of anchor characteristics. As far as we know, this work is the first batch of research on user's word-of-mouth recommendation behavior based on the influencing factors of the anchor's characteristics. Secondly, taking SOR model as the basis of the research model, taking the characteristics of the anchor in SOR model as the stimulus factor, the user's perception experience as the organism factor, and the user's willingness to recommend word of mouth as the reaction factor, expanded the application of this theory. Finally, our research provides practical suggestions and values for the overall development of live broadcast e-commerce, the revenue of live broadcast room of e-commerce, and the user conversion rate.

At the same time, this study is not extremely perfect and there is still room for improvement and development. First of all, due to the limited number of researchers, the conclusions obtained are not perfect, and the scope of the study can be expanded in the follow-up study. In addition, some of the people surveyed in the questionnaire have not formed the habit of live shopping, and their understanding of the experience of the live room is not perfect. In the follow-up study, we can launch a questionnaire for specific people with rich live shopping experience. Finally, when selecting the factors, the selection of the characteristics of the anchor is not perfect. Other characteristics of the anchor, such as the style of the anchor, are not included in the stimulus factors. For the consideration of the organism factors, only the user's perception experience is considered. In the subsequent research, the research model can be improved and a more comprehensive research model can be built.

References

1. The 48th Statistical Report on China's Internet Development. Netw. Commun. (09), 76–81 (2021)
2. Chen, Y.T., Zhang, M., Yuan, S.J., Cao, B.: The transformation mechanism of e-commerce live broadcast user loyalty from the perspective of psychological contract. Enterp. Econ. 41(04), 153–160 (2022). https://doi.org/10.13529/j.cnki.enterprise.economy.2022.04.016
3. Zhong, S.X.: From barbaric growth to live broadcast of word of mouth avalanche with goods: where to go at the tuyere. China's Food Ind. (02), 32–35 (2021)
4. Lovett, M.J., Peres, R., Shachar, R.: On Brands and Word of Mouth. J. Mark. Res. 50(4), 427–444 (2013)
5. Xie, Y., Peng, S.Q.: The influence of brand trust and brand emotion on word-of-mouth communication: the role of attitude and attitude uncertainty. Manage. Rev. 26(2), 80–91 (2014)
6. Berger, J.: Word of mouth and interpersonal communication: a review and directions for future research. J. Consum. Psychol. 24(4), 586–607 (2014)
7. Yang, N.: Research on the influence mechanism of online celebrity live broadcast on consumer brand attitude. J. Central Univ. Finance Econ. (02), 118–128 (2021)
8. Sokolova, K., Kefi, H.: Instagram and YouTube bloggers promote it, why should I buy? How credibility and parasocial interaction influence purchase intentions. J. Retail. Consum. Serv. (1), 1–16 (2019)
9. Feng, X.P., Zhao, C.C.: Anchor types, brand attitudes and purchase intentions – an experimental study based on online live shopping scenes. J. Henan Normal Univ. (Philos. Soc. Sci. Ed.) 48(03), 80–89 (2021)
10. Xiao, K.H., Liu, B.: Opinion leader traits, promotion stimulation and social e-commerce consumers willingness to purchase – a research based on WeChat shoppers. Manag. J/ 34(01), 99–110 (2021)
11. Schmitt, B.H.: Experiential marketing. J. Mark. Manag. 15(1), 53–67 (1999)

12. Feng, C.: Research on the Impact of E-commerce Network Anchor Characteristics on Consumer Attitude. Anhui University, Anhui (2018)
13. Westbrook, R.A.: Product/consumption-based affective responses and postpurchase processes. J. Mark. Res. **24**(3), 258–270 (1987)
14. Anderson, J.R., Lebiere, C.: The atomic components of thought. J. Math. Psychol. **45**(6), 917–923 (1998)
15. Trusov, M., Bucklin, R.E., Pauwels, K.: Effects of word-of-mouth versus traditional marketing: findings from an internet social networking site. J. Mark. (2009)
16. Duan, W., Gu, B., Whinston, A.B.: Do online reviews matter? An empirical investigation of panel data. Decis. Support. Syst. **45**(4), 1007–1016 (2008)
17. Qiang, Y., Sheng, Y.C.: Research on the impact of WeChat business information source characteristics on consumers' purchase intention. Dalian Univ. Technol. J. Sci. (Soc. Sci. Ed.) **38**(02), 27–32 (2017)
18. Yu, X., Xu, Z.L., Guan, W.J.: Research on the impact of online merchants' commodity information presentation on consumers' behavioral intentions – model construction based on social presence theory. Inf. Theory Pract. **40**(10), 80–84 (2017)
19. Eroglu, S.A., Machleit, K.A., Davis, L.M.: Atmospheric qualities of online retailing - a conceptual model and implications. J. Bus. Res. **54**(2), 177–184 (2001)
20. Jiang, M., Zhang, X.C.: Factors influencing consumers' willingness to purchase in the online live broadcast environment of e-commerce based on SOR model. J. Huaibei Normal Univ. (Philos. Soc. Sci. Ed.) **41**(04), 49–57 (2020)
21. Depeng, Z., Shaoxia, C., Jiamin, P.: Formation mechanism of customer word-of-mouth value: research based on the perspective of social impact theory. Forecast **33**(04), 35–41 (2014)
22. Hu, T.Y., Deng, F.M., Wu, X.Y.: Review and prospect of research on influencing factors of consumer electronic word of mouth behavior. J. Henan Univ. (Soc. Sci. Ed.) **60**(05), 45–51 (2020)
23. Chin, W.W., Marcolin, B.L., Newsted, P.R.: A partial least squares latent variable modeling approach for measuring interaction effects: results from a Monte Carlo simulation study and an electronic-mail emotion/adoption study. Inf. Syst. Res. **14**, 189–217 (2003). https://doi.org/10.1287/isre.14.2.189.16018
24. Ringle, C.M., Wende, S., Will, A.: Smart PLS 2.0 (beta). SmartPLS, Hamburg (2005)
25. Pavlou, P.A., Liang, H., Xue, Y.: Understanding and mitigating uncertainty in online exchange relationships: a principal-agent perspective. MIS Q. **31**, 105–136 (2007). https://doi.org/10.2307/25148783
26. Hair, J.F., Black, B., Babin, B., Anderson, R.E., Tatham, R.L.: Multivariate Data Analysis. Pearson, London (2006)
27. Fornell, C., Larcker, D.F.: Evaluating structural equation models with unobservable variables and measurement error. J. Mark. Res. **18**, 39–50 (1981). https://doi.org/10.1177/002224378101800104

Research on M-Commerce Tax Collection and Administration Under Digital Economy

Haiyang Luo[✉], Priyank Zhou, and Qian Wang

Jilin University, 2699 Qianjin Street, Changchun, Jilin, China
LcaHrrYot@163.com

Abstract. Digital economy is a new economic form formed with the high development of information technology. E-commerce is one of the business models of digital economy, and mobile commerce is an extension of e-commerce. With the rapid development and integration of modern information technologies such as the Internet, Internet of Things, and mobile communication, mobile commerce and enterprises have been inseparable.

The rapid development of mobile commerce has brought all kinds of convenience to people's life, but also brought great challenges to the tax collection and administration. It is difficult to define tax jurisdiction, fragmented transactions, and difficult to track bills brought by mobile commerce, which lead to regional tax imbalance. This challenges the tax administration under the traditional economy in the past. Therefore, in combination with regional interests, China's actual situation and the characteristics of mobile commerce, this paper studies the tax administration of mobile commerce in China. Taking tax collection and administration as the power point, this paper puts forward measures for tax collection and administration of mobile commerce under the background of digital economy, and improves relevant tax collection and administration mechanisms, so as to better release the vitality of mobile commerce, drive the development of digital economy, and safeguard tax revenue and fairness of various regions.

Keywords: tax collection and administration · mobile commerce · BEPS · digital economy · digitization

1 Introduction

Nowadays, with the wide popularity of the Internet, mobile commerce has become an essential part of people's life. The access mode of the Internet has expanded from the wired network to the mobile terminal, and the wave of mobile commerce is rising gradually. On August 31, 2022, the China Internet Network Information Center (CNNIC) released the 50th Statistical Report on the Development of the Internet in China in Beijing. According to the report, by June 2022, China had 1.051 billion Internet users and 74.4% of the population had access to the Internet. With 841 million online shoppers in China, accounting for 80% of all Internet users, mobile commerce is increasingly playing an important role in economic activities.

P. Zaphiris et al. (Eds.): HCII 2023, LNCS 14060, pp. 465–474, 2023.
https://doi.org/10.1007/978-3-031-48060-7_35

While mobile commerce has brought rapid development to the society, it also brings challenges to our tax collection and management. First comes BEPS (Base Erosion and Profit Shifting). BEPS means that enterprises make use of the deficiencies in tax rules, differences in tax systems in different regions and loopholes in tax collection and management to formulate tax planning strategies for enterprises, and finally realize the "disappearance" or transfer taxable profits of enterprises. These strategies can minimize the total tax burden. In China, for example, a few regions have allowed eligible companies to collect corporate income tax at the rate of 15%, while the prevailing rate of corporate income tax in most regions remains 25%. In the context of digital economy, enterprises can rely on the rapidity of the digital economy and the convenience of the digital economy platform to achieve more high-frequency mobile transactions, which will lead to more enterprises to choose the digital economy platform to choose the lower collect corporate income tax rate of 15% of the region for trade, to reduce their tax burden. Obviously, mobile commerce provides the space and convenience for national and even global tax planning and profit shifting, and new changes have taken place in the tax avoidance mode of enterprises. This not only leads to huge challenges to tax rules and tax order, but also aggravates the unfairness of tax burden and development across the country and even the world. If China does not pay close attention to the tax collection and administration of mobile commerce, the problem of tax Base Erosion and Profit Shifting will occur, which will lead to the loss of regional tax revenue, and the imbalance of tax collection and administration among different regions will continue to increase.

At the same time, it is difficult to confirm the tax jurisdiction under the economic model of mobile commerce. At present, although the mobile commerce enterprises represented by Didi Outgoing have business activities nationwide, the tax revenue in many provinces is zero. This is mainly because the provinces still use the traditional tax collection and administration system, but the traditional economic tax collection and administration system is not applicable to some mobile commerce. This has resulted in a loss of tax revenue in the province, which needs to be solved urgently.

Finally, under the digital economy, transactions become fragmented and bills are difficult to be tracked in real time. The concealment and ambiguity of tax transaction activities increase the difficulty of tax authorities to obtain taxable information, which leads to the difficulty of applying the traditional tax registration system, and the degree of tax informatization needs to be improved.

The research significance of this paper is as follows: First, the study of mobile commerce tax collection is conducive to improving China's tax collection and administration and maintaining the principle of tax fairness. Otherwise, it is the same sales behavior, but it will be unfair to only collect all receivable on the real economy, which will deal a blow to the real economy and affect the enthusiasm of the real economy development. Secondly, the study of mobile commerce tax collection and administration can avoid tax loss in some regions, ensure the vitality of regional mobile commerce and realize tax increase, boost the development of regional digital economy and promote common prosperity. Third, studying the tax collection and administration of China's mobile commerce is conducive to adapting to the trend of international mobile commerce taxation, promoting the sustainable and healthy development of China's economy, and actively participating in the formulation of tax administration policies can effectively curb the problem of BEPS.

2 Related Concepts

2.1 Mobile Commerce

Concept of Mobile Commerce. Mobile commerce, which first emerged in Finland, combines wireless communication with traditional e-commerce in users' payment and shopping services. Nowadays, with the development of information technology and network economy, mobile commerce has been widely used in payment at the beginning and now relies on mobile terminals to experience online transactions, online medical treatment, information push, offline taxi hailing and other services. Dan (2001) believed that mobile commerce is an extension of traditional e-commerce, which requires wired connection from fixed places to wireless networks and support from mobile terminal devices. Qin Chengde and Wang Rulin (2009) proposed that mobile commerce is a new e-commerce model to carry out various business services based on the data transmission of mobile devices, which can be regarded as a new branch of e-commerce. Fang Hui (2018) believes that mobile commerce is a combination of "mobile" and "business". The definition of Mobile commerce in this paper is the combination of "mobile" and "business". "Mobile" is the means, "business" is the end. "Mobile" means from wired to wireless, from fixed location to no geographical restrictions Mobile e-commerce is defined as the commodity or service transaction based on wireless network by using mobile communication devices such as laptops, mobile phones and personal data assistants. With the help of mobile devices, mobile commerce is no longer limited to fixed places, and users can search and obtain required services or information on the platform anytime and anywhere, which is more flexible and greatly convenient for users to use.

Mobile commerce mode is realized through the following paths: Mobile commerce is an online or offline transaction activity based on mobile terminal equipment, mobile and wireless networks provided by mobile terminal providers and mobile operators. The product provider displays its products, services, digital content and other products to consumers directly through the establishment of its website or the development of mobile apps, or indirectly through intermediary platforms; The consumer selects the product and completes the payment of the product price with the help of financial service providers such as mobile banking and third-party payment. The financial service provider pays the price to the product provider and collects intermediary fees from the payment. After the payment is completed, the product provider shall deliver the purchased products to the consumers. When the traded products are tangible products, the logistics service provider is required to complete the final delivery process. When the traded objects are other products, the product provider can directly deliver the products to the consumers. If the transaction process is conducted through the intermediary platform, the product provider shall pay the intermediary fee to the intermediary platform upon completion of the transaction.

Features of Mobile Commerce. The development of m-commerce has the following characteristics: Firstly, it is highly efficient. With the development of information technology and the improvement of mobile terminal functions, compared with traditional e-commerce, payment functions and information acquisition are more convenient and efficient, prompting more and more users to use m-commerce to complete shopping; Secondly, it is personalized. Compared with traditional e-commerce, it needs to collect more user information, so as to provide users with more accurate services, so as to make customized services and personalized services possible, improve users' sense of experience. Thirdly, it has mobility. Users can browse product and service information anytime and anywhere. At the same time, it can carry out business activities and complete various transactions through mobile devices without the limitation of time and space. Fourth, with positioning, based on the GPS positioning system, the mobile commerce platform can obtain the user's location information in real time under the user's authorization, so as to provide users with corresponding services, namely location-based services (LBS), to help users complete related activities, such as takeaway service, hotel search, route recommendation, etc. The positioning of mobile commerce can help users better meet the corresponding needs.

2.2 Digitalization of Tax Collection and Administration

Tax collection and administration refers to the organization, collection, management and verification of tax by tax authorities in accordance with laws and regulations. At the 13th Forum on Tax Administration (FTA) held in December 2020, the Organization for Economic Cooperation and Development (OECD) released (Tax Administration 3.0: The Digital Transformation of Tax Administration) report proposes ideas for a worldwide digital transformation of tax administration. On March 24, 2021, the General Office of the CPC Central Committee and The General Office of the State Council issued the Opinions on Further Deepening the Reform of Tax Collection and Administration, proposing to promote the digital upgrading and intelligent transformation of tax collection and administration with the concept of data-driven, system integration and overall planning, in order to build a powerful smart tax system. And promote the comprehensive reform of tax law enforcement, service and supervision, and improve the efficiency of tax governance in a holistic and integrated manner.

The understanding of the digitization of tax collection and administration in this paper is to rely on modern technology to change the collection and management mode under the background of digital economy, so as to achieve tax compliance and improve management efficiency. The digitization of tax collection and administration covers at least two aspects: Firstly, at the system level, constantly improve the tax collection and administration system based on modern information means. Second, at the technical level, tax-related information can be processed quickly and efficiently through digital technology, Realize all receivables.

3   Challenges Brought by Mobile Commerce

With the continuous development and popularization of information technology, the development of mobile commerce is more and more rapid. According to the White Paper on the Development of China's Digital Economy (2022), the scale of digital economy reached 45.5 trillion yuan in 2021, with a nominal growth of 16.2% year on year. Digital economy has become an important force driving China's economic growth. However, there are still many problems in mobile commerce based on digital economy.

Mobile commerce has the characteristics of virtuality, cross-regional instant transaction and fuzzy value attribution, which brings great challenges to the prior tax distribution pattern based on the territorial principle. Undeniably, according to the consistency principle, the tax revenue obtained by local governments should be matched with its tax source. However, the development of mobile commerce intensifies the inter-regional tax base flow and tax burden export, which has a great impact on the tax revenue of local governments.

Firstly, through the Internet and other means, mobile commerce reduces the dependence of enterprises on business entities. Enterprises do not need to set up "entities", but only need to pay taxes on the value-added of products and services in the place of registration or origin of enterprises, thus distorting the theoretical distribution pattern of tax revenue. The traditional solution to the deviation between tax revenue and tax source can be corrected by profit distribution method, but in the era of mobile commerce, enterprises only carry out virtual connection between regions, resulting in the applicability of profit distribution method is very low. The current tax collection authority has gradually blurred, no longer applicable.

Secondly, the main body of mobile commerce is mostly online transactions. Based on the confidentiality agreement of various platforms, the main body income is relatively hidden, and the traditional "tax controlled by vote" is invalid. Criminals seize the loophole of "controlling tax by invoice" and evade tax by means of "missing invoice" and "duplicate contracts", resulting in a large loss of tax revenue. In the era of digital economy, the core work of mobile commerce tax control is not invoice, but transaction activities themselves. In the era of mobile commerce, it is difficult for tax authorities to fully grasp taxable information, which may lead to erosion of the tax base of local tax authorities.

The above problems will not only lead to the loss of tax sources in the region, but also lead to the Matthew effect of "the rich getting richer and the poor getting poorer". Under the background of the digital economy era, it is not only necessary to implement the principle of collecting all receivable of the tax Bureau, but also to take "promoting the coordinated development of regions and creating good conditions for promoting common prosperity" as the main line, and realize common prosperity as the overall goal. It is urgent to respond to tax collection and administration.

4 Current Situation of Tax Collection and Administration Under the Background of Mobile Commerce

4.1 Serious Problem of Tax Base Loss

The characteristics of mobile commerce, such as online transaction, transaction channel virtualization, transaction forms hidden, are easy to cause the loss of local tax base. Paperless is an important feature in the background of mobile commerce. Mobile commerce contains a lot of information, such as the product offering method, currency circulation method, the specific amount of the transaction and so on. Compared with entity operation, the flexibility, concealment and virtuality of transaction make it easy to escape from tax regulation, which brings great difficulties to tax collection and management.

Mobile commerce has completed the previous physical currency transaction through the Internet and other online means. Paper invoices are gradually replaced by electronic invoices, and the contents of invoices are stored in the third-party payment platform in the form of electronic data. In the process of trading, the books and vouchers involved in the exchanges of both parties can be paperless, which makes it difficult for tax authorities to trace the traces of the transactions of the two parties involved. In addition, in the process of transaction, from ordering, sales, price payment to final delivery service, all can be completed online. For privacy protection, the third-party payment platform adopts encryption technology to protect the privacy of tax payers and transaction information, and can even tamper with or erase transaction traces with the help of modern technological means. For example, in order to obtain traffic, some merchants brush a large number of orders through false transactions, and it is difficult for tax authorities to obtain relevant electronic vouchers, resulting in higher collection and supervision costs for tax authorities. Therefore, in the context of mobile commerce, it is difficult for tax authorities to obtain tax-related data, which increases the difficulty for tax authorities to "control tax by ticket".

4.2 The Definition Rules of Tax Collection and Administration Power Are Stuck in a Rut

Tax collection and administration power is the premise for local government to realize tax revenue, and its allocation determines which tax authority should carry out the tax revenue. However, in the context of mobile commerce, if we continue to rely on the traditional tax collection and administration definition rules, there will be a serious deviation between the tax and the tax source, so it is urgent to clarify the tax collection and administration power of each region.

Value-added tax, enterprise income tax as the main source of local government tax revenue, mobile commerce is the main tax transfer in the region. The traditional tax law system clearly takes "physical existence" such as the registration place of an enterprise or the location of an organization as the tax place, and takes the principle of origin and the principle of registration as the fundamental way to divide the tax base. However, in the era of mobile commerce, enterprises can provide consumers with cross-province and city-level commodity circulation services through online platforms, which breaks the limitations of the "special store, counter" sales model. Although it greatly reduces the operating cost of enterprises, it separates the place of commodity consumption from the place of organization, which causes a great impact on the division of tax collection and administration power. If the traditional tax authority division rules are still adopted, it will inevitably cause the erosion of the tax base of the destination and contribution. The principle of registration place ignores the cost of public goods and services provided by local governments to cultivate mobile commerce tax sources, and the principle of origin cannot match the tax burden borne by residents in the consumption area with the government tax revenue. It will eventually lead to the occurrence of unfair tax distribution.

At the same time, in the context of m-commerce, m-commerce enterprises rely on the platform to provide information for users. Mobile commerce enterprises collect the data of customers using the platform to form enterprise resources, which can reflect the consumption power and consumption preference of the public through post-processing. When users use the platform to purchase valuable services, they create a large number of customer base and precise positioning of commodities and advertisements for mobile commerce enterprises. The network effect generated by the interaction between users also provides mobile commerce enterprises with competitive advantages and profit benefits, and enterprises are also making extensive use of the marginal utility and interaction between users to find shortcuts for the sale of products and services, such as the delivery of stars and network anchors. The traditional tax collection and administration does not take into account the user's participation in the new model of value creation, so it does not use the value generated by low consumption users, but still uses the profits of the registration place of the enterprise or the location of the organization. Under the action of the identification principle of the "physical existence" of the tax place, the irrationality of the rules on the definition of tax collection and management power becomes more and more prominent.

5 Improve the Means of Tax Collection and Administration

In the era of mobile commerce, it is necessary to build a tax collection and management system compatible with the development of digital economy, so as to give full play to the regulatory role of taxation on the market, reduce the erosion of local tax base, narrow the tax gap between regions, safeguard the stability of tax sources, and boost the development of digital economy.

5.1 Safeguard the Local Tax Base

Improve the Mobile Commerce Registration System. Identifying the identity of tax payers is the starting point of tax collection and administration. Under the background of mobile commerce, the boundary between consumers and producers is becoming increasingly blurred, and the number of tax payers is increasing. It is imperative to improve tax registration, which is the first step to realize the protection of tax base. On the one hand, we should improve the platform user registration system. Detailed and accurate information of users is essential to clarify the identity of taxpayers, which is conducive to maintaining market order and improving the efficiency of tax collection and administration. In mobile commerce model, everyone can be a producer. Therefore, for users who often have flowing funds on their accounts, they need to be forced to register their real names. Our traditional tax registration system requires taxpayers to obtain market main body registration and so on before tax registration. The traditional tax registration system is not conducive to the tax authorities' supervision of numerous small and micro tax sources under the platform economy. Therefore, the identification number can be used as the taxpayer identification number when the taxpayer completes the real-name registration, so as to facilitate the tax authorities to determine the taxpayer.

On the other hand, we should improve the provisions in the *Administrative Measures for Reducing the Burden of Online Transactions* concerning "individuals engaging in labor activities for the convenience of the people without obtaining permission according to law and small and sporadic transactions, and do not need to be registered according to laws and administrative regulations". The current law does not list the items that do not need to be registered for tax purposes, which makes it impossible to adapt to the constantly innovative mobile commerce model. It is necessary to clarify the unified standard of "sporadic" and "small" transactions, and clearly specify which transactions belong to sporadic small transactions. Those not listed in the list will be subject to tax registration. At the same time, mobile commerce practitioners who should have tax registration but fail to do so will be given a time limit to correct and warn them, and punishments will be increased for those who fail to correct repeated teachings.

Improve the Informationization of Tax Collection and Administration. Tax authorities should focus on all aspects of tax collection and administration and promote the establishment of tax information system, mobile commerce trading platform and third-party financial payment platform. For example, the docking of the fiscal and tax system with the enterprise electronic invoice module and the third-party financial database will form a comprehensive platform for sharing factual information and collecting information of all parties, so as to capture the whole process of tax-related information. Tax authorities use big data, cloud computing, blockchain, 5G and other information technology means to solve tax collection and administration obstacles. Cloud computing will record all kinds of transaction information in mobile commerce, extract useful information through big data, and at the same time, decentralize blockchain technology, so that all data in the system can be updated synchronously, realizing the immediacy of information acquisition by tax authorities.

At the same time, we should strengthen system construction and rating classification, downgrade the credit rating of tax payers who conceal, misreport or fail to report, and impose administrative penalties when necessary to form a deterrent force, so as to make efficient and standardized supervision a reality.

Blockchain Innovates Tax Services. While mobile commerce is making great strides forward, collection and management means are also innovated and developed. Information technology is refined into a sharp tool to strengthen tax supervision and inspection technology, prevent enterprises from tampering with tax-related information and providing false materials, improve tax efficiency, and build an intelligent, personalized and convenient tax service system.

Blockchain technology is recognized as the first core technology after the Internet, which is particularly important in promoting the growth of smart taxation. Blockchain electronic invoice realizes the integration of "capital flow and invoice flow", combines invoice issuance with online payment, and gets through the whole process of invoice application, invoice issuing, reimbursement and tax declaration. Blockchain technology is characterized by traceable data sharing, openness and transparency, tamper-proof information, smart contract mechanism, etc. Without the involvement of intermediaries, tax authorities can connect with other departments and directly obtain complete tax-related information. Once an enterprise conducts a transaction, permanent evidence will be left on the chain. This effectively prevents the digital platform malicious modification, falsification of information illegal behavior. Moreover, the law enforcement behavior of tax enforcement personnel is also in a transparent and open situation, which regulates the tax personnel as well as the enterprises.

Therefore, in the future, we can build a "tax chain" integrating enterprise, tax, bank and foreign exchange through blockchain technology. Effectively reduce the tax risks of cross-regional enterprises. Blockchain technology not only improves the access ability and information quality of tax-related information, but also improves taxpayers' tax satisfaction and tax compliance. Tax authorities should deepen the tax application of blockchain technology, make use of the driving role of modern information technology, generate tax declaration data from ledger data on blockchain, realize the whole-process management of tax system -- business model, business process and informatization, and promote the coordination and sharing of tax and fee information among various departments on the premise of ensuring data security. Bridge the information gap between enterprises and tax authorities, effectively solve the problem of information asymmetry of mobile commerce transactions, monitor the behavior of enterprises' mobile commerce transactions, carry out effective supervision and risk prevention and control, realize data value-added, provide a more forward-looking development approach for tax service, and finally achieve the effect of simultaneous promotion of mobile commerce and digital taxation.

5.2   Clarify the Boundaries of Tax Collection and Administration

Determine the Place of Tax Payment. According to the inspiration of relevant tax practice in the international community, the tax place should be detailed. There are two main problems in the judgment of the tax place of mobile commerce: (1) How to judge the tax place when the receiving party of goods and services is an enterprise, and the enterprise has more than one place of operation; (2) How to judge the tax place when the receiving party of goods and services is an individual, due to the mobility of mobile terminals and people. Therefore, the applicability of OECD relevant tax policy opinions is analyzed, as shown in the table:

Users	Method	Applicability
Enterprise	Direct use method (destination of goods and services principle determines tax place)	When the buyer's use of goods and services is obvious (online shopping, etc.)
	Direct delivery method (where the goods and services are provided on site at the place of tax payment)	Goods and services must be provided on site (travel services, etc.)
	Recharging method (the place where the buyer's institution of the products and services is located is the place of tax payment)	The provider of goods and services has the right to recharge the purchaser

(continued)

(*continued*)

Users	Method	Applicability
Individuals	The actual place of performance of the supply may be regarded as the place of tax, provided that all three conditions are met in the presence of both the supplier and the receiver of the service or asset, where the performance is readily identifiable and is consumed at the same time as the actual performance	Although in the context ofmobile commerce, mobile terminals and people have mobility;But three criteria can meet the challenge of "mobility"
	Where consumers often live	Habitual residence does not necessarily represent the location ofmobile commerce sales activity. It is recommended to judge by the place where mobile terminals are used, the place where mobile networks are often used, the address of receiving goods and the address of payment

Therefore, by combining modern technology (GPS positioning), the tax place can be judged in the following ways: (1) When the buyer is an enterprise, the direct use method, direct delivery method and recharge method are adopted. (2) When the buyer is an individual, the tax place can be the place where the seller, the buyer and the commodity are present at the same time, or the place where the consumer's mobile terminal is used, the place where the mobile network is often used, the receiving address, the payment address, etc.

At the same time, in the mobile commerce activities, intermediaries can grasp relatively comprehensive information related to the supply chain, and tax authorities can improve the tax collection rate by mastering comprehensive tax information. Therefore, it is suggested to strengthen the information exchange and sharing between tax authorities and intermediaries based on the current tax collection mode in China. In the context of mobile commerce, intermediaries can be divided into logistics, financial intermediaries, shopping platforms/apps, and operators/mobile terminal providers. By obtaining detailed rules of delivery and use of goods and services, using GPS positioning system to get specific transaction information, according to the above table, clear tax jurisdiction, Realize all receivables.

6 Epilogue

In the context of digital economy, the rapid development of mobile commerce brings opportunities that we cannot deny, but at the same time, it also brings problems such as BEPS, which has a negative impact on local finance. A perfect tax collection and administration system requires not only a sound tax collection and administration system, but also a modern tax collection and administration mode to match it. To realize tax collection and administration reform and integrate information and communication technology, only in this way can we boost the development of mobile commerce and give digital economy a blue sky!

Implementation of ABC Costing Systems Based on Technological Platforms as a Tool to Improve the Decision-Making Process in Credit Unions

Evaristo Navarro[1]([✉]), Alberto Mena[1], Enrique Otalora[1], Kennedy Hurtado[2], and Jisell Trejos[1]

[1] Universidad de la Costa, 58 Street #55 66, Barranquilla, Colombia
{enavarro3,amena4}@cuc.edu.co
[2] Universidad del Atlántico, 30 Street #8-49, Puerto Colombia, Colombia

Abstract. The implementation of new cost systems is extremely important for organizations, especially when they seek to take advantage of new technologies as a tool to improve processes and become more efficient and effective. This study is aimed at recognizing the implementation of ABC costing systems based on technological platforms as a tool for improving the decision-making process in savings and credit cooperatives. At the methodological level, a non-experimental and field research is presented, in which a Likert-type survey is applied to a group of savings and credit cooperatives located in the city of Barranquilla (Colombia). The analysis of the information provided by the applied instrument allowed to establish that for this type of entities the implementation of an activity-based costing system would mean a constant source of competitive advantages and value generation, because it is fully adjusted to the needs of the organization, allowing it to execute the calculation of the CIF with a higher degree of accuracy as a result of the identification of the activities necessary to execute the processes that generate value for the solidarity organization immersed in the cooperative movement.

Keywords: Costing systems · Decision-making process · Savings · Credit

1 Introduction

The implementation of new cost systems is extremely important for organizations, especially when they seek to take advantage of new technologies as a tool to improve processes and become more efficient and effective [1]. Authors emphasize that the importance of ABC cost systems lies in the process of allocating indirect manufacturing costs, since the methodology used under the framework of this cost system is oriented towards activities, processes, products and customers, a situation that generates information based on data that is close to reality, thus providing a high degree of reliability for the financial decision-making process [2].

The importance of implementing an activity-based costing system is based on the fact that by using this type of tool, the organization is broken down into basic processes in order to identify which activities are necessary to carry them out and thus know which of them are generating added value, which activities must be carried out in the production of a good and determine the cost of the activities consumed [3].

Regarding the technological factor, on the one hand, the new technologies based on software, IOT, ICT and 4.0 are very useful tools in any field in which they are applied. Likewise, with respect to the use and benefits of new technologies in the business and accounting environment, it has been shown that they represent benefits such as increased sales, since new technologies and applications generate greater possibilities of capturing new markets, not only in tangible spaces, but also in virtual markets [4].

Once this has been explained, it is mentioned that the present study is developed with the aim of recognizing the implementation of ABC costing systems based on technological platforms as a tool for improving the decision-making process in savings and credit cooperatives; which are located in the department of Atlántico (Colombia) and use software for the management of the ABC Cost System.

2   Theorical Framework

2.1   Decision Making Process

Decision making is an activity which is carried out by senior managers; Much of the success of organizations belonging to today's society is chaired by the ability of managers to make the right decisions at the right time, these decisions are based on models that facilitate a full understanding of the situation in which they are faced is facing the organization; Among the most representative models for decision making are the rational or classical model and non-rational models such as limited rationality, the incrementalist model and the garbage can model.

Classic or rational model for decision-making: For Fernández, the classic model is based on assumptions of an economic nature, because the decisions made by senior leaders will favor the alternative that is economically most advantageous for the organization [5].

Hellriegel and Slocum consider that the rational model for making decisions in the business environment is constituted in a process in which a series of systematized steps are carried out in order to select those alternatives that represent economic advantages for the organization tending to maximize organizational benefits; On the other hand, the rational model implies a broad definition of the problems involved in economic entities, an exhaustive process of gathering and analyzing the information which is exchanged between the entities belonging to the organization with a high degree of objectivity and precision [6]. The foregoing indicates that the rational model for making decisions bases its methodology on the following assumptions (Fig. 1).

2.2   Costing Systems Implementation

At this point, the implementation model of an activity-based cost system defined by Zapata will be taken as a reference, who determines that two stages are necessary in the process of establishing a cost management system based on the ABC model in an organization. Regardless of its nature and size [7].

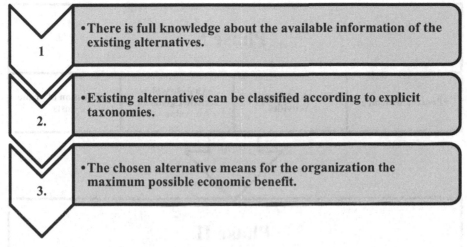

Fig. 1. Decision making assumptions.

Planning Stage: it can be affirmed that planning implies a process that is developed in a preliminary way, in which the parameters and procedures to be carried out in the execution of a job are established; Regarding the implementation of a cost model based on activities, this stage is based on the possibility that economic entities have to consider the feasibility and convenience within corporate processes, and determine the organization of the economic entity in terms of the cost management systems that are used in it and at the same time observe the scope that the use of this type of methodology will have in the context of the company considered individually. The illustration establishes the steps to follow in the planning process to implement a cost system based on activities [8].

Decisive stage: Zapata considers that the implementation or decisive stage will allow the economic entity to establish and maintain a cost system based on activities; the author refers that the process is carried out by executing two relevant phases in the process [7]. In the first instance, the organization must establish the structure of the processes that are part of the cycle of production, commercialization and administration of the economic entity, in order to determine which of them are generating value to the cost objects. Both phases are observed in the following figure (Fig. 2):

3 Material and Method

The present study is developed from the qualitative approach of the investigation with a non-experimental, field and descriptive design; in which, through a six-dimensional survey, recognizing the implementation of ABC costing systems based on technological platforms as a tool for improving the decision-making process in savings and credit cooperatives located in the city of Barranquilla (Colombia).

The sample consists of a total of 80 people who work in the financial and accounting area of credit and savings cooperatives that have management of technological tools

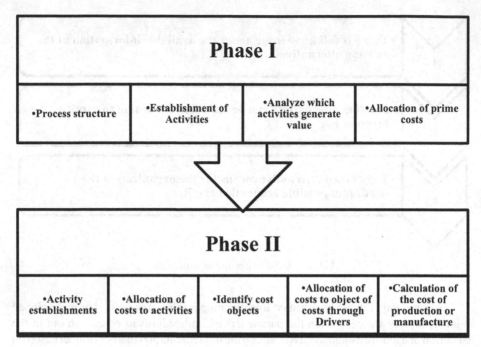

Fig. 2. Costing systems implementation phases.

focused on the ABC cost system. Descriptive statistics are used for the analysis process of the results based on the frequency and percentage of responses obtained on a Likert scale described below:

- Totally disagree.
- In disagreement.
- Neither agree nor disagree.
- Agree.
- Totally agree.

4 Results

The use of software for an ABC cost system is presented in solidarity organizations immersed in cooperatives as an excellent alternative with which decisions can be made with a high degree of efficiency and effectiveness, because it allows to provide data and truthful information related to with direct and indirect manufacturing costs quickly On the other hand, ABC cost system software allows showing the line of key processes that take place within organizations and the activities necessary for them, identifying the peaks and the generation of value in each phase.

In the field collection process towards the cooperatives, questions are addressed to the personnel with accounting functions within said organizations, who have knowledge about the application of the ABC cost system using the various technological tools available in the market.

From this exercise it is possible to determine that there is a degree of acceptance of the ABC cost systems supported by technological tools; especially in relation to the collection of information for decision-making within these institutions of the solidarity economy since they are digital systems adaptable to the reality of each organization. Providing truthful and agile data for the service offer of cooperatives becomes a differential factor with other types of tools (Table 1).

Table 1. There is full knowledge of the necessary activities within the cooperatives thanks to the ABC cost system

Alternatives	Frequency	Percentage
Totally disagree	24	30,0
In disagreement	26	32,5
Neither agree nor disagree	15	18,8
Agree	10	12,5
Totally agree	5	6,3
Total	**80**	**100,0**

From the previous table, it can be seen how 18.8% of those surveyed consider that the ABC cost system based on technological tools allows to know in an optimal way the processes that take place within the cooperatives, while 18.8% state indifference and 62.5% do not agree with this statement (Table 2).

Table 2. The allocation of the CIF considering the resources consumed by the activities generates value in the organization

Alternatives	Frequency	Percentage
Totally disagree	8	10,0
In disagreement	7	8,8
Neither agree nor disagree	9	11,3
Agree	41	51,2
Totally agree	15	18,8
Total	**80**	**100,0**

It can be seen how 70% of those surveyed agree that the allocation of the CIF considering the resources consumed by the activities generates value in the organization, while 11.3% show indifference in this regard and 18.8% disagree with that (Table 3).

According to the previous table, 72.5% of the accountants surveyed mention that the ABC cost system software adapts to the real needs of the cooperative, being versatile in the face of the challenges that these organizations face every day. In turn, 12.5%

Table 3. The ABC cost system software adapts to the real needs of the cooperative

Alternatives	Frequency	Percentage
Totally disagree	8	10,0
In disagreement	12	15,0
Neither agree nor disagree	10	12,5
Agree	40	50,0
Totally agree	10	12,5
Total	**80**	**100,0**

show indifference to this and 25% disagree with the adaptability of these computerized financial systems (Table 4).

Table 4. Having a list of the activities that generate value in the organization is key to assigning the CIF to each one

Alternatives	Frequency	Percentage
Totally disagree	13	16,3
In disagreement	5	6,3
Neither agree nor disagree	2	2,5
Agree	38	47,5
Totally agree	22	27,5
Total	**80**	**100,0**

Once the previous table has been reviewed, it stands out that 75% of all the subjects surveyed consider that having a list of the activities that generate value in the organization is key to assigning the CIF to each one, while 2, 5% mention that they neither agree nor disagree and 22.6% did not agree with the aforementioned statement (Table 5).

Given the statement that implementing a technological tool for the CIF cost system would generate valuable information for decision-making within the cooperatives, it is observed that 60% agree or totally agree, while 2.5% show indifference and 37.5% are not in favor of the aforementioned (Table 6).

As a last question, there is a question about whether the implementation of a cost system software based on activities provides a high degree of confidence in decision-making, where 65.2% of those surveyed agree, 5% neither agree nor disagree and 30% are not in favor of it.

Table 5. The implementation of a technological tool for the CIF cost system will generate valuable information for decision making.

Alternatives	Frequency	Percentage
Totally disagree	7	8,8
In disagreement	23	28,7
Neither agree nor disagree	2	2,5
Agree	28	35,0
Totally agree	20	25,0
Total	**80**	**100,0**

Table 6. The implementation of an activity-based cost system software provides a high degree of confidence in decision making.

Range	Frequency	Percentage
Totally disagree	14	17,5
In disagreement	10	12,5
Neither agree nor disagree	4	5,0
Agree	33	41,3
Totally agree	19	23,8
Total	**80**	**100,0**

5   Conclusions and Discussions

With the findings obtained, it can be denoted in the first instance that certainly the management and development processes within organizations have undergone highly significant changes in recent years [9], where in this case new technologies become effective tools for the success of organizations from communication processes to the financial and accounting field [4, 9].

For an organization, having financial management systems allows an opening to growth and development in the face of globalization, which in the case of countries like Colombia, the relatively recent and late adoption of IFRS has been able to represent a step towards the commercial integration of companies and colombian entities in the global context [10, 11].

However, in the case of savings and credit cooperatives as actors in the solidarity economy, it is essential to have tools that allow them to keep up with the global context and that they can make the best decisions in their daily work as organizations. In this way, the findings allow us to observe how the implementation of an ABC cost system based on a technological tool allows the personnel in charge of said work to have the information for the decisions that must be made in a more agile and transparent way.

Various studies show how the leap from organizational financial systems to technological tools designed for this management greatly increases the effectiveness and competitiveness of organizations [12]. Various studies, in turn, mention the small amount of this type of software in the market [13], which is why the generation of research for the development of new applications in this field is recommended. The development of future research that can measure the effectiveness of these systems and compare them with each other is expected in the future.

References

1. Williams Piedra, T., Sánchez Batista, A.: La gestión de costos ABC y su impacto en la administración de justicia. Revista Cubana de Finanzas y Precios **4**(4), 96–114 (2020)
2. Ramos Farroñan, E.V., Huacchillo Pardo, L.A., Portocarrero Medina, Y.D.: El sistema de costos ABC como estrategia para la toma de decisiones empresarial. Revista Universidad y Sociedad **12**(2), 178–183 (2020)
3. Cervelo, A.: La gestión estratégica de costos: ABC-ABM y la necesidad de otros modelos de costos para la toma de decisiones. Revista iberoamericana de contabilidad de gestión **17**(33), 117–133 (2019)
4. Samper, M.G., Florez, D.G., Borre, J.R., Ramirez, J.: Industry 4.0 for sustainable supply chain management: drivers and barriers. Procedia Comput. Sci. **203**, 644–650 (2022)
5. Fernandez, E.: Introduccion a la administracion. Universitat Politecnica de Valencia, Spain (2005)
6. Hellriegel, D., Slocum, J.: Comportamiento organizacional. Cegage Laerning Editores, Mexico (2009)
7. Zapata, P.: Contabilidad de costos: Herramienta para la toma de decisiones. Mc Graw Hill, Colombia (2007)
8. Jaramillo, S.A., Delgado, J.A.T.: Planeación estratégica y su aporte al desarrollo empresarial. Espíritu emprendedor TES **3**(1), 64–73 (2019)
9. Mendoza-Ocasal, D., Navarro, E., Ramírez, J., García-Tirado, J.: Subjective well-being and its correlation with happiness at work and quality of work life: an organizational vision. Pol. J. Manag. Stud. **26** (2022)
10. Jaimes, R.: Sostenibilidad financiera para las empresas del sector panificador de Pamplona, norte de Santander. Colombia. Dictamen Libre **28**, 33–47 (2021)
11. Parales, J.A., Ramírez, J.A.: Análisis de indicadores de endeudamiento y solvencia enla convergencia a Normas Internacionales de Información Financiera (NIIF) en Colombia. Conocimiento Global **6**(2), 89–102 (2021)
12. Ogundajo, G., Ogunode, O., Awoniyi, O., Iwala, A.: usage of accounting software on cost control of listed deposit money banks in Nigeria. Int. J. Manag. Stud. Soc. Sci. Res. **4** (2022)
13. Alsayegh, M.F.: Activity based costing around the world: adoption, implementation, outcomes and criticism. J. Account. Finan. Emerg. Econ. **6**(1), 251–262 (2020)

Virtual Reality Training System Using an Autonomy Agent for Learning Hospitality Skills of a Retail Store

Akimi Oyanagi[1]([✉]), Kazuma Aoyama[1,2], Kenichiro Ito[1],
Tomohiro Amemiya[1,2], and Michitaka Hirose[3]

[1] Virtual Reality Educational Research Center, The University of Tokyo,
Tokyo, Japan
{oyanagi,aoyama,ito,amemiya}@vr.u-tokyo.ac.jp
[2] Graduate School of Information Science and Technology, The University of Tokyo,
Tokyo, Japan
[3] Research Center for Advanced Science and Technology, The University of Tokyo,
Tokyo, Japan
hirose@vr.u-tokyo.ac.jp

Abstract. Training systems are well known as one practical usage for Virtual Reality. Previous works of hospitality services have mainly focused on some situations which target customers who are face-to-face or whose position is located at their seats in a store. However, there are some types of customer service businesses, such as retail stores, which should serve customers who patrol a store to find desired products. In this study, we developed a VR training system in which customer agents autonomously form a path based on the location of product shelves in the VR store and patrol those paths. We aim to facilitate learning some skills for the hospitality service of a retail store, such as understanding the entire store's perspective, serving customers in need, and not obstructing their paths. Customer agents patrol paths and interact with products by finite state machine system. If agents have an interest during patrolling, they look for shoppers (i.e., trainees) to ask about the location of products. In this paper, we described the autonomy agent and serving systems for trainees in detail.

Keywords: Training Simulator · Immersive Virtual Reality

1 Introduction

Service industries such as hospitality, food and beverage, tourism, and entertainment are major industries in many countries. Therefore, it is necessary to improve customer service skills to provide high-quality services. Generally, employees need on-the-job training to enhance customer service skills, which their supervisors train them through actual work. However, providing on-the-job training when hiring new workers is difficult because of the high financial, time, and human costs involved in providing each individual with the on-the-job training necessary to maintain quality. Thus, there is a dilemma that employers force employees to engage in actual work as soon as possible because they can not pay some costs, even though the service industry wants to train well.

VR training simulators have attracted attention as a solution to this problem, and various positive effects have been reported [1–4]. In recent years, with the low cost of VR equipment and technological developments, training systems utilizing VR technology have been researched and developed in various industries [5]. VR training simulators effectively solve the above limitations because they do not require instructors or monetary costs for the necessary on-site situations. In particular, training simulators using VR technology can more faithfully reproduce work content through immersion and affordance [6]. For this reason, previous works have developed various training simulators for special skills training, such as the industry, disaster response, and military [7–12].

In the service industry, training simulators have also been proposed for medical care, tourism, and education [13–16]. In recent years, some researchers have also studied training simulators for customer service. For example, it includes restaurant customer service and airport ground staff [17,18]. They have assumed the situations when customers are served face-to-face, such as at a cash register, or when multiple customers seated at a particular table are served in parallel, such as in a restaurant. On the other hand, we could also assume that staff serves customers who patrol a retail store to find the desired product. In that case, the simulator requires employees to appropriately provide service to them(e.g., not blocking the path of the customer, promptly going to serve them if they are looking for staff or in trouble).

However, to the authors' knowledge, there have yet to be studies of VR training simulators to improve the skills of serving such autonomously moving customers. Therefore, this study proposes and constructs a VR training simulator to improve customer service skills in retail stores. This paper describes the details and performance of the developed system. Section 2 summarizes previous studies on training simulators and explains the position and contribution of this study. Section 3 discusses the requirements definition of the system proposed in this study. Section 4 summarizes the implemented functions. Section 5 provides a summary. Section 6 summarizes this study, its limitations, and future research.

2   Related Works

Training simulators have been the subject of product development and research for systems enhancing special skills. Users use training simulators in situations that are difficult to replicate in the real world, such as fire, or the limitations of training in the real world, which require skilled staff playing the role of teacher and extensive equipment. Several studies have shown that training simulators can train skills more effectively using immersive VR equipment. It can more faithfully reproduce real-life situations because of immersion and affordance with the environment [6]. Furthermore, the immersive Virtual Reality has more practical effects than traditional media, such as video displays regarding knowledge acquisition and increased self-efficacy [3]. Lui et al. has reported no significant differences between VR and physical space training [2]. In addition, VR-based training is practical for brand attitudes [4].

VR training simulators have been researched and developed for various fields. Many VR training simulators have been developed, mainly to train special skills. For example, previous studies have reported improving skills in driving techniques, machine assembly, underground excavation, and welding operations [7–10]. In addition to exceptional skills training, previous studies have also conducted disaster preparedness. Li et al. reported a training simulator that enables workers to cope with an earthquake without injury [11]. Studies in the service industry aim to transfer medical skills, and VR simulators for suturing, CPR, and other skills have been reported [12,13].

These are all in the construction industry, skills training, and service industries that do not require in-person customer service. On the other hand, in recent years, research on VR training simulators for the hospitality industry has shown promise. For example, in the field of tourism and lodging, they are attracting attention as practical training to help employees acquire guest interaction skills [14]. In education, studies have used collaborative immersive VR platforms to improve classroom management skills [15]. Otsuki et al. proposed and developed a system that can reproduce the customer service work (order taking, cooking, and serving food) in a restaurant in VR and serve multiple customers in parallel [16]. They focus on "awareness" and "priority order judgment", which are difficult to train in an authentic restaurant. Conventional customer service training simulators use interactive agents, but a teacher role is necessary for the actual work to understand the students' behavior. In our previous study, we developed a collaborative VR training simulator to improve the customer service skills of airport ground staff in booking airplane tickets. We used facial capture transmitted facial expressions via a network to train the delicate subtleties of customer service attitudes in the hospitality industry [18]. In addition, Tanikawa et al. also prepare scenarios in which the agents deal with agents with various emotional expressions to train them to deal calmly with customers who are complainers. Furthermore, they monitor the user's biometric information when dealing with the complainer and provide feedback so that the user can deal with the complainer calmly [17].

Thus, previous studies have reported training simulators dealing with face-to-face customer service and multiple customers in parallel. In the case of face-to-face customer service, it is possible to train employees with a skilled trainer, even in physical space. On the other hand, the customer service industry, which deals with many customers, can only be replicated in actual training with the cooperation of customer actors. In the Ohtsuki et al. study, his application can handle many customers in parallel, but the customers are seated (i.e., they are in a fixed position). In retail stores, customers patrol to find desired products (i.e., their positions are updated in real-time). In addition, unlike a restaurant, where the retail customer service business only responds to orders, retail customers behave differently depending on their purchasing intentions and personality traits. The retailer needs to be aware of customer attitudes and respond accordingly. For example, if customers show strong interest in a particular product, they should be encouraged to try it on or bring other product colors from the backyard.

3   Requirements

This study aims to develop a training system for proficiency in customer service skills in retail stores. This section defines the requirements to achieve this objective as follows.

3.1   Customer Agents Autonomously Stroll Around the Store

The application generates the agent at a predefined store visit point. Then the agent strolls the store in search of the desired product.

3.2   Personal Characteristics of Agents and Their Behavior During Strolling

In this paper, we define three types of agents: 1) those with high purchase intent, 2) those with low purchase intent, and 3) those with unknown purchase intent. The high purchase intent type is more willing to walk the center of the store to look at different products and take them. The low purchase intent type is reluctant to purchase a product, as they stare at the product shelves and show no vital interest in it or do not walk around the center of the store very much. The unknown purchase intent type falls between the above two, exploring the store through random routes and using dynamic behaviors, such as picking up a product, and passive behavior, such as just looking at the product shelves.

3.3   Interaction Between Staff (Trainee) and Customer Agents

We summarized the staff's customer service actions toward the customer agents; 1) Staff should not obstruct customer agents. 2) Customer agents look for staff while strolling the store to ask about the location of merchandise. The staff has to serve the customer agent in this case. 3): Then, the customer asks for the location of the merchandise, and the staff should guide the customer to the merchandise shelf. 4): If the customer shows interest in a product, the staff should sales talk and encourage them to purchase.

3.4   Scoring Function for Customer Service Attitude

Based on 3.3, the scoring function awarded points for appropriate customer service behavior while playing the simulator and deducted points for inappropriate responses.

4   Prototype System

We developed our system with Unity Engine 2019.4.36f1. We used The Universal RenderPipeline, officially recommended as lightweight for Unity's graphics rendering pipeline. In this paper, we located 3D models of an apparel store as a retail store from the Unity Asset Store. We show images of the overall view of the VR space, the first-person view from the user when facing a customer agent, and its overhead view in Fig. 1. Our system can adapt other 3D models to any type of customer service business, not limited to apparel stores, as long as it is in a form that allows the user to walk around the store. This section describes the functions designed and implemented to meet the requirements described in Sect. 3.1 and the innovations implemented to make the system more faithful to reality.

Fig. 1. Images of Overview and Perspective from Users

4.1   Agents that Autonomously Roam Around the Store

Before users play with this system, the developer must place the store entrance and product shelves in advance. The store entrance is where the customer agents come to the store. We implemented the manager AI to oversee the customer agents; It can set the maximum of customer who comes to the store and the timing of the next visit. It periodically makes the customer agents if the number of agents in the store is not out of the maximum number of customers. A store visit corresponds to so-called spawning, which in game industry terminology means the appearance of a character in a space. When a customer agent visits a store, it forms a patrol path based on the location of the product shelves. The formation of a patrol route is a random addition to the List collection from all previously placed product shelves. The product shelves are assigned a probability of being set as a patrol route depending on the customer type; as described in Sect. 3, in this case, users with high purchase intent are more likely to choose the product shelves located inside the store, while users with low purchase intent are more likely to choose the product shelves located outside the store. The NavMesh Agent is a Unity AI function that enables the calculation and movement of routes to a given destination.

4.2   Customer Agent Behavior

The customer agent has three states: Strolling State, Interacting with merchandise State and Looking for Staff State. We implemented these transitions with a finite state machine algorithm. When the customer agent reaches a merchandise shelf while strolling, it plays an animation of looking at or taking up the merchandise. Customers with high purchase intent behave as if they are interested in the merchandise through these actions. After finishing the animation, the agent moves again to the following merchandise shelf in the list on the route. It continues until the end of the list, and if the staff does not serve, the agent returns home (i.e., It returns to the store visit position, and manager AI destroys it). When the customer agent reaches one merchandise shelf, it probabilistically transitions to a state where it looks for staff to ask where the desired product is. In this state, the agent abandons the route and begins walking to a random location within a 5-meter radius of itself as its next destination in order to look for staff. When it reaches the destination, it again follows the same procedure to determine the next destination and continues moving. If a customer agent finds a staff in this state, it approaches the staff and asks for the product's location.

4.3   Interaction Between Staff and Customer Agent

The trainee wears a VRHMD and interacts with the VR environment. In doing so, the trainee manipulates the staff avatar. The avatar utilized Final IK, a Unity asset that allows character models to manipulate with Inverse Kinematics. Many VR applications use this asset for manipulating an avatar. A previous study has reported that when a user manipulates an avatar synchronously, the self-perception for that avatar becomes stronger [19]. In this prototype, we solved inverse Kinematics based on the tracked head-mounted display and the positions of both controllers to update the avatar's upper body movements. Final IK automatically updates the lower body motion based on the center of gravity of the character model. The user can move in the direction keyed in using the actual walk and the controller. In addition, the user can hold items on the shelves by pressing the trigger on the controller.

  As mentioned, if the customer agent in the Look For Staff state finds a trainee, the customer agent approach and asks for the location of the merchandise. In response, the appropriate customer service behavior is for the trainee to lead the agent to the desired product shelf and hand the product to the agent. In this case, the staff has to keep the distance between the agent and them within a specific range. The scoring function deducts points for inappropriate behavior if the agent leaves the customer behind. In addition, the trainee can call out to the customer agent who is interacting with the product and perform a sales action to ask about the product the customer is seeking. Currently, the staff can interact with the customer using actual voice through the speech recognition system. For speech recognition, we used Unity's default built-in speech recognition engine. We show An overview diagram of the autonomous agent in Fig. 2.

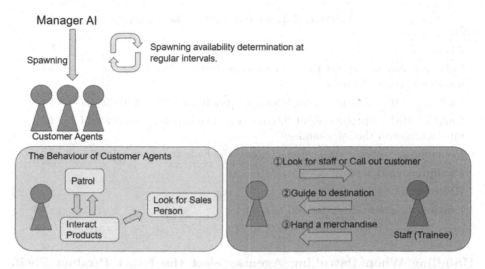

Fig. 2. Summary of autonomous agent movements and customer service interactions

4.4 Scoring System

Through this training simulator, we have developed a function to score whether users have mastered customer service skills. Our system adds or subtracts when the user performs the actions in Table 1. The optimal distance to talk to a customer agent was the social distance (2–3.5 m), which is the distance at which strangers talk to each other, and the correct answer was to maintain the social distance.

4.5 Other Functions

In addition to the above requirements, I will describe the devices implemented to make the customer agent's movements faithful to reality and for the system to work well.

Looking at a Merchandise Shelf While Walking. We used Look Animator, a Unity Asset that allows the character model's head to look in the gazing direction and the weighted bones to rotate in consideration of the gazing direction (i.e., not only the head but also the bones from the neck to the spine are turned in the gazing direction). (i.e., the head and the bones from the neck to the spine are oriented in the gazing direction).

Table 1. Actions and points to be scored

Actions	Points
Inducing customer agents to a merchandise shelf and handing merchandise over to them	30
Calling out the customer agent from appropriate directions and distances	10
Calling out the customer agent interested in merchandise (i.e., State of interacting with the merchandise)	10
Preferentially serving the customer agent who finds trainee in advance	5
Disrupting agent's move	−5
Keep disrupting agent's move	−20
Leaving the customer agent during inducing	−10

Handling When Patrolling Agents Select the Exact Product Shelf. When only functions up to 3 are implemented, when patrolling agents select the exact product shelf, the agent who reached the shelf first will stay there, and other agents will push the agent out. Therefore, the system was set up so several people could be assigned to each product shelf. How many people can be assigned can be changed as a parameter. If a shelf is already full when looking for the next patrol point, the agent will ignore that shelf and move on to the next shelf.

5   Conclusion

In this study, we developed a prototype of a training system for the customer service industry in retail stores to improve service skills, such as understanding customers' location and acquiring customer service skills. In this report, we defined three main requirements and implemented: 1) customer agents strolling in a retail store, 2) their behavior (product interaction, purchase intent), and 3) staff (trainee) customer service functions. In the developed system, customer agents generate a route based on the location of merchandise in the store (e.g., product shelves) when they visit the store. In addition, depending on the agent's predefined purchase intent, it will take different patterns of route formation and exhibit different behaviors toward the products (e.g., just staring at the shelves or picking up the products). The agent probabilistically transitions to a staff-seeking state each time it advances one route. The trainee provides customer service to the staff-seeking customers by calling them from the appropriate direction and guiding them to the product. For this series of procedures, we developed a training simulator that gives points for appropriate behavior and performs self-scoring after the play.

6   Limitation and Future Work

The system implemented in this paper has yet to be evaluated by the staff working in retail shops. Therefore, some specifications may be required before we actually operate the system. In addition, several points still need to be refined regarding functionality. In many cases, there are some staff members in a retail store, and it is necessary to coordinate with other staff members. Since purchase intent constantly fluctuates, customers come to actively stroll the store even though they have a low purchase intent.

We plan to improve that the manager AI increases or decreases the maximum number of spawns and spawning interval to make the task more demanding when it decides trainees have become accustomed to the current task. In addition, with the current implementation, customer agents would be crowded together, for example, when autonomous agents try to pass through a narrow corridor simultaneously. It is not natural behavior in real life.

Furthermore, large-scale language models (LLM) (e.g., Chat GPT) attracted attention as models for generating natural dialogues. This AI agent can generate personality, purpose, and flexible dialogue sentences. In previous works, the agent operates according to a pre-loaded scenario [17]. By incorporating a large-scale language model AI into the agents of this system, it may be possible to develop a training system that represents a variety of customers and more closely resembles actual operations. Staff actively involve sales talks with customers in some occupations, such as apparel stores selling casual clothing. LLM can generate response sentences corresponding to an explanation of clothing trends or introduce limited-edition merchandise. That means it can reproduce chatting regarding a series of procedures for introducing trendy products or determining whether a product suits the customer. In the future, these functions will be expanded and refined.

Acknowledgement. This work was supported by Council for Science, Technology and Innovation, "Cross-ministerial Strategic Innovation Promotion Program (SIP), Big-data and AIenabled Cyberspace Technologies" (funding agency: NEDO).

References

1. Renganayagalu, S., Mallam, S.C., Nazir, S.: Effectiveness of VR head mounted displays in professional training: a systematic review. Technol. Knowl. Learn. **26**(4), 999–1041 (2021). https://doi.org/10.1007/s10758-020-09489-9
2. Lui, T.-W., Goel, L.: Learning effectiveness of 3D virtual reality in hospitality training: a situated cognitive perspective. J. Hosp. Tour. Technol. **13**(3), 441–460 (2022)
3. Meyer, O.A., Omdahl, M.K., Makransky, G.: Investigating the effect of pre-training when learning through immersive virtual reality and video: a media and methods experiment. Comput. Educ. **140**, 103603 (2019)
4. Leung, X.Y., Chen, H., Chang, W., Mhlanga, L.: Is VR game training more effective for hospitality employees? A longitudinal experiment. Tour. Manag. Perspect. **44**, 101020 (2022)

5. Radhakrishnan, U., Koumaditis, K., Chinello, F.: A systematic review of immersive virtual reality for industrial skills training. Behav. Inf. Technol. **40**, 1310–1339 (2021)
6. Dalgarno, B., Lee, M.J.W.: What are the learning afordances of 3-D virtual environments? Br. J. Edu. Technol. **41**(1), 10–32 (2010)
7. Lee, W.-S., Kim, J.-H., Cho, J.-H.: A driving simulator as a virtual reality tool. In: Proceedings IEEE International Conference on Robotics and Automation, pp. 71–76 (1998)
8. Palmas, F., Labode, D., Plecher, D, A., Klinker, G.: Comparison of a gamified and non-gamified virtual reality training assembly task. In: Proceedings of the 11th International Conference on Virtual Worlds and Games for Serious Applications (VS-Games), pp. 1–8 (2019)
9. Zhang, H.: Head-mounted display-based intuitive virtual reality training system for the mining industry. Int. J. Min. Sci. Technol. **27**(4), 717–722 (2017)
10. Papakostas, C., Troussas, C., Krouska, A., Sgouropoulou, C.: User acceptance of augmented reality welding simulator in engineering training. Educ. Inf. Technol. **27**, 791–817 (2021)
11. Li, C., Liang, W., Quigley, C., Zhao, Y., Yu, L.-F.: Earthquake safety training through virtual drills. IEEE Trans. Vis. Comput. Graph. **23**(4), 1275–1284 (2017)
12. Li, L., et al.: Application of virtual reality technology in clinical medicine. Am. J. Transl. Res. **9**(9), 3867–3880 (2017)
13. Almousa, O., et al.: Virtual reality simulation technology for cardiopulmonary resuscitation training: an innovative hybrid system with haptic feedback. Simul. Gaming **50**(1), 6–22 (2019)
14. Nayyar, A., Mahapatra, B., Le, D., Suseendran, G.: Virtual reality (VR) & augmented reality (AR) technologies for tourism and hospitality industry. Int. J. Eng. Technol. **7**(2.21), 156–160 (2018)
15. Lugrin, J.-L., Oberdorfer, S., Latoschik, M.E., Wittmann, A., Seufert, C., Grafe, S.: Vrassisted vs video-assisted teacher training. In: Proceedings of the 25th IEEE Conference on Virtual Reality and 3D User Interfaces (VR) (2018)
16. Otsuki, M., Okuma, T.: Service skills training in restaurants using virtual reality. In: SA 2021 Posters: SIGGRAPH Asia 2021 Posters, Article No. 26, pp. 1–2 (2021)
17. Tanikawa, T., Shiozaki, K., Ban, Y., Aoyama, K., Hirose, M.: Semi-automatic reply avatar for VR training system with adapted scenario to trainee's status. In: Stephanidis, C., et al. (eds.) HCII 2021. LNCS, vol. 13095, pp. 350–355. Springer, Cham (2021). https://doi.org/10.1007/978-3-030-90963-5_26
18. Oyanagi, A., Aoyama, K., Ohmura, R., Tanikawa, T., Hirose, M.: Training simulator for service industry using virtual reality environment. JVRST **25**(1), 78–85 (2020)
19. Slater, M., Pérez Marcos, D., Ehrsson, H., Sanchez-Vives, M.V.: Inducing illusory ownership of a virtual body. Front. Neurosci. **3**, 214–220 (2009)

Effects of the Conversation and Recommendation Mechanism on Chatbots' Recommendation Effectiveness

Xixian Peng[1,2], Lingyi Zhou[1,2], Qingchan Tang[1], and Yuliang Liu[3(✉)]

[1] Department of Data Science and Engineering Management, School of Management,
Zhejiang University, Hangzhou 310058, China
pengxx@zju.edu.cn
[2] Neuromanagement Lab, Zhejiang University, Hangzhou 310058, China
[3] Institute of Artificial Intelligence and Big Data Application, GIIT, Nanning, Guangxi, China
25087137@qq.com

Abstract. This paper delves into the realm of human-chatbot interaction and aims to enhance consumers' experience with chatbots in products recommendation. Through a situational experimental study, we examine the interaction effect of chatbots' conversational interactivity and recommended product relevance on recommendation effectiveness. The results indicate that when recommended product relevance is high, conversational interactivity has a positive effect on recommendation effectiveness, while this effect is reversed when recommended product relevance is low. Moreover, we intend to further examine the emotional appeal and expectations discrepancy consumers form with chatbots in a future study to explain the interplay between conversational interactivity and product relevance.

Keywords: Chatbot · Conversational interactivity · Product relevance · Emotional appeal · Expectations discrepancy

1 Introduction

In recent years, the development of artificial intelligence (AI) technology has led to a significant transformation in various fields, and people's lives are gradually shifting toward a more intelligent direction. One major breakthrough is the emergence of intelligent customer services or AI chatbots. According to the report by StraitRsearch in 2022[1], the global chatbot market growth is projected to reach USD 3.62 Billion by 2030, growing at a CAGR of 23.9%. Chatbots offer lower costs and timely responses compared to traditional customer service, without the need for any human intervention. In today's fast-paced world, this is particularly useful for e-commerce companies that receive a large volume of customer inquiries on a daily basis. Therefore, it's not surprising that chatbot design as well as its influences on consumer behavior have become a key focus of research and development in the e-commerce industry.

---

[1] Chatbot Market Growth is projected to reach USD 3.62 (globenewswire.com).

© The Author(s), under exclusive license to Springer Nature Switzerland AG 2023
P. Zaphiris et al. (Eds.): HCII 2023, LNCS 14060, pp. 493–501, 2023.
https://doi.org/10.1007/978-3-031-48060-7_38

One consistent finding of previous chatbot literature is that conversational interactivity can positively influence user engagement and perceptions of chatbots (Go and Sundar 2019; Schuetzler et al. 2018; Schuetzler et al. 2020). Conversational interactivity refers to the degree to which responses in a dialogue are interrelated and dependent on previous dialogues (Sundar et al. 2014). However, while prior work has examined the role of chatbots' conversational interactivity by focusing on the effects on use intention or acceptance, little exploration and validation of the role of chatbots' conversational interactivity in the scenario of product recommendation have been conducted. The same report by StraitRsearch[2] predicts that the product recommendation landscape of chatbots will acquire the maximum market. Against these backgrounds, the current research aims to examine the impact of a chatbot's conversational interactivity on recommendation effectiveness when recommending products with different levels of relevance. Specifically, drawing on the Computers Are Social Actors (CASA) paradigm and expectations discrepancy theory (Nass et al. 1994; Bhattacherjee 2001), we hypothesize that chatbots' conversational interactivity and recommended products' relevance level will jointly influence consumers' emotions and expectations, ultimately affecting the final recommendation effectiveness.

To examine the proposed effects, a 2 * 2 between-subjects experiment (Study 1) is conducted and the results support the interaction effect between chatbots' conversational interactivity and product relevance on recommendation effectiveness. Study 2 is proposed to delve deeper into the mechanism of consumers' psychological changes during product recommendations by chatbots, focusing on consumers' emotions and expectations. The findings of this research will provide valuable insights into the literature on the design of chatbots as well as recommendation systems.

2 Theoretical Backgrounds and Hypothesis Development

2.1 Chatbots' Conversational Interactivity in Product Recommendation

Conversational interactivity refers to the degree to which responses in a dialogue are interrelated and dependent on previous dialogues (Sundar et al. 2014). Highly interactive conversations can be conceptualized as personalized and human-like interactions, creating a back-and-forth dialogue that resembles a conversation between two individuals. Specifically, when engaged in a conversation, if the other party's response is related to the content of the previous dialogue, the dialogue process can be considered interactive. Although prior studies have examined the positive effects of chatbots' conversational interactivity on users' experience and attitudes toward agents (Go and Sundar 2019; Schuetzler et al. 2018), little research examines this effect in the context of product recommendation.

The self-reference effect (Rogers et al. 1977) proposes that individuals are more likely to be persuaded by memory information associated with the self. The explanation for this phenomenon is that self-relevance stimulates people to process information in detail, enhancing the persuasive effect. In the context of ad recommendation, the self-reference effect explains how an ad's image and textual content affects its persuasiveness.

---

[2] Chatbot Market Growth is projected to reach USD 3.62 (globenewswire.com).

In our context, when a chatbot has highly conversational interactivity, it is considered to be higher anthropomorphic and has stronger communication and response capabilities. Furthermore, according to the self-reference effect, individuals are more likely to be persuaded by memory information associated with the self, which indicates that when the recommended products align with the consumers' needs, consumers will feel more personal relevance and more willing to accept chatbots' recommendation. As explained in more depth later, when the recommended product is relatively irrelevant, consumers' expectations may be disconfirmed, which will weaken or even deteriorate the positive impact of conversational interactivity. Thus, this study hypothesized that:

H1: The positive effect of chatbot's interactivity on recommendation effectiveness depends on product relevance such that the effect is stronger (vs. weaker) when the chatbot recommends highly (vs. weakly) relevant products.

2.2 Consumers' Emotional Appeal to Chatbots

According to the Computers Are Social Actors (CASA) paradigm (Nass et al. 1994), when interacting with computers, humans will consciously pay attention to their social entities (e.g., gender), ascribe a personality to a computer depending on its interaction and generate emotional appeal. Emotional appeal focuses on the fun, playfulness, and emotional value generated by consumers when interacting with chatbots (Babin et al. 1994).

Indeed, several studies have found that consumers enjoyed the experience more when they communicate with more human-like agents. Wang et al. (2007) showed that the social cues of the virtual image can induce people's perception of the sociality of the website, thereby increasing happiness and shopping value. Yang et al. (2013) demonstrated that the level of consumers' intrinsic motivation (enjoyment) is related to the degree of interaction on social media sites. In our context, consumers feel chatbots with high conversational interactivity as human-like. Recommending relevant products is consistent with this human-like image and thus enhance the positive effect of conversational interactivity on emotional appeal. Therefore, we propose that:

H2: When recommending highly relevant products, chatbots' conversational interactivity increases consumers' emotional appeal, which, in turn, enhances recommendation effectiveness.

2.3 Expectations Discrepancy Theory

Before using a product or service, customers develop expectations about the performance of a product, brand, or company. After use, customers evaluate the target's performance and compare it to their pre-encounter expectations (Cadotte et al. 1987). When the target's performance fails to meet their expectations, customers' attitudes change, and this negative variance is called expectation discrepancy (Sundar and Noseworthy 2016). The reasons for the discrepancy of expectations are: higher expectations before use, and poor performance after use. Researches have shown that behaviors that violate expectations not only damage customer satisfaction (Oliver 1980), but also negatively affect subsequent outcomes, including attitudes toward the firm and purchase intentions (Cardello and Sawyer 1992).

Crolic et al. (2021) found that the expectations discrepancy caused by inflated pre-encounter expectations of chatbot efficacy leads to a negative impact on subsequent purchase intentions. Adapting the expectations discrepancy theory into our context, consumers will develop more expectations for a chatbot when the chatbot has higher conversational interactivity, and as a result, if the chatbot recommends an irrelevant product, consumers will generate greater expectations discrepancy, which negatively affects the final recommendation effectiveness. Hence, we propose the following hypothesis:

H3: When recommending weakly relevant products, chatbots' conversational interactivity increases the extent of consumers' expectations discrepancy, which, in turn, reduces recommendation effectiveness.

The conceptual framework is depicted in Fig. 1.

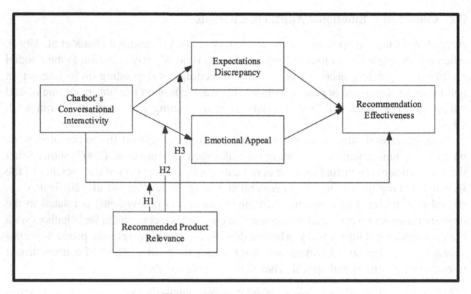

Fig. 1. Conceptual Framework

3 Empirical Overview

We will test our theoretical model through two studies. In Study 1, we will examine the interaction effect of chatbots' conversational interactivity and product relevance on recommendation effectiveness (H1). Study 2 will repeat the finding of Study 1 and test the underlying process mechanisms of emotion and expectation (H2 and H3).

3.1 Study 1

Participants and Design. Study 1 adopted a 2 (conversational interactivity: high vs. low) × 2 (product relevance: high vs. low) between-subjects design. 179 students from a university in China (M_{age} = 23.1 years; female = 60.3%) completed this study for monetary compensation. In the experiment, subjects were randomly assigned to one group.

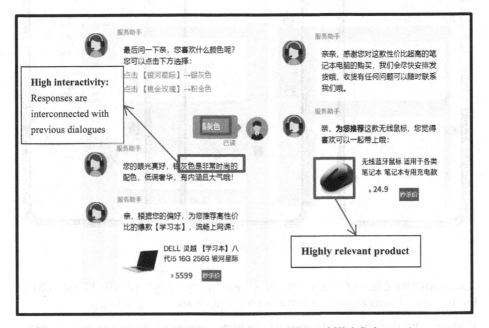

Fig. 2. Experiment Interface (High Interactivity and High Relevance)

Procedure. In this study, we designed an online chatbot and simulated a real online shopping process. Before the experiment started, we described the shopping scene to the participants: in order to meet the needs of daily learning, a laptop computer needs to be purchased, you need to communicate with chatbots to buy the laptop. Then, the participants started to chat with a chatbot. The chatbot introduced itself and asked customers about the laptop's usage, color, and memory. The interactivity of the chatbot was reflected in the feedback based on the customer's answers. For example, when the customer chose silver gray laptop, the highly interactive chatbot replied, "Your taste is really good! Silver gray is a very fashionable color". While low interactive chatbot replied, "Ok, we have known your need". After the customer completed the purchase, the chatbot recommended relevant products (see Fig. 2 and 3).

Measurements. We collected measures of conversational interactivity, product relevance, and recommendation effectiveness (purchase intention). The measurement items were assessed on a 7-point Likert-scale ranging from "strongly disagree" to "strongly agree". The conversational interactivity measurements included five items such as "I feel like I am having an active conversation with the chatbot" (Detenber et al. 2008). The product relevance measures were based on Zeng et al. (2009) and included three items ("relevant", "important" and "means a lot"). The recommendation effectiveness

Fig. 3. Experiment Procedure

consisted of three items ("likely", "willing" and "ready to buy") (Roy and Naidoo 2021). Finally, participants responded to background questions (e.g., gender).

Pretests. We first conducted a pretest to validate our conversational interactivity manipulation with 30 participants who received monetary compensation. Results showed that the conversational interactivity in the low interactivity group (M = 3.58, SD = 0.94) was significantly lower than that in the high interactivity group (M = 5.48, SD = 0.90, p < 0.01), indicating a successful manipulation. Then we conducted another pretest to choose the products related to the laptops. 32 participants completed this pretest and results showed that the relevance between laptop and wireless mouse (M = 6.03, SD = 1.25) and phone case (M = 2.61, SD = 2.25) had a significant difference (p < 0.05). Therefore, the two objects were selected as the products recommended by chatbots.

Results. A 2 (conversational interactivity: high vs. low) × 2 (product relevance: high vs. low) analysis of variance (ANOVA) revealed a significant main effect of product relevance (F = 26.857, p < 0.01) and no main effect of conversational interactivity (F = 0.600, p = 0.440) on recommendation effectiveness, both subsumed by a significant two-way interaction (F = 11.683, p < 0.01). Specifically, in low product relevance group, conversational interactivity had a negative effect on recommendation effectiveness (M_{high} = 2.38, SD = 1.58; M_{low} = 3.32, SD = 1.65, p = 0.008). In contrast, when recommending highly relevant products, recommendation effectiveness in high interactivity group was significantly higher than that in low interactivity group (M_{high} = 4.31, SD = 1.47; M_{low} = 3.73, SD = 1.22, p = 0.043) (see Fig. 4). Thus, H1 is supported.

Discussion. The results of study 1 provide support to H1, which indicates the interaction effect of conversational interactivity and product relevance is significant. Specifically,

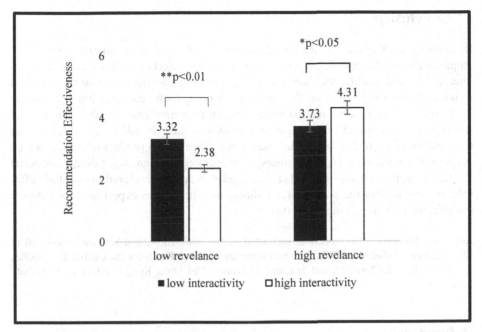

Fig. 4. Interaction Effect of Conversational Interactivity and Product Relevance

when the recommended product relevance is high, conversational interactivity has a positive impact on the recommendation effectiveness, and this effect becomes negative when the degree of relevance is low. In study 2, we will explain this effect in more depth.

3.2 Study 2

According to previous research, the interaction effect of conversational interactivity and product relevance might be explained by consumers' emotional appeal and expectations discrepancy. Hence, the main purpose of Study 2 is to verify the intermediary mechanism in H2 and H3. Similar to Study 1, we will use a between-subjects design to test the hypotheses.

We will add two measurements for consumers' perceptions of emotional appeal and the extent of expectations discrepancy. The items of emotional appeal are derived from Etemad-Sajadi (2016), such as "The interaction with the chatbot is pleasant/funny/enjoyable"; for expectations discrepancy, we will use Bhattacherjee's (2001) scale, including "my experience with using the chatbot was better than what I expected", "the product recommended by the chatbot was better than what I expected" and "overall, most of my expectations from using the chatbot were confirmed".

4 Conclusion

Drawing on the Computers Are Social Actors (CASA) paradigm and expectations discrepancy theory, this research examines the interaction effect of chatbots' conversational interactivity and product relevance on recommendation effectiveness. Our investigation provides fresh perspectives on the significance of chatbots' conversational interactivity in the field of product recommendations, an important and valuable domain that has not received sufficient attention in previous studies. In addition, we reveal that the positive effect of conversational interactivity depends on product relevance, which deepens our understanding of chatbots' conversational design. Regarding managerial implications, the conversation and recommendation designs explored in our study offer valuable insights for the e-commerce industry to improve user experience and enhance the effectiveness of recommendations.

Acknowledgments. This work was supported by the National Natural Science Foundation of China [grant number: 72002193], the Fundamental Research Funds for the Central Universities [grant number: S20230031], and Zhejiang University-The Hong Kong Polytechnic University Joint Center.

References

Babin, B.J., Darden, W.R., Griffin, M.: Work and/or fun: measuring hedonic and utilitarian shopping value. J. Consum. Res. **20**(4), 644–656 (1994)

Bhattacherjee, A.: Understanding information systems continuance: an expectation-confirmation model. MIS Q. **25**(3), 351–370 (2001)

Cadotte, E.R., Woodruff, R.B., Jenkins, R.L.: Expectations and norms in models of consumer satisfaction. J. Mark. Res. **24**(3), 305–314 (1987)

Cardello, A.V., Sawyer, F.M.: Effects of disconfirmed consumer expectations on food acceptability. J. Sens. Stud. **7**(4), 253–277 (1992)

Crolic, C., Thomaz, F., Hadi, R., Stephen, A.T.: Blame the bot: anthropomorphism and anger in customer-chatbot interactions. J. Mark. **86**(1), 132–148 (2021)

Detenber, B., Wijaya, M., Goh, H.: Blogging and online friendships: the role of self-disclosure and perceived reciprocity. In: Communication and Technology Division of the International Communication Association, Montreal, QC, Canada, pp. 22–26 (2008)

Etemad-Sajadi, R.: The impact of online real-time interactivity on patronage intention: the use of avatars. Comput. Hum. Behav. **61**, 227–232 (2016)

Go, E., Sundar, S.S.: Humanizing chatbots: the effects of visual, identity and conversational cues on humanness perceptions. Comput. Hum. Behav. **97**, 304–316 (2019)

Nass, C., Steuer, J., Tauber, E.: Computers are social actors. In: ACM, pp. 72–78 (1994)

Oliver, R.L.: A cognitive model of the antecedents and consequences of satisfaction decisions. J. Mark. Res. **17**, 460–469 (1980)

Rogers, T.B., Kuiper, N.A., Kirker, W.S.: Self-reference and the encoding of personal information. J. Pers. Soc. Psychol. **35**(9), 677–688 (1977)

Roy, R., Naidoo, V.: Enhancing chatbot effectiveness: the role of anthropomorphic conversational styles and time orientation. J. Bus. Res. **126**, 23–34 (2021)

Schuetzler, R.M., Giboney, J.S., Grimes, G.M., Nunamaker Jr., J.F.: The influence of conversational agent embodiment and conversational relevance on socially desirable responding. Decis. Support. Syst. **114**, 94–102 (2018)

Schuetzler, R.M., Grimes, G.M., Scott Giboney, J.: The impact of chatbot conversational skill on engagement and perceived humanness. J. Manag. Inf. Syst. **37**(3), 875–900 (2020)

Sundar, A., Noseworthy, T.J.: Too exciting to fail, too sincere to succeed: the effects of brand personality on sensory disconfirmation. J. Consum. Res. **43**(1), 44–67 (2016)

Sundar, S.S., Bellur, S., Oh, J., Jia, H., Kim, H.-S.: Theoretical importance of contingency in human-computer interaction. Commun. Res. **43**(5), 595–625 (2014)

Wang, L.C., Baker, J., Wagner, J.A., Wakefield, K.: Can a retail web site be social? J. Mark. **71**(3), 143–157 (2007)

Yang, B., Kim, Y., Yoo, C.: The integrated mobile advertising model: the effects of technology-and emotion-based evaluations. J. Bus. Res. **66**(9), 1345–1352 (2013)

Zeng, F., Huang, L., Dou, W.: Social factors in user perceptions and responses to advertising in online social networking communities. J. Interact. Advert. **10**(1), 1–13 (2009)

Machine Learning in Health and Wellness Tourism

Célia M. Q. Ramos[1,2]([envelope]) [iD] and Rashed Isam Ashqar[1] [iD]

[1] ESGHT, CinTurs, University of Algarve, 8005-139 Faro, Portugal
{cmramos,riashqar}@ualg.pt
[2] CEFAGE, Faro, Portugal

Abstract. Health and Wellness Tourism consumers are customers of specific kinds of products, such as luxury hotels, while other perspectives center on recovery, well-being, removing stress, and promoting peer socialization. While others prefer other service categories like personnel health service, health promotion treatments, environment, healthy diet, relaxation, social activities, and the experience of unique tourism resources. The objective of this paper is to identify potential customers through the segmentation of the guests and identify some rules to achieve a specific type of customer. We used Unsupervised Algorithms through the k-Means clustering algorithm by Orange Data Mining and Power BI software. The results of the K-means algorithm identify four clusters: C1 – constituted only by the majority of couples without babies and children, C2 – constituted by Couples with babies and very few children, C3 -Couples with few children, and C4 Couples with several children. Also, we used the Frequent Pattern Mining Algorithm and we found that it is possible to identify some rules that help to learn about consumer behavior.

Keywords: Machine Learning · Data mining · Health and Wellness Tourism · Hospitality

1 Introduction

The need to understand the relationships between customers and the hotel's financial performance is one of the most critical factors for the success and competitiveness of this industry (Gupta and Zeithmal 2006), which is a more demanding dimension when it comes to a hotel, especially in the area of health and wellness tourism, where it is necessary to deal with biometrics and health information. The metrics associated with the concepts of Customer Lifetime Value (CLV) (Venkatesan and Kumar 2004) are no longer enough. Therefore, it is necessary to include new metrics, as well as the concepts of hotel intellectual capital indicators, the metrics that evaluate the customer in the context of social media, combined not only with the simplest statistics but with business intelligence tools, data mining, and machine learning techniques. In this context, in which personal, health, and financial information is stored, processed, and communicated, it is necessary to include considerations associated with handling and communicating customer information safely and ethically, with mechanisms for protecting personal data, such as the premise of blockchain technology, stored by Big Data concepts.

P. Zaphiris et al. (Eds.): HCII 2023, LNCS 14060, pp. 502–518, 2023.
https://doi.org/10.1007/978-3-031-48060-7_39

'Big Data' data analysis has been recognized as one of the most important technology areas of the 21st century and has attracted the attention of many sectors of the economy, as it can generate high returns for companies (Raguseo 2018). Many companies have set up 'Data Science' teams that use large volumes of data to help answer strategic business questions that allow companies to improve performance (Akter et al. 2016). Large multinational companies such as Walmart (the largest North American supermarket chain), Netflix, Rolls Royce, Shell, etc. have invested in a data infrastructure that can then be analyzed to understand consumer habits and develop marketing initiatives to increase sales (Davenport 2013; Marr 2016).

There are many examples in the leisure and hospitality industry that have used advanced data analysis tools to improve operational functioning and create more effective marketing campaigns. Some examples include the use of neural networks to develop a model to predict cancellations of hotel stays (António 2013; Huang 2013); the development of Machine Learning models to predict occupancy rates and forecast hotel demand (Caicedo-Torres 2016); supervised learning algorithms to measure the feeling of hotel reviews by guests (Shi 2011; Raut and Londhe 2014) or the development of Deep Learning algorithms to understand the impact of photos on hotel reviews by guests (Ma et al. 2018), etc.

However, there is no evidence of comprehensive data analysis tools that aggregate the potential data that can be aggregated across hotels such as the Property Management System, the website, check-in data, Restaurant Point of Sales information data, room-service consumption, in-room consumption data, data and services booked (Spa, Golf, Kids Club) among others (Melián-Gonzalez et al. 2016), nor models that add indicators from different areas.

To help Health and Wellness Tourism companies and to improve customer service, it is important to use several types of analyzes that can be explored to improve financial, operational, and marketing (or other) components in Health and Wellness Tourism. The objective is to collect as much data as possible through the different services that guests use (rooms, restaurants, spa, wellness activities, etc.) and online visualization data (company website, online surveys, etc.) to be used by Machine Learning algorithms. These algorithms will be perfected by analysts over time and will provide data and suggest initiatives to the various departments of the wellness company and also automatically update marketing content to be made available to guests.

Current 'Machine Learning' techniques allow the execution of algorithms that create models of knowledge representation automatically based on an existing data set. These algorithms will adjust the results based on new data and have the possibility of making increasingly accurate predictions, without needing to be reprogrammed to react to new variables (Jordan 2015).

The main fundamentals of Machine Learning are the analysis of a sample of data (for example from wellness guests) that will be analyzed and classified by a Machine Learning algorithm, which will then provide a decision on existing data or new data (for example new initiatives to be developed for guests). This paper is structured as follows. Section 2 includes a literature review and theoretical framework about knowledge management and competitive intelligence, subdivided into knowledge management, hospitality competitive intelligence, customer intelligence, and data mining and data analytics associated with health and wellness tourism. Section 3 defines the methodology CRISP-DM used and considers the concept of a Data Mining project. Section 4 presents and discusses the results, and Sect. 5 presents the conclusions, limitations, and opportunities for future work.

2 Knowledge Management and Competitive Intelligence

Organizational performance can be improved through the knowledge management associated with intellectual capital indicators, where the ability to take advantage of all available information can be the most critical component for the success of the modern enterprise (Momeni et al. 2012). An organization's intellectual capital provides the instrument to define strategic actions, whether for innovation or economic growth, through the definition of metrics, which conjugated with a knowledge management system allows the development of new metrics and mechanisms intending to improve the organization's value combined with the assessment of financial performance contributes to successfully amplifying its competitiveness in today's society (Ramos et al. 2023). Intellectual capital can be defined as a mixture of intellectual assets and liabilities (Caddy 2000). Although the definition has not been consensus, many studies consider that there are three major categories of intellectual capital: human capital, structural capital, and relational or customer capital (Manzari et al. 2012; Ramos et al. 2023).

To extract more knowledge from organizational information should be considered the integration between the knowledge management (KM) system and the competitive intelligence (CI) process can create synergies (Momeni et al. 2012), where KM is the most effective way to collect information which is one of the main ways to add value to the business, and is too broad, by another side, the CI is a process to obtain extra knowledge and is too specific. Together with KM and CI, it allows obtaining valuable knowledge for the organization, holistically, from the company to the employees and from the employees to the company, which is something that has a lot of value for the competition and must be protected (Momeni et al. 2012).

2.1 Knowledge Management

Knowledge management systems are developed taking into consideration the focus on learning and knowledge acquisition from the organization, where intellectual capital indicators can be used as metrics to represent the organization's knowledge. To gain competitiveness, in hospitality one of the most important strategies is to manage and acquire customer knowledge, which should be analyzed with three different objectives: (i) to improve the products and services offered by the hotel (information obtained from customers) (ii) to promote the hotel better (information shared with customers), and (iii) about customers, to know the customer preferences (information about customers) (Ramos et al. 2023).

To obtain knowledge about the customers and increase the effectiveness of the hotel strategies the Customer Lifetime Value (CLV) (Venkatesan and Kumar 2004) models applied to the guest data is not sufficient, it is necessary to develop and hotel CRM to "meet customer needs and demands, make the customers highly satisfied, and maintain their loyalties [...] both the efficiency of CRM efforts and the ability of the company in terms of competitiveness may be increased" (Dursun et al. 2016: 153).

The development of a CRM should consider the four CRM dimensions as referred to by Ngai et al. (2009: 2592): "Customer Identification, Customer Attraction, Customer Retention and Customer Development and seven data mining functions: Association, Classification, Clustering, Forecasting, Regression, Sequence Discovery and Visualization".

For each CRM dimension, some activities can be supported by DM techniques such as (i) Customer Identification such as Target Customer Analysis, Customer Segmentation; (ii) Customer Attraction such as Direct Marketing; (iii) Customer Retention such as Loyalty Program, One-to-One Marketing, Complaint Management, and (iv) Customer Development such as Customer Lift Time Cycle, Up/Cross-Selling and Market Basket Analysis (Ngai et al. 2009), as presented in Table 1.

Table 1. Sample of CRM dimensions and potential data mining techniques utility.

CRM dimension	CRM elements	Data Mining technique
Customer identification	Customer segmentation	Classification Clustering Regression
	Target customer	Classification Clustering Visualization
Customer attraction	Direct marketing	Regression Classification Clustering
Customer retention	One to One marketing	Association Classification Clustering Sequence discovery
	Loyalty program	Classification Clustering Regression Sequence discovery
	Complaints management	Clustering Sequence discovery
Customer development	Customer lifetime value	Classification Clustering Forecasting Regression
	Market basket analysis	Association Sequence discovery
	Up/cross-selling	Association Sequence discovery

Source: Adapted from Ngai et al. (2009: 2599).

Data mining techniques can provide more knowledge to generate new opportunities and to understand customer behaviors to define new competitive CRM strategies and to support the decision-maker process in the maximum customer value (Ngai et al. 2009), which is only supported by customer lifetime values and it is not sufficient. However, conjugated with customer capital indicators can achieve new Customer Competitive Intelligence, as long as the combination with data mining techniques is considered.

2.2 Hospitality Competitive Intelligence

Momeni et al. (2012: 3) defined competitive intelligence (CI) as "exclusively focused on the goal of successfully defending the firm from competitive threats and proactively transferring market share from competitors to the bottom line". Therefore, contributes to a long-term competitive advantage while helping decision-makers to evaluate the alternatives they have.

For Köseoglu et al. (2021) competitive intelligence includes six types of intelligence, which hotel managers need to consider: competitor intelligence, market intelligence, business intelligence, customer intelligence, economic intelligence, and competitive technical intelligence (Bulger 2016). Competitor intelligence is related to the competitive set or the competitors that compete with the hotel (Bulger 2016), it can be related to business development (new hotel openings), human resources what the others are doing better than us) or food and beverages (lower prices) (Köseoglu et al. 2020; Köseoglu et al. 2021). Market intelligence is associated with the dynamics that characterize the current market (Bulger 2016), which can be applied to room division, sales, and marketing (obtain new ideas from all around the globe), and new management strategies (Köseoglu et al. 2021; Xiang et al. 2017). Business intelligence considers performance indicators, market share, measurements mainly presented in dashboards or reports about the business (where it is necessary to control deviations and return to equilibrium), sales and marketing (where it is necessary to make adjustments), front office (to monitor and compare our hotel performance with other hotels), and compare the services with new experiences like multisensory service (Köseoglu et al. 2021; Lee et al. 2019). Economic intelligence implies understanding the actual dynamics that happen in the global market, including political and government actions, unemployment, and crisis (Bulger 2016) associated with rooms division (between other markets) and hotel managers (analyzing the government policy and other changes in economic or social aspects) (Köseoglu et al. 2021; Wan and Law 2017). Competitive technical intelligence is an essential intelligence to motivate innovation associated with a product or service (Bulger 2016) and can be related to human resources education, for example, to proportionate rooms to test new concepts, services, and technologies (Chan et al. 2018; Köseoglu et al. 2021).

Customer intelligence is concentrated in a constant and quick way to satisfy customer preferences and trends that can be useful to identify changes in consumer behavior (Bulger 2016). It can be applied to develop new businesses (associated with a specific target), human resources (the customers can help to identify the best), and analyze online reviews to achieve insights about what are the most successful and poor aspects of hotel services among others (Wan and Law 2017; Köseoglu et al. 2021).

2.3 Customer Intelligence and Data Mining

Customer intelligence (CI) can be divided into external and internal (Köseoglu et al. 2021). Associated with external customer intelligence can be considered to create new business, by analyzing customer databases to identify new trends, trade fairs, and specific events; manage the online hotel reputation (Ramos 2022). Concerning internal customers, intelligence can be considered in terms of human resources (to identify the best talents), food and beverage (to manage the gastronomic resources), and in terms of hotel management.

Soldatenko et al. (2023: 2) explained CI as "the customers are the core of the business, and CI could be the resource for the growth of rival superiority and stability". Therefore, if the focus of competitive intelligence in a hotel is the customer will be possible a process analyze and understand the customer's needs and preferences to encourage buying new services and products, and by another side, the hotel achieves its strategy by creating, retaining e and maintaining customer relationships.

In this context to create customer intelligence, conjugated with knowledge management, is necessary to have data about demographics, socioeconomic, or geographic characteristics of the customers are the traditionally and widely used variables for market segmentation (Dursun and Caber 2016), but also travel motivations, destination activities, travel expenditures, among others.

Some recent studies used artificial intelligence for specific issues in hospitality, such as forecast hotel booking cancellations (Sánchez-Medina and Eleazar 2020), examined the features related to guest satisfaction embedded in the textual content of online reviews (Aakash et al. 2021), and establish a prediction model for the development scale of high-star hotels (Zhao and Tsai 2021), supervised learning, text mining, and segmentation machine learning (Alsayat 2023; Lee et al. 2021).

Artificial intelligence (AI) has been receiving significant attention from researchers in all fields including hospitality and tourism, this topic has played an increasingly critical role in transforming the entire business processes and how companies analyze customer and market trends (Lv et al. 2022). Moreover, AI is one of the emerging big data analytics techniques in society, and hospitality, and tourism literature has shown evidence of the potential of using AI algorithms to process and analyze hospitality data (Lee et al. 2021).

2.4 Data Analytics Associated with Health and Wellness Tourism

In contemporary hotel management, taking into consideration that the hoteliers have a huge quantity of guests, that have different needs and preferences, while the profiles and behaviors are also distinct, and in the era of big data, is necessary to consider data analytics for the hotels to take decisions based on data analytics.

Data analytics, from a taxonomical view, presents three main categories: descriptive, predictive, and prescriptive. Descriptive analytics can be used to discover patterns associated with tourism activity, behavior or preferences, and customer segmentation (cluster segmentation). Predictive analytics can deploy sets of statistical techniques to estimate models that predict future tourist visitors' behavior, for example, predicting customer ratings or the number of sales in a specific period (linear regression, logistic regression). And, prescriptive analytics is used to optimize a key performance metric, for example, profit.

Each hotel should understand its customers and identify the segments that can achieve and satisfy their services and products. Each segment implies the identification of different customer groups in their database, which have similar characteristics inside each group.

The Health and Wellness Tourism consumers are a customer of specific kinds of products, such as luxury hotels, while other perspectives center on recovery, well-being, removing stress, and promoting peer socialization (Ahani et al. 2019), while others prefer other service categories like personnel health service, health promotion treatments, environment, healthy diet, relaxation, social activities, the experience of unique tourism resources (Chen et al. 2013). With these guest preferences and specificities, hoteliers should consider data mining techniques to obtain customer competitive intelligence and increase the knowledge about the current, and future candidates to stay at their hotel, where the first task must be to identify the potential customers through the segmentation of the guests, with the objectives to know the hospitality market and identify some rules to achieve a specific type of customers.

3   Methodology

To investigate an objective that is relevant to the process of the hotelier's decision-making, it is essential to use an adequate methodology such as the Cross Industry Standard Process for Data Mining (CRISP-DM) (Chapman et al. 2000; Hamdan and Othman 2022), as presented in Fig. 1.

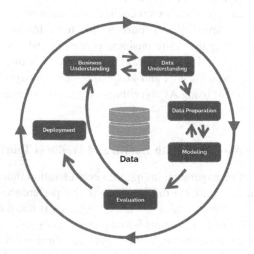

Fig. 1. CRISP-DM Methodology. Source: Hotz (2023).

The CRISP-DM methodology is very flexible, generic, and independent of the technology used to implement the process of knowledge discovery.

The CRISP-DM methodology is divided into six steps: (i) Business understanding, (ii) Data understanding, (iii) Data preparation, (iv) Modeling, (v) Evaluation, and (vi) Deployment. Several steps can be worked together.

3.1 Business Understanding

Health and wellness tourism has seen its importance increase due to the aging of the population; it is a holistic lifestyle that integrates three body-mind-spirit dimensions. This type of tourism is practiced by senior tourists, who are economically secure and see this mode of tourism as a new lifestyle. In parallel and related, medical tourism emerged, which is considered when the tourist travels to another country to receive medical care. Health and wellness tourism is a trend that has led to the economic growth of the destination and is practiced by a small niche of tourists, however, factors that lead to the measurement and evaluation of the destination that practices this type have not yet been identified.

Health and wellness tourism is characterized by several components, where each one will have a specific target audience, so each one will captivate a small group of tourists.

However, the activities associated with the spa have aroused the interest of females of different ages, under the justification of rejuvenation. On the other hand, also motivated by socialization and increased self-esteem, it has led men of different age groups to awaken their interest in this type of tourism. This leads to the conclusion that the reasons may be different depending on the gender and age of the tourists.

The guest data considered in this study belong to the Hotel Booking Demand Dataset (António et al. 2019) although it does not refer to health and wellness tourism guests, it is one of the most complete datasets found by the authors with characteristics of hotel customers. This dataset is made up of booking information for a city hotel and a resort hotel. In total, it consists of 119,390 bookings that arrived between the 1st of July 2015 and the 31st of August 2017, including bookings that effectively arrived and bookings that were cancelled.

3.2 Data Understanding

In this step, an exploratory analysis of the data collected or considered is carried out, identifying problems in the data, the variable type, and a statistical description as presented in Table 2.

3.3 Data Preparation

In this step, the necessary cleaning and transformation of the data is carried out so that comparisons can be made, only the most relevant variables can be identified, and which will be considered in the following steps. Also, it may be necessary to create new variables based on existing ones.

Table 2. Exploratory analysis of the data.

No.	Variable	Variable type	Statistical description
1	*is_canceled (dependent variable, DV)*	Categorical	2 categories: canceled and not canceled
2	*hotel*	Categorical	2 categories: resort hotel and city hotel
3	*lead_time*	Numerical	Number of lead days
4	*arrival_date_year*	Variable related to time	Arrival year: 2015–2017
5	*arrival_date_month*	Variable related to time	Arrival month: 1–12
6	*arrival_date_week_number*	Variable related to time	Arrival week: 1–53
7	*arrival_date_day_of_month*	Variable related to time	Arrival day in the month: 1–31
8	*stays_in_weekend_nights*	Numerical	Number of weekend nights
9	*stays_in_week_nights*	Numerical	Number of weeknights
10	*adults*	Numerical	Number of adults
11	*children*	Numerical	Number of children
12	*babies*	Numerical	Number of babies
13	*meal*	Categorical	4 categories: type of booked meal
14	*country*	Categorical	Customer source country
15	*market_segment*	Categorical	8 categories: market segment designation
16	*distribution_channel*	Categorical	5 categories: booking distribution channel
17	*is_repeated_guest*	Categorical	2 categories: whether is a repeat consumer
18	*previous_cancellations*	Numerical	Number of previous cancellations
19	*previous_bookings_not_canceled*	Numerical	Number of previous bookings not canceled
20	*reserved_room_type*	Categorical	9 categories: reserved room type
21	*booking_changes*	Numerical	Number of booking changes

(*continued*)

Table 2. (*continued*)

No.	Variable	Variable type	Statistical description
22	*deposit_type*	Categorical	3 categories: deposit type
23	*agent*	Categorical	Travel agency ID
24	*days_in_waiting_list*	Numerical	Number of days on the waiting list
25	*customer_typelePara>*	Categorical	4 categories: type of booking
26	*adr*	Numerical	Number of the average daily rate
27	*required_car_parking_spaces*	Numerical	Number of parking spaces
28	*total_of_special_requests*	Numerical	Number of special requests

3.4 Modeling

The modeling stage implies the identification of suitable algorithms for the research problem, which in this investigation are related to achieving two objectives: the segmentation of your guests, with the objectives to know the hospitality market and identify some rules to achieve a specific type of services or products. The first will involve a clustering algorithm and the second association rules.

3.5 Evaluation

The evaluation step is considered to evaluate the model's accuracy results, taking into consideration the objective and the algorithm considered.

3.6 Deployment

The last step will depend on the objective to be achieved, which may imply returning to the first step of the CRISP-DM methodology, it may simply be the preparation of reports with the results obtained, which will be presented in the next section.

4 Results

Considering the steps of the methodology presented above, this section will be presented the results associated with each objective: (i) the segmentation of guests to know the hospitality market and (ii) identifying some rules to achieve a specific of the consumer.

In the data preparation step, only the most relevant variables were selected, and which will be considered in the following steps: *hotel, stays_in_weekend_nights, stays_in_week_nights, adults, children, babies, meal, country, adr, required_car_parking_spaces and total_of_special_requests.* However, it was necessary to create a new variable LenthStay with the sum of two variables: *stays_in_weekend_nights* and *stays_in_week_nights*, to have the complete stay duration.

Since the present investigation intends to analyze health and wellness tourists and how data were obtained according to the characteristics of this type of tourism, in the dataset considered, only reservations were considered that presented a number of *total_of_special_requests* greater than zero, assuming these requests could include specific health and wellness services. It was the way found to overcome the limitation of this study of not having specific data associated with health and wellness tourism reservations.

With these two data preparations, the dataset considered in the research was composed of 49072 rows and ten features, three categorical and the rest numerical.

4.1 Segmentation of Guests to Know Hospitality Market

Currently, Machine Learning techniques allow the execution of algorithms that create models of knowledge representation automatically based on an existing data set. These algorithms will adjust the results based on new data and have the possibility of making increasingly accurate predictions, without needing to be reprogrammed to react to new variables (Zhang 2010; Jordan 2015).

Taking into account the first objective of the study the segmentation of guests to know the hospitality market, an unsupervised algorithm will be considered that will group the data by similar characteristics, since there is no information about the guests.

Unsupervised Algorithms group the data in some format for a better understanding of the structure, which then allows for simplified analysis. Algorithms of this type can analyze data from guests who used wellness services and classify them into interest groups, for example, guests with intensive spa use and/or dietary plans. Knowing about the existence of this customer segment allows the creation of combined products that are of interest to new guests, which allows for increasing revenue per customer. In this case, will be considered a k-means algorithm.

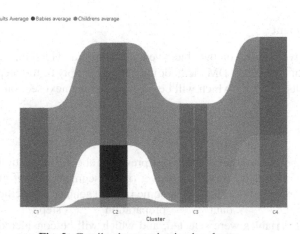

Fig. 2. Family characterization by cluster

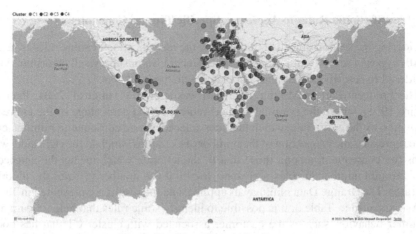

Fig. 3. Booking Clusters by Country

The k-Means clustering algorithm is applied to the data and outputs a new dataset in which the cluster label is added (Arthur and Vassilvitskii 2007). The software considered was Orange Data Mining and Power BI.

The results of the K-means algorithm identify four clusters: C1 – constituted only by the majority of couples without babies and children, C2 – constituted by Couples with babies and very few children, C3 -Couples with few children, and C4 Couples with several children, as presented in Fig. 2. In terms of the distribution by guest clusters in the world can be analyzed in Fig. 3, which shows that the booking considered in the present study belongs to tourists originating from all over the globe. Figure 4 presents the information associated with each cluster, which presents that Cluster C2 is the one that presents more special requests followed by C4, and also has the behavior in terms of the lengths of the stay. However, Cluster C2 is the one that has the biggest *AverageDailyRate* in average followed by C4.

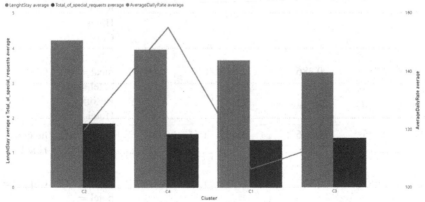

Fig. 4. Booking Clusters by Length of stay, Special requests, and Average daily rate

4.2   Identify Some Rules to Achieve a Specific Type of Consumer.

Considering the second objective of the study the identification of some rules to achieve specific types of services or products for consumers, an unsupervised algorithm will be considered to describe some rules associated with the bookings.

The Frequent Pattern Mining algorithm was applied (Han et al. 2004; Piatetsky-Shapiro 1991), where the minimal support represents the percentage of the entire data set covered by the entire rule, which includes antecedent and consequent; minimal confidence represents the proportion of the number of examples which fit the right side, which means the consequent, among those that fit the left side which means the antecedent; the maximum number of rules represents the limit the number of rules the algorithm generates. The Orange Data mining was applied, and the results are presented in Table 3.

As presented in Table 3, it is possible to identify some rules that help to learn about consumer behavior, such as the customer associated with cluster C1 that has booked a hotel in the city and asked for Bed & Breakfast (BB) meal. The same occurs with a customer classified in cluster C3 that has booked a hotel in the city and wants BB as a meal.

Table 3. Associate rules data mining results.

Support	Confidence	Coverage	Strength	Lift	Leverage	Antecedent	Consequent
0,397	0,721	0,551	1,38	0,949	−0,021	hotel = City Hotel, Cluster = C1	meal = BB
0,397	0,837	0,474	1,724	1,025	0,01	meal = BB, hotel = City Hotel	Cluster = C1
0,215	0,806	0,267	2,849	1,06	0,012	hotel = Resort Hotel, Cluster = C1	meal = BB
0,215	0,752	0,286	2,859	0,92	−0,019	meal = BB, hotel = Resort Hotel	Cluster = C1
0,116	0,996	0,116	5,495	1,557	0,041	meal = SC, Cluster = C1	hotel = City Hotel
0,116	0,951	0,122	6,712	1,164	0,016	meal = SC, hotel = City Hotel	Cluster = C1

(*continued*)

Table 3. (*continued*)

Support	Confidence	Coverage	Strength	Lift	Leverage	Antecedent	Consequent
0,053	0,897	0,059	12,959	1,181	0,008	hotel = City Hotel, Cluster = C4	meal = BB
0,053	0,723	0,073	8,785	1,131	0,006	meal = BB, Cluster = C4	hotel = City Hotel
0,045	0,806	0,056	13,686	1,061	0,003	hotel = Resort Hotel, Cluster = C3	meal = BB
0,038	0,867	0,044	18,775	1,061	0,002	meal = HB, hotel = City Hotel	Cluster = C1
0,019	0,808	0,024	31,892	1,064	0,001	hotel = City Hotel, Cluster = C3	meal = BB
0,01	0,89	0,011	32,356	2,468	0,006	meal = HB, Cluster = C3	hotel = Resort Hotel
0,005	0,811	0,006	119,494	1,067	0	hotel = City Hotel, Cluster = C2	meal = BB
0,003	0,988	0,003	191,299	1,545	0,001	meal = SC, Cluster = C3	hotel = City Hotel
0,003	0,833	0,003	117,993	2,31	0,001	meal = HB, Cluster = C2	hotel = Resort Hotel
0,002	1	0,002	175,238	2,773	0,001	meal = Undefined, Cluster = C1	hotel = Resort Hotel
0,002	1	0,002	326,802	1,564	0,001	meal = SC, Cluster = C4	hotel = City Hotel

(*continued*)

Table 3. (*continued*)

Support	Confidence	Coverage	Strength	Lift	Leverage	Antecedent	Consequent
0,001	0,932	0,001	299,983	2,585	0,001	meal = FB, Cluster = C1	hotel = Resort Hotel
0,001	1	0,001	950,697	1,564	0	meal = SC, Cluster = C2	hotel = City Hotel
0,001	0,926	0,001	1485,296	1,133	0	meal = SC, hotel = Resort Hotel	Cluster = C1

5 Conclusions

The present study aimed to identify and define the Machine Learning algorithms that can most contribute to acquiring intelligence on Health and Wellness Tourism guest data, as well as combining with the potential of Business Intelligence to increase sales, preparing more attractive offers for these customers and improving control of hotel activity in this segment.

In addition, two unsupervised learning algorithms were applied to show that it is possible to segment customers according to their characteristics and identify some behavioral rules. However, there is still much to be investigated, for example, developed and assessed prediction models for review helpfulness using machine learning (ML) algorithms to analyze big data, which can be useful to apply these algorithms to hospitality booking data. The limitation of the present study is the lack of data on reservations made by health and wellness tourists, and also the lack of some sociodemographic data in the data set used to better segment the consumer of this type of tourism.

In terms of future work, the design of new key performance indicators will be considered. In addition, to those associated with intellectual capital that characterizes the relational dimension. This work will include the consolidation of all studies on indicators and characteristics relevant to the Health Tourism area, and work will be developed in order to adapt indicators from other areas, as well as new indicators will be developed.

Acknowledgments. This paper is financed by National Funds provided by FCT- Foundation for Science and Technology through project UIDB/04020/2020 and project Guest-IC I&DT nr. 047399 financed by CRESC ALGARVE2020, PORTUGAL2020 and FEDER.

References

Aakash, A., Tandon, A., Gupta Aggarwal, A.: How features embedded in eWOM predict hotel guest satisfaction: an application of artificial neural networks. J. Hosp. Mark. Manag. **30**(4), 486–507 (2021). https://doi.org/10.1080/19368623.2021.1835597

Ahani, A., Nilashi, M., Ibrahim, O., Sanzogni, L., Weaven, S.: Market segmentation and travel choice prediction in Spa hotels through TripAdvisor's online reviews. Int. J. Hosp. Manag. **80**, 52–77 (2019)

Akter, S., Wamba, S.F., Gunasekaran, A., Dubey, R., Childe, S.J.: How to improve firm performance using big data analytics capability and business strategy alignment? Int. J. Prod. Econ. **182**, 113–131 (2016)

Alsayat, A.: Customer decision-making analysis based on big social data using machine learning: a case study of hotels in Mecca. Neural Comput. Appl. **35**, 4701–4722 (2023). https://doi.org/10.1007/s00521-022-07992-x

Antonio, N., de Almeida, A., Nunes, L.: Hotel booking demand datasets. Data Brief **22**, 41–49 (2019)

Arthur, D., Vassilvitskii, S.: k-means++: the advantages of careful seeding. In: Proceedings of the Eighteenth Annual ACM-SIAM Symposium on Discrete Algorithms. Society for Industrial and Applied Mathematics, Philadelphia, PA, USA, pp. 1027–1035 (2007)

Bulger, N.J.: The evolving role of intelligence: migrating from traditional competitive intelligence to integrated intelligence. Int. J. Intell. Secur. Public Aff. **18**(1), 57–84 (2016)

Caddy, I.: Intellectual capital: recognizing both assets and liabilities. J. Intellect. Cap. **1**(2), 129–146 (2000)

Caicedo-Torres, W., Payares, F.: A machine learning model for occupancy rates and demand forecasting in the hospitality industry. In: Montes y Gómez, M., Escalante, H., Segura, A., Murillo, J. (eds.) IBERAMIA 2016. LNCS, vol. 10022, pp. 201–211. Springer, Cham (2016). https://doi.org/10.1007/978-3-319-47955-2_17

Chan, E.S., Okumus, F., Chan, W.: Barriers to environmental technology adoption in hotels. J. Hosp. Tour. Res. **42**(5), 829–852 (2018)

Chapman, P., et al.: CRISP-DM 1.0 - step-by-step data mining guide, CRISP-DM Consortium (2000)

Chen, K.-H., Liu, H.-H., Chang, F.-H.: Essential customer service factors and the segmentation of older visitors within wellness tourism based on hot springs hotels. Int. J. Hosp. Manag. **35**, 122–132 (2013)

Davenport, H.: Multiplicative Number Theory, vol. 74. Springer, New York (2013). https://doi.org/10.1007/978-1-4757-5927-3

Dursun, A., Caber, M.: Using data mining techniques for profiling profitable hotel customers: an application of RFM analysis. Tour. Manag. Perspect. **18**, 153–160 (2016)

Gupta, S., Zeithaml, V.: Customer metrics and their impact on financial performance. Mark. Sci. **25**(6), 718–739 (2006)

Hamdan, I.Z.P., Othman, M.: Predicting customer loyalty using machine learning for hotel industry. J. Soft Comput. Data Min. **3**(2), 31–42 (2022)

Han, J., Pei, J., Yin, Y., Mao, R.: Mining frequent patterns without candidate generation: a frequent-pattern tree approach. Data Min. Knowl. Disc. **8**, 53–87 (2004)

Hotz, N.: What is CRISP-DM? (2023). https://www.datascience-pm.com/crisp-dm-2/

Jordan, K.: Massive open online course completion rates revisited: assessment, length and attrition. Int. Rev. Res. Open Distrib. Learn. **16**(3), 341–358 (2015)

Köseoglu, M.A., Mehraliyev, F., Altin, M., Okumus, F.: Competitor intelligence and analysis (CIA) model and online reviews: integrating big data text mining with network analysis for strategic analysis. Tour. Rev. **76**(3), 529–552 (2020)

Köseoglu, M.A., Yick, M.Y.Y., Okumus, F.: Coopetition strategies for competitive intelligence practices-evidence from full-service hotels. Int. J. Hosp. Manag. **99**, 103049 (2021)

Lee, M., Kwon, W., Back, K.-J.: Artificial intelligence for hospitality big data analytics: developing a prediction model of restaurant review helpfulness for customer decision-making. Int. J. Contemp. Hosp. Manag. **33**(6), 2117–2136 (2021). https://doi.org/10.1108/IJCHM-06-2020-0587

Lee, M., Lee, S., Koh, Y.: Multisensory experience for enhancing hotel guest experience: empirical evidence from big data analytics. Int. J. Contemp. Hosp. Manag. **31**(11), 4313–4337 (2019)

Lv, H., Shi, S., Gursoy, D.: A look back and a leap forward: a review and synthesis of big data and artificial intelligence literature in hospitality and tourism. J. Hosp. Mark. Manag. **31**(2), 145–175 (2022). https://doi.org/10.1080/19368623.2021.1937434

Ma, Y., Xiang, Z., Du, Q., Fan, W.: Effects of user-provided photos on hotel review helpfulness: an analytical approach with deep leaning. Int. J. Hosp. Manag. **71**, 120–131 (2018)

Manzari, M., Kazemi, M., Nazemi, S., Pooya, A.: Intellectual capital: concepts, components and indicators: a literature review. Manag. Sci. Lett. **2**(7), 2255–2270 (2012)

Marr, B.: Big Data in Practice: How 45 Successful Companies Used Big Data Analytics to Deliver Extraordinary Results. Wiley, New York (2016)

Melián-González, S., Bulchand-Gidumal, J.: A model that connects information technology and hotel performance. Tour. Manag. **53**, 30–37 (2016)

Momeni, A., Fathian, M., Akhavan, P.: Competitive intelligence and knowledge management's affinities and relations: developing a model. Invertis J. Sci. Technol. **5**(1), 1–7 (2012)

Ngai, E.W., Xiu, L., Chau, D.C.: Application of data mining techniques in customer relationship management: a literature review and classification. Expert Syst. Appl. **36**(2), 2592–2602 (2009)

Piatetsky-Shapiro, G.: Discovery, analysis, and presentation of strong rules. Knowl. Discov. Database, 229–248 (1991)

Raguseo, E.: Big data technologies: an empirical investigation on their adoption, benefits and risks for companies. Int. J. Inf. Manag. **38**(1), 187–195 (2018)

Ramos, C.M.: Reputation Intelligence. In: Encyclopedia of Tourism Management and Marketing, pp. 679–681. Edward Elgar Publishing (2022)

Ramos, C.M., Ashqar, R.I., Matos, N., Sousa, C.M.: Capital indicators for hotel customer experience to support strategic management. In: Measuring Consumer Behavior in Hospitality for Enhanced Decision Making, pp. 12–33. IGI Global (2023)

Raut, V.B., Londhe, D.D.: Opinion mining and summarization of hotel reviews. In: 2014 International Conference on Computational Intelligence and Communication Networks, pp. 556–559. IEEE, November 2014

Sánchez-Medina, A.J., Eleazar, C.: Using machine learning and big data for efficient forecasting of hotel booking cancellations. Int. J. Hosp. Manag. **89**, 102546 (2020). https://doi.org/10.1016/j.ijhm.2020.102546

Soldatenko, T.Đ., Ali, F., Yessimzhanova, S.R., Fedorova, T., Aliyeva, N.: From customer intelligence to sustainability: management feature of SMEs in Almaty City. J. Strateg. Mark., 1–15 (2023)

Venkatesan, R., Kumar, V.: A customer lifetime value framework for customer selection and resource allocation strategy. J. Mark. **68**(4), 106–125 (2004)

Wan, S., Law, R.: Leveraging online reviews in the hotel industry. In: Xiang, Z., Fesenmaier, D. (eds.) Analytics in Smart Tourism Design. Tourism on the Verge, pp. 235–252. Springer, Cham (2017). https://doi.org/10.1007/978-3-319-44263-1_14

Xiang, Z., Schwartz, Z., Uysal, M.: Market Intelligence: social media analytics and hotel online reviews. In: Xiang, Z., Fesenmaier, D. (eds.) Analytics in Smart Tourism Design. Tourism on the Verge, pp. 281–295. Springer, Cham (2017). https://doi.org/10.1007/978-3-319-44263-1_16

Zhao, N., Tsai, S.-B.: Research on prediction model of hotels' development scale based on BP artificial neural network algorithm. Math. Probl. Eng. **2021**, 1–12 (2021). https://doi.org/10.1155/2021/6595783

Consumer Behavior in Staffless Stores: A Systematic Literature Review

Marina Staab[✉] [iD], Robert Zimmermann [iD], Patrick Brandtner [iD],
and Oliver Schauer [iD]

University of Applied Sciences Upper Austria, 4400 Steyr, Austria
marina.staab@fh-steyr.at

Abstract. Retail is facing several challenges, resulting in the constant need to adopt. One of such recent adoptions is a new form of physical retail called staffless stores. These stores do not employee staff and instead use state-of-the-art technologies to compensate the lack of staff. This leads to a completely different shopping experience. However, as with any innovation, the success of these stores relies on the consumers' acceptance. Thus, it is critical for retailers to understand which factors influence the consumer behavior of such stores and how consumers react to them. Against this background, the purpose of this structured literature review is to analyze the extant literature on consumer behavior in staffless stores. After extensive initial screening, 22 papers were included in the analysis and synthesis phase of this literature review. We identified two main research streams in the area of staffless stores, namely, technology acceptance and adoption, and consumer experience and value creation. Additionally, we highlight several shortcomings in the current body of knowledge regarding consumer behavior in staffless stores, namely a lack of research regarding concepts, theories, methods, data, and applicability for practitioners. Overall, the review reveals that the topic of consumer behavior in staffless stores is largely under-researched. Based on our findings, we suggest a bouquet of avenues for future research.

Keywords: Staffless Stores · Consumer Behavior · Retail · Customer Experience

1 Introduction

Only a few years ago, physical retail was said to have no future. Thereby, terms like the retail apocalypse were used [1]. Instead, e-commerce was predicted to radically reduce the number of retail stores. However, even as the adoption of e-commerce has accelerated due to the pandemic, physical stores still play an important role to in the retail market. There is at least one aspect of physical retail that provides advantage for customers, which e-commerce cannot replace, i.e., product touch and feel [2], and the instant gratification [3, 4]. In terms of food, additionally ultra convenience is highly important [5]. A recent survey conducted in the DACH region shows that end users are not ready to completely abandon physical stores. For most product categories, consumers continue to prefer physical locations; in particular, half of the Austrian respondents can't even imagine buying grocery online in the future [6].

© The Author(s), under exclusive license to Springer Nature Switzerland AG 2023
P. Zaphiris et al. (Eds.): HCII 2023, LNCS 14060, pp. 519–538, 2023.
https://doi.org/10.1007/978-3-031-48060-7_40

Through new technologies and their infusion into physical retail, this scenario has changed. Yet rumors of the physical store's death are exaggerated [7, 8]. To put this into perspective, by 2025 e-commerce is forecast to account for only 24% of total global retail sales [9, 10] and just 4% of grocery sales [11, 12]. Additionally, successful e-commerce merchants like JD.com recently started opening physical stores [13, 14].

Especially since the first staffless store emerged in 2016 [15, 16], we know how the retail store of the future will look like. This business model is expected to be not just a trend but it will become the future of physical retail [17]. What can be seen as the main characteristic of this kind of store compared to traditional retail stores is that there is no human staff present. According to Berger-Grabner who uses the adjective "staffless" [18] to describe the absence of staff, we refer to this store format as staffless stores hereafter. Staffless stores are physical stores integrated with state-of-the-art technologies [19]. Thus, staffless stores are bridging the physical and the digital world of shopping [20].

From a retailer's perspective, staffless stores seem to be quite promising as they are said to be a lucrative opportunity by entailing lower (operational) costs, enhancing customer satisfaction and retention, and expanding consumer segments [21]. Compared to traditional retail stores, staffless stores do not only mean significant changes in a retail store's atmosphere and services, but also differences in the shopper journey [22]. The customer experience is radically transformed due to the creation of new touchpoints and the reconfiguration of others [17]. While in staffless stores, a customer does not necessarily have to (or much more even can't) interact with a staff member, the interaction/the engagement with the technology is obligatory [23]. Thus, the success of staffless stores relies on the customers' acceptance, manifesting in a continuous usage at them which is determined in how far they are providing satisfying shopping experiences [24, 25]. This task might be especially challenging in the context of staffless stores as they are based on multiple state-of-the-art digital technologies, thereby creating a new offline shopping scenario/environment which is revolutionizing the customer experience [26, 27]. Therefore, gaining knowledge about the consumer behavior in such stores is crucial for retailers for surviving in the competitive retail landscape.

Due to their novelty [28] and futuristic characteristics [29], research findings on other retail in-store technologies (e.g., the singular application of self-checkout in a brick-and-mortar store) are not transferable to staffless stores, thus making it difficult to estimate the consequences on the consumer behavior and calling for research shedding light on this.

Thus, the aim of this paper is to give an overview of the status quo of the literature on staffless stores with focus on consumer behavior, thereby answering the following research questions:

I: How can research streams regarding consumer behavior in staffless stores be classified?
II: What are shortcomings in the current body of knowledge regarding consumer behavior in staffless store research?

The remainder of this study is organized as follows. In the "Background" section we shortly describe our understanding of what staffless stores are. The "Methodology" section presents the steps undertaken for the systematic literature review. It is followed by the description of the results. After that, the main findings are discussed and suggestions for future research are made. Finally, draw a conclusion which includes the limitations.

2 Background: Defining Staffless Stores

Due to the checkout process being one of the biggest pain points in shopping [12, 30] and the ongoing development of new technology providing innovative solutions, the retail industry worldwide is attempting to develop new checkout practices by applying self-service technologies [31, 32]. This is because of the highly competitive environment in the retail industry [33]. Retailers are constantly in need to provide a rich customer experience requiring a frictionless and enjoyable shopping experience. This can be reached by the adoption of cutting-edge customer-oriented store technologies [34].

As such, in the last years several retailers have been implementing different forms of so-called self-checkout (SCO) [35], transferring the performance of the checkout to the consumer. These solutions provide the opportunity for customers to perform the checkout with advanced technology instead having it done by a salesperson [36].

According to Meuter et al.'s definition of self-service technologies, self-checkout can be best described as customers performing the checkout "independent of direct service employee involvement" [37] by using technological interfaces. The term self-checkout indicates that the degree in which the customer is actively involved into the checkout procedure has changed. Compared to the traditional checkout whereby the customer was in a passive role regarding the product registration (scanning) and payment, in the self-checkout the customer is actively involved into this task [38]. Some authors have used the term "quasi-employee" or "partial employee" for describing this [39]. Given this, self-checkout solutions can be understood as all systems whereby the checkout process is undertaken by the customer. Drawing attention to the nature of the relationship, it has changed from a human-human (customer and staff member) interaction to a human-technology relationship [38].

Regarding the function principle of self-checkout, it is distinguished between two systems: stationary or fixed self-checkout (FSCO) and mobile self-checkout (MSCO) [35, 40]. A fixed self-checkout system appears as terminal where the products have to be put on, then have to be scanned and finally can be packed (after having paid for it). Fixed self-checkouts may appear like "unmanned checkout-zones" [41].

With mobile self-checkout the customer scans the products with a mobile device which can either be a retailer-owned device or the customer's own smartphone [40, 42]. In case of the own smartphone, the mobile self-scanning is based on an app. Installing this app is necessary to use the own device [43]. With mobile self-checkout the items can be scanned and directly bagged during the shopping journey. It is completed by using mobile payment services [44]. Self-checkout done by mobile self-scanning and relying on digital payment is also known as "Scan & Go" [45].

Making the customers performing the checkout by themselves leads to frontline staff being in somehow obsolete. Thus, in recent years, stores without any staff emerged [35]. The very first of this kind of staffless stores, named Naraffar, was opened in 2016 in Sweden [46, 47]. Since then, other companies in different countries have launched such stores [48]. But although the opening of the first staffless store was already seven years ago, staffless stores are not widely common yet [31] and so far, most companies engaging in this area operate only a few stores [49].

The staffless stores from different retailers vary in their arrangement, resulting in various concepts. Therefore, it is necessary to categorize them. As such, we suggest differentiating them in the way in which the checkout is performed. In this regard, two types of staffless stores can be distinguished. The first type is based on self-checkout, therefore termed as staffless self-checkout store hereafter. In stores of this type, there is no clerk present and also no traditional cash desk is installed there. But instead, at least some physical equipment for checking out is needed. At stores of the second type, no checkout takes place – neither in the traditional mode nor by self-checkout. This innovative approach which is diminishing the customer's involvement in the checkout to a much lower level was first implemented by Amazon. In 2018, they opened their first "Amazon Go" store [50] which is based on their so-called "just walk out"-technology (JWOT). It eliminates the checkout by leveraging computer vision, sensor fusion and deep learning [51]. JWOT uses an online payment that deducts money from a bank or credit card account through one's smartphone [7]. For specifying this type, sticking to the wording of Capegimini [12] the term staffless checkout-free store is suggested.

In the context of unattended retail Yao et al. mention vending machines [52]. We argue that in a very broad sense, they could be seen as staffless stores. However, vending machines and retail stores differ in some aspects which are: first, when buying at a vending machine, a customer has a non-touch purchase experience. Second, only one item can be selected at a time and a return is not possible if the customer is not satisfied with the taken product(s). In addition to this, the customer has to pay for the selected items in advance (meaning he physically receives the products afterwards) whereas this vice versa at retail stores [53]. To summarize, the assortment being possibly offered at a vending store and the closed room seem to be the only common ground with a staffless retail store. Due to the thus expected difference in the customer's shopping experience, the authors do not include vending stores into the categorization of staffless retail stores.

3 Methodology

The authors have conducted a systematic literature to identify articles containing knowledge regarding consumer behavior in staffless stores. The systematic approach was chosen to ensure the study's objectivity and replicability [54]. For conducting the literature review, we followed the approach of Snyder [55].

The literature search was conducted using the Scopus database in March 2023. This database was chosen because it represents a major database for scientific literature [56]. Also, as we want to review a broad set of literature containing differing perspectives from various domains, we chose Scopus as this database is regarded as multidisciplinary [57].

The following search string was applied in the search fields "article title", "abstract" and, "keywords":

```
((self-service OR "self service" OR self-scanning OR "self
scanning" OR self-checkout OR "self checkout" OR "mobile
checkout" OR staffless OR staff-less OR unstaffed OR unmanned
```

OR unattended OR cashierless OR cashier-less OR cashierfree OR
cashier-free OR checkout-free OR "checkout free" OR autonomous
OR ai-enabled OR amazongo OR "Amazon Go" OR 'just walk out`
OR just-walk-out OR scan&go OR "scan & go" OR "scan and go" OR
grab&go OR "grab&go" OR "grab and go" OR pick&go OR "pick & go"
OR "pick and go" OR "shop and go" OR shop&go OR "shop & go")
AND (retail OR grocery)
AND (behaviour OR behavior OR experience OR loyalty OR satis-
faction OR acceptance OR adoption OR intent* OR willingness))

Table 1. Steps of literature review

Step	Description	Change	Amount
0	original search string: TITLE-ABS-KEY	+504	504
1	pre-defined filter: source type	−58	446
2	pre-defined filter: subject area	−63	383
3	pre-defined filter: publication date	−5	378
4	pre-defined filter: language	−8	370
5	conference reviews	−6	364
6	exclusion of keywords in title	−60	304
7	no full text + Chinese + double	−6	298
8	no thematic match	−284	14
9	failing eligibility in the coding phase	−3	11
10	other relevant	+11	22

This resulted in 504 documents that were published in peer-reviewed journals (337), in conference proceedings (109), in book series (33), in books (16), in trade journals (7) and in reports (2). The selection process is described afterwards and also illustrated in Table 1.

To ensure sufficient quality and actuality only journals and conference proceedings were included leaving 446 articles. Subject areas were applied as next filter for excluding non-relevant research areas, leaving 383 results. Additionally, date filter was applied limiting the results to articles published after 1991 (378 documents). The reason for this is that the first self-checkout was introduced in 1992 [40, 58]; thus, no empirical real-life study could have been conducted before. Finally, the number of results was reduced to by applying a language filter as the authors are only able to understand English and German. Other filters were not applied, leaving 370 papers to review.

Following on, the papers' meta data were exported for further analysis. We excluded 6 results which were conference reviews. Screening the titles for subject-non-relevant terms (deliver, vehicle, drone, logistic, warehouse, energy, aerial, bank, fleet, driving, movement, parking, automotive) excluded further 60 articles.

The remaining 304 documents were thoroughly analyzed if they contain information regarding physical retail store context, staffless stores and if their focus lies on consumer behavior or something else. This was done by reading title and abstract. For those articles for which it was not absolutely clear if they fulfil these criteria by just reading the abstract, the full-text was taken into consideration.

Even after a thorough search, there was, no full text option available for four documents, which is why they were excluded. One article identified as relevant, was excluded due to the full-text being only available in Chinese so that it couldn't be analyzed in detail.

For two studies the search revealed each an older conference paper and an expanded version of this paper in a journal. For those, because of containing the same content only the extended paper was used.

Out of the 298 documents analyzed, we further omitted 284 articles; these articles didn't show any retail context as neither of the words retail or grocery was mentioned nor a typical retail shopping scenario was described. Articles with retail context but having no connection to physical stores were omitted as well as articles tackling physical retail stores but not showing a staffless store scenario. Additionally, articles not analyzing consumer behavior were excluded. By doing so, 14 articles were left matching our criteria.

Two articles did not analyze the consumer behavior empirically but developed conceptual frameworks for understanding factors influencing customers' willingness to use staffless stores [59, 60]. As they don't provide insights into actual consumer behavior, they are not taken into further consideration in the further course of this paper. One article did not correspond to our understanding of staffless store as it dealt with a special version of vending machine [61].

We extended our search by applying forward and backward search. This resulted in 11 articles matching our criteria. Finally, we had a number of 22 articles [19, 21, 22, 28, 31, 48, 62–77].

4   Results

Before giving a detailed overview about our findings regarding consumer behaviour in staffless stores, we first present a general overview of the identified papers (see also Table 2).

The 22 identified papers were published between 2019 and 2023, thereby showing great actuality. The 22 papers were conducted in four different continents, i.e., Asia, Europe, America, and Australia. For one study no region was mentioned. For Asia we found the most studies (n = 13), followed by America (n = 5), Europe (n = 2) and Australia (n = 1).

By looking at the term used for the concept of staffless store, one can notice that several terms are used. As such, the terms AI-enabled checkout and unmanned store are used most frequent (each used in 4 papers), followed from the terms just-walk-out and cashierless store (each used two times). Additional 12 terms were used in the other papers.

Regarding the retail industry, we found one study in which the area was not specified [76], while all others are on grocery.

Eleven articles addressed staffless stores in the checkout-free type [22, 28, 64–68, 71, 72, 74, 76], eight in the self-checkout type [19, 21, 48, 62, 63, 70, 73, 75] and two integrated both types [69, 77]. In one article the mode of checkout is not specified [31].

Besides focusing on different types of staffless stores, some of the studies referred to specific staffless store concepts. This was the case if staffless stores are already operated in the country where the research was undertaken. Otherwise only a fictious scenario was applied.

In addition to information on general aspects of the studies, we want to provide specific details regarding the concept of interest, underlying theory/model, the method for analysis, the study design and the sample size (see Table 3).

The authors used different study designs for researching on their issue. One paper relied on customer interviews [67], one did a case study consisting of a combination of qualitative (observation and interviews) and quantitative (questionnaire) research [66]. Four papers combined online experiments with field studies [28, 71, 72, 74]. Two papers used only online experiments [22, 76]. The other studies relied on surveys, of which 12 were designed as online questionnaire [19, 21, 31, 62–65, 69, 70, 73, 75, 77], one took place physically [68] and one was not specified regarding the mode of data collection [48]. The sample size of the studies ranged from 21 to 2310.

From our literature review, we extracted the main findings from each study and organized them into four themes: (1) consumer attitudes and intentions, (2) consumer motivations and values, (3) customer experience, and (4) consumer characteristics. We present the summary of each theme below, along with evidence from the studies.

Table 2. Literature review – general overview

ID	Year	Type of staffless store	Term for staffless store	Retail industry	Store concept	Country
[64]	2019	checkout-free	just walk out technology (JWOT)	grocery	none (fictious)	Thailand
[74]	2022	checkout-free	AI-enabled checkout	grocery	Amazon Go	US
[65]	2022	checkout-free	cashierless store	grocery	not mentioned	Italy
[22]	2022	checkout-free	cashier-less checkout/AI-enabled checkout	grocery	none (fictious)	Saudi Arabia
[66]	2019	checkout-free	unmanned Store	grocery	X-store	Taiwan
[67]	2022	checkout-free	just-walk-out	grocery	not mentioned	Australia

(*continued*)

Table 2. (*continued*)

ID	Year	Type of staffless store	Term for staffless store	Retail industry	Store concept	Country
[68]	2020	checkout-free	AI-powered automated retail stores	grocery	none (fictious)	India
[72]	2021	checkout-free	AI-enabled checkout	grocery	Amazon Go	US
[71]	2021	checkout-free	AI-enabled checkout	grocery	Amazon Go	US
[28]	2021	checkout-free	AI-enabled checkout	grocery	Amazon Go	US
[76]	2022	checkout-free	AI checkout	retail (not specified)	none (fictious)	not mentioned
[31]	2019	not specified	self-service (convenience) store	grocery	not mentioned	China
[62]	2023	self-checkout	smart store	grocery	Jian 24	China
[19]	2021	self-checkout	smart shop	grocery	Bingo Box	China
[63]	2023	self-checkout	smart retail store	grocery	Bingo Box	China
[75]	2022	self-checkout	unmanned store	grocery	X-store	Taiwan
[48]	2022	self-checkout	intelligent unmanned (convenience) store	grocery	X-store	Taiwan
[70]	2023	self-checkout	smart grocery shopping	grocery	none (fictious)	Canada
[73]	2021	self-checkout	AIoT-based unmanned (convenience) store	grocery	X-store	Taiwan
[21]	2019	self-checkout	unmanned (convenience) store	grocery	Bingo Box	China
[77]	2022	self-checkout and checkout-free	unmanned (convenience) stores	grocery	Bingo Box and TaoCafe	China
[69]	2021	self-checkout and checkout-free	cashierless store	grocery	none (fictious)	Italy

4.1 Consumer Attitudes and Intentions

One of the most common themes that emerged from the literature was consumer attitudes and intentions toward staffless stores. In this regard, attitudes refer to how consumers evaluate these stores in terms of their usefulness, ease of use, enjoyment, trust, risk, and similar aspects. Intentions refer to how likely consumers are to use these stores in the future, or to recommend them to others. Most studies used some variation of the technology acceptance model (TAM) or the unified theory of acceptance and use of technology (UTAUT) to measure these constructs [48, 61, 64, 68–70, 73, 75] (see also Table 3).

It became apparent that perceived usefulness and perceived ease of use were found to be significant predictors of consumer attitudes in staffless stores [19, 64, 68]. Perceived

Table 3. Literature review – study details

ID	What was analyzed	Theory/model	Analysis	Study design	n
64	attitudes, intentions to use	extended TAM	SEM	o. s	400
74	purchase intent, evaluation atmosphere	arousal, attraction misattribution	med	f. s., o. exp.	271, 460, 660
65	perceptions and attitudes	–	desc	o. s	1138
22	purchase intention	Roy adaptation model	med	o. exp.	328
66	experience evaluation	qualia experience, activity theory	quantification theory	c. s	21, 50, 104
67	relationship between customer effort and memorability	–	thematic analysis	interv	30
68	usage intention	extended TRAM	PLS	s. n. s	1250
72	impact of promiscuity on selection of checkout mode and on purchase intent	promiscuity	mod	f. s., o. exp.	271, 531, 610
71	attitudes, purchase intent	self-efficacy, callousness	reg., med	f. s., o. exp.	222, 368, 509
28	patronage likelihood	TTAT	ANOVA, LSD	f. s., o. exp.	177, 246, 397
76	individuals' moral behavior	consumer morality	ANOVA, med	o. exp.	128, 147, 303
31	impact of self-efficacy on customer experience, satisfaction, and loyalty	SERVQUAL model	SEM	o. s	229
62	utilitarian and hedonic motivations promoting purchase intentions	HSAM	PLS	o. s	307
19	utilitarian and hedonic motivations affecting shopping intention	HISAM; TR	PLS	o. s	298

(continued)

Table 3. (*continued*)

ID	What was analyzed	Theory/model	Analysis	Study design	n
63	purchase intention	situational factor framework; TR	PLS	o. s	283
75	impact of expectation psychology, external factors and personal cognition on use intention	extended UTAUT2	desc., reg	o. s	180
48	attitudes and patronage intentions	extended UTAUT	PLS, MAG	s. n. s	430
70	intentions to adopt	extended TAM	SEM	o. s	518
73	influencing factors on purchase intention	extended TAM	MANOVA, SEM	o. s	249
21	experiential outcomes	CX	EFA	o. s	548
77	attitude, continuous usage intention	TR, TP	SEM	o. s	310
69	acceptance, intention to use	UTAUT	PLS	o. s	2310

CX (customer experience), TR (technology readiness), TP (technology paradox), TTAT (Technology threat avoidance theory), LSD (least significant differences), s. n. s. (survey not specified), o. s. (online survey), f. s. (field study), o. exp. (online experiment), c. s. (case study), interv. (interview), diff. (different), mod. (moderation analysis), med. (mediation analysis), reg. (regression), MGA (multi-group analysis), EFA (exploratory factor analysis), desc. (descriptive statistics),
note: studies with more than one n consisted of several sub-studies.

enjoyment, customization, interactivity, and social influence were also found to have positive effects on consumer attitudes in staffless stores [66, 68]. Perceived risk, on the other hand, was found to have a negative effect on consumer attitudes in some studies [48, 73].

Regarding intentions, van Esch et al. [71] found that AI-enabled checkouts led to higher purchase intent than self-service checkouts, but only for consumers who had higher levels of self-efficacy. Thomas-Francois & Somogyi [70] found that different groups of consumers had distinct behavioral attributes toward staffless stores, and that social factors had a major impact on their adoption. Ghazwani et al. [22] found that high convenience in AI-enabled checkouts had a positive effect on purchase intent. Van Esch & Cui [72] found that AI-enabled checkouts stimulated higher purchase intent for low promiscuous consumers, but not for high promiscuous consumers.

4.2 Consumer Motivations and Values

Another theme that emerged from the literature was consumer motivations and values related to staffless stores. Motivations refer to why consumers use these stores or what they seek from them. Values refer to what consumers consider important or beneficial from using these stores. Most studies used some variation of the value theory or the motivation theory to measure these constructs.

The results showed that various motivations exist to use a staffless store (e.g., social norms, convenience, speed, efficiency, flexibility, novelty, curiosity, control, joy, focused immersion, temporal dissociation) [48, 62, 64]. However, one study found that consumer motivations towards using staffless stores is reduced as due to the removal of high interpersonal effort, experiences became more forgettable [67]. Chuawatcharin & Gerdsri [64] found that sticking to social norms positively influences the intention to use staffless stores.

The results also showed that consumer value many things in staffless stores. As such, experience, experiential, utilitarian, and hedonic value, were the values most effected by consumers using staffless stores [21, 31, 62, 75]. In this regard, Chang et al. [62] found that merchandise quality, location convenience, speed of shopping and product recommendation were significant sub-dimensions of utilitarian motivation, while control, curiosity, joy, focused immersion and temporal dissociation constituted hedonic motivation in staffless stores. Ghazwani et al. [22] examined that for consumers valuing high convenience concerns regarding the security of financial transaction is lower which enacts higher purchase intent.

Some studies also found that consumer values affected their attitudes or behaviors toward these stores. As such, Lyu et al. [31] found that experience value was an important factor in consumer acceptance staffless stores and Wu et al. [21] found that experiential quality and experiential desire were significantly positively related to experiential confidence, which in turn affected experiential loyalty to staffless stores.

4.3 Customer Experience

The third theme that emerged from the literature was consumer experiences in regard to staffless stores. These refer to how consumers feel when they use these stores or, in detail, how they perceive the service quality, value, and satisfaction of using these stores.

Results show that consumer experiences were mixed and influenced by various factors. For example, arousal, anxiety, trust, guilt and pride were some of the experiences that consumers reported from using staffless stores [22, 28, 64, 71, 72, 74]. It became apparent that consumer experiences in staffless stores affected their attitudes toward them. As such, Cui et al. [74] found that staffless stores led to a higher level of arousal, which in turn yielded more favorable store atmosphere evaluations and higher purchase intent. However, Chuawatcharin & Gerdsri [64] found that perceived entertainment value, trust, and technology anxiety were not significant in the prediction of staffless store adoption. Giroux et al. [76] found that compared to human checkout, moral intention was less likely to emerge for staffless stores and self-checkout machines. Also, Ghazwani et al. [22] found that financial anxiety mediated the effect of convenience on purchase intent for staffless stores. Van Esch et al. [71] found that the positive effect of staffless stores on purchase intent for low promiscuous consumers was moderated by their level of pride at the checkout. In another study, van Esch et al. [28] found that consumers' receptivity of staffless stores was contingent upon their perceptions of threats associated with it.

4.4 Consumer Characteristics

The last theme that emerged from the literature was consumer characteristics related to staffless stores. Characteristics refer to how consumers differ in terms of their demographics, personality traits, preferences, habits, or other aspects and how these characteristics affect consumer perceptions of or behaviors toward staffless stores.

The results show that many consumer characteristics were researched such as, gender, shopping habits, innovativeness importance, optimism, insecurity, technology readiness, self-efficacy, callousness, promiscuity [19, 28, 31, 64, 68, 71, 72, 74]. It became apparent that consumer characteristics moderated or mediated the effects of consumer perceptions and behaviors toward staffless stores. As such, Lin [48] found that perceived convenience value had a different effect on attitudes toward staffless stores between consumers who had experience of using self-service machines and those who have not. Pillai et al. [68] found that innovativeness and optimism affected the perceived ease and perceived usefulness of staffless stores. Chuawatcharin & Gerdsri [64] found that education, salary and shopping habits have an effect on consumers' acceptance of JWOT. However, Gazzola et al. [65] found that gender was not a differentiating element in determining the importance of the proposed variables.

5 Discussion

In the following the results are discussed in the light of the formulated research questions.

5.1 Classifying Research Streams

Regarding research question I (*How can research streams regarding consumer behavior in staffless stores be classified?*), we propose that research streams regarding consumer behavior in staffless stores can be classified into two main categories: technology acceptance and adoption, and customer experience and value creation.

The first category, technology acceptance and adoption, focuses on how consumers evaluate, adopt, and use staffless stores as a new technology. This category is mainly based on the technology acceptance model (TAM) or the unified theory of acceptance and use of technology (UTAUT), which are widely used frameworks to explain and predict consumer behavior toward new technologies. The main constructs of these frameworks are perceived usefulness, perceived ease of use, perceived enjoyment, social influence, facilitating conditions, attitude, intention, and behavior. Most studies in this category used quantitative methods, such as surveys or experiments, to measure these constructs and test hypotheses or research questions related to them. For example, it was examined how perceived usefulness and perceived ease of use affect consumer attitudes and intentions toward staffless stores [48, 64, 68, 70, 73, 75]. To test how specific aspects of staffless stores, such as checkout mode or store atmosphere, affect consumer purchase intent, experiments were used [22, 28, 71, 72, 74].

The second category, consumer experience and value creation, focuses on how consumers perceive, feel, and benefit from using staffless stores as a service. The main constructs used in this category are utilitarian value, hedonic value, experiential value, convenience, speed, efficiency, flexibility, novelty, curiosity, control, joy, focused immersion, temporal dissociation. Most studies in this category used qualitative methods, such as interviews or observations, to measure these constructs and identify themes or categories related to them. For example, interviews or observations were used to explore how consumers value staffless stores in terms of convenience, efficiency, flexibility, novelty, curiosity, control, freedom, joy and immersive availability [66, 67]. [19, 21, 31, 62, 63, 66, 75] examined how utilitarian value, hedonic value, experiential value, perceived value affect consumer attitudes, intentions, loyalty, or satisfaction toward staffless stores.

However, it has to be noted that these two categories must not be mutually exclusive, and some studies may overlap or combine elements from both categories.

We suggest that these two categories represent the main research streams regarding consumer behavior in staffless stores, and that they can be used as a basis for classifying and comparing different studies in this field. We also suggest that these two categories reflect different perspectives and approaches for studying consumer behavior in staffless stores: one that focuses on the technology aspect, and one that focuses on the service aspect.

5.2 Shortcomings in Literature

Regarding research question II (What are shortcomings in the current body of knowledge regarding consumer behavior in staffless store research?), the following shortcomings could be identified.

The first type of shortcomings relates to the lack of clarity, consistency, and comprehensiveness in the concepts and theories used to study consumer behavior in staffless stores. For example, there is no clear or agreed-upon definition of what constitutes a staffless store, or how it differs from other types of self-service or automated retail stores. There is also no clear or comprehensive framework that integrates all the relevant factors that influence consumer behavior in staffless stores, or that explains how these factors interact with each other. In addition, we find a lack of attention to some important aspects of consumer behavior in staffless stores, such as ethical, social, or environmental implications.

The second type of shortcomings relates to the limitations, biases, and gaps in the methods and data used to study consumer behavior in staffless stores. For example, there is a predominance of quantitative methods over qualitative methods, which may limit the depth and richness of the insights gained from the data. There is also a reliance on convenience samples or laboratory settings, which may limit the generalizability and validity of the findings. In addition, we find a lack of longitudinal or comparative studies, which may limit the understanding of the dynamics and trends of consumer behavior in staffless stores over time or across contexts.

The third type of shortcomings relates to the lack of relevance, applicability, and usefulness of the findings for practitioners and managers who are involved in designing, implementing, or operating staffless stores. For example, there is a lack of practical recommendations or guidelines on how to improve consumer acceptance and satisfaction with staffless stores, or how to overcome consumer resistance or barriers to using staffless stores. There is also a lack of evaluation on the actual performance of staffless stores in terms of, for example, sales, profits, costs, customer loyalty, or customer retention.

All of these shortcomings can be avenues for future research, which are highlighted in the following.

5.3 Future Research Opportunities

Based on the shortcomings identified in the current body of knowledge, we suggest several directions for future research on consumer behavior in staffless stores.

As such, future research could explore more external factors that may affect consumer acceptance and adoption of staffless stores, such as privacy, system quality, personal innovativeness, or ethical, social, or environmental implications. Future research could also apply other types of models or frameworks, such besides TAM and UTAUT to better understand and predict consumer behavior in staffless stores. For future studies we suggest using the motivation, opportunity, and ability (MOA) framework [78], which has been successfully validated in the retail context by Roy et al. [79]. We recommend this because it incorporates motivational resources, thereby improving the predictive power of technology acceptance models. As the MOA framework integrates motivational resources with the innovation adoption framework and user-related factors, it provides an integrated view on the adoption of and shopping effectiveness with staffless stores. Future research could also conduct meta-analysis research to synthesize and compare the findings from different studies in this field.

Also, future research could incorporate more outcome variables that may reflect the performance or impact of staffless stores. Referring to Verhoef et al.'s conceptual model of customer experience creation [80], we find a gap in research on staffless stores for many of its aspects (e.g., assortment, price, basket size, total spend, loyalty, retention, or satisfaction) which we claim to be empirically studied. We suggest studying several factors in terms of their effect on the customers' intention to initially and continuously use staffless stores. Several influencing factors from retail operation, such as increasing traffic and/or interaction with other customers and sales promotion [23], were not considered in these studies. Moreover, other studies found influence on the purchasing behavior for different demographics as well, for example for age, education and income [81, 82]. As age is known to be strongly associated with reduced access to many information technology resources and technologies as well as with limited willingness to engage with new technologies and services [83], it is possible that different generations will react differently to staffless stores [84]. Future research could also explore the role of different shopping scenarios and cultural contexts in influencing consumer behavior in staffless stores. Future research could also conduct studies from the retailer's viewpoint to understand their challenges and opportunities in designing, implementing, or operating staffless stores.

In addition, future research could employ alternative operationalization approaches or methods to measure consumer behavior in staffless stores more accurately and comprehensively. As staffless stores from different retailers have unique business models, including entry, checkout process and core smart technologies; thus, generalizing the results to all staffless store concepts should be done with caution [19]. Future research could thus use more diverse and representative samples or settings to increase the generalizability and validity of the findings. Future research could also conduct longitudinal or comparative studies to capture the dynamics and trends of consumer behavior in staffless stores over time or across contexts.

With respect to potential self-service failures [31], it is crucial to understand the customers reaction to such. In a traditional retail store, where self-service technologies are available, customers prefer an employee to correct the problem and complete the transaction [85]. As in a staffless store, there is no employee to assist the customer or even correct a problem/mistake, the question arises which coping strategies the customers show. As customers invest high levels of effort and time into the checkout action, they might feel annoyed and frustrated when this co-created service fails to meet their expectations, therefore referring to service value co-destruction [86]. So far, neither the positive service quality value of the customers' participating in co-creation nor its destruction has been investigated in the context of staffless stores. Thereby we think of possible spillover effects from (dis-) satisfaction with the staffless store experience to (dis-) satisfaction with the retailer. For example, Robertson et al. demonstrated that user self-service technology satisfaction influences trust in the service provider [87] and Marzocchi and Zammit show that satisfaction with self-scanning use has a positive impact on the customers' opinion of the supermarket [88]. Both aspects of the customer's evaluation (i.e., in case of the task perception on the staffless store concept and in case of the spillover on the retailer) might result in either a positive or a negative spread of word-of-mouth which in turn could be an influencing factor for other customers staffless store usage intention.

Lastly, due to the co-existence of the two different types of staffless stores and none of both being clearly outstanding it would be worth investigating which type is preferred by the customers, i.e., which delivers the better customer experience. Combined with the retailer's perspective in terms of the evaluation of the operational efficiency it should be possible to make predictions which type is likely to be the most successful [29].

6 Conclusion

The main objective of this study was to review the existing literature on consumer behavior in staffless stores, and to identify the main research streams and shortcomings in this field. To do so, we conducted a systematic literature review which yielded in 22 relevant studies.

Based on these, we could identify two main research streams (RQ I) in the area of staffless stores, namely, technology acceptance and adoption, and consumer experience and value creation. Also, we could highlight several shortcomings in the current body of knowledge regarding consumer behavior in staffless stores (RQII), namely a lack of research regarding concepts, theories, methods, data, and applicability for practitioners. Also, we could highlight multiple avenues for future research to fill these knowledge gaps (for details see Sect. 5.3).

As a limitation we have to point out, while our paper gives an overview on the extant papers focusing on consumer behavior in staffless stores in retail and the literature search was done carefully, it cannot be ruled out that we did not cover all the relevant literature on this topic. There may be other studies that we missed or overlooked, or that were published after our search date, that could provide different or additional insights on consumer behavior in staffless stores.

In conclusion, from a theoretical point of view our paper contributes to the scientific literature on consumer behavior in staffless stores by providing a comprehensive and systematic review of the existing studies on this topic. It identifies and classifies the main research streams, themes, and findings in this field, and reveals the gaps and challenges in the current body of knowledge. It also proposes several directions and opportunities for future research on this topic, based on the shortcomings identified in the literature. As such, it offers a clear and coherent overview of the state-of-the-art on this topic. This paper also contributes to the practical knowledge of staffless store design, implementation, and operation by providing relevant and useful insights on how consumers perceive and interact with these stores, and what factors influence their acceptance and behavior. As such, it offers a valuable and applicable source of information and advice for practitioners and managers who are involved in staffless store innovation or automation.

Closing, we want to note that we believe that with the rise of staffless stores retail has ushered in a new era, particularly in the grocery field.

References

1. Helm, S., Kim, S.H., van Riper, S.: Navigating the 'retail apocalypse': a framework of consumer evaluations of the new retail landscape. J. Retail. Consum. Serv. **54**, 101683 (2020)
2. San-Martín, S., González-Benito, Ó., Martos-Partal, M.: To what extent does need for touch affect online perceived quality? Int. J. Retail Distrib. Manag. **45**(9), 950–968 (2017)
3. Rohm, A.J., Swaminathan, V.: A typology of online shoppers based on shopping motivations. J. Bus. Res. **57**(7), 748–757 (2004)
4. PwC, Gondola, and The Retail Academy: Rethinking retail: Rethinking retail: The role of the physical store (2018). https://www.pwc.be/en/documents/20180627-rethinking-retail.pdf
5. Tordjman, K.L., Evans, P., El Bedraoui, H.: Retail Apocalypse: Four Ways Physical Stores Can Survive (2021). https://web-assets.bcg.com/94/96/47b057fd481987004e8950b7818e/bcg-ret ail-apocalypse-apr-2021.pdf
6. KPMG: Online-Shopping: Einkaufsverhalten - wer kauft was, wann, wie (2021). https://www. kpmg.at/upload/MCM/Publikationen/2021/studie-online-shopping-at.pdf
7. Spanke, M.: Retail Isn't Dead. Springer, Cham (2020). https://doi.org/10.1007/978-3-030-36650-6
8. Adhi, P., Burns, T., Davis, A., et al.: A transformation in store. https://www.mckinsey.com/capabilities/operations/our-insights/a-transformation-in-store
9. Lebow, S.: Worldwide ecommerce continues double-digit growth following pandemic push to online, 19 April 2021. https://www.insiderintelligence.com/content/worldwide-ecommerce-continues-double-digit-growth-following-pandemic-push-online
10. Insider Intelligence: Retail Sales Worldwide, 2020–2025 (trillions and % change), 1 January 2022. https://www.insiderintelligence.com/chart/253483/retail-sales-worldwide-2020-2025-trillions-change
11. Fairhurst, M.: Online Grocery Sales Projected to Reach $250B by 2025, According to New Research From Mercatus and Incisiv, 17 September 2020. https://www.mercatus.com/new sroom/online-grocery-sales-projected-to-reach-250b-by-2025-according-to-new-research-from-mercatus-and-incisiv/

12. Jacobs, K., Lindell, P., Rietra, M., et al.: Making the Digital Connection: Why Physical Retail Stores Need a Reboot (2017). https://www.capgemini.com/wp-content/uploads/2017/01/report-making-the-digital-connection.pdf

13. Oliver Wyman: The Future Supermarket: How digital operations will enable a winning customer experience, at much lower cost (2018). https://www.oliverwyman.es/content/dam/oliver-wyman/v2/publications/2018/February/Oliver_Wyman_The_Future_of_Supermarket.pdf

14. RetailDetail EU: JD.com to launch 1,000 stores per day, 17 April 2018. https://www.retaildetail.eu/news/general/jdcom-launch-1000-stores-day/

15. Ahmed, J.U., Ahmed, A., Talukdar, A., et al.: Innovation strategy in retail: the unstaffed digital supermarkets at LIFVS. J. Inf. Technol. Teach. Cases, 204388692211098 (2022)

16. Kitzmann, M.: Nahversorger-Konzept: weltweit erster unbemannter supermarkt in Schweden. Lebensmittel Zeitung (2016)

17. Roe, M., Spanaki, K., Ioannou, A., et al.: Drivers and challenges of internet of things diffusion in smart stores: a field exploration. Technol. Forecast. Soc. Change 178, 121593 (2022)

18. Berger-Grabner, D.: Strategic Retail Management and Brand Management: Trends, Tactics, and Examples. Walter de Gruyter GmbH, Berlin, München, Boston (2021)

19. Chang, Y.-W., Chen, J.: What motivates customers to shop in smart shops? The impacts of smart technology and technology readiness. J. Retail. Consum. Serv. 58, 102325 (2021)

20. Roy, S.K., Balaji, M.S., Sadeque, S., et al.: Constituents and consequences of smart customer experience in retailing. Technol. Forecast. Soc. Change 124, 257–270 (2017)

21. Wu, H.-C., Ai, C.-H., Cheng, C.-C.: Experiential quality, experiential psychological states and experiential outcomes in an unmanned convenience store. J. Retail. Consum. Serv. 51, 409–420 (2019)

22. Ghazwani, S., van Esch, P., Cui, Y., et al.: Artificial intelligence, financial anxiety and cashierless checkouts: a Saudi Arabian perspective. Int. J. Bank Mark. 40(6), 1200–1216 (2022)

23. Chen, S.-C., Shang, S.S.C.: Sustaining user experience in a smart system in the retail industry. Sustainability 13(9), 5090 (2021)

24. Arnold, M.J., Reynolds, K.E., Ponder, N., et al.: Customer delight in a retail context: investigating delightful and terrible shopping experiences. J. Bus. Res. 58(8), 1132–1145 (2005)

25. Bagdare, S., Jain, R.: Measuring retail customer experience. Int. J. Retail Distrib. Manag. 41(10), 790–804 (2013)

26. Fan, X., Ning, N., Deng, N.: The impact of the quality of intelligent experience on smart retail engagement. Mark. Intell. Plan. 38(7), 877–891 (2020)

27. Liu, J.: Autonomous retailing: a frontier for cyber-physical-human systems. In: Lohstroh, M., Derler, P., Sirjani, M. (eds.) Principles of Modeling. LNCS, vol. 10760, pp. 336–35. Springer, Cham (2018). https://doi.org/10.1007/978-3-319-95246-8_20

28. van Esch, P., Cui, Y., Jain, S.P.: Stimulating or intimidating: the effect of AI-enabled in-store communication on consumer patronage likelihood. J. Advert. 50(1), 63–80 (2021)

29. Grewal, D., Noble, S.M., Roggeveen, A.L., et al.: The future of in-store technology. J. Acad. Mark. Sci. 48(1), 96–113 (2020)

30. Ayden: Der Adyen Retail Report Europa: Wie europäische Verbraucher shoppen und was Händler tun können, um in der sich wandelnden Welt des Handels erfolgreich zu sein (2018). https://go.adyen.com/rs/222-DNK-376/images/Retail%20Report%20Europa%202018.pdf

31. Lyu, F., Lim, H.-A., Choi, J.: Customer acceptance of self-service technologies in retail : a case of convenience stores in China. Asia Pac. J. Inf. Syst. 29(3), 428–447 (2019)

32. Rock, S.: Innovativer check out – neue form des bezahlens. In: Knoppe, M., Rock, S., Wild, M. (eds) Der zukunftsfähige Handel, pp. 83–110. Springer, Wiesbaden (2022). https://doi.org/10.1007/978-3-658-36218-8_5

536   M. Staab et al.

33. Chiu, Y.-T.H., Hofer, K.M.: Service innovation and usage intention: a cross-market analysis. J. Serv. Manag. **26**(3), 516–538 (2015)
34. Grewal, D., Kroschke, M., Mende, M., et al.: Frontline cyborgs at your service: how human enhancement technologies affect customer experiences in retail, sales, and service settings. J. Interact. Mark. **51**, 9–25 (2020)
35. Mittelstand-Digital Zentrum Handel: Self-Checkout im Einzelhandel (2023). https://dig italzentrumhandel.de/wp-content/uploads/2023/04/mdzh_infoblatt_self-checkout_a4_dig ital_v6.pdf
36. Aloysius, A., Arora, A., Venkatesh, V.: Shoplifting in mobile checkout settings: cybercrime in retail stores. Inf. Technol. People **32**(5), 1234–1261 (2019)
37. Meuter, M.L., Ostrom, A.L., Roundtree, R.I., et al.: Self-service technologies: understanding customer satisfaction with technology-based service encounters. J. Mark. **64**(3), 50–64 (2000)
38. Hilton, T., Hughes, T., Little, E., et al.: Adopting self-service technology to do more with less. J. Serv. Mark. **27**(1), 3–12 (2013)
39. Anitsal, I., Schumann, D.W.: Toward a conceptualization of customer productivity: the customer's perspective on transforming customer labor into customer outcomes using technology-based self-service options. J. Mark. Theory Pract. **15**(4), 349–363 (2007)
40. Bulmer, S., Elms, J., Moore, S.: Exploring the adoption of self-service checkouts and the associated social obligations of shopping practices. J. Retail. Consum. Serv. **42**, 107–116 (2018)
41. Dekimpe, M.G., Geyskens, I., Gielens, K.: Using technology to bring online convenience to offline shopping. Mark. Lett. **31**(1), 25–29 (2020)
42. EHI Retail institute GmbH: Self-Checkout-Systeme im Handel. https://www.self-checkout-initiative.de/self-checkout/
43. Andriulo, S., Elia, V., Gnoni, M.G.: Mobile self-checkout systems in the FMCG retail sector: a comparison analysis. Int. J. RF Technol. **6**(4), 207–224 (2015)
44. Johnson, V.L., Woolridge, R.W., Bell, J.R.: The impact of consumer confusion on mobile self-checkout adoption. J. Comput. Inf. Syst. **61**(1), 76–86 (2021)
45. PwC: Frictionless retail - the future of shopping (2022). https://www.pwc.co.uk/industries/documents/frictionless-retail-the-future-of-shopping.pdf
46. Rahah Hamidi, S., Muhamad Yusof, M.A., Mohamed Shuhidan, S., et al.: IR4.0: unmanned store apps. Indones. J. Electr. Eng. Comput. Sci. **17**(3), 1540 (2020)
47. Kitzmann, M.: Weltweit erster unbemannter Supermarkt in Schweden. https://www.leb ensmittelzeitung.net/handel/nachrichten/Nahversorger-Konzept-In-Schweden-oeffnet-der-erste-unbemannte-Supermarkt-der-Welt-122496
48. Lin, C.-Y.: Understanding consumer perceptions and attitudes toward smart retail services. J. Serv. Mark. **36**(8), 1015–1030 (2022)
49. Hielscher, H.: Die Revolution im Handel beginnt im Kleinen: mit Geistershops in Kioskgröße. https://www.wiwo.de/unternehmen/handel/einzelhandel-die-revolution-im-han del-beginnt-im-kleinen-mit-geistershops-in-kioskgroesse/28670908.html
50. Rosbach, B., Weber, K.: Just walk out stores: easy going ist im Kommen. Lebensmittel Zeitung (2022)
51. Amazon: Just Walk Out, 20 June 2023. https://justwalkout.com/
52. Yao, L., Shuai, Y., Chen, X., et al.: A two-stage EBM-based approach to evaluate operational performance of unattended convenience store. Int. J. Retail Distrib. Manag. **48**(6), 609–627 (2020)
53. Zhang, H., Li, D., Ji, Y., et al.: Toward new retail: a benchmark dataset for smart unmanned vending machines. IEEE Trans. Ind. Inf. **16**(12), 7722–7731 (2020)
54. Tranfield, D., Denyer, D., Smart, P.: Towards a methodology for developing evidence-informed management knowledge by means of systematic review. Br. J. Manag. **14**(3), 207–222 (2003)

55. Snyder, H.: Literature review as a research methodology: an overview and guidelines. J. Bus. Res. **104**, 333–339 (2019)
56. Kumpulainen, M., Seppänen, M.: Combining web of science and scopus datasets in citation-based literature study. Scientometrics **127**(10), 5613–5631 (2022)
57. Gusenbauer, M., Haddaway, N.R.: Which academic search systems are suitable for systematic reviews or meta-analyses? Evaluating retrieval qualities of Google Scholar, PubMed, and 26 other resources. Res. Synth. Methods **11**(2), 181–217 (2020)
58. Inman, J.J., Nikolova, H.: Shopper-facing retail technology: a retailer adoption decision framework incorporating shopper attitudes and privacy concerns. J. Retail. **93**(1), 7–28 (2017)
59. Junsawang, S., Chaiyasoonthorn, W., Chaveesuk, S.: Willingness to use self-service technologies similar to Amazon go at supermarkets in Thailand. In: Proceedings of the 2020 2nd International Conference on Management Science and Industrial Engineering, pp. 135–139. ACM, New York (2020)
60. Junsawang, S., Chaveesuk, S., Chaiyasoonthorn, W.: Testing and measurement on willingness to use augmented reality, virtual reality, and AI-enabled checkouts. In: 2022 5th International Conference on Artificial Intelligence and Big Data (ICAIBD), pp. 495–500. IEEE (2022)
61. Wu, H.-C., Xu, H., Wu, T.-P.: Service innovation, experiential relationship quality and shopping outcomes in a smart unmanned store. J. Mark. Commun., 1–24 (2022)
62. Chang, Y.-W., Hsu, P.-Y., Chen, J., et al.: Utilitarian and/or hedonic shopping – consumer motivation to purchase in smart stores. Ind. Manag. Data Syst. **123**(3), 821–842 (2023)
63. Chen, J., Chang, Y.-W.: How smart technology empowers consumers in smart retail stores? The perspective of technology readiness and situational factors. Electron. Mark. **33**(1), 1 (2023)
64. Chuawatcharin, R., Gerdsri, N.: Factors influencing the attitudes and behavioural intentions to use just walk out technology among Bangkok consumers. Int. J. Public Sect. Perform. Manag. **5**(2), 146 (2019)
65. Gazzola, P., Grechi, D., Martinelli, I., et al.: The innovation of the cashierless store: a preliminary analysis in Italy. Sustainability **14**(4), 2034 (2022)
66. Lo, Wang: Constructing an evaluation model for user experience in an unmanned store. Sustainability **11**(18), 4965 (2019)
67. Phillips, C., Russell-Bennett, R., Kowalkiewicz, M.: The physical frictionless experience: a slippery slope for experience memorability of retail services? Serv. Ind. J., 1–30 (2022)
68. Pillai, R., Sivathanu, B., Dwivedi, Y.K.: Shopping intention at AI-powered automated retail stores (AIPARS). J. Retail. Consum. Serv. **57**, 102207 (2020)
69. Ponte, D., Bonazzi, S.: Physical supermarkets and digital integration: acceptance of the cashierless concept. Technol. Anal. Strateg. Manag., 1–13 (2021)
70. Thomas-Francois, K., Somogyi, S.: Self-Checkout behaviours at supermarkets: does the technological acceptance model (TAM) predict smart grocery shopping adoption? Int. Rev. Retail Distrib. Consum. Res. **33**(1), 44–66 (2023)
71. van Esch, P., Cui, Y., Jain, S.P.: Self-efficacy and callousness in consumer judgments of AI-enabled checkouts. Psychol. Mark. **38**(7), 1081–1100 (2021)
72. van Esch, P., Cui, Y.: Does consumer promiscuity influence purchase intent? The role of artificial intelligence (AI), change seeking, and pride. J. Assoc. Consum. Res. **6**(3), 394–401 (2021)
73. Wang, I.-C., Liao, C.-W., Lin, K.-P., et al.: Evaluate the consumer acceptance of AIoT-based unmanned convenience stores based on perceived risks and technological acceptance models. Math. Probl. Eng. **2021**, 1–12 (2021)
74. Cui, Y., van Esch, P., Jain, S.P.: Just walk out: the effect of AI-enabled checkouts. Eur. J. Mark. **56**(6), 1650–1683 (2022)
75. Hsu, S.-L.: The Study of consumers' intention to purchase in unmanned stores. J. Econ. Manag. **18**, 1–27 (2022)

76. Giroux, M., Kim, J., Lee, J.C., et al.: Artificial intelligence and declined guilt: retailing morality comparison between human and AI. J. Bus. Ethics JBE **178**(4), 1027–1041 (2022)
77. Park, H.J., Zhang, Y.: Technology readiness and technology paradox of unmanned convenience store users. J. Retail. Consum. Serv. **65**, 102523 (2022)
78. MacInnis, D.J., Moorman, C., Jaworski, B.J.: Enhancing and measuring consumers' motivation, opportunity, and ability to process brand information from ads. J. Mark. **55**(4), 32 (1991)
79. Roy, S.K., Balaji, M.S., Nguyen, B.: Consumer-computer interaction and in-store smart technology (IST) in the retail industry: the role of motivation, opportunity, and ability. J. Mark. Manag. **36**(3–4), 299–333 (2020)
80. Verhoef, P.C., Lemon, K.N., Parasuraman, A., et al.: Customer experience creation: determinants, dynamics and management strategies. J. Retail. **85**(1), 31–41 (2009)
81. Akhter, S.H.: Digital divide and purchase intention: why demographic psychology matters. J. Econ. Psychol. **24**(3), 321–327 (2003)
82. Larson, R.B.: Supermarket self-checkout usage in the United States. Serv. Mark. Q. **40**(2), 141–156 (2019)
83. Lee, S.: Mobile internet services from consumers' perspectives. Int. J. Hum. Comput. Interact. **25**(5), 390–413 (2009)
84. Priporas, C.-V., Stylos, N., Fotiadis, A.K.: Generation Z consumers' expectations of interactions in smart retailing: a future agenda. Comput. Hum. Behav. **77**, 374–381 (2017)
85. Collier, J.E., Breazeale, M., White, A.: Giving back the "self" in self service: customer preferences in self-service failure recovery. J. Serv. Mark. **31**(6), 604–617 (2017)
86. Castillo, D., Canhoto, A.I., Said, E.: The dark side of AI-powered service interactions: exploring the process of co-destruction from the customer perspective. Serv. Ind. J. **41**(13–14), 900–925 (2021)
87. Robertson, N., McDonald, H., Leckie, C., et al.: Examining customer evaluations across different self-service technologies. J. Serv. Mark. **30**(1), 88–102 (2016)
88. Marzocchi, G.L., Zammit, A.: Self-scanning technologies in retail: determinants of adoption. Serv. Ind. J. **26**(6), 651–669 (2006)

Cognitive-Based Design to Influence Structured Financial Planning and Money Management for Young People

Duy Linh Tran[✉]

Goldsmiths University of London, 8 Lewisham Way, London SE14 6NW, UK
dtran003@gold.ac.uk

Abstract. This study aims to develop an interactive digital prototype to help students manage their finances. It explores mental accounting, student money management behavior, and creates design guidelines for personal financial management. By employing various research methods such as usability testing and eye-gaze tracking analysis, valuable insights are gathered to evaluate the effectiveness and user-friendliness of the digital prototype. The results demonstrate significant improvements achieved through the new design, enhancing user engagement and simplifying the process of financial management for students, making financial planning more enjoyable.

Keywords: usability · user-centered design · user experience · eye-gaze tracking · money management · mental accounting · digital budgeting tool

1 Introduction

The absence of money management skills among college students is a major concern; on average, young people worldwide score poorly on financial concepts such as budgeting and saving, which may result in illegal behavior and longer-term debt [1]. To lower the possibility of debt, we need to better understand individual budgeting tendencies. Thus, budgeting is a method of managing personal money to minimize debt growth [2].

This study intends to explore literature reviews in mental accounting, student money management, and existing digital budgeting solutions. It takes a user centered design approach to develop engaging digital interactive prototypes. The goal is to assist young people in managing their money on a regular basis and encourage students to put their financial knowledge into practice.

2 Related Works

2.1 Mental Accounting

Mental accounting is a series of cognitive processes that people use to organize, assess, and monitor their money [3]. Studies have documented that individuals develop two distinct types of labels that influence their behaviour. First, individuals categorise money

© The Author(s), under exclusive license to Springer Nature Switzerland AG 2023
P. Zaphiris et al. (Eds.): HCII 2023, LNCS 14060, pp. 539–549, 2023.
https://doi.org/10.1007/978-3-031-48060-7_41

as relevant to a certain class of products, and then categorise the items as relevant to a particular pool of money. These are referred to as the budget-setting and expense-tracking procedures [4]. These two processes occur simultaneously in our lives, helping individuals to improve their spending self-control and make daily purchase decisions. People often categorise money as significant for certain consumption categories (for example, entertainment, housing, and food) and compare spending against their budget. As they spend money in one category, they use up the money in their account, which makes it less likely that they will buy things in the future [4]. Expense management consists of two steps: First, expenditures must be identified; individuals should be made aware of their spending, which should then be allocated to their appropriate accounts. After a specific event, we check how much money we spent in each category, and how much money we have left to spend for the remainder of the week (or month). Figure 1 visualises the mental model of budget setting and expense tracking.

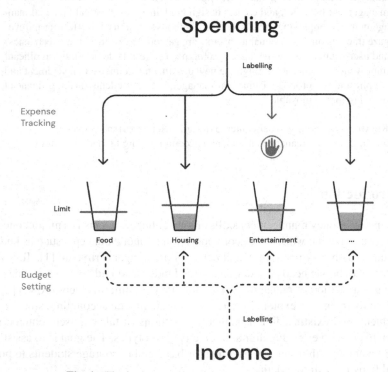

Fig. 1. The budget setting and expense tracking model

2.2 Budget Management in Students

Age, personality, and financial literacy all have a role in how well students manage their financial resources [5]. University students have particular challenges in managing their finances due to their low and inconsistent incomes and high expenses. They may not have a lot of experience with budgeting and managing money. According to Heath and Soll, most students had weekly food and entertainment budgets as well as monthly clothing budgets. These restrictions are likely to have altered considerably when the students find a job at the end of their degrees. Kidwell and Turrisi [6] built the predicted model of budgeting intention using the theory of planned behavior and the theory of social behavior [7]. Negative effects, attitude, subjective norm, past behavior, and perceived control all played a role in people's intentions to keep a budget. These findings suggest that when students believe they have more capacity to budget, they are more likely to do so. In contrast, when students consider they have less control over their finances, they may depend more on their feelings than their cognitive views to determine their overall intentions. Having a budget makes people consider how their money should be spent.

3 Design Guidelines

Any designer of digital solutions must take into account a number of user characteristics. Budgeting is a mentally challenging task that is influenced by a variety of factors. When someone begins managing their money, they should first recognize their financial situation, the balance between their income and expenditure. Understanding the position enables users to evaluate their circumstances in order to develop and commit to a suitable action plan. The design should follow the 3 stages: Aware, Evaluate, and Action

Aware	*Assist people in understanding their financial situation* In order to assist individuals in managing their finances, spending must first be identified and then allocated to the appropriate accounts. Because the process demands attention and memory, the design should first allow users to go back and see, for example, how much money they spent on food in a week or what the proportion of spending on each category is for the month
Evaluate	*Enable people in evaluating their current budget plan* The plan's evaluation is critical since new students, particularly foreign students, struggle to determine if the cost of living in a new country is reasonable for them. The design should allow them to evaluate their plan by providing them enough information, and inform their decision. For example, design should allow them to compare their cost of living to that of other students at their university, so they can estimate how much it will cost them in the future. Everyone has different needs that influence their income and expenditure balance. Instead of indicating whether the budget is high or low, the design assists people in evaluating it based on their own scenario
Action	*Encourage users to put their financial knowledge into practice and stick to the goal* Sticking to a budget involves strong self-control and the formation of a long-term habit that begins with little steps. It is essential that the design assists users in committing to their plan through many ways of behavioral change. For example, the reward system used to incentivize users each time they complete a goal or plan. The design must be engaging and enjoyable so that users will want to engage with it regularly

4 Research Methods

User-centered design (UCD) is an iterative design process that focuses on the users' needs [8]. UCD was adopted in this research to iterate the design.

Guerrilla Testing of Lo-Fi Prototype: A set of paper prototypes is used to conduct Guerilla testing with 3 Goldsmith's students, low-fidelity prototype testing provided quick user responses. It's a good chance to understand students' mental models and how they interact with a new concept.

In-Lab Usability Testing: There were 5 participants who interacted with the interface in the Goldsmiths UX lab. The test's goal is to assess the effectiveness, efficiency, memorability, and learnability of existing and new designs. It also makes practical suggestions for improvement.

Eye-Gaze Tracking Analysis: Eye tracking provides a real-time account of where a person sees without asking them to talk. There are 3 main analysis methods of eye-gaze tracking used to measure UX in this study such as the heatmap to understand more about the visual search experience; gaze plots to understand the visual hierarchy of current and new interfaces and make informed decisions on how to optimize the placement of screen elements, and areas of interest to analyze the users' attention to various visual components.

System Usability Scale (SUS): The System Usability Scale (SUS) is a reliable, quick tool for assessing usability. Five participants were asked to complete questionnaires after interacting with the product and providing feedback to evaluate its system usability score. It enables the researcher to assess the usability perception of interfaces. It also informs me of the overall satisfaction of users after they interact with a new product (Fig. 2).

Fig. 2. Usability testing with eye-gaze tracking was conducted at Goldsmiths UX Lab

5 Results and Analysis

There are three main analysis methods of eye-gaze such as heatmaps, Gaze-plots and areas of interest (AOIs). The results and insights are shown below in Tables 1 and 2.

5.1 Eye Gaze Tracking Analysis

Table 1. Eye-gaze tracking analysis of current design

Screens		Insights
Home-page		• Users scan websites rather than reading all of the content. • Faces tend to attract more fixations than non-face images. • When textual information, particularly titles, is placed next to faces, it receives fewer intense fixations.
Results		• Users actively seek information using a specific strategy. • Users are interested in how much they spend. • They also spent more time looking at total money and status from the system, but an interview revealed that this was due to the label being difficult for them to understand.
Process		• A greater number of fixations indicates that more processing time is required, the object is more difficult to identify. • Users spend a lot of time this screen, one of the main reasons is they have to recall while interacting with the interface

Table 2. Eye-gaze tracking analytics of new design

Screens		Insights

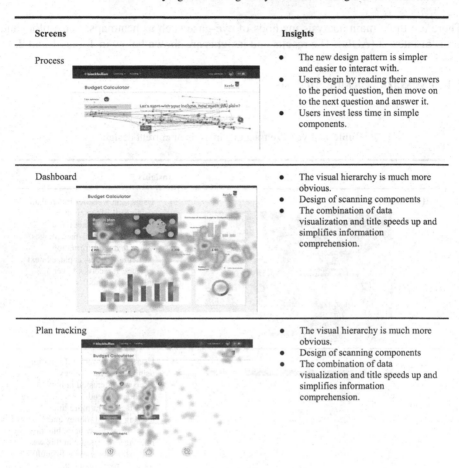

Process
- The new design pattern is simpler and easier to interact with.
- Users begin by reading their answers to the period question, then move on to the next question and answer it.
- Users invest less time in simple components.

Dashboard
- The visual hierarchy is much more obvious.
- Design of scanning components
- The combination of data visualization and title speeds up and simplifies information comprehension.

Plan tracking
- The visual hierarchy is much more obvious.
- Design of scanning components
- The combination of data visualization and title speeds up and simplifies information comprehension.

5.2 Goal-Oriented Plan: Intentions Promote Goals Achievement

In usability testing with the current design, all of the users felt it was really hard to find and create a plan. There was a lack of engagement when users started a new plan (Fig. 3).

When users begin a new plan with the new design, at first, we discuss their goals—the things they want to achieve in their lives, such as setting up an emergency fund, saving more money, getting out of debt, and so on. Research in psychology has shown that setting goals is useful because it helps people get to the right places and do the right things [9].

5.3 New Interactive Patterns: Make the Design More Human

The current design makes data entry appear difficult and complex. There is a lot of input that requires memory and a high level of cognitive overload (Fig. 4).

Before After

Fig. 3. Intentions promote goal achievement design

Before After

Fig. 4. The budget setting process design

The tasks in the new design mimic a human conversation in which the system asks questions and the students respond. When users interact with the interface, they feel more at ease. Data from gaze-plots reveals the new pattern of interaction. The bubble represents where people look, and the size of the bubble represents how much time they spend at each point. Users have to move their eyes back and forth many times to input in the current version, and they spend a long time on screen components, which may cause cognitive overload. In contrast, the eye-movement pattern in the new design is much simpler for users to follow. They first notice their response to the previous question on the left, then read the question and respond to it on the right. It saves a lot of time, and the interaction across the tools is consistent (Fig. 5).

5.4 Design to Empower: Deep Dive to User Behavior

The data from Area of interest (AOIs) provides numerous useful insights into user behaviour. For example, in the result screen, one component with only two words is easy to read, but people spend 3.37 s on it, while a section with 4–5 sentences is read in just 3.81 s (Table 3) (Fig. 6).

According to data gathered from interviews, issues arise after users interact with the interface. For example, users didn't know what the "status" implied, so they viewed it frequently to understand what it meant. On the other hand, the paragraph's content didn't

Before   After

Fig. 5. Data from gaze-plots indicates a pattern of eye movement

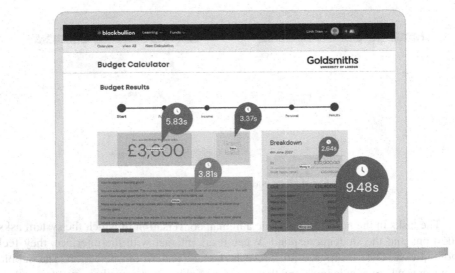

Fig. 6. The area of interest indicates how long the user looks at various interface components

interest them because it didn't meet their needs. The area that gets the most attention is "money out", and interviews show that they care about how money is calculated in their expenses. They want to know how much they spend on each category, and the current design doesn't give them much insight.

In the new design, users are provided with much more insights about their expenses, which aligns with my design strategy, and helps people be aware of and evaluate their situation (Fig. 7).

The new design allows users to compare their cost of living to that of other students at their university, so they can estimate how much it will cost them in the future. Everyone has different needs that influence their income and expenditure balances. Instead of indicating whether the budget is high or low, the design assists people in evaluating it based on their own scenario.

Table 3. Total duration of fixation in 5 defined AOIs

Participant	Education	First time user	Home student	Study type	Areas of Interest (AOI)				
					Advice	Money In	Money out	Status	Total money left
P1	Graduate	Yes	No	FT	5.27	2.02	2.17	5.83	5.30
P2	Graduate	Yes	No	FT	0.72	0.93	3.38	0.32	1.65
P3	Graduate	Yes	No	FT	3.60	6.57	28.46	4.30	8.63
P4	Graduate	Yes	No	FT	5.67	1.03	3.90	3.03	7.73
Average					**3.81**	**2.64**	**9.48**	**3.37**	**5.83**
Share of Total Time (%)					**15.17**	**10.50**	**37.72**	**13.42**	**23.20**

Fig. 7. The new dashboard design

5.5 System Usability Score and User Feedback

The System Usability Scale (SUS) is a trusted, low-cost usability scale that can be used for overall system usability assessments [10]. The new design received positive user feedback. All participants agreed that the new design was more interesting and engaging, and that they would like to use it in the future. Table 2 describes the system usability score based on the survey after users interact with design (Table 4).

System usability score (SUS)

$$SUS = ((Avg\,(x) - 5) + (25 - Avg\,(y))) * 2.5 = 82$$

According to Jeff Sauro [11] the overall average SUS score across is 68. A SUS score of 68 or higher is considered above average, while anything less than 68 is considered below average.

Table 4. Calculation of system usability score

Participant	Q1	Q2	Q3	Q4	Q5	Q6	Q7	Q8	Q9	Q10
P1	5	2	4	1	4	1	4	2	4	2
P2	4	2	4	2	3	1	5	1	4	1
P3	4	3	5	4	5	2	4	2	4	2
P4	3	2	4	1	4	2	5	2	5	1
P5	4	2	5	1	4	2	5	1	5	1
Total	**20**	**11**	**22**	**9**	**20**	**8**	**23**	**8**	**22**	**7**
Sum:	150	Avg								
Odd sum (x)	107	21.4	Odd – questions 1, 3, 5, 7, and 9							
Even sum (y)	43	8.6	Even – questions 2, 4, 6, 8, and 10							

The system usability scale in this research was high, indicating that the new design was regarded as easy-to-use, learnable, and that the users were happy after using the product. Contributing to the improvement of the product's user experience.

6 Conclusion

The research delivered a validated design solution that considers the user, business, and technology. It begins to establish the foundation for how we create useful tools to assist users in financial management. The design has the potential to provide a new approach to user engagement with the tools, making financial planning more enjoyable. The new design incorporates goal-oriented plans, new interactive patterns that mimic human conversation, and deeper insights into user behavior. The system usability score indicates positive user feedback, with participants finding the new design more interesting, engaging, and usable.

The design guidelines were established for personal financial management. These design guidelines can be used to assist designers in developing a theory-practical approach within financial settings, and to help users develop long-term financial management habits. In order to assist individuals in managing their finances, spending must first be identified. It is important that digital tools help users be aware of their financial situation. The next step is to enable people to evaluate their current budget plans. Everyone has different needs that influence their income and expenditure balances. Instead of indicating whether the budget is high or low, the design assists people in evaluating it based on their own scenario. The design should allow them to evaluate their plan by providing them with enough information to inform their decision. Sticking to a budget involves strong self-control and the formation of a long-term habit that begins with little steps. It is essential that the design assist users in committing to their plan through many ways of behavioral change.

The study's findings provide numerous insights into students' money management behaviors. Budgeting is a mentally challenging task that is influenced by a number of variables. Students manage their budgets in a variety of ways. Some students use spreadsheets, while others keep bills and receipts to remind them of their expenses. Some students manage their budgets by keeping a budget diary on their phones. They typically have budgets that are defined over shorter time periods, such as a week or month. Budgeting can be a very emotional process. Some students find it rewarding and a sign of financial independence, while others are extremely worried about not knowing how much they're actually spending, and still others are worried about not being able to pay their bills. These findings identify an opportunity to develop a solution that increases user engagement with the application, simplifies financial management, and instills positive emotions in students.

I believe that future work can enhance these proposed design guidelines and possibly validate this method. Future research may target a broader spectrum of users with diverse characteristics, such as those who are not tech-savvy or who are unfamiliar with online money management concepts.

References

1. Garg, N., Singh, S.: Financial literacy among youth. Int. J. Soc. Econ. **45**(1), 173–186 (2018). https://doi.org/10.1108/IJSE-11-2016-0303
2. Lunt, P.K., Livingstone, S.M.: Everyday explanations for personal debt: a network approach. Br. J. Soc. Psychol. **30**(4), 309–323 (1991)
3. Thaler, R.H.: Mental accounting matters. J. Behav. Decis. Mak. **12**(3), 183–206 (1999). https://doi.org/10.1002/(SICI)1099-0771(199909)
4. Heath, C., Soll, J.B.: Mental budgeting and consumer decisions. J. Consum. Res. **23**(1), 40–52 (1996). https://doi.org/10.1086/209465
5. Norvilitis, J.M., Merwin, M.M., Osberg, T.M., Roehling, P.V., Young, P., Kamas, M.M.: Personality factors, money attitudes, financial knowledge, and credit-card debt in college students. J. Appl. Soc. Psychol. **36**(6), 1395–1413 (2006). https://doi.org/10.1111/j.0021-9029.2006.00065.x
6. Kidwell, B., Turrisi, R.: An examination of college student money management tendencies. J. Econ. Psychol. **25**(5), 601–616 (2004)
7. Triandis, H.C.: The self and social behavior in differing cultural contexts. Psychol. Rev. **96**(3), 506–520 (1989). https://doi.org/10.1037/0033-295X.96.3.506
8. Lillemaa, M.: User-centered design. Bainbridge, W. Encyclopedia of .... (2004). https://www.academia.edu/1012299/User_centered_design
9. Gollwitzer, P.M.: Goal achievement: the role of intentions. Eur. Rev. Soc. Psychol. **4**(1), 141–185 (1993). https://doi.org/10.1080/14792779343000059
10. Brooke, J.: SUS: A quick and dirty usability scale. Usability Eval. Ind. **189** (1995)
11. Andrew, D.: Eye Tracking Methodology (n.d.). https://link.springer.com/book/10.1007/978-1-84628-609-4. Accessed 18 Aug 2022

Digital Marketing: Develop the Scales for Measuring Brand Experience in the Digital Economy

Yubin Xie[1,5], Ronggang Zhou[1,2], Xiaorui Wang[3(✉)], and Beiping Tan[4]

[1] School of Economics and Management, Beihang University, Beijing, China
[2] Key Laboratory of Complex System Analysis, Management and Decision (Beihang University), Ministry of Education, Beijing, China
[3] School of Economics and Management, Beijing University of Chemical Technology, Beijing, China
cecily_wong@126.com
[4] Miaozhen System, Beijing, China
[5] Department of Systems Engineering, City University of Hong Kong, Kowloon, Hong Kong, China

Abstract. Brand experience is crucial in cultivating brand equity, particularly in markets where products and services have become increasingly similar. Based on a theoretical framework of user experience presence, this study aims to develop a scale for measuring brand experience in customer-internet interaction marketing. Three studies were conducted to validate the scale. The first study involved literature analysis and focus group discussions to create an initial lexicon of terms describing brand and product experiences. The second study used expert evaluation and interviews to refine the lexicon, resulting in 57 retained words. The third study included user testing to evaluate the suitability of the words and identified 14 core dimensions, and principal component analysis extracted two dimensions: Inner-Outer and Agency-Pleasure. The scale provides insights into the emotional and rational aspects of brand experiences. This research contributes to understanding and enhancing brand experiences in the digital age.

Keywords: Brand experience · User experience (UX) · Digital marketing · Customer experience management

1 Introduction

Brand experience has long been an important topic of research in the marketing area, as for the vital role it plays in cultivating brand equity [1, 2]. Many previous studies found that positive brand experience arouses affective effects of the customers, such as brand trust and brand authenticity, which then induce brand love and brand attachment [3–5]. In markets where products and services become more and more similar, customers make choices and decisions more based on emotional aspects rather than rational thinking [2]. Thus, providing a better brand experience helps brands access long-term relationships

© The Author(s), under exclusive license to Springer Nature Switzerland AG 2023
P. Zaphiris et al. (Eds.): HCII 2023, LNCS 14060, pp. 550–562, 2023.
https://doi.org/10.1007/978-3-031-48060-7_42

with customers, as well as their loyalty behaviors [6]. In vast traditional brand experience studies, many scales were developed to measure brand experience, and most of them were based on the experience economy theories proposed by Pine and Gilmore [7]. According to Pine and Gilmore, entertainment, education, aesthetics, and escapism from reality are the four main dimensions people pursue in experiences. Brakus et al. [8] reviewed the measurements for brand personality [9], brand community [10], brand trust [11], and brand attachment [12], and proposed methods to measure brand experience. The scale developed by Brakus et al. [8] includes four dimensions: sensory, affective, intellectual, and behavioral. Khan and Rahman [13] developed a 5-dimension scale to measure hotel visitors' brand experience. Nikhashemi, Jebarajakirthy, and Nusair [14] studied how to measure brand experience in the apparel industry and uncovered its influence on brand love.

Nowadays, with the outbreak and fast development of the internet, brand marketing strategies have experienced a dramatic change. The internet erases the wall between brand and customer and provides connecting and information exchange platforms. Customer engagement, as well as the interaction between brand and customer, are enhanced to a great extent. Various studies explored how online brand experience impacts customers' perception and behavior intention. Most of these studies develop the research framework based on traditional brand experience dimensions, among which Brakus et al.'s [8] four-dimension theory were employed the most. Similar conclusions were drawn from these studies. For example, Beig & Nika [15] found how the four dimensions of brand experience (sensory, affective, behavioral and intellectual) impact brand equity (brand awareness, brand association, perceived quality, brand loyalty). However, we hold the opinion that the online brand experience is very different from the traditional brand experience, and this lies in how different the way customers generate and how conveniently they exchange brand information. Indeed, the offline experience still impacts customers' judgment of a brand. But through channels, customers could love or hate a brand more easily [16, 17]. That is why brands take social media marketing activities as a very important thing in brand marketing [18]. Social media marketing was found to have a positive effect on brand trust, brand equity, and brand love [19, 20]. In addition, the online brand committee empowered consumers with the platforms to share knowledge and experiences and participate in community activities, which helps to cultivate brand co-creation, which helps the brand accumulate equity [21]. Thus, online brand experience studies concentrate the online brand communities a lot [21–24].

In this e-marketing environment, brands need to understand what customers experience the brand in this hyper-connected and multi-interactive market, and a scale is needed to help measure the brand experience. However, few studies were found to understand the brand experience based on its difference from traditional brand experience and its characteristics. Moreover, a scale is called to measure the brand experience in custom-internet interaction marketing. This study intends to make efforts to fill this gap and the study aims to develop a scale for measuring brand experience in custom-internet interaction marketing. Based on existing literature, three distinct studies were carried out to validate the scale.

2 Study 1: Item Generation and Selection

Using brand experience and user experience as keywords, we searched the Google Scholar database for 23,300 relevant papers. The scales related to digital brand experience, traditional user experience, human-machine system design, consumer need elements, values, goals, and trust were screened at the consumer experience level and consumer motivation level respectively, and 28 validated scales and evaluation tools were collected and collated, including: Brand Experience Metric Questionnaire [8], SUS System Usability Scale [25], PSSUQ Scale [26], SASSI Scale [27], MOS-X Scale [28], ASQ [29], Computer System Usability Questionnaire (CSUQ) [30], USE Questionnaire [31], WAMMI Analysis Questionnaire [32], ACSI Customer Satisfaction Model [33], CMQ [34], Self-Determination Theory [35], Automation Trust Questionnaire [36], Consumer Values Scale [37], APEC Framework [38], User Product Interaction Model [39], Principles of User Experience [40], Mobile App Usability Framework [41], Microsoft MUG Model [42], Microsoft Corporation Product Response Cards [43], Emotion Thesaurus [44]. A total of 459 topics and 268 adjectives related to describing brand and product experiences were obtained. Eight UX researchers were then recruited to extract the adjectives from the 450 questionnaire questions through focus group discussions. Participants selected each word separately for its suitability for describing brand experiences and for describing product experiences, removing words that more than half of the experts considered unsuitable for describing brand and product experiences, as well as repetitive words and near-synonyms. An initial lexicon of 112 adjectives was created. All items in the thesaurus extraction process were managed in English. They were translated into Chinese using the translation-re-translation method. The actual survey was conducted in Chinese.

3 Study 2: Expert Evaluation and Item Reduction

3.1 Research Method

Participants
In this study, 20 experts working on UX-related research were first invited to assess the applicability of the original thesaurus for brand and product experience. They came from the School of Economics and Management of Beihang University. Each expert was asked to evaluate which of the words in the brand and product experience lexicon proposed in this study were suitable for describing good experiences, which words were suitable for describing bad experiences, and which words were suitable for describing the ideal brand experience. All participants took the survey voluntarily and could terminate the questionnaire at any time. At the end of the survey, each participant will be paid RMB 20.

Research Procedures
The study was conducted by completing an electronic questionnaire offline. First, we asked 20 experts to recall their experiences during their contact with a brand or product, so participants formed an initial perception of the experience. Second, the participants

completed two sections in turn, brand experience, and product experience, to measure the same lexicon repeatedly. In the brand experience section, we first asked participants to recall their recent experience/process of contact with a brand, either by watching a brand live broadcast, or by shopping for a brand's official shop, or by browsing the brand's information on Weibo or WeChat, etc. Participants were then asked which brand brought good and bad experiences, and their reasons, respectively, and were asked to extract the keywords. Participants were then asked to score the appropriateness of each word in terms of its suitability to describe a good or desirable brand experience. The scoring was carried out using a Likert scale, with a scale of 1–5 indicating not appropriate to very appropriate. All words were presented in a randomized form, and some of the words were repeated in the question items to screen and identify invalid questionnaires. In the product experience section, we repeated the above design.

3.2 Analysis and Results

First, we separately calculated the participants' evaluation scores for the brand and product experience lexicon. Separate calculations were also performed for the lexicon of words suitable for describing a good experience and the lexicon of words suitable for describing an ideal experience. To check the validity of the completions, we conducted t-tests on the repeated word scores in each evaluation perspective, which demonstrated significant differences in all evaluation perspectives. In addition, we tested the reliability of the scales, and Cronbach's alpha was above 0.8 for all scales. Therefore, we consider the reliability of the questionnaire to be good. By calculating the mean score for each word, we screened the words that scored greater than 3.0 on all four evaluation structures and merged their common parts. A total of 70 words were retained after merging. After completing the refinement of the thesaurus, we re-contacted the experts who had previously conducted the refinement to confirm the results of the retained words above. The experts concluded that some words in the current lexicon were prone to odd interpretations, similarities in meaning and opposite meanings. Therefore, based on the unified recommendations of the experts and the expert evaluation records collected in the questionnaire, we further trimmed down the lexicon to obtain a brand product experience evaluation lexicon with 57 words (e.g.: Exciting, Convenient, Satisfied, Reliable and so on).

4 Study 3: Questionnaire Survey: Revealed Brand Experience Dimensions

Based on the revised lexicon, we developed a questionnaire for developing the brand experience measurement dimensions and conducted the questionnaire. The questionnaire contained two parts. The first part consisted of questions about the gender, age, education, income, and occupational demographics of the respondents. In the second part we presented the participants with an introductory image of a brand that was derived from this brand's material in digital promotional media. The participants were asked to imagine that they currently needed to buy any product of the type shown in the material and were browsing the websites of the different brands selling the product. We split the word bank into 3 random groups of 19 words each. We asked participants to select 5 words that best described how the brand made them feel and 5 words that were least descriptive. We then tested the words that described how the product under the brand made the user feel similarly to the process described above.

To exclude any bias caused by a single brand stimulus on the user's word choice, six materials were selected for the questionnaire test, containing a new energy car brand, a blind box brand, a beverage brand, a pet brand, a sports brand and a food brand. All these brands have online marketing platforms. In addition, we also differentiated the online marketing channels of the material brands, and all materials came from different online marketing channels. Six materials were designed to be grouped together, and each participant could choose a particular material to evaluate.

The study was reviewed and approved by the Human Research Ethics Committee of the School of Economics and Management at Beihang University. The measurement questionnaire was distributed through an online questionnaire platform and all participants took the survey voluntarily. They could terminate the completion of the questionnaire at any time. A payment will be made upon completion of the questionnaire, which takes approximately 5–8 min to complete.

4.1 Participants

In this study, the data were collected by BrandEx and 2481 questionnaires were distributed from 1591 participants. This included 677 males (42.55%) and 914 females (57.45%), of whom 43 (2.70%) were under 18 years of age, 450 (28.28%) were between 18 and 29 years of age, 739 (46.45%) were between 30 and 39 years of age, 266 (16.72%) were between 40 and 49 years of age, 80 (5.03%) were between 50 and 59 years of age, and 19 (1.19%) were over 60 years of age.

4.2 Data Analysis and Results

Descriptive Statistics
We counted the frequency with which each word was selected. On describing brand experience, 36 words exceeded the mean value of the number of times each word was selected. To describe the product experience, 40 words exceeded the mean of the number of times each word was selected. A paired-sample t-test was conducted on participants' choice of brand experience and product experience lexicons. The results showed no significant difference in participants' choice of words from the two lexicons. Therefore, in the subsequent analysis, we will combine the data from both lexicons for analysis. We plotted the word cloud using the frequency with which each word was selected as a weight and found some differences in the words that were important for brand experience and product experience, as shown in Figs. 1 and 2. For brand experience, participants felt that words such as appealing, interested, satisfied, innovative, friendly, practical, trustworthy, and stylish were more important. They were biased toward describing external characteristics. For product experience, participants felt that satisfied, useful, pleasant, reliable, practical, comfortable, and other words that tend to describe intrinsic characteristics were more important. In summary, participants' descriptions of brand experience favored the

transient experience of direct contact, while descriptions of product experience favored the long-term experience of pragmatism.

Fig. 1. Brand Experience Word Cloud.

Fig. 2. Product Experience Word Cloud.

Construction of a Brand Experience Measurement Model

To explore the dimensional characteristics of the brand experience metrics. We processed 57 words by means of hierarchical clustering, forming a total of 14 categories.

We have named each of the 14 cores as Symbolic, Comfortable, Competence, Functional, Qualitative, Efficient, Creative, Technology, Aesthetic, Joyful, Service, Emotional, Sensory, and Related. Then, we analyzed the linguistic characteristics of the 14 categories of words and found that the statistical clustering results were consistent with the linguistic proxemics feature. Therefore, we concluded that the extraction of statistical clustering was valid. We combined and calculated the 57 words in 14 measurement categories by computing the clustering centers, which we refer to as the cores of brand experience.

To validate the core dimensions of the brand experience, an exploratory factor analysis (EFA) was conducted using the combined 14 core data as the basis. The results of the Bartlett sphericity test indicated the presence of a common factor ($\chi2 = 4836.341$, df = 91, p < 0.01). The results of the Kaiser-Meyer-Olkin suggest that the questionnaire data were suitable for exploratory factor analysis. We enabled the lexicon to be compared in two dimensions by fixing the extraction of two factors, with a cumulative variance explained of 26.65%. The two dimensions were then extracted using principal component analysis to describe the 14 cores.

Figure 3 shows the relationship between the two dimensions and the 14 cores. We called it the Brand experience elements map. We have named the two dimensions: "inner (the letter "I" in the map),, which emphasizes the fundamental functions of the brand, and outer (the letter "O" in the map), which emphasizes the appearance of the brand [45–48], agency (the letter "A" in the map), which emphasizes the basic perception of the brand and pleasure (the letter "P" in the map), which emphasizes the exciting perception of the brand [49, 50]. Based on the characteristics of the words contained in each quadrant. We named the first quadrant Exciting [51, 52], the second quadrant Personality [8, 53], the third quadrant Rational [2, 54], and the fourth quadrant Breaking [55]. We conclude that the cores have a good categorical measure of brand experience.

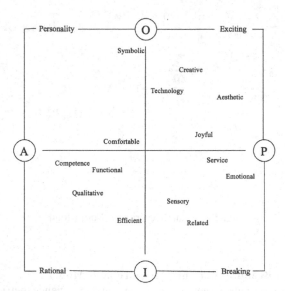

Fig. 3. Brand experience elements map

The dimensions of "inner" and "outer," as well as "agency" and "pleasure." shed light on different aspects of brand experiences in the context of custom-internet interaction marketing. The "inner" dimension emphasizes the fundamental functions of the brand. It delves into how the brand fulfills customers' needs and expectations regarding product performance, reliability, and functionality [56]. This dimension reflects the utilitarian aspects of brand experiences, focusing on the core value proposition and utility that the brand provides to customers [57]. Brands that excel in the "Inner" dimension prioritize delivering high-quality products or services, meeting customer expectations, and providing a seamless user experience. In contrast, the "Outer" dimension highlights the appearance and aesthetic aspects of the brand. It encompasses the brand's visual elements, design, and overall presentation that evoke customers' sensory and emotional responses. The "outer" dimension explores how brands use aesthetics, branding, and visual elements to create an appealing and captivating brand image [58]. This dimension acknowledges the role of sensory and emotional stimuli in shaping brand experiences, as customers are influenced by the visual and sensory cues presented by the brand [59]. The "agency" dimension focuses on the basic perception of the brand, encompassing attributes such as reliability, trustworthiness, and credibility. This dimension emphasizes the role of brand attributes in building customer confidence and trust [60]. Brands that excel in the "agency" dimension establish themselves as reliable and dependable options, instilling in customers a sense of security and assurance [61]. The "pleasure" dimension emphasizes the exciting and enjoyable aspects of the brand experience [62]. This dimension reflects the emotional and hedonic elements of brand interactions, capturing the delight, joy, and positive emotions that customers experience. Brands that excel in the "Pleasure" dimension evoke positive emotions, create memorable experiences, and provide customers with a sense of excitement and pleasure in their interactions [63].

5 Discussion

The three studies conducted in this research have enhanced our understanding of the brand experience and its dimensions in the digital landscape. By synthesizing the literature and employing rigorous research methods, this study provides valuable insights into the measurement and characterization of brand experience. The first study involved literature analysis and focus group discussions to develop an initial lexicon of adjectives. This approach aligns with previous studies that have emphasized the importance of sensory, affective, intellectual, and behavioral dimensions in the measurement of brand experience [8]. The second study employed expert evaluation to refine the lexicon, resulting in a final set of 57 words. The retained words encompass a broad range of dimensions, including symbolism, comfort, competence, aesthetics, and emotionality, reflecting the multidimensional nature of brand experiences. The third study conducted user testing and identified 14 core clusters and two dimensions: "inner" and "outer," as well as "agency" and "pleasure." These findings resonate with prior research that underscores the importance of both rational and emotional aspects in shaping brand experiences [4].

The study also contributes to the existing body of literature by developing a comprehensive scale for measuring brand experience in the digital marketing context. Including multiple dimensions, such as sensory, affective, and cognitive dimensions, allows for a more nuanced understanding of brand experiences. This scale can serve as a valuable tool for marketers seeking to assess and enhance the brand experience provided to customers. By understanding the specific dimensions that influence brand experiences, marketers can tailor their strategies to evoke positive emotional responses, foster brand trust, and cultivate brand attachment [64, 65]. The dimensional and quadrant characteristics retained by principal component analysis including Exciting and Breaking. These dimensions are rarely addressed in traditional brand experiences. They are also rarely mentioned when evaluating some traditional products. Adding these new dimensions showed that the hyperconnected and multi-interactive nature of the digital environment necessitates a deeper understanding of customer experiences and engagement [2]. Marketers can develop strategies that address customers' functional needs, aesthetic preferences, and emotional desires.

Despite the significant contributions of this study, several limitations should be acknowledged. First, the scale development process heavily relied on subjective evaluations and may be influenced by individual biases. Future research could consider incorporating objective measures and conducting cross-validation studies to validate the scale further. Additionally, the current study primarily focused on digital brand experiences, and we have not compared its measurement effects with traditional brand experience scales.

6   Conclusion

Through three studies, this paper has successfully developed a lexicon and structure for evaluating brand experience in a digital medium. Literature analysis and focus group discussions developed an original thesaurus suitable for describing the brand experience. The thesaurus was refined through expert evaluation and interviews. Finally, the brand experience measurement and evaluation lexicon was developed through large sample user testing, and a 2-dimensional digital brand experience metrics model containing 14 cores was identified. It provides a practical and effective tool for digital brand experience measurement and provides strong support for brand experience research in digital media.

Acknowledgments. This study was supported by the National Natural Science Foundation of China (NSFC, 72021001 and 72171015). Thanks a lot to BrandEx for their generous support of the data collection.

Disclosure Statement.   The authors declare that they have no known competing financial interests or personal relationships that could have appeared to influence the work reported in this article.

References

1. Quan, N., Chi, N.T.K.C., Nhung, D., Ngan, N., Phong, L.: The influence of website brand equity, e-brand experience on e-loyalty: the mediating role of e-satisfaction. Manag. Sci. Lett. **10**(1), 63–76 (2020). https://doi.org/10.5267/j.msl.2019.8.015
2. Pina, R., Dias, Á.: The influence of brand experiences on consumer-based brand equity. J. Brand Manag. **28**, 99–115 (2021). https://doi.org/10.1057/s41262-020-00215-5
3. Joshi, R., Garg, P.: Role of brand experience in shaping brand love. Int. J. Consum. Stud. **45**(2), 259–272 (2021). https://doi.org/10.1111/ijcs.12618

4. Kim, R.B., Chao, Y.: Effects of brand experience, brand image and brand trust on brand building process: the case of Chinese millennial generation consumers. J. Int. Stud. **12**(3) (2019)
5. Safeer, A.A., He, Y., Abrar, M.: The influence of brand experience on brand authenticity and brand love: an empirical study from Asian consumers' perspective. Asia Pac. J. Mark. Logist. **33**(5), 1123–1138 (2021). https://doi.org/10.1108/APJML-02-2020-0123
6. Mostafa, R.B., Kasamani, T.: Brand experience and brand loyalty: is it a matter of emotions? Asia Pac. J. Mark. Logist. **33**(4), 1033–1051 (2021). https://doi.org/10.1108/APJML-11-2019-0669
7. Pine, B.J., Gilmore, J.H.: Welcome to the Experience Economy, vol. 76, no. 4, pp. 97–105 (1998). Harvard Business Review Press
8. Brakus, J.J., Schmitt, B.H., Zarantonello, L.: Brand experience: what is it? How is it measured? Does it affect loyalty? J. Mark. **73**(3), 52–68 (2009)
9. Aaker, J.L.: Dimensions of brand personality. J. Mark. Res. **34**(3), 347–356 (1997). https://doi.org/10.1177/002224379703400304
10. McAlexander, J.H., Schouten, J.W., Koenig, H.F.: Building brand community. J. Mark. **66**(1), 38–54 (2002). https://doi.org/10.1509/jmkg.66.1.38.18451
11. Delgado-Ballester, E., Munuera-Aleman, J.L., Yague-Guillen, M.J.: Development and validation of a brand trust scale. Int. J. Mark. Res. **45**(1), 35–54 (2003). https://doi.org/10.1177/14707853030450010
12. Carroll, B.A., Ahuvia, A.C.: Some antecedents and outcomes of brand love. Mark. Lett. **17**, 79–89 (2006). https://doi.org/10.1007/s11002-006-4219-2
13. Khan, I., Rahman, Z.: Development of a scale to measure hotel brand experiences. Int. J. Contemp. Hosp. Manag. (2017). https://doi.org/10.1108/IJCHM-08-2015-0439
14. Nikhashemi, S.R., Jebarajakirthy, C., Nusair, K.: Uncovering the roles of retail brand experience and brand love in the apparel industry: non-linear structural equation modeling approach. J. Retail. Consum. Serv. **48**, 122–135 (2019). https://doi.org/10.1016/j.jretconser.2019.01.014
15. Beig, F.A., Nika, F.A.: Impact of brand experience on brand equity of online shopping portals: a study of select e-commerce sites in the state of Jammu and Kashmir. Glob. Bus. Rev. **23**(1), 156–175 (2022). https://doi.org/10.1177/0972150919836041
16. Brandão, A., Popoli, P.: "I'm hatin'it"! Negative consumer–brand relationships in online anti-brand communities. Eur. J. Mark. (2022). https://doi.org/10.1108/EJM-03-2020-0214
17. Yadav, A., Chakrabarti, S.: Brand hate: a systematic literature review and future research agenda. Int. J. Consum. Stud. **46**(5), 1992–2019 (2022). https://doi.org/10.1111/ijcs.12772
18. Khan, I.: Do brands' social media marketing activities matter? A moderation analysis. J. Retail. Consum. Serv. **64**, 102794 (2022). https://doi.org/10.1016/j.jretconser.2021.102794
19. Haudi, H., et al.: The effect of social media marketing on brand trust, brand equity and brand loyalty. Int. J. Data Netw. Sci. **6**(3), 961–972 (2022). https://doi.org/10.5267/j.ijdns.2022.1.015
20. Hanaysha, J.R.: Impact of social media marketing features on consumer's purchase decision in the fast-food industry: brand trust as a mediator. Int. J. Inf. Manag. Data Insights **2**(2), 100102 (2022). https://doi.org/10.1016/j.jjimei.2022.100102
21. Arya, V., Paul, J., Sethi, D.: Like it or not! Brand communication on social networking sites triggers consumer-based brand equity. Int. J. Consum. Stud. **46**(4), 1381–1398 (2022). https://doi.org/10.1111/ijcs.12763
22. Hsieh, S.H., Lee, C.T., Tseng, T.H.: Psychological empowerment and user satisfaction: investigating the influences of online brand community participation. Inf. Manag. **59**(1), 103570 (2022). https://doi.org/10.1016/j.im.2021.103570
23. Santos, Z.R., Cheung, C.M., Coelho, P.S., Rita, P.: Consumer engagement in social media brand communities: a literature review. Int. J. Inf. Manag. **63**, 102457 (2022). https://doi.org/10.1016/j.ijinfomgt.2021.102457

24. Cui, X., Xie, Q., Zhu, J., Shareef, M.A., Goraya, M.A.S., Akram, M.S.: Understanding the omnichannel customer journey: the effect of online and offline channel interactivity on consumer value co-creation behavior. J. Retail. Consum. Serv. **65**, 102869 (2022). https://doi.org/10.1016/j.jretconser.2021.102869

25. Brooke, J.: SUS-A quick and dirty usability scale. Usability Eval. Ind. **189**(194), 4–7 (1996). https://doi.org/10.1509/jmkg.73.3.052

26. Lewis, J.R.: Psychometric evaluation of the post-study system usability questionnaire: the PSSUQ. In: Proceedings of the Human Factors Society Annual Meeting, vol. 36, no. 16, pp. 1259–1260. Sage Publications, Los Angeles (1992). https://doi.org/10.1177/154193129203601617

27. Hone, K.S., Graham, R.: Towards a tool for the subjective assessment of speech system interfaces (SASSI). Nat. Lang. Eng. **6**(3–4), 287–303 (2000). https://doi.org/10.1017/S135132490000249

28. Polkosky, M.D., Lewis, J.R.: Expanding the MOS: development and psychometric evaluation of the MOS-R and MOS-X. Int. J. Speech Technol. **6**(2), 161–182 (2003). https://doi.org/10.1023/A:1022390615396

29. Riemer, H.A., Chelladurai, P.: Development of the athlete satisfaction questionnaire (ASQ). J. Sport Exerc. Psychol. **20**(2), 127–156 (1998). https://doi.org/10.1123/jsep.20.2.127

30. Lewis, J.R.: Computer system usability questionnaire. Int. J. Hum. Comput. Interact. (1995). https://doi.org/10.1037/t32698-000

31. Lund, A.M.: Measuring usability with the use questionnaire12. Usability Interface **8**(2), 3–6 (2001)

32. Kirakowski, J., Cierlik, B.: Measuring the usability of web sites. In: Proceedings of the Human Factors and Ergonomics Society Annual Meeting, vol. 42, no. 4, pp. 424–428. SAGE Publications, Los Angeles (1998). https://doi.org/10.1177/154193129804200405

33. Angelova, B., Zekiri, J.: Measuring customer satisfaction with service quality using American customer satisfaction model (ACSI Model). Int. J. Acad. Res. Bus. Soc. Sci. **1**(3), 232–258 (2011)

34. Harvey, R.J.: Research Monograph: The Development of the Common-Metric-Questionnaire (CMQ). Personnel Systems & Technologies Corporation (1993). http://www.pstc.com/documents/monograph.pdf

35. Ryan, R.M., Deci, E.L.: Self-determination theory and the facilitation of intrinsic motivation, social development, and well-being. Am. Psychol. **55**(1), 68 (2000). https://doi.org/10.1037/0003-066X.55.1.68

36. Lee, J.D., See, K.A.: Trust in automation: designing for appropriate reliance. Hum. Factors **46**(1), 50–80 (2004). https://doi.org/10.1518/hfes.46.1.50.30392

37. Richins, M.L., Dawson, S.: A consumer values orientation for materialism and its measurement: scale development and validation. J. consum. Res. **19**(3), 303–316 (1992). https://doi.org/10.1086/209304

38. Vyas, D., van der Veer, G.C.: APEC: a framework for designing experience. Spaces, Places & Experience in HCI, pp. 1–4 (2005)

39. Forlizzi, J., Ford, S.: The building blocks of experience: an early framework for interaction designers. In: Proceedings of the 3rd Conference on Designing Interactive Systems: Processes, Practices, Methods, and Techniques, pp. 419–423 (2000)

40. Hartson, R., Pyla, P.S.: The UX Book: Process and Guidelines for Ensuring a Quality User Experience. Elsevier, Amsterdam (2012)

41. Balagtas-Fernandez, F., Hussmann, H.: A methodology and framework to simplify usability analysis of mobile applications. In: 2009 IEEE/ACM International Conference on Automated Software Engineering, pp. 520–524. IEEE (2012). https://doi.org/10.1109/ASE.2009.12

42. Agarwal, R., Venkatesh, V.: Assessing a firm's web presence: a heuristic evaluation procedure for the measurement of usability. Inf. Syst. Res. **13**(2), 168–186 (2002). https://doi.org/10.1287/isre.13.2.168.84
43. To, D.I.H.: Users play cards. We keep score. Magic results! Soc. Tech. Commun., 114 (2011)
44. Puglisi, B., Ackerman, A.: The Emotion Thesaurus: A Writer's Guide to Character Expression, vol. 1. JADD Publishing (2019)
45. Judy, S.: The experiential approach: inner worlds to outer worlds. Eight Approaches Teach. Compos., 37–51 (1980)
46. Xixiang, S., Gilal, R.G., Gilal, F.G.: Brand experience as a contemporary source of brand equity in 21st century: evidence from the Chinese consumer market. Int. J. Educ. Res. **4**(9), 63–76 (2016)
47. Aljukhadar, M., Beriault Poirier, A., Senecal, S.: Imagery makes social media captivating! Aesthetic value in a consumer-as-value-maximizer framework. J. Res. Interact. Mark. **14**(3), 285–303 (2020). https://doi.org/10.1108/JRIM-10-2018-0136
48. Walach, H.: Inner experience–direct access to reality: a complementarist ontology and dual aspect monism support a broader epistemology. Front. Psychol. **11**, 640 (2020). https://doi.org/10.3389/fpsyg.2020.00640
49. Bleier, A., Harmeling, C.M., Palmatier, R.W.: Creating effective online customer experiences. J. Mark. **83**(2), 98–119 (2019). https://doi.org/10.1177/0022242918809930
50. Bannerji, H.: But who speaks for us? Experience and agency in conventional feminist paradigms. In: The Ideological Condition: Selected Essays on History, Race and Gender, pp. 53–80. Brill (2020). https://doi.org/10.1163/9789004441620_005
51. Ramaseshan, B., Stein, A.: Connecting the dots between brand experience and brand loyalty: the mediating role of brand personality and brand relationships. J. Brand Manag. **21**, 664–683 (2014). https://doi.org/10.1057/bm.2014.23
52. Bapat, D.: Impact of brand familiarity on brands experience dimensions for financial services brands. Int. J. Bank Mark. **35**(4), 637–648 (2017). https://doi.org/10.1108/IJBM-05-2016-0066
53. Choi, Y.G., Ok, C., Hyun, S.S.: Evaluating relationships among brand experience, brand personality, brand prestige, brand relationship quality, and brand loyalty: an empirical study of coffeehouse brands (2011)
54. Chuchu, T., Venter de Villiers, M., Chinomona, R.: The influence of store environment on brand attitude, brand experience and purchase intention. S. Afr. J. Bus. Manag. **49**(1), 1–8 (2018). https://hdl.handle.net/10520/EJC-14ba0e2506
55. Demartini, J.F.: The Breakthrough Experience: A Revolutionary New Approach to Personal Transformation. Hay House, Inc. (2002)
56. Su, N., Reynolds, D.: Effects of brand personality dimensions on consumers' perceived self-image congruity and functional congruity with hotel brands. Int. J. Hosp. Manag. **66**, 1–12 (2017). https://doi.org/10.1016/j.ijhm.2017.06.006
57. Jung Choo, H., Moon, H., Kim, H., Yoon, N.: Luxury customer value. J. Fash. Mark. Manag. Int. J. **16**(1), 81–101 (2012). https://doi.org/10.1108/13612021211203041
58. Simonson, A., Schmitt, B.H.: Marketing Aesthetics: The Strategic Management of Brands, Identity, and Image. Simon and Schuster, New York (1997)
59. Zaltman, G.: Rethinking market research: putting people back in. J. Mark. Res. **34**(4), 424–437 (1997). https://doi.org/10.1177/002224379703400402
60. Gray, H.M., Gray, K., Wegner, D.M.: Dimensions of mind perception. Science **315**(5812), 619–619 (2007). https://doi.org/10.1126/science.113447
61. Gilmore, J.H., Pine, B.J.: Authenticity: What Consumers Really Want. Harvard Business Press (2007)

62. Nysveen, H., Pedersen, P.E., Skard, S.: Brand experiences in service organizations: exploring the individual effects of brand experience dimensions. J. Brand Manag. **20**, 404–423 (2013). https://doi.org/10.1057/bm.2012.31

63. Tuerlan, T., Li, S., Scott, N.: Customer emotion research in hospitality and tourism: conceptualization, measurements, antecedents and consequences. Int. J. Contemp. Hosp. Manag. **33**(8), 2741–2772 (2021). https://doi.org/10.1108/IJCHM-11-2020-1257

64. Fan, X., Chai, Z., Deng, N., Dong, X.: Adoption of augmented reality in online retailing and consumers' product attitude: a cognitive perspective. J. Retail. Consum. Serv. **53**, 101986 (2020). https://doi.org/10.1016/j.jretconser.2019.101986

65. Lavoye, V., Mero, J., Tarkiainen, A.: Consumer behavior with augmented reality in retail: a review and research agenda. Int. Rev. Retail Distrib. Consum. Res. **31**(3), 299–329 (2021). https://doi.org/10.1080/09593969.2021.1901765

Design of Chinese Metro Advertising Scene in the Era of Digital Media

Yawen Yang[1] ⓘ, Linda Huang[2](✉) ⓘ, and Junjie Peng[2] ⓘ

[1] Hunan International Economics University (Hunan University), Changsha, China
[2] Changsha University of Science and Technology, Changsha, China
huanglinda@csust.edu.cn

Abstract. With the rise of digital media and the large-scale construction of China's metro, digital media advertising intervenes in the metro space, breaks through traditional advertising forms with strong interactivity and communication capabilities, and provides users with personalized services. This research focuses on 1675 questionnaires on metro advertising scene design and studies the performance characteristics, development trends and user preferences of metro advertising in the digital media era. This paper believes that metro advertising should introduce new technologies brought by digital media, seize the unique advantages of metro scenes, realize the innovation of advertising communication, and improve the situational experience of advertising.

Keywords: Metro · Digital media · Advertising design · Scene

1 Introduction

In the wave of digitalization, computer technology is constantly updated and developed, and digital media is born. Digital media is an emerging media that is different from paper media and is the product of the integration of computer technology, network technology, digital communication technology and culture, art, business and other fields. Digital media relies on traditional media, but also the expansion of traditional media, which is characterized by "fast", "accurate", "full" and "easy" compared with traditional media, which can plug in the wings for the development of various industries. Digital media has distinctive characteristics of the times and has given birth to a large number of new products, new business models and new modes. In the era of digital media, many elements are labeled as digital, such as digital divide, electronic publishing, streaming media, etc. Digital media are also intervening in various spatial scenarios, such as the taxi app born in the travel scenario and the "central kitchen" type of full media created to improve the efficiency of news dissemination.

As a window carrying the city's cultural card, the metro has become an important platform for static advertising with its special spatial structure. However, users' demand for interactive, touchscreen and immersive advertising design has led to the intervention of digital media, a product of the integration of computer technology, network technology, digital communication technology and culture, art, and commerce, into the

P. Zaphiris et al. (Eds.): HCII 2023, LNCS 14060, pp. 563–579, 2023.
https://doi.org/10.1007/978-3-031-48060-7_43

metro space, breaking through traditional advertising forms and providing personalised services to users with its powerful interactivity and communication capabilities.

Currently, urban metro stations in China have distributed a variety of advertising designs such as print billboards, metro charter scene advertising and tunnel dynamic advertising, undertaking the social functions of mass entertainment, commercial promotion, and transmission of culture. However, compared with China, metro advertising design in more urbanized cities abroad brings an upgraded experience inspiring user communication and feedback. Specifically, metro advertising design in these countries has been perfectly integrated into human-computer interaction play, AR, VR and other technologies to contextualize advertising design, giving riders a greater sense of experience and novelty.

This paper finds:

(1) In the metro scene, advertisements can seize users' attention resources, but fail to form long-term memory. Over 70% of users pay attention to the headlines and images of metro advertisements when they take the metro, but there is no linear relationship between user satisfaction and the presence of advertisements.
(2) Metro advertisements in the digital media era tend to be seasonal and interactive and are expected to form an advertising system with unique metro scene characteristics in the future.
(3) Metro advertising can deeply trigger users' various senses, especially the visual. The design of images and colors can best attract users during the period when they enter the station to ride and wait, making it easy to win over outdoor advertising.
(4) The scenes of metro advertising have integrated and immersive characteristics due to their operational status and spatial composition.
(5) Currently, the design of metro advertisements does not change depending on the scene. Forty percent of users think that metro ads are almost indistinguishable from traditional ads, and metro ads cannot give users more information; while 70% of users need to understand more deeply through other means (such as scanning QR codes).

2 Review of the Literature

At present, the following studies related to the design of metro advertising scenes in China in the digital media era have been conducted.

(1) Specific metro advertising design and future planning for a particular city. For example, Cheng Yi-hao et al. (2018) conducted an innovative print advertising design for Qingdao metro, and in order to enrich the visual experience of users, the authors specifically provided improvement directions for Qingdao metro platform promenade advertising, channel promenade advertising, escalator sidewall advertising, and in-car advertising, and hoped to promote the development of Qingdao metro culture through the enrichment of visual presentation. In addition, many scholars have also taken Beijing and Hangzhou metro designs as the main research objects and offered suggestions for the development of metro advertising in each city, but the enthusiasm for this research has been declining in the past three years due to its earlier research background, which failed to link with the digital media era.

(2) Research on the communication strategy of metro advertising in the digital media era. Based on audience survey and spatial environment, Qu Lulu (2022) studied the positioning of metro advertising in terms of product, placement, medium, appeal and the positioning of style; Quan Shui (2017) specifically analyzed the advertising of Harbin Line 1 to explore the development trend and design ideas of the integration of metro advertising and digital media.

(3) Reflections on the excellent performance of metro advertising in other countries based on a specific perspective. Liu (2022) analyzes the specific application, advantages and disadvantages of the concept of "emotional design" in London metro advertisements and believes that the London metro already has its unique British image style and world-leading pioneering artistic attitude, but its obsolete facilities limit the development of advertisements in the digital media era. The author draws lessons from this experience and draws inspiration for the development of metro advertising in China, suggesting that Chinese metro advertising should enhance the artistic expression of advertising, add green modules and build a cultural communication vein in the construction.

3 Method

This study conducted an online questionnaire survey on "metro advertising culture" among 1,675 metro riders of different age groups, focusing on the design of metro advertising in the digital media era. The questionnaire survey covers the basic information of metro riders, their consumption habits of metro services and their basic perceptions of metro advertising culture and explores the relevance of metro culture to the culture of their cities and the transformation of metro advertising in the digital media era. In addition, the study is supplemented by unstructured interviews and field surveys to summarize the experience, summarize and conclude the characteristics embodied in metro advertising, etc.

4 Discussion

4.1 Questionnaire Design and Feedback

4.1.1 Metro Riding and Consumption

(1) Metro user profiling analysis.
As of January 2023, the aggregated metro traffic in China reached 48,938,500, and the number of operating stations reached 5,683. For the purpose of refined marketing and personalized services implemented by metro advertising and consumer demographic characteristics, the study established a portrait model of users who ride the metro based on the personal information filled out by respondents. In terms of gender, the ratio of men to women is relatively even; in terms of age, young users aged 18–25 account for more than half of the users, followed by middle-aged users aged 26–40; the educational background of users is mainly undergraduate, with 72.95% of the surveyed users having a bachelor's degree, master's degree or above; in terms of economic income, nearly the average user has a monthly income of less than 2,000 yuan, and only 10% have a monthly income of more than 10,000 yuan (Figs. 1 and 2).

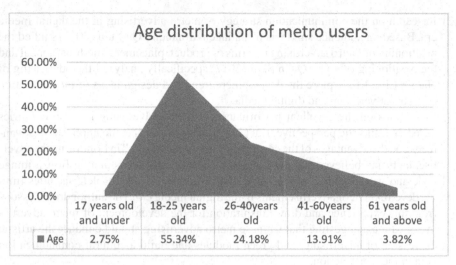

Fig. 1. Age distribution of metro users (Self-designed Form)

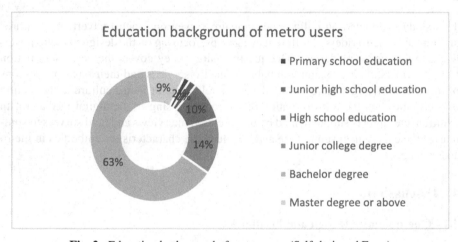

Fig. 2. Education background of metro users (Self-designed Form)

From a comprehensive point of view, the respondents of the questionnaire fit the user profile of metro advertising to a certain extent. They are mostly young people with low income, low consumption ability and good education, indicating that they have a certain degree of cognitive ability and aesthetics of advertising culture and value, which is in line with the user profile of "metro people" in the digital media era.

(2) Metro Riding Habits.
With the development of transportation in China, the metro riding habits of different users vary, and users are not limited to taking the metro in only one city. 43.16% of the respondents choose the metro most often in their daily travels, and the weekly frequency of metro riding is evenly distributed. In terms of the number of metro rides in different

cities, 20% of users have taken the metro in only one city, while 30% of users have taken the metro in three cities or more (Fig. 3).

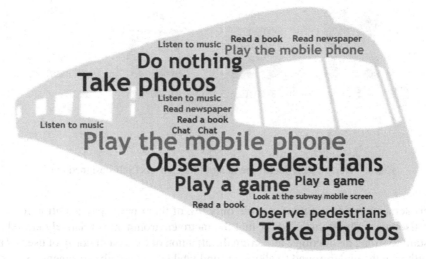

Fig. 3. Word frequency chart of metro users' riding habits (Self-designed Form)

Human behavioral activities can be divided into necessary, spontaneous and social activities. In response to the question "What do you mainly do while waiting and riding in the metro?" 999 passengers chose to "look at my phone" and 242 users "look at the metro mobile screen", while fewer passengers chose to chat, sleep, or take pictures. It's clear that metro users only engage in spontaneous independent activities and engage in less social behavior influenced by the environment. In the age of digital media, users are more likely to spend their metro rides on their own to access information on the screen.

(3) Metro consumption habits.

In response to the question "What is your average daily metro spending?" 38.87% of users spend 3 yuan or less per day, 28.9% spend 3 yuan to 10 yuan, 27.28% spend 10 yuan to 100 yuan, and only less than 10% spend more than 100 yuan. It is worth paying attention to the fact that almost all of the consumption generated by users in the metro is spent on the "cutting edge". The largest share of consumption is spent on metro tickets. According to the scientific analysis of users' consumption composition, the overall score from highest to lowest is as follows: ticket purchase > food and beverage > entertainment > communication > medicine > other > shopping (cultural and creative, clothing, etc.) (Fig. 4).

Analysis of Attention Level of Metro Advertising

(1) Users' attention to metro advertisements.

Regarding "users' attention to metro advertisements", 90% of users said they would pay attention to advertisements inside stations (corridors, platforms, carriages or tunnels) when taking the metro, and about one-third of them would often pay attention to

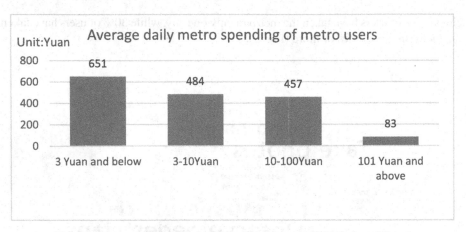

Fig. 4. Average daily metro spending of metro users (Self-designed Form)

advertisements inside the metro, while only 9% of them never pay attention to metro advertisements. The statistics show that the metro environment is relatively closed and resistant to strong distractions, attracting the attention of the vast majority of users. They are either in the underground, walking around while noticing advertisements posted in the corridors, or inadvertently glancing inside kiosks, or browsing LED displays out of boredom while waiting for the metro, or in the immersive environment of the car, paying attention to ads in the cars and tunnels (Fig. 5).

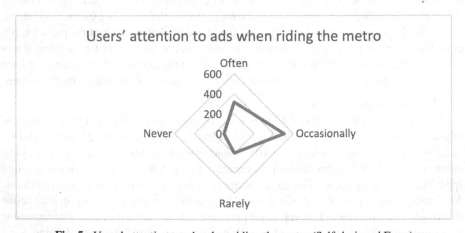

Fig. 5. Users' attention to ads when riding the metro (Self-designed Form)

(2) The degree of attraction of metro advertising elements to users.
The statistical results show that metro advertisement is an extension of human senses, users focus on visual and auditory enjoyment. Metro advertisement is diverse and complex, but there is still audiovisual language combined with better advertisements that stands out and are widely spread. In terms of "the attractiveness of metro advertisements

elements to users", users listed the elements of the advertisement that attract their attention according to their personal preferences. In terms of advertisement formats, video surpasses text and pictures as the format of the most popular advertisement. While in terms of advertisement content, public service ads are the most attractive to users, followed by cultural and travel advertisements, communication advertisements, and food and beverage advertisements. In terms of reasons for advertisements' attention, the top five reasons are attractive picture, attractive title, attractive sound, celebrity effect and eye-catching billboard position. In terms of specific elements, more than half of the users think that color and images give the greatest visual impact and are the reasons why metro advertisements attract their attention (Table 1 and Fig. 6).

Table 1. What types of ads do you generally pay attention to? (Self-designed Form)

Advertising Type	Attention
Public Interest Advertisements	660
Cultural Travel Advertisements	432
Communication Advertisements	303
Restaurant Advertisements	273
Beverage Advertisements	264
City Promotion Advertisements	253
Real Estate Advertisements	214
Recruitment Advertisements	211
Performance Information Advertisements	187
Website Advertisements	144
Shoes and Clothing Advertisements	142
Medical Beauty Advertisements	134

Performance of the Metro Scene in the Eyes of Users

(1) Characteristics of the metro scene.
In response to the question "What do you think is the difference between the metro scene and other transportation scenes?". 80% of users think it is the service mode (e.g. station service, security check, consultation, broadcasting), 53.01% think it is the cultural atmosphere (e.g. special stations, special publications, specific activities), 26.75% think it is the management mode, 27.34% think it is the consumption mode, and only 17.55% think it is the advertising quality. As a public transportation system running mainly in the city, the metro's low pollution, high speed, close frequency and smooth connection along with the high cost of construction and maintenance form the hardware style and cultural characteristics unique to the city metro (Fig. 7).

(2) Metro users' cultural needs.
The questionnaire data shows that 27.39% of users strongly feel about the metro culture, only 3.95% of users do not feel it, and the remaining users do feel it but to a lesser extent.

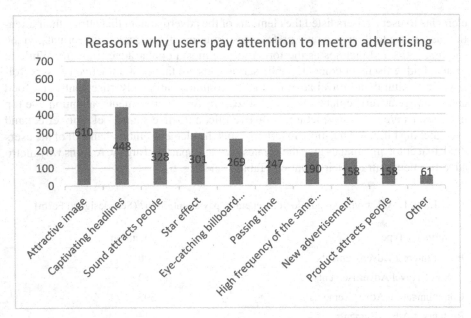

Fig. 6. Reasons why users pay attention to metro advertising (Self-designed Form)

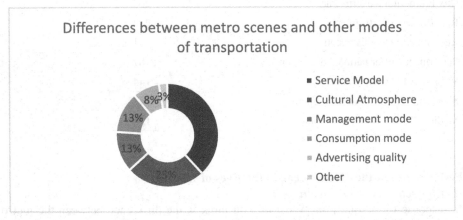

Fig. 7. Differences between metro scenes and other modes of transportation (Self-designed Form)

However, the vast majority of users think that metro culture is important, accounting for 89.82%. In the eyes of users, metro culture should contain a wealth of content. The top ten most supported are city culture (1228 votes), transportation culture (1114 votes), history culture (1013 votes), art culture (747 votes), tourism culture (743 votes), visual culture (608 votes), traditional culture (600 votes), red culture (590 votes), consumer culture (540 votes), and community culture (535 votes). It can be seen that users have an urgent demand for culture in the metro, but due to the limitation of cultural expression or the lack of a wide range of cultural advertising, the current situation of unbalanced supply and demand for culture in metro advertising is caused in order to satisfy the majority of metro users' desire for culture (Fig. 8).

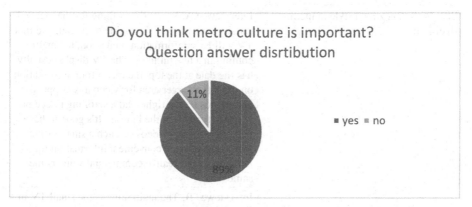

Fig. 8. Do you think metro culture is important? Question answer distribution (Self-designed Form)

4.2 Literature Research and Experience Summary

Metro Advertising Design Features
(1) Integrated.
From oral communication to the invention of printing to the flourishing of camera technology and digital media, the history of advertising has been accompanied by an integrated style. The integrated style here is different from the state of new things eliminating old things under the mere technological innovation, but the use of information technology to organically combine the traditional functions that are independent of each other to achieve the effect of one plus one more than two. The integrated form of metro advertising benefits from the development of digital media technology, and it also represents the form of metro advertising compound, diversified and flexible. The integration of touching copywriting, eye-catching art design, distinctive music and sound effects, dazzling lighting and even texture and smell in special advertisements helps users to awaken their all-round senses (Table 2).

(2) Immersion.
Inspired by sociologist Goffman's "Dramaturgy", communication scientist Meyrowitz developed the concept of "scene" to study the behavioral and psychological effects of "media scene" on people. According to the academic summary, scene is a variety of spatial places for user activities but is not limited to space and has the conditions to meet the integration of space, time and experience. The metro scene, as a combination of residents' living place and social environment, includes traditional physical spaces such as metro carriages and corridors, convenient devices such as ticket windows, automatic gates and escalators, as well as cultural and aesthetic elements such as metro advertisements and safety propaganda. Since the metro scene is located underground, the wrapped

Table 2. Unstructured interviews about metro advertising (Self-designed Form)

Question	Answers
What is the integrated style in metro advertising?	Interviewee A: When I'm waiting for the metro, I usually look at the TV hanging overhead, and this TV will have information on it about the metro coming in a few minutes. The TV display usually has the date at the top, the metro train information on the left, a larger area for video ads or ppt-like picture ads on the right, and a scrolling notice or weather forecast at the bottom. It's good to have text, pictures and videos on such a small display, which can provide convenient information for passengers and realize commercial value at the same time
	Interviewee B: The main thing is the small TV in the carriage, which is an integration of style impact, music and pictures. I think some of the variety shows and soft spots broadcast on TV are quite popular

and enclosed nature of its scenes provides objective and psychological conditions for users to be exposed to advertising in an immersive manner and creates a scenario-based design that advertising operators need to keep in mind (Fig. 9).

Taking the first metro digital art gallery in China as an example, Changsha, the "Media Capital of the World", has seized the immersive characteristics of the metro scene to create the trendy Changsha metro digital art gallery in the 2,000 m² of metro interchange space. Several large-scale steel structure stereoscopic double 8K Super Definition streaming media LED art installations in the metro dynamically present various theme content, forming an underground advertising space with interlaced light and shadow, rich in beauty and technology. The close linkage between the closed metro space and the virtual scene provides an immersive cultural experience for the users who interchange here, enhancing the deep communication between advertising and culture and the cultural atmosphere of the whole city, and achieving a light and shadow effect unmatched by outdoor advertising.

Trends of Metro Advertising Design in the Context of Digital Media
(1) Seasonality.
"Shi ling" comes from the Chinese language, which is an ancient decree on agricultural affairs according to the seasons. As a label of digital media, "change" has driven the design of metro advertising in this era. Whether it is the government's cultural promotion of the city or folklore or commercial advertisers' brand or product advertisements, the trend of seasonality is shown.

As digital media can bring users rapid information content updates, metro advertising is getting updated faster and more ads have started to chase hot spots (such as festivals,

Fig. 9. Metro Digital Art Gallery in Changsha, the "Media Capital of the World"

new policies, popular phrases, popular celebrities, etc.) with strong seasonality and directivity. The most obvious seasonality of metro advertising is to change the style of advertising design according to the seasonal weather or seasons, and product advertising also revolves around the season to create different styles of metro scenes such as winter warmth and summer coolness, which extends to advertising forms, such as when the city is promoting a certain type of culture or when the city holds a large-scale event, all kinds of advertising will take advantage of the situation and design, chasing the current trend or following the general environment around hot spots. In addition, with the gradual evolution of poster ads into digital screens and other electronic technology, the tedious process of tearing and replacing posters in metro ads has been eliminated to a certain extent, and the update of ads can be completed by simple operation in the background, which has improved the efficiency of ads serving, which also facilitates the seasonal change of metro ads.

(2) Interactivity.
Digital media is the presentation medium of metro advertising, and the intersection of its subjective artistic expression and interactive design that favors the user's feelings has formed the trend of interaction in metro advertising today. It is especially important and difficult to disseminate advertisements to effective groups. At this time, the advanced psychological design of users can solve the problem of users' aversion caused by one-way acceptance of metro advertising information before, improve users' sense of experience when collecting users' information, appeals and purchase intentions, and thus guide metro passengers to transform into advertising consumers. With the help of digital media,

interactive advertising provides a platform and hosting space for more information, thus attracting more viewers to choose information points of interest.

Take the creative advertisement jointly created by yogurt brand Ambrosial and the game "Light and Night" on Valentine's Day in 2022 as an example. In addition to the customized product creative display and group photo punching area, the interactive experience area of the "heart phone booth" is placed in the metro corridor to simulate the interactive plot of five male characters accompanying users to make phone calls. The novel form and exquisite interactive device complete the in-depth dialogue with consumers.

However, some of the current metro advertisements with interactive functions do not well integrate the interaction behavior between users and advertisements in the metro scene. The theory of user memory in cognitive psychology includes sensory memory, short-term memory and long-term memory. Some advertisements only mechanically deliver promotional elements to passengers and offer the choice of whether to interact or not. How to make metro users in a hurry stop or pull them into the interactive environment in the shortest time and turn short-term memory into long-term memory is a problem to be considered in interactive metro advertising.

5 Conclusion

In the long term, China will continue to build urban metros on a large scale as urbanization accelerates and population movement increases. As a medium for information dissemination, the survival and development of metro advertising are increasingly dependent on the degree of audience recognition, the widespread use of digital media has significantly increased the audience's demand for accuracy and novelty in information picking.

Firstly, the close connection between metro advertisements and audiences can prompt users to pay part of their attention resources and generate consumption.

Secondly, in the era of digital media, visual culture develops rapidly. Due to the simplification of image reproduction and the convenience of image transmission, the audience affected by visual images has a stronger desire for advertising interaction under the guidance of new technology.

Moreover, the immersive characteristics of the metro scene and the electronic design of advertisements provide a platform and space for displaying more information, thus having the objective conditions to attract more audiences to independently select information points of interest.

Finally, the transformation of the metro, which is still mainly static advertising, has just begun in the era of digital media, and there is a wide space for innovation in technology and art design in the future.

In conclusion, as an important tool of media design, metro advertising should introduce new technologies brought by digital media, integrate three-dimensionality and dynamism in all aspects, so as to realize the innovation of advertising communication and enhance the contextual experience of advertising propaganda.

Based on this, the following improvements are available for reference:

(1) Using digital media technologies such as VR and AR to design interactive advertisements that meet the laws of advertising communication, contemporary user needs and the characteristics of the digital media era.

(2) Increase the proportion of "electronic screens" in metro advertisements, and promote the elimination of advertisements with old forms, imprecise delivery and aesthetics that are not close to users, so as to complete the transformation of metro advertisements into intelligence.

(3) According to the characteristics of the metro space, metro scenes are designed to fit the metro immersion scene. Advertising improves user efficiency through design, and predicting user goals by obtaining user pain points and needs and combining the before and after scenes, such as (Table 3).

Table 3. Key points of metro immersive scene advertising design (Self-designed Form)

Key points of metro immersive scene advertising design					
Characteristics of the metro scene	The metro is underground, with a semi-closed environment	Long continuous routes for entering, exiting, and transferring	Users are bored while waiting for the metro	High flow of people and congestion during peak hours	......
Artistic means	Designing light and shadow effects and LED displays	Using light boxes with lighting effects in the vacant lots	Placing interactive devices that can pass the time and have a promotional effect	Monitoring advertising according to big data, targeting the lots with high efficiency	......

Admittedly, there are still shortcomings in this research. Firstly, no survey has been conducted for different countries or cities to study the characteristics and shortcomings of metro advertising design in different regions. Secondly, this paper does not distinguish between the design of public service advertisements and commercial advertisements, and it would be more beneficial to the future metro advertising design if this can be used as a variable to study the psychology of users in the face of profitable and non-profitable advertisements, so as to derive psychological preferences and analyze the design trends of different types of advertisements in the same scene, it will be more conducive to future metro advertising design.

Appendix

Online Questionnaire Survey on "Metro Advertising Culture"

1: What is your gender? [Single choice]
   A. Male
   B. Female

2: What is your age? [Single choice]
   A. Under 17 years old
   B. 8–25 years old
   C. 26–40 years old
   D. 41–60 years old
   E. 61 years old or above

3: What is your educational background? [Single choice]
   A. Elementary school
   B. Junior high school
   C. High school
   D. Specialist
   E. Undergraduate
   F. Master and above

4: What is your economic income level? [Single choice]
   A. Below 2000 Yuan
   B. 2000–3000 Yuan
   C. 3001–5000 Yuan
   D. 5001–8000 Yuan
   E. 8001–15000 Yuan
   F. 15001–30000 Yuan
   G. 30001 Yuan or more

5: How often do you travel by metro? [Single choice]
   A. More than 1 time a month
   B. 2–3 times a month
   C. 2–4 times a week
   D. More than 4 times a week

6: How much do you spend on the metro every day? [Single choice]
   A. 3 Yuan and below
   B. 3–0 Yuan
   C. 10–100 Yuan
   D. 101 Yuan and above

7: How many regions and cities metro have you ridden? [Single choice]
   A. 0
   B. 1
   C. 2–3
   D. 3 or more

8: Do you feel that the metro varies greatly from city to city? [Single-choice]
   A. Yes

B. No

9: Do you think the metro culture is important? [Single-choice]

A. Yes

B. No

10: Which of the following should be included in the metro culture? [Multiple choice]

A. Transportation culture

B. City culture

C. Community culture

D. Historical culture

E. Art Culture

F. Visual Culture

G. Consumer Culture

H. Tourism Culture

 I. Red Culture

 J. Traditional Culture

K. National culture

11: What do you mainly do while waiting and riding in the metro? [Single choice]

A. Do nothing

B. Look at my cell phone

C. Sleep

D. Read books and newspapers

E. Look at the metro mobile screen

F. Chatting

G. Taking pictures

H. Listening to music

 I. Other

12: What are the elements that attract your attention in the metro space? [Multiple choice]

A. Text ads

B. Video ads

 C Picture ads

D. Logo symbols

E. Station design

F. Supporting facilities

G. Others

13: Why do these elements capture your attention? [Multiple choice]

A. Color

 B Appearance

C. Image

D. Sound

E. Taste

F. Other

14: When you take the metro, do you pay attention to the advertisements inside the station (corridor, platform, carriage or tunnel)? [Single choice]

A. Often

  B. Occasionally
  C. Rarely
  D. Never
15: How much do you care about metro advertisements? [Single choice]
  A. Look at the headlines and images
  B. Read the content of the ads carefully
  C. Browse in a hurry
16: What types of advertisements do you generally pay attention to? [Multiple choice]
  A. Public service advertisements
  B. Cultural and travel advertisements
  C. Communication advertisements
  D. Food and beverage advertisements
  E. Beverage advertisements
  F. City advertisements
  G. Real estate advertisements
  H. Recruitment advertisements
  I. Performance information advertisements
  J. Website advertisements
  K. Shoes and clothes advertisements
  L. Medical beauty advertisements
17: What do you think is the difference between the metro and other means of transportation? [Multiple choice]
  A. Service mode (e.g. station service, security check, consultation, broadcasting)
  B. Cultural atmosphere (e.g. special stations, special publications, specific activities)
  C. Management mode (e.g. state-owned, private, corporate cooperation)
  D. Consumption mode
  E. Advertising quality
  F. Others
18: Do you think the metro culture is important? [Single choice]
  A. Yes
  B. No

References

1. Fang, X., Zhan, Y., Zhang, Z., Zhang, B.: The analysis method of metro passengers' advertising demand from the perspective of user experience. Packag. Eng. **43**(18), 178–183 (2022)
2. Sun, Y.: Research on immersive scene design of digital media art (2021)
3. Fan, H.: Scene use mode of metro media. China Advert. (06), 30–32 (2016)
4. Zhang, L.: Research on the design and management of metro public space (2013)
5. Liu, Z., Sun, H.: The experience of London metro advertising in the context of "emotional design" on China's metro. The development of advertising inspiration. Modern Advert. **444**(08), 48–55+65 (2022)
6. Norman, D.A.: Design Psychology. (US); translated by Mei Qiong. CITIC Press (2003)

7. Huang, Y., Zhang, Y.: Wisdom innovation and development of metro advertising media in the age of intelligence. China Advert. **327**(03), 49–54 (2021)
8. Wang, Z.: Scene accompaniment: the narrative mechanism of native advertising in the era of mobile media. News Knowl. **457**(07), 49–54 (2022)

Author Index

P. Zaphiris et al. (Eds.): HCII 2023, LNCS 14060, pp. 581–583, 2023.
https://doi.org/10.1007/978-3-031-48060-7

Printed in the United States
by Baker & Taylor Publisher Services